"When from these scenes we wander
And twilight shadows fade,
Our memory still will linger
Where light and shadows played..."
Third stanza, *MSU Shadows*

S0-ARF-572

To: Matt... Class of 1991...
True Spartan. Keep The
Spirit Alive!
Bruce McCristal

The Spirit
of
Michigan State

J. Bruce McCristal
Class of 1954

Copyright ©2004 J. Bruce McCristal
Bloomfield Hills, Michigan 48302

First published in the United States of America in 2004 by J. Bruce McCristal

All rights reserved. No part of this book may be used or reproduced in any manner whatsoever without the written permission of the Publisher, except for brief quotations in articles and reviews.

FIRST EDITION

Printed and bound by InnerWorkings LLC in China
Jacket and Interior Design/Layout: The Printed Page, Phoenix, Arizona

ISBN: 1-891143-23-9
Library of Congress Control Number:: 2004094746

McCristal, J. Bruce, 1932
The Spirit of Michigan State: review of Michigan State University history—1855-2004.
Includes bibliographical references and index.
Main entry under title:
The Spirit of Michigan State/J. Bruce McCristal

Books can be ordered, and comments made by accessing the website: www.spiritofmichiganstate.com.

Table of Contents

Michigan State Historical Timeline

MSU's Colleges and Study Programs

Specialty Chapters

Sources, Photographic Credits, and Index

MSU Executive Officers—2004

- M. PETER McPHERSON, President
- LOU ANNA K. SIMON, Provost and Vice President for Academic Affairs
- FRED L. POSTON, Vice President for Finance and Operations and Treasurer
- L. SUSAN CARTER, Secretary of the Board of Trustees and Executive Assistant to the President
- ROBERT J. HUGGETT, Vice President for Research and Graduate Studies
- CHARLES H. WEBB, Vice President for University Development
- STEVEN WEBSTER, Vice President for Governmental Affairs
- LEE JUNE, Vice President for Student Affairs and Services
- ROBERT A. NOTO, General Counsel and Vice President for Legal Affairs
- PAULETTE GRANBERRY RUSSELL, Senior Advisor to the President for Diversity, and Director of Affirmative Action, Compliance and Monitoring
- TERRY DENBOW, Vice President for University Relations
- KEITH WILLIAMS, Executive Director of the MSU Alumni Association

Board of Trustees—2004

- DAVID L. PORTEOUS, Chairman—Reed City, Michigan—Term expires—January 1, 2007.
- JOEL I. FERGUSON, Vice Chairman—Lansing, Michigan—Term expires—January 1, 2005.
- DOLORES M. COOK—Greenville, Michigan—Term expires—January 1, 2007.
- DOROTHY V. GONZALES—East Lansing, Michigan—Term expires—January 1, 2009.
- COLLEEN M. MCNAMARA—Lansing, Michigan—Term expires—January 1, 2011.
- DONALD W. NUGENT—Frankfort, Michigan—Term expires—January 1, 2011.
- RANDALL L. PITTMAN—Ypsilanti, Michigan—Term expires—January 1, 2005.
- G. SCOTT ROMNEY—Detroit, Michigan—Term expires—January 1, 2009.

Trustees Emeriti—2004

- JOHN B. BRUFF, Mount Clemens, Michigan.
- PATRICIA M. CARRIGAN, Ph. D., Bay City, Michigan.
- BOBBY CRIM, Grand Ledge, Michigan.
- MALCOLM G. DADE, JR., Columbia, South Carolina.
- ELIZABETH HOWE, Pleasant Ridge, Michigan.
- RAYMOND W. KROLIKOWSKI, Bloomfield, Michigan.
- CAROLE LICK, Ann Arbor, Michigan.
- BLANCHE MARTIN, D.D.S., East Lansing, Michigan.
- RUSSELL G. MAWBY, Augusta, Michigan.
- FRANK MERRIMAN, Deckerville, Michigan.
- LAWRENCE D. OWEN, East Lansing, Michigan.
- DEAN PRIDGEON, Montgomery, Michigan.
- AUBREY RADCLIFF, Ph.D., East Lansing, Michigan.
- THOMAS REED, DeWitt, Michigan.
- MELANIE REINHOLD-FOSTER, East Lansing, Michigan.
- BARBARA J. SAWYER-KOCH, East Lansing, Michigan.
- JOHN D. SHINGLETON, East Lansing, Michigan.
- MICHAEL J. SMYDRA
- JACK M. STACK, M.D., Frankfort, Michigan.
- BOB TRAXLER, Bay City, Michigan.
- ROBERT E. WEISS, Grand Blanc, Michigan.
- KATHLEEN WILBUR, Okemos, Michigan.
- PATRICK J. WILSON, Traverse City, Michigan.

Academic Definitions & Symbols

Alma Mater

Fostering Mother. The university or school one attended. The official anthem or hymn of a college or university.

Professorial Chair

The custom of endowing an academic chair originated in 16th century England, with just that—a chair. In those days, commoners sat on stools or wooden benches; the gentry sat on cushions. A chair, complete with arms, legs, and a back, was a valuable piece of furniture and an appropriate reward for a teacher who had reached the rank of professor.

"Today, the expression 'endowed chair' is used to mean an academic position supported by the earnings from invested funds. Endowed chairs allow a university to recruit internationally for outstanding faculty beyond the funding provided by the legislative appropriation." (Linda Chadderdon, Information Officer, College of Veterinary Medicine).

Michigan State's endowed professorial chair program is one of President Cecil Mackey's legacy contributions to the university. During his tenure as president, 1979-1985, Mackey initiated the funding for fourteen endowed academic chairs—MSU's first. Since that late beginning, MSU's endowed chair count has risen to 47.

Academic Gowns

In 1895 the Intercollegiate Commission, a group of leading American educators, met at Columbia University to draft a code which would serve to regulate the design of gowns and hoods indicating the various degrees as well as colors to indicate various faculties. This code has been adopted by most colleges and universities in America.

Bachelor's Degree—long, pointed sleeves.

Master's Degree—long, closed sleeves with the arc of a circle near the bottom. The arm goes through a slit, giving the appearance of short sleeves.

Doctor's Degree—gowns are faced with velvet. Sleeves are full, round and open, with three bars of velvet on each sleeve.

Hoods—are lined in the official academic colors of the institution. A chevron introduces a second color of the institution. Colored velvet binds the hoods and indicates the department or faculty to which the degree pertains.

Tenure

The purpose of tenure is to protect ideas. The Tenure System was described at the April 3, 1992, MSU Board of Trustees meeting. "The purpose of tenure is to assure the university staff academic freedom and security to protect the best interests of the university.

"Tenure shall not be considered to protect any person from the loss of his/her position as a result of gross misconduct, such as violation of professional ethics or refusal to perform reasonable duties, incompetence, voluntary withdrawal, or actions which are inimical to the interests of the university.

"A faculty member with the rank of professor in the tenure system is granted tenure (appointment for an indefinite period without terminal date) from the date of appointment at that rank. An associate professor who has not previously served at MSU usually is appointed in the tenure system for a probationary period of four years."

Lovingly dedicated to my parents, King and Alice McCristal

King and Alice McCristal at MSC Dance (1948)

Alice M. McCristal (1908-1974)

Honored for American Red Cross, and Hospital Volunteer Work; Faculty Folk Club Leader.

Dr. King J. McCristal (1907-1993)

Michigan State University

Chair, Professional Education, Physical Education and Recreation Dept., 1953-1961.
Chair, Steering Committee, MSU Academic Senate, 1958-1960.
Distinguished Teacher of the Year for the University and College of Education, 1954.
President, MSU University Club, 1952.
Professor, Associate Professor, Assistant Professor, 1937-1961.
President, Michigan Association for Health, Physical Education and Recreation, 1942.

University of Illinois

Dean, College of Physical Education, 1961-1973; Professor, 1973-75.
Instructor, 1929-1937.
President & Fellow, American Academy of Physical Education, 1974-75.
Honor Fellow, American Association of Health, Physical Education & Recreation, 1966.

Preface

This book has been written for the MSU Family. It is my hope it will serve as a reference point for understanding Michigan State's history and traditions as well as a catalyst for passing on the story of MSU—the birthplace of the widespread democratization of higher education in America. The book's emphasis is on MSU's excellence, leadership, and achievement.

I've been asked, "Why did you write this book?" My answer: "Because I had to." I felt compelled to tell the marvelous story of Michigan State University in a comprehensive way because I didn't believe the many achievements and traditions of the university, its alumni, faculty and students had been pulled together in one place.

My compulsion stems from the fact that my roots and heart are in East Lansing and at Michigan State. My family moved from the University of Illinois to East Lansing in the fall of 1937. My father had been hired by Ralph H. Young, Michigan State's athletic director, to serve as an assistant professor of health, physical education and recreation, a department he would later chair. I went from kindergarten through college in East Lansing, graduating from East Lansing High School in 1950 and Michigan State in 1954 in business and economics.

My earliest recollections of the college campus are pleasant ones. It was an inviting place—an unspoiled, beautiful wonderland for a youngster. It was exciting. There was always something going on.

When I was seven, I remember my dad taking me on a tour of Jenison Gymnasium and Fieldhouse in 1939 while it was under construction. The next year, I recall a tour of the finished facility with Ralph Young as tour guide. He took my family down in the basement, where we were fascinated watching swimmers in the Jenison pool from the underwater window, which allowed the coaches to see how their swimmers performed strokes. I was thrilled watching my first Water Carnival on the Red Cedar River in 1940. My parents took me to my first college football game at Macklin Stadium (now Spartan Stadium) in 1941. I saw my first basketball game at the sparkling new Jenison Fieldhouse in 1942. And, I have vivid memories of watching the fabulous Jennings twins, "Cut" and "Bo," and teammate Bill Maxwell win national wrestling titles for MSC at the NCAA Wrestling Championships held at Jenison Fieldhouse in 1942. "Cut," who would become a surgeon, was once a baby-sitter of mine.

The World Adventure Series, a part of Michigan State's Lecture-Concert Series, was initiated at President Hannah's behest during World War II as a diversion from the stress of war that everyone felt. I was captivated by these entertaining and memorable travelogues which were held in the Auditorium.

Growing up in a faculty family was special. Dinners at home with faculty from many disciplines were evenings of non-stop, stimulating conversation and stories. Close family friends included John and Lauretta Kobs (baseball coach), Charlie and Esther McCaffree (swimming coach), Fendley and Bert Collins (wrestling coach), Dr. Chester and Murial Clark (Dean of veterinary medicine), Dr. Clyde and Caroline Cairy (veterinary medicine professor), and Lowell and Verna Treaster (director of MSC's dept. of information services). Dr. Malcolm and Agnes Trout (dairy science professor and the "father" of homogenized milk) were good friends. Agnes Trout was my piano teacher.

While a student at Michigan State, I spent four years as a part-time aide to Fred W. Stabley, Sr., Michigan State's renowned director of sports information. I watched this "poet in the press box" successfully help promote several great athletes into All-American status. What I learned about public relations from that masterly professional was instrumental in my selection of the public relations field for my career. Nick Vista, who would ultimately succeed Stabley and become a PR legend in his own right, also was a student aide. Nick and I had many good times together, working side-by-side in the Sports Publicity office and at many athletic events.

Additional bonding with MSU occurred through my association with the Alpha Tau Omega fraternity and my "brothers by choice." Among them were Billy Wells and Dave Kaiser, each of whom were key in winning Rose Bowl football games for Michigan State—Wells in 1954 with two touchdown runs (game MVP; MSC 28-UCLA 20), and Kaiser in 1956 with a 41-yard field goal with seven seconds left in the game (MSU 17-UCLA 14). Kaiser would be named to the Rose Bowl Hall of Fame in 2000.

Another fraternity brother, Jack Breslin, was serving as Michigan State's student placement director during my time on campus. As an alum, he was an inspiration and helped us with fraternity activities whenever asked.

Living in East Lansing from 1937 through 1954, I witnessed the dramatic growth of Michigan State from a small college to a great international university. This trajectory into the academic and athletic big-time was propelled by the vision and drive of President John A. Hannah, the greatest university leader of the 20th century. It was an inspiration to watch this transformation, and it imprinted virtually everyone who lived it with great pride in Michigan State.

Later in life, my passion for Michigan State led to appointments as a member of the MSU Alumni Association national board, and as chair and vice-chair of the MSU Development Fund. It was during my service with these organizations that I saw the need for a comprehensive review of Michigan State history, and began work on this book in September of 1992.

Research on the early years of MSU history took place in the MSU Library Archives and Historical Collections. Opening books that dated back to 1850 was like opening the minds and thoughts of great Michigan State educators of the past. Interviews with all of the college deans, several faculty and past MSU presidents also took place on campus. This research involved more than 210 round-trips from Bloomfield Hills to East Lansing and back; more than 130 days spent in the University Archives and Historical Collections; and the taking of 5,000 pages of hand-written notes on MSU history.

Writing was done at my home in Bloomfield Hills, Michigan; at the family summer cabin in Northern Ontario on beautiful Lake Lauzon, near the town of Blind River; and at our winter retreat in Coronado, California.

My major concern in writing this book for the MSU family was to tell the stories of Michigan State University's excellence, leadership and achievement. It's my belief these year-by-year vignettes can engender even greater understanding of the unique Spartan Spirit which makes us proud of our university.

The profits from the publication of this volume will be given to Michigan State University.

Bruce McCristal,
Coronado, California
March 2004

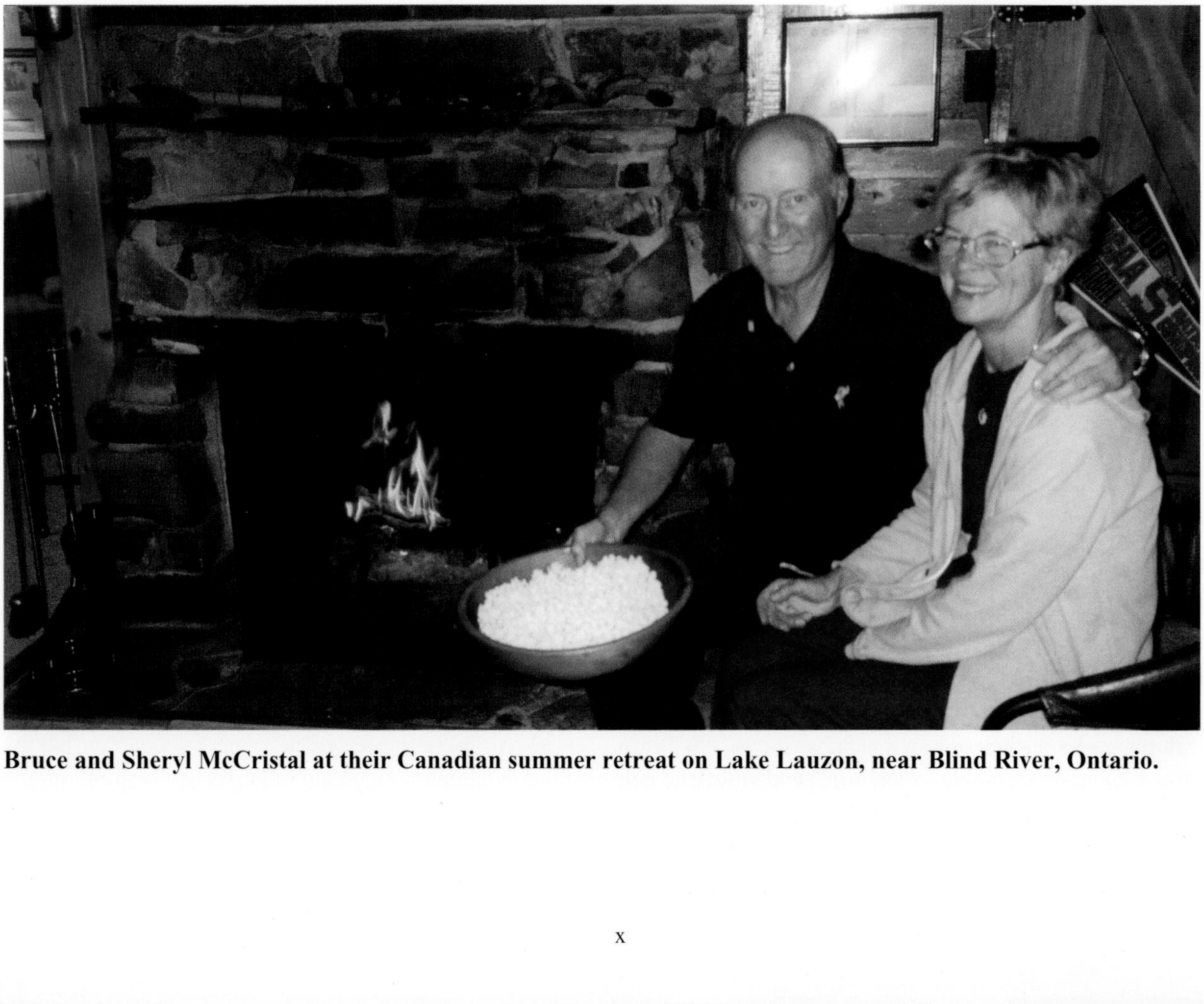

Bruce and Sheryl McCristal at their Canadian summer retreat on Lake Lauzon, near Blind River, Ontario.

Thanks to Those Who Made This Book Possible

This book would not have been possible without major help and encouragement from my wife Sheryl, and a number of generous Michigan State officers, deans, department heads, staff, and friends. I am in their debt and eternally grateful for their support.

Dr. Fred Honhart, director of MSU's Archives and Historical Collections, and his cordial, helpful staff provided invaluable information and guidance. Included were: Dorothy T. Frye, Carl Lee, Whitney Miller, Jeanine Mazak, Sarah Roberts, Portia Vescio, Maria Reviele, and Debbie Hettinger. During more than 130 days spent in the Archives, they tirelessly dug for, and produced needed historical information and photographs, and directed me to other vital sources.

Dr. Charles Webb, vice president for development, and Dr. Keith Williams, executive director of the MSU Alumni Association, both provided important sources of information and made key interviews possible.

Bob Bao, the energetic, outstanding editor of the *MSU Alumni Magazine* since 1983, was a vital help in telling the MSU story between 1983 and 2003. His organized writings, which always focus on the significant activities at MSU, provided a great deal of substantive information on the recent history of the university. Bob was consistently available and ever helpful.

Terry Denbow, vice president of University Relations, and his friendly staff, freely volunteered their help, researching answers to many questions about MSU. Jackie Fondren, executive staff assistant, amiably provided help and hospitality during my many visits. Terry generously provided me with a research desk for which I am most grateful.

John Lewandowski, assistant athletic director/media relations; Becky Olsen, sports information director, key assistant Paulette Martis, and Matt Larson opened the Sports Information files and greatly aided the hunt for detailed sports records, stories and photographs. Paulette's professional organization of MSU's athletic records files makes research there a pleasant chore. Her help went beyond expectations.

Book Reviewers—Seven loyal Spartans agreed to review the book for corrections and additions. It was an honor to have them give their time and effort to help improve the manuscript. Included were: Dr. Gordon Guyer, '50, M.S. '52, Ph.D. '53, MSU president emeritus; Dr. Marylee Davis, '74, Ph.D., secretary of the Board of Trustees emerita and education professor; Barbara Sawyer-Koch, M.A. '90, trustee emerita and former chair; Jack Shingleton, '48, trustee emeritus and placement director emeritus; Dr. Clarence Underwood, '61, M.A. '65, Ph.D. '82, director of athletics emeritus; Duane Vernon, '53, alumni award winner; and Nick Vista, '54, sports information director emeritus. I will be ever grateful to Duane Vernon who went to exceptional lengths in proof-reading and fact checking. He also offered continual encouragement.

Leigh Waltersdorf, manager of alumni records for the MSU Development Fund, who graciously helped many times with accurate alumni names and dates of graduation. Leigh's prodigious effort in building accurate alumni records will be invaluable to MSU for years to come.

Mike Raick, my computer expert and teacher and proprietor of *Be A Computer Whiz* (mdraick@hotmail.com), guided me many times through the tribulations of cyberspace. His advice and problem-solving were invaluable in producing this book.

Jack Seibold, MSU alum and author of the remarkable and prodigious 1,074-page *Spartan Sports Encyclopedia*, was generous in providing accurate information on all of Michigan State's individual NCAA champions, and other athletic facts.

MSU Presidents—Dr. Clifton Wharton, Dr. Edgar Harden, Dr. Walter Adams, Dr. Cecil Mackey, Dr. John A. DiBiaggio, Dr. Gordon Guyer, and M. Peter McPherson—were generous with their time and provided insights into the life and achievements of MSU.

Provosts—Dr. David Scott, and Dr. Lou Anna Simon were helpful with information on MSU's academic affairs.

Steven Webster, vice president for governmental affairs, helped with names of alumni who have served or are serving in the U.S. Congress.

The deans and staffs of MSU's 15 colleges, International Studies & Programs, Urban Affairs Programs; and the director and staff of the Honors College, were selfless in giving their time for interviews and providing any needed information about their particular academic disciplines. I am grateful to these academic leaders and their supporting staffs for the help and encouragement I received. It kept me going.

MSU College sources of information and help included:

College of Agriculture & Natural Resources—Dr. James Anderson, Dr. Fred L. Poston, and Dr. Jeffrey D. Armstrong, Dr. Sylvan Wittwer, Dr. Douglas C. Buhler, Dr. Ronald R. Perry, Dr. Daniel E. Keathley, Dr. Raymond Vlasin, Dr. Kenneth Verburg, Dr. Kirk Heinze, Dr. Mary Harvey, Dr. Maxine Ferris, Donald R. Jost, Dori Card, Kim Hunter, and Becky McAlpine.

College of Arts & Letters—Dr. John Eadie, Dr. Gordon Stewart, Dr. Wendy K. Wilkins; Jo-Ann Vandenbergh, and Barbara Harrison King.

The Eli Broad College of Business and the Eli Broad Graduate School of Management—Dr. Richard Lewis, Dr. James B. Henry, Dr. Robert B. Duncan, Dr. Donald Bowersox, and Kathy Walsh.

College of Communication Arts & Sciences—Dr. Erwin Bettinghaus, James D. Spaniolo, Linda Phillipich, Shirley Braden, Alice Smith, and Phyllis Kacos.

College of Education—Dr. Robert Floden, Dr. Carol Ames, Dr. Cassandra L. Book, Victor M. Inzunza, Kay Wood, and Cindy Casey.

College of Engineering—Dr. Theodore A. Bickert, Dr. Janie M. Fouke, Pam Cosner, and Laura Seeley.

College of Human Ecology—Dr. Julia R. Miller, Dr. Richard Lerner, Julie L. Alchin, Kathy Riel, and Christopher Surian.

College of Human Medicine—Dr. William S. Abbett, Dr. Glen C. Davis, Dr. Ruth B. Hoppe, and Karen Sutberry.

International Studies & Programs—Dr. John K. Hudzik, Dr. Edward Graham, Jay Rodman, and Diana Stetson.

James Madison College—Dr. Ken Waltzer, Dr. William B. Allen, Dr. Sherman W. Garnett, Kim Allan, and Jackie Lee Stewart.

Michigan State University College of Law—Dr. Terrence Blackburn, Chris Hammond, Cyndy Herfindahl, Linda Oswald, and Janet Harvey-Clark.

College of Natural Resources—Dr. Frank Hoppensteadt, Dr. George Leroi, Peter Carrington, and Linda Johnson.

College of Nursing—Dr. Kathleen Bond, Dr. Marilyn Rothert, Pam Martin, and Deborah J. Sudduth.

College of Osteopathic Medicine—Dr. Douglas Wood, Dr. Allen W. Jacobs, Dr. William D. Strampel, Pat Grauer, Colleen Kniffen, Nina Phelps, and Ann Cook.

College of Social Science—Dr. Kenneth E. Corey, Dr. Marietta L. Baba, J.B. McCombs, Maureen Cook, and Joann Elden.

The Honors College—Dr. Donald Lammers, Dr. Ronald C. Fisher, Kathy Rogers, and Tina Stokes.

College of Veterinary Medicine—Dr. John Tasker, Dr. Lonnie J. King, Linda Chadderdon, and Therese Ann Bunn.

Other helpful MSU people included:

Radiology Department—Dr. E. James Potchen, Chair; Dr. Tom Cooper, Assistant Chair; Kevin Henley.

Criminal Justice—Mary Lee Vandermoere.

Engineering & Architectural Services, Physical Plant—Robert Nestle, University Engineer; Lorena Griffin, Physical Plant Engineering Plan.

Planning & Budgets—Dave Byelich, Dee McKay, and Richard Jacobson.

Graduate Studies and Research—Dr. Percy Pierre.

MSU University Club—Richard Bruner.

National Superconducting Cyclotron Laboratory—Orilla McHarris, and Christian Murdock.

University Outreach—Dr. James Votruba.

Student Affairs—Dr. Moses Turner, and Dr. Lee June.

Campus Park & Planning—Jeffrey R. Kacos, Tom Kehler, Gary Parrott, and Karen Wenk.

Instructional Media Center—Steve Jowett and Harley Seeley.

Curator of the W.J. Beal Botanical Garden and Campus Woody Plant Collection—Dr. Frank Telewski.

Horticultural Demonstration Gardens—Douglas Badgero.

Broadcast Marketing—David Brown.

Helpful sources outside of MSU included:

Partners Book Distributors—Sam Spiegel.

Inner Workings (Book Publisher)—Barry Friedland.

The Printed Page (Book Designer)—Lisa Liddy.

City of East Lansing—Carol A. Parry.

Michigan Department of Natural Resources—Harold Herta, '74.

U.S. House of Representatives Historical Legislative Resource Center Library—Colleen Beyer, and Venice Smith.

My most important encouragement and support came from my wife Sheryl, who lived through more than a decade of trips to East Lansing for research and writing; listening to and reading many pages of MSU history; and living with a cluttered study and family room in our Bloomfield Hills, Michigan home. She went beyond what should be expected of anyone living through the birth of book. Without her love, suggestions, and forbearance, the book would not have been born.

Bruce McCristal
Bloomfield Hills, Michigan
June 2004

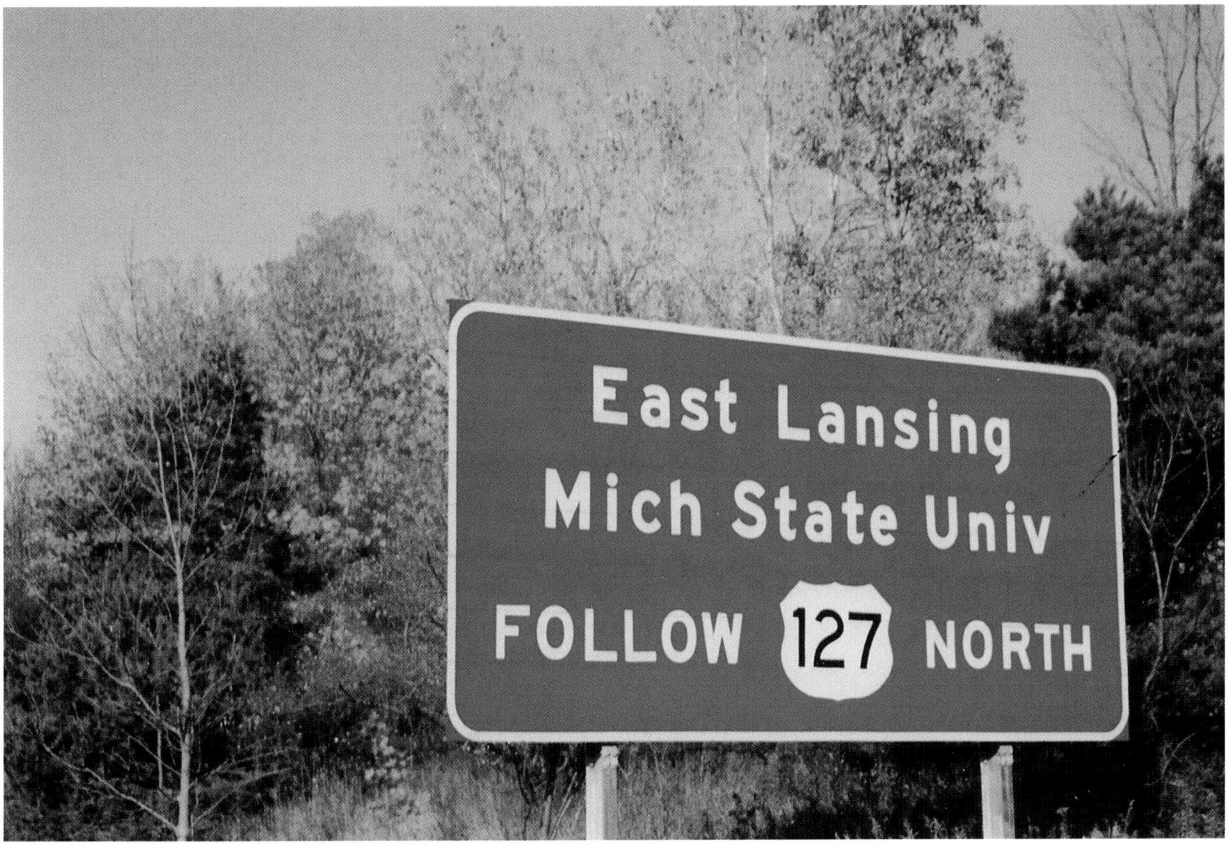

Interstate 96-West Sign Welcomes People to East Lansing and Michigan State University.

East Lansing, Michigan 48823

Founded 1907

Population: 46,525 (2000 Census)

42 Degrees, 44 Minutes North Latitude
84 Degrees, 26 Minutes West Longitude
819.13 Feet Above Sea Level

Michigan State University 48824, 48825

Founded 1855

378,000 Alumni—44,542 Students—4,402 Faculty—9,234 Supporting Staff (2003)

Michigan State's Six Names

Michigan State University—1964
Michigan State University of Agriculture and Applied Science—1955
Michigan State College of Agriculture and Applied Science—1925
Michigan Agriculture College—1909
The State Agricultural College—1861
The Agricultural College of the State of Michigan—1855

Dr. John A. Hannah, Class of 1923

Premier Leader of Higher Education in the 20th Century
Visionary Builder of the Modern Michigan State University
Selected by Six U.S. Presidents to Serve America

Dr. John Alfred Hannah (1902-1991), class of 1923, was the visionary, charismatic leader whose drive and will propelled Michigan State from a small state college to a great international university, known and respected around the globe. Hannah served Michigan State University for 46 years, the last 28 as president (1941-1969). He was the longest-serving president in MSU history.

In 1992, Dr. Ernest Boyer, president of the Carnegie Foundation for the Advancement in Teaching, identified Dr. John Hannah

"as a leader in this century who did more for higher education than any other person."

Dr. John A. Hannah, visionary builder of the modern Michigan State University, was its longest-serving president, 1941-1969. He has been recognized as America's premier leader in higher education in the 20th century. Six U.S. Presidents selected him to serve the nation.

This statement was made at the Association of Governing Boards (universities) annual meeting.

Six U.S. Presidents selected John Hannah to serve the nation—Roosevelt, Truman, Eisenhower, Kennedy, Johnson, and Nixon. President Roosevelt appointed him one of the planners for his White House Conference on Education. Hannah aided President Truman's Point Four Program of technical assistance to less developed areas of the world, which started in 1949. In this role, he was a member of the International Development Advisory Board. President Eisenhower named him Assistant Secretary of Defense for Manpower and Personnel in 1953.

Former Michigan Governor William Milliken stated, **"You will be hard pressed to find another individual whose contributions to American society and international understanding are greater than those of John Hannah.** There's no one I admire or respect more."

John Hannah resigned the MSU presidency in 1969 to become the **Administrator for the U.S. Agency for International Development.** John Macy, former assistant to U.S. Presidents Kennedy and Johnson, said, "By all accounts, **he was the most effective administrator in the history of the Agency for International Development.**"

U.S. President Dwight Eisenhower said of Dr. Hannah's service as U.S. Deputy Secretary of Defense for Personnel, **"It's not generally known, but he was as responsible as any one person for the success of the effort to achieve racial integration in our country's armed forces, both in the ranks and in military housing…I am proud he was an appointee of mine…"**

Hannah was appointed by President Eisenhower as the **first chairman of the U.S. Commission on Civil Rights** in January, 1957. Reverend Theodore M. Hesburgh, C.S.C., president of the University of Notre Dame, 1952-1987, who served on the commission wrote, "Hannah… chaired the body for 12 years. By 1962, it had become clear that **the nation resolved decisively to move towards an unbiased society, and in retrospect, many historians credit the forceful and effective leadership of Hannah with making the change possible."** (*MSU Alumni Magazine,* Winter, 1989).

Other international service by Hannah included:

- **Chairman, U.S. Section—Canadian/U.S.—Permanent Joint Defense Board**, 1954-1963.
- **An original incorporator of Education and World Affairs**, 1962, a private, non-profit educational organization. Purpose: enhance the capabilities of universities, colleges and schools of the U.S. in the area of education and world affairs, including the advancement of teaching and research.
- **Deputy Secretary General for the United Nations** in 1974, planning the World Food Conference in Rome.
- **Executive Director of the United Nations World Food Council**, 1975-1978.
- Key in organizing the **International Fund for Agricultural Development**, with more than $1 billion contributed by nations worldwide.
- **First Chairman, International Fertilizer Development Center**, 1974-1988, (Muscle Shoals, Alabama), a worldwide effort to increase food production in developing countries.
- **Winrock International Institute for Agricultural Development** board member, 1985. (Morrilton, Arkansas).

State service by Hannah included:

- **Michigan Constitutional Convention delegate**, 1961-1962.
- **Chair of the Advisory Committee for State of Michigan Civil Service Reform**, 1979.

National Educational Service

- **President, National Association of State Universities and Land-Grant Colleges**, 1949.

Leadership actions and innovations initiated by John Hannah at Michigan State included:

- Winning Michigan State's entry into the Big Ten Conference—1948.
- Pushing MSU's international outreach into a position of national leadership.
- Establishing the position of Dean of International Programs—first in the nation, 1957.
- Making MSU a leader in Continuing Education.
- Creating the College of Communication Arts in 1956—first of its kind in the nation.
- Establishing the School of Labor and Industrial Relations in 1956—one of the first in the country.
- Directing the establishment of the Honors College in 1958—first among all 74 of America's land-grant colleges and universities.
- Co-Founder of MSU-Oakland, now Oakland University (Rochester, Michigan) in 1957.
- Creating the innovative "Living-Learning" residence halls, which incorporate classrooms, libraries, and faculty offices—1961.
- Establishing MSU's College of Human Medicine in 1964, and the College of Osteopathic Medicine in 1969—both national leaders in producing primary care physicians. With the addition of the these two schools, MSU became the only university in the nation with three medical colleges—Veterinary Medicine, Human Medicine, and Osteopathic Medicine.
- Establishing small residential colleges within the large university. The first was Justin Morrill College in 1965. In 1967, James Madison College, and Lyman Briggs College were launched.
- Winning Michigan State's admission into the prestigious Association of American Universities—a select group of 62 North American institutions known for their premier professional graduate and research programs.

Major Awards

USA Medal of Freedom, 1954—the nation's highest civilian award.

Lifetime Achievement Presidential End Hunger Award sponsored by the Agency for International Development in 1986.

Award of Distinguished Service in International Agriculture, 1983, by the Association of U.S. University Directors of International Agricultural Programs.

Honorary Degrees

Thirty honorary Doctors Degrees were awarded to John Hannah, including the Universities of Michigan, Ohio State, Florida, Maryland, Arizona State, Maine, South Dakota, Howard, Nigeria, Central Michigan, Northern Michigan, Western Michigan, and Michigan State.

"I do the very best I know how…"

A photograph of President Abraham Lincoln hanging on the wall behind John Hannah's desk carried the following Lincoln quote, "I do the very best I know how, the very best I can, and I mean to keep on doing so until the end. If the end brings me out all right, what is said against me won't amount to anything. If the end brings me out wrong, ten angels swearing I was right would make no difference."

"Only people are important…"

John Hannah's signature belief was, "Only people are important, especially poor people." His faithfulness to this principle, truly made Michigan State the "People's University."

A Sesquicentennial Salute:

One Hundred-Fifty Highlights of Michigan State History

▼ **Michigan State was the key leader in establishing America's land-grant colleges (74) which have fostered the widespread democratization of higher education in America.** MSU was the first land-grant college in America, and the model for all others. Joseph Williams, the school's first president, "furnished a good part of the materials for U.S. Representative Justin S. Morrill's speech" (to Congress), which helped sell the Morrill Act creating America's land-grant colleges. Williams also led a national communications campaign to influence U. S. Representatives to pass the bill. These land-grant colleges, which now number 74, opened the door of higher education to the children of farmers, laborers, and all classes across the nation.

▼ **Michigan State was prominent in expanding the mission of universities beyond teaching and research to include service or outreach.** The college was a prime mover in reaching out and sharing newly developed knowledge with the citizens of the state, nation and world, beginning in 1872.

Peter McGrath, past president of the National Association of State Universities and Land-Grant Colleges stated:

"Michigan State is a model and inspiration for the international public service role of our nation's universities."

Today, public service is called outreach. Because of the benefits to society, outreach is now embedded in the mission of higher education in America. (See chapter on International Leader in Outreach, page 291).

▼ **Michigan State was a primary leader in helping establish America's Agricultural Experiment Stations which have been instrumental in applying science to agriculture—making America a world leader in agricultural production as well as in combating crop and farm animal diseases.**

Edwin Willits, the school's fourth president, played an important role in the passage of the Agricultural Experiment Station Act (Hatch Act) in 1887, spending six weeks in Washington, D.C. in 1886 promoting its passage.

Jonathan Snyder, MSU's seventh president, visited Washington, D.C. many times from 1903 to 1906 seeking passage of the Adams Act, which bolstered agricultural research at the nation's land-grant college experiment stations.

▼ **Dr. John A. Hannah, MSU President from 1941-1969, was identified in 1992 "as a leader in this century who did more for higher education than any other person."** The statement was made by Dr. Ernest Boyer, president of the Carnegie Foundation for the Advancement in Teaching at the Association of Governing Boards (of universities) annual meeting. (See Hannah profile on page xiv).

▼ **Seven MSU faculty members have been elected to the National Academy of Sciences—the premier U.S. scientific society and advisor to U.S. Presidents and the U.S. Congress.** (See An Overview Chapter on MSU Leadership, Excellence, and Achievement—1855-2004, page 1).

▼ **Michigan State is the only U.S. university with three medical schools—College of Human Medicine, College of Osteopathic Medicine, and the College of Veterinary Medicine. MSU also has a College of Nursing.**

▼ **MSU graduates have been elected presidents of colleges or universities on at least 107 occasions,** including the following universities—Texas-Austin, Wisconsin-Madison, Nebraska, Alabama, Illinois, Missouri, Massachusetts, Maine, Idaho, Florida State, Colorado State, North Dakota, and New Mexico State. (See chapter on Alumni Achievement, page 292).

▼ **Four MSU graduates have been elected State Governors—George Ariyoshi, '49—Hawaii; James Blanchard, '64, M.A. '65—Michigan; Anthony Earl, '58—Wisconsin; and John Engler, '71—Michigan.** In 1982, Governors Ariyoshi, Blanchard and Earl were serving at the same time. No other university had more state governors.

- **Michigan State students have won national and international championships in 19 different disciplines**—Mathematics...chemical engineering...chamber music...computer programming...journalism... culinary arts...advertising...engineering...debate...oratory...business...business marketing...economics... investing...waste management...international moot court competition... national law student tax challenge...dairy judging...and the college bowl. (See chapter—MSU Students Win National and International Championships, page 315).

- **MSU's nuclear science research and curriculum was vying with the Massachusetts Institute of Technology in 2004 as the top program in America. And, MSU was producing one in every ten nuclear physics Ph.D.'s. in the U.S.**

- **Michigan State Alumni have led hundreds of corporations. MSU graduates have been CEO, chairman, vice chairman, or president of the following corporations**—General Motors, Ford Motor Co., Daimler-Chrysler, Marriott Hotels, Hilton Hotels, Sheraton-North America Hotels, Northwestern Mutual Life, Miller Brewing Co., Ryder Truck, Gerber Products, American Hospital Supply Corp., Gimbel's Department Stores, Lear Siegler, Inc., Guident Corp., Wal-Mart, Libbey-Owen Ford, SCM Allied Paper, Fruehauf Corp., Janus Fund, MVP.com, Herman Miller, Campbell Soup Co., J.C. Penny Co., Burger King, Maytag, Borders Books, Dow Corning, and many others. (See chapter—Alumni Achievement, page 292).

- **Michigan State scientists have developed or released more than 240 varieties of grains, fruits, and vegetables, adding greatly to the world's food supply.** In addition, MSU can be credited with development of the first hybrid corn, creation of the Michigan sugar beet industry, producing the most widely grown peach, greatly increasing bean production, making Michigan No. 1 in blueberries, increasing wheat production by 50 percent, and developing apricots that would grow east of the Rocky Mountains. (For many more examples, see chapter on Feeding the Nation and the World, page 248).

- **"Firsts" are an MSU Tradition**—Michigan State constructed America's first building used solely as a botanical laboratory; first horticultural laboratory; first agricultural laboratory; first bacteriology laboratory; and the first building devoted entirely to chemical work.

- **Ten MSU faculty members have been considered "Fathers" of major discoveries or developments**—A few examples: "Father" of scientific agriculture, "Father" of hybrid corn, "Father" of American horticulture, "Father" of homogenized milk, and "Father" of cisplatin and carboplatin, the most-prescribed anti-cancer drugs in the U.S. (See chapter—The Spirit of Michigan State—An Overview Chapter on MSU Leadership, Excellence and Achievement—1855-2004, page 1).

- **MSU research has produced major disease eradication and crop protection benefits for the nation.** A few examples: conquering Brucellosis (undulant fever), eliminating the swine disease parakeratosis, curbing mint disease which was hindering the chewing gum industry, developing disease-resistant wheat, and creating 2-4-D, which controls broad leaf weeds that hurt crops. (See chapter on Feeding the Nation and World, page 248).

- **MSU students led all U.S. public universities in winning 13 Rhodes Scholarships between 1972 and 1997.** Michigan State also is a top producer of Churchill, Truman, Marshall, Mitchell, and Goldwater Scholars as well as winners of National Science Foundation fellowships. (See chapter on Academic Excellence A Way of Life, page 318).

- **Michigan State became America's first agricultural college when it was founded in 1855.**

- **America's first course in scientific agriculture was offered at Michigan State in 1865.**

- **One in every 131 college graduates in the U.S. is a Michigan State alumnus.** (378,000 living alumni divided into 49.5 million college graduates in the nation—2000 U.S. Census).

- **MSU is a national leader in Minority Opportunity**—A few examples: first major university in the U.S. to elect an African-American as president; first university in the nation to accept American-born Japanese as students during World War II; one of the first universities in the nation to open its doors to the sons and daughters of migrant workers—in 1972. (See chapter—MSU: National Leader in Minority Opportunity, page 321).

- **MSU women and minorities have broken many employment barriers**—The first Asian-American to be elected a state governor; the first African-American to be elected CEO of the U.S. Olympic Committee; the first woman to be selected a member of the Federal Reserve Bank Board; the first woman career foreign service officer to be named a U.S.

ambassador to a foreign country; and the first African-American woman to head a U.S. medical school. (See chapter—MSU: National Leader in Minority Opportunity, page 321).

- **MSU administrators and faculty have helped found and develop three overseas universities—University of Ryukus on Okinawa, University of Nigeria in Africa, and the National University of Science & Technology in Pakistan.** MSU also has been a major partner in establishing universities, colleges, schools, and departments in 20 other nations. (See chapter—International Studies and Programs, page 288).

- **Dr. I. Forest Huddleson, class of 1925, research professor in bacteriology, won the International Veterinary Congress Prize in 1940 for his work to eliminate undulant fever.** Dr. Harry W. Jakeman, chair of the executive board of the American Veterinary Medical Association, stated in the citation, "You have contributed liberally and practically not only to the livestock industry of the world, but also to the protection of human health."

- **MSU was the national leader in formalizing student volunteerism in 1962.** By 1968, Michigan State's Student Education Corps was the largest in the nation with 2,200 volunteers. They tutored and taught young people in south central Michigan. In 1969, **James Tanck,** director of Student Volunteer Programs at MSU, and an alum, was loaned to the White House to help develop a national plan to encourage volunteer programs at the nation's colleges and universities. (See chapter—The Spirit of Michigan State—An Overview Chapter on MSU Leadership, Excellence, and Achievement, page 1).

- **MSU professors and researchers have won hundreds of national and international awards.** The spectrum of honors includes: Pulitzer Prizes, the Peabody Award, Presidential Young Investigator Awards, National Awards from Britain, Sweden, France, Germany, and Russia; Guggenheim Fellowships, U.S. Presidential Faculty Award, Fulbright Awards, Author and Publishers Award, and the Alexander von Humboldt Foundation Award, considered the most prestigious honor for agricultural research in the U.S. (See An Overview Chapter on MSU Leadership, Excellence, and Achievement—1855-2004, page 1).

- **Michigan State could be called "Environmental U."** In the 1870s, the school was a leader in protecting the environment and the public from hazards. **Dr. Robert C. Kedzie and Dr. William J. Beal** called for tree planting to replenish Michigan's forests in the 1870s. In the same decade, Dr. Kedzie fought to protect citizens from highly flammable lighting oils and arsenic-laden Paris Green, a coloring agent used in clothing and wallpaper.

  MSU's Pesticide Research Center (now Center for Integrated Plant Systems), was dedicated in 1970 and led national efforts to seek safe methods for protecting food crops and the public. **The National Food Safety and Toxicology Center**, dedicated on campus in 1997, put MSU in a national leadership position in keeping the country's food supply safe. (See chapter—The Spirit of Michigan State—An Overview Chapter on MSU Leadership, Excellence, and Achievement, page1).

- **MSU, founded in 1855, was the first Michigan college to admit women students—in 1870.** It took Oxford University in England, informally founded in 1180, until 1884 to admit women.

- **The Michigan State campus is one of the world's great arboretums.** The 5,198-acre campus, often called one of the most beautiful in the nation, features 7,800 varieties of trees, shrubs, plants, and flowers. The Beal Botanical Garden, started in 1873, is a living laboratory with more than 5,000 species and varieties of plantings. The garden is the oldest of its kind in America. Unique at MSU are four unspoiled natural areas—the Sanford Natural Area (35 acres), the Red Cedar Natural Area (76 acres), the Baker Woodlot (78 acres), and the Toumey Forest (24 acres). (See chapter—The Campus Beautiful, page 338).

- **Liberty Hyde Bailey, Class of 1882, "Father" of American Horticulture, was the most prolific agricultural writer in history, authoring 75 books and editing 117 others.** Bailey was asked by U.S. President Theodore Roosevelt to chair the new Commission on Country Life in 1907. His commission conducted a national survey and produced the "Report of the Commission on Country Life." This resounding report resulted in passage of the Smith-Lever Act, establishing the Cooperative Extension Services of America's agricultural colleges, and the national 4-H programs. Moreover, the report helped initiate the U.S. Parcel Post system, Rural Free Delivery (Mail), rural electrification, and agricultural education in public schools. (See Bailey biographical sketch, page 34).

- **One of the Nation's first Forestry programs—four years of study—was introduced at Michigan State in 1902.** Among many research contributions, MSU forestry scientists have restored Michigan's Christmas tree industry and developed a system of provanance (improved genotypes) testing that is used worldwide in tree-improvement and testing.

- **MSU developed the "American Spruce"planted at the White House.** Dr. James Hanover developed the tri-hybrid spruce tree (red, white, and blue), named the "American Spruce" in 1976 for America's Bi-Centennial. These trees have been planted on the White House grounds.

- **Dr. Albert J. Cook, class of 1862, and nationally known entomologist, was a U.S. leader in the development of insect spraying to protect crops. The first use of fungicides in America to protect apple trees occurred at Michigan State in 1889.** Professor Levi Rawson Taft introduced the new technique, which dramatically reduced disease in apple trees and helped save Michigan's orchards.

- **Fred P. Alderman, class of 1927 and 1927 track captain, won the 1927 NCAA 100-yard and 220-yard dash titles—the first NCAA individual titles for any Michigan State athlete. In 1928, Alderman became the Spartans' first Olympic gold medal winner as a member of the U.S. 1,600-meter relay team which set an Olympic record of 3:41.1 at the Amsterdam Games.**

- **Dr. Michael F. Thomashow, professor crop and soil sciences and of micro-biology, won the 2001 Alexander von Humboldt Foundation Award, considered the most prestigious recognition for agricultural research in America.** His work held the promise of improving plants' tolerance to cold, and other stresses such as salt and drought. Thomashow is a member of the National Academy of Sciences, the premier scientific society that is advisor to U.S. Presidents and the U.S. Congress.

- **Michigan State's top-ranked School of Hospitality Business was founded in 1927—the second hotel, restaurant and resort management school in the nation.** Graduates of the school have been presidents of Marriott Hotels and Resorts, Hilton Hotels, Sheraton Hotels-North America, Holiday Inn's Food & Lodging Division, Omni Hotels; and general managers of such high-profile hospitality properties as the Broadmoor Hotel-Colorado Springs, Colorado; Boca Raton Hotel & Club—Boca Raton, Florida; Waldorf-Astoria—New York, N.Y.; Raffles International-Singapore; Walt Disney World Hotels—Orlando, Florida; Colonial Williamsburg—Virginia; and the Venetian Hotel—Las Vegas, Nevada. (See Alumni Achievement chapter, page 292).

- **The nation's first, and leading School of Criminal Justice, was founded at Michigan State in 1935 as the School of Police Administration.** Graduates of the school have included two directors of the U.S. Secret Service; the domestic chief of INTERPOL, the international police organization; directors of the Michigan State Police; the chiefs of police of many American cities, and heads of security at corporations.

- **Lyman J. Briggs, Class of 1893, was appointed by U.S. President Franklin Roosevelt in 1939 to lead a top-secret investigation on the feasibility of atomic power and weapons for the nation.** This effort ultimately led to the development of U.S. atomic weapons, which helped end World War II. Briggs and Paul Heyl helped develop the earth-inductor compass which guided Charles Lindbergh's Spirit of St. Louis aircraft from New York to Paris in 1927. Briggs, director of the U.S. Bureau of Standards, was a member of the National Academy of Sciences, and received the U.S. Presidential Medal for Merit. The Lyman J. Briggs School in the College of Natural Science, which is devoted to science education, is named in Briggs honor. (See biographical sketch on Briggs, page 84).

- **Fay Gillis Wells, Class of 1929, was the first woman in the U.S. to parachute from an aircraft—becoming the first female member of the "Caterpillar Club," named for the silkworm that produced the silk for parachutes.** She became a White House correspondent for Storer Broadcasting Co.

- **Harold Furlong, Class of 1918, became Michigan State's first Congressional Medal of Honor winner, the nation's highest recognition it can pay a soldier.** He was a World War I hero, one of only 50 recipients of the award in WWI. **First Lt. Harry L. Martin, Class of 1936, was posthumously awarded the Congressional Medal of Honor** in 1948 for his bravery as a Marine in World War II. **Oscar Johnson, a Michigan State short course graduate in 1948, also won the Congressional Medal of Honor for bravery in WWII.**

- **Ray Stannard Baker, Class of 1889, was Michigan State's first Pulitzer Prize winner.** He won the award in 1940 for his monumental eight-volume *Woodrow Wilson: Life and Letters,* which was published sequentially from 1927 to 1939. Baker was a confidant of U.S. Presidents Theodore Roosevelt and Woodrow Wilson. Six MSU graduates have won Pulitzer Prizes. (See sketch on Baker, page 87).

- **Captain James Gibb, Jr., Class of 1938, won the Distinguished Flying Cross in World War II** for assisting in the rescue mission to bring General Douglas MacArthur out of the Philippines. Nine MSU graduates have won the Distinguished Flying Cross for aerial bravery in WWII and Vietnam.

Michael Thompson, Class of 1970, won two Distinguished Flying Crosses for aerial achievement in Southeast Asia.

- **Florence Hall, Class of 1909, headed the U.S. Women's Land Army of 60,000 farm women during World War II. This nationwide "Crops Corps" worked to prevent a food shortage.**
- **6,379 Spartans served in the U.S. Armed Forces in WWII; 316 were killed; 1,016 received medals or citations.**
- **Joseph Zichis, Class of 1932, M.S. '34, Ph.D. '36, was among the first to develop the chick vaccine for equine encephalitis,** and to propagate hog cholera virus in sheep and rabbits, circa 1944. He showed that antibodies were effective in the prevention and treatment of viral diseases.
- **Howard R. Smith, Class of 1895, "pioneered the program of bovine tuberculosis eradication in the U.S.** By 1951, through his work, cattle condemnations for tuberculosis had been reduced by 98 percent, and the human death rate from non-respiratory tuberculosis, largely of bovine origin, had been reduced by 94 percent." (*MSU Magazine,* September, 1962). He was a professor at the Universities of Minnesota and Nebraska.
- **The nation's first course in Packaging** was offered in the College of Agriculture in 1952. This course evolved into the School of Packaging, the international leader in the field, and the first in the nation to offer graduate degrees. (See chapter on College of Agriculture and Natural Resources, page 245).
- **MSU President John A. Hannah stated in 1952, the Michelite (Michigan elite) bean, developed "by Michigan State crop scientists has resulted in more income for Michigan farmers than has been spent by the college on agricultural research from 1887 to the present time."** (See chapter—Feeding the Nation and the World, page 248).
- **MSU's WKAR-TV was the first educational TV station east of the Mississippi when it began broadcasting on January 15, 1954. In 2004, it stood as the nation's second-oldest public television station.** WKAR's Ready To Learn Service provides more than 600 workshops to parents, teachers and childcare providers each year, aiding 8,000 children throughout Michigan. WKAR-TV was the first to televise an official session of the Michigan legislature. (Story by Jeanie Croope, '73, M.A. '81; *MSU Alumni Magazine,* Winter, 2004).
- **Jaw-Kai Wang, M.C. '56, Ph.D. '58, won the 1991 American Society of Agricultural Engineers' Kishida International Award,** given for professional efforts that improve food production, living conditions, and/or educational levels outside the United States.
- **The College of Communication Arts was established July 1, 1955—the first of its kind in America.** Today, as the College of Communication Arts & Sciences, it is ranked first or second in the nation for its research and quality of programs in advertising, audiology and speech sciences, communication, telecommunication, and journalism. **The College of Communication Arts & Sciences led the nation in scholarly presentations** at the 1989 convention of the Association for Education in Journalism and Mass Communications, and in 2004 remained a center for forward-focused communications research.
- **MSU established the nation's first Office of International Programs and named the first dean of International Programs in the U.S.—Professor Glen L. Taggart—in 1957.** MSU is a national leader in international education with 193 study abroad programs reaching into more than 60 nations on all seven continents. In the 2000-2001 academic year, MSU led the nation with 1,835 students studying abroad. In 2003, MSU had some 3,000 foreign students from 126 countries studying on campus. In addition, some 750 foreign scholars were at MSU doing research and sharing their knowledge and findings in classrooms. **An *Educational Researcher* 1988 report ranked Michigan State number one in international programs**.
- **MSU established the first undergraduate Honors College at any of America's 74 land-grant universities in 1957. Dr. Stanley Idzerda was named its director.** *Money Magazine* in 1994 ranked MSU's Honors College among the finest in the nation. In 2004, under the direction of Dr. Ronald C. Fisher, enrollment in the Honors College reached 2,575.
- **Dr. Edward R. Garrett, '41, M.S. and Ph.D. from MSU, won the 1963 Ebert Prize—the nation's highest pharmaceutical research award—**for "the best published research in all the pharmaceutical sciences" by the American Pharmaceutical Association.
- **In 1959—the year in which Alaska and Hawaii became U.S. States—MSU admitted Miss Alaska, and Miss Hawaii as students. Diane Lee,** freshman liberal arts major entered MSU-Oakland as the 1959 Miss Alaska, a title won in America's Junior Miss Pageant. **Patricia Visser,** freshman business major,

enrolled at East Lansing as the 1959 Miss Hawaii, a title won in the Miss Universe competition.

▼ **MSU led the nation in building "Living-Learning"Residence Halls in 1961.** MSU set a national trend by building classrooms, libraries, laboratories, faculty offices, and assembly areas into new residence halls. By taking many classes inside their own dorms, student learning was made easier and more convenient, creating a small college atmosphere inside a large international university.

▼ **MSU became the first public university to sponsor a program of National Merit Scholarships to attract National Merit Scholars in 1962.** In the fall of 1963, MSU led all universities in the nation with 195 National Merit Scholars enrolled. Following MSU were Harvard—95, MIT—66, Stanford—61, Princeton—50, and Yale—46. By 1972, MSU led all of the nation's universities for the eighth consecutive year with 564 National Merit Scholars enrolled. For the decade 1967-1977, MSU led the nation in National Merit Scholar enrollment. MSU continues to attract large numbers of these scholars.

▼ **MSU pioneered the development of a "Head Start" project, preceding federal legislation to create such a program to improve the early education of culturally deprived children.** Two MSU faculty members were tapped as consultants for the National Planning Committee for Project Head Start.

▼ **Michigan State appointed the nation's first university Ombudsman in 1967** to listen to student complaints about academics and regulations. **James D. Rust** was named the first Ombudsman. In 1969, the Ombudsman stated, "Many of the problems bedeviling the university would disappear or be much mitigated if everyone involved would practice the healing arts of courtesy and kindness."

▼ **Dr. Alfred Day Hershey, B.S. '30, Ph.D. '34, shared the Nobel Prize in 1969 in physiology and medicine.** Dr. Hershey, Max Delbruk of Caltech, and Salvador E. Luria of MIT were called "the three leading figures of bacteriophage research," and were cited "as the original founders of the modern science of molecular biology."

▼ **The College of Osteopathic Medicine was established in 1969** by the Michigan Legislature to help remedy Michigan's shortage of primary care physicians. **Dr. Myron S. Magen was named dean. It was the first state-assisted and university-based Osteopathic College in the nation, and, as such, became the "Flagship" Osteopathic College in the U.S.**

▼ **MSU ranked first in the nation among public universities in National Science Foundation (NSF) awards won during the three-year period—1969-1971**—with the University of Iowa. In 1974, MSU won 18 NSF awards, first among all public universities in the country. MSU has continued to be a national leader in NSF scholarship awards.

▼ **MSU established the first Day Care Center in the Big Ten** for children of married students in 1971.

▼ **Michigan State has won six Big Ten All-Sports titles—1954, 1958, 1962, 1966, 1967, and 1971.** Spartan athletic teams have finished second in the All-Sports competition eleven times, and third, three times.

▼ **Michigan State was the first university in the U.S. to provide medical education to both M.D.s and Doctors of Osteopathy. MSU led U.S. medical education by teaching behavioral sciences in both the College of Human Medicine and the College of Osteopathic Medicine.**

▼ **Ivan Lahaie, '79, was named the Outstanding Radar Engineer of 1991** by the Institute of Electrical & Electronics Engineers. He developed the "passive sensor," which did not use any beams that could alert an enemy that they were being "watched."

▼ **MSU ranked first in the nation in the number of women enrolled on a single campus in the fall of 1972.** MSU's female enrollment was 19,745, followed by Ohio State at 17,635.

▼ **MSU established an Office of Handicapped Students in the fall of 1972 under the direction of James Hamilton, assistant provost for Special Programs.** It was one of the first in the U.S.

▼ **MSU Trustees opened the door to sons and daughters of migrant workers in Michigan in 1972.** They approved a plan making students eligible for "in-state" tuition, provided their parents were employed for a minimum of two months each year for three of the past five years.

▼ **Michigan State's doctoral program for training university administrators was ranked tops in the nation in 1973 and continues as a leader.** Directors and faculty of student personnel programs at 20 universities were surveyed and voted MSU number one. MSU graduates have been elected presidents of colleges or universities on at least 107 occasions.

- **Michigan State's dormitory system was voted No. 1 in the nation** by institutional management competitors nationwide and gave MSU the Award of Distinction in 1973. The Department of Dormitories and Food Services won an Ivy Award from *Institutions/ Volume Feeding* magazine for the quality of its residence hall meals in 1973. **In 1984, MSU's Division of Housing and Food Services won the grand prize for residence hall menus in the National Association of College and University Food Service Menu Competition. In 1986, *Change* magazine ranked MSU's residence halls as "best in the nation"** with Yale University's. MSU is home to the largest residence hall system in America—37 dormitories.

- **Sixty-Five MSU faculty members were serving as presidents of various national professional and academic organizations in 1974.**

- **MSU was selected to develop the first network of international rehabilitation centers in 1974.** Michigan State was chosen as the site by 50 representatives from health agencies, government and industry, because of its leadership in disability programs, research and international outreach.

- **MSU and its College of Agriculture & Natural Resources were leading the fight against world hunger in 1974-1975 and continue to do so.** MSU President Emeritus John A. Hannah led the United Nations World Food Conference in Rome in November, 1974. MSU President Clifton Wharton was head of the Food Advisory Panel created by the U.S. Congress, and Dr. Sylvan Wittwer, MSU's assistant dean of Agriculture, was serving as Chairman of the Board on Agriculture and Renewable Resources of the National Academy of Sciences.

- **MSU's College of Agriculture & Natural Resources was ranked # 1 Internationally in 1976**—topping 57 other U.S. universities in a University of Minnesota survey. The rating was based on 1) Number of foreign students; 2) Number of foreign visiting professors; 3) Number of participants supported by the U.S. Agency for International Development; 4) Number of faculty on overseas assignments; 5) Number of faculty with overseas experience; 6) Number of faculty carrying on international research; 7) Number of campus training programs for foreign groups; and 8) Number of cooperative programs with foreign schools. Today, MSU's College of Agriculture & Natural Resources remains an international leader.

- **MSU's Department of Park & Recreation Resources was named number one in the nation in 1980** by a University of Maryland survey of 250 universities that had outdoor resources and park management programs. MSU continues to lead in this field.

- **MSU dedicated the National Superconducting Cyclotron Laboratory—the world's first—in September, 1982.** Dr. Henry Blosser, director of the laboratory, stated, "This cyclotron and this laboratory will go on to be the leading center in the world for research in the present frontier of nuclear physics."

- **The U.S. Department of Education awarded its Certificate of Excellence for Research on Teaching to Michigan State in 1983.** It was described as a "one-of-a-kind" award by the Department of Education.

- **MSU students won the National Invitational College Bowl Championship for the second consecutive year in 1983,** defeating 17 other university teams, including five from the Big Ten. MSU was the only university to have won the title more than once. Ability to answer questions on virtually any subject determined the winning team.

- **Morton B. Panish, M.S. '52, Ph.D. '54, senior scientist at Bell Laboratories, was inducted into the National Academy of Engineering and won Japan's $61,000 Computer and Communications Award in 1986.** Panish's work on hetero-structure lasers with Japanese scientist Izuo Hagashi led to laser printers, bar code readers, digital signals in CD players, auto-focus cameras, and fiber-optic communication. Panish held 12 patents and had published 140 technical papers.

- **Donald F. Keck, '62, M.S. '64, Ph.D. '67, Corning Glass Works scientist developed, with two other researchers, a method for transmitting laser light through optical fiber in 1989.**

- **The World's first medical superconducting cyclotron was designed by MSU physicist Dr. Henry Blosser, and built at MSU's National Superconducting Cyclotron Laboratory in 1990.** It was delivered to Harper Hospital in Detroit to provide an efficient, inexpensive method of neutron therapy for the treatment of cancers that resist conventional radiation.

- **Two MSU graduates were elected to lead General Motors Corporation in 1990. Robert C. Stempel, MBA '70, became chairman and CEO, and Robert J. Schultz, '53, MBA '69, was selected vice chairman.** MSU graduates also have served as CEO and vice chairman of Ford Motor Company, and presidents of Daimler-Chrysler, Mazda Motor-Japan, Porsche

Cars-North America, and Toyota Motor Manufacturing-North America. (See chapter on Alumni Achievement).

- **Joseph Penicone, assistant professor of radiology, and James Siebert, chief engineer for MSU's radiology department, pioneered a method using superconducting magnets and radio waves to give physicians a picture of the body's blood flow from any angle.**

- **Eli Broad, Class of 1954, founder and CEO of Kaufman & Broad, Inc., gave $20 million to the College of Business in 1991—the largest private gift to a public university up to that time.** Since then, Broad has continued to generously support MSU with major gifts. The College of Business and the Graduate School of Management have been named in Broad's honor.

- **The third and final U.S. Presidential Debate of 1992, staged by MSU at the university's Wharton Center, featured President George H.W. Bush, William J. Clinton, and Ross Perot. It drew the largest debate global TV audience in history—nearly one billion people.** The event was praised by the National Debate Commission and press corps. They said MSU had provided the best-organized, smoothest running debate venue in their experience.

- **Dr. Chris Somerville, MSU plant scientist, and colleagues, discovered how to produce plastics from plants. *Time* magazine ranked their work among the top ten stories of 1992.**

- **MSU First Lady Joanne McPherson led the establishment of MSU Safe Place (MSU's Domestic Violence Shelter)—the first on-campus facility of its kind in the nation.**

- **MSU's International Travel/Study Program was named one of the three best in the nation by the Association of Continuing Higher Education in 1994.** MSU's Annual Odyssey to Oxford University in England, developed by Dr. Charles McKee, is considered a national model.

- **Three Spartans were owners of professional athletic teams in 1994. Drayton McLane, MBA '59,** vice chairman of Wal-Mart stores, was owner of the Houston Astros baseball team. **Harley Hotchkiss, '51**, owner of Spartan Resources in Calgary, Alberta, was part owner of the Calgary Flames NHL hockey team. **Earvin "Magic" Johnson, former MSU All-American,** Los Angeles Laker star and business entrepreneur, was part owner of the Los Angeles Lakers NBA basketball team.

- **The staff of Michigan State's daily newspaper—The *State News*—has won the National Pacemaker Award for the outstanding college newspaper in America eight times—more than any other university**.

- **H-Net, which supported more than 100 free electronics, interactive humanities and social science newsletters around the globe, was created at MSU in the early 1990s to bring together the world's top scholars in those fields.** H-Net is housed in the College of Arts & Letters.

- **MSU scientists and educators won the "Computer Software Innovation of the Year" honor at the Discover Awards for Technological Innovations conference in 1995.** They created the Personal Communicator, a hyper-media CD-ROM software program to enhance deaf students' communication with others. Leading team members included **Carrie Heeter**, director of MSU's Communication Technology Laboratory; **David Stewart**, associate professor for special education; and **Patrick Dickson**, professor of educational psychology.

- **The College of Education's graduate programs in elementary and secondary education were rated best in the nation for the tenth consecutive year in 2004 by *U.S. News & World Report.*** Overall, the college had eight graduate programs ranked in the top nine.

- **Steve Smith, former MSU basketball All-American, Atlanta Hawks star, and U.S. Olympic gold medal winner on Dream Team III, gave $2.5 million to MSU for its new Student-Athlete Academic Support Center in 1997. The facility has been named for his mother, Clara Bell Smith.** The gift was the largest ever given to an American university by a professional athlete.

- **The National Voice Library—with 8,000 recordings dating to the beginnings of sound recording—was brought to MSU in 1962 by Dr. Richard C. Chapin, Director of MSU Libraries.** Chapin persuaded G. Robert Vincent, collector and curator of the nation's foremost voice library, to locate it permanently at MSU. It is housed in the university's main library.

- **Stanley Ikenberry, M.A. '57, Ph.D. '60, regent professor and president emeritus of the University of Illinois, was elected president of the American Council on Education in 1997. In this position, Ikenberry became the spokesman for U.S. education to the U.S. Congress.**

- **Charles Fisher, '71, M.D. '73, director of Cleveland Clinic's Critical Care Research Unit in 1997, helped develop many drugs, such as Centoxin, which helped cut death rates from septic shock.** He served as a Lt. Colonel and Deputy Command Surgeon of the U.S. Special Operations forces, and was sent on missions known only by command officers and the President of the United States.

- **MSU's participation in the Southern Astrophysical Research (SOAR) project was hailed by MSU astronomer Timothy Beers in 1999 as "securing MSU's place in the worldwide astronomical community."** MSU, the University of North Carolina, the National Optical Astronomy Observatories ultimately teamed to establish the 4.2-meter telescope on a 9,000-foot mountain in the Chilean Andes.

- **The Smithsonian Institution gave its 2000 Computer World Award, considered the most prestigious information technology recognition in the nation, to MSU.** The award was for a joint School of Music and Artificial Language Laboratory project, which enables persons with physical disabilities to express themselves in music and singing.

- **The College of Natural Science LON-CAPA project won the 2003 Computer World Honors 21st Century Achievement Award for "best IT (Information Technology) application in the world in education and academia." Gerd Kortemeyer** was director of the project which "dramatically enhanced the delivery of virtual education" (*MSU Alumni Magazine,* Summer, 2003).

- **Paraj Mandrekar, '93, Promega Corporation genetic research scientist, helped develop two forensic DNA processing kits that were named among the year's (2003) top technologies by *R & D Magazine.***

- **The College of Agriculture & Natural Resources (CANR) was the only one of 15 premier agricultural colleges with all 13 of its departments ranked in the top ten nationally by a 1994 survey conducted by Penn State.** Among the CANR departments, Animal Science, Crop and Soil Sciences, Park & Recreation Resources, and the School of Packaging were considered the best in the country. The departments of Agricultural Economics, Entomology, and Horticulture were ranked either # 1 or # 2 in the nation.

- **The College of Arts and Letters has produced seven of Michigan State's 16 Rhodes Scholars.** Graduates of the college have included Richard Ford, '66, Pulitzer Prize winner for the novel *Independence Day;* Frank Price, '51, former president of Columbia and Universal Pictures; Bill Mechanic, '73, CEO of Fox Film Entertainment (20th Century Fox); Tom Gale,'66, M.A. '67, MBA '78, former Daimler-Chrysler executive vice president; John Kornblum, '64, former U.S. Ambassador to the Federal Republic of Germany; and William D. Brohn, '55, who orchestrated the music for *Miss Saigon, Crazy for You, and Ragtime.*

- **The College of Engineering, is home to the nation's premier Composite Materials and Structure Center.** The college is a national leader in automotive engineering, bio-engineering, composite materials research and development, manufacturing and processing engineering, and environmental management and protection.

- **The College of Human Ecology is internationally recognized for world-class programs in merchandising management, dietetics, nutritional science, child development, family and consumer sciences, and interior design.** The merchandising management program is the only one in the nation with an international emphasis. The MSU Central School Child Development Laboratories are recognized as one of the top two such laboratories in America.

- **The College of Human Medicine is consistently ranked among the top ten of 144 U.S. medical schools in the U.S. in its training of primary care physicians. MSU's College of Human Medicine was rated "best in the nation" by the country's intern-residency directors, all of whom were surveyed.** The college revolutionized medical education by incorporating social science, the humanities, and the bio-psycho social disciplines into the curriculum. This gained MSU a national reputation for producing "caring physicians." The college also pioneered Problem-Based Learning—featuring small groups of students discussing cases from both biomedical and psycho-social perspectives. Harvard University instituted this approach to their medical training after a visit to MSU by the dean of the Harvard Medical School. For three consecutive years, the American Academy of Family Physicians presented the college its highest recognition—the Gold Achievement Award—for graduating a high percentage of doctors who choose family practice residency as their specialty.

- **Rujuta M. Bhatt, '93 James Madison and Bio-Chemistry graduate, won Rhodes, Marshall, and Truman Scholarships in 1993.** She is a graduate of the Harvard Medical School.

- **University of Chicago scholar Allan Bloom, author of the book *The Closing of the American Mind,* and former visiting professor at MSU's James Madison College, once noted that the brightest students he had ever taught "were not from Harvard or Yale, but from James Madison College."** James Madison College has produced five Rhodes Scholars, six Marshall Scholars, eight Truman Scholars, ten Fulbright Scholars, five National Science Foundation Fellows, and MSU's first George Mitchell Scholar and first Carnegie Junior Fellow.

- **Michigan State's College of Law is home to America's first Trial Practice Institute located at any law school, and home to the National Trial Advocacy Competition**. The college has a national reputation as one of the leading appellate advocacy programs in the nation.

- **The world-renowned Juilliard String Quartet became artists-in-residence at MSU in 1977** for a minimum of three years, leaving their home base for the first time in 30 years. Robert Mann of the Quartet said, "We've come to regard certain places as very strong islands of interest in the arts and East Lansing is one." The quartet stayed at MSU for several years beyond their original commitment, teaching and performing.

- **Five Michigan State College of Law students became the first U.S. team to win the Philip C. Jessep International Moot Court Competition (2003). They defeated teams from Georgetown, Harvard, the University of Michigan, and Columbia University.**

- **MSU's Debate Team won four National Tournaments in 2004.** They defeated top-ranked University of California-Berkeley to win the **2004 National Debate Tournament, the ultimate prize of intercollegiate debate held at Catholic University in Washington, D.C.** They also scored 22 consecutive debate victories in competition at the University of Southern California and California State-Fullerton. The team prevailed over teams from Harvard, Cal-Berkeley, University of Texas-Austin, and Dartmouth. **They also won the Dartmouth College Annual Herbert L. James Debates, to which only the seven most-accomplished debate teams in the nation are invited.** The MSU team defeated teams from Harvard, Cal-Berkeley, Dartmouth, Northwestern, Georgia, and Emory universities. (See MSU Students Win National and International Championships in Many Disciplines).

- **Dr. William F. Jackson, DVM '47, M.S. '49, was presented the National Gamma Award as "the most outstanding veterinarian in the United States" in 1968.**

- **The College of Natural Science graduates have included a Nobel Prize winner and four of MSU's Rhodes Scholars. MSU's National Superconducting Cyclotron Laboratory—staffed 80 percent by College of Natural Science faculty—has earned international recognition for its active program of basic research in nuclear physics and for its innovation in cyclotron design.**

- **The College of Nursing pioneered primary care graduate education in Michigan, and is a leader in faculty practice.**

- **The College of Osteopathic Medicine was ranked fourth in the nation, out of 144 medical schools, for its primary care education in the April, 2003 *U.S. News & World Report.*** It was the first osteopathic college where a person could earn a Doctor of Osteopathic medical degree (D.O.) as well as a Ph.D. in biological sciences. And, it was the first osteopathic school in the nation approved by the American Osteopathic Association to administer both residency and internship programs. The college's educational system is considered a national model.

- **The College of Social Science has pioneered many firsts, including—1) The concept of police-community relations (Community Policing); 2) The study of highway safety; and 3) The development of the field of industrial security.** The college is nationally known for its leadership programs in Anthropology, Criminal Justice, Economics, Geography, Labor and Industrial Relations, Political Science, Psychology, Social Work, and Sociology. The School of Criminal Justice was the nation's first and is the acknowledged leader in its field. The department of psychology's industrial/organizational psychology program was ranked # 1 in the nation by *U.S. News & World Report.* The department of sociology is a recognized world leader in international migration research, and one of the top two programs nationally in scholarly resources dedicated to race and ethnicity issues.

- **The College of Veterinary Medicine ranks among the top five veterinary schools (of 28) in the U.S.** It is home to world-renowned Large-Animal and Small Animal Clinical facilities. Its laboratory for Comparative Orthopedic Research is a national leader in the basic science investigation of musculo-skeletal tissues in all species. The college's Small Animal orthopedics expertise ranks among the best in the nation, where surgical techniques developed for use on animals have been refined and applied to human surgery.

- **MSU ranks fifth among all universities in U.S. Peace Corps volunteers—1,900 as of 2003.**
- **Seven internationally focused centers at Michigan State are designated National Resource and Language Resource Centers by the U.S. Department of Education.** Centers include: African Studies, Asian Studies, Center for Latin American & Caribbean Studies, Center for Advanced Studies of International Development, Center for International Business Education and Research, Women and International Development Program, and the Center for Language Education and Research. **MSU's African Studies Center was described in 1982 as a model National Resource Center** in African Studies at the National Advisory Board for International Programs.
- **Three MSU graduates have served as U.S. Presidential Cabinet members—Frederick H. Mueller, Class of 1914, Secretary of Commerce; David Stockman, '68, Director of the Office of Management and Budget; and Spencer Abraham, '74, Secretary of Energy.**
- **Three MSU graduates have been elected U.S. Senators representing the State of** Michigan—Donald W. Riegle, MBA '61; Spencer Abraham, '74; and Debbie Stabenow, '72, MSW '75.
- **Kalmal Ahmed El-Ganzoury, Ph.D. '72, served as Egypt's Prime Minister.** He was named to that position in 1996 by Egyptian president Hosni Mubarak.
- **Seven MSU alumni have served as U.S. Ambassadors to foreign nations.** (See Alumni Achievement chapter, page 292).
- **MSU alumni have served as White House physician, White House press secretary, U.S. drug czar, director of the U.S. census, director of the U.S. Mint, director of the National Park System, head of the U.S. Forest Service, head of the Agency for International Development, administrator for the National Highway Traffic Safety Administration, chief naturalist for the U.S. Fish and Wildlife Service, and chief of U.S. Agricultural Extension**. (See Alumni Achievement chapter, page 292).
- **MSU alumni have won four Academy Awards, seven Emmy Awards, two Grammy Awards, a Toni Award, a Peabody Award, and two Desk Dram Awards for musical arrangement.** (See Alumni Achievement chapter, page 292).
- **President Emeritus Dr. John A. Hannah, Class of 1923, won the singular U.S. Presidential Hunger Award in 1986 for "Lifetime Achievement." He also was given the USA Medal of Freedom—the nation's highest civilian award.**
- **Verghese Kurien, M.A. '48, chairman of India's National Development Board, was named the 1989 World Food Prize Laureate for making an outstanding contribution toward improving the world food supply.**
- **MSU graduates have been:**

  —Dean of the Wharton School of Business at the University of Pennsylvania.

  —Dean of the Military Medicine Education Institute and vice president of the Uniformed Services University of Health & Sciences (Defense Department's military medical school).

  —Director of the Cleveland Clinic's Critical Care Unit.

  —Chair of the Radiation Oncology department at the Memorial Sloan-Kettering Cancer Center.

  —Chair of the Nutrition Department at the Harvard School for Public Health.

  (See Alumni Achievement chapter, page 292).
- **TV and Radio Networks that have been headed by MSU graduates include**—CBS Broadcasting, Universal TV, USA Network, Cox Broadcasting, Twentieth Television, HGTV, Food Network, Do-It-Yourself Network, Children's TV Workshop, and Buena Vista Home Entertainment. (See Alumni Achievement chapter, page 292).
- **Amir Kahn, M.S. '49, M.S. '52, Ph.D. '67, agricultural engineer with the International Rice Research Institute, won the International Inventor's Award for 1986.** It was presented by H.M. King Carl Gustaf of Sweden. Kahn invented an axial flow thresher heavily used in rice producing nations.
- **Dawn Kuchar, '87, was selected Ambassador for Walt Disney World out of a cast of 35,000 employees.**
- **Hollywood Movie Studios that have been headed by MSU graduates include**—Columbia Pictures, Universal Pictures, and Fox Film Entertainment (Twentieth Century Fox). (See Alumni Achievement chapter, page 292).

- **Michigan State graduates have led the production or written the screenplays for the following movies**—*Titanic, Spiderman, Witness, The Big Chill, Kramer vs. Kramer, The X Files, Pocahontas, The Star Wars Trilogy, Top Gun, Legal Eagles, Dick Tracy, The Deer Hunter,* and many more. (See Alumni Achievement chapter, page 292).

- **Twenty-Four MSU graduates have achieved the military rank of General or Admiral.** (See Alumni Achievement chapter, page 292).

- **MSU News Media leaders have included the publisher of *Time Magazine*, general manager of the *Washington Times*, and the publisher and editor of the *Detroit Free Press*.** (See Alumni Achievement, page 292).

- **George Levitt, Ph.D. '57, won the National Medal of Technology in 1993—the highest award bestowed by the President of the United States for extraordinary achievements in technology.** Levitt discovered a family of herbicides that were environmentally friendly and less toxic than salt.

- **Peter Morris, M.A. '90, won the North American Scrabble Open in 1998, which was considered the world championship.**

- **Nancy Ann Fleming, '65, won the 1961 Miss America and Miss Michigan titles.** She graduated in 1965 with honors and a 3.8 grade point average. Including Fleming, five MSU alumna have won the Miss Michigan title. Other graduates have won the Miss Alaska, Miss Arkansas, Miss Hawaii, and Miss Thailand titles. (See Alumni Achievement chapter, page 292).

- **Michigan State has won 24 team national championships in ten different sports as well as 104 individual NCAA titles. Spartans have won 23 Olympic medals, ten of them gold. Former MSU athletes have been World Series, Super Bowl, National Basketball Association, Stanley Cup, and America's Cup champions. MSU is one of just five universities to have won National Championships in both football and basketball. MSU is the only school to have won multiple National Championships in football, basketball, and ice hockey.** (See Spartan Sports Success chapter, page 380).

- **Thirty-Eight Spartan athletes, coaches and sports administrators are members of National or International Halls of Fame. Twenty-eight Spartans are in the Michigan Sports Hall of Fame.** (See Spartan Sports Success chapter, page 380).

- **Michigan State graduates and former faculty have buildings named for them at the following universities**—Cornell, Nebraska, Illinois, Missouri, New Hampshire, Maine, Northern Michigan, Ferris State, Eastern Michigan, Oakland, and Michigan State. The football field in Arizona State's Sun Devil stadium is named for an MSU graduate. (See Buildings and Places Named for MSU People, page 324).

- **The National Gallery of The Spoken Word is located at MSU's College of Arts & Letters.** The gallery, underwritten by a $3.6 million grant from the National Science Foundation, revolutionizes audiotape repositories nationwide. It is a fully searchable online data base of spoken word collections, spanning the 20th century. It's the first large-scale repository of its kind.

- **MSU athletes Earvin "Magic" Johnson, Steve Garvey, and Kirk Gibson were among sports figures appearing on the most *Sports Illustrated* covers in the magazine's first 50 years.** In 2004, the magazine reported Johnson had been on 22 covers, Steve Garvey three, and Kirk Gibson three. Johnson was tied with Kareem Abdul Jabbar and Jack Nicklaus for the third most covers. Michael Jordan was first with 49 covers, and Muhammad Ali second with 37 covers.

- **Dr. Barnett Rosenberg, MSU biophysicist and founder of MSU's Biophysics Department, led an MSU scientific team in the discovery and development of two anti-cancer drugs—Cisplatin (approved by the Federal Drug Administration in 1978) and Carboplatin (approved in the mid-1980s). These became the most-prescribed anti-cancer drugs in the nation.** More than $300 million in royalties flowed to Michigan State's Foundation from Cisplatin and Carboplatin patents by the year 2004.

- **Two MSU alumna have been named the National Suzy Favor Female Athlete of the Year.** In 1984, Judi Brown, 1984 Olympic silver medal winner of the 400-meter hurdles and 1983 NCAA champion in the same event, won the award. In 1991, Julie Farrell-Ovenhouse, NCAA record-setting 3-meter diving champion, won the Favor award. Brown and Farrell-Ovenhouse each were named Big Ten Woman Athlete of the Year.

- **MSU's Debate Team won the 2002 National Championship, officially know as the Cross Examination Debate Association Seasonal National Championship. It was MSU's third title in seven years.** In the competition, Harvard finished 25th, and the University of Michigan, 26th.

- **Dr. William J. Beal, MSU's nationally recognized botanist, is known as the "Father" of hybrid corn, seed-testing, and Michigan Forestry.** Beal started the campus botanical garden named for him in 1873. It is the oldest, continuously operating botanical garden of its kind in the U.S. (See biographical sketch on Beal, page 26).

- **Dr. Robert C. Kedzie, founder of Michigan State's chemistry department in 1863, was a national leader in conservation, protection of the environment, and consumer advocacy a century before such efforts became popular. Kedzie was the "Father" of the Michigan sugar beet industry,** and warned the public in 1875 of the hazards of drinking water pollution, poisonous Paris Green—an arsenic-laden coloring agent, and flammable oils used for lamp lighting. (See biographical sketch on Kedzie, page 23).

- **Michigan State authors have included Pulitzer Prize winners Ray Stannard Baker, Class of 1889, for his 8-volume biography *Woodrow Wilson: Life and Letters* (1940); English Professor Russell Nye for *George Bancroft, Brahmin Rebel* (1944); and Richard Ford, '66, for the novel *Independence Day* (1996). Professor Georg Borgstrom, internationally known food scientist, authored *Hungry Planet* which was named one of the 50 most important books of the year in 1986. Craig Jones, '67, wrote *Blood Secrets* (1979), which was a Book of the Month Club selection. Gary Gildner, '60, M.A. '61, won the 1986 National Magazine Award in Fiction—the highest honor in the magazine world. Pete Gent, '64, former MSU basketball player and Dallas Cowboy wide receiver, authored best-seller *North Dallas 40* in 1972. It sold more than two million copies.**

- **MSU is home to the only accredited Journalism School in Michigan.**

- **The Accounting Department at MSU's Eli Broad College of Business educates more Michigan Certified Public Accountants than any other university.**

- **Michigan State is the largest single-campus university in Michigan, with 44,542 students (fall of 2003).**

- **Frank Johnson, class of 1895, rose to chief engineer of Ford Motor Company's Lincoln Division in 1926. He was key in the design of the famous Ford Model "A" car.**

- **Six MSU graduates have won Pulitzer Prizes as journalists or authors.**

- **Thirteen MSU alumni have been inducted into the Michigan Journalism Hall of Fame.**

Cowles House—the President and First Lady's Home at MSU.
Built in 1857, it is the oldest structure on campus, and a state historic site.

An Overview Chapter on MSU Leadership, Excellence, and Achievement–1855-2004

Leader in Democratizing U.S. Higher Education

Michigan State's pioneering leaders were at the center of the revolution that democratized higher education in America. These gritty believers battled from 1849 to 1855 to establish the nation's first agricultural college, opening the doors of advanced education to the children of farmers and the working class. It was the birth of the "Spirit of Michigan State."

Then these early educational advocates fought for the passage of the Morrill Act, which would create the uniquely American land-grant colleges and universities of which there are now 74. Michigan State served as the model from which the land-grant colleges were created, and was, indeed, the "Mother" of all land-grant colleges.

When President Abraham Lincoln signed the Morrill Act into law on July 2, 1862, it was a landmark event in the history of higher education in the United States. It signaled the widespread democratization of higher education, welcoming the seven-eighths of the population previously excluded from such pursuits. It reaffirmed the meaning and Spirit of Michigan State.

This event was a monumental contribution to the future of the nation, unlocking the brain power of the sons and daughters of toil—putting a college education within their reach. This immense liberating wave washed across America over the next decades, creating armies of trained minds that helped launch the United States into world leadership. Today, the productive graduates of the land-grant colleges and universities number in the millions and stand in leadership positions across the spectrum of human activity.

Tiny School to Major International University

Founded in 1855, Michigan State has grown from 81 students, eight faculty, 16 courses of study, a 676-acre campus, and an annual budget of $20,000 when its doors opened in 1857, to an internationally respected major university. By 2003, MSU claimed 378,000 alumni, 44,542 students, 4,402 faculty, 9,234 supporting staff, 15 colleges

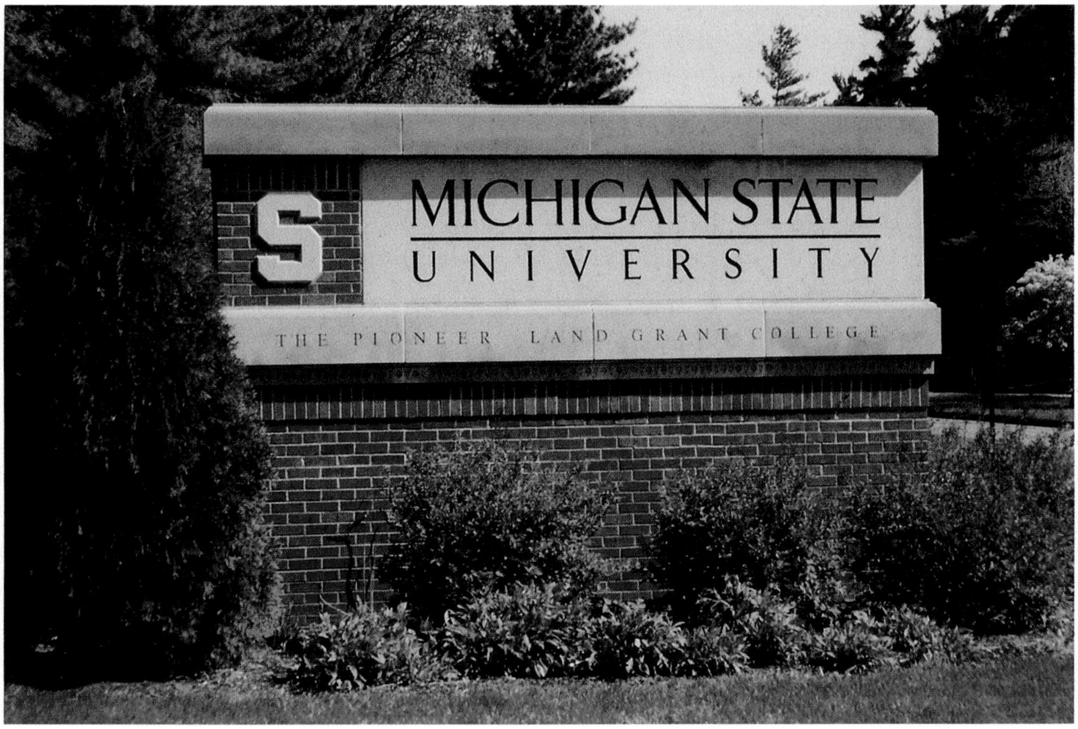

Five campus entrance signs are gifts of the classes of 1981, 1982, 1983, and 1987. They all are inscribed with Michigan State's historic educational distinction: "The Pioneer Land Grant College."

offering degrees in 278 different academic subjects, a 5,198-acre campus, and an annual budget of $1.4 billion (2004).

Small Agricultural School—1857 to 1909

From 1857 to 1909, Michigan State was a small agricultural school with a strong scientific curriculum as well as a liberal arts component that was unusual among colleges at that time. Courses included engineering and mechanics, veterinary training, home economics, biology, geology, astronomy, physics, laboratory science, entomology, ethics, logic, psychology, ancient history, English language and literature, economics, geography, and constitutional law. Enrollment was small, growing from 81 in 1857 to 1,494 in 1909.

Regional State College—1910 to 1945

Michigan State grew into a regional state college between 1910 and 1945. Dozens of departments, divisions and schools were added, including the divisions of applied science and liberal arts, and the schools of veterinary medicine, science and arts, hotel administration, police administration, business administration, and education. Enrollment grew from 1,568 in 1910 to 5,284 in 1945.

International University—1946 to 2003

Michigan State blossomed into university status—both academically and in enrollment—following World War II. The enrollment explosion occurred in the fall of 1946 with the return of the war veterans who were fortified with their GI Bill of Rights scholarships. Enrollment soared to 13,282—two and one half times the 1945 total of 5,284. From that point on, MSU was considered a large university.

MSU's emergence from a small school to great university was exemplified by the 3,148 degrees granted to the Class of 1949. That class alone was equivalent to 12 percent of all graduating classes in the entire history of the institution. And, the 3,148 degrees were more than were granted in the sixty-year period, 1857-1917. Between 1946 and 2003, Michigan State steadily expanded its academic offerings. A student can now major in 278 different disciplines, which are taught in 15 colleges. Many specializations also are available, including International Studies and Programs, The Honors College, and a full spectrum of graduate studies. Enrollment grew from 15,208 in 1947 to 44,542 in 2003. From 1969 to 2003, MSU enrollment has topped 40,000 in all but one year. On several occasions, MSU's enrollment has ranked the university as the second largest, single-campus student body in America.

One in Every 131 College Graduates in the United States is an MSU Alumnus

Michigan State had 378,000 living alumni in 2003, out of 49,516,000 university graduates in the nation (2000 U.S. Census). These figures translate into a startling fact—one in every 131 university graduates in the United States is an MSU alum.

Traditional copper lanterns dot the beautiful Michigan State campus.

MSU: Educational Entrepreneur

Today, Michigan State is renowned as an innovator in teaching, research, international outreach, and the development of leaders. Pioneering began at MSU with its founding in 1855 as the nation's first agricultural college, which then served as the model for America's 74 land-grant colleges and universities.

"At Michigan State Breaking With Tradition is a Tradition"

The late, legendary Dr. John A. Hannah, MSU's president from 1941 to 1969, validated the innovative culture by encouraging faculty, administrators, and students to try new ideas; to take chances, to create new educational vistas, and to work cooperatively. That mentality has continued to thrive at East Lansing. Former U.S. President Gerald Ford at the 1998 dedication of Michigan State

MSU Library fountains and reflecting pool were gifts of the Class of 1964; the fountain system, a gift of the Class of 1968; and the fountain renovation, a gift of the Class of 1983.

University-Detroit College of Law, stated, **"It's no exaggeration to say that at Michigan State University, breaking with tradition is a tradition."** His statement embodied the "Spirit of Michigan State."

Michigan State's Leadership in Scientific Agriculture Education & Research: Key in Nourishing America's Food Production Machine; and Helping Free Most Americans to Pursue Other Occupations

Leadership emanating from the East Lansing campus was key in securing the passage of the Morrill Act in 1862—which created the Land-Grant colleges and universities in America (74); and in winning passage of the Hatch Act in 1887—which established the nation's Agricultural Experiment Station.

In retrospect, America should be grateful for the work of Michigan State Presidents—Joseph Williams, to pass the Morrill Act; and Edwin Willits, to pass the Hatch Act.

These two powerful pieces of legislation nourished the development of scientific agricultural knowledge that has made America's food production **"machine" the envy of the world.** As a result, Americans spend a smaller percentage of their personal budgets for food than any people on earth. And, the great advances in agriculture have freed nearly 98 percent of the U.S. working-age population to pursue occupations other than food production.

Today, Americans spend about 12 to 14 percent of their earnings for food, compared with other nations, where people use 30 to 80 percent of their income to sustain physical life.

"Firsts" An MSU Tradition

MSU offered the country's first course in scientific agriculture. It was a leader in establishing outreach—the sharing of new knowledge with citizens of the state, nation and world—as a major part of a university's mission. **Michigan State built the nation's:**

- **first structure used solely as a botanical laboratory,**
- **first horticultural laboratory,**
- **first agricultural laboratory,**
- **first bacteriology laboratory, and**
- **first building devoted entirely to chemical work.**

It is known nationwide as a place where inter-disciplinary faculty cooperation is extremely high.

Michigan State has pioneered in offering educational and research opportunities in agriculture, hotel, restaurant and resort management, criminal justice, packaging, communication arts and sciences, international studies, nuclear physics, primary medical care, pesticide research, food safety, urban affairs studies, research on teaching, teacher education, plant and soil science, plant biology, microbial ecology, magnetic resonance imaging (MRI), and legal trial practice.

MSU: The Only University with Three Medical Colleges

Michigan State is the only university in the nation with three medical colleges and a college of nursing—all recognized nationally.

50-Plus MSU Academic Programs Top Ranked

Nationally ranked MSU academic programs include—Agricultural economics; animal science, crop and soil sciences; parks & recreation resources; entomology; horticulture; packaging; music; African languages; hotel, restaurant and resort management; marketing and supply chain management; accounting; telecommunications; journalism; advertising; audiology & speech sciences; elementary and secondary education; educational administration; composite materials research and development; child development; dietetics; merchandising management; interior design; nutritional science; family and consumer sciences; primary care medical training; family practice medical training; pre-law and public policy; trial practice legal training; plant sciences; structural biology and chemistry; nuclear and high-energy physics; materials and environmental sciences; genetics; ecology; evolutionary biology and behavior; cellular and molecular biology; neuroscience; anthropology; criminal justice; economics; geography; labor and industrial relations; political science; psychology; social work; sociology; osteopathic medicine; veterinary medicine; international studies and programs; and urban affairs programs.

By 2003, MSU's nuclear science research and curriculum was vying with MIT as the top program in America, producing one of every ten nuclear physics Ph.D.s in the U.S.

MSU: Member of the Association of American Universities

The university is a member of the prestigious Association of American Universities—an organization comprised of the nation's 62 premier graduate education and research institutions.

Producing Leaders: A Michigan State Culture

MSU graduates have included three U.S. Presidential cabinet members, four state governors, three U.S. senators, seven U.S. ambassadors, Federal Reserve Board members, a Nobel Prize winner, Pulitzer Prize winners, Academy Award winners, Emmy and Grammy Award winners, 107 university and college presidents, hundreds of corporate CEOs—including the heads of five auto companies, nine hotel corporations, five TV networks, and two movie studios. MSU Spartans have been members of Super Bowl, NBA, World Series, Stanley Cup, and America's Cup championship teams. Twenty-three graduates have won Olympic medals—ten of them gold.

MSU: Leader in Minority Opportunity

A strong commitment to equal rights, and opportunity for minorities and the disadvantaged is ingrained in the "Spirit of Michigan State." **MSU is the:**

- **first major U.S. university to select an African-American as president,**
- **first university to accept Japanese-Americans as students during World War II,**
- **first university in the Big Ten to select a woman as provost, and**
- **first university to create an on-campus shelter for victims of domestic violence.**

MSU graduates include the:

- **first Asian-American to be elected a state governor**
- **first African-American to be selected CEO of the U.S. Olympic Committee**
- **first woman career foreign service officer to be named a U.S. ambassador**
- **first woman to be selected a member of the Federal Reserve Bank Board**
- **first African-American women to head a medical school in the U.S., and**
- **first African-American female to serve as director of media relations for the President of the United States.**

(See chapter on MSU: National Leader in Minority Opportunity, page 321)

Michigan State Students have won National Championships in 19 disciplines:

Mathematics, chemical engineering, computer programming, journalism, chamber music, culinary arts, advertising, engineering, international law moot court competition, debate, oratory, business, business marketing, economics, investing, national law student tax challenge, dairy judging, environmental waste management, and college bowl. The latest successes were winning the 2004 National Debate title, the 2003 National Collegiate Chamber Music competition, the 2003 International Law Moot Court competition, and 2004 National Law Student Tax Challenge.

(See chapter on MSU Students Win National and International Championships, page 315)

Award-Winning Faculty Leadership

MSU professors and scientists have been national leaders since the early days of the institution.

Michigan State faculty and alumni have been proclaimed:

- **The "father" of scientific agriculture— Dr. Manly Miles.**
- **The "father" of hybrid corn, seed-testing, and Michigan Forestry —Dr. William J. Beal.**
- **The "father" of the Michigan sugar beet industry—Dr. Robert C. Kedzie.**
- **The "father" of American horticulture— Dr. Liberty Hyde Bailey.**
- **The "father" of homogenized milk— Dr. G. Malcolm Trout.**
- **The "father" of American veterinary public health—Dr. James H. Steele.**
- **The "father" of the herbicide 2 4-D, a major aid in controlling broad leaf weeds— Dr. Harold B. Tukey.**
- **The "father" of cisplatin and carboplatin, the most-prescribed anti-cancer drugs in the U.S.—Dr. Barnett Rosenberg.**
- **The "father" of community policing in America—Dr. Robert C. Trojanowicz, and**
- **The "father" of the National Superconducting Cyclotron Laboratory–Dr. Henry Blosser.**

Seven faculty members have been elected to the National Academy of Sciences, the premiere U.S. scientific society and advisor to U.S. Presidents and Congress:

- **Dr. N. Edward Tolbert**, bio-chemistry—1984
- **Dr. James Dye**, chair of the chemistry department—1989
- **Dr. Hans Kende**, leading plant researcher—1992
- **Dr. Richard L. Witter**, clinical professor of veterinary pathology—1998
- **Dr. Jan A. D. Zeevaart**, professor, MSU-U.S. Department of Energy plant research laboratory—1998
- **Dr. James Tiedje**, University distinguished professor of crop and soil sciences and director of the National Science Foundation Technology Center for Microbial Ecology—2003
- **Dr. Michael Thomashow**, professor of crop and soil sciences and of micro-biology, and member of the Energy Plant Research Laboratory—2003

In one year alone—1974—sixty-five MSU faculty members were serving as presidents of national academic and professional associations.

MSU professors and researchers have won hundreds of international and national awards—including:

Pulitzer Prizes, the Peabody Award, National Cancer Institute Award, Guggenheim Fellowships, National Academy of Science Fellows, Presidential Young Investigator Awards, National Awards from Britain, Sweden, France, Germany, and Russia; Sloan Foundation Research Fellowship Award, American Association for the Advancement of Science Fellowships, American Council on Education Fellows, American Chemical Society Award, Fulbright Awards, U.S. Presidential Faculty Award, American Academy of Nursing membership, Distinguished Contribution in Nursing Science Award, Columbia University Journalism Award, Distinguished Advertising Educator Award, American Society of Composers, Authors and Publishers Award; American Academy of Arts and Sciences Fellow, and the Alexander von Humboldt Foundation Award, considered the most prestigious honor for agricultural research in the United States.

MSU Students—Leaders in Winning Major Scholarships

Between 1972 and 1997, MSU students won 13 Rhodes Scholarships—more than any other public university in America—bringing MSU's Rhodes' total to 16. Spartans also have won 15 Churchill Scholarships, 13 Truman Scholarships, eight Marshall Scholarships, four Woodrow Wilson Scholarships, two Danforth Scholarships, several Mellon Fellowships, a Mitchell Scholarship, and a Goldwater Scholarship. MSU has led the Big Ten Conference in producing National Science Foundation Fellowship winners on many occasions, and has been highly ranked in this category among all public universities.

Michigan State led all universities in attracting National Merit Scholars, starting in 1963 with a total of 195. By 1974, MSU had 462 National Merit Scholars on campus, leading all public universities, and was second only to America's oldest private university: Harvard. From that time forward, MSU has continued to attract large numbers of National Merit Scholars.

(See chapter on Academic Excellence: A Way of Life, page 318)

International Leader in Outreach

Michigan State pioneered in extending the mission of higher education beyond teaching and research. Energetic faculty have done this by reaching out to share existing and new-found knowledge with the people of the state, nation, and world to help them solve problems.

Peter McGrath, past president of the National Association of State Universities and Land-Grant Colleges, stated:

"Michigan State is a model and inspiration for the international public service role of our nation's universities."

Faculty outreach began in 1872, when professors formed a class in chemical manipulations to help public school teachers be more effective in chemistry education. The class was free.

The First Farmers' Institutes to share the latest scientific agricultural knowledge were held at six locations in Michigan in 1876.

By 1895, Farmers' Institutes reached into all 67 Michigan counties (now 83).

Extension Schools were established in every Michigan County in 1918 to bring the best agricultural information more directly to farmers. County (Agricultural) Agents already were located in virtually every county. The county agent had local knowledge of farming conditions, and could combine this with the research findings provided by Extension scientists at the college.

Since then, MSU's educational mission has reached around the globe. Faculty and administrative know-how have helped create three overseas and one domestic university—Ryukus University, Okinawa (1951); University of Nigeria, Africa (1960); the National University of Science & Technology, Pakistan (1990s); and Oakland University, Rochester, Michigan (1957).

Moreover, MSU was a major partner in establishing universities, colleges, schools and departments in nineteen other nations—Argentina, Bangladesh, Brazil, Colombia, Costa Rica, Guatemala, India, Indonesia, Iran, Malaysia, Mexico, Nepal, Peru, Philippines, Taiwan, Tanzania, Thailand, Turkey, and Vietnam.

MSU has had more faculty working overseas than any other American university for more than 50 years.

Providing Leadership, Teaching and Research Expertise

Providing leadership for universities around the globe is one of MSU's greatest contributions. On more than 107 occasions Michigan State alumni have been chosen college and university presidents in 37 different states, the District of Columbia, and four foreign countries. MSU faculty and administrators also have been named university presidents on dozens of occasions. Hundreds of MSU alumni and faculty have served as deans and department heads at universities from coast to coast, and worldwide. MSU faculty have helped launch universities on three different continents. As early as 1910, eleven of the nation's 57 Agricultural Experiment Stations—the furnaces of agricultural research—were directed by Michigan State graduates.

3,000 Research Projects Funded at $295 Million

MSU ranked in the top seven percent of 623 universities in 2003 research expenditures according to a report by the National Science Foundation. Michigan State had more than 3,000 externally funded research projects with support totaling $295 million, and aimed at medical, technological, social and economic benefits for the state, nation and world.

MSU's Inter-Disciplinary Culture of Cooperation

Embedded in the Spirit of the Michigan State faculty is an unparalleled culture of inter-disciplinary cooperation.

Dr. James Anderson, retired Dean of Agriculture and Natural Resources, described MSU in 1992 as "The best place I've seen for working together. In the 1950s money flowed in, but faculty didn't guard their turf, they worked together. We established that research is a holistic look at a total problem—inter-disciplinary. The nation would be further ahead with the holistic research approach, if all schools were like MSU. Problems today are so complex that they cut across disciplines. We have team after team here at MSU working in an inter-disciplinary fashion. Our mission is to be out there solving problems. We are very practical. MSU is a great place to work and live."

Dr. Fred L. Poston, MSU vice president for finance and operations and former Dean of Agriculture and Natural Resources, has stated, "You can work with any other faculty member in any other college, without question. There are few impediments to cross-disciplinary work. We have units that report to multiple deans. The joint relationships have created a culture with little turf protection. Because we all are moving across lines, this leads to happier groups of teachers and researchers. It's unique among land-grant schools... probably all schools."

Dr. Kenneth Corey, Dean of the College of Social Science in 1992, affirmed the inter-disciplinary environment, stating, "There are low boundaries between colleges and departments (at MSU) and high permeability."

Feeding the Nation and World

Michigan State's contributions to feeding America and the world are exceptional. Dr. Manly Miles introduced the nation's first course in scientific agriculture at the college in

1865, opening the avenues of research into greater food production and protection. Through the years, MSU scientists have developed and released more than 240 varieties of grains, fruits and vegetables. These breakthroughs have improved the yield, quality and disease- and insect-resistance of dozens of crops important to Michigan and the world.

(See chapter on Feeding the Nation and the World, page 248)

Disease Eradication and Crop Protection

Agricultural and other research efforts at MSU also have produced major disease eradication and crop protection benefits for the nation.

Brucellosis (undulant fever), parakeratosis (swine disease), Fabry's disease (a rare and fatal disease caused by kidney failure), Marek's disease (a poultry cancer), and amoebic dysentery all have been alleviated or eliminated through MSU research.

Disease-resistant wheat, control of cherry leaf spot, and the protection of the Christmas tree industry from the pine shoot needle, are just a few of the successes in crop-protection resulting from MSU research discoveries.

A major facility for fighting disease–the $58-million **Diagnostic Center for Population and Animal Health**—opened on south campus early in 2004. It is a world-class facility, and the only one in Michigan. The first center was established in the College of Veterinary Medicine in the mid-1970s, and in 2002 was running more than one million diagnostic tests a year and received more than 500 requests for service per day. Dr. Lonnie King, Dean of the College of Veterinary Medicine stated in 2003, "Over the past two decades, we have entered into an unprecedented era of infectious diseases. More than 30 emerging or re-emerging diseases have either produced epidemics or serious health problems." "Of these 30 diseases, 75 percent are zoonotic—that is, they are transmitted to people either directly or indirectly through animals and their products (such as SARS and Monkey Pox)." (*MSU Alumni Magazine*, Winter 2003, by Linda Chadderdon, Pattie McNiel and Kirsten Khire).

(See chapter on Feeding the Nation and the World, page 248)

Michigan State University: "Volunteer U"

A culture of student volunteerism has existed at Michigan State for more than a century. MSU became a national leader in formalizing student volunteerism in 1962 with the creation of its Student Education Corps—a part of the "Spirit of Michigan State." This program reached out with more than 2,000 students who mentored young people in

Promenade and mini-park between Anthony and Erickson Halls, links North and South Shaw Lanes and stands on the site of the old Judging Pavilion, torn down in 1997. Twelve limestone columns incorporate bricks from the pavilion and support the nostalgic copper lanterns that punctuate the campus.

ten schools in Lansing, Flint, Pontiac, Morrice, and Holt, Michigan. This effort received national recognition in the *Congressional Record, New York Times*, and *Newsweek.*

By 1968, MSU's Student Education Corps was the largest in the nation with 2,200 volunteers, and became the nucleus for establishing the MSU Office of Volunteer Programs under the Student Affairs Office. James Tanck, an MSU graduate, was named director. This was the first student volunteer organization in the nation supported by a university. The program received national attention in 1969 when an amazing 17,239 student volunteers were being transported to places of service in the East Lansing-Lansing region.

It was then that the White House asked for MSU's help in developing a national plan to encourage volunteer programs at colleges and universities. James Tanck, director of student volunteer programs, was loaned to the Federal Government. MSU's volunteer program won a National Volunteer Effort award from America's First Lady Pat Nixon in 1970. In 1974, MSU was leading the nation in Peace Corps volunteers, and today stands among the top six universities in that category.

"Learning to Serve and Serving to Learn" became the operative motto of the Office of Volunteer Programs in 1978, when it changed its name to the Service Learning Center. The working objective was to "inform and prepare students for career and civic involvement through community service."

MSU students initiated the **"Adopt-A-Grandparent"** program, which has now migrated to campuses nationwide. They also created the **"Into the Streets"** and **"Just A Friend"** programs to provide meaningful community and educational service.

In 2002, the MSU Service Learning Center placed 6,000 students in semester-long commitments to community service, and another 2,000 students in short-term projects, such as community-cleanups. Thousands more students in residence halls and fraternities and sororities also volunteer their time in community outreach. The center also encourages and provides Alternative Spring-Break Service opportunities in the U.S. and overseas. Instead of partying, students make a commitment to serving others.

MSU faculty are reinforcing the giving concept by incorporating service learning into their curriculums to further encourage student volunteerism.

MSU Solidifies Claim As "Environmental U"

Nearly a century prior to the nation's environmental awakening and the first national Earth Day in April of 1970, MSU was a leader in protecting the environment, an attitude reflecting the "Spirit of Michigan State." In the 1870s, Dr. Robert C. Kedzie, chemistry professor, and Dr. William J. Beal, botany professor, called for tree planting to replenish the Michigan forests lost to lumbering. In the same decade, Dr. Kedzie also fought to protect citizens from highly flammable lighting oils and arsenic-laden Paris Green, a coloring agent used in clothing and wallpaper.

In 1970, MSU President Clifton Wharton announced the establishment of a Center for Environmental Quality. The Center's program and policy board was to consist of various college deans. Its Interdisciplinary Teaching and Research Committee, selected by the deans, was to develop recommendations for new curricula in the environmental quality area.

MSU's Pesticide Research Center (now Center for Integrated Plant Systems), a $2 million facility, was dedicated in 1970. It led national efforts to seek safe methods of protecting food crops and the public. It was another milestone in the University's nearly century-long involvement with agricultural pest control and pesticide problems. The new center was the culmination of an inter-disciplinary pesticide research program involving 17 departments, which was launched in 1964.

The National Food Safety and Toxicology Center, a 115,000 square-foot facility, was dedicated at Michigan State in October, 1997. It solidified MSU's position as a national leader in keeping the country's food supply safe.

MSU: "Advancing Knowledge" and "Transforming Lives"

In the 21st century, Michigan State University will continue to break with tradition by expanding its entrepreneurial educational culture. In keeping with the definition of the newly launched $1.2 billion Campaign for MSU (2002-2007), the nation's pioneer land-grant university will maintain its focus on "Advancing Knowledge," and "Transforming Lives."

Michigan State University Historical Timeline

1849-1855

Selling the Need for an Agricultural College—A five-year battle to create America's first agricultural college was waged between 1849 and 1855. The cause was advanced by leaders of the Michigan Agricultural Society and several prominent citizens. A persistent communications onslaught, pushing for agricultural education in Michigan began in 1849.

The Honorable E.H. Lothrop, orator for the first (Michigan) State Fair, proclaimed in 1849, "We dot our land with seminaries of law, medicine and theology, but agriculture 'as yet has no seminary in which to teach her sons the most valuable of all arts.'"

Michigan Lt. Governor William M. Fenton addressed the Calhoun County Agricultural Society on September 20, 1849, pleading for "education in the science and practice of agriculture."

Joseph Williams, who would become Michigan State's first president and was president of the Michigan Agricultural Society, made a strong address to the Kalamazoo Agricultural Society on October 11, 1849, urging farmers "to educate themselves and their children."

Bela Hubbard (Hubbard Halls), a Detroit geologist and farm owner, wrote the first resolution calling for an agricultural college. It was passed on December 19, 1849 by the Michigan Agricultural Society's executive committee.

Resolution for Agricultural College Put Into State Constitution

Hubbard followed with a January 1, 1850 memorandum to the Michigan legislature calling for agricultural education, "The day has forever gone by when an enlightened liberal education was deemed useless for a farmer. Agriculture has risen into a science which demands not alone bodily labor, but active, vigorous, cultivated intellect."

Williams, as president of the Michigan Agricultural Society and a member of the State's 1850 Constitutional Convention, led the work to embed the call for an agricultural college in the constitution. On June 10, 1850, at the convention, Samuel Clark moved "that the committee on education be instructed to inquire into the expediency of providing for the establishment of an agricultural school." The essence of the resolution was put into the State Constitution of 1850.

Planting the Seed of the Land-Grant Concept and The Morrill Act

Soon the state legislature responded. In 1850, it passed a joint resolution, asking the U.S. Congress "for a gift of 300,000 acres of land for the support of agricultural schools in Michigan." Congress didn't take action. But, this was the precursor of the Morrill Act, which 12 years later would give each state 30,000 acres of land for each senator and representative in Congress for the support of schools of agriculture and the mechanic arts. With the passage of the Morrill Act in 1862, Michigan—with two senators and six representatives—would receive 240,000 acres of federal land, located primarily in the northern part of the Lower Peninsula.

"Praying for the Establishment of a State Agricultural College"

In 1852, the Michigan Agricultural Society presented another memorandum to the state legislature, "praying for the establishment of a State Agricultural College." As the idea of an agricultural school was discussed, the question arose, "Should it be under the direction of the University in Ann Arbor, or the State Normal School at Ypsilanti (now Eastern Michigan University), or should it be an entirely separate institution?"

John C. Holmes Argues for "Stand-Alone" Agricultural College

Chief advocate for a separate college was the Michigan Agricultural Society and its secretary, John C. Holmes **(Holmes Halls)**. The Normal School and the University of Michigan opposed this idea. Both institutions argued they would offer superior education at less cost. Holmes countered with a report commissioned by the State of Massachusetts legislature, governor and council. The Massachusetts study examined European agricultural schools and recommended against connecting agricultural schools with universities. The report pointed out cogently that "it was necessary to teach the practice as well as the theory of agriculture." Neither the Normal School or the University of Michigan were prepared to do this.

The Final Sales Push for a Separate Agricultural College

Two years later, in December of 1854, Holmes kept pushing the idea of a separate agricultural school with the Michigan Agricultural Society. At his own expense, he spent much of the winter of 1854-1855 in Lansing, lobbying for the passage of legislation creating the college.

Member S.M. Bartlett of Monroe wrote the following resolution: "Resolved that an agricultural college should be separate from any other institution."

Next, Justus Gage prepared a memorandum to the legislature, "Praying for an appropriation sufficient to purchase a body of land suitable for an experimental farm and for the erection of buildings for an agricultural school separate from any other institution of learning." John Holmes, over his own signature, circulated this appeal statewide. Momentum for the school built after this information campaign.

1855

Birth of America's First Agricultural College—Michigan Governor Kinsley S. Bingham recommended establishing an agricultural college in his January 4, 1855 state-of-the-state message to the legislature. A senate bill for an agricultural college passed 24-5 on February 9, 1855, and also passed the house, 52-13, the same day. Governor Bingham signed the bill creating an Agricultural College for the State of Michigan on February 12, 1855 (Act No. 130). It was America's first agricultural college, and the pioneer, and "Mother" of all Land-Grant Colleges in the United States.

$5,000 Faculty and Free Tuition

Section 5 of Act 130 called for a faculty to be paid a total of no more than $5,000, and free tuition for state students.

Campus Site Selected: "A Judicious and Admirable Location"—On June 16, 1855, the Michigan State Agricultural Society executive committee selected a 676 57/100th acre tract for the campus, and called it "...a judicious and admirable location." The college grounds were located three and one-half miles directly east of the State Capitol Building, right down what is now Michigan Avenue.

Members of the committee were A.Y. Moore, president; J.C. Holmes, secretary; S.M. Bartlett; Payne K. Leach; James Bayley; Justus Gage; and John Starkweather.

In the center of the college land was the farm of B. Robert Burcham **(Burcham Drive)**. Burcham had built a log cabin in 1851 on the site of the present Music Building and had cleared three acres of land, which was later used as an athletic and drill field. This is now Walter Adams Field (formerly Landon Field), where the MSU Marching Band does its pre-game warm-ups on football Saturdays.

1856

First Two Campus Buildings Constructed—College Hall—a 55' x 100' three-story brick structure, and a Boarding Hall (later nicknamed "Saints' Rest")—a 43' x 82' three-story brick building—were constructed in 1856-57. They were located in an "oak opening" on the highest point of the college grounds. College Hall stood on the site of Beaumont Tower. The Boarding Hall stood just east of today's Museum (formerly the Library).

1857

Joseph R. Williams Named First President of the College (served 1857-1859)—Joseph R. Williams (1808-1861), a renaissance man of his time, was selected by the State Board of Education to be the first president of the new college. He was an 1831 Phi Beta Kappa graduate of Harvard University. Williams was an attorney, a merchant, miller, and a gentleman farmer from Constantine, Michigan.

He served as president of the Michigan Agricultural Society, and at the 1850 Michigan Constitutional Convention, led the effort to write the need for an agricultural college into the fundamental laws and principles of the state. He was a writer and in the mid-1850s served as editor of the *Toledo Blade* newspaper. He helped found the Ohio Republican Party. He twice ran unsuccessfully for the U.S. Senate in Michigan. In 1860, he was elected to the Michigan Senate, and was later elected unanimously, president pro tem of that body. He became acting Michigan Lt. Governor when James Birney resigned from that position.

Joseph R. Williams, First President

President Williams speaking of the College at its dedication...

"Established on no precedent, it is alike a pioneer in the march of men and the march of mind."

The College was dedicated on May 13, 1857 in the chapel of the new College Hall. Michigan's governor, state officials, faculty, the first class of students, and a large contingent of citizens from around the state were present.

Newly appointed president Joseph R. Williams delivered an eloquent address on the importance of the work of America's pioneer agricultural school. The speech included some of the most profound quotes in the history of Michigan State. "Perfect as our educational systems are, for a long time, a great vacuum has remained to be filled. **By reason of tradition, neglect and prejudice, seven-eighths of the race, on whose toil all subsist, have been deemed unworthy of mental cultivation."**

"That the agricultural masses have felt keenly this great want is evinced by the simultaneous creation of Agricultural Societies and Periodicals, and the craving for more abundant knowledge. Here, on the very margins of the cultivated portions of our country, where the 'forests primeval' are just vanishing, the youthful and vigorous State of Michigan, first among her sister states, dedicates this Institution to the instruction of men who are devoted exclusively to the cultivation of the earth. **Established on no precedent, it is alike a pioneer in the march of men and the march of mind."**

Williams stated, "A great advantage of such colleges as this will be that the farmer will learn to observe, learn to think, learn to learn. **Every man who acquires the information attainable in a college like ours, should become a perpetual teacher and example in his vicinity." Thus, President Williams laid down the principle of sharing new found knowledge—a forerunner of outreach for which Michigan State has become internationally renowned.**

"A farmer is a citizen, obliged to bear his portion of public burdens. He should speak and write with ease and vigor. He should be qualified to keep farm accounts. A farmer should be a chemist, a farmer should receive instruction in the veterinary art, entomology, and the principles of natural philosophy. A farmer should perpetually bear in mind that one generation of men hold the earth in trust for the next. (The result) of enlightening the whole agricultural population (will be) that leisure will be afforded for still wider individual improvement."

He continued, **"the Institution should be good enough for the proudest, and cheap enough for the poorest."** Williams concluded, "As to this youthful State belongs the honor of establishing the Pioneer State Institution of the kind, initiating what may prove one of the significant movements of the age, may she enjoy the glory of its complete and ultimate triumph."

Governor Kinsley S. Bingham pronounced, "Gentlemen, if this experiment shall prove successful, **Michigan**, first in many other matters of progress and improvement, **will be justly entitled to the high honor of having first established a College to teach the theory and practice of Agriculture.** One of the highest objects to be attained by the establishment of an Agricultural College is to elevate and dignify the character of labor. This can only be attained by increased amount of knowledge, by making the laborer intelligent."

Governor Bingham then directed his remarks to the faculty: **"the young men placed under your instruction will be reared to become men of thought and men of action**; that you will instill in their minds, both by precept and practice, a proper sense of the dignity and respectability of labor that they will here learn that the habits of industry will promote purity of morals, and that purity of morals and purity of life is the only guarantee to usefulness and happiness."

Faculty & Staff of Nine; Total Payroll: $5,000

The first faculty and staff included Joseph R. Williams, president and director of the farm; Calvin Tracy, professor of mathematics; Lewis R. Fisk, professor of chemistry; Dr. Henry Goadby, professor of animal and vegetable physiology, and entomology; D.P. Mayhew, professor of natural science; Robert D. Weeks, professor of English literature, farm economy, and secretary of the college; John C. Holmes **(Holmes Halls)**, professor of horticulture, and college treasurer; Enoch Bancker, assistant in

College Hall, completed in 1857, was the first place scientific agriculture was taught in America. It was razed in 1918, and stood on the site of Beaumont Tower. Photo–1892.

"Saints' Rest," completed in 1857, was the first dormitory. Students help clean up "the most desolate scene."

chemistry; and James M. Shearer, steward. **Total payroll for the faculty and staff: $5,000.**

Faculty Row Begun

Four brick homes were built along what is now West Circle Drive for the president and professors. This was the beginning of "Faculty Row." Today, only Cowles House, the president's home, still exists.

Classes and Student Labor Began on May 14, 1857

The next day classes and a pioneering experiment in advanced education began. Over the next few weeks 18 students were added to the original 63, and the boarding hall was filled to capacity, with four young men to a room.

Life was without amenities. Each room in the Boarding Hall was heated by a pot-bellied stove. There was no running water, no electric lights, no telephones, no indoor toilets or bath facilities. The school had no gymnasium or athletic program. There were no local restaurants or theaters. And, there were no coeds.

Students attended classes for four hours each morning, and then performed three hours required labor on the campus in the afternoon. Work included chopping down trees, wrenching stumps from the ground using ox-power, splitting rails, building fences, laying tiles to drain swampy areas, repairing the leaking roof of College Hall, and helping build four faculty homes. Pay ranged from five to ten cents an hour.

Among the college rules were several admonitions, "There will be chapel exercises every morning and religious services every Sunday. Spiritous liquors will not be allowed upon the premises. The use of tobacco will be discouraged. Exact conformity to the hours of study and labor will be required."

Board was to "be charged at a cost, not exceeding $2.50 per term. It is a subject of regret, that the exorbitant ruling prices of all articles of consumption will make the board high during the first term of the institution."

"A Most Desolate Scene"

The campus grounds were not a pretty picture at that time. In Dr. William J. Beal's book, *History of the Michigan Agricultural College* (1915), the setting was described. Charles Jay Monroe was a student at the 1857 dedication of the college and would later become president of the State Board of Agriculture (Board of Trustees). At the 1907

continued on page 14

MSU: Key In Helping Establish America's Land-Grant Colleges

Joseph R. Williams, Michigan State's first president, was a key leader in winning passage of the Morrill Act, which created America's land-grant colleges and universities in 1862. This movement led to the widespread democratization of higher learning in America.

Williams spent a great deal of time in Washington, D.C. during the winter of 1857-1858, lobbying face-to-face with Congressmen for passage of the Morrill Act. According to Albert E. Macomber, a Toledo attorney and former Michigan Agricultural College student (1857-1859), Williams "furnished a good part of the materials of Representative Morrill's speech, made on the introduction of that bill in the U.S. House of Representatives. The speech was full and elaborate, and as the Congressional Record shows was the only carefully prepared speech made at any time in either house on that question." (*History of the Agricultural College of Michigan* by Dr. William J. Beal).

At one point, it looked as if the Morrill bill would fail. Madison Kuhn's book, *Michigan State—The First Hundred Years*, states, "Congressman Walbridge may have saved the project by a vigorous minority report, a half of which, Morrill later wrote, was furnished by Williams." The bill was narrowly approved by the U.S. House and then postponed in the Senate.

Perhaps Williams' greatest contribution to the passage of the Morrill Act was his national communications campaign. His talents as a political practitioner and editor of the *Toledo Blade* became evident. He organized the mailing of 5,000 copies of a sixty-page booklet, titled, "The Agricultural College of the State of Michigan," to editors, agricultural societies, and opinion leaders nationwide. The support the bill received was rallied by his efforts. Even the Bill itself was matured and revised at his suggestions. The booklet included addresses given at the college's dedication, and an overview of the new institution.

In addition, Williams wrote a persuasive pamphlet urging editors to promote the Morrill Bill. Hundreds of these circulars were addressed and mailed by students at the college (Michigan State). Newspapers across the country responded by writing supportive editorials.

Williams' leadership was pointed out in William J. Beal's 1915 book, *History of the Michigan Agricultural College*: "*The Southern Farmer* of Virginia, and the *Scientific Artisan* of Cincinnati, reported: The honorable J.R. Williams, President of the Agricultural College of Michigan, which is now in successful operation, is an able and zealous advocate in the cause of agricultural education, and no man has done more, or as much, to promote the passage of the law."

"Not a few Representatives in Washington, last winter, voted for the Agricultural College Bill, because of instructions received from their constituents, who were aroused to the necessity of doing so by the efforts of President Williams. The elaborate speech of Mr. Morrill, in Congress, winter before last, was prepared principally from information derived from him, and a large portion of the support which that bill received, was rallied by his efforts. Even the Bill itself was matured and revised at his suggestions."

MSU vs. Illinois in Winning the Land-Grant Legislation

In 1967, the University of Illinois, in its centennial year, released a book on the life of Jonathan Baldwin Turner, a native of Illinois, who was given prime credit for the passage of the Morrill Act. There is no doubt Turner deserves a portion of the credit for the success of the Land-Grant Bill. Nonetheless, the author of this book challenges the Illinois leadership claim by pointing out that it was the State of Michigan that first petitioned the U.S. Congress for land grants in 1850—two years before Illinois did. It was Michigan, led by Joseph R. Williams, that established the nation's first agricultural college in 1855—the model for America's land-grant institutions.

It was Williams who helped strategize on how to get the land-grant bill passed in both houses, and who made major contributions to Morrill's successful Congressional address on the subject. And, it was Williams who lobbied Congressmen face-to-face, and organized a national communications campaign to influence U.S. representatives to pass the bill.

Moreover, Michigan's Agricultural College was established 12 years before the University of Illinois, and greatly aided the University of Illinois in its early years by providing it with outstanding faculty, including Dr. Manly Miles, who at M.A.C. was the first professor of scientific agriculture in the U.S., as well as Dr. Eugene Davenport and Dr. Herbert W. Mumford. Buildings on the University of Illinois campus quadrangle are named for Davenport and Mumford, both of whom became Deans of Agriculture at the Champaign, Illinois campus. Davenport was dean—1895-1922 (Davenport Hall).

Mumford was dean—1922-1938 (Mumford Hall).

semi-centennial of the opening of the College, Monroe spoke about the early days: "A few acres had been slashed down and the logs and brush cleared. On every hand were old stubs and partially burned trees so that at every point of the compass you beheld dead and blackened trees which presented **a most desolate scene**."

1858 **A Well-Rounded Education: Science and Liberal Arts**—Being the first agricultural college in the country, there were no models to follow. Yet, the faculty challenged the students in 1858 with analytical chemistry, trigonometry, surveying, ancient history, and rhetoric. **Professor L.R. Fisk's course in analytical chemistry preceded by one year the teaching of similar courses at Harvard and the University of Michigan.**

English Professor T.C. Abbot, a future president of the college, led the development of a sound curriculum in the summer of 1858, asking each faculty member to draft a proposed course of study. The synthesis of those outlines emerged in September of that year into a challenging four-year study program.

Madison Kuhn's book, *Michigan State—The First Hundred Years,* states, "Three five-hour courses were required each term. About two-thirds of the work was in science: over two years of mathematics, a year of mechanics and engineering, a year of biology (later expanded), and a term each of geology, astronomy, and physics. Laboratory science was emphasized to an extent almost unknown outside a medical school. Dr. Henry Goadby, a physician, offered a pioneer course in entomology and brought the first microscopes to the college. The other third was in liberal arts: ethics, logic, psychology, ancient history, English language and literature, economics, geography, and constitutional law."

This program required more science and liberal arts than most undergraduate students were required to study at other colleges. Science had been substituted for the classic languages. Kuhn states, "This was one of the distinctive contributions of the land-grant college movement." **Dr. C.E. Bessey** (Bessey Hall), nationally-known botanist, faculty member and alumnus, **stated in 1907, "Forty years ago, this was the only college in the West in which one could study all of the great sciences."**

The idea was to give students a solid grounding in the sciences so they could solve day-to-day agricultural problems and, at the same time, give them a liberal arts education so they would be critical-thinking, articulate, effective citizens.

Supporting the educational process was a small library on the third floor of College Hall. It housed 200 agricultural society reports and government documents collected by John C. Holmes. These were augmented by some 1,000 books and publications President Williams solicited from members of Congress, government agencies, book publishers, and others. These were the first recorded gifts to the college.

Professor John C. Holmes planted the first evergreens on campus, according to Harold Lautner's book, *From An Oak Opening.* These included Norway spruce, white pine, Austrian and Scots pine, and red cedars.

Seventy students were hit with malaria in 1858.

College Broke, Survival in Question; Williams Lobbies for Morrill Act

The College was broke by end of 1858—$13,000 in the red. Survival of the institution was in question. Dedicated faculty, with a keen interest in students, kept the school alive.

Williams Lobbies for Morrill Act—The college board sent Joseph R. Williams to Washington, D.C. in 1858 to help Vermont Representative Justin Morrill sell Congress on passing the bill that would create America's land-grant college system.

President Joseph Williams spent much of the winter of 1858 in Washington, D.C., lobbying face-to-face with Congressmen for passage of the Morrill Act, which would create the land-grant colleges. **He assisted Congressman Justin Morrill (Morrill Hall)** with his speech on the subject. He then led a national communications campaign to win passage of the Morrill Act. M.A.C. students helped with mailings to newspapers nationwide.

Enrollment was 98.

President Williams Asked to Resign; Lewis R. Fisk named Second President (served 1859-1862); Legislator Calls for Closing the College—A false notion existed among some legislators that the college should sustain itself from the earnings of crops grown on the school grounds. The college's request for $38,500 in funding was therefore not well received. **A state representative introduced legislation in 1859 to close the college and move agricultural education to the University of Michigan. It was defeated 51-21.** This was the first of six closing threats the school would endure between 1859 and 1869. 1859

The State Board of Education mistakenly asked president Joseph Williams to resign. The Board was at fault for college debt, administrative meddling, and a miss-guided quest for a two-year course of study. The college president was even precluded from membership on, or even attendance at Board meetings.

Lewis R. Fisk (1825-1901), professor of chemistry, was named president pro tem—the school's second president. Fisk was an 1850 graduate of the University of Michigan. He had a D.D. degree from Albion College, and an LLD. Degree from Michigan. He was a minister and had served from 1850 to 1853 as a professor at Wesleyan Seminary & Female Collegiate Institute; from 1853 to 1856 as a professor at the State Normal School in Ypsilanti, and from 1856 to 1859 as a professor at M.A.C.

President Fisk…

"productive agriculture demands a high grade of intelligence."

In 1859, "Dr. Asa Gray, professor of natural history at Harvard University, donated a large box of perennial herbs from the botanical garden in Cambridge, Massachusetts to the college horticulture department," (From An Oak Opening by Harold Lautner). In addition, "seedsmen, florists, and nurserymen of New York donated hardy plants, bulbs and trees, including magnolia, panlonia, wigelia, and salisburia."

Faculty records of 1859 recorded, "On the motion of Professor Abbot, (the faculty) voted that the steward be notified that the burning of camphine or spirits as a light is considered dangerous, and is forbidden by the faculty, and that he take measures to supply students with candles, and that they be notified of this rule." (*Wolverine,* 1901).

Manly Miles, M.D. **(Manly Miles Building)**, joined the faculty. He would become the first professor in the United States to teach scientific agriculture.

Enrollment for 1859 was 49.

1860 **T.C. Abbot** returned to the college as professor of rural engineering after a short absence. Abbot and president pro-tem Lewis Fisk polled students on their curriculum preference: the four-year scientific and liberal education program, or the State Board of Education proposal for a two-year plan, which stripped both science and humanities from course work. Students unanimously choose the four-year plan.

Lewis R. Fisk, Second President

The first bridge to span the Red Cedar River was authorized by the college board. It was 150 feet long, 16 feet wide, with wood piles and planking. It was located at the current site of the Farm Lane bridge, and cost $750.00.

Enrollment was 66.

Williams Helps Reorganize the College—Joseph R. **1861**
Williams, former M.A.C. president and now a state senator, shepherded a bill through the Michigan legislature that created the **State Board of Agriculture as the ruling body of the college**, and assured a four-year curriculum providing for a scientific and liberal arts education. Importantly, the bill also secured the needed authority for the college president, making him an ex-officio member of the board, and "Chief Executive Officer" of the College.

Rumors revived that the college would be shut down and a department of agriculture established at the University of Michigan, to save money. The threat faded when the new Board proclaimed a new school term opening on April 17, 1861.

Samuel Alexander, a junior, entered the Union Army, becoming the school's first student ever to go to war.

The entire M.A.C. senior class of 1861, the college's first graduating class—seven men—enlisted for service in the Civil War.

The graduates and their status after serving in the Civil War, was as follows: A.F. Allen, farmer, Butler, Missouri; A. Bayley, farmer, Troy, Michigan; L.V. Beebe, insurance agent, Utica, New York; **H.D. Benham, died in the**

The Class of 1861—the school's first—L to R: H.D. Benham, L.V. Beebe, A.N. Prentiss, G.A. Dickey, A.F. Allen, A. Bayley, and C.E. Hollister.

army; G.A. Dickey, killed in the Battle of Gettysburg; C.E. Hollister, farmer, Laingsburg, Michigan; and A.N. Prentiss, professor of botany, Cornell University, Ithaca, New York. Prentiss would later join the faculty in East Lansing.

Judge Hezekiah Wells **(Wells Hall)** of Kalamazoo was named a member of the State Board of Agriculture (Board of Trustees). He would serve on the board until 1883, 14 of those years as president. Wells was passionately devoted to the college. Enrollment was 69.

1862

Theophilus C. Abbot (1826-1892), Named Third President of the College (served 1862-1884)—Abbot was an 1845 graduate of Colby University in Waterville, Maine, and was selected as the third president of the college in December 1862. His election was a major step in the survival of the college, although unknown at the time. Abbot had taught at Bangor Theological Seminary in Maine; Colby University; Berrien Springs, Michigan schools; and the Union School in Ann Arbor before his appointment in 1858 as a professor of English at M.A.C.

President Abbot...

"There is special need of educational work for farmers."

T.C. Abbot's human touch, love of the students and inspired leadership of a small, but talented faculty carried the college through its darkest days. His dedicated work secured the college's place as the leader among America's land-grant colleges. Abbot would serve as president for 22 years (1862-1884), second only to the 28-year tenure of President John A. Hannah (1941-1969).

President Abraham Lincoln signed the Morrill Act (Land-Grant Act) on July 2, 1862. It read; "...to teach such branches of learning as are related to agriculture and the mechanic arts...in order to promote the liberal and practical education of the industrial classes in the several pursuits and professions of life."

The Morrill Act rewarded the great lobbying and communications efforts made by M.A.C. President Williams in the late 1850s. Tragically, Williams, who struggled with asthma and poor health all of his life, died on June 15, 1861 in Toledo, Ohio at age 53. He missed by 12 months and two weeks witnessing the signing of the act that created the nation's land-grant colleges.

Congressman Henry Dixon of Utah, who proposed the Centennial Recognition of the Land-Grant Act in 1962, stated that **President Lincoln "lighted a candle during the darkest days..." by signing the Morrill Act.** "In 1862, one American in 1,500 went to college. Today (1962), the ratio is one in three, thanks chiefly to the Morrill Act." (*MSU Magazine*, February, 1962).

A diphtheria epidemic hit the college in 1862, killing five students. This episode, combined with previous malaria shutdowns of the school, hurt the attractiveness of the college.

Oscar Clute, class of 1862, "...delivered the first commencement oration made at an Agricultural College in America. He married Mary Merrylees, sister-in-law of President Abbot." (From *The Harrow*, school yearbook, 1889). Clute would become the first alumnus to serve as president of M.A.C., in 1889.

Enrollment was 60.

Theophilus C. Abbot, Third President

1863

School's First War Death—Gilbert A. Dickey, class of 1861 and second lieutenant in the Michigan 24th Infantry, was killed on the opening day of the Battle of Gettysburg, July 1, 1863. He was the first school student to die in any war. It is ironic that 92 years later, the motto of Michigan State's centennial celebration in 1955, would be selected from President Abraham Lincoln's classic Gettysburg address, **"...it is for us, the living, to be here dedicated to the unfinished work."**

College Existence Threatened Again—Because of lack of funding and the fact scores of students enlisted in the Army, and many more were needed on farms, the existence of the college was threatened again. In Madison Kuhn's book, *Michigan State—The First Hundred Years*, he wrote, **"a strong effort was made in the 1863 legislature to transfer the college and its land grant to Ann Arbor."** Students started to make plans to move to other colleges as they believed the college would be shuttered. This threat never materialized.

Landscaping improvements are obvious in this 1865 view of "Saints' Rest."

Dr. Robert C. Kedzie (Kedzie Halls) joined the faculty as professor of chemistry. In Madison Kuhn's book, *Michigan State—The First Hundred Years*, it was reported that Kedzie "had been taken prisoner at Shiloh (during the Civil War) after refusing to leave the wounded of his (Army) hospital."

Oscar Clute, Class of 1862, became an instructor in pure and applied mathematics. He would become the fifth president of the college in 1889, the first graduate of the school to attain that position.

Enrollment was 62.

1864

College a Leader in Agricultural Education—Despite the college's struggles, President Abbot's 1864 report on the college, stated, "The details of our plans (the building of an agricultural college) are eagerly sought for by persons in other states, and as a general thing, are approved by those who give them their attention.

"The Commissioner of Agriculture in Washington (D.C.) has examined and endorsed our general plan. Intelligent farmers and educationists who have visited the college, express themselves pleased with the plan, and what they see of its workings."

Reflecting Michigan State's long-held love of its campus, Abbot stated, "The grounds should be made a model of taste."

Military training was added to the curriculum, which included lectures on military hygiene and field fortifications.

The college budget for 1863-1864 was $14,551.79. President Abbot was paid $1,634.45.

Enrollment was 88.

1865

Dr. Manly Miles (Manly Miles Building) introduced America's first course in scientific agriculture at the College. He also initiated America's first scientific agricultural tests to determine the effectiveness of fertilizers on crops.

Albert N. Prentiss, professor and head of the horticulture department, "produced a new variety of tomato of superior quality."

The college apple orchard planted in 1858, first bore fruit in 1865.

Ninety-six faculty, students, and members of the State Board of Agriculture served the nation in the Civil War.

Fifteen alumni died in the Civil War—Sidney M. Abbott, 1861, Isaac B. Bailey, w 1861; William M. Begole, w 1864; Henry D. Benham, w 1861; Isaac M.D. Benham, w 1861; Otis W. Carpenter, w1864; Alpheus W. Carr, w 1861; Gilbert A. Dickey, w 1861; Charles T. Foster, w 1861; William M. Greene, w 1861; Cornelius Paulding, w 1861; Edward M. Prutzman, w 1864; Sidney S. Sessions, w 1862; John D. Skinner, w 1861; and William A. Smith, w 1861.

Another legislative proposal was made to transfer the school to Ann Arbor.

The Honorable Ezra Cornell of Ithaca, New York—co-founder of Cornell University—gave the college a South Down ram.

Baseball was introduced at the college. The team was known as the Stars.

Enrollment was 108.

Dr. Manly Miles—First Professor of Scientific Agriculture In America

**Dr. Manly Miles,
"Father" of Scientific Agriculture**

Dr. Manly Miles, M.D. (1826-1898), the "Father" of scientific agriculture in America, joined the State Agricultural College faculty in 1860 to teach zoology, animal physiology, geology and entomology. He revolutionized agricultural education in America by introducing the nation's first course in the application of science to agriculture in 1865.

Professor Byron D. Halsted of the New Jersey Agricultural College Experiment Station, who had been a student under Miles, characterized him as "Having been a full man who knew his subjects deeply and fondly. In those days, I am safe in writing, he represented the forefront of advanced agriculture in America." (*History of the Michigan Agricultural College,* 1915).

Miles believed "Every farm operation was the result of generations of successful experience. It was the scientist's duty to discover the biological or chemical processes which made those practices effective. By that understanding, one might distinguish the best techniques from those that were merely good, and might modify even the best. Miles was the leader in blending textbook education with practical observation and experimentation. As he learned to bridge the gap between farm and laboratory, he became, as a vice president of the University of Illinois, later remarked, 'the only professor of scientific agriculture in America.'" (*Michigan State: The First One Hundred Years, 1955).*

In 1875, Dr. Miles left the college to join the faculty of the University of Illinois. An editorial in the *Michigan Farmer* said of Miles, "We doubt very much if his place could be filled, in every way, by any two men picked out of any collegiate institution in or out of the country." (*Michigan State: The First One Hundred Years, 1955).*

Dr. Miles was the author of several books: *Stock Breeding; Experiments with Indian Corn; Silos and Ensilage;* and *Land Drainage.*

Dr. Miles grew up on a farm near Flint, Michigan and earned his M.D. degree from Rush Medical College in 1850 (now Rush Graduate School of Medicine at the University of Chicago).

1866

President Abbot defended the experimental nature of the college. Abbot lamented the fact that some people expected perfection of the new agricultural college in East Lansing. He stated, "Such persons forget the present classical college (traditional college) is the joint product of numerous college systems, experimenting through more than five hundred years; it is the result of the efforts of the first thinkers and educators in all lands, giving their best efforts to this educational problem—of mistakes rectified and errors rejected."

"We have the satisfaction of knowing that it (the College) stands before the country not only as the pioneer of its class, but also as having demonstrated many important truths of which other institutions are availing themselves. Indeed, it is a fact that these **agricultural colleges (in the U.S.) which give the greatest promise of success are using the Michigan Agricultural College as a model."**

Enrollment was 97.

1867

Appropriations Shortfall; Another Closing Threat—In President Abbot's annual report, he indicated legislative appropriations would only defray current expenses and would not allow for badly needed new buildings and other improvements.

Once more there was strong legislative backing to shut down the college and move it to Ann Arbor. Again, the Michigan Agricultural Society battled for an autonomous agricultural school.

Joseph Harris, editor of the *Genesee Farmer,* visited the college in June, 1867, reported, "...a finer set of young men I never saw together. Leaving science entirely out of the question, what he (the student) sees of good cultivation, good implements and machines, improved breeds of cattle, sheep and pigs, will go far towards making him a good farmer." "... may the day soon come—and it is coming very fast—when trained minds and skilled hands shall banish drudgery from American farms."

Dr. C.E. Bessey, Class of 1869, well-known botanist and faculty member, spoke of the year 1867 at the 1907 fiftieth anniversary of the opening of the college: **"Forty years ago this was the only college in the West in which one could study all of the great sciences in any manner** and it is greatly to her credit that, with the possible exception of Harvard University, this college then gave the most extended and thorough course in botany in this country."

Daniel Strange, Class of 1867, speaking years later about the college, stated, **"We dwelt in a sacred nearness to our teachers (Professors Abbot, Kedzie, Miles, Clute and Prentiss) that never can obtain in a larger institution.** We were invited into their families and welcomed into their libraries or to private interviews at all times. **Their personalities impressed us and were stamped upon us for all time."**

First Williams Hall, a dormitory built in 1869, was named in honor of Joseph Williams, first president of the college. It burned to the ground in 1919.

The Horticulture Department started a nursery to supply trees for the campus.

Enrollment for 1867 was 82.

1868

Single Dormitory Bursts With Students—Crowding of the Boarding Hall ("Saints' Rest") was noted by President Abbot in his 1868 report, "The number of applications for admission having been largely in excess of the number that could be accommodated with rooms (required) in most instances, four, and sometimes five students per room."

Attendance reached 82 students—76 from Michigan, representing 26 counties, and six from other states. Abbot wrote, "Sixty, or three-fourths, are sons of farmers, and the larger part of them work to teach in the winter (prior to the summer vacations, which occurred later), to earn means for defraying their college expenses."

Enrollment was 82.

1869

The Turning Point in the Survival of the College—A final attempt to move the school to Ann Arbor arose in the legislature in 1869, but was squelched. It was the sixth and final threat to close the college that had emanated from the legislature since 1859. The Michigan Agricultural Society effectively continued its vigorous support of the college.

The Survival of the college was foretold by two significant events—first, University of Michigan opposition to the college folded. And, second, legislative appropriations included funds for the annual operating budget as well as $30,000 for a desperately needed dormitory, as well as funds for a new farm house. According to Kuhn's book, *Michigan State: The First One Hundred Years*, University of Michigan regents finally realized that moving the agricultural school to Ann Arbor would "subject them to pressure from a group of rural leaders," which they did not want.

First Williams Hall Built—The $30,000 appropriation built a new Boarding Hall which was four stories tall, had a Mansard roof and a tower 100 feet tall. It was heated by steam. The hall was later named for the college's first president Joseph R. Williams. It was located between College Hall and the Boarding House (Saint's Rest), on the site of the present Museum.

Campus Care—President Abbot reported, "The grounds around the new Boarding Hall and the farmhouse will be graded and put in order in the coming season. Improvements have progressed in the getting out of stumps, the building of fences, the eradication of bushes, clearing fields of rubbish, and bringing the land into grass as rapidly as the character of the season would allow."

Enrollment was 132.

1870

First Women College Students in Michigan—Ten women students—the first admitted to any college in Michigan—were enrolled at East Lansing in 1870. They ranged in age from 16 to 23. President Abbot wrote in his diary about his faculty poll on admitting women to the College: "To town from 4-6 (pm). All about the application of girls for admission to the College. Saw faculty in succession, except Professor Cook. All thought we ought not to reject them." ("First Ten Years of Co-edism at Michigan State, by Frances Ayres, class of 1925, in February, 1931 *MSC Record*.) Following the coeds' first year, President Abbot commented, "They studied chemistry, botany, horticulture, floriculture, trigonometry, surveying, entomology, bookkeeping, and other branches. Their progress was rapid, and their improvement marked."

The ten coeds were: Isabelle Allen, Catherine Bacon, Ella Brock, Mary Daniels, Harriett Dexter, Gertrude Howe, Emma Hume, Mary Jones, Elizabeth Sessions, and Catherine Steele. Abbot stated that a hall was needed for the women. It would take 30 years to realize that dream.

It took Oxford University in England—one of the oldest universities in the world–until 1884 to admit women.

The first money from the Morrill Act—$2,779.89—was received by the college. It was generated from interest on the sale of portions of the 240,000 acres granted to the college in 1862. Seemingly a small amount, the funds were enough to pay the annual salaries of the college president and a full professor.

Retaining talented faculty members—a concern even today—was first mentioned in 1870. President Abbot wrote, "The college is in constant danger of losing professors from the fact that salaries in this state are much lower than is frequently offered them in other states. Men competent to fill chairs in agricultural colleges are hard, and for some places, almost impossible to find."

Dr. William J. Beal, who would become a giant in the field of botany, joined the faculty as a lecturer in botany and horticulture.

Enrollment was 141.

1871

U of M President Angell Calls the College "Unrivaled"—President Abbot was awarded an LL.D. degree by the University of Michigan in June, 1871. It was only the seventh honorary doctor's degree the U of M had awarded.

University of Michigan President James B. Angell delivered the commencement address at M.A.C. in November of 1871. He said, "You have enjoyed facilities for the study of scientific agriculture, superior to those offered by any similar institution in the land, for I can say that the Michigan State Agricultural College stands unrivaled. This lays upon you a heavy responsibility."

In the November 16, 1871 *Detroit Free Press*, President Angell was quoted, **"The Agricultural College of Michigan is recognized as the best of its kind in the U.S."**

J.J. Thomas wrote in 1871 in *Country Gentleman*, **"The Agricultural College of the State of Michigan has long stood in the front rank of the most efficient institutions of the kind in the world."**

A chemical laboratory costing $10,000 was built to Chemical Professor Dr. Robert Kedzie's specifications. He had researched the nine best labs in the country and one in Germany. Ventilation hoods, a modern innovation for that era, were placed over laboratory tables. Following World War II, this yellow brick building served as the university library annex and a lecture hall. It was located on the site of the present library and was razed in 1955 when the new library was built.

A.S. Welch, president of Iowa State Agricultural College, donated two volumes on the Geology of Iowa to the college library.

The Kew Gardens of England donated 200 varieties of tree seeds and 70 grass seeds to the college.

Enrollment was 131.

1872

First Outreach and Ozone Observations—Principals of union (high) schools appeared on campus in the summer of 1872 requesting lessons in analytical chemistry and chemical manipulations. The faculty responded by forming a class in chemical manipulations, which was free to teachers of public schools. It was the first formal outreach by the college.

With the current concern regarding the earth's ozone layer, it is remarkable to note that M.A.C. faculty members were making observations on ozone in 1872 "to determine its influence on the atmospheric conditions and fluctuations on health and disease."

All examinations given to students were to be executed in writing. Enrollment was 143.

1873

Dr. Dr. William J. Beal Starts Oldest Continuing Botanical Garden in U.S.—To help his students learn through observation, Dr. Beal, professor of botany, started planting a botanical garden in the ravine across from today's Music Building. This living laboratory is the oldest, continuing botanical garden of its kind in America. Today it features more than 5,000 plant species and varieties.

Dr. William J. Beal, "Father" of Hybrid Corn, observing the botanical garden he started in 1873. It is the oldest continuing garden of its kind in the U.S.

Beal Leads the Nation in Labeling Trees & Plants—Beal was ubiquitous with his planting. He created miniature arboretums around the campus. Moreover, Beal labeled and catalogued hundreds of trees and plants to aid his students. It is believed this was the first tree and plant labeling program on any college campus in the nation. Today, this identification program is the most extensive in America. The Royal Gardens of Kew, England donated 200 varieties of tree seeds, and 70 varieties of grass seeds to the college for planting in 1873.

A beautiful president's residence was built on Faculty Row, near the top of the Beal Street hill, on a site where the west end of Gilchrist Hall now stands.

For health reasons, President Abbot was granted a leave of absence to go to Europe from May, 1873 to May, 1874. Professor G.T. Fairchild **(Fairchild Auditorium)** was named Acting President.

Enrollment dropped to 121 from 143 the previous year due to "financial troubles that disturbed all classes (of people)."

1874

Commencement Address: "Does Education Pay?"—George P. Hays, President of Washington & Jefferson College, gave the first recorded commencement address at the college, titled, "Does Education Pay" on November 8, 1874. There were 21 graduates in the audience. He stated, "a common school (high school) education adds 25 to 50 percent to a man's money-making power," and that a higher education (college) will add in the same proportion.

According to 1870 U.S. census figures, only 17,824 men out of 2,611,796, ages 18 to 24, went to college—or one in 146. He pointed out that of the 302 members in the U.S. House of Representatives, 138 were college graduates, and another 55 had received more or less education. Of the 72 members in the U.S. Senate, 35 were college graduates, and 15 others had more or less education. Of the 15 men who had been President of the United States. 13 were college men, and two were "self-made."

Hays said, "A college education costs from $1,500 to $2,500—at your college here, but a little over $700—and any man worth a snap can in one year after get his $1,000." Hays made two cogent points—first, **"It is college life that educates. College students criticize unmercifully, and though mortifying, it is extremely healthy to the subject;" and second, "Knowledge is said to be power, but one half of knowledge is in its prompt recall**...it is important for farmers to be able to tell what they know, and to speak in public as any professional man."

President Abbot wrote in his annual report, "I think it a great credit to the college that it has infused into its graduates a great desire for further knowledge. We are one of the very few institutions that yearly retain a portion of their graduates for further study."

The first graduate courses were contemplated in 1874 "to submit to the Board for their approval."

President Abbot reported that "More than half of the students were members of the College Christian Union, which has sustained meetings, lectures, a Sunday school, and is possessed of a growing library, periodicals, and maps."

Chemistry Professor Dr. Robert C. Kedzie, in his report to the president, referred to his "evening 'chemical

President's home, # 1 Faculty Row, opened in 1874 near the top of Beal Street Hill, then known as "President's Hill." It stood on the site where the west end of Gilchrist Hall now stands. The home later served as a senior women's dorm, the College Hospital until 1940 when Olin Health Center was built, and a home economics practice house. It was razed in 1946.

conversations' with students, to understand what his students understood."

Kedzie accepted a position on the State Board of Health, working on his own vacation time. He also served as a member of the Michigan Section of State Medicine and Public Hygiene of the American Medical Association.

The effect of coeds on the men was noted by a male student in 1874: "Right opposite me at the dining table were three of the five coeds. Oh, they were beautiful! Belle Allen, fair, titian-haired and with rosy cheeks and a skin like alabaster; Mollie Jones, with a smile so winning and such charm and so pretty; and Libby Sessions, dainty and brunette, with hair inclined to curl and eyes so black and lustrous! (They seemed beings apart, a little but not much lower than angels, and far above the boys)." (*MSC Record*, February 1931, "First Ten Years of Co-edism at Michigan State" by Frances Ayers, Class of 1925).

A generous gift from the Ilgenfritz Nursery Company in Monroe, Michigan included 35 apple trees, five peach trees, 20 plumb trees, 13 ornamental trees, and 200 apple stocks.

William H. Marston was secretary of the State Board of Agriculture (Board of Trustees).

Enrollment was 156.

Class of 1875 at "The Rock," gift of the Class of 1873, which now stands northeast of Farm Lane bridge.

1875

Dr. Robert Kedzie: Pioneer in Public Health and Consumer Protection—Dr. Robert C. Kedzie, chemistry professor and a member of the Michigan State Board of Health, made a remarkable address to the Michigan House of Representatives on March 16, 1875 on public health and consumer protection issues.

Working on his own time, he had inspected the illuminating oils of the day (no electric lights) to prevent highly volatile ones from going on sale. He called for a bill to protect the public.

He had studied ventilation in public buildings, including prisons statewide, and emphasized, "The foul air in an unventilated room stupefies the brain and prevents all proper mental activity. Your own legislative halls need pure air." He suggested to the legislators that building codes be passed requiring ventilation to be included in new building plans.

He called their attention to the poisonous substance Paris green, which was then being used in wall paper and dress fabrics as a coloring agent. Kedzie analyzed the paper and found that Paris green coloring contained arsenic. The courageous professor called for an end to the use of Paris green as a coloring agent even though there was business opposition to this idea.

"Drinking the Drippings of Death"—He also discussed the dangers of digging drinking water wells close to outhouses and graveyards. He had tracked the causes of severe sickness and typhoid in Grand Rapids and Lansing to wells too close to contaminating sources. Speaking of wells in Grand Rapids near a graveyard, he said, "Who can doubt that these unfortunate families have been drinking the very drippings of death."

College Plan Copied by Other Schools—Kudos flowed to the college in 1875. President Abbot reported, "Massachusetts (Agricultural College) sent each of her three presidents to visit our College, and to copy in great part our plans." Maine (Agricultural College) sent its acting president and a professor to the campus, and copied plans. "President White of Cornell (University) has been here twice, and always refers to the College as one of the best."

President Abbot Tells of the Burden of Office—"The executive duties of the office of president, and its correspondence, are enough to tax the best abilities of one man, but I have shared in the burden of overwork which the poverty of the institution imposes on all its officers a burden complained of only that the multiplicity of duties impairs the quality of work that is done."

Heavy Faculty Workload Explained—The extraordinary work effort of the small faculty was responsible for the College's new found success and recognition. Professor Beal wrote, "No one who has not been inside as one of the faculty of an agricultural college such as the one at (East) Lansing in 1875, can have any adequate conception of the unceasing work and worry it requires. Growing crops take no vacations in the summer, and to a far larger extent than in older colleges and in classical schools, the faculty of an agricultural college must be on duty all year round."

The first Farmers' Institutes were proposed in 1875 by Dr. Kedzie to share new found agricultural knowledge with the practicing farmers of the state who could not come to the campus. This practical outreach added greatly to the work of many professors. The next year, institutes were held in several cities.

The students, under the authority of the faculty, formed an organization for self-government at the beginning of the 1875 school year.

The total payroll for nine faculty and staff in 1875 was $15,850. T.C. Abbot, President and Professor of Mental Philosophy and Logic, was paid $3,000; Dr. Robert Kedzie, Professor of Chemistry and Curator of the Laboratory, $2,000; William J. Beal, Professor of Botany, $2,000; Rolla C. Carpenter, Instructor in Mathematics and Civil Engineering, $1,000; and Robert F. Kedzie, Assistant in Chemistry and Kedzie's son, $600.

In the 1875 commencement address, Michigan Governor Bagley told the graduates that "their education was given them by the State, not for their own personal and selfish ends, but as a trust to be used for the good of the community in which each one dwelt, and of the State of Michigan."

Enrollment for 1875 was 164.

Dr. Robert C. Kedzie

"Father" of Michigan's Sugar Beet Industry
Leader In American Consumer Advocacy

Dr. Robert C. Kedzie (1823-1902) (Kedzie Halls, Kedzie Street), joined the college faculty in 1863 as chemistry professor, and served 39 years until his death in 1902.

Kedzie was a national leader in conservation, protection of the environment and consumer advocacy, nearly a century before such efforts became popular.

In an 1867 address, Kedzie railed against the "useless and thoughtless destruction of one of the most beautiful of God's gifts to man—trees." He won a seat in the Michigan legislature and authored a bill that granted tax breaks to anyone who planted trees along the state's roadways. This law resulted in the planting of thousands of trees.

He delivered a remarkable address to the Michigan House of Representatives on March 16, 1875. It was titled, "The Relations of Chemistry to Agriculture and Public Health." The professional physician and chemist stated, **"Sickness is something more than a private calamity to the individual and family, it is a damage to the commonwealth."**

Kedzie reviewed his recent research activities with the law-makers. He told them about the poisonous substance Paris green, which was then being used as a coloring agent in wall paper and dress fabrics. He called for an end to the use of Paris green, which contained arsenic, even though there was business opposition to the idea. He had studied the foul air in unventilated public buildings, and recommended that building codes be passed requiring ventilation in new building plans. He had tracked the causes of severe sickness and typhoid in Grand Rapids and Lansing to drinking wells that were located to close to outhouses or graveyards, and suggested pubic education.

Kedzie proclaimed, **"among a free people, the surest, if not the quickest way, to remove any great evil is to clearly point out the evil itself, its extent, its effects."**

Kedzie was a superb researcher, master teacher, and inspiring lecturer. He gave his view of teaching in 1891, "To hold students to thorough work, to inspire enthusiasm in their studies, to induce scholarly habits and good principles, and thus fit them for life's work are the chief duties of a teacher."

He authored the *Handbook of Qualitative Analysis* in 1869. The book ran through four editions and was used to instruct students for three decades.

In 1875, Kedzie also proposed Farmers' Institutes to share new-found agricultural knowledge with the farmers of the state. This gave real impetus to the college's leadership outreach efforts.

In 1878, Kedzie warned of and predicted the eventual pollution of the Detroit River by human sewage and other sources.

Kedzie challenged the producers of phony fertilizers in 1883. He analyzed a fertilizer named "Farmer's Favorite." It was made from furnace slag and salt, and had no value. He provided the *Detroit Free Press* with his analysis, which resulted in killing the sales of the useless concoction. Kedzie was threatened with a $50,000 law suit by the company,

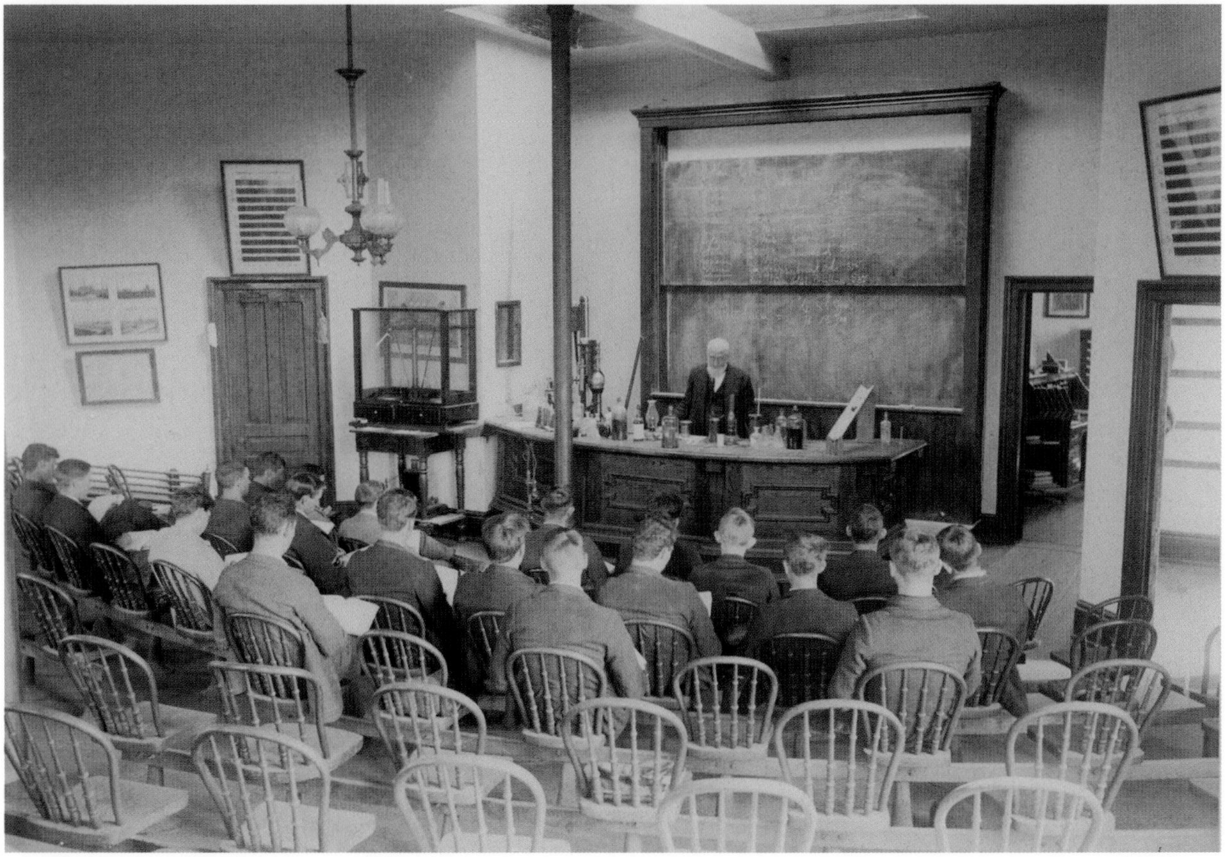

Dr. Robert C. Kedzie, "Father" of the Michigan sugar beet industry and master teacher, lecturing in 1892 to students in the Chemical Laboratory, built to his specifications in 1871. It stood on the site of today's Library.

but the suit was never pursued. His consumer advocacy resulted in "a law requiring the inspection and regulation of commercial fertilizers." (*Michigan History* magazine, January/February, 1989).

Kedzie crowned his notable career by creating the Michigan sugar beet industry. In 1890, he supervised the importation of 1,760 pounds of sugar beet seed from France and Germany. The seeds were distributed free of charge to farmers, with instructions on how to plant and cultivate sugar beets. He thus created Michigan's sugar beet industry.

According to the January/February 1989 *Michigan History* magazine, "On Kedzie's advice, the legislature passed a 'sugar beet' bounty of one cent per pound on beet sugar processed in Michigan. This stimulated business men to build sugar beet processing plants and soon the industry took off." By 1989, Michigan ranked fifth in the nation in sugar beet production.

Among his many national leadership positions, Kedzie served as president of the American Public Health Association (1882), president of the Society for Promotion of Agricultural Science (1887-1889), president of the Association of Agricultural Colleges and Experiment Stations (1899), and vice president of the American Medical Association.

Kedzie had three sons. William became a chemistry professor at Oberlin College in Ohio. Robert became a chemical professor at Mississippi State. Frank joined the Michigan Agricultural College faculty in 1880, succeeded his father in 1902, and was elected president of M.A.C. in 1915.

On November 7, 1902—the day of Dr. Kedzie's funeral—no classes were held at M.A.C. At the funeral services, held in the college Armory (site of the Music Building), Dr. Victor C. Vaughn, dean of medicine and surgery at the University of Michigan, eulogized, **"I know of no man who has done so much for the betterment of human life."**

1876

First Farmers' Institutes Held—Following an 1875 proposal by Dr. Kedzie, the college, for the first time took its agricultural knowledge on the road to share with the farmers of the state. Institutes were held in Adrian, Allegan, Armada, Coldwater, Decatur, and Rochester. Information was shared on crops, fertilizers, even lightning rods. These meetings featured local involvement and participation—"two local speakers to one from the College," according to Kuhn's book. This two-way communication was unique in college outreach.

"Saints' Rest" Burns to Ground—The school's first dormitory, called the Boarding Hall or "Saints' Rest" (named for a popular religious book of the time), burned to the ground in December. It was valued at $15,000, and was uninsured. A worn concrete square on the sidewalk east of the Museum and south of Linton Hall, marks the spot where Saints Rest stood.

At the U.S. Centennial Exhibition in Philadelphia in 1876, the college displayed a large map of the campus, a manuscript history of the institution, 120 kinds of grasses, 258 varieties of potatoes, and 1,115 specimens of woods collected by Dr. Beal in Michigan. The potato and woods collections both won awards. It probably was the first time the college had been represented at a national forum.

Good Accounting; No Insurance—The college accounted in detail for assets, but had no insurance due to the legislature. In each annual report there was painstaking accounting for everything on campus. The 1876 College Accounts review covered 61 pages. As an example, on page 59: "Inventory of the Department of Mathematics and Engineering—Book Case A, Shelf No. 3: model of ordinary plow, models of corn plows."

No insurance was kept on college buildings or property because the legislature cut these proposed expenditures from the school budget. This "penny-wise" mentality was costly. The Botany Laboratory would burn to the ground in 1890, uninsured.

President Abbot emphasized the importance of communications skills: "The attaining of accuracy and clearness in the expression of one's knowledge and opinions is too valuable an acquisition, both on its own account and for its reflex influence on the habits of observation and thought, to be made subordinate to other studies."

No matter how busy President Abbot was with his administrative and teaching duties, he responded to the students' desire for more knowledge. He wrote in 1876: "I have read with them (students) on Friday evenings (in his own home) the first three books of Milton's *Paradise Lost*. This reading was at their earnest and reiterated request." Enrollment was 154, six of whom were women.

1877

Dr. William J. Beal Develops Hybrid Corn—A monumental agricultural research break-through was developed by Dr. Beal in 1877. Kuhn's book (*Michigan State: The First Hundred Years*) recounts how Beal planted alternating rows of two different yellow dent strains of corn in a field east of what is now the Old Horticulture Building. "He removed the tassels of (one strain), so that its silk was fertilized by the pollen of the (other strain)."

"In 1878, ears of corn from the cross (fertilization) were planted." "Beal's cross-fertilization yielded fifty-three percent more (production) than (the corn) surrounding the field. Thus, he had improved yield, not by securing a new variety, but as he wrote, by adding 'vigor to the race.'"

Nation's First Seed Testing Laboratory—In 1877, Beal also "established the first seed-testing laboratory in the country."

The College is First in Reforestation Efforts—From the Civil War to the Spanish-American War, Michigan was the nation's leading producer of lumber for industry and building the railroads. Lumber from Michigan rebuilt Chicago after its great fire in 1871. At the peak of the logging era, about 1888, Michigan's forests provided one quarter of the nation's lumber—three times more than any other state.

"A Tree for a Tree" Program—As early as the 1870s the faculty at the college realized the threat of the de-forestation of Michigan. Dr. Kedzie, chemistry professor and Dr. William Beal, professor of botany and forestry, wrote at length deploring the rapid disappearance of Michigan's forests and urging farmers to plant trees. Kedzie and Beal encouraged farmers to plant trees. In 1877, a forest nursery was established on campus to provide farmers with saplings at cost. By 1933, Michigan State's tree nurseries produced 1.3 million trees for the U.S. Forest Service and Civilian Conservation Corps to plant in Michigan, with the goal of "A Tree for a Tree" to preserve and sustain the state's woodlands.

First Wells Hall Built—A $25,000 legislative appropriation provided the funds for a new three-story brick dormitory with room for 130 students. The dorm was named in honor of Hezekiah Wells, long-serving president of the State Board of Agriculture and fighter for the college's needs. It was located on the site of the current library.

Enrollment was 239.

Picturesque First Wells Hall was built in 1877. It was named in honor of Judge Hezekiah Wells, long-serving president of the State Board of Agriculture (Trustees). The Second Wells Hall was built in 1906, and the Third in 1967.

Dr. William J. Beal

"Father" of Hybrid Corn, Seed-Testing, and Michigan Forestry; American Environmental and Science Pioneer

Dr. William J. Beal (1833-1924) **(Beal Botanical Gardens; Beal Street)**, joined the faculty in 1870 and served for 40 years.

In 1873, he started what is now the oldest, continuously operating botanical garden of its kind in the United States. He did this to help his students learn through observation. One of the visual gems at Michigan State, the serene gardens cover five acres in a ravine across from the Music Building, and house more than 5,000 different plants.

Beal made an immense contribution to the nation and world when he successfully cross-fertilized corn in 1877. This experiment created the miracle of hybrid corn and greatly increased crop yields. He also "established the first seed-testing laboratory in the country," according to Madison Kuhn's book, *Michigan State: The First One Hundred Years*. In 1878, "Beal's cross-fertilization (of corn) yielded 53 percent more (production)." Dr. John Winburne, dean emeritus of MSU's University College, commented on the "Father" of hybrid corn in the *MSU News Bulletin* (May 15, 1980), "His primary work on hybridization, I believe, was one factor in reducing the number of persons needed on farms to feed the country."

In 1878, Beal cross-bred wax beans, producing a better flavor and higher yields.

Beal was ubiquitous with his plantings, creating miniature arboretums around the campus. He planted 150 species of trees and shrubs on a two-acre site north of Campbell Hall, and east of Mayo Hall. In 1896, he planted the two-acre "Beal Pinetum," a plantation of Norway Spruce, along the Red Cedar River, east of Hagadorn Road. These were but two of his many campus plantations.

To aid his students, Beal labeled and catalogued hundreds of trees and plants, believed to be the first such program on any college campus in the country. This label identification program today is the most extensive in America.

Dr. William J. Beal, "Father" of Michigan Forestry, views his botanical garden, started in 1873. It is set in the ravine next to the Library. Photograph circa 1880s.

"Upon his recommendation, the State Board of Agriculture (Board of Trustees), voted to cut no more of the woods at the Agricultural College, leaving approximately 150 acres" (May 1973 *Michigan Science* in Action magazine). As a result, MSU today has two rare forestry education resources—the Baker Woodlot, a 73-acre beech-maple forest (southeast corner of Farm Lane and Service Roads); and the 35-acre Sanford Natural Area (along the Red Cedar River between Hagadorn Road and Bogue Street).

Beal was "a teaching pioneer" and maverick. "He promoted the inductive, or laboratory method of learning. His students learned by examining nature first, and secondly, from texts and lectures." (*Michigan Science* magazine, May 1973). An 1880 lecture by Beal, titled *The New Botany*, was later published as a book. It was called "one of the five best internationally published books on teaching botany" in 1891.

Like Dr. Robert C. Kedzie, Beal was a conservationist and early environmentalist. He constantly promoted tree preservation and planting. He directed the establishment of experimental plantations of trees near Grayling, Oscoda, Harrison, Baldwin, and Walton, Michigan. He was the first to teach forestry at M.A.C., and served as the first director of the State Forestry Commission in 1888.

"Dr. Beal pioneered methods of silviculture (the cultivation of forest trees), including site preparation; planting, transplanting and cultivation of forest trees; development of forest nurseries; evaluation testing for performance of both native (trees) and introduced timber tree species under the variable climate and soil conditions of Michigan; and tree seed storage and viability. His early suggestions...had an early impact on reforestation of Michigan, as did his advocacy toward forestry, conservation, and forest legislation." (Dr. Frank W. Telewski, Curator, W.J. Beal Botanical Garden, in *The Beginning of An Artificial Forestry in Mid-19th Century Michigan—The Contributions of W.J. Beal to Silviculture).*

Beal was the first president of the American Association for the Advancement of the Science of Agriculture—1880; the first president of the botanists of the U.S. Agricultural Experiment Stations—1888; and the first president of the Michigan Academy of Science—1894.

Beal was born in Adrian, Michigan, earned a degree in zoology at the University of Michigan, then studied botany and zoology under the renowned Asa Gray and Louis Agassiz at Harvard.

1878

Educational Mission: Access to the Poorest; College Reputation Grows—"The students who come to us," President Abbot declared, "are for the most part dependent on their own earnings. We desire to retain this class of students, a class who may not have had the opportunity to go further than the minimum laid down by the law of the State." It was an affirmation of the Spirit of Michigan State.

Abbot proudly reported examples of M.A.C.'s growing reputation. "The college engaged the largest share of attention of the National Educational Society in the centennial year at Baltimore." He cited how **Mr. Gilmore, president of Johns Hopkins University**, visited the industrial schools (agriculture & mechanics) of the country as U.S. Special Commissioner several years ago. **"In his report he speaks of this college, alone of all, as having a well assured success."**

James McDonal, *Edinburgh Scotsman*, visited the U.S. to study cattle raising. **He selected the Michigan Agricultural College to describe at length, and called it, "one of the oldest and best." Moreover, officers of the colleges of Maryland, West Virginia, Indiana, Ohio, Arkansas, and Minnesota had visited the M.A.C. campus to study the college's organization and curriculum.**

Some 280 giant elm trees that graced the Grand River and Michigan Avenue median for more than 80 years were planted in the fall of 1878.

The college budget was $58,525. Faculty salaries totaled $15,523.72. Interesting line items: President's office expense—$80.97; diplomas—$150; improvement of the Red Cedar River—$35.93.

Enrollment was 230.

1879

First Woman Graduate; Telegraph Line Reaches Campus—Eva Diann Coryell (Mrs. William McBain), Class of 1879, was the first woman to graduate from the college.

Although kerosene lamps were still used to light classrooms and student rooms, and professors carried kerosene lanterns to find their way across campus after late hours in the labs, modern communication reached the campus. Kuhn's book states, "A telegraph line, extended to the campus in 1879, brought daily weather predictions which the Kedzie's relayed (to the campus family) by hanging flags outside the chemistry laboratory."

Always experimenting, Professor Beal "buried 20 pint bottles, each containing 1000 seeds of 20 plant species, mostly weeds, planning that one bottle be dug up every fifth year." These were placed near the Class of 1873 rock (which was then located just west of Linton Hall, and is now near the northeast corner of the Farm Lane bridge). Kuhn's book reads, "in 1905, eleven of the 20 species germinated and in 1950, when Professor H.T. Darlington dug the eleventh bottle (the interval had been widened to ten years), three kinds grew."

With an economic downturn, the college budget dropped to $45,249.72. Professors salaries were cut from $2,000 to $1,800.

Enrollment was 232.

1880

Beal First President of the American Association for the Advancement of the Science of Agriculture. The college's good national reputation was evident when Dr. Kedzie, Dr. Beal, and Professor Cook helped organize the American Association for the Advancement of the Science of Agriculture in Boston in 1880. Professor Beal was elected as the association's first president.

Two buildings went up in 1880—the first structure in the nation built solely as a Botanical Laboratory, and the Observatory. The laboratory—a beautifully ornamental wooden structure—was built on the north edge of the ravine overlooking the Beal Botanical gardens. It burned to the ground in 1890.

An ice house, 30' x 20' x 14', which would hold 200 tons of ice, was built near the Red Cedar dam.

Abbot reported on a poor faculty to student ratio at the college. He said that at the University of Michigan, and at the Iowa and Kansas Agricultural Colleges, it was one instructor to 13 students. At Cornell it was one to 10. At M.A.C., it was one to 30 in 1880. He also wrote, "The college is cramped for rooms for its classes, collections and work."

The college budget for 1880 was increased to $62,652.13. Enrollment was 221.

1881

Library-Museum (Linton Hall) Constructed: Steam Heat and Telephones Arrive—The long-sought Library-Museum was built in 1881. It is a classic old building with distinctive spire, and housed the president's office. Today it is often photographed from the west because of the picturesque view across a sweeping lawn and walkways. Located inside Circle Drive West, the building is named after **Robert S. Linton**, the long-time Registrar of the university, who introduced the perforated IBM card to help automate student registration in 1939.

Linton Hall was enlarged after World War II and was home to President John A. Hannah's office and Board Room until 1968, when the Hannah Administration Building was completed.

Centralized steam heat came to the campus in the spring of 1881.

Dr. Kedzie first brought telephone technology to the college by stringing a line between his office and Faculty Row home. Kuhn's research indicates a Lansing telephone

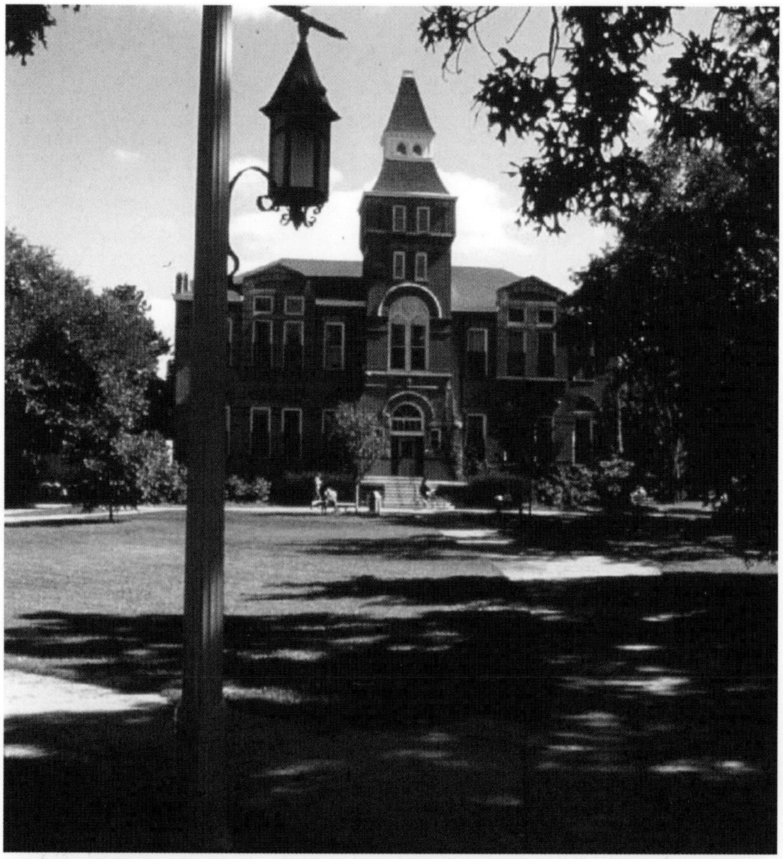

Linton Hall was built in 1881 as the Library-Museum. Now it's home to the College of Arts and Letters, and Graduate Studies.

company put up poles and lines to connect two telephones on the campus in 1881.

Enrollment for 1881 was 216.

1882

Abbot Calls for Greater Fire Protection—"I desire to call attention to the fact that we are without efficient means of fire protection," Abbot declared in his annual report. He wrote, "Cost of a complete system of water works, including a large steam pump, a large tank in the tower of Williams Hall, pipes, hydrants, hose & carts, would cost about $6,000, or about two percent (of the value) of the property protected." The concern was real. Fire had destroyed the college's first dormitory—"Saints Rest," in 1876. Fire would take other buildings in 1890, 1905, 1916, and 1919.

Lautner's book *From an Oak Opening* referred to President Abbot's comments about the campus in 1882, "There are in the park no straight rows of buildings or trees, but its more than 30 buildings are separated by undulating lawns, shallow ravines and groups of trees."

Enrollment was 185.

1883

First Appearance of Forestry and Veterinary Medicine; First Female Staff Member—Because of his deep interest in the environment and the preservation of the State's woodlands, the teaching of Forestry was added to Dr. Beal's workload.

Professor E.A.A. Granger, who had been a veterinary professor at the Ontario Agricultural College, was appointed to teach a one-year course in veterinary science.

For the first time, changes in the curriculum allowed seniors to select each term, three of the five courses they would study.

Beautiful fountain, gift of the Class of 1883, was last used in the Horticulture gardens formerly located behind the Old Horticulture Building.

Mrs. Mary J.C. Merrill, class of 1881, was named Librarian, and thus became the first female staff member at the school.

A student-proposed club system of boarding was put into operation. Students divided themselves into five dining clubs, each with its own steward. Meals improved and board was cut from $3.00 to $2.50 per month.

A water works, with high-pressure pumps, and a 300-gallon tank in the Williams Hall tower, was installed at a cost of $4,267.

The first "water closets" (flush toilets) on campus were installed in the Museum and Library (Linton Hall) at a cost of $350.

The Class of 1883 gave the college a beautiful fountain, which in the 1950s was located in the horticultural garden east of today's Old Horticulture building.

The library housed 6,135 volumes.

Enrollment was 171.

1884

President Abbot—The Survival Leader—Resigns—The man most responsible for the survival of the college in its infancy, T.C. Abbot, resigned the presidency in 1884, after serving for 22 years. He remained as acting president until July 1, 1885, when his successor took over. He was the inspirational leader who kept a small, tightly-knit, hard-working faculty together through the dark days, when the institution's existence was being challenged regularly.

Abbot's human and ethical standards paid big dividends for the college. He said, **"I laid it down as a rule that no opposition to the college should be held to be a ground of ill feeling against any person, and now I have the pleasure of seeing former opponents of the college amongst its warm friends..."**

The U.S. Government authorized a Post Office at the college in 1884. It was designated Agricultural College, Michigan. Robert G. Baird, Secretary of the Board, was appointed postmaster.

The State Fish Commission designated the college as a station and promised to form ponds and introduce fish in them.

Dr. Kedzie introduced the first electric lighting on campus, "using a gasoline engine to turn a dynamo in the chemistry lab."

"Intercollegiate athletic competition began in 1884, with participation in a field meet at Olivet College, and another at home to which the University of Michigan baseball team came," according to Kuhn's book *Michigan State: The First Hundred Years.*

The Library housed 8,000 volumes. Enrollment for 1884 was 173.

College Band in 1884. First Wells Hall in left background

1885

Edwin Willits Elected the College's Fourth President (served 1885-1889)—Edwin Willits (1830-1896), an 1855 graduate of the University of Michigan, took office as the fourth president of M.A.C. on July 1, 1885. In the mold of the college's first president, Joseph Williams, Willits was a "Renaissance man." He was 54, and most recently had been president of the State Normal School (now Eastern Michigan University). He had been a school teacher, an attorney, a county prosecutor, editor of the *Monroe Commercial* newspaper, Postmaster of Monroe, State Board of Education member for 12 years, and had won three terms in the U.S. House of Representatives. He was a very effective lobbyist for school appropriations, and led the greatest burst of campus building construction in the 19th century.

Edwin Willits, Fourth President

President Willits...

"The Agricultural College has been a potent factor in the dominion of scientific investigation."

"Drudgery without intelligence is slavery! Manual labor with intelligence is freedom!"

"... the best legacy we can leave to a son is a willingness to work."

The Armory was built in 1885. It served as a drill hall, gymnasium and auditorium. It occupied the site of the current Music Building.

Three important buildings went up during 1885. A **Mechanical Laboratory** (Engineering Department), with shops and classrooms, was built on the site of the current Olds Hall for $10,800. A **Veterinary Laboratory** ($5,400) was erected east of the Mechanical Laboratory on what is now the front lawn of the Hannah Administration Building. A long-sought **Armory** ($6,000) was constructed on the site of the present Music Building. The Armory served as a military drill hall, education hall, a gymnasium, an auditorium for commencement ceremonies, visiting lecturers, dances, and other events.

In his inaugural address President Willits referred to the work of the early leaders of the college as **"heroic persistency"** which kept the school alive. He stated he had visited alumni meetings at other colleges, "but never had witnessed so lively an interest" (in a school as he saw among alumni of M.A.C.). He also pointed out, **"The Michigan Agricultural Society said in regard to one special investigation by Dr. Kedzie that 'it has saved the farmers of this State more than the Agricultural College ever cost.'"**

President Willits was asked by the U.S. Commissioner of Agriculture to read his paper on *Industrial Education* at the convention of the nation's Agricultural Colleges and Experiment Stations held in Washington, D.C. on July 8, 1885.

Sharing newly discovered scientific knowledge with farmers through Agricultural Bulletins, an established practice at the college, was formalized into law in 1885.

Liberty Hyde Bailey (Bailey School, Bailey Street, Bailey Hall) was appointed Professor of Horticulture & Landscape Gardening. An 1882 M.A.C graduate, he would become renowned as the "Father of Horticulture" in the U.S., the most prolific agricultural author in the nation, the designer of the first Horticultural Lab in the nation, a leader in establishing 4-H Clubs, and distinguished faculty member at Cornell University, where a building would be named in his honor.

Enrollment for 1885 was 295.

1886

M.A.C. Admission Standards Match the Military Academies—A suggestion that the college admission standards be raised was not accepted by President Willits. He wrote, "I'm clearly of the opinion there should be no change. The standard is practically the same as that at the Military Academy at West Point and the Naval Academy at Annapolis."

ROTC cadets practice drills in 1886. Flag pole in front of Armory was purchased with a $150 gift from a United Kingdom student.

MSU Presidents Helped Establish and Support America's Agricultural Experiment Stations

MSU's fourth and seventh presidents worked effectively to help influence Congress to establish and support Agricultural Experiment Stations nationwide. The research generated by these stations has led to immense gains in agricultural productivity and quality, making the U.S. the world's premier food producer.

Edwin Willits, MSU's fourth president, played an important role in the passage of the Agricultural Experiment Station Act (Hatch Act) in 1887. This act provided the agricultural research dollars that enabled the nation's land-grant colleges to develop superior crop varieties and growing techniques, as well as combating crop and farm animal diseases. This stimulus energized the application of science to agriculture, making America the "Bread Basket" of the world.

The State Board of Agriculture (Board of Trustees) directed President Willits to spend six weeks in Washington, D.C. in 1886 to help promote the passage of the Agricultural Experiment Station Bill by Congress. The bill was passed by the 48th Congress and signed into law by President Grover Cleveland on March 1, 1887. It provided each agricultural college experiment station with $15,000 annually for research.

Jonathan L. Snyder, MSU's seventh president, visited Washington, D.C. many times from 1903 to 1906 seeking passage of the Adams Act, which bolstered agricultural research at the nation's land-grant college experiment stations. This act provided an additional $5,000 for research the first year, with an increase of $2,000 per year until a total of $30,000 a year had been added to the $15,000 received annually from the Hatch Act (Agricultural Experiment Station Act) of 1887.

Introduction of engineering education, then called mechanic arts, was one of Willits' major contributions. The new Mechanic Arts Building, with labs and lecture rooms, and constructed for 75 students, was immediately filled to capacity.

The Board directed President Willits to spend six weeks in Washington, D.C. to help promote the passage of the Agricultural Experiment Station Bill by Congress. The bill was successfully passed by the Agricultural Committees of the House and the Senate, but was not signed into law.

A two-year student from England gave the college a gift of $150 in gratitude for the "wonderful facilities for scientific study free of charge." President Willits said the student wished to remain anonymous, and that the gift would purchase a 100-foot flag pole to be erected in front of the Armory.

The 1886 college budget was $88,686.49. Salaries for 21 faculty totaled $29,250, with the president being paid $3,200; two professors $2,000; and six other professors $1,800.

Student enrollment was 323. The library held 9,820 books and publications.

1887

Willits' Work Rewarded with Passage of Ag Experiment Station Act. The Agricultural Experiment State Act that President Willits and others had labored to pass in the 48th Congress in 1885-1886, was overwhelmingly accepted by the 49th Congress, and signed into law by President Grover Cleveland on March 1, 1887. Thus, for the second time in three decades, an M.A.C. president had been key in passing leadership laws to provide for the nation's agricultural education and research.

Known as the Hatch Act, the bill established agricultural experiment stations at all of the land-grant colleges in the United States, and provided each with $15,000 annually for research. This was highly significant in extending and improving scientific research in agriculture.

The Hatch Act stated: "...it shall be the object and duty of such experiment stations to conduct original researches or verify experiments on the physiology of plants and animals; the diseases to which they are severally subject, with the remedies for the same..."

An 1887 State Law, Act No. 259, designated **the State Board of Agriculture to serve as an Independent Forestry Commission.** Section 2 called for, "an inquiry into the extent to which the forests of Michigan are being destroyed by fires, used by wasteful cutting for consumption, or for the purpose of clearing lands for tillage or pasturage."

Dr. Beal, the college's first forestry professor, said of the commission, "They do believe most emphatically in teaching children and young people a respect for growing trees, developing in them a love for the planting and growing of trees, and opening to them a knowledge of the influences trees and forests have upon people and the modification of civilization as affected by the deforestation of a country."

Wearing green as a school color was first recorded in 1887, when fans wore green ribbons at a field event. Perhaps the selection of green flowed from the nature of the school's focus on successfully growing plants, crops and trees—mostly green.

The college budget for 1887 was $56,685.92. Enrollment was 312.

First Abbot Hall, built in 1888 for $10,000, stood on the site of the Music Practice Building. It overlooked "Sleepy Hollow," foreground, a campus beauty spot to this day. In 1894, 10,000 plants were laid out in beds in the hollow. Abbot, first housed men and later women—when it was called "The Abbey." It was razed in 1967.

1888

Three New Buildings; First Horticulture Lab in U.S.—Three new buildings were completed in 1888, equaling the record three constructed in 1885. The first building and laboratory in the nation devoted wholly to horticulture was built at a cost of $7,000. It was designed by M.A.C. graduate Liberty Hyde Bailey and still stands on West Circle Drive. Today it is known as Eustace-Cole Hall (Dr. Harry J. Eustace was chair of horticulture, 1908-1919), and is home to the Honors College.

A sixty-student dormitory, costing $10,000, was erected on a site just east of today's Music Building. It was **named for President Emeritus Theophilus C. Abbot**. It was razed in 1968.

Howard Terrace, eight-apartment instructors' residence costing $10,000, also was built in 1888. **Named for Sanford Howard**, the first Secretary of the State Board of Agriculture, it was located on the site of today's Human Ecology Building (formerly Home Economics). It was torn down in 1922.

On January 26, 1888, the college created its Agricultural Experiment Station on campus.

Due to the importance of weather forecasting in growing all things, a **State Weather Service** was established on campus in 1888. A new Farm Lane bridge, made of iron, was constructed over the Red Cedar River.

The Junior Hop, major social event of the year, originated in 1888. "Of those who danced (at the J-Hop) in 1895, it was reported that the 'gray dawn of morning caught them still in the dizzy whirl of the waltz.'"

The college budget for 1888 was $111,064.93, excluding the three new buildings, which were purchased from 1887 appropriations. Enrollment was 340.

Eustace-Cole Hall, nation's first Horticultural Laboratory, built in 1888 for $7,000, is home to the Honors College.

Liberty Hyde Bailey, Class of 1882

"Father" of American Horticulture and 4-H Programs
Most Prolific Agricultural Writer In History

Dr. Liberty Hyde Bailey, "Father" of American Horticulture, pictured at age 90, still doing research.

Liberty Hyde Bailey (1858-1954), Class of 1882, **(Bailey Hall, Bailey School, Bailey Street)** was born in South Haven, Michigan.

In his career, Bailey earned the title, "Father" of American Horticulture, rural sociology, 4-H programs, and agricultural journalism.

He arrived at Michigan Agricultural College in 1877, his belongings bundled in a piece of carpeting. As a student he founded the *Speculum*, the student quarterly newspaper.

After graduation, Bailey spent two years—1883-1885—as an assistant to Dr. Asa Gray the famed Harvard University botanist. In 1885, he returned to M.A.C. to head the horticulture department. He designed the first horticultural laboratory in the U.S. It was completed in 1888, and stands today in renovated splendor as Eustace-Cole Hall on Circle Drive, home of MSU's Honors College. The desk Bailey used at M.A.C. still resides on campus in the office of Dr. Ron Perry, chairperson, Department of Horticulture (2003), located in the Plant and Soil Sciences building.

Cornell University attracted Bailey in 1888 to chair practical and experimental horticulture. By 1903, he was named dean of the college of agriculture. He retired in 1913 to research, write, and explore for new plant specimens. **The Bailey Hortitorium stands on the Cornell campus** as a tribute to Dean Bailey.

Bailey became the most prolific agricultural writer in history, authoring 75 books himself, editing 117 books by 99 authors between 1890 and 1940, and writing and editing 700 scientific papers. Bailey's books included: *Standard Cyclopedia of Horticulture, Manual of Cultivated Plants,* and *Outlook to Nature.*

In 1907, Bailey met and dined with U.S. President Theodore Roosevelt at the 50th anniversary of the opening of M.A.C. At that time, Bailey was president of the Association of Agricultural Colleges and Experiment Stations, and spoke at the celebration, as did Roosevelt, who was the keynote speaker.

On his return to Washington, D.C., President Roosevelt asked Bailey to chair the new Commission on Country Life, whose task was to determine why people were leaving their farms for city life, and make recommendations for rural improvements.

Bailey conducted a national survey and produced the **"Report of the Commission on Country Life,"** which had a major impact on rural reform. **Results included: passage of the Smith-Lever Act, establishing the Cooperative Extension Services of America's agricultural colleges, and the national 4-H programs. Moreover, the report helped initiate the U.S. Parcel Post system, Rural Free Delivery, rural electrification, and agricultural education in public schools.** Bailey also wrote a book on the subject, *The Country Life Movement in the U.S.*

Bailey was still doing research at age 91. He died on Christmas Day, 1954 at age 96.

A U.S. Postage Stamp honoring Bailey was issued in 1958 on the 100th anniversary of his birthday.

The Liberty Hyde Bailey Museum in his hometown of South Haven, Michigan, a tribute to his life work, was designated a National Historic Site in 1984.

1889

Oscar Clute, Class of 1862, Named Fifth President (served 1889-1893)—President Willits resigned in April, 1889 to become Assistant Secretary of Agriculture for the United States. Oscar Clute (1837-1902), a member of the college's second graduating class—1862—was elected the school's fifth president. He was the first M.A.C. graduate to become its president. He served in Howlett's Engineers during the Civil War. He taught mathematics at M.A.C. between 1862 and 1866, and received an M.S. degree from the college in 1864. He graduated from Meadville Theological Seminary in 1867, and served as a minister in the Unitarian Church of New Jersey, Iowa, and California from 1868 until 1889.

President Clute...

"The Michigan Agricultural College had its origins in the minds of men who were firm believers in a new order in education."

Oscar Clute, Fifth President

The Entomology Building, first agricultural laboratory in the nation, was erected on campus in 1889. Located on West Circle Drive across from Linton Hall, the building is **named in honor of Professor Albert J. Cook**, Class of 1862, who returned to campus as a math instructor. He was a nationally known entomologist and a leader in the development of insect spraying.

Leadership in the use of fungicides to spray apple trees in 1889 was provided by Levi Rawson Taft, Liberty Hyde Bailey's successor. A campus marker at East Circle Drive near the Collingwood Entrance proclaims Taft as **"first in Michigan, a pioneer in America."** His efforts dramatically reduced disease in apple trees and helped save Michigan's orchards.

A heated bathhouse with ten tubs and hot and cold water was built for the students at a cost of $600. The students raised $300 as a loan to launch the project.

The college budget for 1889 was $103,558.81. Enrollment hit a record 369.

1890

Heavy Faculty Losses—Leadership in producing top agricultural scientists and engineers, combined with a low pay scale, continued to deplete the college's professorial ranks.

R.C. Carpenter left to chair Practical and Experimental Engineering at Cornell, increasing the number of M.A.C. graduates on the Ithaca, New York faculty to five.

Albert B. Cordley, Class of 1888 and zoology instructor, was appointed Professor of Entomology at the Vermont Agricultural College.

C.S. Crandall, Class of 1873 and foreman of horticulture, was named Professor of Botany and Horticulture at the Colorado Agricultural College.

G.L. Teller, assistant chemist, was promoted to Adjunct Professor of Agriculture and Chemistry at the Arkansas Industrial University.

L.H. Dewey, Class of 1888, appointed Assistant Botanist of the Department of Agriculture, Washington, D.C.

C.B. Walton, Class of 1887 and assistant in Botany, named Botanist at the Experiment Station in North Dakota.

James Wiseman, foreman of the iron shop, accepted a position in a manufacturing company in Chicago.

The Botanical Laboratory erected in 1880, burned to the ground. The *Botanical Gazette* in 1885 had called it, **"the most imposing building erected for botanical instruction in the country."**

The 1890 college budget was $99,411.24. Enrollment was 360. At graduation 31 bachelor's degrees were awarded. Receiving master's of science degrees were Charles B. Collingwood **(Collingwood Drive and Campus Entrance)**, who would become a judge; and Kumaroku Shoshima, a graduate of the Imperial College of Agriculture, Tokio, (actual spelling in the annual report) Japan.

1891

The Detroit College of Law Founded in Detroit—It became the Michigan State University-Detroit College of Law in 1996, when it moved to the East Lansing campus. Today it is the nation's oldest continuously operating independent law school, and through 2001, had produced 8,000 graduates.

Mrs. Linda Landon (Landon Hall) began her 41-year career as college librarian in 1891. Here she works in the Library-Museum built in 1881, now Linton Hall. She also taught English at M.A.C. Landon was valedictorian at Niles High School (Michigan).

To replace the Botanical Laboratory which burned in 1890, the legislature appropriated $10,000. **The new building was completed in 1892**, is located on West Circle Drive opposite Linton Hall, and today is known as **Old Botany**.

A report on the Agricultural Experiment Station said that a kerosene emulsion "insecticide is becoming so important in the work of fighting our insect foes that any new facts concerning its manufacture and use will be eagerly studied by every enterprising fruit grower and farmer."

Newly found agricultural knowledge was shared with state farmers through 69 college agricultural bulletins.

Eugene Davenport, class of 1878 and professor of agriculture, was named president of the first agricultural school in South America–Escola Agricola de Sao Paulo at Piracicabo, Brazil.

Mrs. Linda Landon (Landon Hall) began a 41-year career as college librarian. She developed the first cataloging system for classifying books and had "a deep interest in students." There were 16,466 volumes in her care in 1891.

The college budget for 1891 was $99,516.07. Enrollment totaled 345.

Dr. Robert C. Kedzie on the Duties of a Teacher—1891

In a classic statement, appropriate to this day, Professor Robert C. Kedzie wrote about the duties of a teacher.

"The first duty of the teacher is in his classroom…to hold students to thorough work, to inspire enthusiasm in their studies, to induce scholarly habits and good principles, and thus fit them for life's work are the chief duties of a teacher."

1892

Laboratory Method: Prime Instruction Method—"In all the departments of our college," President Clute declared, "the instruction is largely carried on by the laboratory method. The 'labor-atory' is the place for labor. The student labors at what he is to learn, applying such principles as he has already learned." He also said "textbooks and the word of the live teacher were an indispensable force in teaching (because) the teacher explains, enforces, (and) enlarges on the text."

The experimental farm at the college had 350 acres in crops, producing hay, wheat, oats, corn, potatoes, silage, and other items. In addition, there were ten acres of vegetable gardens, five acres of small fruit plants, and 35 acres planted in orchards, producing apples, pears, cherries and plums. Farm animals included cattle, horses, sheep, and swine.

Agricultural Experiment Station bulletins distributed to farmers included Insecticides and Fungicides, Roots vs. Sileage for Fattening Lambs, Potato Tests, Fertilizer Analysis, and Vegetable Tests. Each bulletin had a circulation of 7,000.

To ease the evening darkness, President Clute had 25 kerosene lanterns placed on posts located along the most traveled campus walkways. Strategic electric lighting was yet to come.

Woodland covered 160 acres of the college property, and the campus park and buildings occupied 100 acres.

Budget for the year was $119,151.46. Enrollment was 355.

1893

Lewis G. Gorton Named Sixth President (served 1893-1896)—On August 20, 1893, President Clute resigned to accept the presidency of the Florida Agricultural College. Lewis G. Gorton (1859-1933), 33, an 1879 graduate of Michigan Normal College (Eastern Michigan University), was named president of M.A.C. He had an M.S. degree from South Dakota Agricultural College, and first taught at the Michigan Military Academy. He then served as principal of the Duffield and Bishop Schools in Detroit.

President Gorton...

"The work of education should be so conducted as to make a well-rounded soul."

He was selected because of his youth, educational experience, and the ability to maintain student discipline. Gorton stood six foot three and weighed 250. He related well with the students, won their confidence, and had "fewer disciplinary cases in his two years (as president) than in any similar period."

At the 1893 Columbian Exposition (World's Fair) in Chicago, the college won four medals of excellence for its exhibits. Most impressive was the collection of 800 pieces of wax fruit and vegetables created by Mrs. Stanley Porter. The replicas were so natural that many viewers did not believe they were artificial.

Professor Beal alluded to professorial competition in 1893. He wrote, "For a long time three of us pulled together, and pulled apart, Kedzie, Cook, and Beal. We were a restless triumvirate, each ambitious for his department and what he believed was for the good of the college. We were criticized, and received hard knocks from those in high authority."

The first concrete sidewalks (then called artificial stone), three to six feet wide, were poured between every important building on the campus.

Lizzie McSweeney became the first female graduate of the Detroit College of Law, which would become the Michigan State University-Detroit College of Law in 1996, when it moved to the East Lansing campus.

Notable was the increase in the 1893 budget to $140, 356.48 from $119,151.46 the year before. Included was a $300 item for a Wells Hall privy.

Enrollment was 308, with 44 students graduating on August 18, 1893.

Lewis G. Gorton, Sixth President

1894

First Campus Hospital Built—Contagious diseases, such as measles or mumps, spread easily in the early days of the college because there was no hospital in which to isolate sick students. A few students might catch a disease and "before it had run its course, the entire student body would be affected." The Board was concerned about the educational process and the bad publicity. A small hospital was built next to Grand River Avenue, on the site of the Union Building. It contained seven rooms, two bathrooms, and cost $3,500.

A special dairy course was offered during the first six weeks of the year. It was the beginning of laboratory work in dairying.

Professor Kedzie and the Chemical Department were often called upon to determine the presence and kind of poisons in substances. In one case three cows had died after eating a wheat bran mix. Kedzie found the wheat bran to contain "an astonishing amount of white arsenic." His investigation showed the arsenic had been scattered in the mill to kill rats and mice, and then was carelessly swept up with other material and mixed with the bran.

Campus Cycling Club—The famed, old-fashioned high-wheel bicycle so often symbolizing the "Gay Nineties," gave way to the modern, chain-driven rear wheel and created a new bicycle fad. An M.A.C. Cycling Club was formed by the faculty and students. "The club used dues and contributions to build a gravel path along the north side of Michigan Avenue."

Some 10,000 plants were laid out in beds in Sleepy Hollow, just south of today's Music Practice Building.

Trolley to Lansing heads west on Michigan Ave. at Beal Street campus entrance, circa 1894. President's home is visible on "President's Hill."

As a part of the early educational outreach, the college printed and distributed 7,000 circulars on agricultural subjects for reading by farmers. In addition, 500 books were circulated.

The 1894 budget was $119,790.47. Enrollment was 406.

1895

President Gorton Asked to Resign; College in Crisis—A convergence of problems in the fall of 1895—economic depression, faculty losses, public complaints, and "above all, confused goals," led the Board to give President Gorton a "leave of absence, which was never terminated, after he refused to resign."

The troubles of the school were addressed at a September 10, 1895 Board meeting through a communication and resolution by Professor Garfield, "It is a lamentable fact that we are not getting our annual supply of students from the farms of the State in such proportions as we ought."

"We are not commanding the confidence of those engaged in agricultural pursuits that we have a right to expect, and it is possible there may be some radical defect in our system which will account for this lack of cooperation."

Garfield then resolved that a "Committee of the faculty consisting of Dr. Howard Edwards, Professor C.D. Smith, and Professor Frank S. Kedzie, is hereby selected to carefully inquire into the causes which have contributed to the seeming lack of popularity of our college." The committee reported its findings in 1896.

Charles J. Monroe served as president pro-tempore of M.A.C. from December, 1895 to February, 1896. He was a member of the college board of directors from 1895 to 1907.

Formalization of the Farmers' Institutes occurred in 1895 when the legislature appropriated $5,000 for this twenty-year-old program. Kenyon L. Butterfield, an 1891 graduate of the college and future president of the school, was selected as superintendent of the program. Butterfield was instrumental in staging institutes in every one of the state's 67 counties (now 83). He concluded the year's educational sessions with a state-wide "Round-Up" of farm leaders in Grand Rapids. This large state gathering became the model for the annual Farmers' Week, which was held every February on campus.

An electric light plant was installed for lighting "the grounds, library, corridors of dormitories, barns, and some laboratories." Most of the work was done by students.

Eugene Davenport, class of 1878, was named Dean of Agriculture at the University of Illinois. Davenport Hall, built in 1901 and named in his honor, still stands on the Illinois campus.

Charles R. Webb became the first African-American graduate of the Detroit College of Law, which would become the Michigan State University-Detroit

College of Law in 1996, when it moved to the East Lansing campus.

Budget for the year was $108,730.96. Enrollment was 356.

There were 19,668 volumes, 4,631 pamphlets, and 250 Sunday school books in the library.

1896

Jonathan L. Snyder Named Seventh President (served 1896-1915)—President Lewis G. Gorton resigned on December 31, 1895. Jonathan LeMoyne Snyder (1859-1918), 36, who earned a B.A. degree in 1886 and Ph.D. in 1891 from Westminster College, New Wilmington, Pennsylvania, was named the college's seventh president. He taught at Fairview School near Slippery Rock, Pennsylvania and then became principal of the 5th Ward School in Allegheny, Pennsylvania. He had a part in founding Slippery Rock State College. His farming background, tough discipline, and innovative education concepts led to his election as president.

President Snyder…

"There is no fixed standard or position for anyone. Merit is the only test. Fourteen sons of tillers of the soil have filled the (U.S.) presidential chair."

Special Report on College Problems Presented—The special committee formed in 1895 to investigate the problems of the school, reported in 1896. The attendance problem was starkly apparent by comparing 1895 enrollments at other Michigan colleges with that of M.A.C.: University of Michigan—2,850, The Normal School (now Eastern Michigan)—930, Albion College—650, Olivet College—400, Michigan Agricultural College—356.

Committee research found interest in agricultural education had stagnated, remained stationary for 20 years, but was a condition that existed across America.

A rise in the importance of and interest in the mechanical course (engineering) was a factor.

The depressed condition of agriculture led even farmers to push their sons towards the cities and other professions. A major shift in the population from the farm to the city was occurring. In 1880, the rural population of Michigan was 1,096,533, almost double the city population. By 1894, the population of Michigan cities was within 80,000 of equaling that of the rural districts.

The introspective report said farmers were ignorant of the work being done at the college. The faculty committee assumed the blame on behalf of the college, stating, "The reason for this ignorance lies in our omission to advertise." At the time, the college spent only $590 per year for advertising, and that included the publication of the catalog of courses.

High schools were manned by teachers from the University of Michigan, who logically directed students to their school. District schools were controlled by graduates from the Normal School (EMU) and they used their influence for that institution. M.A.C. had no "feeders" to send secondary students on to East Lansing.

Jonathan L. Snyder, Seventh President

Antagonism by the press was noted as a problem. The report stated, "much of this is due to previously noted ignorance of what the college is and what it is doing. The cases where an editor has visited the college and become acquainted with the spirit here, and afterwards attacked the institution, are rare indeed." Stating a modern communications principle, the committee declared that "the college should demand that facts shall be truthfully presented and that misstatements be corrected."

The final problem delineated was that too much cash was required of students when they entered college. Advanced payments ran from $75 to $100, a great deal of money for a teenager at that time.

Ten recommendations to rectify the problems were offered by the committee:

1. "A clear definition of the character of our agricultural and mechanical courses be given, and a continuous

Mary A. Mayo led the initiative for a women's course at M.A.C. which was launched in 1896.

campaign of advertising and education among the people be begun and kept up;

2. Earlier years of the curriculum be made more technical; get practical quicker; teach skills that offer direct financial value;

3. Special winter courses be organized;

4. That the long vacation (from school) occur in the summer;

5. Effort be made to infuse the country schools with an interest in agricultural pursuits;

6. That a ladies course (curriculum) be organized;

7. That a short preparatory course of six months be established (for incoming students in need);

8. That the matriculation fee be reduced to one dollar (from five), or entirely abolished;

9. That the dormitory system be abolished (this proposal was not accepted); and

10. That we advertise extensively."

An 1896 advertisement for the college stated, "We have better equipment for Scientific Practical Investigation along Agricultural and Mechanical lines than any similar Institution in the country. We have a teaching force of thirty professors and instructors. We have a library containing over 18,000 volumes, 8 laboratories, fully equipped. Three large dormitories, all located in one of the Most Beautiful Parks in Michigan. Tuition is free to residents of the State; $5.00 per term to non-residents. Board in clubs costs about $2.50 per week."

Women's Course Requested—Mrs. Mary A. Mayo (Mayo Hall), a leader in the Michigan Grange and among state farm wives, requested a women's course at the college.

Mary Mayo…

"Thinking parents of today are anxious that their daughters shall be as thoroughly trained for the practical work of their lives as are their sons."

Her campaigning, plus the recommendation of the faculty study committee and professorial sentiment toward higher education for women, resulted in the introduction of a women's curriculum in 1896.

E.M. Shelton, class of 1871, was the agricultural advisor to the government of Queensland, Australia.

Football was introduced in 1896. The four-game schedule included Lansing High School, Kalamazoo College, and Alma College. The lone victory was a 10-0 win over Lansing High School. The team had no coach.

The college budget for 1896 was $115,406.29, and included $3,231.55 for electricity, $1,754.05 for lighting (first mention), and $3,000 for water closets in Abbot, Williams and Wells Halls.

Enrollment totaled 398.

1897

Inequitable Funding Versus Other State Schools—Because the college had received the State's land-grant of 240,000 acres from the Morrill Act of 1862, the legislature adopted the attitude that its obligation to the school for annual appropriations was considerably less than to the other state schools. The law-makers believed the trust fund created from land sales would eventually generate enough income to pay the full cost of annual operations at the college. This was a misconception. The $569,951.10 in the trust fund in 1897 produced just $39,009.66 of interest income, only 32 percent of that year's budget of $121,273.23. The legislators appropriated money for building repairs, student labor and farmers' institutes, but nothing for normal operations.

The per student appropriation was $65 for the University of Michigan; $58 for the Normal School (EMU), and just $29 for M.A.C.

The new women's curriculum included English, mathematics, history, literature, French, German, botany, chemistry, entomology, natural philosophy, home-making, and even free piano lessons. Forty-five coeds were enrolled. **The college catalog of 1897 stated that "women were subject to only such restraints as would be expected in a well-regulated Christian family."**

To accommodate farmers who could not devote four years to studying agriculture, the college introduced specialized winter short courses, lasting six weeks. Offerings

Professor Edith F. McDermott leads cooking class (1897) in Old Abbot hall (site of Music Practice Building).

included dairying, live stock husbandry, fruit culture, floriculture, and vegetable gardening.

The college's long winter vacation was moved to the summer to accommodate students working on their family farms.

The college budget of $121,273.23 included $5,000 for a new electric light plant.

Enrollment totaled 464, with 11 graduate students. The library housed 20,000 volumes.

1898

Communication and Excursions Yield Record Enrollment—Using lessons learned from the 1896 study of school problems, the college dramatically increased its communications, advertising, and special programs to reach prospective students and the public.

Kenyon L. Butterfield, college field agent, initiated a comprehensive mailing program, distributing 5,000 college calendars, 18,000 envelope catalogues, 10,000 copies of the college yearbook (farmer's almanac), 5,000 copies of the regular college catalogue, and 6,000 special editions of the *College Record* to young people in the state. Also sent were thousands of special circulars.

President Snyder carried on extensive correspondence with high school students. Every request for the college catalogue was honored and sent with a personal letter.

College news stories and advertising appeared in some of the state's religious and educational publications.

Railroad excursions from Michigan cities brought 3,000 people to the campus. President Snyder wrote, "As is usual with persons who visit the college for the first time, they were very **happily surprised at the beauty of the campus**, and the number and character of the buildings."

There was a huge payoff from the public and community relations activities. New students enrolling in the fall jumped from 135 in 1897 to 244 in 1898, a record.

Dr. Robert C. Kedzie "helped with the planning of Michigan's first sugar beet factory in 1898," according to

Organic chemistry laboratory in 1898. It stood on the site of today's Library.

Kuhn's book. Kedzie was the "Father" of Michigan's sugar beet industry. He had "imported sugar beet seed from Germany, distributed it to farmers," thus creating a new stream of agricultural revenue for the state.

President Snyder stated in his annual report, **"Though not a sectarian institution, the faculty is composed of Christian men and women who do not feel their responsibility ends with classroom instruction. They realize that better than knowledge gained from books or in the laboratory is a strong Christian character..."**

The 1898 college budget was $142,163.02, including $1,000 for a cold storage fruit house. Student dormitory room rent ranged from $4.92 to $7.75 per term. Meals averaged between $1.45 and $2.46 per week.

Enrollment was 528.

1899

First College Coach a Minister—L. Whitney Watkins, Class of 1893, who was appointed a Board member in 1899, proposed that an athletic coach be hired for the college. This idea met resistance from the Board because "many coaches were reputedly so intent on victory and therefore so accustomed to dishonest practice, that they would be a pernicious influence on the campus."

President Snyder side-stepped this issue by proposing the appointment of Reverend Charles O. Bemies, a Western Theological Seminary graduate, as the sports coach, who might also lead chapel services and the Y.M.C.A. He was hired, and served until 1901.

Bemies immediately created the Department of Physical Culture, and **introduced intercollegiate basketball to M.A.C.**

All students in the Women's Department were required to take gymnastics exercises, led by Miss Ronan. Exercise could be avoided only with an excuse from the president.

As the college's reputation grew, a staggering number of information requests were mailed to faculty members by farmers and the general public. Dr. Robert C. Kedzie, head of the Chemical Department, wrote "Many persons do not realize how much they are asking in making such inquiries. A communication came to me from Saugatuck containing 143 questions. To answer all of them would require the work of an expert for a whole month. They do not realize the work of the Chemical Department is to teach chemistry and to make investigations that will be of value to the public."

Student church preferences were dominated by four denominations: Methodist—49; Congregational—43 Baptist—21; and Presbyterian—15. Interestingly, these were the four founding denominations of East Lansing's People's Church.

At the commencement exercises, president Jonathan Snyder told the 29 graduates, **"In looking back, the four years seem to have vanished almost as in the night."**

The 1899 college budget was $137,001.70. Enrollment reached a record 627.

1900

Women's Building Completed; Booker T. Washington Delivers Commencement Address—Completion of a magnificent Women's Building (now Morrill Hall) marked the turn of the century. Discussed for thirty years, the new $95,000 structure ($12,000 for furnishings) was the most expensive ever built at M.A.C. It was state-of-the art, including offices, a four-room suite for the Department of Domestic Art, a kitchen laboratory, dining room, recitation room, kitchen and serving room on the third floor, a two-story gymnasium, music rooms, waiting and reception rooms, toilet and bathrooms, and large, well-ventilated rooms for 120 young women.

A $15,000 Dairy Building also was constructed in 1900. It was later designated the Forestry Building and is located on West Circle Drive. Today it is named **Chittenden Hall, for Alfred K. Chittenden, the third head of Forestry**.

Board member L. Whitney Watkins suggested the college purchase a 13-acre site south of, and along the banks of the Red Cedar River (Old College Field and Kobs

Class of 1900 members gather in 1930 at Fountain they gave to the college. It's located on the walk between Linton Hall and the Museum.

Women's Building completed in 1900 is now named Morrill Hall for the Congressman whose bill led to the creation of the Land-Grant Colleges and Universities in America.

Field) for athletic grounds. This sprawling area was developed into a football field with grandstand, a baseball diamond, and a quarter-mile track. Today, this attractive area serves as the home for Spartan baseball, the site of varsity soccer, women's softball, and as an intramural sports field.

President Snyder's annual report alluded to a heightened interest in engineering education, "The bright boy can see there is likely to be a great demand for well trained men in mechanical and electrical engineering. Steam and electric power will be utilized to a greater extent in the future…"

A 1¾-mile railroad track was built by the Pere Marquette Railroad from Trowbridge Road on to the campus and crossing the Red Cedar River to the land behind today's Library and Olds Hall. It was used to transport some 3,000 tons of coal annually to the site of the old college power plant.

With a mission to educate "the poorest and the proudest," the college could not have selected a more appropriate commencement speaker for opening the Twentieth Century, than Booker T. Washington, the leading black educator in the United States.

There were 25 graduating seniors in the audience of nearly 1,000 that were gathered in the Armory (Music Building site). Washington, founder of the famous Tuskegee Institute, stirred them for nearly an hour with his address, "Solving the Negro Problem in the Black Belt of the South."

The college budget for 1900 topped $200,000 for the first time, reaching $206,613.39.

There were 54 officers, faculty and staff; and the enrollment was 652.

1901

Annual State Funding for Buildings Approved—To provide regular funding for buildings, the Board asked the legislature for a tax of 1/15th of a mill on taxable property in the state. A House of Representatives committee, chaired by Mr. B.A. Nevins, Class of 1874, decided to make an appeal for 1/10th of a mill and limit annual support from the tax to $100,000. The bill passed both houses and was signed into law. As the 1/10th mill tax represented about $110,000, the college was assured of receiving $100,000 per year. After funding institutes, student labor, the U.P. experiment station and repairs, it was believed some $60,000 to $70,000 would be left each year for new buildings or additions.

The Department of Bacteriology was created, and **Professor C. E. Marshall (Marshall-Adams Hall)**, was named department head.

The largest gathering of women's organizations in state history helped dedicate the new Women's Building (Morrill Hall) on October 25. More than 1,000 people attended. Addresses included "The 20th Century Girl" by Mrs. Ella Rockwood; and "College Woman" by Mrs. Martha A. Keating of Muskeon, president of the State Federation of Women's Clubs.

Maude Gilchrist (Gilchrist Hall) became the first dean of the Women's Department. She would serve as dean until 1913. Gilchrist insisted that music, art and literature were as essential as domestic science in training the homemaker.

Maude Gilchrist, first Dean of Women (1901-1913)

In late fall "the new athletic field (Old College Field; Kobs Field) was graded and a quarter-mile bicycle track with embankments at the curves was laid out..."

Miss Rowena Ketchum, a trained nurse, was placed in charge of the college hospital.

At a livestock show in Chicago, M.A.C. students won three firsts—including a grand championship for dressed carcasses—as well as two seconds and three third prizes.

By 1901, Dr. Beal and his students had planted and catalogued over 600 species of native and experimental trees on the campus. All of the trees and shrubs on campus were listed alphabetically by their scientific and common names, and their campus location noted to aid botany, forestry and horticulture students. The listing, prepared by Dr. Beal, ran for 21 pages in the college's 1901 annual report.

Students studying in dorm room—circa 1902.

The 1901 college budget was $236,698.22. Enrollment was reported as 689.

1902

Fifth Year Added to Agriculture and Women's Courses—To match the quality of bachelor's degrees at other colleges, a fifth year was added to the agricultural and women's curriculums. "Home Nursing" was added to the women's course.

Forestry Program: One of Nation's First—Charles W. Garfield, class of 1870 and Michigan lumber baron, who served on the State Forestry Commission, funded a four-year degree program in forestry—one of the first in the nation. The course was launched "to render valuable service to the state in taking care of and developing large tracts of unproductive land," through forest planting, management, and preservation.

Ernest E. Bogue (Bogue Street), a graduate of Ohio State and Harvard, arrived from Ohio State to start the forestry department and serve as professor.

First Lighted Athletic Field—Pressed for athletic and physical fitness facilities, the Department of Physical Culture—with vision far ahead of 1902—requested electric lights for Old College Field to allow more playing time during the fall term.

Ice from the Red Cedar was deemed "impure and dangerously so." With the new rail spur into campus, "relatively pure ice could be brought in by rail car from Lake Odessa at a slight increase in cost."

M.A.C.'s horticultural and landscaping expertise was engaged in laying out shrubbery beds on the north, west and south sides of the State Capitol in Lansing, and planting 4,000 bedding plants, and 1,000 hearty shrubs in them.

The Board approved building a pedestrian and vehicular bridge across the Red Cedar River to access Old College Field (Kalamazoo Street Bridge). It was built in 1903.

Dr. Robert C. Kedzie (Kedzie Hall), long-time professor and head of Chemistry, died on November 2, 1902. His son, Professor Frank C. Kedzie, would become president of the college in 1915.

Robert S. Shaw (Shaw Hall, Shaw Lane, Shaw Estates) was named Professor of Agriculture and Superintendent of the Farm. He would be elected president in 1928.

In Grand Rapids, Michigan, John A. Hannah **(Hannah Administration Building)** was born. He would graduate from the college in 1923, become Secretary of the Board in 1935, marry President Shaw's daughter Sarah in 1938, and succeed Shaw as president in 1941.

Miss Louise Freyhofer joined the faculty as a piano teacher for the women's program. President Jonathan Snyder believed "the complete homemaker must have had music training. Therefore, two years of music were required and the training was free." Freyhofer started with 116 pupils and taught for 17 years. Eventually, she needed three assistants. (*MSU Magazine*, February, 1962)

The college budget was reduced to $193,964.82 due to an economic downturn.

A record 854 students were enrolled, and 59 graduated—the largest class in history. Ohio State President W.O. Thompson delivered the commencement address.

Nation's first bacteriology laboratory was completed in 1903. Today it is named Marshall-Adams Hall, and is home to the Economics Dept.

1903

The Nation's First Bacteriology Research & Teaching Building was completed at a cost of $27,000. It was set back from Old Botany, and Eustace-Cole Hall on West Circle Drive. Now Marshall-Adams Hall, it is named in honor of Dr. Charles E. Marshall, first Bacteriology Department head, and Dr. Walter Adams, MSU's 13th president and distinguished economics professor, whose office was located there for many years.

Chester L. Brewer, an Owosso native, Wisconsin graduate, and successful Albion College coach, was named Professor of Physical Culture and head coach for all sports. It was during Brewer's tenure that green and white athletic uniforms were introduced.

Miss Maude Gilchrist, dean of the Women's Department, was appointed "expert in charge of household economics at the Louisiana Purchase Exposition."

Spraying of 480 campus elm trees with a solution of lime, salt and sulfur, recommended by the college's Agricultural Experiment Station, showed "very gratifying" results. "A scale insect had been feeding on the elms for a decade." This probably was the precursor to the Dutch Elm disease that hit later in the century.

A badly needed new bathhouse with a small swimming pool, the school's first, was built adjoining the Armory (Music Building site). It served 375 young men, and included 15 shower baths and two tub baths. A controversial one-time fee of $1.50 was required for a student to use the facility.

"Movable bleachers, added to the new grandstand" at College Field brought seating capacity for athletic events to more than 1,000.

Franklin Wells, President of the Board for 20 years, a member for 30, died July 3. Thus ended a 42-year period in which a man named Wells **(Wells Hall)** was a member of the State Board of Agriculture—Judge Hezekiah G. Wells, 1861 to 1883, and Franklin Wells, 1873 to 1903. The two men were passionately devoted to the college, and between them served as President of the Board a total of 34 years: Hezekiah—14, and Franklin—20. Each, in his time, was credited with keeping the college alive and prospering. President Snyder said of Franklin Wells, "...his own personal business was never closer to his heart than the interests of this institution have been."

Elida Yakeley (Yakeley Hall) was named secretary to the president.

Liberty Hyde Bailey, class of 1882, was named Dean of Agriculture at Cornell University.

1903 Garden Party by M.A.C. First Lady Snyder. Ladies are pictured just across the drive from the President's home–# 1 Faculty Row—which was located on the site of the west end of Gilchrist Hall.

Elida Yakeley, named secretary to President Snyder in 1903, became M.A.C.'s first Registrar of Students in 1908, and served in that position for 30 years. Yakeley Hall, built in 1948, is named in her honor.

The 1903 college budget was $269,461.88.

Enrollment was a record 917. The graduating class of 60, plus two master's degree recipients, also was a record.

1904

Harry F. Moon: M.A.C.'s First Nationally Recognized Athlete; Enrollment Passes 1,000—At the 1904 World Collegiate Track Championships, held in St. Louis, Missouri, M.A.C.'s Harry F. Moon was runner-up in the 100- and 200-meter races. He was one of the nation's first sprinters to run the 100-yard dash in ten seconds. M.A.C. tied the University of Illinois for third place in the meet.

E.S. Bartlett, a freshman, won the $125 trophy in the college class sheep-shearing competition at the 1904 St. Louis Exposition (World's Fair). Dr. Beal cited this win as but one example of student "victories too numerous to record" over past years in athletics, oratory, livestock, fruit and flower judging, etc.

Dr. Clarence B. Smith, class of 1894, co-authored *The Farmer's Cyclopedia of Agriculture.*

C.D. Smith, Dean of Special Courses, reported that campus short courses offered farmers were resulting in better quality butter and cheese production in the state.

Mr. Bert Wermuth, class of 1902, was named the first full-time secretary of the college's YMCA, which had "a strong and vigorous" program. Faculty and students raised $992.75 to support the position.

The 1904 budget was $250,161.57—the first to reach the quarter-million level. Making up for cutting President Snyder's salary to $2,000 in 1903, the Board jumped his pay to $5,000 in 1904—as much money as the entire faculty was paid when the school opened in 1857.

Enrollment went over 1,000 for the first time—1,009.

1905

Wells Hall Burns—In the early morning of February 11, 1905, Wells Hall burned to the ground. Students on the third floor were driven by smoke down the outside fire escapes. No one was injured.

A student relief fund was started to help those who had lost clothing, military (ROTC) uniforms, and books. Some $1,100 was raised to help the displaced students. In a magnanimous gesture, the students who needed help asked that the money only be loaned to them, with the expectation it would be repaid after they graduated. This money thus became the basis for an on-going student loan fund at the college.

A seventh member was added to the six-member State Board of Agriculture (Trustees) by the state legislature, with the direction that the member "must be a resident of the Northern Peninsula."

Railroad Institutes—an innovative outreach effort—were inaugurated in 1905. Special trains consisting of two passenger coaches and one baggage car, carried college lecturers to 47 different towns. Each stop lasted a little more than an hour. Lectures focused on one subject—corn production, for example. Following the lecture in the passenger coaches, farmers would walk to the baggage car where scientific exhibits were displayed.

Horticulture Professor U.P. Hedrick made a well-founded protest against the assignment of campus "housekeeping" chores to his department. "The non-professional work of delivering ice, hauling coal, caring for garbage, and doing the general utility work of the college community has been most annoying and burdensome at times. I again protest against the continuation of this disagreeable, non-horticultural work."

In response, **Thomas Gunson (Gunson Street)** was named Superintendent of Grounds, relieving the Horticulture Department of these duties.

A. R. Sawyer, professor of physics and engineering, reported, "There is considerable demand on the part of students for more instruction in electricity…"

Ray Stannard Baker (Baker Hall), class of 1889 and star reporter for *McClure's* magazine, interviewed U.S. President Theodore Roosevelt at his Sagamore Hill, N.Y. summer home. Baker, who would win a Pulitzer Prize in 1940 for his eight-volume biography of Woodrow Wilson, was called on by Roosevelt on several occasions for his feedback on the sentiment of the American people.

Eight thousand trees were planted on campus.

J. Willard Bolte, class of 1905, reported in 1964 (*MSU Alumni Magazine*, May 1964) that it cost his dad a little less than $1,200 to put him through a four-year course at M.A.C. Room cost $17 for a three-month term; board was $2.31 per week for 21 meals.

M.A.C. defeated Notre Dame in a dual track meet, 75-51.

Stately Wells Hall—built in 1877—burned to the ground in 1905. Other fires destroyed campus buildings in 1876, 1890, 1916, and 1919.

The 1905 budget rose to $332,331.36—the first above $300,000.

Enrollment dropped to 950, due to the Wells Hall fire. A record 75 men and women graduated on June 21, 1905.

1906

President Snyder Helps Pass Adams Act—To bolster agricultural research at the land-grant college Experiment Stations, the Adams Act was passed in 1906. It provided an additional $5,000 for research the first year, with an increase to $2,000 each succeeding year until a total of $30,000 per year was available. President Snyder, as a member of the executive committee of the National Association of Agricultural Colleges and Experiment Stations, visited Washington, D.C. many times over a three-year period to help pass the Adams legislation. He thus became the third M.A.C. President to have a critical role in passing significant legislation for American agricultural education, research and outreach. Adams was a Wisconsin Congressman.

"Sacred Space" Preserved inside West Circle Drive—O.C. Simonds, noted Chicago landscape architect, was hired to look over the campus with a view to suggesting a plan for the placement of future buildings. His major recommendation was that no new buildings be placed on the inner campus—the "Sacred Space" (inside West Circle Drive). Simonds wrote, "but I would regard all the ground included within the area marked by a dotted red line on the accompanying map (inside West Circle Drive), as sacred space from which all buildings must forever be excluded. **This area contains beautifully rolling land with a pleasing arrangement of trees I am sure, that feature of the college (is the one) which is most pleasantly and affectionately remembered by the students after they leave their Alma Mater."**

President Snyder reported that the Board approved the idea and wrote, "If this policy is followed, the M.A.C. campus will go down to future generations as "a thing of beauty and a joy forever."" In actuality, this outsider's recommendation just reinforced what had been the practice and belief of the leaders of the school.

Ray Stannard Baker, Class of 1889, and reporter for *McClure's Magazine*, was asked by U.S. President Theodore Roosevelt to review the galley proofs of the president's forthcoming address to the U.S. Congress. He became a confidant of Presidents Teddy Roosevelt and Woodrow Wilson.

An automatic telephone system was installed at the college and connected to the Citizens Telephone Company of Lansing, Michigan.

Circle Drive Macadamized—Professor Fletcher reported "the main campus drive (West Circle Drive) was macadamized (laying and rolling successive layers of broken stone) from the Chemical Laboratory (site of the Library) to Howard Terrace (site of the Human Ecology Building)."

Second Wells Hall Built—Learning from the fire that destroyed the first Wells Hall in 1905, the administration built the second Wells Hall differently. It was erected in six sections, or wards, each separated by fireproof walls. Each section had its own outside entrance. The dormitory housed 156 students, and was a popular living quarters. It stood until 1955, when razed to provide space for the current library.

Dr. Howard Edwards, professor of English, was selected as President of Rhode Island College of Agriculture and Mechanic Arts.

College's First 49 Years: 1,218 Graduates—The 1906 annual report recapped the school's first 49 years (1857-1906) of educational production, stating that 1,218 people had received bachelor of science degrees, and that 6,000 students had received instruction. President Snyder also noted that there had not been a death among the active teaching force during the entire 49 years of the college's existence.

The 1906 college budget was $333,612.96. Enrollment was 1,001. The graduating class of 1906 numbered 74.

President Theodore Roosevelt keynoting the college's 50th anniversary on May 31, 1907. He spoke with no public address system to 20,000 gathered on the Drill Field (now Walter Adams Field, across from Gilchrist and Yakeley Halls). The date printed on the photograph is inaccurate.

1907

Semi-Centennial of the Dedication of the College—A remarkably sophisticated three-day celebration of the 50th anniversary of the opening of the college was staged May 29-31, 1907. President Snyder described the event in the *Annual Report of the State Board of Agriculture.*

U.S. President Theodore Roosevelt was invited to be the keynote speaker 13 and one-half months ahead of the event. After full consideration, he said "it was his desire to make one address to the farmers of the country while he was in office, and probably this would be the proper occasion."

Invitations were ordered from Tiffany of New York, and "mailed to all alumni and former students…to prominent citizens of the state, and to other educational institutions as well as organizations in foreign lands."

President Roosevelt and his party arrived in Lansing in his private railroad car at 10 am, Friday, May 31, 1907. After visiting the State Capitol and addressing the legislature, Mr. Roosevelt and his party were driven to the college in ten open top REO (R.E. Olds) cars. Ransom E. Olds, founder of the Oldsmobile and REO car companies, wore a derby hat and chauffeured President Snyder and the nation's Chief Executive. Both rode in the back seat wearing silk top hats. The car preceding the President carried the Lansing chief of police and four Secret Service agents. Three news correspondents representing the principal news agencies of the day also were traveling with the president. "A company of cavalry escorted the entourage from the Capitol" to the campus. Olds then drove President Roosevelt around the circle drive past the Armory, Williams Hall, the Library, past Faculty Row to President Snyder's home, arriving precisely at noon. "Immediately after sixty distinguished guests entered the president's home, the calvary encircled the house and no one was permitted to come near unless he was properly vouched for."

In the early morning, prior to Roosevelt's arrival, President Snyder had crawled under the speaker's platform to make sure there was no hidden bomb. Following a five-course luncheon in President Snyder's home (located where the west end of Gilchrist Hall stands), President Roosevelt emerged. On the walk to the speaker's platform he stopped to plant an elm tree, which was an inch and a quarter thick and seven feet tall. Forty years later it succumbed to Dutch Elm disease.

On this sunny final day of May, Roosevelt climbed the platform atop the slight hill that slopes down to Walter Adams Field (first called the Drill Field; then called Landon

U.S. President Theodore Roosevelt (back seat-left) arrives on campus for M.A.C.'s 50th anniversary in 1907 REO car. He, President Jonathan Snyder (back seat-right), and Mr. Loeb, Roosevelt's secretary, (front seat-right) were driven by Ransom E. Olds (front seat-left), founder of Oldsmobile and REO car companies.

Field) precisely at 2 pm, and began addressing the crowd of 20,000 people. There was no public address system. His voice alone had to carry the crowd. President Snyder said Roosevelt spoke from "a manuscript in large type on one side of the paper." Snyder reported the President held the manuscript in one hand, but did not follow it closely, frequently gesturing with both hands. "He spoke quite slowly in a high penetrating voice, and was heard by nearly all present." The speech ran one hour and 15 minutes and "held the closest attention of the audience throughout." Following the talk, the crowd sang "America."

Myrtle Craig Mowbray, Class of 1907, First Black Graduate

Then the Class of 1907, a record 96 students, was asked to come forward to receive their diplomas. To their delight, the parchments were handed to them by the President of the United States, who visibly enjoyed this duty. **Included among the graduates was Myrtle Craig, (later, Myrtle Craig Mowbray), the first black to graduate from the college**. She was one of only four black students on campus, and the only black woman. There were 15 women graduates in the class of 1907.

The first two days of the celebration included a special session of the American Association of Agricultural Colleges and Experiment Stations; an alumni banquet, a meeting to honor the builders of the college, the oratorio "Elijah," a dress parade by the student military battalion, a students' parade, the illumination of the campus, and a public reception.

On Thursday and Friday evenings the campus glowed. Aided by the new lighting system, the Women's Building, the Library, Williams Hall, College Hall, the new Engineering Building, and Abbot Hall were outlined with incandescent lights. Strings of lights ran along the tops and edges of the roofs and down the buildings' corners—presenting a striking scene for those days. The entire length of "Faculty Row" (West Circle Drive from Cowles House to today's Williams Hall) was wired and hung with colorful Japanese lanterns every few feet.

The school's first Alma Mater was written for the occasion by Addison Makepeace Brown, Secretary of the State Board of Agriculture (Board of Trustees) and former State Senator. Titled, "Close Beside The Winding Cedar," it was set to the music of the famous Cornell University alma mater, "High Above Cayuga's Waters." This beautiful song

First Williams Hall lighted for the 1907 Semi-Centennial celebration. Five other campus buildings also were outlined with lights, creating a dramatic evening scene.

would be used until 1949, when students voted for "MSU Shadows" as the official alma mater. The lyrics were poignant:

"Close beside the winding Cedar's
Sloping banks of green
Spreads thy campus Alma Mater,
Fairest ever seen.

"Swell the chorus! Let it echo
Over hill and vale
Hail to thee our loving mother,
M.A.C. all hail!

"Backward through the hazy distance
Troop the days of yore,
Scenes and faces float before us,
Cherished more and more."

Preparations for the Semi-Centennial were meticulous. Three giant tents were rented and erected on the drill field, now Walter Adams Field. One was 100 feet by 200 feet; two others were 70 feet by 130 feet. They were used for jubilee events, dining rooms, and the provisions committee. A small tent was set up for the press. Folding chairs were imported from Detroit, Grand Rapids, and Ionia. The college constructed a large number of wooden benches. If bad weather had forced the Roosevelt speech into the tents, a crowd of 6,000 could have been seated.

A new Engineering Building (located where the Olds Hall of Engineering now stands) was completed in 1907 at a cost of $110,000. It featured more than 40 laboratories and recitation rooms, and was considered the finest structure on campus.

East Lansing Incorporated As a City—Some 800 people lived in the village just north of the campus in 1907. The first subdivision, called "Collegeville," had been plotted by Professors Beal and R.C. Carpenter in 1877. In 1907, Charles B. Collingwood (Collingwood Drive), Class of 1885, and postmaster, suggested incorporation of the village as a city. A poll was taken to select a name for the new city. Collegeville, Agricultural College, Oakwood, College Park, Montrose, and East Lansing, all received votes, but College Park was the favorite.

However, the legislature—with no feel for the charm of connecting the city name with the college—selected East Lansing because "it was a practical name and its close proximity to Lansing." The bill for incorporation was signed by Governor Fred M. Warner, May 8, 1907.

The first fraternity house built off-campus was constructed in 1907 by the Eclectic Society (The Tics). It was a fine three-story red brick house, built on a hill on

Eclectic Society "Tic" house (Alpha Tau Omega since 1940)—was the first fraternity built off-campus (1907) at 451 Evergreen. MSU structures named after members of the fraternity include Beaumont Tower, Jenison Gymnasium & Fieldhouse, Butterfield Hall, and the Breslin Student Events Center. Photo: 1954.

Grandstands at Old College Field in 1909. M.A.C. tied Michigan, 0-0, here in football in 1908, the Wolverines first appearance on campus.

Evergreen Street. In 1940, the Eclectic Society became the Epsilon Eta Chapter of Alpha Tau Omega.

The college budget for 1907 was $438,558.21. Enrollment was 1,191.

1908

New Department of Agricultural Education Wins National Recognition—A Department of Agricultural Education was established to meet a growing demand for agricultural education in public schools. Professor Walter H. French, who had been serving as Deputy State Superintendent of Public Instruction, was named department head. At the National Education Association meeting in Cleveland, that organization's president said this development was one of the most important progressive movements of the year.

A new Michigan Constitution, ratified in 1908, provided that college Board members should be elected, not appointed by the Governor.

A twenty percent increase in enrollment for 1908 was attributed in part to the high visibility the college received during its 1907 semi-centennial. Attendance rose to 1,370.

On the day of the 1908 commencement, **the corner stone of the new Agricultural Hall was laid** by Board member A.J. Doherty. A sealed copper box containing a college catalog and other documents was placed inside the corner stone.

With the rapid increase in enrollment, President Snyder expressed his concerns of preserving a democratic social standing among all students. He felt dormitory life was a democratizing influence on students. But with the college unable to provide enough dorm rooms, the literary societies (fraternities) were building their own living and boarding houses. Snyder's suggestion was to build new well-lighted, well-ventilated dormitories with modern sanitary facilities for men. As it turned out, no new dormitory would be built on campus for another 23 years, when Mary Mayo Hall was built in 1931.

President Snyder reported, "The addition of the women's department (which occurred in 1896) had improved the social side of college life. The young men became neater in appearance and more refined in manners."

"M.A.C.'s first annual barbecue was held on a Friday evening in October, 1908 in the hollow (Sleepy Hollow) in front of Wells Hall (next to the Music Practice Building)." "The college band began festivities with a concert," which was punctuated by talks by football team members and Secretary of the Board Addison Brown. Three cooks from the Hotel Downey started carving the ox, which had been roasting all day, at 8:30 pm. "Seniors were served first—a cup of cider and a generous ox sandwich."

Professor Robert S. Shaw was appointed Dean over Agriculture, Horticulture, Veterinary Science, and Forestry.

Professor Clinton D. Smith, director of the Agricultural Experiment Station, resigned to become president of the Luiz de Queiroz College of Agriculture at Piracicaba, Brazil.

The football team was undefeated and tied the University of Michigan, 0-0, in East Lansing, before the largest home crowd in history (1,000+). It was Michigan's first football appearance at M.A.C.

The 1908 college budget was $385,204.63. Enrollment was 1,370, and the graduating class numbered 84. Miss Jane Addams, LL.D. of Hull House in Chicago gave the commencement address on June 23 in the Armory.

1909

Name Changed Officially to Michigan Agricultural College—Although the college had been called the Michigan Agricultural College (M.A.C.) for several years, the name was made official in 1909. Previous names were: The Agricultural College of the State of Michigan—1855; and the State Agricultural College—1861.

In the last week of **December, 1909, Agricultural Hall was completed**. It cost $182,000 and was the finest building on campus. President Snyder commented on "the perfectness of lighting (large windows), of which there is great abundance. Artificial lighting has been well provided for by tungsten lamps." The building was heated by radiators with heat from the college power plant, which was regulated by thermostats. Two elevator shafts were built in, and an electric elevator installed in one of them. A two-story extension behind the hall was a stock judging pavilion, which seated 1,200. The large room also was used for many college events.

A U.S. Weather Service building, costing $12,000 to $15,000, was built on campus just west of the current Abbot Street entrance. It was demolished in 1948.

To clarify sentiment on the question of dormitories versus fraternities, the Honorable R.D. Graham, president of the State Board of Agriculture, initiated a survey of 700 alumni. Replies were received from 278, of whom 218 were opposed to fraternities, 35 favored them, and 25 were neutral. This poll led to a board resolution stating, "In accord with the expressed sentiment of between 80 and 90 percent of the alumni heard from, be it resolved, that it shall be the policy of this institution to foster the dormitory system of housing students, and that efforts will be made to increase as rapidly as possible dorm accommodations, eating halls, and quarters for social purposes." The sentiment of the resolution, however, wasn't backed by new dormitory construction until 1931.

The Forestry Department sold 250, 730 trees to those interested in forestry throughout the state. More than 27,000 trees were given away to public institutions. And, 8,053 trees were planted in the college woods.

Natural gas was piped from Lansing to the campus in 1909. It was introduced into some campus laboratories and homes, and some residences in East Lansing.

The annual student carnival or circus, initiated in 1906, was described in the *M.A.C. Record* of April 13, 1909. "The Armory and vicinity were converted into a veritable hippodrome...The circus opened at 1:30 pm with a magnificent street parade with three bands accompanied by the usual complement of clowns and rough riders." The parade circled the campus, then returned to the Armory. "The Armory was divided into booths where various special acts were pulled off, including the Salome dance hall... and along the north side, 'dainty delicious delicacies were deftly dispensed by the demure damsels of the dean's department'."

Dr. Frederick B. Mumford, class of 1891, was named Dean of Agriculture at the University of Missouri. Mumford Hall, built in 1923 was named in his honor in 1930. It still stands on the Missouri campus.

Lloyd C. Emmons (Emmons Hall), was named Instructor in Mathematics.

The college budget for 1909 was $500,661.74, the first to cross the half-million mark. Faculty and staff numbered 127. Enrollment jumped 16 percent to 1,494, a new high.

There were 98 graduates, a record.

1910

Division of Veterinary Medicine Established—A Division of Veterinary Medicine was established in response to demands from several quarters. Dr. Richard P. Lyman, M.D.V., Harvard University, was selected as the first Dean. M.A.C.'s veterinary course started with a four-year curriculum, at a time when three-year programs were being offered at most other colleges.

College Produces Researchers for the Nation—A list of M.A.C. men who had risen to responsible research positions at other institutions was printed in 1910. It revealed that eleven of the nation's 57 agricultural experiment stations were directed by men educated at M.A.C. Their geographic spread was nationwide: **Alaska**—C.C. Georgeson, **Colorado**—L.G. Carpenter, **Connecticut**—L.A. Clinton, **Idaho**—E.E. Elliott, **Illinois**—E. Davenport, **Michigan**—Charles E. Marshall, **Missouri**—F.B. Mumford, **Nebraska**—E.A. Burnett, **New York**—L.H. Bailey, **Ohio**—C.E. Thorne, and **Wyoming**—J.D. Towar.

Dean Bissell (Engineering) voiced concern over the distance between professors and students. He declared, "With the growth of the college, this problem becomes of greater and greater moment." And this was said when the student body was 1,568!

Dr. Blaisdell called for better pre-college English preparation for students. "Among these essentials in English education are terminal punctuation, capitalization, and the form of a business letter." In its short courses, the college started teaching business letter writing, which was very successful.

Chester L. Brewer, coach and Professor of Physical Culture, stated, "A great effort was made during the year to interest as large a number of young men in some sort of work in the Department of Physical Culture."

Faculty salaries amounted to $138,747.14 of the school budget of $452,508.05 in 1910.

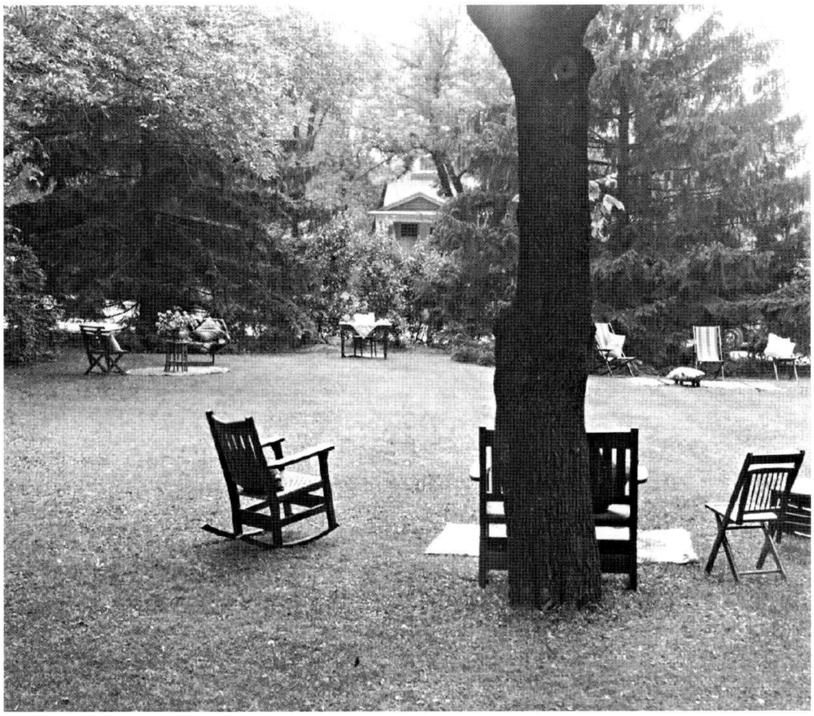

Yard of President and Mrs. Snyder's home—Faculty Row # 1—set for a garden party in 1910. Gilchrist Hall now stands on the site.

Enrollment rose eleven percent to 1,568. There were 92 in the graduating class.

Dr. James B. Angell, President Emeritus of the University of Michigan, delivered the commencement address. He had previously addressed the graduating class of 1871.

1911

College Grows to Thirty Departments—For its first 30 years (1857-1887), the school's annual reports included just four to six departments. In the 1911 annual report, 30 departments were represented, most of them added between 1901 and 1911.

President Snyder was effusive about the progress the college had made over its first fifty-plus years. "You old fellows of 1870, and earlier, think of this college in 1911, with 1,700 students, and a corresponding increase in the number of faculty! Witness a military parade of 700 to 900 men in uniform. Visit the library of 33,000 books and 466 periodicals, American and foreign! See the large numbers of good buildings, trees and extensive lawns in place of charred logs and stumps or ragged fields!"

Dr. C.E. Marshall (**Marshall-Adams Hall; Marshall Street**), bacteriology department head, working with others, produced a bacteriology text book for use in agricultural colleges.

John F. Macklin (Macklin Stadium; now **Spartan Stadium**) was named athletic director and football coach, succeeding Chester L. Brewer. Macklin was a University of Pennsylvania graduate.

The 1911 college budget totaled $445,411.63. Key salaries were $5,000 for the President; $3,000 for the Deans of Engineering, Bacteriology, and Agriculture, and the Professor of Chemistry; $2,500 for the Professor of Veterinary Science; $2,400 for the Professor of Physical Culture; $2,250 for the Secretary of the Board; $1,700 for the Dean of Home Economics; and $1,100 for the Editor of the M.A.C. Record.

First Graduating Class Over 100—Enrollment grew to 1,702, and the graduating class totaled 128, the first to surpass 100.

Remarkable October 27, 1911 night photo of Annual Student Barbecue in front of Wells Hall (site of Library).

1912

Frosh-Soph Tug-of-War across the Red Cedar River—1912.

Outreach and the Synergy of Knowledge Sharing—Professor Robert S. Shaw, Dean of Agriculture, told how knowledge sharing with farmers in one area led to improvements in many other areas. He cited an example: "Members were pledged for one specific purpose only—improved cattle breeding. Soon, however, they were figuring on rations and purchasing cotton seed meal; records of the production of individual cows were being kept; silos were being erected; commercial fertilizers were being used; improved varieties of grain grown and the general horizon widened by extending the scope of reading in the home."

Veterinary Medicine Dean Richard P. Lyman reported that our "school of instruction is now justified in claiming a place in the front rank of veterinary institutions."

In a call for a half dozen new buildings, President Snyder stated, "One-half million dollars could very properly be expended at once on new buildings without any show of extravagance or possibility of exceeding any pressing needs."

The college lecture-concert series was inaugurated in 1912. The first programs were held in the college Armory (Music Building site), where 700 folding chairs were put in place for the audience. To support the program, the State Board of Agriculture authorized a blanket tax of two dollars per term, or six dollars per year for student activities. Five dollars were to go to the Committee on Athletics, and one dollar to the Committee on Liberal Arts. The first year featured five lectures. This was the beginning of what would grow into MSU's comprehensive performing arts offerings.

A theatre-style lecture room for 250 and a laboratory for 286 students were added to the Chemical Building. This building served as the Library Annex following World War II, and many students attended lectures there.

M.A.C.'s first football victory over a Big Ten team occurred on Thanksgiving Day in Columbus, Ohio, when the Aggies stunned the Buckeyes, 35-20, after trailing 20-14 at halftime. Arriving back at the Lansing railroad station following the game, students and the college band marched to the Capitol building and lined the front steps in celebration.

Charles McKenney, class of 1881, was elected President of Michigan State Normal College (now Eastern Michigan University).

Dr. T. C. Blaisdell, professor of English, was named President of Alma College (Michigan).

John W. Beaumont (Beaumont Tower), Class of 1882, was elected to the Board. As an undergraduate he was a member of the Eclectic Society (now ATO). He became an attorney, taught at the Detroit College of Law, which now resides on the MSU campus.

Charles E. Ferris, class of 1890, was named Dean of Engineering at the University of Tennessee.

Student demographics showed ten foreign students—four from China, three from Russia, two from South America, and one from Canada; and students from 13 states outside of Michigan—22 from New York, 17 from Ohio, seven from Illinois, five from Pennsylvania, three from Indiana, three from Maryland, and one each from Connecticut, Massachusetts, Missouri, Montana, New Mexico, Wisconsin, and West Virginia.

The college budget for 1912 was $477,628.28. Enrollment was 1,643. The graduating class numbered 165—66 in agriculture, 54 in engineering, 30 in home economics, and 15 in forestry.

1913

336 Acres Added to the Campus—The Board purchased the 336-acre C.C. Woodbury farm which lay south of the Red Cedar River and adjacent to Old College Field in 1913. This acreage included the sites of Demonstration Hall, Jenison Gymnasium and Fieldhouse, and the western end of the current Old College Field. The purchase enabled the expansion of the athletic field and development of a new drill area. With the added land, the campus grew to 1,020 acres, double the size of many of today's college and university campuses.

A blue-ribbon committee was appointed to develop plans for locating future buildings on campus. Four of the five committee members now have buildings on campus that bear their names: Harry J. Eustace (Eustace-Cole Hall), Professor and Head of Horticulture; Robert S. Shaw (Shaw

M.A.C. fullback "Carp" Julian scores first touchdown in M.A.C.'s first victory over the Michigan Wolverines, 12-7, in Ann Arbor in 1913. Goal posts were situated on the goal line in those days. Julian was a member of the Eclectic Society, now Alpha Tau Omega.

Hall; Shaw Lane), Dean of Agriculture; Frank S. Kedzie (Kedzie Laboratories was named for Kedzie's father, Dr. Robert C.), Professor of Chemistry; and Board member John W. Beaumont (Beaumont Tower). The fifth person was I. Roy Waterbury, a Board member.

Frank F. Rogers, class of 1883, was named Michigan State Highway Commissioner.

The Alumni Association was reorganized in 1913 as "the M.A.C. Association, opening its membership to all former students."

First Undefeated, Untied Football Team—Coach John Macklin's M.A.C. football team ran through seven opponents undefeated and untied, a first for the college. The team handed Michigan its only loss of the season, 12-7, at Ann Arbor. It was the first victory over Michigan. Fullback George "Carp"Julian, an Eclectic Society (ATO) member, scored the first touchdown. Another season highlight was the defeat of defending Big Ten champion Wisconsin, 12-7 in Madison.

A celebration triggered by the victory at Michigan "began in Ann Arbor on Saturday afternoon, and ended Monday night with a bonfire before the Capitol Building in Lansing."

Maude Gilchrist (Gilchrist Hall), Dean of the Women's Department and Home Economics, resigned after 12 years to return to her alma mater—Wellesley, as an Associate Professor of Botany.

The college budget for 1913 was $514,001.17. Enrollment was 1,534, and there were 195 graduates.

1914

Remarkable Research and Outreach Help Michigan Citizens—Research and problem-solving to help Michigan citizens reached a remarkable level by 1914.

The Agricultural Experiment Station was filling research and knowledge needs in the areas of animal and dairy husbandry, soils, farm crops, farm mechanics, and other lines of agricultural work.

The Bacteriology Department was investigating the bacteriological factors in the "keeping qualities" (preservation) of butter and milk.

The Division of Soil Physics was investigating soil temperatures and their effect on soluble salts in moisture movements in soils.

The Department of Entomology published a three-year study on how contact-insecticides kill. Their scientists were combating the Tamarack sawfly by the introduction of parasites.

The Botanical Department was investigating plant diseases, including apple canker.

The Horticulture Department was experimenting with fertilizers for potatoes and tomatoes; and with sprays to control destructive fungous diseases and insects that attacked

Dusty road to Lansing (Michigan Ave.)—before paving in 1916.

New Dairy Building, built in 1914, east of Agricultural Hall, is now gone. It was home to the popular "Dairy Store" ice cream cones for decades.

plums, cherries, peaches, apples, raspberries, muskmelons and tomatoes.

The Division of Chemistry made an exhaustive study of acid soils and the most economical form of lime to correct acidity. Their researchers also investigated the cause of small infertile areas in fields. Moreover, the chemistry laboratory was required by law to analyze all fertilizers in the state.

The Farm Crops Division was selecting and breeding corn, wheat, oats, barley, rye, field beans, cow peas, alfalfa, clover, timothy and orchard grass. This work produced improved wheat, corn, barley, oats and alfalfa.

The Forestry Division maintained a 29-acre forestry nursery which nurtured 250,000 young hardwood trees and two million conifers. A full-time staff member advised farmers on woodland management and encouraged them to plant new trees, which the nursery furnished at cost.

The Dairy Department was in charge of five cow testing associations in the state to monitor for any diseases. Staff members tested from 600 to 700 herds during the year, and helped place Michigan as the third ranking dairy state.

The Animal Husbandry Department maintained experimental herds of beef cattle, sheep and swine, which were outstanding specimens. Surplus from the herd was sold at reasonable rates to farmers.

The Department of Agricultural Education was introducing agricultural teaching in the public schools.

The Department of Home Economics was producing well-trained home-makers who were teaching domestic science and domestic art in high schools and grammar schools.

The Poultry Department stimulated the state poultry industry.

The Veterinary Division regularly sent doctors to farms where there was a serious outbreak of disease among animals.

The Farm Mechanics Department assisted in planning farm buildings and fencing, and ran tests and offered advice on farm machinery.

A new $55,000 Dairy Building was completed. It stood immediately east of Agricultural Hall. For years it was the home of the popular "Dairy Store" ice cream cones. The first Dairy Building, erected in 1900 on West Circle Drive, was turned over to the Forestry Department.

A Summer School was inaugurated, and included conferences for "Rural Leadership," for "Housekeepers," for "Teachers of Domestic Science and Domestic Art," for the Home Economics Section of the State Federation of Women's Clubs, for high school Teachers of Agriculture, and for the Granges.

Professor Alfred K. Chittenden (Chittenden Hall), a Yale graduate, replaced Fred Baker as head of the Forestry Department.

The Married Students' Association was formed "to improve the opportunities of the members for an enjoyable time during their college life." Meetings included a short literary program and a social hour. (Wolverine, 1915).

The college budget for 1914 was $591,184.25. Enrollment was 1,455. There was a record graduating class of 211.

1915

Frank S. Kedzie Becomes M.A.C.'s Eighth President (served 1915-1921)—Frank S. Kedzie (1857-1935), M.A.C. Class of 1877 and Professor of Chemistry, was selected the eighth president of Michigan Agricultural College in 1915, when Jonathan LeMoyne Snyder retired. Frank Kedzie was born in Vermontville, Michigan the day prior to the opening of the college in 1857. When his father joined the faculty as Professor of Chemistry in 1863, six-year old Frank moved into a home on Faculty Row, and literally grew up on the M.A.C. campus.

Kedzie studied medicine with a Lansing physician; joined the faculty in chemistry in 1880; and earned a master's degree at Friedreich Wilhelm University in Berlin, Germany in 1890.

"The Grand Old Man of Michigan State College"...

...was how the *Detroit Free Press* described Frank Kedzie when he retired in 1932 after 52 years of service (1880-1932). He was affectionately known by students as "Uncle Frank."

Jonathan Snyder, in his 19 years as chief executive officer, was a strong and successful leader. Enrollment increased from 400 to as high as 1,700. Fixed income for the college grew from $80,000 to $800,000. New buildings valued at $700,000 plus had been erected. The Women's Division, the Veterinary Division, and the Forestry Department had been added. And service to state citizens through off- and on-campus teaching and knowledge sharing, soared.

In 1915, M.A.C. graduates were to be accepted "without condition to the Graduate Schools of the Universities of Wisconsin, Illinois, Missouri, Indiana, Ohio State, Michigan and Chicago." This was welcome recognition of M.A.C.'s academic credentials.

Helping eradicate tuberculosis and warning of contaminated well water were 1915 Bacteriology Department outreach projects to improve public health in the state.

Dr. Ward Giltner (Giltner Hall), department head, reported a system of tuberculin tests had been initiated and were being promoted statewide to eradicate tuberculosis. Analysis of well water from 42 rural community wells revealed that 67% were polluted with sewage bacteria, 79% polluted with soil bacteria, and 55% polluted with both bacteria.

A new Veterinary Science Building (now part of Giltner Hall) was completed in 1915 at a cost of $25,000. Already a leader among the few Veterinary Medicine schools in the nation, the new facility put the program equal with the best.

Frank S. Kedzie, Eighth President

Campus lectures included, "Highway Construction" by K.I. Sawyer of Lansing, Michigan; "Marketing Fruit in Detroit," by C.A. Bingham of Birmingham, Michigan; "Convenient Kitchens" by Mr. C.W. Foulk of Columbus, Ohio; and "Sex Hygiene," by Dr. Exner of New York City.

A Student Employment Bureau was opened in September under the direction of Donald C. Heffley, general secretary of the college YMCA. Some 130 employers, including college divisions, hired 225 students. In all, 1,178 jobs were reported to the bureau.

Ernest E. Alden, Class of 1915 remembered, "Roomed in Williams Hall—'Bedbug Alley.' The bunk beds had legs resting in a can of oil away from the walls (to prevent bugs from getting into the bed)."

In December 1915, Dr. William J. Beal's *History of the Agricultural College of Michigan* was published. It was a thorough review of the college history from 1855 through 1913.

The school's first Alumni Homecoming was originated in 1915.

M.A.C. Band proudly marches down Ann Arbor street after M.A.C.'s 24-0 football victory over the University of Michigan–1915.

Numbered football jerseys were worn, and programs printed, for the first time in school history. M.A.C.'s football team shocked the University of Michigan in Ann Arbor, defeating the Wolverines, 24-0. Fullback Jerry DePrato gained 153 yards rushing and receiving, scored all three touchdowns as well as drop-kicking a 23-yard field goal. Halfback and end Blake Miller gained 115 yards. DePrato and Miller became M.A.C.'s first All-Americans.

The college budget for 1915 was $637,172.47. Enrollment totaled 1,499, and the graduating class numbered 244. Dr. David Starr Jordan, chancellor of Stanford University, delivered the commencement address.

1916

Engineering Building Burns; R.E. Olds Gives $100,000 to Rebuild—Out of disaster came the first great private gift to M.A.C. On Sunday morning, March 5, 1916, fire roared through the Engineering Building, destroying a proud structure, just nine years old. **University of Michigan advocates pounced on the crisis as an opportunity to move all engineering education to Ann Arbor**. They argued it would be less expensive to enlarge the engineering facilities at the university than to rebuild in East Lansing.

Kedzie Keeps Engineering Education at M.A.C. Alive—President Kedzie struck quickly, and demonstrated first-rate crisis management skills in preserving M.A.C.'s engineering autonomy. He immediately called the faculty together to earmark rooms for carrying on the engineering classes. On the afternoon of the day of the fire, he met with "engineering students" and announced the places where classes would meet on Monday morning, and warned, "it is up to you men to keep a stiff upper lip. It lies with you as to whether or not the engineering department will live."

On Monday afternoon—the day after the fire—Kedzie wired Ransom E. Olds, founder of Oldsmobile and the REO Motor Company, who was vacationing in Florida, with an appeal for help in rebuilding the engineering facility. Previously, Kedzie had talked with Olds about giving a building to M.A.C. And, Olds remembered that Kedzie's father had loaned the Olds family money when they were struggling to launch their motor car business.

On April 29, 1916, Kedzie received a letter from R.E. Olds, declaring he "would give $100,000 towards the reconstruction of the Engineering Building at the Michigan Agricultural College." Olds wrote, **"I have great faith in the college and see no reason why it should not become one of the foremost colleges in the United States."** It was the largest private gift the college had ever received, and remained so for 12 years.

Reminiscing on Dr. Kedzie, Lynn J. Pardee, Class of 1916, remembered, "Dr. Kedzie blocked the door of his classroom so students entered one by one. As they entered, he asked their name. From that day on, he always remembered names, and called on each student personally."

Campus view–1916. Williams Hall (far left), Library-Museum (now Linton Hall; center-right), Women's Building (now Morrill Hall; upper right-center), Howard Terrace (left of Women's Building; on site of the Human Ecology Building).

Reflecting the onset of the technical era, two new scientific departments were created in 1916: The Department of Physics, with Associate Professor C.W. Chapman in charge; and, The Department of Electrical Engineering, with Professor A.R. Sawyer named head.

In a similar vein, a course in Chemical Engineering was established.

Scarlet fever hit the campus and affected 13 students. Dr. Ward Giltner, Professor of Bacteriology, and Dr. O.H. Bruegel, East Lansing City Health Officer, moved quickly to quarantine those who had symptoms. Fortunately, none died, and all recovered.

Ayesha Raven Laidlaw, Class of 1916, recalled that "A blizzard prevented streetcars from running (between the campus and Lansing) the night of the J-Hop. So horses and sleighs took couples to the dance (at the Masonic Hall in Lansing)." She also remembered, "East Lansing had one store, a combination drug and grocery."

Olds Hall of Engineering, built with a $100,000 gift from R.E. Olds, founder of Oldsmobile & REO car companies, was M.A.C.'s largest private gift to that time—completed 1917.

The Prudden Highway—A concrete road, nearly two miles long, running from Harrison Road in East Lansing to the eastern limits of Lansing—was constructed for $25,000 between August and the end of November. It was "fostered and largely financed by W.K. Prudden, class of 1878."

The 1916 college budget soared to $839,090.62, more than $200,000 higher than the previous year. Enrollment totaled 1,516, and the graduating class numbered 265.

1917

Students Enlist for World War I—U.S. President Woodrow Wilson declared war with Germany simultaneously with the opening of the spring term in 1917. Seniors who desired to enlist in the Officers' Training Camps were granted their diplomas. Juniors who entered training camp were given credit for spring term work.

The "opening of the college (1917-1918 academic year) was postponed from September 26 to October 10, permitting students to complete the harvest work (on family farms)."

Higher food prices were a consequence of World War I, which had been raging since 1914. There was a concern on campus that high food costs could affect attendance at the college. However, the efficiency of the Student Boarding System held costs down—averaging $3.26 per term for men, and just $3.11 per term for women. During the war, the College Extension Service helped promote and develop greater food production statewide in cooperation with the State's Food Preparedness Committee.

Vocational Agricultural Education, a concept M.A.C. launched in 1908, was promoted in Congress with the passage of the Smith-Hughes Bill on February 23, 1917, which provided funding. This led to the creation of the State Board for Vocational Education by the Michigan legislature. President Kedzie stated, "The college will...be called on to exert still greater efforts toward developing in Michigan's secondary and rural schools instruction in elementary principles of agriculture."

The new Engineering Building, named in honor of R.E. Olds, was completed during the year at a cost of $155,000. Professor G.W. Bissell, Dean of Engineering, reported that a portrait of Mr. Olds had been permanently hung in his office.

President Kedzie reported on future planning in his 1917 report. "The teaching force of the college remained at their posts during most of the month of June...several conferences were held by...groups of teachers discussing the general aims and work of the staff. An outline has been made of plans which I hope will lead to a closer contact between the different divisions...so unity of action may be assured and that each one of us may feel he is recognized as an integral part of M.A.C., and as such is responsible for the up-building of the college."

Frank E. Robson, class of 1878, was named general counsel for the Michigan Central Railroad.

An Alumni Secretary's Office was created in October, 1917. Card-file records of alumni addresses and occupations were organized and updated.

The first million dollar budget was recorded in 1917: $1,207,598.65. Enrollment was 1,116, and the graduating class totaled 282.

1918

Influenza Epidemic Kills 18 on Campus—On October 11, 1918, the virulent worldwide influenza epidemic—which killed between 21 and 100 million people around the globe (*The Great Influenza* by John M. Barry, Published by Viking—a member of the Penguin Group USA, Inc., 2004)—hit the East Lansing campus. Seventeen male students and one male faculty member died from the flu. The epidemic killed 675,000 Americans—more than died in all of the 20th century wars.

The disease first flared in an Army detachment that was in training on campus, and lived in temporary barracks that had been erected on the site of Berkey Hall. The Army Medical Corps and the College Health Officer moved quickly to restrict the spread of flu. Army trainees were moved from the barracks to the new gymnasium, now IM Circle. The barracks cubicles were used as quarantine hospital rooms.

The young women students were segregated from the young men in all classes for six weeks. This action prevented the spread of disease to the Women's Building. As a result there were only two mild cases among the coeds, with no deaths.

Florence Kugel Scofield, Class of 1920, recalled, "Because of the flu epidemic, we wore face masks to get in classes, and had to have passes to get on campus and into buildings."

U. Florine Folks Plumb, Class of 1920, wrote, "At the end of World War I (November 11, 1918), the student body took streetcars to Lansing and 'promenaded' around the Capitol while eating popcorn. Noisy, but not devilish."

Ray Stannard Baker, Class of 1889, was appointed a special commissioner of the U.S. Department of State by U.S. President Woodrow Wilson.

The college accepted a U.S. War Department request to train a detachment of 518 Student Army Training Corps (S.A.T.C.) men in the care, repair, and handling of motor trucks. Eight barracks and two mess halls were constructed immediately east of the Horticulture Building (now Eustace-Cole Hall) to accommodate up to 1,400 men. Four faculty members spent six weeks at an Officers' Training School at Fort Sheridan, Illinois for training in military instruction.

A total of 980 M.A.C. students, faculty, and alumni—295 of them officers—were in the armed forces by mid-1918. Some 425 were serving overseas in the American Expeditionary Forces. The Aviation Section of the Signal Corps had 82 M.A.C. men. Seven of the college's men had lost their lives by mid-1918. Six had been seriously wounded in action of the western front of the war. **Two M.A.C. men were awarded the French Cross of War for bravery in action in France.**

All four classes and every one of the societies (fraternities and sororities) purchased Liberty Loans to help finance the war.

The long-sought Gymnasium Building (now IM Circle) was completed during 1918 at a cost of $200,000. Its major features were a large gymnasium, with overhanging running track, a large indoor swimming pool, and plenty of classrooms and office space. It became the home of basketball, indoor sports, and large social events, such as the J-Hop.

Old College Hall Collapses—Restoration and preservation of Old College Hall (site of Beaumont Tower), as a Student Union, was a dream of the older alumni. The building was vested with major historic significance as the first structure at the pioneer land-grant college in the country, and birthplace of the first scientific agricultural teaching in America.

An Alumni Association committee, headed by Judge William L. Carpenter, received approval from the Board to undertake the restoration. When the work began, it was discovered the brick walls were hollow, the brick strength inferior, and that the hall rested on wood plank footings. Restoration was halted. Then, "on an August evening in 1918, while a band played the national anthem at a war trainees' retreat on the drill field (now Walter Adams Field), large portions of the west and south walls collapsed."

Shortly afterwards, the building was razed.

East Lansing High School was selected as the student practice teaching venue for instruction in home economics and agriculture.

Gymnasium, now IM-Circle, served men and women from 1918 to 1940. It became the Women's Gym in 1940 when the men moved into Jenison Gymnasium and Fieldhouse.

M.A.C. Defeats Notre Dame, Rockne, and "The Gipper"—In driving rain and mud on Old College Field, M.A.C.'s football team defeated the first Notre Dame team coached by Knute Rockne on November 16, 1918. Rockne's star player was the legendary George Gipp. The Aggies won 13-7, handing Rockne his only defeat of the season, and the only loss Notre Dame would suffer until 1921. George Gauthier was in his first and only season as the M.A.C. head coach. He was the first M.A.C. graduate to hold the head coaching position. He went on to become athletic director and coach of several sports at Ohio Wesleyan.

Robert D. Graham, chairman of the State Board of Agriculture and his wife, donated 50 acres of land in Kent County to the college for "an up-to-date, scientific and practical horticulture experiment and demonstration station."

The college budget for 1918 was $1,088,182.08. Enrollment dropped to 1,125 due to World War I. Fewer than 100 of the graduating class of 180 were present to receive their diplomas because of the war.

1919

Ex-U.S. President Taft Visits Campus—Former U.S. President William Howard Taft delivered a lecture on the League of Nations before the assembled student body and faculty in the new Gymnasium (IM Circle) on April 6, 1919. Earlier in the day, he spoke to the Michigan legislature.

Memorial Tree Grove Honors World War I Dead—In honor of the forty M.A.C. men who gave their lives in World War I, a memorial grove of 40 trees was planted at commencement on the lawn that slopes downward immediately west of the current site of Williams Hall (built in 1937). Names of the dead are on a metal plaque placed on a large rectangular stone which sits in the grove.

In a final accounting, it was determined that **1,400 M.A.C. men served in World War I.** Some 20 graduates and former students were presented decorations from the U.S., British and French governments.

Harold Furlong, Class of 1918, was awarded the Congressional Medal of Honor, the highest recognition the nation can pay a soldier. Fewer than 50 of these awards were made during WWI.

Williams Hall burned to the ground on January 1, 1919. It was the oldest dormitory on campus, having been built in 1869, and the first to be heated by steam. President Kedzie voiced hope that East Lansing cafes, dining halls, private homes, and the Wells Hall facilities would be able to handle the feeding and housing of the students driven from Williams.

College establishes Health Service and appoints Health Officer—Undoubtedly influenced by the horrendous flu epidemic of 1918, Dr. Ward Giltner, bacteriology department head, recommended the appointment of Dr. O.H. Bruegel, Health Officer for East Lansing, as Medical Officer for M.A.C. Dr. Bruegel had been of great service

Dr. Ward Giltner (Giltner Hall) at his desk in 1919. He was named Dean of Veterinary Medicine in 1923.

during the 1918 crisis and was hired at a salary of $1,200. "The faculty also took steps to establish a college Health Service."

Physical training for all students was mandated by faculty vote, starting in the fall of 1919.

M.A.C.'s ROTC unit was ranked for the first time among "Distinguished Colleges" by action of the U.S. War Department.

Electrically controlled clocks were installed in several campus buildings.

Frank H. Sanford (Sanford Natural Area), was hired as Associate Professor of Forestry.

The 1919 college budget was $1,322,473. Enrollment was 1,401. The graduating class numbered 130.

1920

Mrs. Dora Stockman Elected First Woman Board Member—Mrs. Dora Stockman of Lansing was elected the first woman member of the State Board of Agriculture, and as a result was the first woman to hold an elective office in Michigan. She also was the first woman in the U.S. to be on a Board of Control of a Land-Grant institution.

By 1920, the Union Memorial Building fund had reached $151,103, with $103,600 from alumni, $38,403 from students, and $9,100 from faculty. At the M.A.C. Association meeting, alumni resolved to raise the fund to $300,000, and maybe $500,000.

Home Economics added an elective course in Advanced Nutrition. Elements of the course involved the participation of the Departments of Chemistry, Bacteriology, Botany, Physiology, Drawing, Mathematics, and Physics. It was an early example of inter-disciplinary education. Forty-one senior women elected the course and did well in it.

U. Florine Folks Plumb, class of 1920, remembered the "Tug-of-war each spring; freshmen vs. sophomores, across the Red Cedar."

Florence Kugel Scofield, class of 1920, recalled the "Rule for dancing: had to see daylight between partners."

The college budget for 1920 was $1,481,303.50. Women's salaries were improving: Dean of Women—$3,300; Dean of Home Economics—$2,800; Dean of Women's Dormitories—$2,600; and Librarian—$2,400. Top men's salaries were: President—$7,000; Director of Physical Culture—$4,500; Deans of Agriculture, Engineering, and Veterinary Science—$4,200 each; and Secretary of the Board—$4,000.

Enrollment was 1,411, and the graduating class numbered 274.

1921

President Kedzie Resigns; David Friday Named Ninth President (served 1921-1923)—Flat attendance at M.A.C. following World War I caused concern. Other land-grant institutions were enjoying greater enrollment from the flood of post-war students. It was determined that majors in agriculture, engineering, and home economics weren't enough. High school graduates wanted more options.

Professors Bessey, Plant, and Ryder developed a new science and arts curriculum in the winter of 1920-21, which "offered majors and minors in ten departments ranging from bacteriology to German." This was fine-tuned by the faculty and then presented to the Board under the title of Applied Science. The new program attracted 98 freshmen the first year it was offered.

President Friday…

"It is in the public interest to furnish opportunity to all classes (of people)."

The static attendance, however, had alumni concerned and the 1921 legislature threatened to withhold a building appropriation unless there was a change in the college administration.

President Kedzie retired in September 1921, and was appointed Dean of the new Division of Applied Science. The *Alumni Recorder* wrote, "we greatly dislike to bid farewell to President Kedzie. The Kedzie smile will be missed from the corner of the Library Building (now Linton Hall, where the President's office was located)."

David L. Friday (1876-1945), an agriculturist and economist of national repute, was selected as the ninth President of M.A.C. The Board hoped he would have answers to the farmers' problems resulting from the post-WWI agricultural depression. He had served Michigan Governor Alex J. Groesbeck as a budget specialist, and had worked in the effort to win appropriations for M.A.C.'s forthcoming Library and Home Economics Buildings.

He was a University of Michigan graduate and an instructor in their economics department until moving to East Lansing to assume the presidency.

Due to his work on the Congressional Commission of Agricultural Inquiry, Friday did not assume the presidency until March of 1922. **Dean of Agriculture Robert S. Shaw** served as Acting President from September 1921 until President Friday arrived.

Clarence Beaman Smith, class of 1894, was named Chief of the Agricultural Extension Work for the United States.

Phillip B. Woodworth, class of 1886, was elected president of Rose Polytechnic Institute at Terre Haute, Indiana. In 1893, Woodworth married a daughter of M.A.C. president emeritus Oscar Clute.

Charles W. Garfield, class of 1870, master's 1873, honorary LL.D., 1917, was noted as one of the founders of the Michigan Horticultural Society. He was often called the "Father of Michigan Forestry." He was the director of the American Playground Association, president of the Grand Rapids Savings Bank, and served 12 years on the State Board of Agriculture.

David Friday, Ninth President

A course in Hospital Nutrition Problems was begun in cooperation with Sparrow Hospital in Lansing. Students worked in the hospital diet kitchen under the direction of the staff.

Besides the Women's Building, which housed 85 coeds, 58 freshmen women were living in Abbot Hall (old Abbot

M.A.C. 1921 Homecoming parade on Circle Drive.

on the site of the Music Practice Building), and 60 in Howard Terrace (on the site of the Human Ecology Building). In addition, Waterbury House, College Cottage, College Residence, and Senior House—all located in East Lansing—housed 26, 18, 14, and 18 women, respectively.

Dean of Women Eudora H. Savage reported all of the women students were members of the Women's Self-Governing Association.

The 1921 college budget was $1,912,151.23. Enrollment was 1,629. Degrees were granted to 225 graduates.

1922

President Friday Strengthens Academic Programs—Shortly after his arrival in mid-March, 1922, President Friday suggested the Engineering curriculum should be opened up to include courses in accounting, business law, economics, and industrial management. These program expansions were agreed to by the Board.

Some twenty economics courses were added to the curriculum. These were not only for engineers. Eight courses were initiated in agricultural economics. The updated curriculum reflected the fact the agricultural engineering professions needed to recognize the disciplines of accounting, management, and marketing.

Friday also encouraged the expansion of graduate studies. Some sixty graduate courses were introduced across a majority of the college departments. Graduate assistantships were increased from four to 23. Doctor of Philosophy tracks were introduced in seven departments: Bacteriology, Botany, Chemistry, Entomology, Farm Crops, Horticulture, and Soils.

President Friday believed fruit-growing should be one of Michigan's strengths. This probably was partially influenced by the fact he grew up on a farm which was in the fruit belt near Benton Harbor. He also knew that other crops—like wheat—had been overproduced. Michigan fruit production had some natural advantages. He encouraged the doubling of the Horticulture faculty, from five to ten, and made a new Horticulture Building a priority.

First College Radio Station—A "sending station" (radio transmission) was set up in the Engineering Building to experiment with the transmission of radio signals. Professor A.R. Sawyer reported, "A great day for M.A.C. will dawn when the departments actually use broadcasting signals for imparting public information." In May, using the call letters 8YG, "President Friday spoke to alumni groups assembled throughout the region."

First Radio Agricultural Outreach in the Nation—Professor Howard C. Rather (**Rather Hall**) broadcast agricultural information over the air waves in March of 1922 from radio station WWJ in Detroit. It was the first recorded use of radio to extend agricultural knowledge to citizens in the state or nation.

The Utilities Commission asked the college to maintain a Standards Laboratory for certifying the accuracy of measuring instruments used by the Public Utilities of the state.

The Home Economics Department conducted a major study in "Problems of Nutrition" with the children of the Franklin and Walnut public schools in Lansing.

Land acquisition—a habit practiced by Robert S. Shaw, Dean of Agriculture, Acting President, and later President—and later passed on to his son-in-law John A. Hannah—added 200 acres to the 1,020 acres already owned by the college.

Dr. Victor R. Gardner, class of 1905 and chair of horticulture, and professor F.C. Bradford authored with H.J. Hooker, Jr. the *Fundamentals of Fruit Production* in 1922.

Students spell M.A.C. at 1922 J-Hop in the Gymnasium (now IM-circle).

It became the standard text in advanced pomology until 1952.

DeGay Ernst set a world record in the 40-yard dash—4.56 seconds. Ernst was captain of the track team in 1922-1923. He held eight M.A.C. track records in dash and hurdle events.

DeGay Ernst set a world record in the 40-yard dash—4.56 seconds—1922.

Reid L. Rayner, Class of 1922, recalled that "Freshmen men were not allowed to date," and that the detested Brown freshman beanie—worn the first year—was burned at the end of the freshman year. The beanies had different colored buttons to indicate the college course one was taking.

Clark L. Brody (Brody Hall), Class of 1904, and **Melville B. McPherson** (Grandfather of MSU's nineteenth President, M. Peter McPherson) assumed their elected positions on the Board.

The college budget for 1922 was $1,792,399. The President received a dramatic increase in salary from $8,000 to $12,000. Enrollment was 1,611. Degrees were granted to 249 graduates.

1923

Friday Resigns As President; Shaw Becomes Acting President—President Friday's management style was not popular with the faculty. They had been used to the "hands-on" attention to detail at any hour by Presidents Snyder and Kedzie. Friday posted office hours of 11 am to 12:30 pm daily and issued decisions via staff members, rather than discussing them face-to-face with faculty.

Friday also alienated farm groups which expected him to reorder research and outreach work from increasing crop production to helping them market their products. As an economist, he believed crop prices were dictated by international economic conditions, and that trying to replace wholesalers and retailers with farm cooperatives would not improve the return to farmers. "He suggested efficient farmers were prospering, that inefficient ones must learn to produce at a profit." That belief, plus "his efforts to dissolve the close relationship between county agricultural agents and the Farm Bureau's cooperative marketing agencies" were not well received.

Friday resigned at the end of May, 1923. Agricultural Dean Robert S. Shaw was once again named Acting President.

Use of electricity was spreading rapidly. Proposals to extend huge bus bars across the country to create giant power grids promised to lower electrical costs. The Engineering Division and Department of Electrical Engineering were working on courses to prepare students to participate in this growth.

WKAR Radio Established—WKAR was established as the college radio station in 1923, and its first broadcast in March carried an hour of the student produced Union Opera, "Campus Nights."

James B. Hasselman, a publicist, was named the station's first director and **may have been the first college sportscaster in the nation**. He broadcast the college basketball games from a phone booth situated on the elevated running track overhanging the gymnasium floor.

Seven majors were offered in Home Economics: General, Foods & Nutrition, Clothing, Textiles, Related Arts, Vocational Management, and Institutional Management. The latter major included tearoom management, cafeteria management, advanced cookery, accounting and marketing. This course probably was the forerunner of hotel, restaurant and institutional management, now known as the School of Hospitality Business.

The Home Economics Department required its students to take their meals at the Women's Commons or the College Residence starting with the spring term of 1923. This nutritional directive was given because so many students were eating at irregular hours and not choosing good foods.

Ground was broken for the Union Building by W.K. Prudden in June, 1923. Although only $130,000 had been raised for the building, estimated to cost $650,000, it was hoped the ground-breaking would stimulate new pledges.

"When that didn't happen, W.O. Hedrick and Alumni Secretary Robert J. McCarthy led a dramatic **'Excavation Week'** in November, 1923." It was similar to an old-fashioned barn-raising. Students, faculty, and even Board members, came to the site with shovels and helped dig the hole that would accommodate the basement foundation.

"Excavation Week"—November, 1923—Students, Faculty, even Board Members, volunteered to dig the hole for the Union Building foundation.

New 14,000-seat football stadium was completed in 1923. The grandstands were later incorporated into enlargements that resulted in Spartan Stadium. Aerial photo taken in 1929. Beaumont Tower, built in 1928, is above and to the right of the stadium. Note all the parked cars, upper left hand corner. It was the "Roaring Twenties."

Competition was encouraged among teams. The Eclectic Society (now Alpha Tau Omega) excavators arrived dressed as a chain gang in striped prison costumes. Coeds served coffee and doughnuts. Music was played by the college military and Swartz Creek bands. Deans and Board members, including Mrs. Dora Stockman, came and shoveled one wagon load of dirt. It would take another 18 months before the building was completed.

All students were given small pox vaccinations in January to head off an epidemic from the one case that was reported on campus. During winter term, epidemics of influenza and scarlet fever hit the campus.

New Football Stadium—The football program moved to a new 14,000-seat stadium from Old College Field in 1923. The new facility cost $160,000 and was the foundation of the current Spartan Stadium.

The First Complete Play-by-Play Movies of Football Games in the U.S. were filmed by Everett N. Huby at M.A.C. in 1923. (*MSC Record*, August 1, 1954).

T. Glen Phillips (Phillips Hall), Class of 1902 and Landscape Architect and City Planner for Detroit, was hired as a consultant on campus planning. For a salary of $1,000, he was to visit the campus monthly to confer with Board members on where to locate new buildings, and on the layout and design of the college grounds.

At the National Fruit Show in Council Bluffs, Iowa, an M.A.C. team won second place honors in its first national competition.

June Night Pageant Evolves Into Water Carnival—An annual June night pageant was performed outdoors in the Forest of Arden on campus (located on the lawn northwest of Linton Hall) between 1919 and 1922. "In 1923, the pageant was moved to the Red Cedar River and combined with the annual canoe-tilting competition to create the first Water Carnival. Single canoes, each decorated by a fraternity or sorority to represent a popular song, floated toward the bridge, while its occupants sang the lyrics."

Karl H. McDonel (McDonel Halls) was named Assistant to the Director of the Division of Extension.

Ralph H. Young (Ralph Young Fund and Ralph Young Track & Field) was named Professor of Physical Education and Director of Athletics.

The college budget for 1923 was $1,943,521. Enrollment was 1,609. Degrees were granted to 292 graduates.

1924

Kenyon L. Butterfield Named Tenth President (served 1924-1928)—Kenyon L. Butterfield (1868-1935) **(Butterfield Hall; Butterfield Drive)**, Class of 1891 and President of the University of Massachusetts, was chosen by the Board as the tenth president of M.A.C. on May 21, 1924. Prior to Butterfield's selection, Dean of Agriculture Robert

S. Shaw had served just four days short of a year as Acting President.

Butterfield was the third graduate of M.A.C. to rise to the presidency (Oscar Clute and Frank Kedzie being the others). He was a natural leader. As a student, he had been elected president "of his class, the Y.M.C.A., the *Speculum* board (college magazine), the Eclectic Society (now ATO) and more."

He had deep roots in the history and culture of the college. "His grandfather Ira H. Butterfield, helped to found the college. His father, Ira H. Butterfield, Jr. served as a member, and Secretary of the State Board of Agriculture from 1889 to 1899."

Butterfield served on the M.A.C. staff and was superintendent of the Farmers' Institutes. He received an M.A. degree from the University of Michigan in 1902. He was elected President of Rhode Island College of Agriculture in 1903, and President of Massachusetts Agricultural College in 1906. He received an LL.D. degree from the Massachusetts school in 1910.

U.S. President Theodore Roosevelt made Butterfield a member of the Country Life Commission, and "he (Butterfield) founded and presided over the American Country Life Association." He was an advisor to U.S. President Woodrow Wilson's staff on rural credit, and to the Chinese government on superior agricultural techniques.

President Butterfield...

"let us give students a large view of the place of one's life work; both the material and the ambition to broaden their lives..."

Butterfield was strong on preparing people for specific occupations, but with a general and liberal education component.

In the greatest and most expensive burst of construction in the school's history to that time, four major buildings and a power house were going up or would be completed in 1924.

The $350,000 **Library (now the Museum)** was being erected on the site of old Williams Hall. This modern structure included offices for the president.

The $350,000 **Home Economics Building (now Human Ecology)** was completed in winter term on the site of the old Howard Terrace apartments, which had been torn down in 1922.

The new $400,000 **Horticulture Building (now Old Horticulture)** was underway on a site just east of the Bacteriology Building (now Marshall Hall). Horticulture Halls of Fame honoring great horticulturists would be created on three floors—1st floor, Michigan honorees; 2nd floor, U.S. honorees; 3rd floor, international honorees.

Work on the $650,000 **Union Building** at the corner of Abbot Road and Grand River Ave. would continue throughout the year.

A new **Power House** for central heating of campus buildings was completed at a cost of $150,000.

Frederick B. Mumford, class 1891 and Dean of Agriculture at the University of Missouri, "drafted the Purnell Act passed by the U.S. Congress in 1924. This act provided for increased appropriations to land-grant colleges for research in rural economics, rural sociology, and land economics." (*Wolverine,* 1930).

Mumford was honored in 1924 by having his portrait hung in the Saddle and Sirloin Club gallery in Chicago, top recognition in the animal industry field. A building named in his honor stands on the University of Missouri campus.

Kenyon L. Butterfield, Tenth President

During the year, there was a flap over the State Administrative Board holding up monies for extension work and in the process interfering with governance by the State Board of Agriculture. A judicial opinion stated, "...the Constitution of 1850 wisely provided against legislative interference by placing its exclusive management in the hands of a constitutional board elected by the people. **The Agricultural College and the University of Michigan are constitutionally immune from such legislation. The legislature has no control over them.**" A committee of students strongly requested that student-staff convocations be held regularly to improve communication. The meetings were credited with developing a spirit of cooperation between students and the administration and a loyalty and helpfulness.

A 125-acre farm adjoining the south campus was purchased by the college with a $20,625 appropriation from the legislature.

Alpha Phi was granted permission to build the first sorority house off-campus.

Mary F. Cook, class of 1924, experienced a stunning surprise that year, which was described by her daughter Mary M. Cowles, class of 1950 on the occasion of her 50th reunion in 2000. Cowles wrote, "I remember my mother telling the story about when she was living in Morrill Hall, then the Women's Building. The R.O.T.C. then used the field next to the Music Building (now Walter Adams Field) for cannon target practice. A shell missed its target and proceeded through the wall of my mother's room, and embedded itself in an interior wall. Mom was in the room, unhurt. I guess it caused quite a stir on campus."

Shortly after Dean Robert S. Shaw was named acting president in May of 1923, it was discovered that the college accounts had been overdrawn the previous year by $125,000. Shaw reported in 1924 "…the entire staff accepted the situation cheerfully and rendered valuable service throughout the entire year by way of effecting still further savings in order to restore the treasury to an even balance." He praised the board for "maintaining salaries, and even advancing those whose efforts merited recognition." By July 1, 1924, through Shaw's effective, steady leadership, the college budget was back in the black by $65,628.95.

The 1924 college budget passed the two million mark at $2,044,529.79. Enrollment reached 1,873 and the graduating class numbered 292. The library housed 51,103 volumes.

1925

Michigan State College of Agriculture & Applied Science—Michigan Senator Norman B. Horton, Class of 1902, proposed in a bill that the school's name be changed from Michigan Agricultural College to Michigan State College of Agriculture and Applied Science. The bill passed on May 13, 1925.

The name change had been contemplated since 1912. It was driven by the fact the school had broadened its offerings far beyond agriculture, to mechanical and electrical engineering, home economics, veterinary medicine, chemistry, physics, bacteriology, botany, horticulture, applied sciences, languages, liberal arts and more.

Dairy Students Win National Title—Department of Dairy Husbandry students scored the highest among 24 colleges and universities at the National Students' Judging Contest at the National Dairy Show in Milwaukee. Their scores were tops in all classes of cattle judged. Frank Williamson won the sweepstakes prize and was awarded a $400 scholarship. Other team members were E.S. Weisner, and R.P. Britsman.

Department of Poultry Husbandry students won the Annual Judging Contest at the Coliseum Poultry Show in Chicago, in competition with eight other colleges. Team members included Clyde Norton, Frank Williamson, Ralph Meek and Richard Weine.

The girls debate team from the Department of English and Modern Languages won four of five debates with other colleges. Myrtle Lewton, Florence Albright, Dorothy Robinson, Alberta Bates, Elizabeth Sackett, and Jetta Thompson comprised the team.

A course in Business Administration was initiated in the Division of Liberal Arts and was described as different from any other in the country. Economics was the backbone of the course, supplemented by English, Mathematics, History and Political Science, Science, Sociology, and Foreign Language.

A comprehensive freshman orientation program was introduced in the fall of 1925. Melville B. McPherson of Lowell was elected chairman of the Board (grandfather of M. Peter McPherson, MSU's 19th president).

Robert S. Linton (Linton Hall), a critic teacher in Vocational Education, joined the faculty.

John Herman Kobs (Kobs Field) was named an Instructor in Physical Education. Kobs would serve Michigan State for 39 years as baseball coach, and as ice hockey coach and as an assistant football coach.

The 1925 college budget was $2,484,364.41. Enrollment was 2,314. Degrees were granted to 343 graduates. Students came from 21 states, the District of Columbia, and eight foreign countries.

1926

Michigan State Teams Named "Spartans"—When the school name changed to Michigan State College in 1925, calling the athletic teams "Aggies" was inappropriate. In a naming competition, "Michigan Staters," was the popular choice. However, *Lansing State Journal* sportswriter George A. Alderton thought Michigan Staters too cumbersome for news columns and headlines. Alderton and "Dale Stafford of the *Capital News*, dug through the rejected entries and chose a name submitted by Perry J. Fremont: 'Spartans.'"

When traveling with the Michigan State baseball team on its first southern tour, Alderton used the name "Spartans" in an April 2, 1926 story. Soon thereafter, the *State News* used the name, and it took.

Alderton said that **"When the young men of ancient Sparta went off to war, they were told to come home with their shield on high, or come home carried on it."**

Interestingly, **"Congressman Morrill promised in 1858 that his bill** (the Morrill Act creating the Land-Grant Colleges) **would found schools like that in Michigan,**

schools like those 'of ancient Sparta' whose graduates would know how to sustain American institutions with American vigor."

Dr. Ward Giltner, Dean of Veterinary Medicine, introduced a new course in 1926 to train medical technicians.

A "General Campus Plan" was produced by campus planner T. Glen Phillips **(Phillips Hall)** in 1926. In a remarkably visionary plan, Phillips "reserved ample space for dormitories, academic buildings, athletics and agriculture." Harold Lautner's wonderful book on the campus, *From an Oak Opening,* described the planning insight: "...the most saleable aspect of Phillips plan was his informal spacious placement of buildings and groups of buildings, all with 'studied random effect.'"

Phillips kept the "Sacred Space" inside West Circle Drive sacrosanct. "He tied blocks and super-blocks of buildings together with a curving road system." Phillips' plan retained the charm of the old while providing a layout that would give Michigan State the beauty and free-flowing, innovative informality of its future campus.

A Home Economics summer course, Home Economics 23, "Food Sales and Service," **attracted national attention** among home economics professionals.

Frank Johnson, class of 1895, was named chief engineer of Ford Motor Company's Lincoln Division. He was key in the design of many Lincolns, and the famous Ford Model "A."

Professor Dwight T. Ewing of the Engineering Department developed successful chromium plating techniques in conjunction with the REO Motor Car Company. This discovery added to the beauty and preservation of automotive bumpers and trim.

Rural electrification was being studied by the college, working with Consumers Power Company. An experimental line strung between Mason and Danville was accessed by farmers along the route, many of whom "made arrangements to install and use electrical equipment."

Louise H. Campbell (Campbell Hall), the school's "State Home Demonstration Leader, introduced the annual Farm Women's Week in 1926."

Engineering Professor Slaughter studied the disposal of creamery wastes to reduce the problem of stream pollution. This was some 44 years before America's first Earth Day in 1970.

Future President John A. Hannah, age 24, was praised for his work in the Poultry Husbandry Department. "He has placed the poultry extension work on a very high plane...the organization of the Michigan State Poultry Improvement Association and the organization of the Record of Performance Work were special pieces of work that desire recognition." This was the first appearance of Hannah's name in the annual board report.

Through lease or purchase, 315 acres were added to the south campus.

The first mention of a Publicity Department occurred in the 1926 board report. A staff of five operated on a total budget of $11,760.

Emory V. Houk, Class of 1926, recalled, "Some outfitted their rooms with a 'cat's-whisker', galena crystal, and a ground to the fire escape and some form of receiver to make a radio which would pick up the college transmitter."

Six East Lansing landmarks were constructed in 1926: Peoples Church, the Tea Pot Flower Shop on campus, the Campus Hotel (later North Hall), the Hunt Food Shop, the State Theatre, and the new East Lansing High School on Abbott Road (later the Hannah Middle School, and now the Hannah Community Center).

Richard Miles Olin (Olin Health Center) was named Director of the College Health Service.

The college budget for 1926 reached $2,738,064.69. Receipts from students (both tuition and fees) totaled $264,133.84. Enrollment was 2,534. Degrees were granted to 373 graduates.

Louise H. Campbell led MSC's home economics outreach in the 1920s, and promoted education for farm women.

1927

Legislature Increases College Tax Support—In 1927, the legislature allowed the school's funding from the education mill tax to rise above a previous cap of $1,000,000 annually to $1,541,958. **The beautiful Kedzie Chemical Building,** named in honor of the school's first chemistry professor, Dr. Robert C. Kedzie, was constructed at a cost of $590,000. It featured the finest ventilation system of any chemical facility in the nation and housed dozens of individual laboratories and classrooms.

The Kedzie Chemical Laboratories, opened in 1927, honored Dr. Robert C. Kedzie, the school's first chemistry professor, early consumer protection advocate, and "Father" of Michigan's sugar beet industry.

Demonstration Hall was built at a cost of $300,000. It housed offices, classrooms, a gymnasium, and a demonstration riding arena—from which it took its name. It also was to be used for the demonstration of agricultural stock and implements. The arena accommodated crowds of up to 6,000 for concerts, and commencement exercises. For basketball games, and later ice hockey matches, it could seat about 4,500, but sight lines were poor and blocked in some areas by steel pillars.

Studies on the destruction of vitamins in the blanching and processing of peas were conducted by the Home Economics Department.

From its nurseries, the Forestry Department shipped 716,000 trees for planting throughout the state.

A 1927 survey revealed annual student expenditures averaged $654, ranging from $398 to $1,141. Although having a reputation as being rich, fraternity members only spent $45 more per year than other students.

First Michigan State NCAA Titles—Fred P. Alderman, a world-class sprinter, Class of 1927, won the 100, 220 and 440-yard dashes in the NCAA, Western Conference, and IC4A meets. He was the first Spartan to win an individual national championship in any sport. **He also was co-holder of the world's indoor 300-yard dash record, at 31.2 seconds.**

Ray Stannard Baker, Class of 1889, published the first of his massive eight-volume biography of Woodrow Wilson. The eighth volume was released in 1939. In 1940, Baker won the Pulitzer Prize for his monumental work.

A four-year course in Physical Education and Athletic Coaching for men was offered for the first time in 1927.

Nation's Second Hotel Administration School Born—Twelve members of the Hotel Men's Association education committee visited M.S.C. on December 14, 1927 to propose that the college establish a course in Hotel Management. These leaders included Messrs. Klare of the Statler Hotel in Detroit; Pantlind of the Pantlind Hotel in Grand Rapids; and Doherty of the Doherty Hotel in Clare, Michigan.

They met with President Kenyon Butterfield and a faculty committee of nine. They were enthusiastic about the idea. As a result, a Hotel Administration course—the second in the nation (Cornell first)—was initiated in the spring of 1928. Today, this academic discipline is known as the School of Hospitality Business, which includes hotel, restaurant, resort, and institutional administration. It is recognized as one of the two top schools of its kind in America.

The 1927 college budget passed the $3 million milestone: $3,196,126.29. Enrollment rose to 2,800. Degrees were granted to 363 graduates.

1928

Robert S. Shaw—"The Canny Scot"—Named Eleventh President (served 1928-1941)—President Kenyon L. Butterfield and the Board became embroiled in a number of issues—a college budget deficit, off-campus education, a recommended "self-study" of the institution, and executive authority in day-to-day operations.

A budget deficit of $224,708 was being blamed on Butterfield. He countered that by law the Secretary of the Board was the business manager, and that, he (Butterfield), had no responsibility for expenditures. John D. Willard, Director of Continuing Education, directed off-campus education consisting of correspondence courses, speaking engagements, and some extension classes. Confusion was created regarding off-campus continuing education versus extension work. The "legislators, farm bureau officers and county supervisors preferred to spend money where there would be a clear financial return," such as improved crop programs.

President Shaw at the dedication of Beaumont Tower in 1929…

"I would like to have associated with this idea of inspiration, the idea of the matter of standards. Inspired to do what? Inspired to advance and to elevate and to live up to higher standards—scholastically, socially, morally and spiritually in all our affairs."

Butterfield recommended a "self-study" of the institution which was to result in a vision-mission plan. This threatened certain departments and professors who feared their efficiency would be called into question.

Finally, there was a tug of war over who ran the school's day-to-day operations—the President or the Secretary to the State Board of Agriculture. Butterfield said, the Board, in effect, allowed two "Presidents."

While Butterfield was on a trip to Palestine, the Board fired John Phelan, Dean of the College; Dr. Clara Powell, Advisor of Women; and John D. Willard, Director of Continuing Education. Butterfield protested this action in a printed statement dated December 5, 1928, saying the matter was not handled fairly or with recognized practices of management, or common law justice. He pointed out that the Board had hired Phelan and Powell unanimously, had never criticized any of the three they fired, and gave no reason for their dismissal.

Butterfield wrote, "The newspapers published a vast amount of misinformation which was not in accordance with Board records, but which remained uncorrected by the Board."

Butterfield's tenure ended when the Board asked him to resign at their May meeting.

Robert S. Shaw (1871-1953) **(Shaw Hall; Shaw Lane, Shaw Estates),** 1893 graduate of the Ontario Agricultural College, was elected Michigan State's eleventh president on May 22, 1928.

Robert S. Shaw, Eleventh President

He came to the U.S. in 1898, serving as an Assistant Professor of Agriculture at Montana State College. He joined the M.A.C. faculty in 1902 as Professor of Agriculture and was named Dean of Agriculture in 1908. During the three times he served as the college's Acting President, Shaw had shown sound and frugal management, always bringing the budget into the black. He had won the confidence of the Board and was well thought of by the faculty and students.

Beaumont Tower, the landmark structure on the Michigan State campus, was built in 1928. The tower stands on the site of Old College Hall (1857-1918), which was the first building on campus, and the first place where scientific agriculture was taught in America. The tower was a gift of John Beaumont, Class of 1882, member of the Eclectic Society (ATO), and Detroit attorney who also served on the State Board of Agriculture. In Detroit, Beaumont served as a professor at the Detroit College of Law, which moved to the MSU campus in 1996 (now Michigan State University College of Law).

Elisabeth W. Conrad, Dean of Women, 1928-1945.

Elisabeth W. Conrad (Conrad Hall) was named Dean of Women and Assistant Professor of French. She served as dean from 1928 to 1945.

Beaumont Tower was completed in 1928. It commands the highest ground on campus, and stands on the site of Old College Hall, where scientific agriculture was first taught in America. Built in 1857, Old College Hall was razed in 1918.

Edgar A. Burnett, class of 1887, was elected chancellor of the University of Nebraska. He had been Dean of Agriculture at Nebraska from 1909 to 1928. Burnett Hall stands in his honor at Nebraska.

Kellogg Gift Largest in School History—The Kellogg Company gave Michigan State its W.K. Kellogg Experimental Farm and Bird Sanctuary in December, 1928. This magnificent gift consisted of 860 acres, including the 90-acre Bird Sanctuary with its Wintergreen Lake. The land value was estimated at $300,000. In addition a $265,000 endowment was donated for the upkeep of the properties. It was the largest gift in school history.

G. Malcolm Trout (Malcolm Trout Building of Food Science and Human Nutrition) was hired as Assistant Professor of Dairy Husbandry. Within a few years, Trout developed and became the "Father" of homogenized milk.

East Lansing's First Traffic Light—A sign that East Lansing's rural environment was ending, was the installation of the city's first traffic light at the corner of Abbot Road and Grand River Avenue in 1928.

The 50-acre Tommerell Farm was purchased on January 1, 1928, adding to the south campus.

Fred P. Alderman became Michigan State's first Olympic gold medal winner as a member of the record-setting U.S. 1,600-meter relay team at the 1928 Olympics in Amsterdam.

The college budget was $3,218,867.87 in 1928. Enrollment was 2,813. Degrees were granted to 388 graduates.

1929

Department of Journalism & Publications Established; Enrollment Passes 3,000—The only accredited Journalism School in Michigan was established as the Department of Journalism and Publications in 1929. The purpose was to coordinate activities in the fields of journalism, publications and public information. This was the first formalization of a public relations function at the college.

The State College Club, forerunner of today's University Club, was founded. For forty years, this faculty club, met regularly for luncheons in three rooms on the third floor of the Union Building. MSC President Robert S. Shaw was the club's first president.

Grover C. Dillman, class of 1913, was appointed Michigan State Highway Commissioner.

Fay Gillis Wells, graduated in the winter term of 1929. She would become a White House correspondent for Storer Broadcasting. She was one of the first female pilots in the U.S., and with Amelia Earhart, founded the Ninety-Nine Club, an association of women pilots. Wells became the first women member of the "Caterpillar Club," bailing out of an airplane and being saved by the silk parachute.

Fay Gillis Wells, w '29, first female pilot to parachute from an aircraft, later became White House correspondent for Storer Broadcasting Company.

Coeds on walkway near Beaumont Tower—1929.

With the larger display areas at Demonstration Hall, Farmers' Week drew a record crowd of 7,000.

The Physics department took over the old Chemistry building, which was remodeled for $35,000.

Home Economics department research discovered that yellow corn was higher in vitamin A content than white corn.

Five concerts were presented to students as a part of a new Michigan State concert series, which later would become the Lecture-Concert Series. Cost of a season ticket was $1.50.

The Girls Glee Club was organized. Their first appearance at the lighting of the campus Christmas tree on December 17 was postponed due to inclement weather.

The first May Morning Sing was presented by the two glee clubs at the foot of Beaumont Tower in 1929. In the early morning beauty enhanced by flowering trees and tulip beds, this tradition became a favorite at Michigan State.

Intramural sports competition involved 1,203 men and women.

The 1929 college budget was $3,514,172.15. Enrollment was 3,019. Degrees were granted to 480 graduates. Library volumes grew to 69,642.

1930

Enrollment Rises Despite the Depression—Despite the economic depression, enrollment rose to 3,211, an all-time high.

To improve potato plant breeding, potato varieties and the handling and storing of potatoes, a 40-acre **Potato Experiment Station was established** in Lake City, Michigan. The Farm Crops Department ran the program.

As a sign of the times, Civil Engineering 450, The Design and Construction of Airports, was offered as the department's only new course in 1930.

Operating out of a new $55,000 Poultry Building, the Poultry Husbandry Department opened research on: 1) Developing a Spartan Starter Chick as a part of chick rearing experimentation, 2) Using artificial heat in egg-laying houses, 3) Testing barley as a substitute for corn in poultry diet, and 4) Executing a breeding and rearing program which resulted in larger eggs and higher production.

College concert programs included the Chicago Civic Opera and the Minneapolis Symphony.

Frank F. Rogers, class of 1883, Michigan Highway Commissioner (1905-1929), was honored with the placement of a highway monument on June 4, 1930, at the intersection of US 2 and US 31 near St. Ignace, Michigan.

Harry F. Johnson, Class of 1930, recalled, "Drove a Ford touring car to campus; used to remove the steering wheel and take it to class with me."

MSC defeated Michigan, 27-26 in a January 15 basketball game that drew 6,000 fans to Demonstration Hall—the largest crowd in school history up to that time. It was billed as the dedication game for Dem Hall, and played on a new sectionalized, removable hardwood floor. MSC's Roger Grove was the game's star, hitting four late field goals, including one from near center court. The lead changed hands seven times in the final five minutes.

William H. Berkey (Berkey Hall) of Cassopolis, Michigan was elected to the Board.

Ernest Lee Anthony (Anthony Hall) was named Professor of Dairy Husbandry. Later in his career he would become Dean of Agriculture.

The 1930 college budget was $3,610,932.37, down because of the economic depression. Enrollment was 3,211. Degrees were granted to 518 graduates.

Dr. G. Malcolm Trout

"Father" of Homogenized Milk

Dr. G. Malcolm Trout,
"Father" of Homogenized Milk

Dr. G. Malcolm Trout (1896-1990) (Trout Food Science & Human Nutrition Building), joined the Michigan State's Dairy Faculty In 1928.

In the early 1930s, Trout made homogenized milk possible by linking the processes of pasteurization and homogenization. By pasteurizing milk before forcing it through a screen at high pressure to break down fat globules, the fat and milk were kept from separating.

Trout said on his 90th birthday, "We wouldn't have a milk industry today if it weren't for homogenization. Because the cream would have churned; you'd have plugs on top of the bottle, and kids wouldn't drink the milk."

Working closely with the dairy industry, trout developed new processes to make cheese, yogurt, and other products. He became a national expert in milk flavors, cheese manufacturing, and daily product quality control.

Trout authored or co-authored more than 200 papers, articles and bulletins on dairy technology. He authored the book, *Homogenized Milk: A Review and Guide* (1950); and co-authored two others, *Milk Pasteurization* (1968); and *Judging Dairy Products* (1934).

Among Dr. Trout's many honors were the Borden Award in 1945, the Milk Industry Foundation Award for teaching excellence in 1957, the American Dairy Association's highest award in 1964, the Medal of Distinction from the University of Helsinki, Finland, in 1965, the American Dairy Science Association special award in 1982, named a fellow by the Institute of Food Technologists in 1987, and named an honorary Michigan State alumnus in 1989.

Trout earned bachelor's and master's degrees from Iowa State University, and a doctorate from Cornell University. He served in the U.S. Army's 330th Field Artillery unit in France in World War I.

March 7, 1986 was proclaimed "Malcolm Trout Day" in Michigan. On that occasion, **Dr. Trout commented on the transference of devotion from one's alma mater to MSU** (in his case from Iowa State to Michigan State). He said it was a phenomenon he had witnessed many times in his 57 years on campus. **"This magnetic drawing power remains one of MSU's strongest, if not fully appreciated assets."**

1931

MSC Accredited by Association of American Universities—Accreditation of Michigan State by the Association of American Universities in November, 1931 was the outstanding achievement of the year. Immediately, universities and colleges that formally did not accept MSC graduates without question, now did so. The academic recognition also opened the way for petitioning the American Association of University Women for membership.

In 1931, the Board made the President's position stronger by giving him a key role in the budget planning process. Moreover, the Board approved William H. Berkey's motion that **"as a general policy, the President of Michigan State College shall have the direction and the supervision of the affairs of the Institution subject to the general supervision of the Board."** This undoubtedly was a reaction to the troubles that emanated from the split responsibilities that existed when Kenyon Butterfield was President.

Shaw Initiates Innovative Financing for Dormitories—The shortage of on-campus housing for coeds was finally addressed in 1931. President Shaw and the Board used innovative financing to build the new 246-resident Mary Mayo Hall. Because the Michigan Attorney General ruled the Board could not obligate itself with bond financing, "the Detroit Security and Trust Company sold six percent certificates and erected the dormitory, which it leased to the college. From the income of the rooms and dining halls, the college paid a rental fee with which the trustee redeemed coupons and gradually retired the bonds." This successful private financing—a first in university construction—led MSC to build many more buildings at no cost to the taxpayers, to be repaid by their earnings.

The Veterinary Science Division dedicated a new building to the service of Animal Husbandry in particular, and of human welfare in general.

Bang's disease, an infectious scourge affecting cattle and causing spontaneous abortions, was fought by the Animal Pathology Department. Their medical strategy was to test the blood of animals to identify those infected, and to eliminate infected cattle from herds. Education efforts reached all but four of Michigan's counties.

Music Department faculty traveled to rural schools and gave classroom instruction in singing, rhythmic drills, folk dances, and music appreciation in seven counties: Saginaw, Clinton, Eaton, Genesee, Lapeer, Livingston, and Kalamazoo.

Michigan State's land-acquisition strategy would pay off for years to come. Between 1890 and 1931, the college acquired 32 pieces of property statewide. Most of the land was purchased, but several acquisitions were gifts. Fifteen of the parcels, ranging from one to 309 acres, added to the contiguous campus property.

President Shaw was especially aggressive in acquiring adjacent land. In the 1928-1931 period, he oversaw 12 additions to the college holdings. Shaw's wise forward vision is why Michigan State University today has a 5,192-acre campus, and additional lands around the state, totaling more than 17,000 acres. His son-in-law, John Hannah, continued the practice during his tenure as MSU's 12th president.

Genetics and Conservation Given Recognition—The Department of Zoology reported that two strong zoological currents should be recognized: 1. The practical and theoretical importance of the new science of genetics for animal and human life, and 2. An increasing appreciation for the elements of nature and a consequent desire to conserve them.

Clara (Hantel) Brucker, Class of 1930, became Michigan's First Lady in 1931.

WKAR radio began broadcasting an afternoon "Homemakers' Hour," featuring short talks on Home Economics.

Mrs. Wilbur M. Brucker (Clara Hantel), '30, became the first MSC graduate to be Michigan's First Lady. Her husband took office as Michigan's Governor on January 1, 1931.

MSC Band Has Picture Taken With U.S. President Herbert Hoover—Willliam D. Colegrove, Class of 1931, recalled the 1930 football trip to Washington, D.C. when MSC played Georgetown in the first night game in Michigan State history. The "band had their picture taken with President Hoover. I stood next to the President in this picture."

Willis R. Stacey, Class of 1931, recalled attending "the Varsity Hop at the Masonic Temple (Lansing); Duke Ellington's band played."

Wallace B. Fox, Class of 1931, remembered "President Shaw's remarks to the freshmen class: **"Write to your parents at least once a week."**

Richard W. Toolan, Class of 1931, recalled, "While working cleaning out underground tunnels during Christmas vacation, we located a manhole under a huge evergreen tree near the girl's dorm. The tunnel opened into the dorm basement. Used to sneak in girls after hours."

First Flight for a Collegiate Basketball Team—Head basketball coach Ben Van Alstyne and five players flew to Milwaukee in a passenger bi-plane to play Marquette. It is believed to be the first flight in the nation by a collegiate team. The players were: Dee Pinneo, Art Haga, Randall Boeskool, Edward Scott,

Nation's first flight for a college basketball team–Coach Ben VanAlstyne (3rd from right) leads Spartan Five on flight to Marquette game in Milwaukee.

and Roger Grove. With only five players, there were no substitutions.

A winning percentage of .941 was posted by the basketball team, winning 16 of 17 games, the best record ever.

The Beal Botanical Garden attracted 40,000 visitors during the year.

The Michigan Press Association comprised of Michigan weekly newspapers, established its office within the Publications Department on campus.

Mrs. Alfred G. (Matilda R.) Wilson (Wilson Hall; Wilson Road) was elected to the State Board of Agriculture (Trustees) in April, 1931 to replace Mrs. Dora Stockman, whose term was to expire on December 31, 1931.

Enrollment totaled 3,299. The graduating class numbered 557.

1932

Economic Depression Hits Hard; Grand Jury Probes College—The depths of the economic depression hit in 1932. More than 25 percent of the nation's employees were out of work. Farm prices were half what they had been in 1928.

The Michigan Legislature cut appropriations by 15 percent at a special session. MSC had to trim $250,000 from it s 1932-33 budget. To save the faculty from layoff, the Board reduced department allocations by 12 percent and faculty salaries by seven percent.

Adding to the operating problems caused by the depression, was a grand jury investigation (of the college) requested by five Ingham County citizens in August, 1932. The allegations were: "That salaries were paid as deposits in the local bank in which college staff were officers; that the Secretary of the Board had attempted to sell a horse to the college, which would have been illegal; that a faculty group had offered its Nickerson farm to the college at an excessive price; that campus planning was performed at a high fee by a Detroit landscape architect, rather than a college department; and that the Michigan State Institute of Music and Allied Arts used campus buildings, received fees from the college for student lessons, and profited in other ways from its connection with the Music Department."

Circuit Judge Leland W. Carr sat as a one-man jury. The Board requested that Michigan's Assistant Attorney General Joseph A. Baldwin conduct a separate inquiry. No misconduct or financial malfeasance was found by Carr or Baldwin.

Because of large unemployment in the state, there were heavy demands on the Division of Agriculture staff in the areas of gardening, poultry raising, and the use of farm produce, meats, fruits and vegetables. The agricultural faculty helped Michigan industries in their efforts to promote extensive gardening projects to feed families.

W.K. Kellogg continued his generosity toward Michigan State by donating the 280-acre Kellogg Reforestation Tract in Kalamazoo County to the school's Forestry Department.

Florence L. Hall, class of 1909, Hon. Home Economics, 1932, was supervisor of home economics extension work in the 12 eastern states for the U.S. Department of Agriculture.

In 1932, the Board established 32 alumni scholarships (one for each of the state's senatorial districts). High school graduates who finished in the top fifth of their classes were nominated for these scholarships by alumni.

MSC Professor Lewis Richards gave a harpsichord concert at the White House for U.S. President Herbert Hoover, and Canadian Prime Minister Ramsay MacDonald.

Robert A. Campbell, Class of 1932, remembered "During the depression days, ate lots of celery, cabbage—cheap and filling."

Marion Lee Aylesworth, Class of 1932, wrote, "Depression, no new clothes; senior year didn't buy books, but used the library text books."

Enrollment was 3,139. Degrees were granted to 549 graduates. The library grew to 82,630 volumes.

1933

The Depression Bites Deeper—The legislature cut the Michigan State "appropriation to one million dollars, 39 percent below the 1930-31 level." Moreover, the state was $400,000 in arrears in payments to the college, "and another $300,000 of college funds were frozen in closed banks."

Responding with resourcefulness, President Shaw had money delivered to the campus "by armored car to pay salaries in cash: one-half at the close of the month, and one-half at mid-month."

Shaw cared about his faculty and staff. Although the 1933-34 budget was trimmed by 13 percent, faculty salaries were reduced on average only seven percent. Yet, it was the second salary cut in two years. **Shaw remarked, "the human element was to be considered even more than the financial."**

Shaw reported, "I can with all sincerity commend the loyalty and helpfulness of the faculty and staff during these two years; they have cheerfully shouldered their financial burdens and heavier duties and have maintained the high quality of instruction and research for which the college stands."

Michigan State's reserve fund was $386,880 in June, 1932. For the 1933-1934 year, it was drawn down by five percent to aid the college budget.

Home Economics Division faculty lectured on low-cost meals throughout the state. Welfare agencies appealed to the college for help in planning minimum-cost meals. The bulletin, "Low Cost Meals for the Family" was revised and widely distributed.

Food from farm homes allowed MSC coeds living in low-cost rooms, and cooking in groups, to cut meal expenses to one dollar or less per week.

Keeping some 90 women students employed, who had to work for room and board to stay in school was difficult. Student labor was viewed as expensive when unemployed plant laborers were ready to work for 15 cents or less per hour.

Dean of Women Elisabeth W. Conrad reported, "There seemed to be in the student mind an intense feeling that college life should proceed as usual. A total of 211 dances were held during the year, exclusive of afternoon 'tea dances' and Union Building dances, held every two weeks."

Lyman J. Briggs, class of 1893, was appointed Director of the U.S. Bureau of Standards by U.S. President Franklin D. Roosevelt. "When Roosevelt came into the presidency in 1933, he was asked if he would name 'a good Democrat' to direct the Bureau." FDR retorted, "I haven't the slightest idea whether Dr. Briggs is a Republican or Democrat; all I know is that he's the best man for the job." (*Lyman Briggs—A Biography* by Tony Lush).

Dr. H.E. Van Norman, class of 1897, was supervising operations at Chicago's 1933 World's Fair, called the "Century of Progress."

The Library (now Museum), which opened in 1924, was nearing its book-holding capacity.

Robert Miller was chosen as one of ten students out of 50,000 nationwide to compete in the final auditions of the Atwater-Kent Radio Contests in New York.

Beatrice Brody, a student, won first place in a regional opera competition for Michigan, Indiana, and Ohio.

Clarence W. Van Lopik, Class of 1933, remembered, "Students mailed soiled laundry home in brown cloth laundry cases. They received clean laundry in boxes from home a week or so later with food (and other goodies)."

The Union Grill Menu featured two eggs on toast—20 cents, eggs with fried ham—30 cents, raisin-walnut sweet roll—10 cents, and buttered toast—5 cents.

Football tickets were priced at $1.00, $1.65, and $2.00, depending on the opponent.

For state forest planting, the Forestry Department furnished at cost 2,437,181 trees during the year.

Total enrollment was 2,794. At graduation, 649 degrees were granted, including one that was honorary.

President and Board Responsible for Business Policies—In a state law passed on October 17, 1934, all business policies of the college were put wholly in the hands of the President and the Board. Duties of the Business Manager were vested in the Comptroller, who reported to the President. **The Secretary of the Board was made Property Custodian, in charge of Buildings & Grounds**; and the Dean of Engineering was named the Institutional Engineering Consultant.

The Date on College Seal Changed to 1855—The date on the College Seal was changed in December, 1934 to the founding date, 1855, from 1857, when the school was opened and dedicated. For historical purposes, the 1855 date was legitimate and appropriate. As a result, Michigan State fairly claims the distinction of being the oldest agricultural college in the nation, and the pioneer land-grant institution.

With enrollment suffering during the depression, a faculty committee led by John Hannah and Lloyd Emmons mobilized a campaign of high school visits, distribution of booklets, contacts by alumni, radio talks, and distribution of news releases to weekly newspapers statewide to attract new students. By the fall of 1934, there were five percent more college students nationally than the previous year. But at Michigan State, there were 19 percent more!

In response to the national economic crisis, student course fees per term were reduced from $35 to $32.50 for 1932-33. They were further lowered in 1933-34 to $30. Meal prices in the women's dormitories and room rent for freshmen men in Wells Hall were reduced. Sympathetic faculty from several departments offered students free tutoring. Some 500 students were employed doing part-time work for the college. The Federal Emergency Relief

The date on the Michigan State College seal was changed to 1855, the founding date, from 1857, the opening and dedication date, in December, 1934. This beautiful wood-carved seal appears above the east entrance to Linton Hall, which housed the president's office from 1938 to 1968.

Administration also provided part-time work, paying $15 per month. Short-term emergency and long-term loans were available to students, to be repaid after graduation.

President Shaw stated that more competition for jobs and the possibility of unemployment looming ahead "have produced a noticeably more practical, work-a-day atmosphere in campus life. **College is now a means to an end for all—not a stop-gap for some as before."**

A booklet titled, *Ready For Business,* listing business administration graduates, was published by the Department of Economics. It was financed by the students and sent to 600 business men. All of the students who later answered a questionnaire on their experience, "reported they had found employment."

Treatment for Amoebic Dysentery Found by MSC Researchers—A specific treatment for amoebic dysentery—neoarsphenamin—was found by the Animal Pathology Section after two decades of research.

A yellow, disease-resistant strain of celery was developed by the Botany Section.

P.J. Hoffmaster, class of 1918, was named State Director of Conservation.

Frank T. DuByne, Class of 1934, wrote, "Professors helped in 'bread and butter' situations by offering work when needed, especially Dr. Malcolm Trout."

Florence M. Findley, Class of 1934, remembered, "Earned money working the switchboard at the dormitory nights and Sundays. Also earned a little money mending runs in silk hose for girls in the dorm."

Dorothy McDonald Parsons, Class of 1934, recalled, "(President) Shaw's emphasis on friendliness and speaking to students on campus when walking to and from classes."

Charles Bachman, new Head Football Coach, introduced black and gold uniforms. It was said the coach wanted to put his stamp on the team and he brought the color gold with him from his days as a player at Notre Dame. The team would wear those colors until 1947.

The football team defeated the University of Michigan, 16-0, the first of four consecutive wins over the Wolverines. MSC halfback Kurt Warmbein scored one of the touchdowns on a 35-yard run.

Following the win over Michigan, NBC radio requested permission to broadcast the MSC-Carnegie Tech game from East Lansing. **It was the first national broadcast of a Spartan game**, and featured the legendary Graham McNamee doing the play-by-play over NBC's Blue Network.

A travel advertisement aimed at alumni in the November, 1934 *M.S.C. Record* offered an 85-day, first class "Round the World" cruise for $810 from the Dollar Steamship Lines and American Mail Line.

The college budget for 1934 was $2,157,212, allocated to three areas: Education—$1,387,412 (65%); Extension—$413,238 (20%); and Research—$356,561 (15%). Enrollment totaled 3,323. Graduates numbered 565.

1935

John A. Hannah Appointed Secretary of the Board—One of the great educational leadership careers in the nation's history was launched on January 1, 1935, when John A. Hannah was appointed Secretary of the State Board of Agriculture (Board of Trustees), making him a corporate officer of the college. The title Secretary was a misnomer, because it was a power position at Michigan State with full responsibility for all of the buildings and grounds, campus construction, regular interaction with the state legislature, and involvement in major campus decisions.

It was the springboard from which Hannah became Michigan State's greatest builder and father of the modern University. His visionary strategies literally catapulted the institution from a small college to a great University, internationally known and respected. After serving as Secretary of the Board for six years, he was elected President of the school in 1941 at age 38, and served as chief executive officer for 28 years, resigning in 1969.

Pre-World War II Building Program Planned—In his new position, Hannah, and President Shaw, in 1935, began formulating a significant building program for the

John A. Hannah was named Secretary of the Board in 1935 at age 33.

college. Included were plans for men's dormitories—Abbot and Mason Halls, women's dormitories—Williams and Campbell Halls, Jenison Gymnasium and Fieldhouse, the Music Building, the Auditorium, and the Olin Health Center. Hannah and Shaw's energetic management assured that all of these structures would be standing by 1940.

MSC Founds Nation's First Police Administration School—Michigan State led the nation by offering a five-year course in Police Administration (now Criminal Justice) in 1935. The course was developed in cooperation with the Michigan Crime Commission and the Michigan State Police.

Charles W. Garfield, a distinguished alum, was honored by the board by having a piece of land next to the Beal Botanical Garden designated the Charles W. Garfield Botanical Garden.

James F. Thomson, class of 1911, was appointed director of the Michigan Agricultural Dept.

Grover C. Dillman, class of 1913, was appointed Michigan Welfare Director early in the year. But by November, he was in another position, elected president of Michigan College of Mining and Technology (Now Michigan Technological University).

Dr. Eugene B. Elliott, class of 1924, was appointed Michigan's Superintendent of Public Instruction.

Because the Alumni Office was suffering from falling income, the Board assumed the financing for all Alumni Office activities in July, 1935. The *MSC Record* had been published by the Alumni Association and distributed to only 2,500 of the 10,000 school graduates. This responsibility was transferred to the Department of Journalism and Publications and the quarterly publication was sent to all graduates free of charge.

Ten bells for Beaumont Tower were purchased for $2,640 and added to the original 13. This increased the playing range of the carillon. Gillett & Johnston, an English firm, installed the bells.

Football Stadium Named for Macklin—John F. Macklin, who first brought Michigan State into football prominence as head coach from 1911-1915, was honored by having the football stadium and field named for him on November 9, 1935. The stadium press box was enclosed and broadcast booths added.

The 1935 *Wolverine* (yearbook) listing of key faculty included eight who would have campus buildings named for them: Robert S. Shaw, president; John A. Hannah, secretary of the Board; Elida Yakeley, registrar; Ernest L. Anthony, dean of agriculture; Ernest A. Bessey, dean of the graduate school; Elisabeth Conrad, dean of women; Lloyd C. Emmons, dean of liberal arts; and Ward Giltner, dean of veterinary science.

Forestry Club members erected a log cabin in honor of the late professor A.K. Chittenden. It was located on the site of the present Erickson Hall, and dedicated November 9, 1935. It served as a recreational venue for many campus groups for years.

Russell Hurd, Class of 1935, told of a Depression story on campus. "First student: 'I had a letter from Mom today.' 2nd student: 'What did she say?' 1st student: 'She said, "Please send money. Dad just lost his paper route."'"

At Coral Gables a 12-ounce beer on tap cost 10 cents; a tuna sandwich—15 cents.

The football team posted a 25-6 victory over Michigan, a second straight win.

President Shaw was the master manager of finances. Although the college's legislative appropriation was cut by $640,284 for 1935, he had built a reserve fund of $480,000, which was used in part to keep the college going.

Enrollment totaled 3,991. Degrees were granted to 599 graduates. The library housed 105,413 volumes.

1936

Union Building and Stadium Enlarged—An annex was added to the Union Building in 1936 to provide 12 additional classrooms; a home for the Art Department; and headquarters for the *Wolverine* student yearbook, and the *State News*.

The football stadium floor was lowered and the running track removed to accommodate the addition of an inner oval of 12 rows of permanent seats. **This raised the seating capacity from 14,000 to 23,000.** A new running track **(now the Ralph H. Young Track & Field)** was constructed just west of the stadium.

George C. Humphrey, class of 1901 and professor of animal husbandry at the University of Wisconsin, was honored with an oil portrait in the gallery at the Saddle and Sirloin Club of the Union Stock Yards of Chicago. The national recognition was by the American Society of Animal Production at the International Livestock Exposition.

C. Earl Webb, class of 1912 and executive engineer with the American Bridge Co., prepared the procedures for erecting the cantilever span and towers for the 8 1/4-mile San Francisco-Oakland Bay Bridge, which took three years and four months to build prior to its opening on November 12, 1936.

A Master of Music degree was offered for the first time by the Music Department.

The football team made it three in a row in Ann Arbor, defeating Michigan, 21-7.

A Spartan Women's League booklet of the 1930s, "We Like It Done This Way," offered suggestions for men's appearance—"Men with baggy trousers and a haircut resembling Tarzan's don't make any girl's heart thump. A clean-shaven appearance is more collegiate than an unkempt chin and cheek."

Henry Ford, founder of Ford Motor Company, was given an honorary Doctor of Engineering degree at MSC's 1936 commencement ceremonies.

Enrollment totaled 4,608. Degrees were granted to 630 graduates.

1937

Legislature Doubles MSC's Appropriation; Enrollment Over 5,000—In 1935, the University of Michigan was receiving triple the state money that was given to Michigan State. The appropriation formula was .730 mills for the U of M, and just .243 for MSC.

Hannah Sells Legislature on Increased Funding for MSC—John Hannah, as Secretary of the Board, dug for facts to point out the inequity of this kind of state financing. In 1936, the enrollments were 9,300 for U of M, and 4,608 for MSC. Hannah reported to the legislature that in the three previous years, Michigan State had 1,395 freshmen from the State of Michigan, while the University of Michigan had only 892.

These arguments rang true with the legislature. In 1937, they doubled MSC's appropriation to .47 mills. This change led to a record $2,500,000 appropriation for Michigan State for 1937-38. Still, U of M led MSC by almost two to one in state funding. In response to a record enrollment of 5,212 in the fall of 1937, MSC hired 40 new instructors and restored most of the depression salary cuts.

The Federal Government's Social Security system adopted in 1935 did not include public college employees. Encouraged by greater state funding, the Board in 1937, introduced **a pension system for MSC faculty and staff** that would allow retirement at 65. The minimum pension was $480 annually, and the maximum $1,500.

The Horace H. Rackham and Mary A. Rackham Fund gave Michigan State a trust endowment of $500,000 "for conducting research in the general agricultural field, with special emphasis toward finding individual uses, other than food, for farm produce." It was the largest private grant ever received by MSC up to that time.

By 1936, the State Attorney General allowed the Board to sell revenue bonds to finance **Sarah Langdon Williams Hall**, named in honor of the wife of the school's first president. The $550,000 women's dorm was completed in 1937, housed 250 coeds, and was self-liquidating.

MSC purchased the Campus Hotel at 215 Louis Street, refurbished it, and opened it as North Hall. It served as a dorm for 86.

Women's Building Renamed Morrill Hall—The Women's Building was converted to general offices and classrooms and officially renamed Morrill Hall in honor of Congressman Justin Morrill, whose bill created America's Land-Grant colleges and universities. It was a women's residence hall from 1900-1937. Unofficially, the building was referred to as Morrill Hall as early as 1919 in a picture caption in the school's yearbook—the *Wolverine.*

Hannah "Seizes the Day" to Launch New Dormitories—To give the sagging economy a shot in the arm, the Public Works Administration, in late 1937, initiated a program contributing 45 percent of "the cost of approved buildings erected by public agencies." With an aggressive building plan already in hand, John Hannah and Michigan State seized the day. Abbot and Mason Halls for men and Campbell Hall for women, were begun immediately. Because of MSC's sound reputation for paying its debts, financial institutions were ready to finance the 55 percent non-government portion of new buildings.

WKAR Called "College of the Air"—*The Christian Science Monitor* of June 21, 1937 ran a front-page story about MSC's radio station WKAR, calling the station a "College of the Air." In a national survey by the National Committee on Education by Radio, WKAR was placed among the leaders in the field. Robert J. Coleman was the director of WKAR radio.

NBC radio's "Varsity Show" was broadcast coast-to-coast from MSC's gymnasium (now IM Circle), and featured the MSC Concert Band and Glee Club.

Dr. C.F. Huffman, dairy professor, received the **Borden Merit Award of $1,000 "for the most outstanding contribution to dairy production in the past five years."**

Assistant Professor King J. McCristal introduced an Adapted Sports course to provide physical education and recreational activities for physically handicapped students in 1937. Even blind students were taught how to hit and maintain a rhythm with a punching bag. It was one of the leadership efforts in the nation to care for the physical and emotional needs of handicapped college students.

John W., Class of 1882, and Elizabeth Beaumont—donors of MSU's landmark Beaumont Tower.

Magnificent Band Shell, a gift of the Class of 1937, sat on the north bank of the Red Cedar River and faced a sloping lawn now occupied by Bessey Hall (1961). Completed in 1938, the Band Shell was a concert, graduation and pep rally venue. It was razed in 1960.

John W. Beaumont, class of 1882, who gave the school Beaumont Tower, made his last visit to the campus and saw for the first and only time his gift to the college. Beaumont, in a wheel chair, was wheeled to the balcony at Morrill Hall where he listened to a carillon concert dedicated to him.

Herbert E. Marsh, class of 1908, was elected president of the University of Redlands (California), where he had been dean of men.

George Gauthier, class of 1915, Ohio Wesleyan University athletic director and football coach, was nicknamed "The little giant of Ohio football." He was 5'7". "During the last decade his Ohio Wesleyan team won 89, lost 44 and tied nine." (*MSC Record*, Feb. 1937). Gauthier was the first M.A.C. graduate to serve as Michigan State football coach (1918), and basketball coach (1916-1920). He also starred on M.A.C. football and basketball teams as an undergraduate.

Miss Sarah Shaw, class of 1932 and daughter of MSC president Robert Shaw, was engaged to John A. Hannah, class of 1923 and Secretary of the State Board of Agriculture (Board of Trustees).

MSC's Michelite Beans Cover the State—"Michelite beans (Michigan elite) bred by MSC's Professor E.E. Down in the 1920s and tested with the aid of staff members in soils, plant pathology, entomology, and home economics (for cooking quality), were released in 1937. Four years later, **they covered 40 percent of the state's navy** bean acreage because yield was higher and because a smaller percentage of culls reduced the sorting costs. **Michelite beans (were) estimated to have increased farm income by a sum greater than the entire cost of the Agricultural Experiment Station since its founding in 1888."** (*Michigan State: The First Hundred Years* by Madison Kuhn).

"Michigan cherry canners will not buy cherries (25,000 to 30,000 tons per year) unless the fruit is sprayed according to recommendations from MSC's entomology department," the February 25, 1937 *M.S.C. Record* reported.

Olga Gelzer became the first woman editor of the *State News* in 1937. After publishing only one edition per week during the economically depressed years of 1935 and 1936, the paper increased to three issues per week in 1937, and added staff.

"On That Autumn Evening...the Moon Shining on Beaumont Tower..." Donald W. Kilbourn, '41, recalled on the 50th anniversary of his graduation in 1991, "My most memorable experience at Michigan State occurred the first Saturday night I was on campus in September 1937, near Beaumont Tower. A few days previously, I had resigned from a job that required me to be on my feet for some 70 hours a week. After working three years at a salary of $15 a week, I decided there must be something better, a decision that led me to Michigan State, where I expected to remain a year or two before my meager funds would be exhausted.

"On that beautiful autumn evening, the moon shining down on Beaumont Tower, I suddenly realized how fortunate I was to be alive, to be a part of this pristine campus, to be away from the drudgery I had known for so long. I recall weeping quietly, something I hadn't done since childhood. **In the joy of that rare 'peak' experience, I made a vow. A vow that resulted in three degrees from MSU.** Through the years, a daughter and a son also graduated from State and in a few months, two granddaughters will become MSU alumnae."

The Spartan football team beat the U of M in Ann Arbor, 19-14, for a fourth consecutive win over the Wolverines. The crowd of 71,800 was the largest ever to watch MSC play football.

Athletic Director Ralph H. Young was honored by having MSC's new track and field layout just west of Macklin Stadium dedicated in his honor in the spring of 1937.

The Forestry Club placed a plaque at the base of the "Huntington Elm" which had been planted thirty years before by U.S. President Theodore Roosevelt on the occasion of the 50th anniversary of the school's opening in 1857. (MSU founded in 1855). The elm stood on the site of the west end of Gilchrist Hall, and succumbed to Dutch Elm disease in 1947, when it was cut down.

For the first time enrollment passed the 5,000 mark. There were 5,212 students enrolled. At graduation, 632 degrees were granted.

1938

MSC Budget Jumps Nearly $1 Million to $3.8 Million—The 1937-38 budget jumped to $3,805,543.36 from $2,817,640.77 the previous academic year.

Mason Hall, named after the state's first and youngest governor, **Stevens T. Mason,** was completed at a cost of $550,000. Mason was acting governor of the Michigan Territory at age 21 in 1834, and was labeled the "Boy Governor."

The Judging Pavilion was erected on a site between today's Anthony and Erickson Halls.

MSC deeded 50 acres of land to the U.S. Department of Agriculture for a Federal Poultry Research Laboratory ($250,000) at the corner of Mt. Hope and Harrison.

Donald C. McSorley, '38, won the 1938 American Society of Mechanical Engineers Undergraduate Student Award for the best technical paper of the year of any mechanical engineering student in the U.S.

Dr. W.A. Taylor, class of 1888, retired as the Chief of the U.S. Department of Agriculture Bureau of Plant Industry.

Abbot Road Campus Entrance Sculpture, a gift of the Class of 1938.

Harvey Woodstra tied World Records in the 60- and 70-yard high hurdles—1938.

Professor W.L. Mallman led the Bacteriology Department in studies of the domestic water supply, swimming pool waters and routine examinations of silverware, glassware and dishes in restaurants, boarding clubs, fraternity and sorority houses in East Lansing throughout the year, in the interest of public health.

Athletic Director Ralph H. Young led the establishment of the NCAA Cross Country championships. This annual title event was held on the Michigan State campus every year from 1938 to 1964. Since 1964, the championships have been rotated among universities nationwide.

MSC hurdler Harvey Woodstra tied world records in the 60-yard high hurdles at 7.4 seconds, and the 70-yard high hurdles at 8.6 seconds.

To make way for the Periodical Reading Room in the Library (now the Museum), the President's suite of offices was moved to Linton Hall in 1938.

A two-credit course in Traffic Efficiency and Automobile Operation was offered in the summer session, primarily for high school teachers.

A non-credit first-time course in marriage was offered to senior women only by the Women's Physical Education Department.

Class of 1938 Gift: Abbot Road Entrance Sculpture—This eleven-foot tall stone sculpture welcomes people entering the MSU campus at the Abbot Road entrance. The figures depict an early agricultural scene, a man standing beside a horse; a woman sitting, holding a sheaf of wheat. The wheat also symbolized home economics. The cultural arts are represented by the fluted Grecian column on the left side. From either side of the monument extend curved stone block arms in a gesture of welcome. **"Theme of the figures may be interpreted as guidance,"** according to Sylvester Jerry, director of the Federal art project.

Arthur N. Breyer, Class of 1938, recalled that "The football team 'pulled' against a champion heavy-weight pair of draft horses in Demonstration Hall during Farmer's Week (February) and won."

Enrollment reached 5,835. The graduating class totaled 793.

1939

Five New Buildings Completed; MSC Wins Its First NCAA Team Title—Buildings completed in 1939 were: Abbot Hall, a men's dormitory—$525,000; Campbell Hall, a women's dormitory—$500,000; Olin Memorial Health Center—$250,000; the Music Building—$230,000; the Livestock Judging Pavilion—$175,000; and an addition to the Veterinary Clinic—$133,000.

Ray Stannard Baker, Class of 1889, published the final volume of his 8-volume biography of Woodrow Wilson, which would win the Pulitzer Prize in 1940.

Dr. Lyman J. Briggs, Class of 1893, Director of the National Bureau of Standards and a nationally respected physicist, **was asked by U.S. President Franklin D. Roosevelt in October, 1939 to lead the Advisory Committee on Uranium in a top-secret investigation to determine the feasibility of producing atomic power and an atomic weapon.** Briggs' committee reported back to the White House in November, 1939 that both atomic power and weaponry were possible. The Uranium Committee became a sub-committee of the National Defense Research

Campus aerial view—1939: Macklin Stadium—lower left-center; Demonstration Hall—upper middle-center; Jenison Gymnasium & Fieldhouse under construction—right of Dem Hall; Old College Field—right of Jenison.

Committee (NDRC), and was later designated the S-1 Section of the NDRC. Later, the project was transferred to the Office of Scientific Research and Development. The Manhattan Project took over the operation in the summer of 1942 to launch the development of the A-bomb.

A Highway Research Laboratory was established in the Engineering Building as a cooperative effort between the Engineering Division and the State Highway Department.

Civilian Pilot Training Comes to MSC—The Civil Aeronautics Authority was given approval by the faculty to introduce civilian pilot training on campus on September 8, 1939, one week after Germany invaded Poland, starting World War II. Engineering Dean H.B. Dirks was named coordinator. This was a prelude to the forthcoming U.S. need for World War II military pilots.

Michigan State's News Service produced 359 articles for newspapers during the year. A weekly check of some 230 newspapers revealed that 11,438 stories on MSC appeared in 1939, and almost universally, there was no change in content or headlines.

There were five cooperatives housing 76 women in the 1938-39 school year. All of the women were required to cook. The average cost per student was $5.25 per week for meals.

Michigan State's cross country team won the NCAA championship—the Spartans' first national title in any sport. The NCAA meet was held on MSC's campus.

WKAR radio broadcast all Spartan football games, and the home baseball games.

Clark Brody **(Brody Hall)** was elected to the Board.

At commencement, **Ransom E. Olds**, founder of Oldsmobile and REO Motors, was presented an honorary Doctor of Engineering degree at the MSC commencement by President Shaw.

The 1939 college budget was $3,812,736.31, which included $526,729.12 in student fees.

Enrollment for 1939 was 6,650. Students hailed from 45 states, Washington, D.C., and ten foreign countries.

Degrees were granted to 968.

Lyman J. Briggs, Class of 1893

Appointed by U.S. President Franklin Roosevelt to Lead Investigation on the Feasibility of Atomic Power and Weapons

Lyman J. Briggs (1874-1963), class of 1893, **(Lyman Briggs School at MSU),** was born on a farm north of Battle Creek, Michigan on May 7, 1874. Briggs never attended high school, but entered Michigan Agricultural College by examination at the age of 15.

Lyman J. Briggs, Class of 1893, led U.S. investigations on feasibility of Atomic Power and Weapons in 1939.

Four years later, he graduated second in his class. At M.A.C., he wrote articles for *The Speculum* (student publication); became captain of the cadet R.O.T.C. corps; and helped win permission for the Union Literary Society to build a house on campus.

He received his masters' degree in physics at the University of Michigan in 1895. In 1896, he took a position as a physicist at the Bureau of Soils with the U.S. Department of Agriculture, and pursued his Ph.D. at Johns Hopkins University, which he earned in 1901. "He did pioneering work in the field of soil physics from 1896 to 1917." (All quotes in this biographical sketch are from *Lyman Briggs A Biography* by Tony Lush).

The U.S. Department of Commerce requested the U.S. Department of Agriculture to release Briggs in 1917 to help organize a division within the National Bureau of Standards for the certification of gauges for the manufacture of munitions. He also worked on a stable zenith instrument which increased the accuracy of naval gunsights by overcoming the problems of ocean pitch and roll. And, he helped develop a wind tunnel at the Bureau of Standards capable of generating air speeds of 90 miles an hour. A later tunnel, developed in 1919, produced airspeeds of 150 miles per hour.

By 1920, Briggs was given a permanent appointment with the National Bureau of Standards as chief of the

Mechanics and Sound Division. **He and Dr. Paul R. Heyl "invented the earth inductor compass that eventually was used by Charles Lindbergh" in his immortal trans-Atlantic flight in 1927.**

Briggs was named Acting Director of the U.S. Bureau of Standards in 1932. **"When Franklin D. Roosevelt took office as president in 1933, he was asked if he would name 'a good Democrat to direct the Bureau. FDR said, 'I haven't the slightest idea whether Dr. Briggs is a Republican or Democrat; all I know is that he's the best man for the job.'"**

Briggs became a member of the National Advisory Committee on Aeronautics (forerunner of the National Aeronautics and Space Administration) in 1933, and was elected its vice chair in 1942. He helped create two balloons that broke altitude records—Explorer I and Explorer II. These soared to 11.5 and 13.7 miles, respectively.

"In October, 1939—less than a year after the discovery of uranium fission—Briggs was called to the White House (by President Roosevelt) and given the responsibility for a top-secret investigation into the possibilities of atomic power. This Advisory Committee on Uranium, with Briggs as chair and with Col. Keith Adamson, U.S. Army Ordnance, and Commander Gilbert Hoover, Navy Bureau of Ordnance, as members, reported back to the President in November, 1939 that both atomic power and a bomb were possible."

The Uranium Committee became a sub-committee of the newly established National Defense Research Section, and later was designated the S-1 Section. "Just prior to the attack on Pearl Harbor on December 7, 1941, the S-1 Committee recommended a determined effort to produce an atomic weapon. Soon thereafter, the project was transferred to the Office of Scientific Research and Development (OSRD). Briggs remained chair until the committee became the executive committee of the OSRD. The Manhattan Project took over the operation in the summer of 1942."

Dr. Vannevar Bush, who led the Manhattan Project and development of the atomic bomb described Briggs' contribution: "There were thousands of men involved in the atomic energy program in a thousand ways. Lyman Briggs carried his post well. Never unduly excited, calm, facing the appalling future with determination, he often served as **a balance wheel and a staunch support."**

Briggs held honorary degrees from six universities. He was a member of the National Academy of Sciences, and winner of the Academy's Magellan Award. He received the U.S. Presidential Medal for Merit. The U.S. Department of Commerce gave Briggs its Exceptional Services Gold Medal for outstanding contributions to science and humanity. National Geographic presented its Franklin L. Burr Award to Briggs in 1954 and 1962 for his contributions to science.

The Lyman Briggs School in MSU's College of Natural Science, which is heavily devoted to science education, stands as a tribute to Briggs remarkable life and career.

1940

Auditorium and Jenison Gymnasium & Fieldhouse Completed; Ray Stannard Baker, Class of 1889, Wins Pulitzer Prize—Two one-million dollar buildings—the first on campus—were completed: the Auditorium at $1,025,000, and Jenison Gymnasium & Fieldhouse at $1,100,000.

U.S. First Lady Eleanor Roosevelt made an address to dedicate the Auditorium in March. John A. Hannah, Secretary to the State Board of Agriculture (Board of Trustees), introduced her. **Mrs. Roosevelt told Secretary Hannah, "These wonderful state universities are a constant surprise and a matter of great pride to me..."** (*MSC Record*, April 1940).

In the first basketball game played in the new Jenison Fieldhouse, MSC defeated Tennessee, 29-20, on January 6, 1940. John Hannah, Secretary of the Board with responsibility for all MSC buildings, commented on the new Jenison Gymnasium and Fieldhouse, "This is undoubtedly the finest building in the world devoted to athletic purposes." *(MSC Record*, April, 1940).

Ray Stannard Baker, Class of 1889, was awarded the Pulitzer Prize for his eight-volume biography *Woodrow Wilson: Life and Letters*, which was produced and published over the 12-year period of 1927 to 1939. The *New York Times* reported, "They (the 8 volumes) represent one

U.S. First Lady Eleanor Roosevelt and Secretary of the MSC Board John Hannah at the 1940 dedication of MSC's new Auditorium.

Jenison Gymnasium and Fieldhouse opened in 1940. All-time record basketball crowd was 15,384 in 1948, when MSC lost to National Champion Kentucky, 47–45.

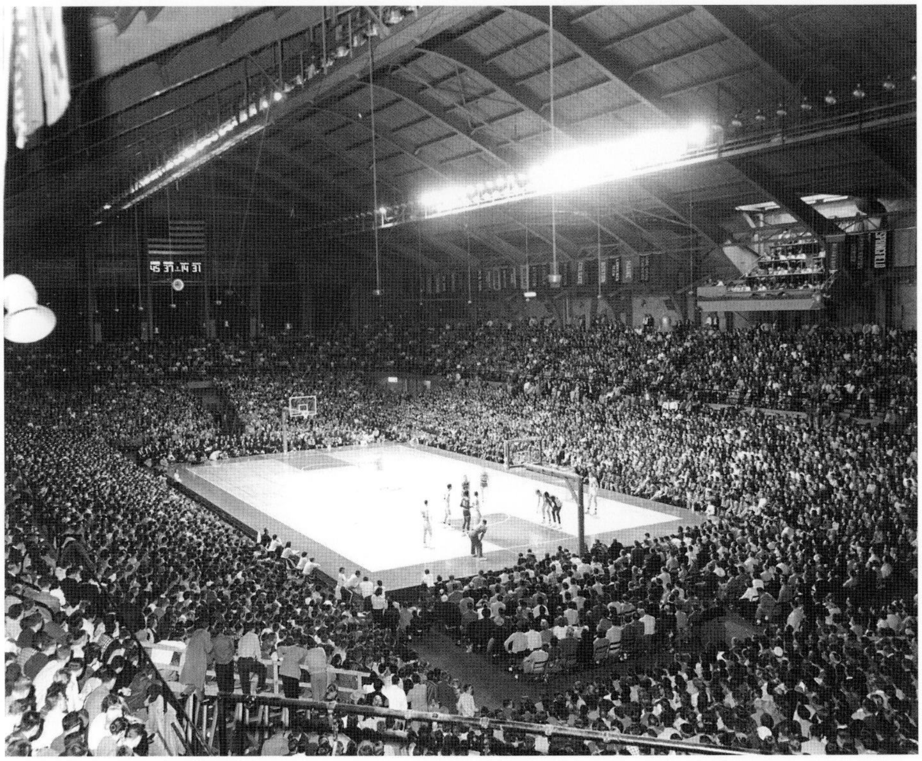

type of American biography at its best." (*MSC Record*, July, 1940).

A.L. Bibbins, Class of 1915, considered America's outstanding seedsman and agricultural industrialist—was president of G.L.F. Mills, Inc., the largest manufacturer of dairy and poultry feeds in the world. The auditorium in the G.L.F. School of Cooperative Administration was named **Bibbins Hall** in his honor on October 15, 1940. The building sits just opposite the Cornell University campus in Ithaca, New York.

Dr. I. Forest Huddleson, Class of 1925, bacteriology research professor, won the **International Veterinary Congress prize for 1940** for his work aimed at curbing undulant fever. The award stated, "You have contributed liberally and practically not only to the livestock industry of the world, but also to the protection of human health."

Continued land acquisition by Shaw and Hannah expanded the contiguous campus acreage to 2,500—creating one of the largest campuses in the nation.

The Walter T. Best Women's Club of Leland, Michigan deeded their club house and property to Michigan State for use in education. A summer school for art students was held in the charming Lake Michigan village in the summer of 1940.

Ormand E. Hunt gave MSC a tract of land in the City of Ann Arbor consisting of a subdivision. The land was to be sold and the funds used for scholarships for needy students in agriculture and horticulture.

WKAR radio moved its studios from the Home Economics Building (now Human Ecology) to the Auditorium, right above the main entrance.

MSC Auditorium, capacity 5,000—dedicated in 1940.

Benjamin H. Anibal, class of 1909, was vice president of engineering for Pontiac Motor Division of General Motors.

Captain Jack Knight, Class of 1915, was United Airlines flight educational director.

Mary Jane Stuart Spalding, '40, recalled, "My fondest memories of college were how it taught me to organize effectively, to be responsible for myself, to continue my studies and to look forward to learning something new each day."

Roy Fehr, track captain, won the NCAA two-mile championship in 9:18.9.

The 14 hotel rooms in the Union building were completely reconditioned and refurbished. These served visitors to the campus for years. John Hannah lived in one of these rooms prior to his marriage in 1938.

The 1940 college budget was $3,990,693.41. Enrollment of regular students totaled 6,776.

The graduating Class of 1940 was the first to surpass 1,000, with 1,134 degrees granted.

Ray Stannard Baker, Class of 1889

Confidant to U.S. Presidents; Pulitzer Prize Winner

Ray Stannard Baker, Class of 1889
1940 Pulitzer Prize Winner

Ray Stannard Baker (1870-1946), Class of 1889, **(Baker Hall)**, was born in Lansing, Michigan in 1870, and chose M.A.C. because it was the only college that would accept a 15-year old, and charged no tuition. He served as editor of *The Speculum*, the college newspaper; graduated with more honors than anyone in his class; and later was presented with M.A.C.'s first Alumni Award for Distinguished Service.

After graduation, Baker launched his career in journalism as a reporter for the *Chicago News Record*. In 1896, Baker married Jessie Beal, daughter of Dr. William J. Beal, M.A.C.'s renowned professor and botanist (Beal Botanical Gardens; Beal Street).

While a reporter for *McClure's* magazine from 1898 to 1906, Baker won the confidence of U.S. President Theodore Roosevelt. He interviewed Roosevelt on many occasions, and in 1906, while on assignment at the president's *Sagamore Hill* summer residence at Oyster Bay, Long Island, was asked by Mr. Roosevelt to review the galley proofs of the president's forthcoming address to Congress.

Baker left *McClure's* in 1906 and purchased, with some colleagues, the *American Magazine.*

He met future president Woodrow Wilson in 1910, and campaigned for Wilson's presidential bid in 1912 and 1916. In 1918, President Wilson appointed Baker as a special commissioner of the U.S. State Department. He was to secretly probe the rumored unrest of French, Great Britain and Italian citizens. Baker earned entry into the socially and politically elite circles in Europe and reported back to Wilson via diplomatic pouches.

President Wilson appointed Baker director of the press bureau of the U.S. contingent to the Paris Peace Conference in 1919. When the U.S. Senate refused to ratify the peace treaty, Baker defended Wilson against his critics.

The *MSU News* of February 11, 1976 reported, "In the last letter written by Wilson, the ailing ex-president told Baker that the writer should be the politician's biographer." Wilson wrote, "Every time you disclose your mind to me you increase my admiration and affection for you. I shall regard you as my preferred creditor, and shall expect to afford you the first—and if necessary, exclusive—access to those papers. I would rather have your interpretation of them than of anybody else I know. Pray accept assurance of my unqualified confidence and affectionate regard." Wilson was so weak when he wrote the letter to Baker that he was unable to sign it.

Baker started work on his extensive eight-volume *Woodrow Wilson: Life and Letters* in 1925. This monumental biography was published sequentially between 1927 and 1939. Baker was awarded the Pulitzer Prize for his portrait of Wilson in 1940.

1941

John A. Hannah Elected Michigan State's twelfth President (served 1941-1969)—On July 1, 1941, John Alfred Hannah (1902-1991)—age 38—took office as the twelfth President of Michigan State, launching one of the great educational leadership careers in the history of U.S. universities. With unparalleled vision and salesmanship, he propelled Michigan State from a small agricultural college to a great university respected and recognized internationally.

He was replacing another giant in MSC's history—Robert S. Shaw, nearly 70, who had served 13 years as chief executive officer, had been Acting President three times, and was Hannah's father-in-law.

Hannah had been a student at Grand Rapids Junior College and the University of Michigan before moving to Michigan State, where he graduated in 1923. He joined the Michigan State extension service right out of college as a poultry specialist. In 1933, he was named managing director of the National Poultry Breeders and Hatchery Committee. A year later he returned to M.S.C., and in 1935 was named Secretary of the State Board of Agriculture, where for six years he led the largest building program in the history of the school, up to that time.

President Hannah...

"Only people are important, especially poor people"

"Knowledge should not be worshiped itself as a god, but put to work for mankind."

Hannah statement at Commencement Addresses:

"From now on Michigan State will always be part of you, and you will be a part of Michigan State. Remember, your education was made possible by the people of Michigan—rich and poor alike. This wasn't an entitlement; somebody had to sweat for it."

A *Lansing State Journal* editorial stated, "The judgement is that he (Hannah) will get for State whatsoever it may need and make even the poor taxpayer and his agent, the legislator, like it."

Hannah was friendly and very approachable. Students affectionately called him "Uncle John." As a speaker, he had a commanding presence, with a deep resonant voice that captivated audiences. He was eminently persuasive, particularly when selling the school's needs to the Michigan legislature.

In a memorable coincidence, Mr. and Mrs. Hannah moved into the President's House (now Cowles House) at Number One Abbot Road on December 7, 1941—Pearl Harbor Day. For Mrs. Hannah, it was a return to Faculty Row, where, as Sarah May Shaw, she had grown up as the daughter of the Dean of Agriculture, and later, the President. She earned bachelor's and master's degrees in chemistry at Michigan State, and was married to John Hannah in 1938.

President Emeritus Shaw, in a nostalgic farewell, said, "Memories of the beautiful campus can never be effaced. May it continue to appeal to and stimulate the aesthetic taste so that we may be inspired to leave the world more beautiful for our having lived in it."

John A. Hannah, Twelfth President

John W. Beaumont, class of 1882, Hon. Dr. of Letters, 1932, who gave Beaumont Tower to the university, died on July 17, 1941. He had served as a Naval Reserve in the Spanish-American War. A Detroit attorney, he was Judge Advocate for the Michigan National Guard; taught at the Detroit College of Law, now on the MSU campus; and served on the State Board of Agriculture (Board of Trustees) from 1912 to 1924.

MSC Responds to War Food Needs—The Farm Crops and Horticulture Departments aided in the development

Robert Shaw, left, turns the MSC Presidency over to his son-in-law John A. Hannah on July 1, 1941 on the Linton Hall steps. Linton housed the president's office 1938 to 1968.

and growth of crop seeds that were cut off from Europe by World War II. Many important seeds, such as chicory and spinach, formerly imported from Europe, were successfully grown in various parts of Michigan with the aid of MSC experts.

The Engineering Division, in response to the Engineering Defense Training Act to speed the nation's defense program, developed short engineering courses in Materials Inspection and Testing, Drawing, Shop Math and Processes, and Production Supervision.

A Radio Broadcasting department was established in the All-College Division, with R.J. Coleman as director.

Curtis Beachum was praised for his highly professional management of Mason-Abbot Halls by the Dean of Men.

George Sidney Alderton, sports writer for the *Lansing State Journal*, was hired as MSC's athletic publicity writer. He brought a professional touch to the sports information function. Under his direction, facts books on the football, basketball, and baseball teams were produced for sports writers covering Michigan State athletics.

Three WKAR radio student announcers resigned to take positions with radio stations WWJ, WXYZ, and WJLB in Detroit. This brought to eleven the number of students, who because of their training at WKAR, landed positions in the broadcasting industry.

The 1941 NCAA swimming championships were held in the new Jenison Gymnasium pool.

The MSC Intrafraternity Council won the National Intrafraternity Conference Award for the most outstanding program of activities of any similar group in the U.S. or Canada. Membership of the 17 social fraternities on campus totaled 1,000, including actives and pledges.

MSC was ranked the 15th largest university in the nation in a 1941 *New York Times* article. Interestingly, the top five schools in enrollment were members of the Big Ten: 1. Minnesota–13,617; 2. Illinois–13,547; 3. Ohio State–12,760; 4. Wisconsin–11,291; and 5. Michigan–10,908. Penn State, not then in the conference, was 12th–7,195, and Michigan State was listed 15th–6,756.

The contents page of *The MSC Record* of January, 1941 carried the statement, "A magazine for State's 16,000 Alumni." Today (2004), MSU has 378,000 living alumni.

Actual student enrollment for 1941 was 6,342. Graduate students numbered 456. At commencement, 1,175 degrees were granted, including 77 master's, 13 doctoral, and 51 doctor's of veterinary medicine.

The Library grew to 176,430 volumes.

1942

Michigan State Goes to War—World War II gripped the campus in 1942. After Congress declared war on Japan on December 8, 1941, and Germany shortly thereafter, the all-out national war effort, military training, and stress of a world conflict enveloped every activity at Michigan State.

A War Service Information Bureau was established early in 1942 by President Hannah to keep MSC faculty and students informed about Selective Service activities and war service enlistments.

MSC offered the broadcast facilities of WKAR radio to the Governor of Michigan and the Michigan Defense Council for any service they might require.

The Agricultural Division modified courses and introduced accelerated and specialized courses **to help with national defense priorities**. A new course in camouflage was offered by the Department of Landscape and was very popular.

The Liberal Arts Division developed new courses in Economics of War, Current History, Navigation, Spherical Trigonometry, Psychological War, and the Portuguese and Russian languages.

Civilian pilot training (a prelude to military flight training) was conducted at Capital City Airport for 163 students, with the ground school instruction held on campus.

Veterinary students were authorized to apply for commissions as 2nd lieutenants in the Medical Administration Rescue Corps.

The Agricultural Engineering Department focused on machinery to produce necessary food, which required a minimum of metals (which were needed for war materials);

safe food storage; accident prevention training; and time and labor saving methods.

The Animal Husbandry Department worked on improvements with meat and milk-producing animals for the Food for Defense Program.

Agriculture Dean Anthony and members of his faculty engaged several hundred students in 1942 to help harvest sugar beets.

Campus groups provided variety show entertainment at Camp Custer, Michigan, and later when the war wounded returned home, at Percy Jones Hospital in Battle Creek, Michigan.

On a voluntary basis, students organized classes in "Arabic, Japanese, Morse-code and plane-spotting, bandage rolling, home nursing, and first aid."

Ruth Ann Henry, '45, recalled that "World War II had a sobering effect on us all."

Hannah Reassures Students About Their Future—President Hannah met with students at the end of the 1942 winter term to reassure them about the future. He told them "some pessimists tell us that civilization is going to be wiped out by the war. That is not likely to happen. Even if the war is long and costly, most of us who fight in it are going to return. We are going to marry and raise families and live normal lives. We have a fundamental, personal stake in winning this war."

Three MSC 1942 NCAA Wrestling Champions—William Maxwell, 136 lbs, center; flanked by Jennings twins; Burl (Bo), 128 lbs, L; and Merle (Cut), 121 lbs, R.

President Hannah promised in December, 1942 that MSC "would continue to offer all course requirements for women students, and for men who due to age or physical disability may be ineligible for military service."

"Don't Bring Cars to Campus"—In September, 1942, President Hannah sent a request to the parents of all students that they not be given automobiles for the coming college year. This was in keeping with the nationwide effort to conserve on gasoline for the war effort.

Glen Wagner, '42, won first place in the National Oratorical Pi Kappa Delta tournament held in Minneapolis. He competed against speakers from 50 colleges and universities.

Dr. Lawrence T. Clark, class of 1904, was serving as managing director of the research and biological laboratories at the pharmaceutical firm Parke Davis & Co. in Detroit.

Donald A. Stroh, class of 1915, was promoted to Brigadier General in the U.S. Army.

***The State News* became a daily newspaper in 1942.** Because of the paper shortage, it was reduced to tabloid size. The paper also became a member of the *Associated Press*.

A Department of Alumni Relations was created by board action on July 1, 1942.

To bring world travel to the campus and to give people relief from the war, **the World Adventure film series was initiated in the winter of 1942.** These Saturday night shows were so popular they had to be moved from the 600-seat Fairchild Theater to the main Auditorium, which seated up to 5,000.

A Coke date (Coca Cola) at the Union grill "became a war casualty." Emery Foster, Union manager, "announced (February 3, 1942) that no more Cokes would be served due to the sugar shortage" caused by World War II. *The State News* reported, "the Union Grill has long held a position as the foremost single distribution center of Cokes in the Middle West…"

Spartan wrestlers win three NCAA titles—The Jennings twins—Merle "Cut," and Burl "Bo," won NCAA wrestling titles at 121 and 128 pounds, respectively. Bill Maxwell also won an NCAA title at 136 pounds. The NCAA championships were held in Jenison Fieldhouse, with MSC the team runner-up.

Michigan State Football Team Produces "Miracle" Upset—Great Lakes Naval Training Station's football team came to play Michigan State in East Lansing in the fall of 1942. The war-time service team was heavily favored because it was loaded with college All-Americans and professional players who were in training at Great Lakes. Among their players were Bruce Smith, 6', 193-pound 1941 Heisman-trophy winner and National Player of the Year, as well as Bob Swieger, 6', 215-pound All-American halfback. Both had starred for Minnesota's 1940 and 1941 national championship teams.

No sports writer gave Michigan State a chance. MSC entered the game with a 1-2 record. It was such a long-shot that MSC Head Football Coach Charley Bachman declared at the Lansing Rotary Club the day before the game, that if the Spartans won, he would wade across the Red Cedar River on Sunday, the day after the contest. The Spartans rose to the occasion, shutting out Great Lakes 14-0 before a Homecoming crowd of 12,000.

Lansing State Journal sports writer George Alderton—who named the Spartans—wrote, "Michigan State scored one of the nation's major football upsets Saturday. State's united front worked in what in many a football huddle this weekend, will be regarded as a miracle."

The next day at high noon, a huge crowd gathered at the Kalamazoo Street bridge to watch Bachman fulfill his promise. The picture of the coach wading hip-deep across the river made the newswires and appeared in newspapers nationwide.

Stadium Refreshments–5, 10, and 15 Cents—The 1942 MSC football programs carried an advertisement on stadium refreshments: Sandwiches, peanuts, hot dogs, coffee, pop and cigars were all ten cents. Cigarettes cost 15 cents, and chewing gum was five cents.

Forest H. Akers (Forest Akers Golf Courses; Akers Hall; and Akers Gym) of Detroit, was elected to the Board.

Enrollment was 6,319. At graduation, 1,143 degrees were granted.

1943

14 MSC Men Die in the War; 4,074 Students in the Military—Fourteen students and alumni were killed in the war in the first six months of 1943. Alumni Director Glen O. Stewart reported that 4,073 students were serving in the armed services.

Four Spartans were awarded the Distinguished Flying Cross. Lt. Douglas MacDonald, '42, for rescue of Army pilots; Capt. James Gibb, Jr., '38, for rescue mission bringing General Douglas MacArthur out of the Philippines and heroic action in the Pacific War Theater; Robert Zant, '39, for bravery in aerial combat; and Captain Leon Williamson, '39, for meritorious achievement with the Marine Air Corps.

Ernest H. Burt, '14, was serving as a Brigadier General in the Army.

Donald A. Stroh, '15, was promoted to Brigadier General in the Army.

Florence Hall, Class of 1909, headed the U.S. Women's Land Army of 60,000 farm women working in the "Crop Corps," to prevent a WWII food shortage.

Florence Hall, 1909, was appointed head of the Women's Land Army, directing 60,000 women farm workers in the "Crop Corps," designed to beat the war food shortage threat.

President Hannah proposed a memorial certificate to be sent to the families of former students killed in the war.

Michigan State became one of the leading college military training centers in the U.S. in 1943, with nearly 3,500 uniformed soldiers on campus. There were 1,500 Army Air Corps cadets who were "to receive five months of intensive general education before entering pre-flight schools." They were taught physics, geography, mathematics through trigonometry, the history of war, and an English course that combined writing, speaking and literature. They were housed in Mason and Abbot Halls.

An Army Specialized Training Program for engineers brought 1,150 trainees to East Lansing. Some 300 Area Foreign Language students were being trained in the language and culture of Western Europe to be ready to occupy territory taken by the Allied Forces.

The success of these highly compressed courses had an impact on faculty thinking about teaching and education. Student grasp of liberal arts education in a short, intense course led to the development of Michigan State's Basic College in 1944.

One hundred fifty veterinarians and 250 Junior Reserve Officer Training Candidates were at the college for additional training before going to Officer Candidate Schools.

Throughout the campus, cadets could be seen marching to class in uniform and heard singing "Off We Go Into the Wild Blue Yonder" and "On The Banks of the Red Cedar."

A pleasant surprise to the professors was the seriousness of the military students. They were focused, respectful, and highly motivated. They liked the school and campus, and many returned to Michigan State on the GI Bill following the war.

Army Air Corps cadets stream into Abbot Hall in 1943 to begin war training.

Off campus, Michigan State was offering 27 Engineering War Training courses in ten cities around the state to 1,600 students.

Producing enough food for the armed forces and the civilian population was a huge concern during World War II. Lack of food on the home front had done Germany in during World War I.

MSC's Division of Agriculture focused on food production and preservation. Research on food preservation by drying was passed on to Michigan citizens.

The Michigan Defense Council requested the services of **P.R. Krone,** assistant professor of floriculture, to direct the operations of Victory Gardens in Michigan.

"Victory Gardens" to supplement the food supply were planted on campus and maintained by students and faculty.

A wartime emergency course to train farm women to do farm work was inaugurated, with the cost of housing and maintenance paid for by the Kellogg Foundation.

The Home Economics Department worked with Michigan housewives on canning larger and larger quantities of homegrown vegetables.

"Your War Notebook," a daily WKAR radio broadcast kept listeners up to date on the war.

With board approval, the college took over the operation of all fraternity and cooperative houses during the war for housing servicemen or civilian students.

MSC Welcomes Japanese as Students—While the Federal Government was herding American-born Japanese into internment camps during World War II, President Hannah put Michigan State on record as willing to accept American-born Japanese who had been employed for six months in Michigan as students in the college on the same basis as other residents of Michigan. The Board approved this action.

International Studies Program Launched—The Institute of Foreign Studies—the beginning of Michigan State's leadership international studies program—was launched in the fall of 1943 with Dr. S.C. Lee as its director.

A Central Placement Office was opened in the fall. MSC sent letters to 823 companies, 300 of whom made requests for graduating students.

The American Hotel Association Testing Laboratory was moved to the campus during the year. This reinforced the national leadership stature of the Hotel Administration program at MSC.

Chuck Davey and Bill Zurakowski each won individual NCAA boxing titles.

Merle "Cut" Jennings and Bill Maxwell each won National AAU wrestling titles.

Athletics Discontinued—Because of the ban on participation in intercollegiate athletics by members of the armed forces in training on campus, the Board proposed on August 5, 1943 that consideration should be given to discontinuing intercollegiate athletic for the duration of the war. The 1943 football season was cancelled.

President Hannah initiated the first separate *President's Annual Report* in November, 1943. It was titled, "Michigan State College in War Time." Over the years, his annual report won national praise.

Due to the war, regular enrollment dropped to 3,463 in 1943. At the same time, there were some 3,500 servicemen in military training on campus. At graduation, 1,183 degrees were granted, including 59 master's, 7 doctoral, and 55 D.V.M.s.

1944

5,400 MSC Men and Women in the Armed Forces; 69 Killed—Michigan State men and women—5,400 strong—were serving in the United States Armed Forces in 1944. Through June of that year, 69 Spartans were reported killed in military service—30 in war action, 25 in Army Air Corps flight training in the U.S.; the remainder in accidents.

Hannah: "We've Been Asked to Make Tanks and Automobiles"—The college was frenetic with activity, offering both accelerated military training and regular civilian education. President Hannah's analogy of the dual educational role was that "universities and colleges have been asked to 'make tanks and automobiles' at the same time." Michigan State responded by operating on a continuous, year-around basis. The combined military and civilian student bodies pushed enrollment to an all-time high of 11,708. This included 3,801 regular students, and 361 short course students. Military trainees numbered 8,395—4,753 from the Army Air Corps and 3,642 from the Army. Civilian male students dropped to 643—the lowest in 30 years.

Hannah Reached Out to Servicemen's Families—With a look to the future, President John Hannah sent a personal message on 7,500 cards to the families and wives of most of the military trainees on campus. Some 15,000 picture postcards of Abbot and Mason Halls were given to the soldiers on their arrival to mail to parents, wives and friends.

A small folder entitled "At Michigan State We Sing," with facts about the school was given to 7,500 trainees. An 8-page brochure containing a certificate of achievement, views of aircrew soldiers in training, and a statement about the academic opportunities at MSC was prepared by the Publications Department and sent to 5,000 parents and wives.

Professor Russell B. Nye won the 1944 Pulitzer Prize for biography.

In addition, **the MSC Alumni Office mailed thousands of personal letters to alumni in the Armed Services and their families.**

This friendly outreach impressed many soldiers and their families. The good feelings generated about Michigan State, in addition to a pleasant experience on campus, led many veterans to return to East Lansing with their GI Bill of Rights scholarships following World War II.

President Franklin D. Roosevelt Signed the GI Bill of Rights into Law on June 22, 1944, two weeks after the Allied Forces' D-Day assault on the beaches of Normandy, France. The bill is considered the second most important educational legislation in the nation's history—behind the Morrill Act which created the land-grant colleges. The GI Bill would provide college tuition for more than two million returning military veterans as well as $65 per month for living expenses per single person, or $90 per month for married students.

Lessons Learned from Military Training Led to Basic College—Faculty ferment for a change in the college curriculum bubbled as a result of the precisely prescribed training required by the military that they witnessed and participated in. Large numbers of traditional students received no grounding in the liberal arts disciplines. Although the military training was heavy on technical subjects, the Army still required trainees to study geography, literature and history.

On December 15, 1943, President Hannah hired Floyd W. Reeves of the University of Chicago to spend six weeks on campus to study the curriculum and consult on potential changes. At a March, 1944 meeting, Hannah focused on "the need for a fundamental revision in the educational philosophy of the institution." **Hannah believed that every entering freshman was at MSC "in order to become an educated man or woman: a person with social poise, with 'a good control of his native tongue able to speak, to read and write with reasonable fluency,' with an 'understanding and appreciation of literature and art and music,' with a reasonable comprehension of the laws of nature and the laws of men, with 'an appreciation of the spiritual values without which no life is complete and adequate, 'and finally the knowledge and skills that will help one make a living.'"**

Reeves "proposed a program of basic general education, required rather than optional, for all freshmen and sophomores and taught by a distinct faculty." The faculty agreed to putting a program in place by the fall of 1944. Hannah selected Howard C. Rather as chairman of an implementation committee which worked full-time on the new Basic College program. Seven basic courses were proposed: Written and Spoken English, Biological Science, Physical Science, Social Science, Effective Living, History of Civilization, and Literature and Fine Arts.

***Detroit News* writer Allen Schoenfield** reported on the new Basic College, **"Breaking sharply with accepted pedagogical theory and practice, Michigan State College has staged a revolt of such significance and magnitude that it may influence the course of higher education in the United States for generations to come."**

The course was introduced in the fall of 1944, with Howard Rather as Dean of the new Basic College.

"A food technology curriculum, created in the School of Agriculture in 1944, was designed to train people in the scientific processing or manufacturing of dairy, meat, cereal, fruit, and vegetable products."

English Professor Russell B. Nye won the 1944 Pulitzer Prize for biography with his book, *George Bancroft, Brahmin Rebel.*

Joseph Zichis, '32, M.S. '34, Ph.D. '36, founded Markham Laboratories in Chicago. He was **among the first to develop the chick vaccine for equine encephalitis**, and to propagate hog cholera virus in sheep and rabbits. He showed that antibodies were effective in the prevention and treatment of viral diseases.

The War Food Administration allocated $44,450 to MSC's Cooperative Extension Service for an emergency food production and conservation program.

The "Beaumont Library" was installed in the former Library (now Museum) Browsing Room. It consisted of the 1,800-volume gift of the late John W. Beaumont **(Beaumont Tower),** class of 1882.

On April 7, 1944, MSC's Athletic Council recommended the resumption of athletic competition in all sports effective July 1, 1944.

Because of the shortage of men on campus, women marched in the band for the first time and provided most of the cheerleaders.

Sarah Van Hoosen Jones (Van-Hoosen Hall) of Rochester, Michigan was elected to the Board.

President Hannah was awarded an honorary doctor of laws degree from the University of Michigan in February, 1944.

Regular civilian student enrollment for 1944 was 3,801. At graduation, 692 degrees were granted, including 50 master's, nine doctor's, and 57 D.V.M. sheepskins. For the second time in Michigan State history, women outnumbered male graduates. The first time was in 1919, following World War I.

1945

6,379 Spartans in Armed Services; 316 Killed; 1,016 Receive Medals or Citations; MSC Swimmers Win National AAU Title—World War II finally ended in August of 1945. The war record of Michigan State alumni and former students was exemplary. In 1945, 6,379 Spartans were serving in the four service branches—4,786 in the Army, which included the Army Air Corps; 1,385 in the Navy; 175 in the Marines; and 33 in the Coast Guard.

Five percent of those serving—316—gave the ultimate sacrifice to their nation, laying down their lives for our freedom. They died at locations around the world: Germany, Italy, France, England, Scotland, Belgium, Holland, Czechoslovakia, the Mediterranean, China, India, Guam, Saipan, Leyte Island, New Guinea, Luzon, Tinian Island, Iwo Jima, Okinawa, and the Philippines.

Medals and citations for bravery and outstanding service were received by 1,016 Michigan State men and women.

War Effect: "Willingness to Disregard Precedent"—President Hannah in his 1945 report said the war "had a stimulating effect upon our faculty and staff. It created a willingness to disregard precedent." He said the Basic College was an outgrowth of the wartime stimulus of accelerated learning on campus.

Of the 3,000 to 4,000 veterans anticipated to arrive following the war, 660 already were on campus. One third of the veterans were married, and there was no housing for them. MSC had taken over a trailer camp in South Lansing for 50 families, and plans were underway to provide housing for 350 additional families.

Women on campus outnumbered civilian men students three to one in the spring of 1945. There were 3,400 women enrolled by fall term, 1945. "Coed enrollment grew by 90 percent" in the five years preceding World

East Lansing Business District—Grand River Ave. looking east—1945.

The Spartan Statue, the world's largest free-standing ceramic figure, was unveiled in June 1945.

War II, and by another 40 percent "in the five years ending in June, 1945."

Post-War Building Program Takes Off—Taking action on the housing issue, Hannah and the Board borrowed $6 million to build three women's and two men's dorms, the first unit of a married housing project, and a major addition to the Union Building. Financing was to be repaid from the earnings of the buildings. Construction of Snyder and Phillips Halls began in the fall of 1945.

No New Academic Buildings Since 1929—Needed academic and classroom buildings as well as laboratories, could not be financed through self-liquidating bonds, because there was no revenue stream generated by such facilities. It would take legislative appropriations. President Hannah noted there had been no new academic buildings provided by the state since 1929. He was pleased the most recent legislature had made $700,000 available for a classroom building. This would help build Berkey Hall, which ultimately would run $1,000,000.

Hannah's call for needed facilities included new buildings for Agricultural Engineering, Electrical Engineering, Chemistry, Civil Engineering and Chemical Engineering, and Veterinary Medicine. Building additions were needed for Home Economics, Agricultural Hall, the Art Department, the Forestry Department, and Business Administration. A new Library was an urgent need, as was an expansion of the Power Plant.

It was an astonishing list of needs. But John Hannah justified all these requests by stating, "The parents (voters) of Michigan send their sons and daughters to MSC expecting there will be available to them adequate opportunities for a university education. If needed facilities are lacking, the students are cheated and the state suffers through the inadequate training of its future leaders."

Nine MSC graduates took office as State Senators and Representatives–Senators: G. Edward Bonine, '23; Harold Tripp, '16; Carl F. Delano, '12 short course; and George Girrbach, '24. Representatives–John W. Thompson, 1900; Albert W. Dimmers, '26; Dora Stockman, Hon. Dr. of Science, '34; Howard Estes, '17; and Arthur C. Mackinnon, 1895.

Dale Stafford, '31, was serving as managing editor of the *Detroit Free Press*.

The Spartan Statue, a ten-foot figure fashioned from red Ohio clay by Professor Leonard Jungwirth, and fired in a Grand Ledge, Michigan kiln, was unveiled during commencement week, 1945. It is the largest free-standing ceramic figure in the world. Rumor has circulated that Jack Breslin **(Breslin Center)** was the model for the mighty Spartan.

Charles McCaffree's MSC swimming team won the National Senior AAU outdoor swimming championship in 1945.

Gale Mikles, 17-year old freshman, won the 1945 National AAU wrestling title at 145 pounds.

Nick Kerbawy, MSC sports information director, developed a sports news service aimed at Michigan newspapers and out-state publications. As a result, media coverage of MSC sports stories increased 407 percent over the previous year. Kerbawy later went on to become General Manager of the Detroit Lions football team, and found the Michigan Sports Hall of Fame, now housed in Cobo Hall in Detroit.

Michigan State did not field a marching band in the fall of 1945. Instead, local high school bands performed at home football games.

Winfred G. Armstrong (Armstrong Hall) of Niles, Michigan, was elected to the Board.

Regular student enrollment was 5,284 in 1945. The 598 degrees granted during the year was the lowest number in a decade. It was the calm before the storm.

1946

Explosive Growth; Enrollment More Than Doubles in One Year—A fifty-year pent-up demand for new buildings was released in the 1945-1946 school year. Hannah wrote in his nationally recognized annual report, "From 1900 to 1945, the State of Michigan appropriated $4 million for buildings and capital equipment at MSC. During that period, enrollment was growing from 600 to 7,000 (regular plus part-time students), and now in a single year, that has nearly doubled and reached 13,282."

Hannah continued, "One year ago it was predicted MSC might be called on to provide educational opportunities for as many as 3,000 or 4,000 veterans in the fall of 1946. We find instead of 4,000 veterans, we have 8,265 enrolled, and a total enrollment of 13,282." The student ratio swung from three to one women to three to one men.

World's Largest One-Room Dormitory—Probably the world's largest one-room dormitory for men was created in 1946 on the Jenison Gymnasium floor (second level), by placing double-deck beds for 500 students. Getting a good night's sleep there was not easy.

Edwin Bozian, '50, remembered, "all PA announcements (in the gym) were preceded by 'Now Hear This.'" Donald D. Juchartz, '51, recalled, "If you don't think having 300 alarm clocks going off in the morning, all at slightly different times was an experience, you haven't lived."

Mary Jane Osborne Teage, '50, wrote, "The massive number of returning veterans (fall of 1946) who chose to use the GI Bill (Government college scholarship) made a heavenly but unequal ratio that fall term. Our freshman class, as I recall, had 4,500 men—mostly veterans—and only 500 freshmen women. Nice! I admit being enthralled by those leather bomber jackets (worn by B-17 and B-24 bomber crews on the WWII raids over Germany)."

Campus Planning Given a Top Priority—Hannah brought Harold W. Lautner, '25, to the campus in 1946 to succeed Glenn Phillips as campus planner. Lautner had been in Washington, D.C. during the war, planning war housing in the Division of Defense Housing. Lautner, in his book *From an Oak Opening*, wrote, "No other university is known to me that equals Michigan State for its foresight immediately after the war, in creating its own permanent campus planning office with clear responsibility to answer the daily and long-term needs for expanding its physical plant. Surely no institution carried out its plans more efficiently and with greater vigor. This was entirely due to a president who understood the building process and the professions that could make and carry out plans."

Lautner wrote, "Over the years, working with President Hannah, I was often reminded of Daniel H. Burnham, architect, city planner and co-author of the early 1900s visionary plan for Chicago." Burnham made a statement on planning that is classic. It personified John Hannah: **"Make no little plans, they have no magic to stir men's blood, and probably themselves will not be realized. Make big plans, aim high in hope and work, remembering that a noble, logical diagram will never die, but long after we are gone will be a living thing asserting itself with ever growing insistency."**

Creation of the Red Cedar River Corridor—One of the finest contributions to the beauty of the Michigan

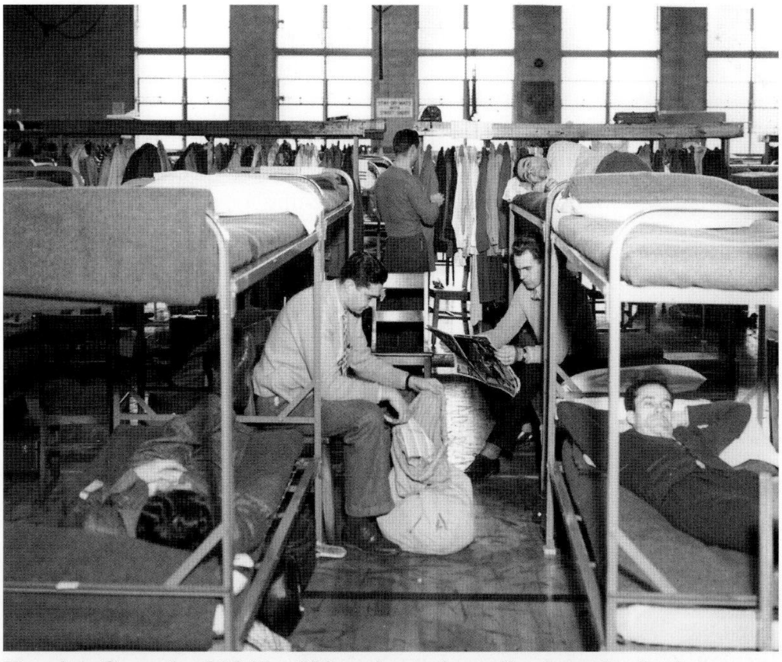

Housing Crunch of 1946—500 male students lived on the Jenison Gymnasium floor in double-deck beds, waiting for Snyder and Phillips Halls to open.

State campus started in 1946 when Harold Lautner suggested creating the Red Cedar Corridor. Lautner wanted to clean and landscape "the entire flood-plain of the Red Cedar River from Harrison Road to Bogue Street as a first step in exploiting the natural beauty of the stream in every way incorporating it into the campus scene to the north. One way to achieve this goal was to face new buildings toward the river."

It took twenty years to accomplish the creation of this ribbon of beauty through the heart of the campus—a visual delight, and one of the most pleasant walks at MSU.

Construction of Landon Hall, a women's dorm, was begun in 1946. So was the building of faculty and married student apartment buildings, which were named for alumni who died in World War II. MSC borrowed another $3 million for buildings.

MSC Leads the Nation in Student & Married Housing—To handle the burgeoning student population, the college moved 500 house trailers on campus. Service buildings, including laundries and playgrounds for children were constructed near the trailers.

One hundred and four Quonset huts were erected to house 1,456 men. Each unit accommodated 14 men, sleeping in partitioned double-deck bunks. They studied in an open room at the end of the Quonset. Showers and washbasins were provided in a separate building, a daunting trip in the cold of winter. A large Quonset dining hall and Quonset snack bar were built next to these living quarters. Fred P. Adolph, Jr., class of 1950, recalled, "I was in Quonset Hut 30. Saturday night party-goers would throw beer bottles in the air to bounce off the metal roofs."

Forty Girls in a Room—Rosemary Rolls Colston, '50, recalled, "I lived on the top floor of the Union. Forty girls in one room with a long pipe holding all our clothes. We shared desks in the hall and two showers."

"Fertile Valley" is Born—Barracks apartments for 1,100 family units were provided by the Federal Public Housing Authority (FPHA), and covered 130 acres of the west end of the campus along Harrison Road and south of Kalamazoo Street. When these apartments filled with married students, and new families were begun, this area was dubbed "Fertile Valley" by its inhabitants.

Two large military overseas hospital units were given to the college by the FPHA to house 240 students. Fifty faculty dwelling units were erected—31 Quonsets and 19 overseas British Empire type houses.

Veteran Students Create Own Society—"Many of the (veterans) wives worked in Lansing or in campus offices;

Canoeing the Red Cedar in 1946 to promote the first Water Carnival since 1941: Left canoe—Mary Stewart, Detroit; and Bob Schweitzer, Owosso; Right canoe—Gloria Patton, Saginaw; and Bob Argyle, Midland.

some of the men worked split-shifts at Oldsmobile to support their families, sharing the eight-hours with a neighbor across the court. Couples sat with one another's children and organized, with help from the Kellogg Foundation, a nursery school in a double Quonset."

The veterans "organized a city council to regulate their affairs, and to negotiate with the institution. They formed a cooperative store, which saved a mile's walk. Spartan Wives, advised by the Adult Education staff, conducted classes in dramatics, interior decoration, and child care." They also nurtured neat flower beds and planters, and vegetable gardens.

One alum wrote, "Married housing units were equipped with ice boxes, not refrigerators. One memory is gathering snow from the yard for the box, thus saving on ice."

Louis O. Schulte, '50, recalled, "The veterans (on campus) added a sense of maturity and determination that was good for the student body."

Students between classes—Winter 1946; Ag Hall in background.

"Pushing Hubby Through" Degree—"Wives of veterinary students attended special evening classes to understand their husband's profession; to them the school faculty awarded a special degree of P.H.T.—'Pushing Hubby Through.'"

Thirteen large structures that had housed high explosives during the war were erected south of the Red Cedar River as classroom buildings—the birth of "South Campus." These long buildings were split by a hallway, with classrooms and offices located on each side. Later, nine small metal units were added to this complex. These "temporary" classrooms were used into the mid-1950s.

Because of inadequate classroom and laboratory space, the college extended the working day from 7 am to 10 pm.

Comprehensive Exams Speeded Graduation—MSC's Board of Examiners gave 8,800 comprehensive exams during the 1946 school year, saving the equivalent of a year of class time for 275 students.

With the return of war veterans to campus, the tradition of no smoking was frequently violated. A student vote eliminated the ban on smoking.

MSC's Department of Information Services sent 3,800 news releases to the *Associated Press, United Press, International News Service*, and to daily and weekly newspapers nationwide. This effort resulted in 118,000 stories on Michigan State appearing in various news media, a 30 percent increase over the previous year.

Faculty Row # 1—which had served as the president's home from 1875 to 1915, a women's dormitory 1915 to 1925, the college hospital from 1925 to 1939, and a home management practice house from 1939 to 1946, was razed in 1946 to make way for Gilchrist-Yakeley Halls.

A Creative Spartan Gets into the "Big House"—Late in the fall of 1946, the University of Michigan was to play Army at Michigan Stadium in Ann Arbor. The Army football team was undefeated and was ranked No. 1 in the nation.

Their backfield included the 1945 Heisman trophy winner, fullback Felix "Doc" Blanchard, and the man who would win the Heisman for 1946, halfback Glenn Davis. This was one of the two top games of the year (the other: Army-Notre Dame).

A creative Michigan State student decided he wanted to see the game. But he didn't have a ticket. He had a buddy who was a gate guard at Michigan Stadium. He arrived in Ann Arbor a couple hours before the game. His buddy slipped his official armband off and handed it through the fence so the Spartan could get inside. Once he had returned the armband to his friend, the Spartan still had a problem—he didn't have a ticket to occupy a seat, and the game was a total sell-out.

The Spartan walked into the stadium, down the steps to the playing field, over to the Army team bench, and sat down. When the Army team came on the field, Head Coach Col. Earl "Red" Blaik, an imposing personality, questioned the young man why he was sitting on the end of the Army bench. The creative Spartan replied, "The University of Michigan has asked me to sit here to keep autograph seekers away from Blanchard and Davis." Blaik was pleased with Michigan's thoughtfulness. He introduced the "autograph guard" to the Army team. The creative Spartan watched the entire game right next to the playing field, seated next to the Cadets. Army won the game 20-13. Never underestimate the ingenuity of a Spartan!

The Spartan track team won the prestigious Drake Relays.

The 1946 enrollment of 13,282 was more than double the 1945 enrollment of 5,284, and was an all-time high. Degrees granted during the year totaled 739, including 70 master's, 3 doctor's and 43 D.V.M.'s.

The glory of MSU's "Sacred Space" inside West Circle Drive is enjoyed by three strolling coeds—spring term 1946.

1947

Michigan State on the Move; Morale High—Fall term 1947 opened with a record enrollment of 15,208 students. President Hannah proclaimed, "I doubt that even the oldest professor emeritus can recall when morale on this campus has been at such a high pitch, when there was so much evidence of a general determination to solve complex problems and push ahead courageously."

"This spirit has been shared by students, faculty and administrative staff alike, and as a result, inconveniences, crowding, long hours, and lack of adequate facilities have not been the onerous burdens they would have been had such high morale been lacking."

Of course, the high morale was a by-product of Hannah's great leadership and his ability to communicate his robust vision of the transformation of Michigan State from a small college to a great university. He met weekly with his administrative staff, deans and key faculty, and monthly with student leaders. He showed them future building plans and discussed new faculty additions to engage them in a shared vision of MSC's great growth and potential.

In President Hannah's 1947 report, he pointed to the Michigan legislature's 1946 special session approval for seven buildings: Berkey Hall, Agricultural Engineering (Farrall Hall), Electrical Engineering (now Computer Center), Physics & Mathematics (now Physics-Astronomy), Natural Science, Home Management Labs (now Paolucci Building), and a Steam Generating Plant. These were the first state appropriations for academic or non-revenue buildings since 1928.

Landon Hall opened during spring term. Gilchrist and Yakeley Halls were nearing completion.

South campus was born with the placement of eleven World War II ammunition storehouses, converted to classrooms, south of the Red Cedar. They were billed as "temporary" but were used for nearly a decade.

Hannah praised the returning veterans, referring to their "eager interest." "Not only are they setting a fast pace for the non-veteran student; they are stimulating their instructors to greater exertions and accomplishments."

Alfred R. Bransdorfer, '50, remembered Hannah's accessibility to students, "You could greet President Hannah as he walked to his office from his home after lunch."

Daily evidence of a tremendous building program, the energy of bright new and older faculty, a vigorous student body populated with veterans who regularly challenged their professors, and a revived athletic program, created an excitement about being at Michigan State. The members of the Spartan family were part of a revolution in higher education and MSC was the premier change-agent in the nation.

MSC baseball team plays "canoe baseball" on flooded Old College Field (now Kobs Field in 1947).

1947 aerial view of temporary student housing: 104 Quonset Huts—upper left; Barracks Apartments for 1,100 family units—foreground and upper center; Jenison Gymnasium & Fieldhouse and Dem Hall—upper right.

Jim Denison, newly hired Administrative Assistant to the President, in charge of public relations, recommended that large signs be placed in front of all the new buildings being financed with borrowed funds. They read, **"Constructed Without Expense to the Public—Financed by Borrowed Funds to be Repaid by the Earnings of the Building."** This was excellent PR strategy, eased taxpayers minds, and won photo-caption coverage in *Time* magazine.

"Hand Me The Quick-Growing Ivy"—Although the campus was torn up with prodigious building activity, John Hannah never lost his love for maintaining and enhancing its beauty. Even before buildings were completed, landscaping crews were on site putting in lawns, trees and shrubs. "Hand me the quick-growing ivy," became the operative phrase to describe Hannah's dedication to instant beautification.

WKAR radio station received Federal Communications Commission approval for FM (frequency modulation) broadcasting as a non-commercial, educational station.

To save money, students "organized and operated their own co-op store on campus."

Hannah's Strategy for Big Ten Membership—Membership in the Big Ten Conference had long been a goal of President Hannah. The big question mark was whether Michigan State could compete in football. The 23,000-seat Macklin Field (25,000 with bleachers; now Spartan Stadium) was a shortcoming. Most of the Big Ten stadiums seated 50,000 or more.

Hannah's strategy was two-fold. He brought Clarence L. "Biggie" Munn, age 38, in as head football coach in 1947, and launched plans to double the size of the stadium to 51,000 before the 1948 season. Munn's team won seven and lost two in 1947, beginning the most successful football coaching tenure in Michigan State history. When he retired early in 1954 to become Athletic Director, his football winning percentage was .857.

MSC fans were uplifted at the first home football game in 1947 when the Spartans took the field in sparkling new green and white uniforms, returning MSC to its true colors, and ending 14 seasons of wearing black jerseys and gold pants.

Special bleachers were purchased to increase the capacity of Jenison Fieldhouse to 13,000 for basketball games. This was prior to fire marshall restrictions on the capacity of Jenison.

James D. Towar, 1885, who had served as acting president of the University of Wyoming and director of the

Three 1947 NCAA Champions–George Hoogerhyde (L)–swimming, 1,500-meter freestyle; Chuck Davey (C)–boxing, 135 pounds; Gale Mikles (R)–wrestling, 155 pounds.

University of Wyoming Agricultural Experiment Station, died on September 28, 1947.

Harry Wismer, '37 and sports director for ABC radio since 1942, was named the nation's outstanding sportscaster by *Sporting News* for the fourth consecutive year, 1944-1947.

Roberta Applegate, '40, was appointed as press secretary to Michigan Governor Kim Sigler, the first woman ever to hold that position. She was the daughter of Professor and Mrs. A.A. Applegate.

Barbara Tanner, a junior, was named the "Ideal American Coed," in a *Ladies Home Journal* poll.

Nine players from John Kobs 1947 MSC baseball team went to the professional ranks. Robin Roberts was the most prominent, becoming a consistent 20-game winner with the Philadelphia Phillies, and later winning a place in Baseball's Hall of Fame.

George Hoogerhyde won the NCAA 1,500-meter freestyle swimming title.

Charles Davey won the NCAA 135-pound boxing title, his second national championship.

Gale Mikles won the NCAA 155-pound wrestling title, his second national championship.

Glenora Irwin Anderson, Ph.D. '50, recalled, "In the forties, pleasures were simple. The event of the day was to go for coffee at 9 pm every night. Coffee with cream was 7 cents a cup, and black coffee was 5 cents. I still drink black coffee."

Donald D. Juchartz, Class of 1951, recalled a talk by President Hannah to his freshman class in the fall of 1947—"Only half your education will be in the classroom the other half will be outside the classroom."

Ted Haskell, '49, remembered, "the 1947 flood of the Red Cedar. The MSC baseball team played a game on Old College Field (now Kobs Field) in canoes. The steam tunnels under the campus flooded and we had no heat or electricity for several days."

Enrollment was 15,208. At commencement, 1,443 degrees were granted, including 170 master's, 12 doctorates, and 40 D.V.M.'s. The library housed 209,483 volumes.

1948

Michigan State Voted Into the Big Ten—A Landmark Event in the History of the University. A multi-year pursuit of membership in the Big Ten (Western Conference) was rewarded on December 12, 1948, when the Big Ten presidents and faculty representatives voted Michigan State into conference membership. This was a major step into big-time athletic competition and into the inner circle of academic respectability in the nation. MSC replaced the University of Chicago which had dropped out of the conference in 1946.

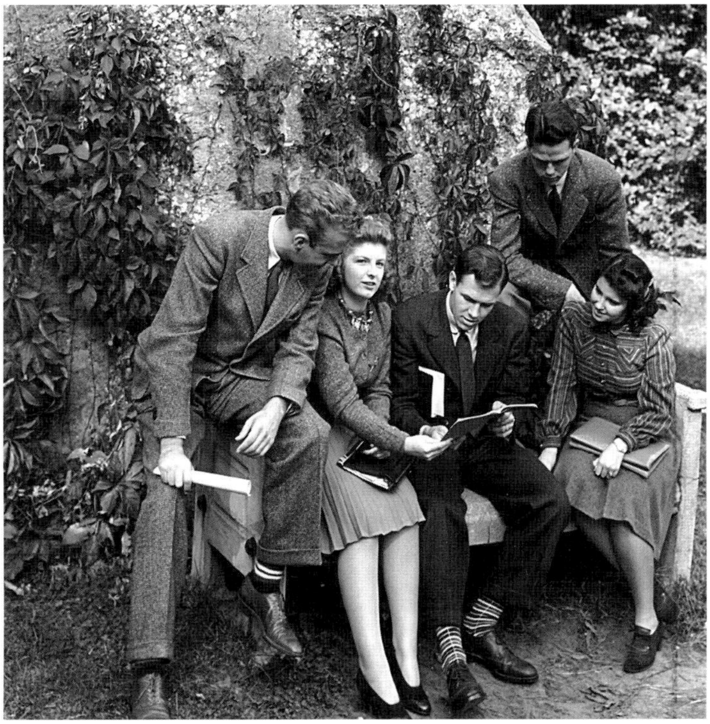

"Engagement Rock and Bench"—1940s–located just north of Beaumont Tower—was where many "MSU mergers" started. "The Rock"—a gift of the Class of 1873—was first located northwest of Linton Hall. Today it sits at the northeast corner of Farm Lane Bridge, where it is a billboard for painted messages.

Critical to selling MSC's entry into the conference was the friendship President John Hannah had cultivated with Dr. Louis Morrill, president of the University of Minnesota. It was Morrill who championed MSC's cause with the other conference schools. After a Big Ten review, formal membership was approved May 20, 1949. (See chapter, The Big Ten Conference: Important in MSU's Development, page 372.)

"It Was A Scoop; No Eastern Paper Bothered to Hold Their Press Run." Ron Linton, '51, *State News* reporter, described the tension during the vote on entry into the Big Ten. "We camped outside the meeting room where the vote was being taken in the College Inn in Chicago. We got a jump on everyone by getting a signal from inside. Andy Anderson made the first call to the *State News* to give the thumbs up, and I got on the phone to give more detail. It was late at night and it was a scoop because no other eastern morning papers bothered to hold their press run. Linton went on to become editor of the *State News*.

"The Greatest Edition of the *State News* Ever!" Meanwhile George W. Krause, '51, *State News* staffer, described what went on in East Lansing that night. "About two dozen of us huddled in the office of Harold Fuller's Campus Press—home of the *State News* back then. Finally, the phone rang. We were in! What joy! This was not a regular publication night. I believe it was a Saturday night. We took bundles of extras and scattered them throughout East Lansing and Lansing shouting and selling the greatest edition of the *State News* ever!"

Sang The Alma Mater on Cowles House Porch—Leroy (Lee) Conley, '50, remembered that on "December 12, 1948 when MSC was admitted to the Big Ten Conference, I was one of the students who stood on the porch of Cowles House and sang the Alma Mater until Dr. Hannah came out on the deck and spoke to us."

Basic College A Pioneering Success—The first class to enter the Basic College in 1944, graduated in 1948. President Hannah reported, "This was an event of significance to higher education in general, for it made possible the first testing of the results of the theory of general education that was put into practice in 1944. This theory, which has come to be identified with MSC, has brought more distinction to this institution as an educational pioneer."

New curricula were being developed for Metallurgical Engineering, Police Science, Journalism, and there was a new six-year program in Veterinary Medicine.

Hannah pointed with pride to the work of MSC's Cooperative Extension specialists, county agents, home demonstration agents, and 4-H club agents, who since 1914, had been "helping rural people help themselves." He said the program was "keeping the rural population up-to-date with economic trends and advice on farm

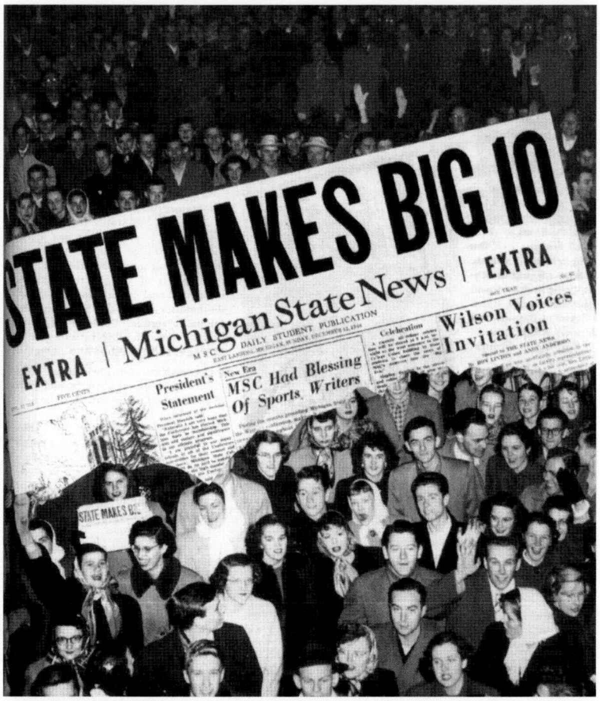

Major milestone in MSU history was entrance into the Big 10 Conference. Students celebrated in front of the President's home.

management problems." This outreach made "the entire state the campus of MSC."

Hannah Shared The Growth Vision with his leadership group. Lautner wrote in *From an Oak Opening*, "The President (Hannah) held weekly luncheon or board room meetings attended by the secretary of board, vice president for business and finance, manager of dormitories and food services, head of buildings and utilities, dean of the department of the building under construction, architects, engineers, and contractors. I remember one meeting where 75 were present. Hannah introduced each person by name and responsibility with no mistakes. Such meetings were great morale builders and drew everyone together on one team." "Throughout the years from 1946 on, the president started faculty meetings by describing progress on the building program."

Dr. Claude Bryan (Bryan Hall) was named Dean of Veterinary Medicine.

First Lt. Harry L. Martin, '36, was posthumously awarded the Congressional Medal of Honor—the nation's highest military decoration—for his bravery in World War II in the U.S. Marine Corps.

Oscar Johnson, an MSC short course graduate in '48, also was awarded the Congressional Medal of Honor.

Alfred Iddles, 1912, was elected president of Babock & Wilcox Company, the world's largest manufacturer of steam boilers.

1948 MSC-Michigan game draws first capacity crowd in newly enlarged, 51,000-seat Macklin Stadium (now Spartan Stadium). National champion U of M won the game 13-7. Ralph Young Track & Field–left corner.

Bonnie Atwell, journalism senior, was one of three first place winners in a National Advertising competition conducted by Gamma Alpha Chi, national advertising sorority.

Barbara Tanner, 20-year old senior, was selected as the National "Sweetheart of Sigma Chi" fraternity. The title included a Hollywood screen test, a 45-inch trophy, and diamond-studded Sigma Chi pin.

Karl Schlademan's MSC cross country team won an unprecedented three national titles: NCAA, Senior AAU, and IC4A. It was the second NCAA cross country title.

Seven Michigan State men won places on the 1948 U.S. Olympic team—in boxing, swimming, walking and wrestling.

Leland Merrill, '42, won an Olympic bronze medal in welterweight wrestling.

Dick Dickenson won the NCAA 136.5-pound wrestling title.

Robin Roberts signed a $25,000 contract to pitch for the Philadelphia Phillies.

Senior Barbara Tanner was chosen National "Sweetheart of Sigma Chi" fraternity in 1948.

Students protest 1948 ankle-length skirts by Christian Dior. Note signs: "Long Hemline, No Dateline;" "You'll Stag It! If You Drag it!"

Enrollment smashed all records, with 16,019 students registered during the 1947-1948 school year. The 1948 graduating class was the largest in school history, totaling 2,154, including 256 master's degrees, 22 doctorates, and 45 D.V.M. degrees.

Remarkably, the 2,154 graduates in 1948 pumped the total Michigan State alumni body by nearly ten percent.

Geographically, the student body came from 82 Michigan counties, 47 states, four U.S. territories, and 38 foreign nations.

1949

Graduating Class Equals 12% of All Degrees Ever Granted—Total enrollment in the 1948-1949 academic year rose to a record 16,243. At commencement, a record 3,148 degrees were granted—2,715 baccalaureate, 338 master's, 31 doctoral, and 64 D.V.M.s.

The 1949 graduating class was 46 percent larger than 1948's, and was equivalent to twelve percent of all the graduating classes in the entire history of the institution. In fact, the 3,148 degrees were more than the total granted in the sixty-year period 1857-1917.

President Hannah proclaimed in the April *MSC Record*, **"That Michigan State is never content with past accomplishments but is always diligent in self-improvement and in searching out new opportunities to be of service is one of its finest and best traditions."**

The Board's $30-million post-war building program was nearing completion in the 1948-49 school year. Seven buildings and facilities had recently been opened—the **Natural Science Building, largest of its kind in the world;** Electrical Engineering; Physics and Mathematics; a large addition to the Union; the doubling of Macklin Stadium's capacity to 51,000; a Greenhouse range on Farm Lane; and the construction of the ice skating rink in Demonstration Hall.

When added to Berkey Hall, Agricultural Engineering, the Home Management Laboratories, and the steam-generating plant—all built post-war—there were seven academic, laboratory, and service buildings financed at a cost of $11,600,000 by the state. **Berkey Hall was the largest building in the world devoted exclusively to classrooms.**

The State Board of Agriculture financed all other capital improvements—a total of $18,700,000—on a self-liquidating basis. These structures included five dormitories— Snyder, Phillips, Landon, Yakeley, and Gilchrist, as well as the stadium addition, the Dem Hall skating rink, and the Union addition. Even with all the new dormitories, living was crowded. Dorm rooms planned for two, were occupied by three. The recreation rooms in all of the women's dorms were being used as sleeping quarters for up to ten young ladies.

A special course in military intelligence was offered in MSC's ROTC curriculum, one of six colleges in the U.S. selected by the U.S. Army headquarters.

Dr. Christopher M. Granger, 1907, was in charge of all national forests for the U.S. Forest Service.

Don Francisco, 1914, was a vice president and director of the J. Walter Thompson advertising agency in New York, the nation's largest in billings.

Student camp-out on steps of Jenison Gymnasium to buy tickets to the 1949 MSC-Notre Dame football game. National champion N.D. won the game, 34-21, but State's competitive showing signaled a move into the big time.

Muriel Read McGuire, '49, wrote, "I was glad our dorms were not coed. I remember vividly the call 'Man on the Floor' whenever a male ventured upon our (dorm) floor."

Dorothy Silver Chamow, '49, recalled, "Curfew for girls was 10 pm week nights; midnight on Friday."

William L. Davidson, 1913, was named director of the newly created MSC Fund. It was the beginning of a permanent, long-range fund-raising program for the school.

Milton Baron, campus landscape architect, "Redesigned the Horticultural Garden with new cross-walks and garden plots that related to desirable new pedestrian routes between the new Natural Science Building and Berkey Hall," according to Lautner.

A twenty-year, 35 percent decline in state appropriations per student (in 1948 dollars) was noted by President Hannah. He reported, "In 1929, this college received a state appropriation equivalent to $462 per student; in 1948-1949, this was down to $407 per student, which would buy no more than $232 bought in 1929!" MSC, Hannah said, was particularly hard hit by this decline because of the huge enrollment increase.

"For Here Began The Great Experiment in Public Education..." President Hannah stated, "The cost of education is already so high thousands of capable Michigan high school graduates give up all hope of attending a college...this has a poignant significance **for here began the great experiment in public education. It was to prove that given an equal education, the boy from the farm or shop could go as far and do as much as the son of the wealthy, privileged family."**

MSC Shadows Selected as the Alma Mater—A 1949 Student Council campus poll selected "MSC Shadows" (now "MSU Shadows") as the Alma Mater, replacing "Close Beside the Winding Cedar," which was written in 1907 by Addison Makepiece Brown, Secretary of the State Board of Agriculture. The vote for "MSC Shadows" was 6,000 to 2,000.

The lyrics of the 1907 song were sung to the tune of the famous Cornell University Alma Mater, "High Above Cayuga's Waters." The lyrics of the first alma mater were compelling:

> "Close beside the winding Cedar's
> Sloping banks of green,
> Spreads thy campus Alma Mater,
> Fairest ever seen.
>
> Swell the chorus! Let it echo
> Over hill and vale,

Michigan Governor G. Mennen "Soapy" Williams waves checkered flag to start 1949 Junior 500 Push Cart Race around West Circle Drive. Start-finish line was in front of the Women's Gymnasium (now IM-Circle).

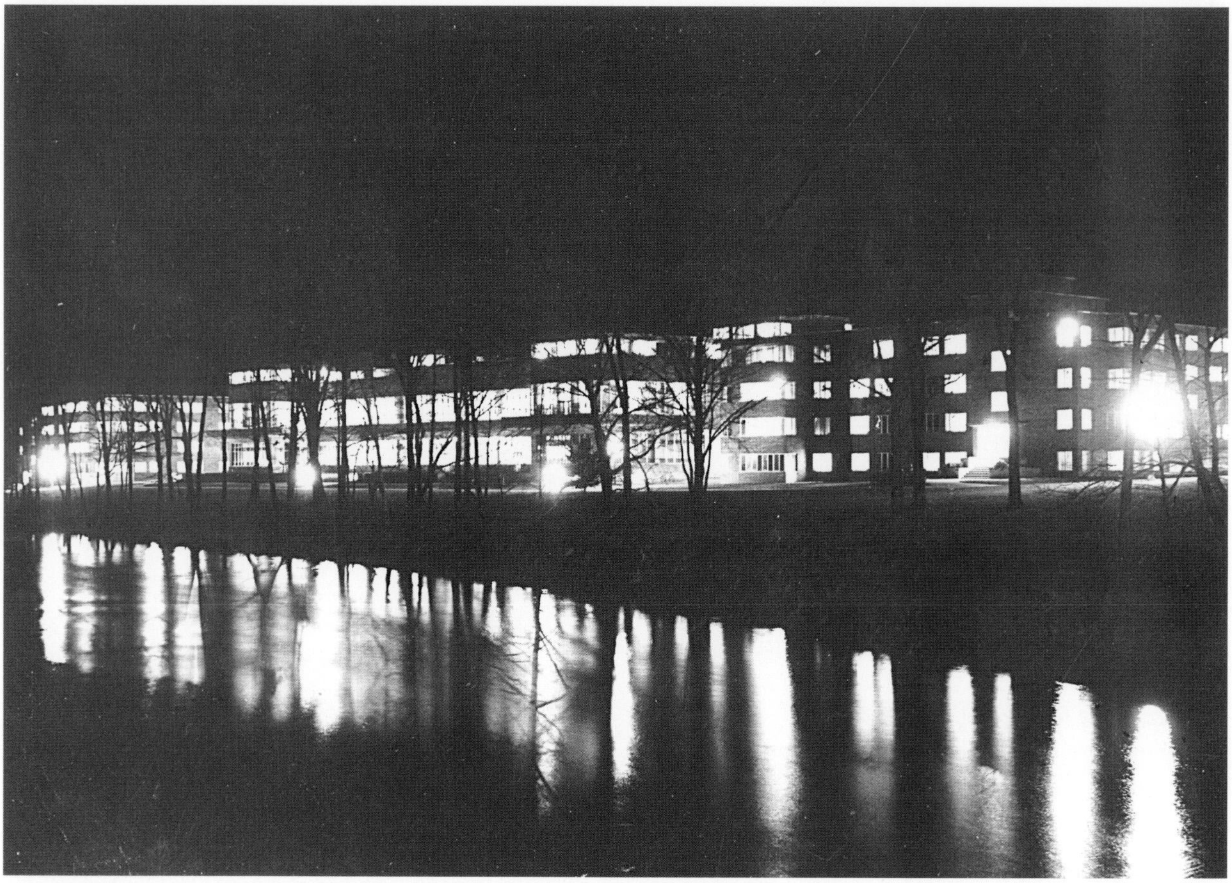

Shaw Hall, nation's largest dormitory, with a capacity of 1,500 students, opened in 1949-1950 school year.

Hail to thee our loving mother,
M.A.C., all hail!

Backward through the hazy distance,
Troop the days of yore,
Scenes and faces float before us,
Cherished more and more."

"MSU Shadows" is set to the music "from the opera *Lucia.*" Bernard P. Traynor, football line coach, wrote the lyrics in 1927:

"MSU, we love thy shadows
When twilight silence falls,
Flushing deep and softly paling
O'er ivy covered halls,

Beneath the pines we'll gather
To give our faith so true,
Sing our love for Alma Mater
And thy praises MSU.

When from these scenes we wander
And twilight shadows fade,
Our memory still will linger
Where light and shadows played;

In the evening oft we'll gather
And pledge our faith anew,
Sing our love for Alma Mater
And thy praises MSU."

The MSC cross country team won its second consecutive NCAA title, its third in school history.

Fred Johnson tied the world record in the 65-yard low hurdles and won the NCAA Long-jump at 25', 2".

Michigan State hosted the 1949 NCAA Boxing Tournament in Jenison Fieldhouse.

MSC boxer Chuck Davey won his unprecedented fourth NCAA boxing crown at this event. He also won the LaRowe trophy as the outstanding boxer in the NCAA tournament for the third time. **Davey was the first boxer to win the award more than once**.

MSC's football team finished #14 in national rankings, with a 6-2-2 record, losing only to National Champion Notre Dame, and Michigan.

Louis E. Durkee, '49, showed his engineering creativity in 1949 by bringing a 1901 curved dash Oldsmobile to life and watching it run away. He described the incident for his 50th class reunion in 1999: "One day in 1949, I discovered (the car) under a pile of stuff in the mechanical engineering shop." Durkee called Mr. Olds, who was still living, to get information on the car. Olds said the car had been put together with leftover parts at the plant, but he couldn't make it run before giving it to the

Chuck Davey presented his third LaRowe trophy as the outstanding boxer in the NCAA tournament by former Michigan Governor Harry F. Kelly, Sr. Davey was the first boxer to win the trophy more than once.

college. Durkee "tried and tried and finally got the car running. I had put the car in gear so it would not roll." While talking to his roommate, who had arrived to watch, "there was a very loud explosion and flames shot out from beneath the car. Suddenly, my friend shouted, 'look out, here she comes.' The car came out of the garage, turned right, and went up the alleyway, bounced down the curb, crossed the street, jumped the curb on the other side and was going up the lawn of the library (now the Museum). We chased it on foot and finally caught it and got it back to the garage."

President Hannah was elected "to a three-year term as president and executive committee chairman of what became, in part through his initiative, the Association of State Universities and Land-Grant Colleges." (Paul L. Dressel—*College to University—The Hannah Years at Michigan State, 1935-1969,* Michigan State University Publications, 1987).

Bricking Up the U-M's Engineering Arch—One of the all-time student pranks occurred on the eve of the Michigan State-Michigan football game in 1949. A dozen students decided they would brick up the engineering arch at the University of Michigan campus.

The Spartan students got the measurements of the arch and then practiced bricking it shut. They fine-tuned their system so they could do it in seven minutes. In the early morning hours of "Arch Day," they rolled into Ann Arbor and started putting the bricks in place. But this time, they also were spreading mortar as they placed the bricks. This added time to the process. And, before they could complete their wall, the Ann Arbor police caught them. They were put on social probation for the rest of the term.

A *Chicago Tribune* Sunday story featured photographs of Spartan coeds Barbara Tanner, 1949, and sophomore Ruth Hawley, who were selected among the five most photogenic discoveries of the year by *Tribune* photographer Andew Pavlin. The article was titled, "Five Co-eds and a Dream Girl."

David E. Lilienthal, Chairman of the Atomic Energy Commission, gave the commencement address in Jenison Fieldhouse. Dr. Newell A. McCune, Class of 1901, Minister Emeritus of Peoples Church in East Lansing, and Lilienthal were granted honorary degrees.

Student enrollment reached 16,243–another record. And, a record 3,148 degrees were conferred during the academic year.

1950

Return to Normalcy—After the great post-war burst of building and the invasion of veterans, Michigan State settled into its most normal operation since World War II.

Nonetheless, President Hannah warned against complacency, "Without difficulties, without headaches, without heartaches, MSC would soon become complacent and self-satisfied. As it is, unresolved difficulties keep us awake, and alert and growing."

With the incessant growth of new knowledge, curriculum upgrading, and academic reorganization—constant change was a reality.

U of M seeks Hannah as Its President—John Hannah's incredible leadership of Michigan State had attracted the attention of the University of Michigan on several occasions. U of M administrators had visited the East Lansing campus more than once "to see what Hannah was doing."

At a 1950 luncheon in Ann Arbor, **Dr. Melvin Buschman, '43, M.A. '47, Ph.D. '60**, then an assistant principal at East Grand Rapids High School, sat at the same table with U of M president Alexander Ruthven. Dr. Ruthven mentioned he would be stepping down from the presidency within a year. Buschman asked Ruthven, "who do you want as your next president?" Ruthven replied, "John Hannah, and I'm asking two of our regents to discuss the idea with him."

Ruthven admired Hannah's tremendous foresight. As an example, during World War II, Hannah was already planning for Michigan State's expansion. When the war ended, construction equipment blanketed the East Lansing campus, and new buildings were going up everywhere. While MSC was building, many other university presidents were playing "catch-up." Buschman told the author that two Michigan regents did visit East Lansing to invite Hannah to come to the U of M as president. However, Hannah's roots, loyalty, and dynamic forward vision for Michigan State kept him in East Lansing. Buschman retired from MSU as professor emeritus in graduate education and educational administration.

A Nursing curriculum was introduced in the School of Science & Arts.

A new Division of Conservation created a leading program in preserving the environment.

A Division of Hotel, Restaurant and Institutional Management was established—expanding the scope of hospitality education, in which MSC was a national leader.

Police Administration was now training coeds, a pioneering step by the leading police education program in the U.S.

Bacteriology, in which MSC had a worldwide reputation, was enhanced with modern facilities in the new Veterinary Medicine Building.

Elementary Education enrollment topped 1,000, with MSC the leading provider of elementary teachers in Michigan.

MSC began preliminary steps to use television as a teaching medium—a pioneering experiment.

A high school engineering program designed to create interest in the profession was offered by MSC, and was showing promise.

Shaw Hall, the largest college dormitory in the U.S., opened during the school year. It housed 1,050 men and was slated to accommodate up to 1,500.

Mary Termohlen, 18, blue-eyed 5'10" blonde sophomore home economics major from Washington, D.C.—1950 Homecoming Queen, and Kappa Kappa Gamma member.

Head football coach Biggie Munn admires U of M goal post brought to his front door by students after State beat Michigan, 14-7 at Ann Arbor—1950.

President Hannah commented on the Korean War, which erupted in June of 1950. He said everything would be fine **"provided we keep our eyes on the eternal objective of improving the lot of mankind through the discovery and dissemination of knowledge, and continue to be guided by the rule of self-less service, MSC will live and grow and wax stronger with the years."**

"Golden Era" of Football Kicks Off—Michigan State's "Golden Era" of football started in the fall of 1950. Biggie Munn's Spartans defeated Michigan for the first time in 13 years, 14-7 before a sell-out crowd of 97,039 at Ann Arbor on September 29. In their first appearance ever on TV, MSC thrilled a regional audience with a sensational 36-33 win over Notre Dame on October 28 at South Bend before a capacity crowd of 57,886. The Spartans finished the season with 8 wins, one loss, and a No. 7 national ranking. They ended the season with six consecutive wins—the start of the legendary 28-game winning streak that would carry into the middle of the 1953 season. Halfback Everett "Sonny" Grandelius, and end Dorne Dibble were named football All-Americans for 1950.

An October 14, 1950 *Saturday Evening Post* article titled, "The Big Ten's Surprise Package," by Stanley Frank stated, "...The brethren who ganged up on Michigan (to vote State into the Big Ten)—Minnesota, Ohio State, Illinois, Northwestern, Wisconsin, Iowa, Purdue, and Indiana—are just beginning to realize that the big baby they adopted (Michigan State) already is a full-grown menace."

Five Athletic Teams in Top Ten Nationally—Five MSC athletic teams finished in the top ten nationally in 1950: Cross Country–#2; Boxing–# 3; Gymnastics–#5; Swimming–# 5; and Football # 7.

World Record Two-Mile Relay Team–L-R: Bill Mack, Don Makielski, Warren Druetzler, and Dave Peppard–ran two miles in world record 7:31.4 at the 1950 Coliseum Relays in L. A.

MSC's Two-Mile Relay Team set a World Record of 7:31.4 at the Coliseum Relays in Los Angeles, beating the old record of 7:34.6, established in 1941. Team members were: Bill Mack, Don Makielski, Warren Druetzler, and Dave Peppard.

"Is Michigan State the College of Beautiful Women," was the title of a December 10, 1950 *Parade Magazine* article. Renowned band leader Woody Herman said, "This school has the most beautiful girls in the country." Bob Gail, a mid-western band leader agreed, saying, "They're really stunning."

"Book bags were unknown. You carried your books under your arm." (Alfred R. Bransdorfer, '50).

Stanley C. (Jack) and Marjorie (Dunlap) Johnston recalled, "The year-end comprehensive exams were sheer terror!"

Student enrollment was 14,993. There were 349 students from 50 foreign nations.

At commencement, a record 4,069 degrees were granted, a 22 percent increase over the previous year. Included were 427 master's, 38 doctorates, and 68 D.V.M.'s. U.S. Vice President Alben W. Barkley spoke at commencement and was awarded an honorary degree.

1951 **Kellogg Center Completed; National Champions in Football and Boxing**—Kellogg Center for Continuing Education—**the finest hotel-restaurant training laboratory, and the finest adult education center in the nation**—was opened September 23, 1951.

The Continuing Education program under Special Courses & Conferences Director Edgar L. Harden, a future MSU president, served 70,588 people. This adult education outreach involved 33 special courses, 29 evening classes, 157 conferences, 168 visiting delegations, and 40 miscellaneous meetings. Another 8,619 business and industry employees were reached through classes in insurance, real estate and industrial management.

In its greatest season in history up to that time, the Michigan State football team went undefeated in nine games, and won national championship recognition. Tennessee also was rated as national champion, but did not play as difficult a schedule as MSC. The Spartans defeated Michigan at Ann Arbor, 25-0 before a sell-out crowd of 97,000.

At Columbus, Ohio before 82,640 fans, MSC scored twice in the final minutes of the fourth quarter to beat Ohio State, 24-20, in what many Spartan fans consider the most exciting game in Michigan State history. Prior to the game OSU was ranked No. 2 in the nation, and MSC, No. 1.

National recognition for the Michigan State football program was won on a late November afternoon in East Lansing. Notre Dame came to town with a 6-1

Spartan fullback Dick Panin races 88 yards to score on MSC's first play of 1951 Notre Dame game, won by MSC, 35-0 in East Lansing. It was a signature moment in Michigan State's rise to football prominence, crushing the # 1 Irish in the Spartans' first nationally televised game.

Spartans' First Big Ten Title in any sport—Tennis, 1951. Champions—L to R: Wally Kau, Capt. Len Brose, Dave Mills, Dick Rieger, Keith Kimble, John Sahratian, and Ken Kimble. Sahratian, 2nd from R, won the 1994 National 60-and over, hard-court tennis singles title.

record and was ranked No. 1 in the nation. MSC was 6-0, and ranked No. 2. **It was MSC's first game on national TV,** and drew an audience equivalent to one-sixth of the U.S. population. On Michigan State's first play from scrimmage, fullback Dick Panin, burst through a wide hole in the Irish line and sprinted 88 yards for a touchdown. The Spartans won the game 35-0, handing legendary head coach Frank Leahy (four national championships) the worst defeat of his career. Michigan State was on the football map.

W.K. Kellogg's country estate overlooking Gull Lake, Michigan, valued at $1,000,000, was given to Michigan State.

Coach George Makris led the boxing team to its first NCAA championship. Spartan boxers Chuck Speiser and Gerald "Jed" Black won NCAA titles at 175- and 145-pounds, respectively. MSC hosted the NCAA tournament at Jenison Fieldhouse.

Seven MSC teams were ranked in the top ten nationally in 1951. In addition to the National Champion football and boxing teams, the rankings were: Swimming—No. 2; Track—No. 4; Wrestling—No. 5; Fencing—No. 7; and Gymnastics—No. 7.

Michigan State's first Big Ten title in any sport was won by the 1951 tennis team. It was the first year in which MSC was eligible to compete in the conference (except football, which would begin in 1953). The team was undefeated in ten dual meets.

Warren Druetzler won the NCAA mile run championship.

MSC's Four-Mile Relay Team set a Drake Relays Record of 17:21.2, beating the old record by 12 seconds. Team members were: Jim Kepford, John Walter, Don Makielski, and Warren Druetzler.

Michigan State was selected by the American Council on Education, at the insistence of the U.S. Department of Defense, to foster and develop the newly created University of Ryukus on the Island of Okinawa in Asian Pacific.

Taking the campus to still another continent, MSC entered a cooperative agreement to upgrade teaching and research at two agricultural colleges in Colombia, South America.

MSC established an American Studies program and a Far East & Asian Russian Studies curriculum.

A $100,000 campus-wide TV network was completed, making MSC a national leader in on-campus video communication.

An Evening College was opened in response to demands from Lansing area citizens.

Howard R. Smith, class of 1895, "pioneered the program of bovine tuberculosis eradication in the U.S. By 1951, through his work, cattle condemnations for tuberculosis had been reduced 98 percent, and the human death rate from non-respiratory tuberculosis, largely of bovine origin, had been reduced by 94 percent." He served as a

Boxing Coach George Makris holds 1951 NCAA Team Championship trophy–Michigan State's first. Spartan NCAA champions—Chuck Speiser, L, 175-lbs., and "Jed" Black, R, 145-lbs.

professor at the University of Nebraska and the University of Minnesota. (*MSU Magazine*, September, 1962).

Mary Lonn Trapp, '54, was the National Cherry Queen, and was selected as MSC's 1951 Homecoming Queen.

Fourteen soprano bells were added to the Beaumont Tower carillon.

Placement Director John F. Schlueter reported there were 6,000 interviews conducted on campus by 406 corporations.

Enrollment was 13,593. During the year 3,741 degrees were granted, including 482 master's, 54 doctorates, and 85 D.V.M.'s.

The 1951 commencement exercises were held outdoors for the first time in 12 years—in Macklin Stadium. Honorary doctorates were awarded to Dr. Alexander V. Ruthven, retiring U. of Michigan president; and Nelson A. Rockefeller, chairman of U.S. President Truman's Point Four advisory committee, who delivered the commencement address.

1952

Alumni Memorial Chapel and Giltner Hall Dedicated; National Football and Cross Country Champions—The Alumni Memorial Chapel was dedicated on Alumni Day, June 7, 1952. Inscribed on the corner stone of the chapel is this tribute: **"In Honor of Those Who Served Their Country and In Memory of Those Who Made the Supreme Sacrifice."** On the interior walls of this beautiful chapel, which has been the site of many campus weddings, are stone remnants from many European cathedrals.

Giltner Hall, a $2,400,000 Veterinary Medicine and Bacteriology Center, was dedicated in 1952. **It was the finest Vet Med facility in the nation**, containing 60 teaching and research laboratories, five operating rooms, and X-ray rooms.

The nation's first course in Packaging was offered in the College of Agriculture in 1952. This course evolved into the School of Packaging, the international leader in the field, and the first in the nation to offer graduate degrees.

Michigan State's football team reached the pinnacle again in 1952, winning its second consecutive national championship. The Spartans were undefeated in nine games, running their consecutive win streak to 24 games. They beat Michigan, Notre Dame and Penn State along the way.

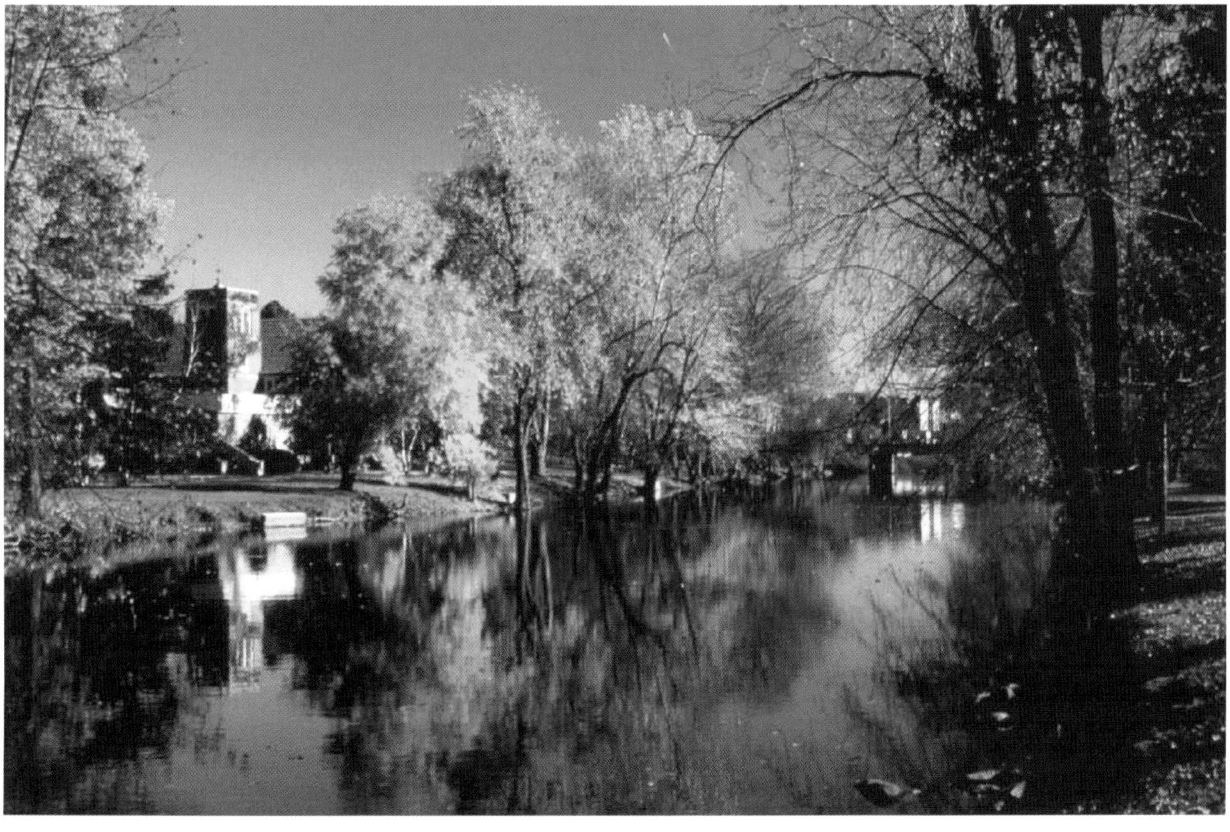

Alumni Memorial Chapel, reflected in the Red Cedar, was dedicated on June 7, 1952. Inscribed on the chapel entrance wall are the names of 487 alumni and former students killed in conflicts stretching from the Civil War to the present. The chapel is the site of many campus weddings and memorial services.

Karl Schlademan's great cross country team again won three national titles—NCAA, AAU, and IC4A. It was the harriers fourth NCAA championship.

Six MSC athletic teams were ranked in the top ten nationally—Football–No.1; Cross Country—No. 1; Boxing—No. 2; Fencing—No. 4; Swimming—No. 4; and Gymnastics—No. 6.

Swimmer Clarke Scholes, Big Ten and NCAA 100-yard freestyle champion, **won the Olympic gold medal in the 100-meter freestyle and set a new Olympic record** at the 1952 Games in Helsinki, Finland. Seven other Spartans were Olympic team members in other sports.

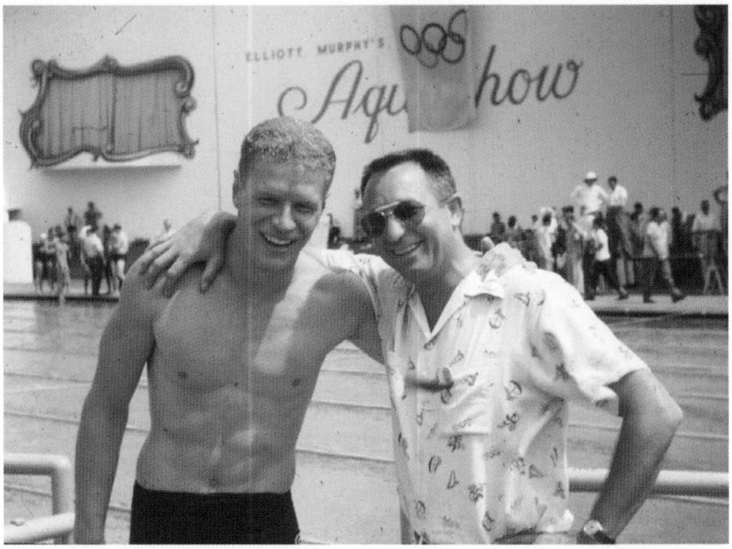

1952 Olympic 100-Meter Gold Medal Winner Clarke Scholes, (L) with MSC swimming coach Charlie McCaffree at Olympic trials in Flushing Meadows, N.Y. Scholes set a new 100-meter record at the Helsinki, Finland Olympic Games. MSU's indoor and outdoor varsity swimming pools are named for McCaffree.

In recognition of its role in **training more teachers than any institution in Michigan, and in leading all Big Ten universities in the production of teachers**, the Department of Education gained status, being elevated to the School of Education.

Reflecting on Michigan State's outreach with Cooperative Extension services and to overseas educational institutions, and the new Continuing Education thrust for adults, President Hannah proclaimed, **"If this university had a motto it would be 'Service,' for MSC was created for the purpose of service alone."** Referring to benefits of MSC's leadership educational outreach and that of other universities, Hannah wrote, **"Without these contributions… it is questionable whether America would have attained the pinnacle of strength on which she stands, and inherited the leadership of the free world which is now her privilege and her burden."**

Hannah stated that **the Michelite bean developed "by Michigan State crop scientists has resulted in more income for Michigan farmers than has been spent by the college on agricultural research from 1887 to the present time."**

Marvin D. Livingood, '52, wrote, "I proposed on the banks of the Red Cedar River. We were married the following spring near campus. Now four years past our Golden Anniversary, I count Agnes as one of the greatest gifts MSU ever gave me."

The 1952 college budget was $27,754, 038. Enrollment was 14,085. At graduation, 3,300 degrees were granted.

The Library reached a milestone of 500,000 volumes.

1953

President Hannah Named U.S. Deputy Secretary of Defense; Concern for Students Emphasized; MSC Wins First Big Ten Football Title—Dr. John A. Hannah was tapped by U.S. President Dwight Eisenhower to be Deputy Secretary of Defense in charge of manpower and personnel. President Hannah was granted a year's leave of absence.

Michigan State's reputation as a caring and friendly institution was evidenced in a number of programs aimed at helping students in their adjustment to college life.

Improvement Services were instituted to salvage students capable of doing college work, but who were inadequately prepared in writing, reading, mathematics, or speech. President Hannah stated that this program prevented "a tremendous waste of human resources."

A Personal Adjustment Clinic was established in the Olin Health Center to help troubled students deal with campus life. The staff included two mental hygienists and a part-time psychiatrist, and M.D.

Student Counseling Services were placed under the jurisdiction of the Dean of the Basic College, which was the entry point for all students.

Dormitory staffs were reorganized to make dorm life and services more satisfactory and helpful. Resident hall advisors redoubled efforts to insure that every student found living quarters with a congenial group.

President Hannah already was warning that the school should be preparing for the enrollment surge that would come with the baby boom which would hit the campus in the early 1960s.

In its first season of eligibility in Big Ten competition, the football team tied Illinois for the conference championship, and then was voted the Big Ten representative to compete in the 1954 Rose Bowl game.

The Spartans ran their nation-leading football winning streak to 28 games before losing a heartbreaker

Students play "Donkey Basketball" at the Judging Pavilion (now gone), Dec., 1953.

Dee Means, class of '53 and a senior, was elected Miss Big Ten and Miss MSC in 1953. As reigning Conference Queen, she rode the Big Ten float in the 1954 Tournament of Roses Parade with Michigan State's cheerleaders.

at Purdue, 6-0. Michigan was beaten for the fourth consecutive year, 14-6, before 51,000 at East Lansing. Ohio State was beaten 20-17 before a sell-out, 80,000+ crowd in Columbus. It marked the second time in three years that MSC had beaten Michigan and Ohio State on consecutive Saturdays, a feat accomplished by no other school.

The regular season ended with 8 wins, one loss, and a No. 3 national ranking. In their 28-game winning streak, which stretched from the middle of the 1950 season to the middle of the 1953 season, the team came from behind 18 times to win games. The 1950-1953 "Golden Era" of Spartan football saw 34 victories out of 36 games. And, Head Coach Biggie Munn and his staff produced 14 All-Americans. Few universities have experienced such success in a four-year period.

Continuing the athletic excellence of the early 1950s, **Michigan State had six teams ranked in the top ten nationally**: Football—No. 3; Boxing—No. 4; Swimming—No. 5; Cross Country—No. 6; Gymnastics—No. 7; and Wrestling—No. 8.

President Hannah emphasized, **"this college continues to be dedicated to the one-time radical theory, first put into practice here, that knowledge should not be worshiped itself as a god, but put to work for mankind."**

MSC added to the importance of Continuing Education by creating the title, Dean of Continuing Education. President Hannah stated, **"...in the years to come, the**

function of providing education services of widely varied kinds for those not enrolled… in formal degree programs may come to rival in importance and accomplishment the traditional functions of on-campus teaching." According to the president's annual report, 43,271 people were enrolled in Continuing Education courses, workshops and conferences the previous year. An additional 77,744 citizens were served through meetings and exhibitions provided by MSC.

Charles Dwight Curtiss, class of 1911, was serving as deputy commissioner of the U.S. Bureau of Public Roads.

Dr. Gus Turbeville, Ph.D., '48, elected president of Northland College, Ashland, Wisconsin.

Jean Mathieson, '49, won a Fulbright Scholarship to study in Australia.

Alma Routsong Brodie, '49, authored the novel *The Gradual Joy* (Houghton Mifflin Co, 1953), a novel about a young couple going through college on the G.I. Bill of Rights. The story was set in the MSC trailer village.

Dr. Lloyd M. Turk, was named director of the Michigan Agricultural Experiment Station. He had been head of the soil science department. Turk, co-author of *Fundamentals of Soil Science*, a popular text book, had authored many publications.

Alvie L. Smith, news editor in the Department of Information Services, was named director of Michigan State's centennial observance scheduled for 1955. He led the planning of a prodigious celebration which won MSU world-wide recognition.

Dr. G.M. Gilbert, associate professor of psychology, who served as prison psychologist at the Nuremburg War Trials, 1945-46, authored the best-seller *Nuremburg Diary*.

Dee Means, class of 1953 and a senior from Schenectady, N.Y., was elected Miss MSC and Miss Big Ten. She was a member of Kappa Alpha Theta sorority.

Campus view looking northwest–early 1950s. Shaw Hall–foreground facing Red Cedar River—and barns immediately below; Auditorium—center; Natural Science—above & right of Auditorium; Berkey Hall—above Natural Science. Note Power Plant smokestack—upper left—then located on North Campus; and the Band Shell (white arch, left center) and its expansive, sloping lawn just across Farm Lane from the Auditorium.

The Department of Information Services won national first place honors for "PR Achievement Through the Press" by the American College Public Relations Association.

Standing committees of the Faculty numbered 40, covering such activities and issues as: English, educational research, athletic council, audio visual aids, course and curriculum changes, evaluation of credits from foreign universities, honorary degrees, lecture-concert series, library, museums, orientation and freshman week, out-of-state admissions and fees, patents, scholarships, social affairs, special lectures, television, and tenure rules.

Campus cultural events included the Boston and Chicago symphonies, the New York City Opera Company, vocalist Rise Stevens, and Vladimir Horowitz.

Two-thirds of the 14,609 regular students—10,000—found part-time job opportunities on campus through the Placement Bureau. Working your way through school was typical of the Michigan State student body. **The work ethic on the East Lansing campus qualified MSC as "Hardwork U."**

President Emeritus Robert S. Shaw (Shaw Hall; Shaw Lane; Shaw Estates), former Dean of Agriculture, and one of the great builders of Michigan State, died on February 7, 1953.

The 1953 college budget was $31,105,503. Enrollment was 14,609. At commencement, 3,132 degrees were awarded.

Janice Somers, sophomore, won the 1954 Miss Michigan, Miss Big Ten and Miss MSC titles.

1954

First Nursing Class Graduates; WKAR-TV Begins Broadcasting; MSC Wins Rose Bowl—The first graduating class of the School of Nursing was outstanding. The entire Class of 1954 scored between the 92nd and 99th percentile in state examinations, and ranked exceptionally high in national achievement tests. It was a proud beginning for a nationally prominent program.

WKAR-TV—the first educational TV station east of the Mississippi—and the fourth to be operated by an American university, began broadcasting on January 15, 1954. MSC's programming was generally considered the finest produced by an educational institution. The 1954 commencement ceremonies, June 6th in Macklin Stadium, were the first ever televised, carried by WKAR-TV.

On New Year's Day 1954, Michigan State's football team won the Rose Bowl game in an exciting come-from-behind win over UCLA, 28-20. Halfback Billy Wells scored two touchdowns for the Spartans, one a 62-yard punt return, and was voted the game's most valuable player. Michigan State had 14,000 fans at the game, the largest contingent ever to represent a Big Ten team at the Rose Bowl. A ticket to the 1954 Rose Bowl cost $5.50, but the student price was $2.29. In the Tournament of Roses Parade, Dee Means, Miss MSC and Miss Big Ten, waved to parade fans from the Big Ten float which was adorned with MSC cheerleaders.

Billy Wells was not only the star of the game, but the center of the most interesting story of the Rose Bowl adventure. MSC Sports Information Director Fred Stabley learned from Wells at a pre-game practice in East Lansing, that Billy would like a date with Debbie Reynolds, his favorite movie star, when the team got to Los Angeles. Billy was a good dancer and admired Debbie's dancing ability. Unknown to Billy, Stabley contacted Big Ten representatives in L.A. who sponsored an annual pre-game dinner for the visiting

Halfback Billy Wells is stunned by hug from Debbie Reynolds at Pre-game Rose Bowl dinner. Wells wish for a date with Reynolds after the game was arranged by Bob Hope, dinner emcee. Wells scored two TDs in MSC's 28-20 win over UCLA and was voted Rose Bowl MVP.

Students do the "Hokey-Pokey" at the 1954 J-Hop in the Auditorium.

Big Ten team. These dinners always featured Bob Hope as the emcee.

At the dinner, two nights before the Rose Bowl, Bob Hope asked Billy Wells to join him on stage for a soft shoe routine. Billy, who was totally uninhibited, was in the middle of several dance steps when Debbie Reynolds slipped through the stage curtains, glided behind Billy and put her arms around him. Wells was stunned and thrilled. Debbie joined him at his dinner table, and Hope announced that he had arranged a date for Billy with Debbie following the game. Hope would pay for the whole evening. Billy got game tickets for Debbie and her parents. They watched him win the game and MVP honors. Then came a great evening of celebration. It was a once-in-a-lifetime experience.

Name Change Proposal Shot Down—A proposal to change the school's name from Michigan State College to Michigan State University was sent by the Board to the State Legislature. The Board report for 1954 stated, "Due to unexpectedly violent opposition of the University of Michigan the proposal was eventually withdrawn in the interests of educational harmony."

The University of Michigan Board of Regents stated that giving Michigan State the University designation "...is an infringement on the University's name, is probably unconstitutional, and has implications for higher education in Michigan that are not spelled out." (*MSC Record*, January, 1954). This reasoning was utter nonsense. The *Michigan Daily*, U-M student newspaper, did not support the U-M Regents, and the U-M student legislature voted down a proposal to support the Regent's opposition to the name change. More than 8,000 MSC students signed a petition that was sent to the legislature requesting the name change.

MSC leaders pointed out that there were many states in which two schools were designated universities—such as Ohio University and Ohio State University, which had co-existed as universities for 75 years. The *MSC Record* (January, 1954) mused, "...it is the feeling of Michigan State officials that the people of Michigan would be...able to cope with the mental problem involved (differentiating between the two universities)."

The naming battle went into 1955 where it was resolved to Michigan State's satisfaction.

MSC's international educational leadership was evident. The U.S. government invited MSC to help establish the first school of business administration in Brazil. A total of 192 technicians from 43 countries were on campus for training. Three hundred foreign students from 52 nations were studying at MSC, ranking the school among the highest overseas enrollments in the U.S.

The Veterinary Medicine graduate study program exceeded that of any college in the nation, with 127 students studying in five departments.

Four new graduate programs were initiated during the year—a Ph.D. in Philosophy; a master's in Landscape Architecture; a master's in Hotel, Restaurant and General Institutional Management; and a master's of science in Agricultural Engineering.

A curriculum in Public Relations was being developed by the Department of Journalism.

A new Listening Comprehension course was initiated. President Hannah reported, "So far as is known, MSC is the only institution in the U.S. that requires all students to take a course in listening, one hour a week for one academic year."

The course in Packaging was the only one of its kind in America.

MSC moved to the front ranks of teacher education in the U.S., producing 1,002 certified teachers.

Ronald K. Evans, 1912, retired as an executive vice president of General Motors Corp. He had earlier served six years as general manager of GM's Adam Opel car subsidiary in Germany.

P. Eduard Geldhof, 1914, was vice president of engineering and research for Whirlpool Corporation. He held more than 100 patents on home laundry equipment.

Arthur F. Vinson, E.E. '29, was elected vice president of manufacturing for General Electric.

Janice Somers, '56 and a sophomore, won the Miss Big Ten and Miss Michigan titles.

Bob Hoke won the NCAA 157-pound wrestling title.

Herb Odom won the NCAA 147-pound boxing title.

Five MSC athletic teams finished in the top ten nationally: Baseball—No.3; Gymnastics—No. 5; Boxing—No. 6; Wrestling—No. 6; and Swimming—No. 8.

Ralph H. Young (Ralph H. Young Track & Field) retired after 31 years of distinguished service as Director of Athletics. Young built the Michigan State athletic program into a national all-sports powerhouse. In 1950, five MSC teams finished in the top ten nationally; in 1951 it was seven; in 1952-six; in 1953-six; and in 1954-five. This remarkable record was the result of Young's excellent selection and nurturing of head coaches–eight of whom were inducted into National Halls of Fame for their coaching—Fendley Collins, wrestling; Ben VanAlstyne, basketball; John H. Kobs, baseball; Biggie Munn, football; Charles McCaffree, swimming; Charles Bachman, football; Pete Newell, basketball; and Amo Bessone, hockey.

In addition, Young selected George Szypula, gymnastics coach, and George Makris, boxing coach, both of whom led Michigan State to NCAA team titles.

Moreover, Young's excellent human relations and public relations skills greatly aided Michigan State's bid to gain Big Ten membership.

Biggie Munn (Munn Arena), retired as Head Football Coach and was named Athletic Director.

Hugh "Duffy" Daugherty (Daugherty Football Building), Munn's line coach for seven years, was named Head Football Coach.

The 1954 college budget was $34,001,219. Enrollment was 15,525. At the June 6, 1954 commencement–tenth anniversary to the day of the WWII D-Day invasion of France–2,888 degrees were presented. **These were the last degrees to carry the name Michigan State College.** WKAR-TV made it the first commencement ever televised.

1955

Centennial Year: It's Michigan State University! National Boxing and Cross Country Champions—An inspiring, year-long Centennial Celebration was capped by legislative action which gave Michigan State **the University designation** it had earned and deserved. Alumni and friends bombarded the legislature with letters, telegrams, phone calls and personal contacts urging them to support the name-change bill, and they did.

The Centennial Celebration was an exquisitely planned series of elaborate and meaningful events that dominated the school year. Alvie L. Smith, director of MSC's news bureau, was director of the Centennial program, which had 500-member faculty, and 300-member student committees. Smith would go on to become a top communications executive with General Motors.

Theme of the Centennial was appropriately borrowed from Abraham Lincoln's Gettysburg Address: **"It is for us the living to be dedicated here to the unfinished work."** It was Lincoln, of course, who signed the Morrill Act into law in 1862, creating America's land-grant colleges, of which Michigan State was the first.

One thousand world leaders in education, government, business, science and industry came to the campus on February 12, 1955 to celebrate Founders' Day, the 100th anniversary of the founding of the Pioneer Land-Grant College. Dr. James B. Conant, President Emeritus of Harvard University and then U.S. High Commissioner for Germany, addressed a major convocation in the afternoon. Not only was Michigan State the first Agricultural College in America, it served importantly as the "Mother" and the model for the land-grant system of colleges and universities.

A special commemorative U.S. Postage Stamp was presented to the Presidents of Michigan State and Penn

Lone coed returning to her dorm—1955. Union in background.

State honoring the Centennials of both institutions. Michigan State was founded February 12, 1855, and Penn State on February 22, 1855. The stamp proclaimed, **"First of the Land-Grant Colleges." It was the first U.S. postage stamp ever to honor any U.S. college or university.**

Jackson & Perkins released its "Spartan" rose in 1955 in honor of MSU's centennial.

Universities across the globe sent MSU congratulatory proclamations on the centennial milestone.

Other major events that punctuated the Centennial Year were: eleven scholarly symposia, **the largest exposition of farm machinery in the history of the U.S.**, many national conferences, a musical production titled "Michigan Dream," a Centennial alumni birthday party, and a student Homecoming parade titled, "A March of Memories."

In all, the 40 elegantly orchestrated Centennial Celebration events were seen and participated in by an estimated 1,000,000 people. Coverage of the year-long effort by radio, TV, newspapers and magazines reached 60 million persons around the world.

The College of Communication Arts was established July 1, 1955. It was the first of its kind in the nation. It brought together: journalism, advertising, rhetoric and public address, radio, TV, drama, speech correction and audiology.

President Hannah recognized Professor Durward B. Varner, "who served with great distinction as the Director of the Cooperative Extension Service," by making him the first person at MSU to be given the title vice president. Varner was appointed Vice President for Off-Campus Education & Director of the Continuing Education Service.

Mrs. Ruby Niebauer, College of Home Economics, won two international film awards—one for an educational film (Italy), and one at the Annual Film Festival at Stamford, Connecticut.

MSC's boxing and cross country teams each won NCAA titles in 1955. It was MSU's second NCAA boxing title; and the fifth NCAA cross country title. The football team was ranked number one in the nation by

First U.S. postage stamp to honor any college or university.

"A March of Memories"—1955 Student Centennial-Homecoming Parade—drew 100,000+ spectators. Grand Prize float—"A Guide to Our Goals"—was produced by SAE and Chi Omega. MSU President Hannah (not shown) rode in the parade with Spartan great Robin Roberts, Philadelphia Phillies' Baseball Hall of Fame pitcher.

Boand, and second by the Associated Press and United Press International.

The 1955 college budget was $37,854,341. Enrollment was 17,176. During the year, 2,908 degrees were granted.

Admiral Arthur W. Radford, Chairman of the U.S. Joint Chiefs of Staff, made the 1955 commencement address before 20,000 in Macklin Stadium. **The 2,908 graduates received the first diplomas reading: "Michigan State University."**

James H. Steele, DVM 1941

"Father" of American Veterinary Public Health
U.S. Assistant Surgeon General for Veterinary Affairs

Dr. James H. Steele, '41 DVM,
"Father" of American Veterinary Public Health

Dr. James H. Steele, DVM, class of 1941, has been recognized as the "Father" of American Veterinary Public Health.

He earned this designation through his leadership in the veterinary profession, which included **founding, or co-founding the American Veterinary Medical Association's Section on Public Health; the American Board of Veterinary Public Health (now the American College of Veterinary Preventive Medicine); the American Veterinary Epidemiological Society; and the Conference of Public Health Veterinarians. He is a worldwide medical pioneer.**

After graduating with his veterinary medicine degree at Michigan State in 1941, Steele earned a master of public health degree from Harvard University in 1942.

His first position was with the Ohio State Health Department, followed by a tour of duty with the U.S. Public Health Service. Next, Steele served with the Communicable Disease Center (now Center for Disease Control) Atlanta, Georgia, starting in 1947. There, he established the nation's first veterinary public health program.

Steele also served as a professor of environmental health at the University of Texas-Houston, and as director of the Institute for Environmental Health for the University of Texas School of Public Health, from which he retired as professor emeritus.

Later in his career, after serving at the U.S. Public Health Service, Dr. Steele rose to become the U.S. Assistant Surgeon General for Veterinary Affairs.

He served as vice president of the American Association of World Health from 1965 to 1985. He served on the U.S. President's Commission on Consumer Affairs from 1969 to 1989, and on many international fronts, including the Pan American Health Organization and the World Health Organization, and helped establish veterinary health programs from Latin America to Russia.

Steele's national honors include the Public Health Service's Meritorious Service Medal, the Distinguished Service Award from the Public Health Service, and the Bronfman Award from the American Public Health Association.

Honors given to Steele by Michigan State University include, MSU College of Veterinary Medicine Distinguished Alumnus Award in 1973; MSU's Distinguished Alumnus Award in 1958; and an MSU Centennial Award for Distinguished Service in 1955.

1956 **New Library Opened; Rose Bowl Champions; NCAA Cross Country Champions**—Michigan State's long-sought, first-class Library building opened in January, 1956. It was the nation's fifth largest library in terms of floor space under a single roof. On January 13, the flow of books from the old Library (now the Museum) to the ultra-modern facility began. On average, 7,000 volumes were moved each day.

The move was timed so that no book was out of circulation more than 30 minutes. On one day, 17,000 volumes were moved when 140 student volunteers formed a human chain from the old Library, across West Circle Drive, and into the new building. They passed books by hand like an old-time bucket brigade. The entire transfer of 765,187 books was completed on April 6, 1956.

New Year's Day 1956 saw the Spartans win their second Rose Bowl game in three years, defeating UCLA, 17-14 in dramatic fashion. With seconds remaining in the game and the score tied 14-14, MSU's future two-time Super Bowl Champion quarterback Earl Morrall declared in the huddle, "Dave Kaiser is going to kick the field goal." MSU lined up for the field goal. Dave Kaiser took a practice kick, swinging his right leg through the normal kicking motion. To his surprise the ball was snapped unexpectedly. Morrall caught the ball and placed it on the 31 yard line. Kaiser quickly backed up and took a one-step kick into the ball. He said, "I saw it go toward the goal posts. I turned my back to the goal posts to watch the official behind me to see if it would be good. It was! I was jumped on by team captain Buck Nystrom, followed by the entire team." Kaiser, who played offensive and defensive end, said, "It was the hardest I was hit all day." It was a 41-yard victory kick! MSU 17, UCLA 14.

The game was television's all-time, top-rated college football bowl game, gaining a 67 percent share of the national TV audience. In 2000, Dave Kaiser was named to the Rose Bowl Hall of Fame, the first Spartan so honored.

The MSU cross country team won its sixth NCAA title.

Major curriculum changes were made in the College of Engineering to focus on teaching the science of engineering, leaving to industry the teaching of the art of engineering.

Beautiful new Library opened in 1956 was the nation's fifth largest in square footage under one roof. Fountain and reflecting pool were gifts of the class of 1964, the decorative fountain system was a gift of the class of 1968, and the fountain renovation—a gift of the class of 1983. Today the Library houses a Cyber Café and an Electronic Resources Help room to aid student computer searches of databases. The main Library and 11 on-campus branches house 4.5 million volumes and provide 8,500 electronic journal links, 300 online indexes, and 600 other electronic texts and links.

President Hannah wrote in his annual report, **"Research is not an expense—it is our best investment in the future."**

He also reported, "An ingenious dairy researcher at the Michigan Agricultural Experiment Station and a veterinarian surgeon combined talents to make **the most substantial advance in the science of dairy cattle nutrition in 25 years**. Researchers are now able to determine how much of the food intake is absorbed through the stomach walls before it reaches the intestines, a heretofore relatively unknown area of dairy nutrition."

MSU horticultural researchers discovered that spraying tomato seedlings with N-arylphtalanic acid doubled the early yield in tomato crops.

Another MSU research team comprised of an agricultural chemist, a veterinarian, and a swine nutritionist, developed a way to prevent a swine disease called parakeratosis.

Other MSU researchers developed a high-yielding bush-type bean as well as a high-yield, scab-resistant potato variety called the Onaway.

The Labor & Industrial Relations Center and the Highway Traffic Safety Center were established as functions of the Continuing Education Service.

A broadcast "first" was initiated by WKAR radio: a 5-minute daily report on the activities of the Michigan legislature.

Dr. Floyd W. Owen (Owen Hall), '02 and '30, died leaving MSU an estate of $420,000 to be used "for a building and faculty club." He had been president of the Crescent Co. of Detroit, and managing director of a large Australian and New Zealand firm.

Buildings completed during the year included the tall, sound-proof Music Practice Building, and the final three dormitories in the Brody complex.

The south end of Macklin Stadium (now Spartan Stadium) was elevated to match the height of the east and west stands, adding 9,000 seats and upping the capacity to 60,000.

The Dean of Students addressed a perennial issue: "Automobiles present the most difficult problem. They have given more difficulty to universities perhaps than any other single thing."

The MSU Fund's name was changed to the MSU Development Fund.

The 1956 university budget was $44,848,578. Enrollment totaled 18,806. Nearly a quarter of the students were married. At commencement, 3,051 degrees were granted.

1957

Nation's First Dean of International Programs; Meadow Brook Farms Given to MSU—Michigan State led the nation in establishing the first Office of International Programs and naming the first dean—Professor Glen L. Taggart—in 1957. Today, MSU still is a national leader in International Programs, with 193 programs in 60 different countries, on seven continents.

MSU's Honors College was established with Dr. Stanley Idzerda as its director. It was the first undergraduate honors program at any of America's 74 land-grant universities.

A doctorate program for the College of Home Economics was approved.

An annual Canadian-American seminar was initiated.

One of the premier gifts ever received by Michigan State was given to the university in 1957 by Mr. and Mrs. Alfred G. Wilson of Rochester, Michigan. They gave their magnificent 1,600-acre Meadow Brook Farms and Estate and $2 million with which to establish a university in Oakland County, Michigan. The estate included the classic 1927, 110-room Meadow Brook Hall mansion, and an 18-hole golf course which had been built by one of the founders of the Dodge Motor Company, later a part of the Chrysler Corporation.

MSU lost no time in tapping **Durward B. Varner**, its vice president of Off-Campus education, to be the **first Chancellor and builder of MSU-Oakland**, a four-year university located on the Meadowbrook estate. In 1970, MSU gave up its administration of MSU-Oakland, and it became Oakland University. Today the school serves 16,000 students.

Michigan Legislature cuts its support for higher education—President Hannah lamented the Michigan legislature's refusal to authorize any capital improvements on any college or university campus for the 1957-58 fiscal year.

Pinning serenade by SAE fraternity at Tau Beta Phi sorority—1957.

The football stadium was double-decked in 1957, adding 16,000 seats, increasing capacity from 60,000 to 76,000. The name was changed from Macklin to Spartan Stadium. The triple-decked, 80-yard long pressbox was named for Fred W. Stabley, Sr., MSU sports information director (SID), 1948-1980, and SID Hall of Fame member.

Hannah reported, "(MSU) tried to build new classrooms and laboratories with a portion of income from student fees. This passed both houses of the legislature…but was eliminated in conference committee."

"The legislature (also insisted) that fees charged to students be raised substantially. This runs counter to the historic philosophy that education should be made available to Michigan young people at a minimum cost."

Additionally, "…the legislature (insisted) that the cost of water, lights and other utilities be charged against income from dormitories and married housing units, which had the effect of forcing a substantial increase in rates charged to students…"

Anthony Hall and an addition to the Olin Health Center were completed.

A Restaurant Equipment Testing & Research Laboratory was established in Brody Hall in conjunction with the National Restaurant Association.

The Men's Intramural Building (IM-West) was opened, as was a new swimming pool addition to the Women's Gymnasium (IM-Circle).

From Macklin to Spartan Stadium—Eight-thousand-seat second decks were added to both sides of the football stadium, increasing capacity from 60,000 to 76,000. At the same time, **the name was changed to Spartan Stadium.**

The 1957 football team was voted national champion by Billingsley, Dunkel, and Sagarin, and ranked third by the AP and UPI.

Forddy Anderson's Spartan basketball team tied for the Big Ten title with Indiana, **and advanced to its first NCAA Final Four appearance**. The team lost in

All-American "Jumping" Johnny Green leaps for rebound. He led MSU to its first NCAA Final Four.

triple-overtime to eventual national champion North Carolina, 74-70.

Karl Schlademan's cross country team won the Big Ten title and finished second in the NCAA championships.

Charley McCaffree's swimming team won the Big Ten title and finished third in the NCAA championships.

The 1957 university budget was $49,534,853. Enrollment was 18,965. U.S. Vice President Richard M. Nixon gave the 1957 commencement address to the 3,740 graduates.

1958

MSU-Oakland Launched; NCAA Cross Country and Gymnastics Champions—Ground was broken for the first building at Michigan State University-Oakland on May 2, 1958 in Rochester, Michigan.

President Hannah reacted strongly to legislative budget cuts amounting to $1,015,000. He declared, "...this stunning decision was symptomatic of a growing national misapprehension that many other things are more **important** than good, sound education for our talented young people. Suffice it to say that if this illusion persists, it bodes ill for our country and its future."

WKAR Radio won the George Foster Peabody Award for public service for a series of highway safety programs produced with MSU's Highway Traffic Safety Center. **This was the first time since 1942 that a university had won this national award.**

Liberty Hyde Bailey (Bailey Hall), class of 1882, was honored with a U.S. postage stamp, issued on the 100th anniversary of his birth. Bailey was the "Father" of American horticulture, and the most prolific agricultural author in U.S. history, producing 75 books, and editing 117 others.

MSU dairy scientists devised a new high-temperature method of milk pasteurization which would extend the life of refrigerated milk by some 11 days.

A Ph.D. program was approved for the College of Communication Arts.

A Science and Mathematics Teaching Center was established by the College of Science and Arts in cooperation with the College of Education.

New campus structures opened in 1958 included: the **Education Building**, one of the finest education centers in the nation; the world-class **Student Services Building;** and **Van Hoosen Hall**, named for Dr. Sarah Van Hoosen Jones, an apartment residence for women; and **500 more married apartments—bringing the total to 2,124, leading all other colleges and universities in married housing.**

Father Jerome MacEachin, St. Thomas Aquinas parish priest and MSU football team chaplain, raised $700,000 to build the St. John's student center on M.A.C.

World-class Student Services Building, completed in 1958, houses America's finest University Placement Center, Student Government, and offices of the *State News* and *The Red Cedar Log* (yearbook).

Avenue. In winning Catholic alumni contributions, he pointed out to them that **MSU had more Catholic students than the University of Notre Dame.**

MSU provided 10,000 campus student parking spaces—a space-to-student ratio surpassing all other Big Ten universities. Some 42 percent of the student body had cars registered.

The first 18 holes of **Forest Akers Golf Course opened.**

The cross country team won the NCAA, IC4A and Big Ten titles. It was the harriers seventh NCAA championship.

Gymnastics coach George Szypula led the gymnastics team to their first NCAA title.

Soccer coach Gene Kenney led the MSU team to their third consecutive undefeated regular season. In 1956, 1957, and 1958, the Spartan kickers won 19, lost 0, and tied 3.

The 1958 university budget was $55,835,646. Enrollment was 18,531. At commencement, 3,979 degrees were granted.

1959

Kresge Art Center MSU-Oakland opened; NCAA Cross Country Champions—The beautiful Kresge Art Center and Museum opened in 1959. This facility is home to the Department of Art of the College of Arts and Letters, as well as a popular art museum and gallery.

Coeds exit Mason Hall for the tennis courts–1958.

Calling for a date "1958 Style"—before room and cell phones.

Michigan State University-Oakland opened its doors in the fall of 1959 with a freshman class of 500. *Time* magazine described MSU-O as "a top-drawer liberal arts college."

Durward B. "Woody" Varner and his wife Paula, the new Chancellor and First Lady of MSU-O, were the perfect choice to energize the building of the university. During their tenure, **the Varners inaugurated the Meadowbrook Music Festival and the Meadowbrook Theatre, the home of Michigan's only resident theatre group**. These are two of the most popular venues in Southeastern Michigan. What the Varners built is today an educational treasure for Oakland County residents and 16,000 students (2003). In 1970, Woody and Paula Varner went on to lead the University of Nebraska-Lincoln.

The legislature reduced the university budget by $1,000,000. President Hannah reported, "Salary increases were foregone; step increases suspended; budgets reduced; travel curtailed; and equipment funds slashed." He wrote, "…some of our able, experienced teachers and research workers accepted offers from universities outside of Michigan." Hannah stated, "(I)…question whether the people of Michigan really appreciated the tremendous importance of higher education and the value of the work done by those who teach their sons and daughters, pursue the research for new truths, and seek ways to apply accumulated knowledge for the benefit of mankind."

The position of Provost was created, "with responsibility for both on-campus and off-campus academic affairs." Dr. Paul A. Miller, a distinguished sociologist, who had

Kresge Art Center opened in 1959. It houses the Kresge Art Museum, and Department of Art studios, classrooms and offices.

served as director of the Cooperative Extension Service, was named the first Provost.

The College of Veterinary Medicine led the nation in graduate enrollment.

The pioneering College of Communication Arts established two departments that are leaders in American education: The Department of Advertising, and the Department of Television-Radio-Film.

Frederick H. Mueller, '14, was appointed U.S. Secretary of Commerce by U.S. President Dwight Eisenhower. He was MSU's first Presidential Cabinet member.

Hazen S. Stevens, '42, was elected president of U.S. Van Lines at age 39 in 1959. Stevens was the first president of the Epsilon Eta Chapter of Alpha Tau Omega at State in 1940, when the fraternity changed its status from the local Eclectic Society to ATO.

Diane Lee, freshman liberal arts major, entered MSU-Oakland as the **1959 Miss Alaska**, a title won in America's Junior Miss Pageant.

Patricia Visser, freshman business major, enrolled at the East Lansing campus as the **1959 Miss Hawaii**, a title won in the Miss Universe competition.

Graduate students at MSU increased from 359 in 1940 to 3,638 at the beginning of the 1958-1959 academic year—a ten-fold increase.

President Hannah said educators in other parts of the country referred to **MSU's men's residence hall program as "the best and most advanced."** The reference was to the quality of rooms, food, out-of-class recreation, study facilities, and social events.

The College of Business and Public Service established a Doctor of Business Administration degree.

Life magazine reported it used a greater number of stories from MSU during the year than from any other college or university in the U.S.

The Wall Street Journal of November 21, 1959 reported, "the career carnival at Michigan State University, one of the oldest and largest throughout the country, (generated) 4,000 fall interviews and 7,000 winter interviews (for students)."

MSU's cross country team won its eighth NCAA title as well as the IC4A title.

The ice hockey team was runner-up in the NCAA championships.

The name of the governing Board of the University was changed from The State Board of Agriculture to The Board of Trustees.

"Life in the Union grill became such an institution that the Union Board...awarded the title of 'Grillhound of the Week,'" according to Patricia Grauer writing on 'The

Frederick H. Mueller, '14, sworn in as U.S. Secretary of Commerce by Attorney General William Rogers as President Dwight Eisenhower observes–1959.

Fifties at MSC' in the March issue of the *MSU Alumni Association Magazine.*

The 1959 university budget was $56,471,680. Enrollment was 19,217.

Canadian Prime Minister John Diefenbaker gave the graduation address. A total of 3,990 degrees were granted.

1960

Committee on the Future of the University Reports; Future President John F. Kennedy Visits Campus—President Hannah's Committee on the Future of the University, formed in 1959 and chaired by Professor Dale E. Hathaway of the Department of Agricultural Economics, reported more than 60 specific recommendations for university operations, objectives, and philosophy.

In the area of forward vision, the committee said MSU should aspire to be a university which:

1. Achieves international distinction by emphasizing research, graduate and professional programs,

2. Develops and maintains vigorous 4-year undergraduate programs and off-campus programs of every-increasing quality, and

3. Carefully selects the programs in which it will be distinguished and allocates its resources in the fashion that will best achieve them.

The committee also defined several broad goals:

1. Focus attention on the development of graduate and advanced professional programs and on the development of undergraduate programs which build upon them.

2. Emphasize the advancement of knowledge through research.

3. Give higher priority to the development of the fundamental areas of knowledge and to the relationship of these areas to the problems of men.

4. Place greater emphasis on the liberal education components of all undergraduate curricula.

As a result of the recommendations, an Educational Policy Committee was formed to work with the provost on educational concerns. And, five-year plans—under the direction of the provost—were developed for all colleges and departments.

Campaigning U.S. Presidential candidate John F. Kennedy visited the campus in October, 1960, three weeks prior to his election as President of the United States. *MSU Alumni Association Magazine,* reported, "...some 12,000 students greeted him (Kennedy) with the kind of enthusiasm that later generations reserved for rock stars."

After three consecutive years of cutting university budgets, the legislature increased appropriations to MSU, allowing faculty salary increases, and step increases to classified personnel.

Owen Graduate Center was opened as a residence hall for 476 graduate students. A gift of $420,000 from Floyd W. Owen, Class of 1902, made the building possible.

A Biological Research Center was opened.

A complex of buildings at MSU's Kellogg Gull Lake Biological Research Station were put into service, making this complex one of the finest in America.

Owen Graduate Center opened in 1960 and housed 476 graduate students.

The Saturday Evening Post of February 13, 1960, proclaimed, **"Michigan State University—America's first state agricultural college—is now turning itself into one of the country's first universities in total service to the world and in pursuit of total knowledge.** It is inconceivable that any alert human being could not find his interest at this university. It has the only Dean of International Programs in the world. Its faculty members go out to Brazil, Okinawa, Vietnam, Pakistan clearing the corners of the earth for more abundant and democratic development."

President Hannah reported, **"We had more faculty members at work overseas last year than any other American university."**

In eastern Nigeria, MSU worked to support the opening of the University of Nigeria at Nsukka in the fall of 1960. Leadership was provided by Professor George Johnson.

MSU provided agricultural education counsel to the faculty and students of the National Taiwan University.

The College of Engineering was inaugurating a graduate level project at the Guindy Engineering College at Madras, India; and at Poona College of Engineering at Bombay, India.

Dr. Clyde F. Cairy, Veterinary Medicine professor, was elected president of the American Society of Veterinary Physiologists and Pharmacologists.

Russell F. Gustke, '41, U.S. Air Force Brigadier General, was serving as commander of Ellington Air Force Base, Texas. He had been wing commander of the 440th Fighter Bomb Wing. Gustke flew 165 combat missions in P-38s and P-51s in the European Theater in World War II.

The College of Agriculture created a Food Science Department, under Dr. Bernard S. Schweigert.

The University College, formerly Basic College, prepared to offer a "Great Issues" course.

The Board of Trustees recommended "the desirability of establishing a medical school."

Dr. Gordon A. Sabine, Dean of the College of Communication Arts, was named MSU's vice president for special projects.

Gene Grazia and Weldon Olson won Olympic gold medals as members of the champion U.S. hockey team, which defeated Russia.

A mile of 18-inch wide concrete bike paths were set on campus.

The popular and beautiful Band Shell—a gift of the class of 1937—was torn down to make way for Bessey Hall. This treasured facility, which backed up to the Red Cedar and looked up a sweeping lawn, was the scene of many outdoor band and symphony concerts, fraternity and sorority sings, pep rallies, and graduation ceremonies. A monument recognizing this gem was placed at the southwest corner of Bessey Hall along the Red Cedar walkway.

The University budget for 1960 was $61,540,906. Enrollment reached 21,157, topping the twenty thousand mark for the first time. At commencement, 4,239 degrees were awarded.

Former U.S. President Harry S. Truman delivered the commencement address.

1961

MSU Leads Nation in Building "Living-Learning" Residence Halls—To improve the campus learning environment and make greater academic use of residence halls, MSU set a national trend by building classrooms, libraries, laboratories, faculty offices, and assembly areas into new dormitories. The creation of "Living-Learning" residences, where students took many classes, made learning easier and more convenient. It also created a small college atmosphere inside a large international university.

The Albert H. and Sarah A. Case Halls, located at Shaw and Chestnut, were the first "Living-Learning" units, and were completed in 1961. Albert H. Case was a 1902 graduate of M.A.C., and captain of the 1901 football team. His wife, Sarah Avery Case, also graduated from M.A.C., and taught physical training to women students at the college in the early 1900s.

President Hannah once again questioned the legislature's reticence to fund the university's growing needs. He wrote, "It is a...paradox that Michigan committed itself as a state to the principle of low tuition in public institutions at the very beginnings of its history when its financial resources were scanty and precarious, and is questioning that principle in these days when it is possessed of resources beyond the fondest dreams of its founders."

Hannah pointed out that "The university had raised tuition 55 percent since 1954" to cover underfunded costs. To operate with reduced support, fees for non-Michigan students were raised to $750; the Highway Traffic Safety Center was closed; support for the Upper Peninsula Experiment Station was withdrawn; the Cooperative Extension Service budget was cut $100,000; all non-academic department expenditures were cut ten percent; and students were required to pay $1 per quarter for the student newspaper and $1 for each university catalog.

The National Mathematics Championship (Annual Putnam competition) was won by MSU over 124 other colleges and universities in the U.S. and Canada. Finishing behind MSU were MIT, Caltech, Harvard, and Dartmouth. The MSU team included Frederick J. Gilman, senior physics major from East Lansing; Robert E. Greene, sophomore mathematics major from Knoxville, TN; and Richard D. Freeman, senior mathematics major from Midland, MI. Gilman graduated with an all-A record for 202 credits of un-repeated work—the first MSU student to do so.

Ten MSU students were selected for Woodrow Wilson Fellowships in 1961.

Nancy Ann Fleming, Miss America and Miss Michigan for 1961 enrolled at MSU. The Montague, MI freshman majored in home economics and communication arts. She would graduate with honors and a 3.8 GPA in 1965.

Frederick C. Belen, '37, was named U.S. Assistant Postmaster General, heading the Bureau of Operations, with responsibility for 35,200 post offices and 560,000 postal employees.

Dr. Leland G. Merrill, Jr., '42, who captained the 1942 wrestling team and won a wrestling bronze medal in the 1948 Olympics, was named dean of the College of Agriculture at Rutgers University.

H.C. "Dutch" Diehl, class of 1918, was managing director of Trans-American Refrigerated Services, a national network of refrigerated warehouse firms.

G.F. "Brick" Dressell, '24, elected president of Ethyl-Dow Chemical Co.

Dr. Karl G. Merrill, M.A. '38, vice president emeritus of Ferris State University, had a dormitory at the university named in his honor—Merrill Hall.

John S. Pingel, '39, former All-American halfback and Lt. Col. in WWII, was executive vice president of Ross Roy Advertising in Detroit.

Nancy Ann Fleming, Miss America and Miss Michigan for 1961, enrolled at MSU. She was a freshman from Montague, Michigan.

The new **Eugene C. Eppley Center opened**. It housed Graduate Studies in the Service Industries as well as the Graduate School of Business. The Eppley Foundation, established by Omaha, Nebraska hotel chain owner, gave $1.5 million toward the construction of the building.

Bessey Hall, named for Dr. Ernest Bessey, world-famous botanist and first dean of MSU's Undergraduate School, was opened and was to house the University College.

The College of Science and Arts was split into three new colleges: Arts & Letters, Natural Science, and Social Science.

The Department of Biochemistry was established by the Colleges of Agriculture and Science & Arts.

A Learning Resources Center was established in the College of Education Building to encourage the use of closed-circuit TV (CCTV), film, teaching machines, and programmed studies. Twenty classrooms in the building were wired for CCTV. Major buildings on campus also were linked by coaxial cable, opening the possibility of extensive use of CCTV.

A new Dairy Teaching & Research Center, and an Endocrine Research Unit were opened by the College of Agriculture.

Jack Breslin was named Secretary of the Board of Trustees. Jack Shingleton, director emeritus of Placement and Student Services and Trustee emeritus, said of Breslin in 2002, "He was President Hannah's closest confidant, and was like a son to him."

President Hannah reported "In the fall of 1959, 43 percent of freshmen had ranked in the upper quartile of their graduating classes." In 1960, 60 percent were so ranked. He projected that 73 percent of the entering freshmen would be in the upper quartile in 1961.

The Board of Trustees voted to put ROTC (Reserve Officer Training Corps.) on a voluntary basis starting in 1963.

Retired General Douglas MacArthur delivered the commencement address, and gave a warm tribute to Michigan State. He stated, **"no institution of learning is more devotedly dedicating its full strength to the preservation of those fundamental principles upon which this nation was conceived and nurtured to greatness."**

The university budget for 1961 was $66,195,226. Enrollment was 22,724. At commencement 4,274 degrees were granted.

1962

Record Female Enrollment—A record 40.7 percent of the 25,040 students enrolled at Michigan State in 1962 were women. **MSU led all other Big Ten universities in the number of women enrolled in undergraduate classes**, and in the number of women housed on campus.

President Hannah reported that the cost of education would continue to grow. He said, "Most of the increase is directly related to the rate of expansion of human knowledge, which we aid and abet to the best of our ability."

Hannah wrote, "...the legislature strongly recommended that an increase in tuition and fees be imposed to meet the impending deficit. Trustees resisted as best they could (but) increased fees $15 per term for Michigan residents and $40 per term for non-residents." MSU's $324 fee for three terms compared unfavorably with Indiana—$235, Purdue—$240, Illinois—$270, and Michigan, which

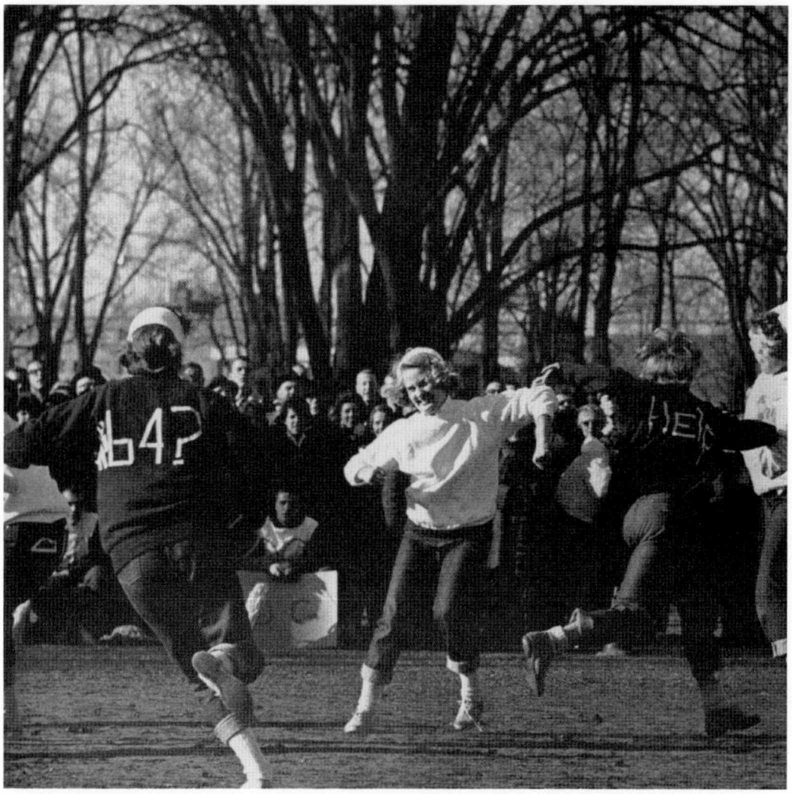

Record MSU coed enrollment of 11,768 in 1962 led all other Big Ten universities, as did the number of women living on campus. Above: Annual Powder Puff Bowl between Delta Gamma and Gamma Phi Beta sororities. (*Wolverine*–1962).

had a range of $280 for freshmen and sophomores, and $310 for juniors and seniors.

"Several faculty served with distinction as consultants and administrators for the Michigan Constitutional Convention—Dr. William H. Combs, dean of University Services; William H. Roe, professor of education; Charles R. Adrian, professor of political science; and Charles Press, assistant professor of political science."

On July 2, 1962—the 100th anniversary of the passage of the Morrill Act, which created America's land-grant colleges and universities—Congressman Henry Dixon of Utah declared in the *Congressional Record*: "Lincoln (who signed the Act into law during the Civil War) lighted a candle during the darkest days…" Dixon stated, **"In 1862, one American in 1,500 went to college. Today the ratio is one in three, thanks chiefly to the Morrill Act."**

A report by the National Manpower Council described the Morrill Act as "The most important single Government step…in the training of scientific and professional personnel."

"In 1962, Land Grant universities enrolled 20 percent of the nation's college population and granted 40 percent of all doctor's degrees; and conferred about 50 percent of all doctorates in the sciences, health professions, and engineering; all of those in agriculture and 25 percent in arts and languages, business and commerce, and education itself. They also trained one-half of all regular and reserve officers entering the armed forces."

It should be a matter of great pride with the MSU family that **it was Joseph Williams, Michigan State's first President and its Board members who were a driving force behind the passage of the Morrill Act. And, it was Michigan State that was the first Land-Grant university, and indeed, the "Mother" of all the Land-Grant colleges and universities in America.**

Gerald A. Behn, '39, was Chief of the White House Secret Service Detail, with responsibility for guarding the President. He was featured on the cover of the January, 1962 *MSU Alumni Magazine* following President John F. Kennedy down the steps from Air Force One.

John W. Henderson, M.A. '50, Education doctorate '58, was elected president of Iowa Wesleyan College.

Dr. Arthur W. Farrall, chair of Agricultural Engineering for 17 years, was elected president of the American Society of Agricultural Engineers, an association of 6,000 members.

The Wilson Residence Halls, located at Shaw Lane and Chestnut, opened in the fall of 1962. They were named for Matilda R. Wilson, a member of the Board of the university from 1932 to 1937, and Alfred G. Wilson, a Detroit philanthropist. The Wilsons gave MSU their 1,600-acre Meadowbrook Farms and Hall to MSU in 1957.

Some 12,000 students lived in university dormitories, the largest on-campus housing in America.

In its pioneering tradition, MSU was the first public university to sponsor a program of Merit Scholarships to attract National Merit Scholars.

The National Voice Library, with 8,000 recorded voices dating back to the beginnings of sound recording, was brought to MSU by Dr. Richard Chapin, Director of the Library. Chapin persuaded G. Robert Vincent, collector and curator of the nation's foremost voice library, to locate it permanently at MSU and run it. It was housed in the Library.

A State Senate Committee called for MSU to abandon its Labor and Industrial Relations Center on the grounds that it was biased in favor of union labor. A minority report on the issue took the exact opposite view. The MSU Trustees stood firm, and took action to establish a School of

Labor and Industrial Relations within the College of Social Science to insure greater academic control.

Dr. Gordon E. Guyer, future MSU president, was named chair of the department of entomology.

Last temporary campus housing torn down—"Faculty Village," 50 temporary housing units erected after World War II, were removed from the campus.' It was the last of the temporary housing.

Doing what no other football team in history had accomplished, the 1962 Spartan gridders defeated Notre Dame for the seventh consecutive time, 31-7; and defeated Michigan for the fourth consecutive time, 28-0.

The 1962 university budget was $69,007,764. Enrollment was 25,040. At commencement, 4,600 degrees were granted. The Library grew to 897, 612 volumes.

1963

Michigan State Reinvents its Curriculum—Overhauling the university's course and curriculum structure overshadowed all other faculty work in 1963. This plan—the Educational Development Program—evolved from the 1960 report on "The Future of the University." "From the beginning, the total faculty was engaged in the discussion of the program."

President Hannah said the overhaul was urgent because of the: Explosion of knowledge, increasing number of students, impending shortage of qualified faculty, mounting demands for educated manpower, and insufficient financial resources.

Provost Dr. Clifford Erickson, who died of a heart attack on March 23, 1963, led the effort to attain the objectives of the restructuring. The steps included: more efficient use of faculty; re-organization of courses and curricula; improvement of instructional techniques; and placing more responsibility upon students for their own learning.

The Dean of the University College pointed to characteristics the university wanted to inculcate in students: ability to engage in responsible thought; possession of a desire to learn throughout life; and (a) realization that what happens in distant parts of the world will be important throughout their lives.

President Hannah stated in his annual report, "In all modesty, **MSU is one of a handful of institutions to recognize that tremendous changes are coming about in education at every level.**"

Building on its leadership in offering Merit Scholarships in 1962, **MSU set a national record in attracting National Merit Scholars in the fall of 1963, leading all universities in the nation**. A total of 195 came to the campus, double the number entering all other Big Ten universities combined. Following MSU in National Merit Scholars were Harvard—95, MIT—66, Stanford—61, Princeton—50, and Yale—46.

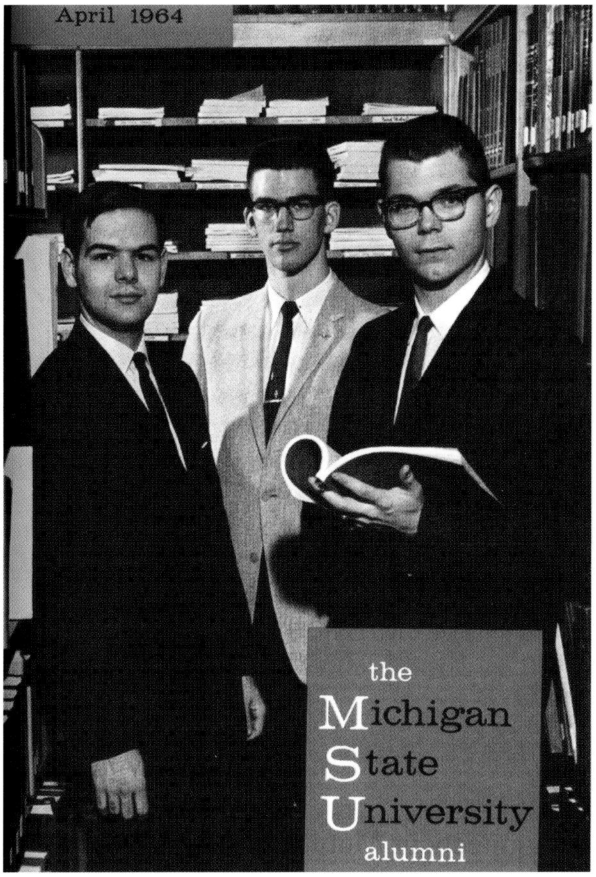

**1963 National Mathematics Champions—
L to R: Robert E. Greene, Knoxville, TN senior; Stephen E. Crick, Livonia, MI junior; and William A. Webb, Wyckoff, NJ sophomore, defeated 198 other college teams, including Caltech and MIT.**

An MSU team won the National Mathematics Championship (Annual Putnam competition) for the second time in three years. Team members were: Robert E. Greene, Knoxville, Tennessee senior; Stephen E. Crick, Livonia, MI junior; and William A. Webb, Wyckoff, NJ sophomore. The Spartans finished ahead of 198 other colleges and universities. Right behind MSU were: Brooklyn College, University of Pennsylvania, Caltech, and MIT.

Dr. Edward R. Garrett, '41, also M.S. and Ph.D. from MSU, won the Ebert Prize—the nation's highest pharmaceutical research award—for "the best published research in all the pharmaceutical sciences" by the American Pharmaceutical Association.

Elwin D. Farwell, '43, M.S. '47, was elected president of Luther College in Decorah, Iowa.

A Computer Center was established in the Electrical Engineering Building and featured a new 3600 computer, which was considered "the most advanced at any university."

Wonders Halls, located on West Shaw at Birch Road, were completed during 1963. They were named for Wallace

The Beal Botanical Garden, home to 5,000 species and varieties of plants, was judged "without question, the outstanding campus-located botanical garden in the country" by the Michigan Horticultural Society—1963.

K. Wonders and Grace Wonders. Wallace Wonders, Class of 1902, was a generous contributor to MSU.

McDonel Halls, located on East Shaw Lane near Hagadorn Road, were opened in 1963. They were named for Karl H. and Irma N. McDonel. McDonel was Secretary of the Board from 1941 until retirement in 1960.

An Asian Studies Center was established.

"The Beal Botanical Garden was judged by the Michigan Horticultural Society to be 'without question, **the outstanding campus-located botanical garden in the country.'"**

Coach Charles Schmitter led the Spartan fencing team to its first Big Ten title. Individual conference champions were Dick Schloener in foil, and Lou Salamone in sabre.

At the Big Ten indoor track championships, Bob Moreland won the 60-yard dash in 6.1 seconds, and Sherman Lewis won the long jump.

In the fall of 1963, the Spartans became the only football team in history to defeat Notre Dame in eight consecutive games; and only the second team to go eight years without losing to Michigan—recording six wins and two ties. State beat Notre Dame, 12-7, and tied Michigan, 7-7.

MSU and Illinois were to play for the Big Ten football title in East Lansing on Saturday, November 23, 1963. Each had a 4-1-1 record in conference play. In a stunning turn of events that shocked the nation, President John F. Kennedy was assassinated in Dallas on November 22. On Saturday, some 90 minutes before kickoff, the game was postponed until Thanksgiving Day, the following Thursday. The Fighting Illini returned to East Lansing, and defeated MSU, 13-0, taking the Big Ten title and the trip to the Rose Bowl.

The 1963 university budget was $79,050,548. Enrollment reached 27,597. At commencement, 4,831 degrees were awarded.

1964

College of Human Medicine Founded; MSU Becomes Largest Single-Campus University in the State—MSU's College of Human Medicine was founded in 1964. It was the first new medical school to be established in Michigan in nearly a century, and was approved as a two-year, pre-clinical medical school. Dr. Andrew D. Hunt, an outstanding member of the Stanford University medical faculty was appointed the first dean. The college would later receive state approval to grant the four-year MD degree, and graduated its first class in 1972.

MSU became the largest single-campus educational institution in the state when enrollment jumped to 31,268. This surpassed the University of Michigan-Ann Arbor campus enrollment—27,790—for the first time. The long-heralded flood of "Baby Boomer" students was a reality.

Student Enrollment

	Michigan State	Michigan
1900	652	3,303
1910	1,568	4,755
1920	1,411	8,560
1930	3,211	10,107
1940	6,776	12,875
1950	14,993	19,487
1960	21,157	23,851
1964	31,268	27,790
1970	40,511	34,702
1980	44,940	35,670
1990	42,785	36,306
2000	43,366	38,103
2001	44,227	38,248

For the first four decades of the 20th Century, the University of Michigan enrollment ranged from five to two times larger than MSU's.

The University's final name change was made in 1964—from Michigan State University of Agriculture and Applied Science to Michigan State University.

It was the sixth name, preceded by:

- ▼ The Agricultural College of the State of Michigan—1855,
- ▼ The State Agricultural College—1861,
- ▼ Michigan Agricultural College—1909,
- ▼ Michigan State College of Agriculture and Applied Science—1925, and
- ▼ Michigan State University of Agriculture and Applied Science—1955.

Clarence Haston Shaver, class of 1920, was serving as chairman of U.S. Gypsum Co.

John C. Mackie, '42, was elected to the U.S. House of Representatives from Michigan's 7th Congressional District. He had previously served as Michigan Highway Commissioner.

Earl Hoekenga, '39, was named chair and CEO of Ryder Truck Lines.

Verghese Karien, M.S. '48, won the Ramon Magasay Award, in recognition of those Asians who exemplify greatness of spirit, integrity, devotion to liberty, and service to the public. The award included $10,000 and a gold medal.

Dale Cooper was recognized for being a two-time NCAA and Big Ten gymnastics champion in the still rings event.

The world's largest known collection of woody plant species and varieties–4,898–were growing on campus in 1964. This was in addition to the 5,000 species and varieties of plants growing in the Beal Botanical Garden.

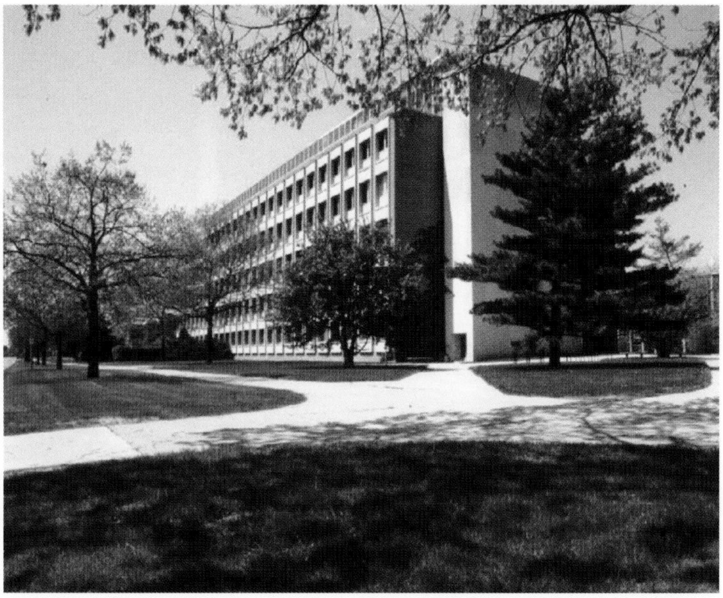

Bio-Chemistry was one of six major buildings to rise in 1964.

Six major buildings went up during 1964. The new **Chemistry Building, Biochemistry Building, and the International Center** were academic facilities financed by the state.

Akers and Fee Halls were financed with self-liquidating bonds.

Abrams Planetarium, financed with private gifts, was dedicated.

The International Center featured a "Con-Con Room"—which contained "furniture used by the delegates to the historical State Constitutional Convention held in 1962-1963."

At MSU's Agricultural Experiment Station, agricultural scientists were finishing research work that would end the gypsy moth scourge.

A new program in business administration was established by MSU in Turkey.

An International Communications Center was established by the College of Communication Arts.

The College of Education, a major source of teachers for Michigan, had student teaching centers in 79 school systems throughout the state.

The Highway Traffic Center, previously eliminated by the legislature, was reactivated by the 1964 legislature at the behest of Michigan Governor George Romney.

MSU's Library acquired its one millionth volume in 1964.

The largest known collection of woody plant species and varieties—4,898—were growing on campus.

MSU's soccer team was undefeated in regular season play.

The 1964 university budget was $84,794,858. Enrollment totaled 31,268. At commencement, 5,940 degrees were awarded.

1965

National Football Champions; 10 New Buildings Constructed; Cyclotron First Operated—The Spartan football team was undefeated and untied in ten regular season games, winning the National Championship and the Big Ten title. **They led the nation in rushing and scoring defense**, holding ten opponents to an average of just 45.6 yards rushing per game, and an average of just 6.2 points per game.

MSU's football team did what no other school in history had done—holding Michigan, Ohio State, and Notre Dame to negative rushing yardage. In the games with MSU, Michigan lost 51 yards, Ohio State 22 yards, Notre Dame 12 yards. The chant, "Kill Bubba, Kill," rang out from the student section in Spartan Stadium. They were referring to giant 6'8", 285-pound defensive end Charles "Bubba" Smith, a terror on defense, and a true giant in those days. He would become an All-Pro tackle and movie actor.

It was a season of victories over many of the storied football programs in America. The Spartans beat UCLA, 13-3; Penn State, 23-0; Michigan, 24-7; Ohio State, 32-7, and Notre Dame, 12-3.

Eight team members won All-American honors: Bob Apisa, fullback; Ron Goovert, linebacker; Clint Jones, halfback; Steve Juday, quarterback; Harold Lucas, middle guard; Charles "Bubba" Smith, defensive end; Gene Washington, end; and George Webster, linebacker.

Head football coach Duffy Daugherty was selected as Coach of the Year by the Football Writers Association of America, becoming **the first coach to be selected twice for the honor: 1955 and 1965.**

MSU's Marching Band played in President Lyndon B. Johnson's inaugural parade on January 20, 1965 in Washington, D.C. It was the only band invited from Michigan, and led the Michigan section of the parade. Oldsmobile paid the entire cost of the band's trip.

Regina Gabriel Frisbie, '35, had been serving as director of home economic services for the W.K. Kellogg Co. since 1949. She had been a past president of the Michigan Dietetic Association.

Dr. James H. Steele, DVM '41, was chief veterinary officer for the U.S. Public Health Service.

John St. John, '43, was president of the Minute Maid Division of Coca Cola Company.

Jack Shingleton, '48, director of the MSU Placement Bureau, was praised by corporate recruiters for running "the finest placement bureau in the nation."

Harold E. Sponberg, Ph.D. '52, was elected president of Eastern Michigan University.

John W. Henderson, Ed.D. '58, was elected president of Washburn University, Topeka, Kansas.

In an incredible burst of construction energy, eleven new buildings were sprouting on campus in 1965. This put more buildings on campus in one year than the school had in its inventory in its first 30 years.

Buildings under construction included: a **new Veterinary Clinic**, the **Packaging Laboratory**, **Psychology Research**, **Conrad Hall, Natural Resources, Food Science and Human Nutrition, the Plant Biology Laboratories, the John C. Holmes Halls, and the Theodore B. Simon Power Plant. Additions also were being made to the Kresge Art Center and Owen Graduate Center.**

Conrad Hall, named for Elisabeth Conrad, former Dean of Women, was completed in 1965. It houses the MSU Archives & Historical Collections, and a large lecture hall.

MSU put its first cyclotron, a type of particle accelerator, into operation.

The **"Living-Learning" program** operating in Case, Wilson, Wonders, Akers, Fee, McDonel, and Brody Halls was working. Dr. H.H. Kimber, Director of the Arts & Letters program in Akers Hall, said it was **designed "to create in the residence hall by means of precept and example an atmosphere conducive to serious study and the enrichment and elevation of the educational environment."** This pioneering program drew great interest from other large universities, who adopted the idea.

President Hannah pointed out, "...even first term freshmen in the University College are not only taught by full professors, they are given easy access to their offices, especially in the residence halls."

MSU's first venture into the small, semi-autonomous residential college was the creation of Justin Morrill College, which would offer a four-year broad, liberal education. The experiment was to provide a small college atmosphere supported by the advantages of a large university. Snyder-Phillips Halls were to house the student body and the faculty offices of the new college. Some 400 freshmen were accepted in 1965.

MSU led the nation in developing a "Head Start" project, preceding federal legislation to create such a program. Two MSU faculty members were tapped as consultants for the National Planning Committee for Project Head Start.

MSU students established the "Just a Friend" program. Volunteers, a part of the University's Student Education Corps, mentored and taught youngsters in local schools.

MSU's leadership model in "Living-Learning" residence halls was adopted by large universities across the country—"creating an atmosphere conducive to serious study."

The National Center on Police & Community Relations—a leading initiative to promote community policing—was established at MSU with a $100,000 grant from the Field Foundation. It was directed by the School of Police Administration & Public Safety.

The Mott Institute for Community Improvement was established with a $3 million grant from the Mott Foundation.

A Rural Manpower Center, first of its kind in the nation, was established with a $50,000 appropriation by the Michigan legislature.

Dr. Sylvan H. Wittwer, professor of horticulture, succeeded Dr. Lloyd M. Turk as director of the Agricultural Experiment Station.

Professor Georg Gorgstrom, MSU's internationally recognized food scientist, produced the book, *The Hungry Planet* in 1965.

The American Library Association named it **one of the 50 most important books of the year.**

Dr. John D. Wilson, class of 1953, Rhodes Scholar and former defensive halfback, was named Director of MSU's Honors College.

With the expansion of the campus, distances between classes were growing. Two actions were taken: 1. **Inauguration of a campus bus service**, and 2. **Extending the period between classes from 10 minutes to 20.**

"Bike freeways" were laid out on campus to help handle 8,000 bike riders.

MSU's 1965 budget was $99,203,453. A surge of 4,183 additional students lifted MSU's enrollment to 35,451. At graduation, 6,423 degrees were granted.

1966

Department of TV & Radio Ranked No. 1 in Graduate Education; National Champions in Football and Ice Hockey—MSU's Department of TV & Radio was ranked number one nationally in graduate education.

"Game of the Century"—MSU 10, Notre Dame 10—On November 19, 1966, Michigan State's undefeated football team met Notre Dame's undefeated Fighting Irish in a game at Spartan Stadium that grabbed the nation's attention. MSU was ranked No. 2 in the polls, and Notre Dame was No. 1. Many sports enthusiasts still call it the "Game of the Century." ABC-TV was scheduled to telecast the game only on a regional basis. Football fans nationwide went crazy. ABC received an unprecedented 50,000 letters requesting that the game be televised nationally. ABC responded by televising the game on a tape-delayed basis to that part of the country that previously was to be blacked out.

***The Wall Street Journal* carried a front-page story on the game**, the day before. MSU Sports Information Director Fred Stabley, Sr., squeezed 754 sports writers and broadcasters into the Spartan Stadium press box, now named in Stabley's honor. It was the largest press turnout for a college game in history, and would be the largest even when compared with Super Bowls for years to come.

Mike Celizic, a 1970 Notre Dame graduate and sports columnist for *The Record* of Bergen County, New Jersey, wrote a 320-page book on the game in 1992, titled, *The Biggest Game of Them All; Notre Dame, Michigan State, and the Fall of 1966* (Simon & Schuster, 1992). He wrote, **"Notre Dame-Michigan State was the Super Bowl before the Super Bowl became what it is today."** Celizic also described the madness that surrounded the game. "Mike Schrems of Saginaw offered to sell his liquor store, which had done $65,000 worth of business in 1965, for four tickets, plus $1,700 for the beer in the storeroom, and $4,000 for goodwill."

Richard Paisley of Cleveland, Ohio wrote MSU ticket manager Bill Beardsley, asking, "If President Johnson phoned or wrote you for a ticket, I'm sure you would be able to send him one. Well, President Johnson will not be there. So why not send me the ticket you would have for him?'" Beardsley checked to see that President Johnson would not attend, and then sent a ticket to Paisley. The story was reported by United Press International, the Associated Press, *Detroit Free Press*, CBS and NBC.

(Reprinted with the permission of Simon & Schuster from *The Biggest Game of Them All: Notre Dame, Michigan State and the Fall of 1966* by Mike Celizic).

Colleges and high schools across the country changed the starting times of their games so as not to conflict with the monumental clash between Michigan State and Notre Dame. Catholic priests altered the times they would hear confessions so they and their parishioners could watch the game. Michigan's hunting season opened on game day, and the woods were virtually empty as hunters stayed home to see the Spartans and Irish play for the national championship.

The football talent that took the field on game day was awesome. **Twenty-five of the players were, or would become, All-Americans.** Ten of the players would be first-round draft picks in the National Football League, and 33 of those that saw action that day would play in the NFL.

The game turned out to be a titanic struggle that ended in a 10-10 tie. Many of the players that day said it was the hardest-hitting game they had ever experienced. Notre Dame coach Ara Parseghian received heavy national criticism for sitting on the ball in the final two minutes, running the clock out with the score tied 10-10. *Sports Illustrated* ran a story titled, "Tie, tie for old Notre Dame." MSU head coach Duffy Daugherty lamented after the game, that a tie was "like kissing your sister."

MSU finished the season with nine wins, no losses and a tie, and was selected National Champion by NFF, Football Research, Helms, and Poling. Notre Dame also was selected national champion by other rating services.

The MSU ice hockey team, led by coach Amo Bessone, won its first NCAA championship in 1966. His teams went to three Final Fours. In 1959, the Spartans lost a heartbreaker in the championship game, 4-3 in overtime to North Dakota. They finished third in 1967.

President Hannah addressed the issue of "...unrest within society itself as time-honored values, morality, principles, and religious concepts were confronted with the most formidable challenges any of us can remember. A few (students) arrive already intoxicated with the pleasure of defying authority and the fun of shocking their elders. Their youth and inexperience do not let them see that what might be appropriate in the streets of the city is not necessarily appropriate in a university.

"For example, coercion except by strength of reason is unacceptable in a scholarly community dedicated to the pursuit of truth by the road of reason, leaving emotion to those who would rather fight than think. Most students know this, or learn it quickly."

Coach Amo Bessone led MSU to its first NCAA ice hockey title in 1966.

Dr. Hiroshi Naito, class of 1920, was president of Tokyo University of Agriculture.

Edward Q. Moulton, '47, was elected president of the University of North Dakota.

Christian E.W. Baker, DVM '55, was president of Cuttington College & Divinity School in Liberia.

The entering freshmen class was labeled the "most aided" in the state by President Hannah. The new class received "...two million dollars in scholarships, grants, loans and guaranteed jobs." Moreover, he stated in his annual report, "Last year students borrowed $3.1 million to continue their education. There were loans to 2,511 (students) under the National Defense Education Act, to 2,362 from university funds; and to 1,403 under the Michigan Higher Education Assistance program, the United Student Aid program, and the U.S. Loan Program for Cuban Refugees."

For the second consecutive year, the College of Education prepared more teachers than any other American institution.

MSU worked with the South Vietnamese government, training people in Police Administration. A sensational west coast magazine made allegations that MSU had aided and abetted the U.S. Central Intelligence Agency in clandestine work. The charges were unfounded and unsubstantiated. President Hannah reported, "there were scores of errors in the story," and that MSU had responded with facts that were distributed nationwide. Hannah said, "we were greatly encouraged by the private letters of support and understanding that came in from other universities and the amazing lack of demonstrated interest on the part of the general public."

One result of this episode was the establishment of a "...faculty committee to review our overseas projects and advise on the suitability of new proposals."

Building construction included **Hubbard Halls, Urban Planning & Landscape Architecture, a new Veterinary Clinic, an Activities Center at MSU's Hidden Lake Gardens in Lenawee County, additions to Owen Hall, Kresge Art Center, and Kedzie Laboratories,** as well as **228 apartments for married students**.

MSU's national leadership in "Living-Learning" was evident across campus. The residence halls incorporated 50 classrooms, 22 laboratories, seven auditoriums, four libraries, 245 faculty offices, and 14 conference rooms—all for academic purposes.

The second Wells Hall, a popular dormitory built in 1906, was razed to make way for an addition to the Library.

MSU helped with the development of business administration courses at 15 Brazilian universities and centers.

Within the Institute of International Business Studies, a Market Development Center was established "to bring about a better understanding of the role of marketing in international development." The program was directed by Professor Charles C. Slater and undertaken with the U.S. Agency for International Development.

The Institute of International Agriculture and Nutrition was established with the College of Agriculture, under the direction of Dr. Kirk Lawton.

A computer sciences major was initiated.

"...the Educational Policy Committee and the Standing Committee of the Academic Council recommended the university seek approval from the State Board of Education for a law school at the University." It would take until 1996 for MSU to acquire a law school—the Michigan State University-Detroit College of Law.

A national survey showed that as of 1964, MSU stood 12th in the U.S. in the number of doctorates granted. In 1965, MSU ranked 5th among state universities and land-grant colleges in doctor's degrees awarded.

The 1966 university budget reached $119,665,909—the first over $100 million. Enrollment jumped to 38,107—second in the nation in main campus (as opposed to multi-campus) headcount. **The freshmen class numbered 10,389—larger than the total enrollment at Michigan State in any one of its first 91 years.** At commencement, 7,035 degrees were awarded.

1967

Greater Academic Freedom for MSU Students; James Madison and Lyman Briggs Colleges Established; NCAA Soccer and Wrestling Champions—In one of the most significant events of the year, students gained a greater voice in decisions affecting them through the adoption of the report on Academic Freedom of Students at MSU. The Faculty Committee on Student Affairs prepared the final report, which resulted from extensive hearings, discussion and review by the Associated Students of MSU.

President Hannah pointed out the benefits of the prolonged exercise, "Students learned that faculty members and administrators are willing to listen to them, although they may not always agree. Faculty and administrators learned that students often have good ideas to offer, ideas too good to be discarded on the ground they threaten tradition and the status quo. (Students) learned, too, the faculty is not prepared to accept students as contributing partners in all areas, especially those touching on professional standards and prerogatives."

As a result of the report on Academic Freedom for Students at MSU, **Michigan State led the nation in appointing an Ombudsman** to listen to student complaints and criticisms about regulations and their enforcement. James D. Rust was appointed MSU's first Ombudsman.

As a part of the student push for greater freedom, regulations governing women's hours were extensively liberalized. Freshmen women living in residence halls or sororities would be required to sign in by specified times. All other women were free to return to their residences whenever they desired.

President Hannah stated the university's on-going and contemporary mission: **"...it is not enough to prepare the individual to be a productive member of the community; the university must identify the needs of the community itself, and seek ways to satisfy them more effectively."**

MSU reached out "... to make educational opportunities available to young people in disadvantaged cultural, ethnic, and economics groups..." **"Nearly 100 high school graduates, nearly all black, were identified, encouraged to continue their educations, admitted to MSU, and granted massive financial aid in an attempt to help disadvantaged youths."**

Two new semi-autonomous residential colleges were established at MSU in 1967. **The James Madison College**, devoted to pre-law and public policy education, was launched and housed in the Case Residential Halls. Dr. Herbert Garfinkel was named Dean.

The Lyman Briggs College (now School), focused on education in the physical sciences, and was given a home in Holmes Hall. **Dr. Fred B. Dutton** was named Dean.

MSU's College of Home Economics continued its leadership in developing the national Head Start program, and was named one of ten National Centers for evaluating research relating to the program.

An MSU student team won the National Mathematics Championship (Putnam Competition) for the third time in seven years. Finishing behind MSU were: Caltech, Harvard, MIT, and Michigan. Professor Fritz Herzog coached the champions.

Dr. William H. Sewell, B.A. '33, M.A. '34, was elected chancellor of the University of Wisconsin-Madison.

Stephen M. Rogers, '33, was president of the Herald Company, publisher of the Syracuse, N.Y. *Herald-Journal* and *Herald-American*.

Don A. Jones, '33, was promoted to Rear Admiral in the Coast & Geodetic Survey.

Holden Hall-East was one of five buildings erected in 1967.

Harold C. MacDonald, '40, was named vice president for Car Engineering and Product Development, Ford Motor Company.

Charles Fairbanks, '55, was named head football coach at the University of Oklahoma.

Reverend Douglas Trout, Ph.D. '65, was elected president of Tusculum College, Greeneville, TN.

A record 20.4 inches of snow fell in 24 hours on January 26 and 27, 1967. Classes and university operations were suspended for two full days.

Five more major buildings were completed in 1967: **Wells**

Hall, **Holden Halls**, **Baker Hall,** and the **Instructional Media Center.**

Agricultural Engineering and Soil Science researchers found a way to increase yields on crops such as beans and cucumbers by more than 100 percent. They did it by putting a thin layer of asphalt under the surface of sandy soils, which doubled the capacity of the soil to hold water. This discovery opened the possibility of using millions of acres of dry soils throughout the world for food production.

MSU scientists developed and introduced the apricot variety "Goldcot," which was expected to open the first successful apricot production east of the Rockies.

MSU researchers discovered "that the protein content of several food and forage crops could be increased from 25 to 80 percent by the application of simazine, a chemical weed killer, to the soil at planting…"

The U.S. Naval Academy selected the College of Engineering as a center for electrical engineering graduate training.

The name of the College of Agriculture was changed to the College of Agriculture and Natural Resources.

MSU's soccer and wrestling teams won NCAA championships.

Financial support of students by the university was substantial. President Hannah reported, "The university made loans amounting to $4.9 million to 9,989 students last year; it paid $4.3 million in wages to 16,151 students, and an additional $5.7 million to 2,342 graduate student assistants."

The 1967 university budget totaled $142,156,918. Student enrollment reached 38,758—81% from Michigan, 16% from other states, and 3% from other countries. A total of 7,595 degrees were awarded.

1968

State Support Less Than Half of University Income; NCAA Soccer Champions—President Hannah stated in his annual report, "Once we looked to the State of Michigan as the source of most of our monetary support. Appropriations now represent far less than half of the total university revenues. More and more of the total state tax money being invested in education is being shifted to support elementary and secondary schools, and more and more of the cost of higher education is being shifted to the students and their parents."

A sit-in by students and non-students at the Administration Building in June was triggered by state police arrests of several individuals on charges of selling marijuana. The Academic Council supported the actions taken by the university administration, because the demonstrators had refused to use ample avenues of protest that exist under university regulations. The Trustees then issued a statement reaffirming the university's traditional tolerance of dissent and orderly demonstration, and the long-standing policy against interference with the orderly conduct of university operations.

A committee empowered by President Hannah to study what MSU should do in the field of civil rights, equal opportunity and harmonious race relations, recommended:

1) An all-out effort to increase the number of black students, both graduate and undergraduate,

2) The university would intensify its search for qualified black faculty and staff,

3) The establishment of a Center for Race & Urban Affairs at MSU, and

4) Every encouragement given to voluntary programs involving students and faculty in the area of harmonious race relations and equal opportunity.

President Hannah reported, **"Studies conducted by MSU over the years have led to the establishment of 14 community colleges in Michigan."**

The *State News* won first place honors in the annual national judging of university newspapers by the American Newspaper Publisher's Association. This "Pacemaker"award was the sixth number one finish in seven years for the State News. At that time no other university paper in the U.S. had won more than two of these awards.

Dr. William F. Jackson, DVM '47, was presented the National Gamma Award as "the most outstanding veterinarian in the U.S."

Major General Donald V. Bennett, MSU student 1933-35, was named the 47th Superintendent of the U.S. Military Academy at West Point, N.Y.

Howard James, '58, chief of the *Christian Science Monitor's* midwest news bureau in Chicago, **won the 1968 Pulitzer Prize** for 13 articles on "Crisis in the Courts," published in a book by David McKay Co.

Clarence A. Boonstra, '36, was U.S. Ambassador to Costa Rica.

David H. Stroud, '58, was elected president of the National Live Stock and Meat Board, Chicago.

Walter E. Boek, '48, Ph.D. '53, was president of the National Graduate University (outside Washington, D.C.), a private school for those pursuing doctoral or post-doctoral degrees.

Eleftherios S. Kanellakis, M.A. '62, Brigadier General in Greece's Royal Hellenic Air Force, was chief of Air Force Justice, Athens, Greece.

Dr. Robert L. Ewigleben, B.S. '52, M.A. '55, Ed.D. '59, was elected president of the College of San Mateo, California.

Sheldon Moyer, '44, was elected president of D.P. Brother & Co. Advertising, Chicago.

MSU's Volunteer Student Education Corps—the largest in the nation—established in 1962—had 2,200 students enrolled. These student volunteers tutored and

New Administration Building, named for President John A. Hannah, was completed in 1968. The front lawn was planted with the turf from Spartan Stadium, which was converted to artificial turf.

taught young people in 72 schools throughout south central Michigan.

Doctoral programs were added in Russian Languages & Studies, Systems Science and Linguistics.

The College of Home Economics ranked first in the nation in granting master's degrees.

MSU's chapter of Phi Beta Kappa—nationally, the most-respected undergraduate honors society for liberal arts students—was formed in 1968.

On-campus buildings constructed included a new **Administration Building, a Music Practice Building, and the Speech & Hearing Clinic.** A large addition to the Library also was completed. A Plant Conservatory Building at MSU's Hidden Lake Gardens in Lenawee County was made possible by a gift from the Herrick-Cobb families.

Head soccer coach Gene Kenney led the Spartans to their second consecutive NCAA title. In addition to two NCAA titles, Kenney's teams twice finished second, and twice third in NCAA competition for a total of six "Final Fours." **His 1956-1968 record was 120 wins, 13 losses and 13 ties—a 90 percent winning record, unmatched by any other coach in MSU history.**

In 1968, the grass turf in Spartan Stadium was removed and replaced with synthetic Tartan Turf. The grass from the stadium was transplanted as the lawn in front of the new Administration Building. Thus, nostalgic Spartan football fans can still see the grass on which the 1965 and 1966 MSU National Champions played.

The 1968 university budget was $148,525,152. Student enrollment was 39,949. At commencement, 8,485 degrees were awarded.

Dr. William Harrison Pipes

MSU'S First African-American Full Professor

Dr. William H. Pipes

Dr. William Harrison Pipes, (1912-1981), emeritus professor of American Thought and Language, was the first African-American to be named a full professor at Michigan State. He joined the faculty in 1957 and was named a full professor in 1968.

Pipes was the son of a cotton plantation sharecropper in Inverness, Mississippi. He worked his way through Tuskegee Institute high school and college in Alabama. He earned a master's degree at Atlanta University, and became the first African-American in the U.S. to earn a Ph.D. in speech—at the University of Michigan.

Dr. Pipes served as president of Alcorn College from 1945 to 1949. He was academic dean and professor of English and speech at Philander Smith College, Little Rock, Arkansas, from 1949 to 1956. And, he was a guest lecturer in English and speech at Wayne State University; Fort Valley State College, Georgia; West Kentucky State College; Langston University, Oklahoma; and Southern University, Louisiana in 1956 and 1957.

Dr. Pipes authored several books, including: *The English Major*; *Say Amen, Brother*; *Is God Dead?*; and *Death of an "Uncle Tom."*

1969

President Hannah Resigns; Walter Adams Named thirteenth MSU CEO; Dr. Alfred Day Hershey, '30, Ph.D., '34, Wins Nobel Prize—President John A. Hannah, educational giant and visionary builder of MSU, resigned on April 1, 1969 to become Administrator of the U.S. Agency for International Development. Hannah had served for 28 years as president, and was recognized nationally as the 20th century's finest higher education leader.

At the 1992 Association of Governing Boards (Universities) annual meeting, **Dr. Ernest Boyer, President of the Carnegie Foundation for the Advancement in Teaching, identified Dr. John Hannah "as a leader in this century who did more for higher education than any other person."**

U.S. President Dwight Eisenhower wrote of **Dr. Hannah's service as U.S. Deputy Secretary of Defense for Personnel, "It's not generally known, but he was as responsible as any one person for the success of the effort to achieve racial integration in our country's armed forces, both in the ranks and in military housing...I am proud he was an appointee of mine..."**

At Hannah's retirement party, Durward "Woody" Varner, chancellor of MSU-Oakland, stated, **"...of the 98,492 diplomas awarded in the history of this institution...our honored guest tonight has personally signed 89,062 of them."** It was Dr. Hannah's belief that if a person invested four years in earning a degree, the least he could do was personally sign the diploma.

Little known publicly was the disconnect between the board of trustees and President Hannah at that time. Lautner in his book *From an Oak Opening* described the situation, "Several members elected to the board of trustees in the early 1960s seemed to have little or no interest in the institution, and politics became the first order of the day. Slowly, Hannah lost the total support of the board." This was undoubtedly a key factor in Hannah's resignation.

The issue of publicly elected boards was raised at that time and again in the early 1980s. A discussion of this issue appears under the year 1981.

From the time of his graduation from M.A.C. in 1923 to his retirement in 1969, John Hannah dedicated 46 years of his life to the development, growth and excellence of Michigan State University.

Upon his retirement, a joint session of the Michigan Legislature was convened to honor Dr. Hannah. **In his last remarks to the law-makers, he continued building MSU by making a final request: that they authorize MSU's College of Human Medicine as a four-year medical school. They did!**

Dr. Walter Adams (1922-1998), distinguished professor of economics at MSU, was named Acting President, thus becoming MSU's thirteenth chief executive officer **(served April 1-December 31, 1969)**. Adams had a B.A. degree from Brooklyn College (1942), and MA and Ph.D. degrees from Yale (1946 and 1947). He joined the MSU faculty in 1947.

Dr. Walter Adams…

"The Land-Grant philosophy is a reflection of what John Hannah taught me. It's the radical notion of affording educational opportunity to people who otherwise would not have it. This is a uniquely indigenous, American ideal in contrast to the European notion of higher education essentially for the aristocracy and upper bourgeoisie. The land-grant philosophy is the notion of opportunity no matter where you start from. It is the democratic idea of vertical mobility. That made me a believer. That was what Michigan State was all about."

"Teaching is a calling, not a job. You teach values by example."

Dr. Walter Adams, Thirteenth President

Adams stated he would not be a candidate for the presidency, preferring to return to teaching as soon as a new president was selected. He took office on April Fool's Day, 1969. He served until the end of the year and dealt with crisis after crisis on campus. He handled confrontations with white radicals, sit-ins by black students, Vietnam demonstrations, ROTC protests, a strike by university employees, heated debates over open admission and quota policies, angry demands by alumni, parents and legislators, and attacks by the news media.

Adams remarked, "There is no solution to a crisis; one can only hope to endure and surmount it."

Adams quick wit and self-deprecating style won the respect of students, faculty and alumni. He was one of the most popular classroom professors on campus. He taught his famous Economics 444 course for 45 years. Adams said, "The students all bitched about me being an autocrat: no lateness to class; read the assignment; be prepared to be called on; written examinations; and no curve. **I told them, 'you're reaching for excellence.' When they left the course, they referred to themselves as 'veterans of Econ 444.' There was a pride there."**

Dr. Alfred Day Hershey, B.S. in Bacteriology, Class of 1930, and Ph.D. in Chemistry, 1934, won the 1969 Nobel Prize in Physiology or Medicine. He shared the $75,000 prize with Max Delbruck of Caltech, and S.E. Luria of MIT. Their work involved "the pursuit of the elusive mechanism of replication of genetic material—a mechanism fundamental to man and creature." **Their pioneering research resulted in a better understanding of the nature of viruses and laid the foundation for studies of such diseases as rabies, encephalitis and the common cold.**

Dr. and Mrs. Ernest Hart of Medina, N.Y. gave MSU a $64,300 Schlicker Organ to the School of Music. Dr. Hart, class of 1914, had been president and chairman of FMC Corporation.

MSU's baseball field was named in honor of John H. Kobs in 1969. He served as Spartan baseball coach for 39 years—1925-1963. His teams posted 35 winning seasons. He was inducted into the College Baseball Coaches Hall of Fame in 1966.

Joseph F. Kerigan, '66 MBA, was serving as vice president and group executive of Chrysler Corporation's car assembly and stamping group.

Dr. John D. Wilson, '53, Ph.D. '65, associate provost and director of undergraduate education, resigned to become president of Wells College, Aurora, NY.

Dr. Adrian R. Chamberlain, '51 was elected president of Colorado State University.

Frank A. Banks, '61, MBA '62, was general manager of the Waldorf-Astoria Hotel, New York.

E. Genevieve Gillette, class of 1920, was appointed by President Lyndon Johnson to the Citizens Advisory Committee on Recreation and Natural Beauty. She was known as "Miss Michigan State Parks." Gillette founded and was first president of the Michigan Parks Association (1955); was the first woman president of the Michigan Horticultural Society (1958); and led the battle for state and national parks across Michigan. She had also won the Park and Conservationist of the Year Award from the National Wildlife Federation.

Dr. William J. Westcott, DVM '43, was serving as president of the American Animal Hospital Association.

Robert G. Clark, Jr. '59, became the first African-American elected to the Mississippi legislature since Reconstruction following the Civil War. He championed laws to make junior college education available to every young person in Mississippi.

Dr. Barnett Rosenberg, Department of Biophysics, discovered that certain platinum compounds inhibit the growth of cancer in experimental animals. This was the precursor of the development of Cisplatin, which was to become the most-prescribed anti-cancer drug in the nation.

MSU's College of Osteopathic Medicine was established by an Act of the Michigan legislature to help remedy Michigan's shortage of primary care physicians. It was the first state-assisted and university-based osteopathic college in the nation, and, as such became the "flagship" osteopathic college in America. Dr. Myron S. Magen was named Dean.

The Center for Urban Affairs and Equal Opportunity Programs was established. This center evolved into MSU's Urban Affairs Programs, which were unique in America. These programs addressed issues of race, urban inequality and social justice, housing and land development, and economic and fiscal concerns. Dr. Robert L. Green, professor of education, was named director of the center.

A planning committee established by the president and the board, proposed three campus buildings: l. An All-Events Building to seat at least 15,000 for basketball,

Profusion of color greets visitors to the Center for Integrated Plant Systems. Built in 1969, the facility was originally known as the Pesticide Research Center.

Dr. John A. Hannah, MSU President, 1941-1969, visionary builder of MSU, in front of the Administration Building named in his honor.

concerts, and conventions; 2. A Communications Arts Building; and, 3. A Music Hall Auditorium. It would take between 12 and 20 years to see these structures become reality—Communication Arts & Sciences Building—1981; Wharton Center for the Performing Arts—1982; and Breslin Student Events Center—1989.

MSU chemical engineering students won first and second place in the national competition sponsored by the American Institute of Chemical Engineering, competing against 100 other universities.

Dr. Howard R. Neville, Provost, resigned to become president of Claremont College, Claremont, CA.

Dr. William Kelly, director of the Honors College, resigned to become president of Mary Baldwin College, Staunton, VA.

James Tanck, Director of Student Volunteer Programs at MSU, and an alum, was loaned to the White House to help develop a national plan to encourage volunteer programs at the nation's colleges and universities. At MSU, "The trustees provided funds to transport 17,293 student volunteers to places of social service within the East Lansing region."

MSU's Ombudsman reported, "...the largest number of problems taken to the Ombudsman for mediation counseling related to academic problems. **Many of the problems bedeviling the university would disappear or be much mitigated if everyone involved would practice the healing arts of kindness and courtesy.**"

Sue Tushingham McNary, popular Coronado, California artist known for her dramatic color paintings of the renowned Hotel Del Coronado, as well as landscape, garden and sailing scenes, studied at MSU's Department of Art in 1969 and 1970.

The College of Business created a new major in Tourism.

The College of Engineering established a Department of Computer Science.

With 684 National Merit Scholars enrolled, MSU led the nation in this category for the sixth consecutive year.

The new **Plant Biology Laboratories Building** was completed during 1969, and the **Pesticide Research Center** was nearing completion. Construction was started on the **Observatory** for the Department of Astronomy. A three-story addition to **Wells Hall** for the mathematics library and staff offices was underway.

A Christmas dinner dance for Faculty Folk Club, Faculty Club, Faculty Women's Association and the Newcomers Club at Kellogg Center cost $6.25 per person.

The 1969 university budget was $158,022,945. Enrollment passed 40,000 for the first time, reaching 40,820. Record black student enrollment of 1,007, was up from 700 the previous year. **The university began "to put indirect restrictions on enrollment...to stay within its resources."** Applications from Michigan residents beginning with the 1970 academic year had to be submitted by the end of January, and out-state applications had to be in by December 15, 1969. At commencement, 9,743 degrees were granted.

John Hannah's 1969 annual report, his last, marked the end of these insightful commentaries on Michigan State's moving history.

Dr. Alfred Day Hershey, B.S. '30, Ph.D. '34

Nobel Prize Winner In Physiology and Medicine
A Founder of Molecular Biology

Dr. Alfred Day Hershey, '30, Ph.D. '34
1969 Nobel Prize Winner

Dr. Alfred Day Hershey, B.S. '30, Ph.D. '34, became Michigan State's first Nobel laureate in 1969, sharing the prize in physiology and medicine with Max Delbruk of Caltech, and Salvador E. Luria of M.I.T.

The three men were cited for "their discoveries which give deeper insight into the nature of viruses and virus diseases and provide increased understanding of the mechanism of inheritance and the mechanisms that control the development, growth and function of tissues and organs. The work of the three researchers, centering on bacteriophage—a type of virus that infects bacteria rather than ordinary cells—since around 1940 has had a great impact on biology in general. It called them 'the three leading figures of bacteriophage research.'" (*Detroit Free Press*, Oct. 17, 1969).

The Nobel winners also were cited "as the original founders of the modern science of molecular biology."

Dr. Hershey, who at the time of the Nobel award was director of the Carnegie Institute's Genetic Laboratory, told about the influence MSU had on him. "I had a fellowship under (I.F.) Huddleson. It was his idea to go into the chemistry of Brucella (the bacteria that causes brucellosis, or undulant fever). Huddleson asked me to work a deal with chemistry for a joint degree. The Nobel laureate described his entry into the chemical investigation of Brucella as the key to his future work which led to the Nobel Prize." (Philip E. Miller, *MSU Faculty News*, Oct. 28, 1969).

Dr. Hershey also won the Lasker Award in 1958 from the American Public Health Association.

Dr. Hershey was born in Owosso, Michigan in 1908. He earned his bachelor's degree in microbiology, '30; and his doctorate in chemistry,'34—both from MSU. He served on the faculty of Washington University (St. Louis) before joining the Carnegie Institution's genetics department. Hershey's brother, the late Robert Hershey, was a professor in MSU's foods and nutrition department.

1970 **Clifton R. Wharton, Jr. Elected MSU's fourteenth President (served 1970-1977)**—Dr. Clifton R. Wharton, Jr. (b. 1926) was elected MSU's fourteenth president, effective January 1, 1970. He was the **first African-American president of any major university in the United States.**

Dr. Clifton R. Wharton, Jr., Fourteenth President

Prior to being elected, Wharton had been serving as vice president of the Agricultural Development Council, a Rockefeller Family Foundation. He served with the council for 13 years and had directed programs in Vietnam, Thailand, and Cambodia. He also taught and conducted research as a visiting professor at the Universities of Malaysia and Singapore.

Wharton entered Harvard University at age 16, and graduated in 1947 with a B.A. in history. "At Harvard...he helped found the National Student Association, which developed into a major force and lobby for students nationwide," according to a report by George Bullard in the *MSU Alumni Association Magazine.* "During World War II, he trained as a pilot at the home base of the famed Tuskegee airmen—talented black Army officers who took flight training near...Tuskegee Institute in Alabama." The war ended before he won his pilot's wings.

He received a master's degree from Johns Hopkins University's School of Advanced International Studies, and later earned M.A. and Ph.D. degrees in economics from the University of Chicago.

Dr. Wharton in a December 10, 1977 Farewell Commencement Address:

"In 1862, the Morrill Act (Creating the land-grant colleges) ushered in the most revolutionary reform in the history of education in the United States. It issued the land-grant mandate: to promote 'the liberal and practical education of the agricultural and industrial classes in the several pursuits and professions of life.'" "MSU came into being seven years before the Morrill Act and was in fact the mold from which the entire land-grant system was cast. We were pioneers then, and we are pioneers now."

An MSU team of Biochemistry researchers discovered a new way to detect and treat the rare and fatal Fabry's disease, a cause of kidney failure. The team consisted of Richard L. Anderson, Carol Mapes, and Charles C. Sweeley.

MSU Biophysicist Barnett Rosenberg led a team of researchers that discovered a platinum compound which halted the growth of cancer cells. This discovery, which would lead to an important new cancer-fighting drug, was submitted to the National Cancer Institute.

President Wharton announced the establishment of a Center for Environmental Quality—a national leadership initiative. Its Interdisciplinary Teaching and Research Committee, selected by the various college deans, was to develop recommendations for new curricula in the environmental quality area.

Oakland University, launched by Michigan State as MSU-Oakland in Rochester, Michigan in 1959, became an independent university. This action was approved by the MSU trustees in March, 1970, and by vote of the Michigan legislature on July 1, 1970.

Many Spartans regret this decision because of the effective presence Oakland University gave MSU in Oakland County, a flourishing business corridor and Michigan's most affluent county. Moreover, the loss of the school's elegant Meadow Brook Hall could have been a ready venue for conferences and fund-raising events.

MSU's University Club—an impressive dining and entertainment facility for MSU faculty, alumni, and townspeople—was completed in 1970. It was launched with $600,000 in gifts from alums Forest Akers and Floyd

MSU's University Club, a premier U.S. faculty club, opened in 1970.

Owen, and carried a mortgage of $1.2 million. At the time the site for the club was selected, East Lansing was "dry." Club members wanted to be able to have alcoholic beverages served. Therefore, the club was located just inside Lansing, which was "wet." In November 1968, East Lansing citizens voted two to one for lifting the ban on alcoholic beverages, rendering the club location a non-issue.

The University Club was founded in 1929 as the State College Club, and was primarily a faculty social organization. For forty years, the club met regularly for luncheons in three rooms on the third floor of the Union Building. Dr. Robert S. Shaw, MSC president, 1928-1941, was the club's first president. In the early years, retiring presidents of the State College Club (now University Club), were given a commemorative gavel that was fashioned from a giant timber that had been preserved from Old College Hall—the first building constructed on campus (1857-1918), now the site of Beaumont Tower.

Melvin C. Holm, '38, was elected CEO of the Carrier Corporation, Syracuse, N.Y.

Major Monte L. Stuck, '59, U.S. Air Force major, won the Distinguished Flying Cross for heroic aerial achievement in Southeast Asia.

Dr. Warren W. Brandt, '44, was elected the first president of Virginia Commonwealth University.

MSU dedicated its new $2 million Pesticide Research Center, thus leading national efforts to seek safe methods of protecting food crops and the public.

The College of Home Economics changed its name to the College of Human Ecology, the second university to do so. Cornell University was the first. Jeanette Lee, Dean of the College said, "We deal with individuals in a family environment, and the family as a unit in the larger environment of the community and society. We look at the family, or an individual, as an ecosystem."

The School of Police Administration was renamed the School of Criminal Justice. The name change stemmed from the fact the school did not serve a "police academy" function. Instead, the school was stressing the social sciences, law, public administration, and scientific investigation procedures.

The *State News* won its seventh Pacemaker Award for outstanding college journalism, in competition with 700 college newspapers nationwide. Only two college dailies received this top recognition in 1970.

Dr. Walter L. Mallmann's career-long work in assessing and protecting water and food supplies was recognized by the *MSU Faculty News* (Jan. 6, 1970): "The sanitary quality of the food and water that are consumed today have undoubtedly been influenced by Mallmann's teaching, research and public service. One of his students in a 1928 course in antiseptics and disinfectants was Alfred D. Hershey, winner of the 1969 Nobel Prize in medicine and physiology."

Tenure was explained by Assistant Provost Herman King. He said, "the tenure system (in America) was not invented by faculty, nor was it invented to protect people. **It is a device of society to protect ideas."**

Three of the 35 residence halls—Mary Mayo, Shaw, and Williams Halls—began a coed living experiment, placing men and women on different floors. MSU students had petitioned the Trustees to try different living environments, and it was approved in the fall of 1970. At that time, Shaw Hall already had women living on top floors and men on the lower floors. Coed living in separate wings of dormitories had been in existence since 1961.

Behavior changes noted as a result of coed living: "tremendous sociability" throughout the halls; students seemed to respond maturely on the morality issue, men decorated their rooms more, rooms were noticeably cleaner, some increase in noise levels—primarily on weekends, and masculine desire to protect females at Shaw Hall had emerged strongly.

In May of 1970, MSU students joined students from more than 400 college campuses in a nationwide strike against the Vietnam War. The first day of the strike, Wednesday, May 6, classroom attendance at MSU was down 23 percent; the second day, May 7, attendance was 31 percent below normal; and on Friday, May 8, no classes were held on campus.

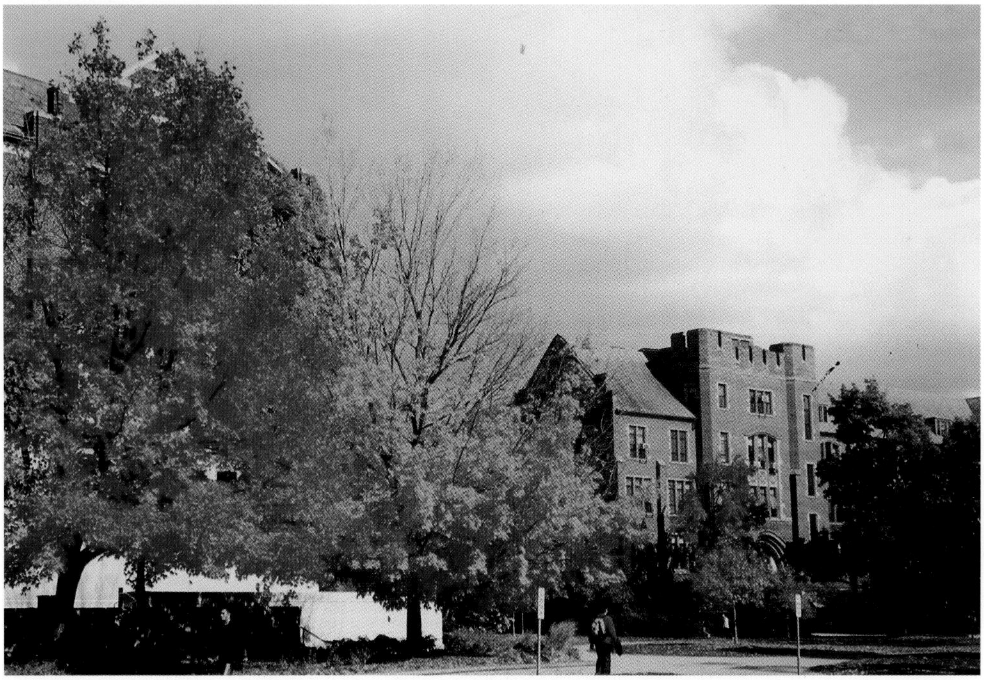

The College of Home Economics was renamed The College of Human Ecology in 1970. Its building, constructed in 1924, is now called Human Ecology.

It's notable that attendance in the Colleges of Veterinary Medicine, Natural Science, Engineering, and Agriculture and Natural Resources, remained essentially normal. Justin Morrill College of liberal arts had the lowest attendance, with 75 percent of the students missing.

The Geriatric Six Plus One—Popular Campus Dixieland Band—was organized by Professor Maury Crane, director of MSU's Voice Library. The group included Owen Reed, professor music, piano and flugelhorn; Owen Brainard, professor of art, drums; Bill Faunce, professor of sociology, trumpet; Bennett Sandefur, retired professor of geology and assistant dean of the College of Natural Science, banjo and guitar; Bob Snidnell, professor of music, piano, trombone and bass; Waldo Keller, professor of veterinary medicine, trumpet; Maury Crane, clarinet; and MSU alumnus Don Thornberg, an Oldsmobile executive, trombone and bass.

A survey of black, senior, and freshmen students revealed general satisfaction with MSU, particularly "friendly people, helpfulness, the atmosphere and the available assistance." Seniors rated the university high in modernity (80%), friendliness (70%), concern with social problems (84%), teaching quality and faculty accessibility (71%). Dissatisfaction was voiced regarding courses, residence halls, and academic advising. The survey was conducted for the Office of the Vice President for Special Projects by Dr. Bradley S. Greenberg, associate professor of communication.

MSU's official, lighted Christmas tree was curtailed as an economy measure. This brought to an end a 45-year tradition that began in 1924. The *MSU Alumni Magazine* (Feb. 1971) reported, "The campus Christmas tree was lighted in 1924 in front of the Women's Building (now Morrill Hall). The 65-foot tree was used through 1929. From 1930 through 1934, a tree in front of the Home Economics Building (now Human Ecology) was used." Then, from 1935 through 1969, a beautiful pine near the Abbot Street entrance to the campus was decorated. For 1970, a decorated tree was put up in the Union Building lounge.

At the December 5, 1970 commencement, **Durward "Woody" Varner**, chancellor of MSU-Oakland and soon to be chancellor of the University of Nebraska, told MSU graduates, **"Leave with a commitment."**

The 1970 university budget was $168,748,578. Enrollment was 40,511. At commencement, 9,979 degrees were awarded.

1971

Students Gain Participation in Academic Governance—Following two years of debate, the Taylor Report was approved, allowing students participation in academic governance. The report recommendation increased the number of students on the 133-member Academic Council from three non-voting members to 31 members with voting rights. The Council reported to the Academic Senate.

The report stated, "...each of the university departments, schools, and units whose work concerns students 'shall develop patterns for the significant involvement of its students in the decision-making processes by which policy is formed.'"

Fourteen MSU graduate programs were ranked in the nation's top 30 for quality by an American Council on Education survey of 6,000 faculty members throughout the U.S. Twelve graduate departments were ranked in the highest category: Sociology, Zoology, Psychology, Chemistry, Electrical Engineering, Physiology, Micro-Biology, Biochemistry, Molecular Biology, Entomology, Population Biology, and Development Biology. Another dozen departments placed in the second highest category.

MSU ranked first in the nation among public universities in National Science Foundation (NSF) awards won during the three year period—1969 through 1971, tying the University of Iowa by averaging 2.1 fellowships per 100 students. In total number of NSF awards granted during the three-year period, MSU was fifth among all public and private universities—ranked just behind Caltech, MIT, Harvard and Cornell—all private schools. The report on NSF awards, written by Harvard scientists Paul Doty and Dorothy Zinberg, appeared in the 1973 winter issue of *American Scientist.*

MSU students were second in the nation in the number of Woodrow Wilson fellowships won.

President Wharton described an action-packed year of confrontations, saying, "I've had the works—demonstrations, sit-ins, student riots—there's been everything you could imagine. We even had a wildcat strike. This is one of the most total jobs I've ever run across. You are on demand at all times for every conceivable kind of decision."

He, of course, was referring to the multiple-constituency nature of being the president of a state-assisted university with a politically elected board. Demands can come from students, faculty, staff, alumni, trustees, legislators, the governor, citizens, the news media, and more. Wharton pointed out that university presidential tenures had dropped on average from eight years to five.

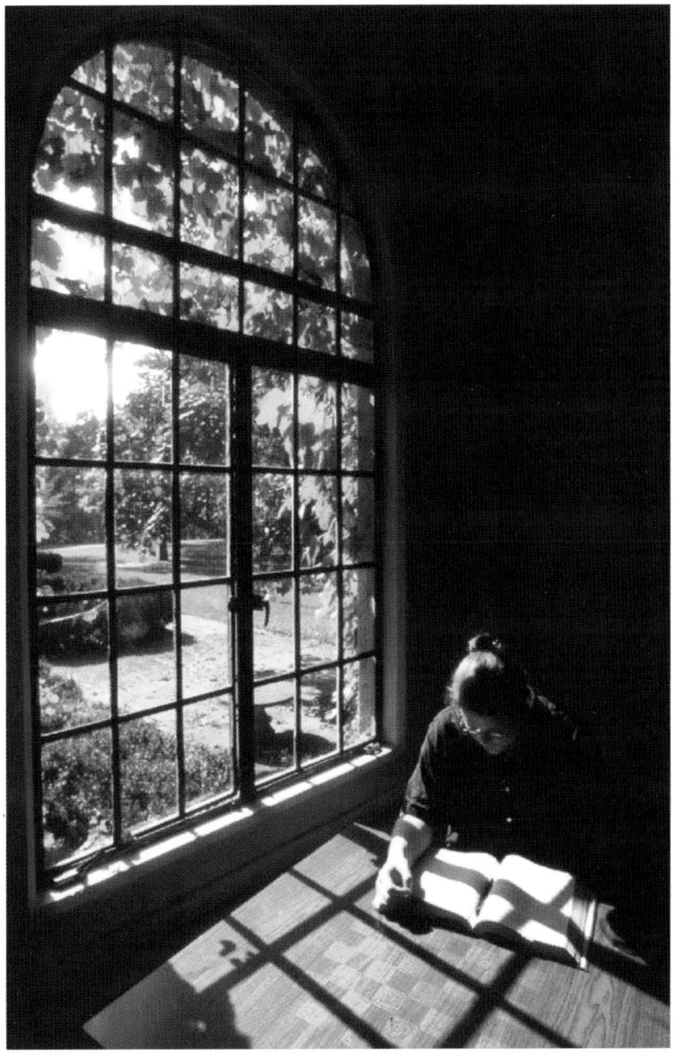

"Studying up a Storm" at Williams Hall. MSU students ranked 1st in the nation in winning National Science Foundation awards, 1969-1971.

"When President Clifton and First Lady Dolores Wharton traveled to the Far East in 1971, wherever they went—Japan, Korea, Taiwan, or the Philippines, their alumni hosts included graduates of MSU's School of Hotel, Restaurant and Institutional Management (who were running the hotels where they stayed)," as reported by Bob Bao in the *MSU Alumni Association Magazine.*

True to its pioneering tradition, **MSU established a Day Care Center for its married students—the first comprehensive facility of its kind in the Big Ten.**

Lyman L. Frimodig, retired MSU Athletic General Manager, and **Fred W. Stabley, Sr.**, MSU Sports Information Director, combined to produce the book *Spartan Saga*, which reviewed 115 years of athletics at Michigan State.

George R. Ariyoshi, '49, was elected Lt. Governor of Hawaii, the first Asian-American to serve in that capacity.

Dr. David K. Berlo, '53, was serving as president of Illinois State University.

Charles Cioffi, '61, M.A. '62, had strong supporting roles in the movies *Klute* and *Shaft.*

Dr. Hugh Jerome Scott, Ed.D. '66, was named Superintendent of Schools for Washington, D.C.

Director of Bands Ken Bloomquist used the 100th anniversary of the Spartan Marching Band to launch an **Alumni Band Association**. In the fall of 1971, Bloomquist gathered 140 alumni for a pre-football game practice session. Participants included alumni going back to 1919. The tradition has grown to the point where 400 alumni musicians show up each fall for their annual football halftime show.

The Life Sciences I Building for the College of Human Medicine was completed. Fee Halls were remodeled to accommodate offices and medical teaching laboratories for the College of Human Medicine and the College of Osteopathic Medicine.

The College of Human Medicine added the third and fourth years of medical education, which would lead to the first Doctor of Medicine degrees at MSU in 1972.

Credit card use was extended to all areas of the campus in January, 1971.

A legislative effort to enforce uniform teaching loads in all institutions of higher learning was one of six intrusions mentioned in **President Wharton's first State-of-the-University message.** He was emphatic, **"Who we have on this campus, who we promote, who we admit, what we teach, and what we research are all public concerns but decisions on these issues must be made with the university. Not by outside parties, and not in the political arena."**

With the approval of the *State News* articles of incorporation, the Trustees officially cut the university's ties to the newspaper, making it an independent operation.

Addressing campus unrest during 1971—which included anti-"Chicago Seven" verdict, anti-ROTC, anti-Cambodia, and anti-Kent State shootings protests and led to some destruction of property—George Bullard, editor of the *State News,* wrote, "Unfortunately, many citizens did not distinguish between the 50 radicals and 39,950 other students who did not turn dissent into destruction."

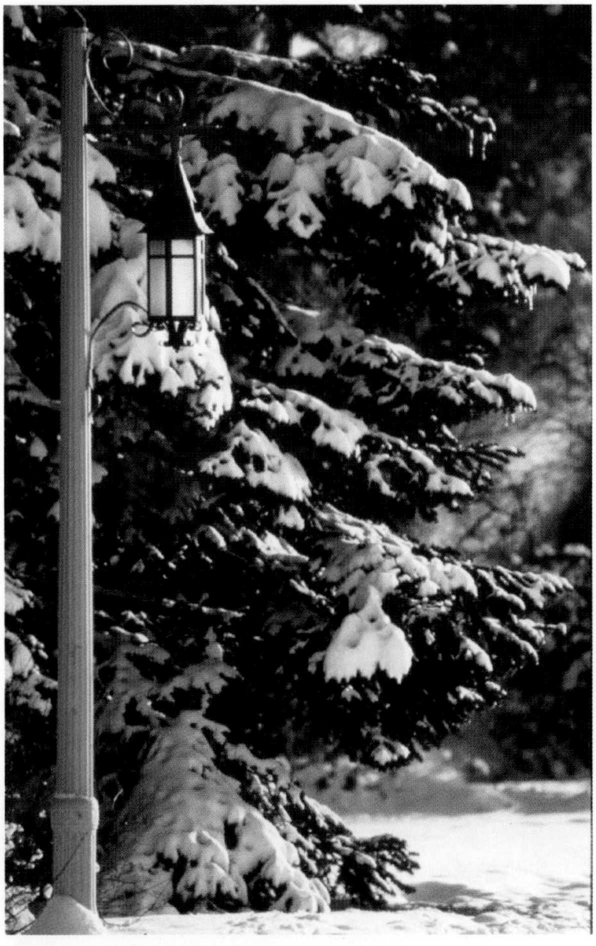

Historic Lanterns punctuate the campus scene.

MSU won the Big Ten All-Sports competition in the 1970-1971 school year with team championships in five sports: cross country, fencing, hockey, wrestling, and baseball.

Since beginning Big Ten sports participation in 1951, the Spartans had won six All-Sports titles; finished second eleven times; third three times, and fifth once. MSU's first place finishes were in: 1954, 1958, 1962, 1966, 1967, and 1971.

Spartan halfback Eric "The Flea" Allen set an NCAA and Big Ten single game rushing record of 350 yards at Purdue. MSU won the game 43-10, setting school records of 573 rushing yards, and 698 total yards.

The "Freaks," long-haired students, beat the "Pigs," East Lansing Policemen, 12-7 in a football game attended by 25,000 at Spartan Stadium. Ticket proceeds were given to leukemia research and treatment at St. Jude's Hospital in Memphis, Tennessee.

The former East Lansing High School building on Abbott Road was renamed the John A. Hannah Middle School. It is now the Hannah Community Center.

Some 46 percent of all MSU students received annual financial support, averaging $554 per student.

The 1971 university budget was $174,468,335. Enrollment was 41,649. At commencement, 10,850 degrees were awarded.

1972

MSU Reaches Out to Disadvantaged, Minorities and Women—President Wharton's Commission on Admission and Student Body Composition reported that "MSU should enroll more disadvantaged and minority students, redouble its efforts to work with the state's community colleges." The Women's Steering Committee of the Commission developed a 29-page "action plan" for equal opportunity that proposed 21 recommendations for changes in policy or procedure—12 of them specifically for women. Included were appointment of a director of women's athletics, an Office of Women's Affairs, and creation of a Women's Advisory Council.

In the fall of 1972, two women were admitted to the MSU Marching Band. They were the first females to win positions in the band, with the exception of World War II years, when there was a shortage of men on campus.

MSU's pro-active stance on equal opportunity increased minority enrollment from 2,064 in 1971 to 3,024 in 1972. This represented 7.2 percent of the university's 41,378 students. As a result, **MSU was among just a few major universities in the nation with more than 3,000 minority students.**

President Wharton outlined several university priorities in his State-of-the-University address: expanded medical education programs, new colleges of law and

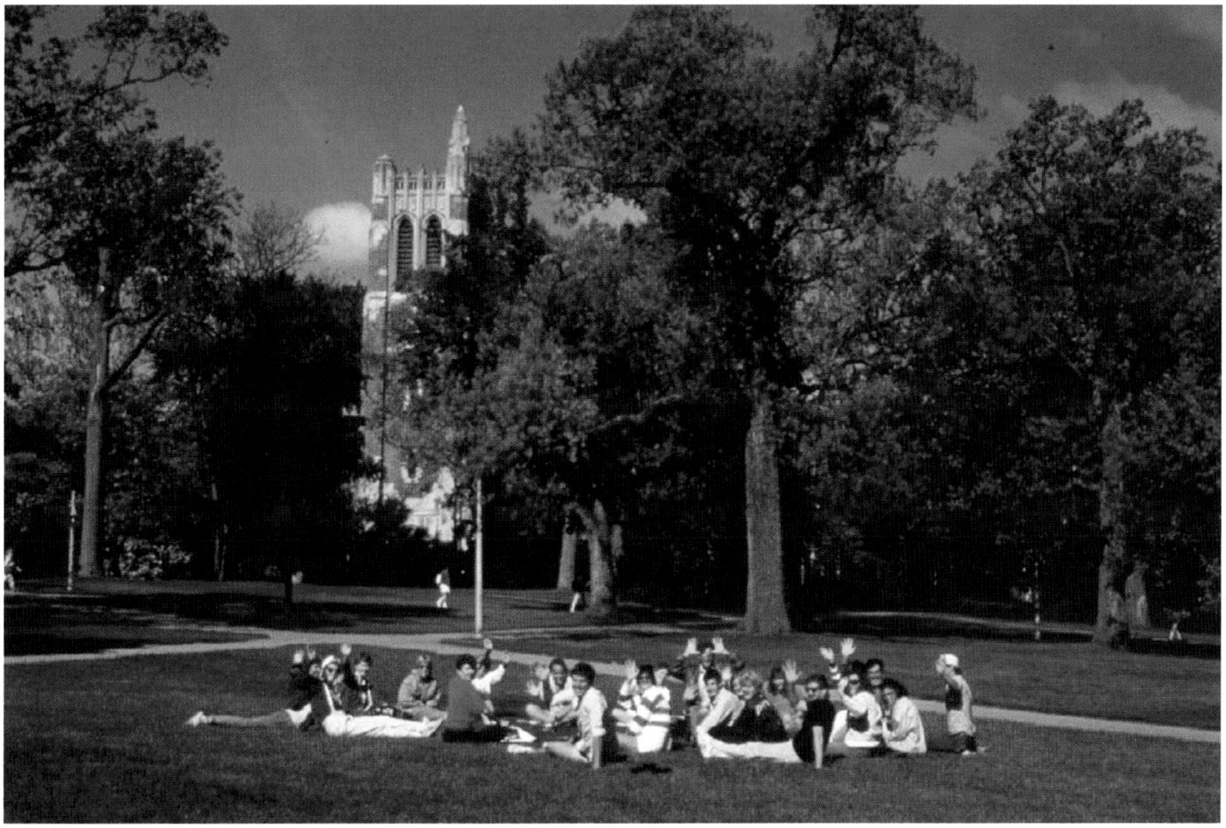

Students luxuriate in front of Beaumont Tower in late spring sunshine, inside MSU's "Sacred Space."

urban development, wider efforts on behalf of the poor, greater funding and support for environmental programs, and even stronger emphasis on the academic foundation of the university—the basic disciplines.

In early February, **the Big Ten was accused of blatant segregation by three black MSU administrators** —Dr. Robert L. Green, Director of the Center for Urban Affairs; Joseph H. McMillan, Director Equal Opportunity Programs; and Thomas Gunnings, Assistant Director of Minority Housing. They demanded the appointment of blacks to administrative positions.

These administrators laid out seven recommendations to the Big Ten faculty representatives and athletic directors in Chicago on March 7, 1972. Recommendations included: Establishment of a Big Ten equal opportunity committee, selection of more black officials for athletic events, a fifth year of financial support for athletes, hiring of a black associate commissioner of the conference, hiring of black counselors by universities—focusing on the needs of black athletes. Following the meeting, Dr. Green stated, "Mr. Duke (Big Ten Commissioner) assured me they will give full consideration to each concern raised and recommendations offered through our report." MSU Trustees voted 5 to 3, criticizing Green's methods, but supporting his purposes.

In late February, **a group of MSU black athletes made seven demands of the university and the athletic department**. Within a month, MSU Executive Vice President Jack Breslin announced agreement on the seven points. The agreement called for MSU to encourage the appointment of more black officials, coaches and trainers in the Big Ten; to name two athletes to the search committee reviewing athletic director candidates; and to form a "racially sensitive" grievance committee in the department of athletics.

Alan L. VerPlanck, senior English major, won a Rhodes Scholarship, MSU's fourth.

Dick Cooper, Class of 1969, a reporter with the *Rochester* (N.Y.) *Times Union* newspaper, teamed with John Machacek to win a Pulitzer Prize for reporting on the Attica (N.Y.) prison riot of 1971.

William Kostecke, '51, was serving as president of the Miller Brewing Company.

Harold L. Neal, Jr., '46, was serving as president of ABC Radio.

James Caan, '60, was nominated for an Oscar and an Emmy in 1972 for his roles in the movies *The Godfather* and *Brian's Song.*

Don A. Jones, '33, U.S. Navy Rear Admiral, was appointed director of the National Ocean Survey for the National Oceanic & Atmospheric Administration.

Joseph A. Marino, '60, named president of the Braun North America Division of Gillette Co.

Fred S. Wojtalik, '52, was awarded the National Aeronautics and Space Administration's Exceptional Service Medal for work on the development of the Lunar Roving Vehicles which drove on the moon.

George E. Willis, '42, was elected president of Lincoln Electric Co., Cleveland, Ohio.

William E. Engbretson, '50, was elected the first president of Governor's State University, Chicago.

John Rosencrans, '47, was serving as president of Eisenhower College.

MSU led all of the nation's universities in the number of National Merit Scholars enrolled for the eighth consecutive year—564.

For three days in May, some 3,000 to 4,000 students and non-students—less than ten percent of MSU's enrollment—protested the Vietnam War. In East Lansing, Grand River Ave. was blockaded repeatedly, causing traffic to be routed around the downtown area. Students attempted to take over the Administration Building and other sensitive areas. Protestors pitched tents along Grand River Ave. and built fires on the street. By week's end, 74 people had been arrested, 30 of them students.

President Wharton did not accede to a student demand that MSU be closed for a week as a war protest. He stated, "The Board of Trustees recently adopted two resolutions condemning the expansion of the Vietnam War and I sent these resolutions to President Nixon."

In keeping with its tradition of innovation, **MSU established an Office of Handicapped Students in the fall of 1972**, under the direction of James Hamilton, Assistant Provost for Special Programs.

In a pioneering inter-disciplinary effort, **MSU had become the first university in the U.S. to provide medical education to both M.D.s and Doctors of Osteopathy. MSU led the nation in the study of behavioral sciences for both medical programs.**

MSU ranked first in the nation in the number of women and first-time freshmen enrolled in the fall of 1972. The survey by the National Association of State Universities and Land-Grant Colleges showed MSU's female enrollment at 19,745, followed by Ohio State at 17,635. First-time freshmen numbered 6,894, again followed by Ohio State with 6,463

MSU Trustees opened the door to the sons and daughters of migrant workers in Michigan. They approved a plan making students eligible for "in-state" tuition, provided their parents were employed for a minimum of two months each year for three of the past five years.

The age of majority in Michigan was changed from 21 to 18 through an amendment to the State Constitution. This altered the political complexion of elections in East Lansing and social habits, too, because thousands of students could now vote as well as purchase alcoholic beverages.

J. Burt Smith, assistant athletic director since 1965, was named athletic director, replacing Biggie Munn who retired after suffering a stroke.

Coach Grady Peninger led MSU's wrestling team to its seventh consecutive Big Ten title. Three Spartans won individual NCAA titles: Greg Johnson, his third consecutive, at 118 pounds; and brothers Tom and Pat Milkovich, at 141, and 122 pounds, respectively. MSU's team was NCAA runner-up.

The Spartan wrestling team defeated defending NCAA champion Oklahoma State, 20-15 in a dual meet before an overflow crowd at the IM-West building. Those who attended said it was the most exciting wrestling match in MSU history.

World records were set by MSU sprinters Herb Washington and Marshall Dill at the Spartan Relays at Jenison Fieldhouse. Washington, a senior, won the 60-yard dash in 5.8 seconds, beating the world record of 5.9 seconds. Dill, a freshman, won the 300-yard dash in 29.5, beating the previous world record of 29.8.

Ken Popejoy won the NCAA indoor mile run title in 4:02.9. The MSU track team won the Big Ten indoor title, and was NCAA indoor runner-up.

Judy Spraggs, a junior, placed first in the North American Skating Championships, winning three of five races. She had been senior women's state champion for two years.

Mike Robinson, basketball guard, became the first Spartan to win the Big 10 scoring title, averaging 27.2 points in 14 conference games.

In Duffy Daugherty's last year as coach, the Spartan football team beat undefeated Ohio State at Spartan Stadium, 19-12. Dirk Krijt, called the "Little Dutch Treat," kicked four first half field goals. It was OSU's only loss in 1972.

Carol M. Davis was appointed by MSU as the first Assistant Athletic Director for Women in the Big Ten.

Lyman Frimodig, MSU's only ten-letter athlete (baseball, basketball, football) and 41-year athletic department staff member, died in 1972. He was MSU athletic business manager for decades, served four terms as East Lansing's mayor, and was a teammate of Notre Dame's legendary George Gipp at Larium, Michigan High School in the Upper Peninsula.

The 1972 university budget was $182,428,900. Enrollment was 41,378. An all-time record 11,100 degrees were granted during the year.

1973

College of Urban Development Opens: First in Nation—The College of Urban Development opened at MSU in the fall of 1973. It was the first of its kind in the nation, and offered a series of courses emphasizing the problems of urban living as well as racial and ethnic studies.

Dr. Robert L. Green was named acting dean. He emphasized, "A dedication to the eradication of urban problems must permeate university courses and field work."

President Wharton called for the university to "...re-dedicate itself to lifelong education," a discipline in which MSU already was a national leader. In his State-of-the University address, Wharton called for "regular sabbaticals for scientists, scholars and executives; catch-up and updating opportunities for professionals; training and re-training for homemakers and others who wish to enter or re-enter the job market; and enrichment opportunities for the disadvantaged." His remarks were "...based on the work of the MSU Task Force on Lifelong Education, which had completed a year-long study."

Wharton declared, "The very heart of the land-grant concept lies in its requirement that new knowledge and insight to be available to the widest public as soon as possible."

Michigan State's doctoral program for training university administrators was ranked tops in the nation. Directors and faculty members of student personnel programs at 20 colleges and universities were surveyed and gave MSU the number one position.

MSU's Department of Dormitories and Food Services won an Ivy Award from *Institutions/Volume Feeding* magazine for the quality of its residence hall meals. Institutional management competitors nationwide **voted the MSU dormitory system No. 1** and gave MSU the Award of Distinction.

Michigan State's Volunteer Bureau attracted more than 1,000 student volunteers who gave between three to five hours a week to helping the elderly, the young, the physically handicapped, and mothers on Aid to Dependent Children assistance. **Their motto was: "People Need."**

MSU's Waste Control Authority, established in 1971 and headed by Mark Rosenblatt, was initiating recycling and clean-up programs. **It was the first university organization of its kind in the nation.** Student involvement was key in MSU's newspaper recycling project which also was run by the Authority. It was the largest such effort by any university—handling 8 tons of paper per week from dormitories.

Dr. Ben Burmester, director of the U.S. Department of Agriculture's Regional Poultry Research Laboratory on the MSU campus, **won the Browning Award "...for the most outstanding achievement in the improvement of food sources anywhere in the world."** Burmester's team

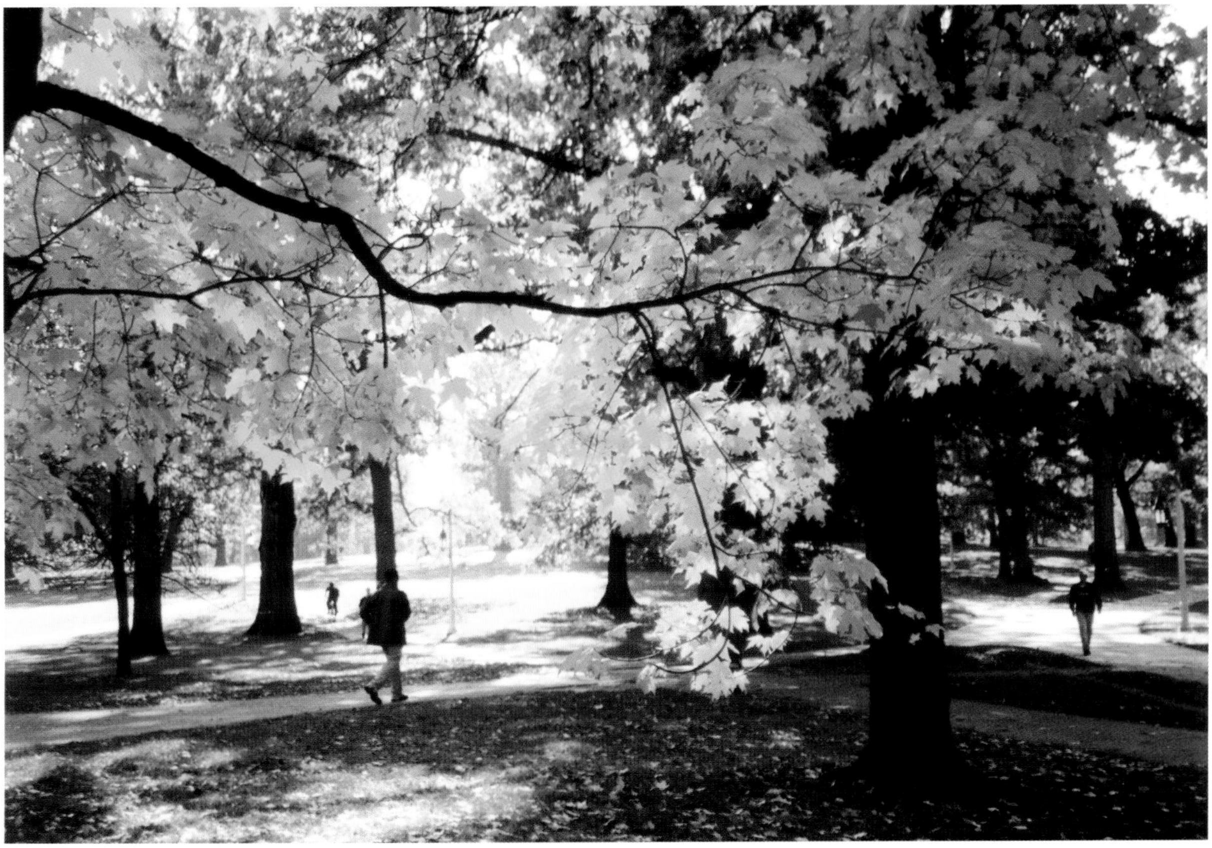

The haze of a fall afternoon envelopes the central campus–one of America's botanical jewels.

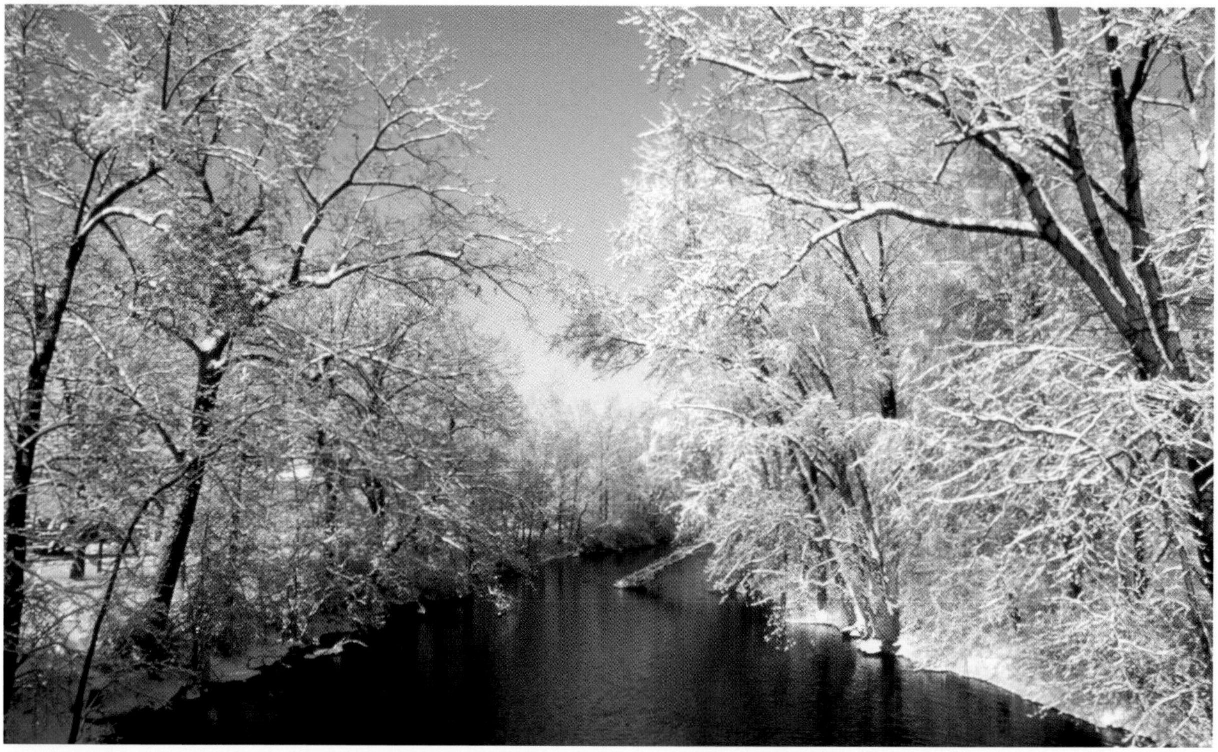

Powdered snow decorates the tree-lined Red Cedar River. In 1905, 8,000 trees were planted on campus, including a row of trees on both sides of the river from the Kalamazoo Street bridge to the Farm Lane bridge.

developed an anti-cancer vaccine for chickens. He made the vaccine available for commercial production to help reduce the annual $200 million loss in poultry meat and eggs. The vaccine prevented Marek's disease, a malignant disease in the lymph system in chickens.

Four College of Education faculty were presidents of national and international organizations: Dr. Cole S. Brembeck, president, Comparative and International Education Society; Dr. William K. Durr, president, International Reading Association; Dr. Robert L. Ebel, president, American Education Research Association; and Dr. Floyd G. Parker, president, Council of Education Facility Planners International.

Jack Meyers, '51, was serving as publisher of *Sports Illustrated.*

Coy G. Ecklund, '38, was elected president of the Equitable Life Assurance Society of New York.

William H. Bricker, '54, was serving as president of Diamond Shamrock Corporation.

Charles W. Bachman, '48, Honeywell Corp. senior scientist and son of former Spartan football coach Charles Bachman, won the A.N. Twining Award from the Association of Computing Machinery for outstanding contributions to data base technology.

Dr. Gary L. Seevers, '59, M.A. '66, Ph.D. '68, was nominated to one of three seats on President Nixon's Council of Economic Advisors.

Michael J. Dul, '73 and landscape architecture graduate, designed the memorial honoring the 300th anniversary of missionary explorer Father Marquette, who died in 1675. The memorial was to be built in 1974 near the north end of the Mackinac Bridge at the Straits of Mackinaw.

Edith Stern, M.S. '70, once the youngest coed in the nation at age 12, took her first job at age 20 as a senior associate programmer at IBM's development laboratory in Boca Raton, Florida.

Martha Smith, '74, a Detroit model, was *Playboy Magazine*'s July playmate of the month.

Spartan Bonnie Lauer, 22, from Berkley, Michigan, won the Women's NCAA golf championship. At MSU, she was Michigan Amateur Champion in 1970 and 1972; won medalist honors in four consecutive Midwest Collegiate playoffs, and was medalist in the 1971 Western Amateur.

MSU telephone operators were tested regularly by students and outside callers. Student questions included, "How do I get my hide-a-bed down?" "How long do you bake a potato?" "Could I speak to Mary? She drives a red Chevy." Correct spelling of words was a common request by students without dictionaries.

Brad Van Pelt won the Maxwell Trophy as the nation's top football player.

Mike Robinson won the Big Ten basketball scoring title for the second consecutive year.

Tom Milkovich won his fourth straight Big Ten individual wrestling title.

Marshall Dill set an NCAA record in the 220-yard dash in 20.9 seconds.

Ken Popejoy ran the fastest mile in Big Ten history: 3 minutes and 57 seconds.

President Wharton reported, "The Governor has endorsed MSU's request for the establishment of a College of Law..." This dream would not materialize until the Detroit College of Law moved to MSU in 1996.

MSU was assigned the zip code 48824. Faculty apartments, University and Spartan Villages, the Cherry Lane apartments, and the MSU Alumni Association were designated 48823.

Charles Washburn, proprietor of the popular Smoke Shop on Grand River Avenue, which he opened in 1916 and operated until 1960, died at age 80.

MSU had 18,600 parking spaces on campus—more spaces than the enrollments of most schools. Still, finding a place to park on campus could be frustrating.

The 1973 university budget was $193,158,868. Enrollment was 41,649. A total of 10,831 degrees were granted during the year.

1974

MSU Continued to Flex Its Academic Brainpower and Faculty Leadership—President Wharton pointed to MSU's academic success and faculty leadership:

1. MSU students won 18 National Science Foundation graduate fellowships, placing it first in the Big Ten and first among all public universities in the country. Only Harvard, Yale, and MIT had more NSF awards.

2. MSU had 462 National Merit Scholars enrolled, tops among all public universities, and second only to Harvard.

3. Senior Roy Pea was named MSU's fifth Rhodes Scholar, and the second student in three years to win this scholarship. Two students won prized Danforth Scholarships.

4. Sixty-five MSU faculty members were serving as presidents of various national professional and academic organizations.

5. Two faculty members won rare Guggenheim Fellowships.

MSU's Cooperative Extension Service made more than three million contacts with Michigan citizens during 1974. These contacts included 535,000 through its family living programs in nutrition, family finance, and health and resource management.

MSU's flagship youth program—4H—reached 210,000 boys and girls.

Munn Ice Arena was built in 1974 at a cost of $3.5 million dollars. It honors Clarence L. "Biggie" Munn, MSU football coach (1947-1953) and athletic director (1954-1971). Built strictly for hockey, it seats 6,470, but accommodated 7,121 fans for a game with Michigan on March 1, 2001.

MSU was selected to develop the first network of international rehabilitation centers. Michigan State was chosen as the site by 50 representatives from health agencies, government and industry, because of its leadership in disability programs, research and international outreach.

MSU junior Eric Gentile, who lost the use of his limbs in a 1967 motorcycle accident, **coined the word "handicapper"** to describe himself. He said it had a better connotation than "disabled" or "crippled." "Handicapper" has since been adopted by disabled people as a favored description.

Professor Oscar Tosi was "...perfecting a scientific method which identified people by mapping their voice patterns. Tosi was a leading authority in the field. Karl Kryter, Stanford Research Institute, said '...he (Tosi) had more data than anybody else has ever collected in dealing with voice ID.'" Bill Iddings reported the story in the *MSU Alumni Association Magazine.*

MSU reached out to help upgrade the Michigan wine industry, which was sixth in the nation, producing two million gallons annually. **Professor Stan Howell**, associate professor of horticulture, led the research and development, which was funded by the Michigan Wine Institute and sponsored by the MSU Agricultural Extension Service. Bob Bao, *MSU Alumni Association Magazine,* reported the story, quoting Howell, "The Michigan wine industry is capable of producing wines that would make Baron Rothschild envious."

MSU Ombudsman Jim Rust declared, "I think MSU is great, and the distinguishing thing is the vitality. I don't know if there ever has been a university so bursting with energy. We've always been willing to try new things."

MSU First Lady Dolores Wharton "...visited every dormitory on campus and ate with the students. Twice Mrs. Wharton has spent a week living in a residence hall...in McDonel and Snyder-Phillips." Pam Robinson of the *East Lansing Towne Courier* reported the story.

MSU opened a new residence hall living option, allowing men and women to reside on the same hall floors starting in September 1974. Just 125 rooms were set aside for the option, or just 1.5 percent of MSU's 9,000 residence hall rooms.

A residence hall campaign to cut food waste was launched under the slogan, **"Take all you want, eat all you take."** The program drew national attention and inquiries from several universities and the U.S. Army.

Bob Leonard, Class of 1963, and a sound engineer for Universal City Studios, won a special scientific Oscar from the Academy of Motion Picture Arts for the invention of Sensurround, a low frequency sound system that "surrounds your senses."

President emeritus John A. Hannah, age 72 and class of 1923, was tapped by the United Nations to organize the World Food Conference, held in November, 1974.

Jack Breslin, '46, MSU executive vice president and secretary of the board of trustees, was praised by Charles Zollar, chair of the Michigan Senate Appropriations Committee: "Jack Breslin is the most efficient of any of the lobbyists. I couldn't recommend anybody higher, and I don't know him on a social basis. He's never bought me a drink. He just provides the information in a way that even legislators understand it. I know the university would never have been as successful in the State Legislature if it were not for the efforts of Jack Breslin."

Dr. William Lukash, '52, Navy Rear Admiral, was named chief White House physician and President Gerald Ford's personal doctor.

Jerald F. terHorst, '45, was named White House press secretary.

H. Stewart Knight, '48, was appointed head of the U.S. Secret Service.

Don Johnson, '51, was elected president and CEO of J. Walter Thompson Co., the world's largest advertising agency.

James H. Quello, '35, former general manager of WJR-Radio, Detroit, was named a member of the Federal Communications Commission.

Clifford M. Kirtland, '45, president of Cox Broadcasting Corp., Atlanta, was appointed to the board of the Federal Reserve Bank of Atlanta.

John W. Fitzgerald, '47, was named to the Michigan Supreme Court.

Karl Eitel, '51, was serving as general manager of the famous Broadmoor Hotel, Colorado Springs, Colorado.

First Lt. Michael L. Thompson, '70, received his second Distinguished Flying Cross for aerial achievement in Southeast Asia.

Dr. H. Charles Moore, M.A. '65, Ph.D. '70, elected president of Kirksville College of Osteopathic Medicine, Kirksville, MO.

Dr. Frank H. Blackington, III, Ph.D. '60, named president of the University of Pennsylvania at Johnstown.

Dr. Beverly White Miller, M.A. '57, elected president of The College of St. Benedictine, St. Joseph, Minnesota.

Dr. Howard A. Tanner, '47, M.S. '50, Ph.D. '52, was named director of the Michigan Department of Natural Resources. He had been MSU's director of natural resources.

Stuart A. Lassen, '54, was named president of the Lassen Pontiac, Buick, Cadillac dealership in Battle Creek, Michigan. Lassen had served as dealer since 1966 for the automotive retail operation, which had been founded in 1931.

Gustav Henry Poesch, '30, was elected to the **Floriculture Hall of Fame** for "contributions to the advancement of floriculture in America." He was vice president of Fred C. Gloeckner & Co., New York.

George Taylor, a blind summa cum laude 1964 graduate, with a masters degree in 1966, was writing and editing technical publications at the Army Tank-Automotive Command in Detroit.

Colleen House, '73, a 22-year old Republican, won a seat in the Michigan House of Representatives. She became the second youngest person ever to serve in the legislature.

The *MSU Alumni Association Magazine* won five awards at the National Conference of the American Alumni Council.

Students establish *Guinness Book of World Records* non-stop bridge game record. "At Snyder Hall, a group of bridge fanatics" played non-stop for 205 hours, breaking the old world record of 176 hours, 45 minutes, set in Scotland in 1971. Anchor man for the Spartan team was Larry "60-Hour" Wickett.

"At the Meridian Mall in Okemos...Jannie MacKercher and Rick Young jitterbugged for 50 consecutive hours" winning a marathon dance contest staged for the National Multiple Sclerosis Society. They outlasted 500 other contestants.

MSU Upsets Undefeated, No. 1 Ohio State—In one of its greatest upsets of all time, the Spartan football team stunned the undefeated No.1 Ohio State Buckeyes before a packed Spartan Stadium and a regional television audience on November 9, 1974. Ron Karle, editor, *MSU Alumni Association Magazine,* wrote about a game to remember. OSU had won 19 straight games. Midway in the fourth quarter of this November 9th game, Ohio State was leading 13-3. With five and one half minutes left, Spartan quarterback Charlie Baggett hit end Mike Jones with a perfect 50-yard touchdown pass to cut the lead to 13-9.

After the next series of plays, OSU punted to MSU's 12 yard line. The next play ranks among the most memorable of all time at MSU. With 3:21 left in the game, sophomore fullback Levi Jackson blasted off tackle, dashed past the Buckeye linebackers, cut to the west sideline and out-sprinted the OSU secondary on the way to an 88-yard touchdown run. The explosive roar of the crowd was the loudest the author has ever experienced. MSU kicked the extra point and led 16-13.

Ohio State then moved the ball to the MSU six yard line in the final seconds of the game. The ball was snapped to Brian Baschnagel who ran it into the end zone. The head linesman signaled touchdown. But the field and back judges both signaled that time had run out before the ball was snapped. Both teams thought they had won. The crowd was confused.

MSU fans stormed the field, covering it from goal line to goal line. Wayne Duke, Big Ten Commissioner, was in the press box and took the initiative to get to the officials to get a clear reading on their decision. Meanwhile, MSU

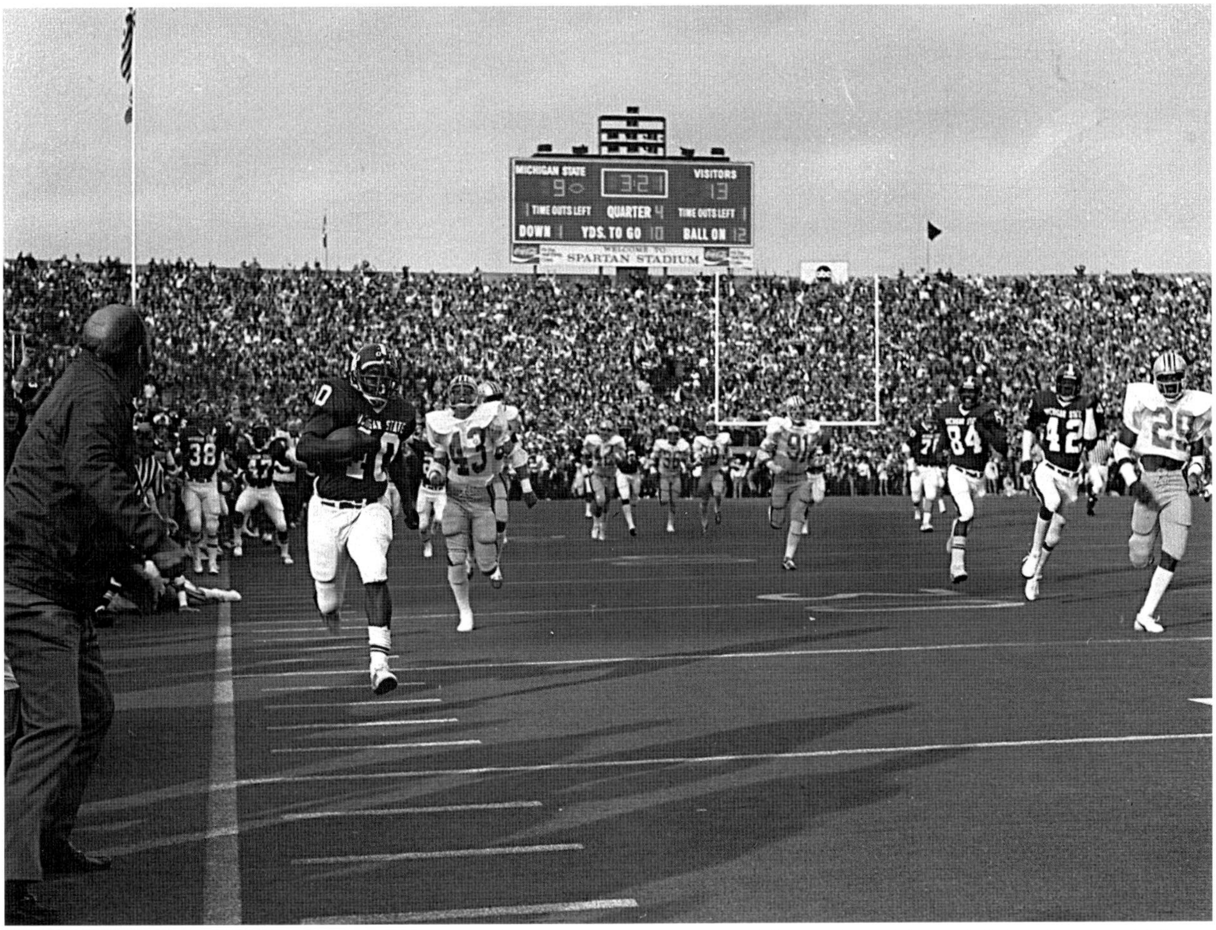

MSU fullback Levi Jackson sprints 88 yards for fourth quarter touchdown that defeated # 1 unbeaten Ohio State, 16-13, before a regional TV audience and 78,533 Spartan Stadium fans on November 9, 1974. This unforgettable run ranks among the five most exciting plays in Michigan State football history.

fans roamed the field and tore down both goal posts. "One enterprising student, apparently anticipating victory, had the foresight to bring an acetylene torch to the game providing professional assistance in...dismantling the goal posts." Other fans remained standing at their seats awaiting the outcome. Duke finally tracked the officials to their rooms in Kellogg Center, and was told the OSU touchdown did not count, and MSU was the winner.

Forty-six minutes after the game concluded, Duke announced on the Spartan Stadium public address system that the final score was MSU 16, OSU 13. Again, there was bedlam among Spartan fans. It was the most unusual finish to a major football game anyone had ever seen.

Ohio State football coach Woody Hayes declared, "A great, great season was smashed to smithereens."

***Sports Illustrated* proclaimed, "a group of undernourished and culturally deprived Michigan State Spartans scored one of the epic, colossal, classic, shocking upsets in the history of men and boys."**

Mike Robinson, All-American 5' 11" basketball guard, set an MSU career scoring record of 1,717 points. He won the France Pomeroy Naismith Award as the **"Nation's Most Outstanding Basketball Player Under Six Feet."**

Steve Garvey, '72, and Mike Marshall, '65, M.A. '67, Los Angeles Dodgers teammates, helped the National League win the All-Star baseball game versus the American League, 7-2. Garvey, the game's MVP, had two hits, one RBI and one run. Marshall pitched two no-hit innings.

Los Angeles Dodger relief pitcher Mike Marshall, Class of 1965, won the coveted Cy Young Award as the best National League pitcher. He was the first relief pitcher in history to win the award.

Three Spartans played in the 1974 World Series—Steve Garvey, '72, L.A. Dodgers first baseman, who **won the National League's MVP award**; **Mike Marshall, '65**, L.A. Dodgers relief pitcher; and **Herb Washington, '73, Oakland Athletics, baseball's first and only designated runner.** Washington was considered the world's fastest human, with 9.2 second speed in the 100 yard dash. Oakland won the World Series.

The 1974 university budget was $209,334,369. Enrollment was 43,459. Graduates during the year numbered 10,298.

1975

MSU and its College of Agriculture & Natural Resources Were Leaders in Fighting World Hunger—One half billion of the planet's four billion people were hungry every day in 1975, and one billion were undernourished. Ten thousand people were starving to death each day around the world.

MSU's contributions to feeding the world were unrivaled:

1. MSU President Emeritus John A. Hannah led the United Nations World Food Conference in Rome, held in November, 1974.

2. President Wharton was head of the Food Advisory Panel created by the U.S. Congress, and was editor of Subsistence Agriculture and Economic Development.

3. Dr. Sylvan Wittwer, MSU's Assistant Dean of Agriculture, was serving as Chairman of the Board on Agriculture and Renewable Resources of the National Academy of Sciences. The National Science Foundation asked Wittwer to prepare a plan to increase food and fiber production. As Director of MSU's Agricultural Experiment Station, he supervised 450 agricultural research projects that were run on a $9 million budget.

4. MSU's Institute of International Agriculture transmitted agricultural knowledge to 50 nations.

5. More than 150 MSU faculty had international experience and were working on the problems of the underdeveloped countries.

6. MSU's Center for Responsive Learning in the College of Agriculture was visited regularly by foreign agricultural policy makers to learn how to attack their agricultural problems.

7. Michigan State in its history had developed more than 200 varieties of agricultural crops and products that increased the quality and quantity of food produced.

Dr. Armand Hunter, director of MSU's Continuing Education Service, was named the first Dean of Lifelong Education Programs.

Science professor John Newton Moore "began including the theory of creation by God in his introductory science courses. His was **the first serious treatment of Biblical creation in a science course at a public university.**" Moore stated, "I feel that it is high time that taxpayers be assured that their young people hear a fair presentation of both sides of the issue. These people who are evolutionists have been getting away with monopolistic practices."

Biggie Munn (Munn Arena), MSU's winningest football coach and athletic director, died on March 18, 1975 at age 66. His coaching put Michigan State into the big time in college football. **His .857 winning percentage is the finest in MSU football history**. His teams won two national championships—1951 and 1952; MSU's first Big Ten title—1953; and first Rose Bowl title—1954.

Munn was athletic director from 1954 to 1971. He had to retire in 1971 due to a stroke.

He held the entire athletic staff to high expectations for excellence. His outstanding motivation of coaches and athletes produced a winning tradition of national proportions.

During his tenure as athletic director, MSU athletes won individual NCAA titles in seven sports, an all-time record—up to that time—matched only by Navy in the NCAA's 100-year history. Moreover, during his administration, MSU won NCAA team titles in six different sports, an achievement bettered by no institution, and matched by just a few.

Under Munn's leadership, MSU won Big Ten titles in every conference sport, a feat no other university in the Big Ten had accomplished. He was voted into the College Football Hall of Fame in 1959.

Munn lived by a philosophy he repeated to his players, **"The difference between good and great is a little extra effort."** Jack Heppinstall, MSU's legendary athletic trainer, who served from 1914 to 1959, stated, "Biggie was a great handler of men. He could get more out of men than they had in them." This statement was reported by George T. Trumbull, Jr. in the *MSU Alumni Association Magazine.*

Jack Shingleton was named acting athletic director. He replaced Burt Smith, who had succeeded Biggie Munn as A.D.

George Ariyoshi, '49, was elected Governor of Hawaii. He was the first Asian-American and first MSU graduate to become a state governor.

Fred Stabley, Sr., MSU sports information director, published *The Spartans,* the story of MSU football. It was $7.95.

George R. Ariyoshi, age 48, Class of 1949, became the first Asian-American governor in the nation when he was elected Governor of Hawaii in 1975. He was the first MSU graduate to become a state governor.

J. Frank Witter, D.V.M., Class of 1932, was honored by the University of Maine when they named their new million-dollar animal research complex the "J. Frank Witter Animal Science Center." He had served on the Maine faculty for many years—15 as head of Animal Pathology.

Dr. Richard A. Rann, D.V.M. '50, was promoted to Brigadier General, U.S. Air Force, and commander of the 127th Tactical Fighter Wing, Michigan National Air Guard.

Sherrie Payne, '66, joined the Motown trio "The Supremes" in 1975. She was a medical technology graduate and taught in Grayling, Michigan. Between concerts she composed songs—250 of them. The religious singer said, "He's guiding my hands and making my fingers move."

Charles Weddle, M.A. '38, had developed 61 different varieties of flowers over the three decades following World War II, which won him 21 different medals.

Edmund C. Arnold, '54, designed the 6-column newspaper format which was being adopted by publications across the country. He was chair and professor at the graphic arts and publishing department at Syracuse University, and had published 16 books on journalism and graphic design.

George Weeks, '55, was named executive secretary to Michigan Governor William Milliken after serving for six years as his press secretary.

Paul Hunt, a senior chemistry major and Alumni Distinguished Scholar, won a Rhodes Scholarship—MSU's sixth, and the third in four years.

The Board of Trustees on July 28, 1978 unanimously approved the Alumni Association becoming a corporation of the State of Michigan. The new designation, effective July 1, 1979, was to "...create an organization run by the membership, yet serving as a partner with the university."

After 65 years of carrying the name *Wolverine*, the MSU yearbook was renamed the *Red Cedar Log*. Michael Dover, a senior research assistant, submitted the winning name. Other suggestions were: Spartan, Shadows, Green & White, Reflections, and Spartaniety.

A study of 3,000 alumni "...indicated MSU had made substantial contributions to their lives. Ranking first and second were, **'...developed my ability to think and express myself' and '...expanded my tolerance for people and ideas.'"**

On Thursday, April 3, 1975, thirteen inches of snow fell on the campus in 15 hours, and **MSU shut down for only the second time in history**. The most popular sport was using dorm food trays as "mini" toboggans for sliding down the sloped roof of Munn Arena.

Campus parking tickets brought in $102,000 from September 1977 to March 1978. All of the money went into a fund to upgrade campus streets, sidewalks, parking lots and lighting.

"Ten of MSU's 12 varsity basketball players—all blacks—walked out of a team meeting prior to the Indiana game (January 4, 1975) in protest of the starting lineup which included white freshman Jeff Tropf," as reported by Bob Bao in the *MSU Alumni Association Magazine.* "Head coach Gus Ganakas had no choice but to suspend the ten dissenting players for their action. Ganakas played a collection of junior varsity players and Jeff Tropf. Indiana was No. 1 in the nation and won the game 107-55. Tropf scored 21 for MSU. The next week, all ten players were reinstated, and MSU beat Ohio State, 88-84."

The 1975 university budget was $ 230,361,708. Enrollment was a record 44,580.

During the year, 10,262 degrees were awarded.

1976

College of Agriculture & Natural Resources Ranked # 1 Internationally; MSU Chosen for International Handicapped Center; Women's Softball Team Wins the National Championship—The College of Agriculture & Natural Resources was ranked No. 1 internationally—topping 58 other U.S. universities in a University of Minnesota survey. The rating was based on: 1. Number of foreign students, 2. Number of visiting foreign professors, 3. Number of participants supported by the U.S. Agency for International Development, 4. Number of faculty on overseas assignments, 5. Number of faculty with overseas experience, 6. Number of faculty carrying on international research, 7. Number of campus training programs for foreign groups, and 8. Number of cooperative programs with foreign schools.

MSU's women's softball team swept through five tournament games to win the National Championship. Coach Diane Ulibarri's team compiled a 23-4 overall record, greatly aided by pitcher Gloria Becksford's 16 wins and a single loss.

MSU was selected as the home of an international center for research, information and training in the rehabilitation of handicapped individuals. Dr. John Jordan, professor of rehabilitation, was named to head the program—a cooperative effort of the College of Education and the College of Osteopathic Medicine. MSU won the center as the result of 15 years work in handicapped research and rehabilitation.

President Wharton reported some 2,800 research projects were on-going at MSU, "producing data on topics ranging from cancer causes to improved soybean production."

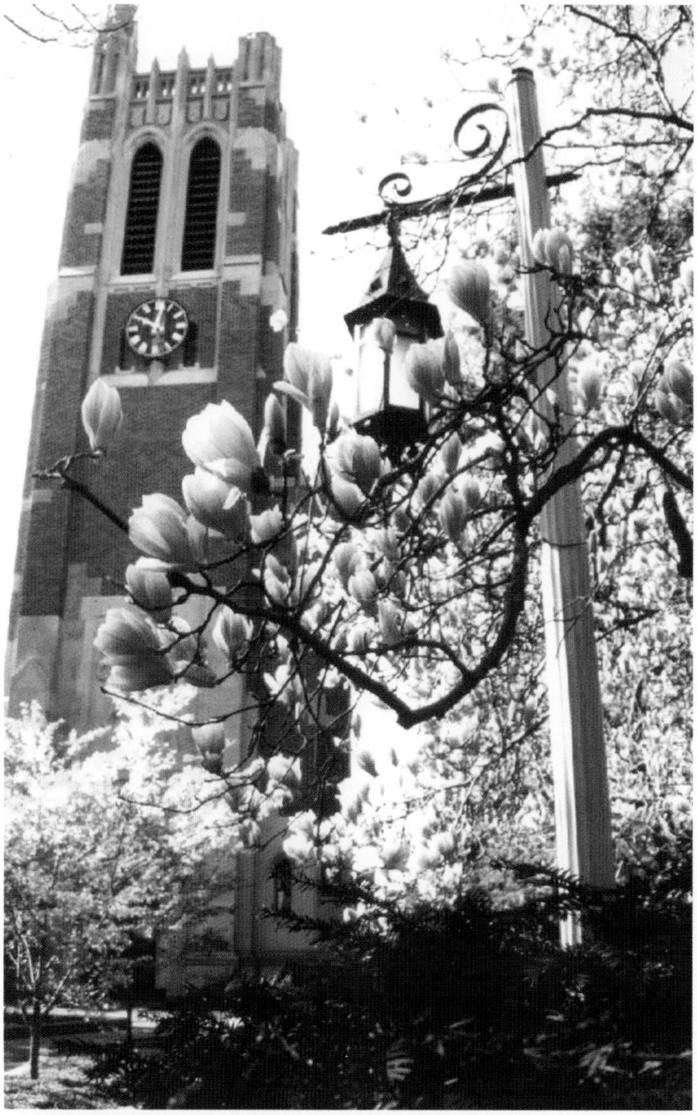

Beaumont Tower bathed in magnolia blossoms.

MSU led the higher education community in adopting an affirmative action policy for the employment and advancement of the physically handicapped.

Dr. Judith Lanier, assistant director of teacher education and associate professor of curriculum and instruction, **and Dr. Lee Shulman**, professor of psychology, **"convinced the National Institute of Education to grant the university $3.5 million to fund the nation's most comprehensive program of research on teaching."**

The Clinical Sciences Building—an $18.4 million complex—opened. The new facility housed the largest campus outpatient care facility, an animal resources laboratory, and a faculty office tower.

The *New York Times* praised MSU's College of Human Medicine, calling it "The College of the Bedside Manner." Reporter Boyce Rensberger wrote, "In a time when people increasingly criticize the impersonality of doctors…MSU's College of Human Medicine is devoting a major effort to turning out doctors who are not only up-to-date but who combine the warmth of the old-time family doctor with a grasp of the often-neglected social and environmental factors in illness."

Senior Pat Milkovich won his third Big Ten wrestling title, and became the only Big Ten wrestler in history to make the NCAA finals four times. He finished his career with 90 victories, second all-time at MSU. His brother Tom held the school record with 93 wins in the 1970-1973 period.

Dennis Lewin, '65, won three successive **Emmy Awards** as director of production coordination for ABC-TV's "Wide World of Sports" program.

Frank Kush, Class of 1952 and former All-American guard, was named **College Football Coach of the Year** by the American Football Coaches Association for leading Arizona State to a perfect 12-0 season in 1975.

Jack Barksdale, '50, was serving as president of the Holiday Inns Food & Lodging Division.

Lou Hagopian, '47, was serving as chairman and CEO of N.W. Ayer ABH International, the oldest advertising agency in the U.S.

Michael J. Ketchum, '54, was serving as president & CEO of Ohio Blue Shield.

Steve Holtzman, philosophy major, won a Rhodes Scholarship. He was MSU's seventh recipient of the prestigious award, and the fourth in five years.

Robin Fields, an 18-year old freshman, arrived on campus as the outgoing **Miss Arkansas** of 1975.

Dr. Derek T.A. Lamport, Professor at MSU's Energy Research & Development plant laboratory, and **Dr. Bryan H. Wildenthall**, Professor of Physics and Associate Director of the MSU Cyclotron Laboratory, **won prestigious Guggenheim Foundation Fellowships.**

Professor John Eulenberg, linguistics and computer service, "developed a talking computer" that enabled handicapped people to express words via a modified keyboard that included "a matrix of phrases."

MSU was put on a three-year NCAA probation, to end on January 18, 1979, for football recruiting violations. Of 34 charges, the university admitted to 14. Ron Karle, editor of the *MSU Alumni Magazine*, reported on the controversy. The penalty cost MSU all football appearances on TV or in bowl games, and ten recruits in 1976 and five in 1977. The charges turned on the credibility of MSU assistant football coaches Howard Weyers and Charles Butler versus statements by four Ohio State football players.

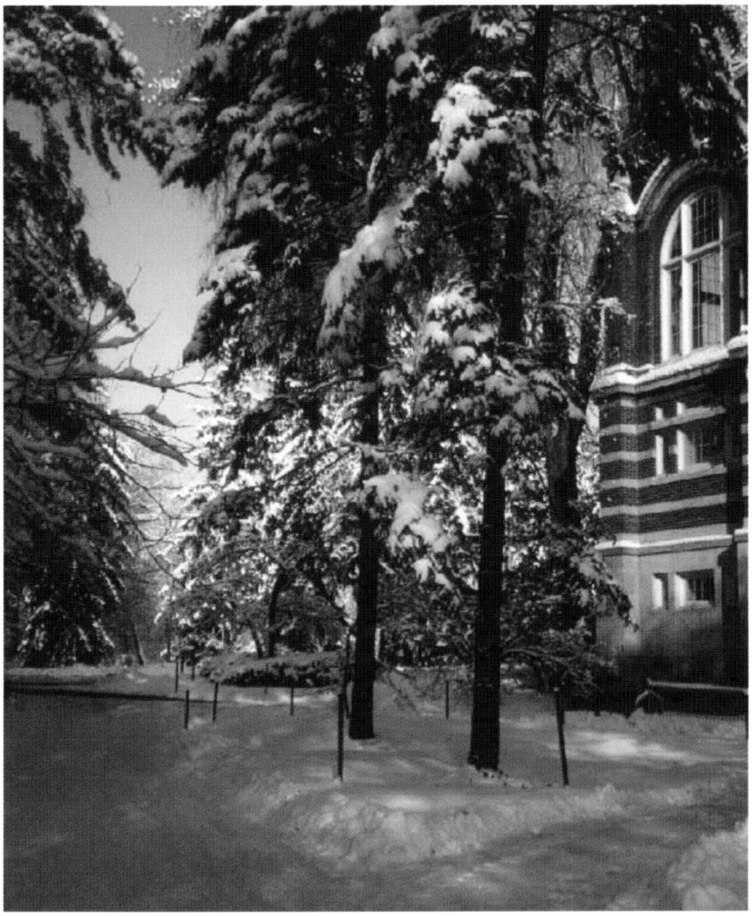

Snow trail along the Red Cedar behind IM-Circle.

MSU insisted on polygraph examinations for the two coaches with the understanding the results would be used in the case. "Results of the tests fully supported the coaches' denials of the allegations. Yet, the NCAA chose to accept the statements of the Ohio State players." The OSU players never submitted to polygraph tests.

"Trustee John Bruff, an attorney and member of President Wharton's Select Committee (on the probation issue), took issue with the procedure. 'I was very disturbed as were all the members of the MSU committee, as to the complete absence of due process in the hearings. The rules of evidence weren't followed and hearsay was admitted. I was appalled.'"

The Select Committee reported that NCAA investigator David Burst used threats, intimidation, and vulgarity while interviewing athletes, and leaked confidential information to the news media. They also stated the NCAA would not provide MSU with the details of its charges, and that it relied on a "farcical" appeal process.

Actual violations included lending equipment to four high school players in the Ohio North-South game who had already committed to MSU; loaning a car to an MSU player to drive around campus, and giving two MSU players a ride to Cleveland so they could be home for Thanksgiving. Two student athletes made two visits each to campus instead of the permitted one. Subsequently, the NCAA dismissed 38 alleged infractions.

Jud Heathcote, 48, was named head basketball coach, replacing Gus Ganakas. He had been head coach at the University of Montana.

Darryl Rogers, 40, was named head football coach, replacing Denny Stolz. Rogers had been head coach at San Jose State.

Smoking Banned on Campus—Following a student referendum that voted 7,411 to 1,980 to ban smoking in "all areas in which organized academic activity is taking place," the Trustees voted seven to one to enforce such a ban. Sam Gingrich, MSU fire safety officer who arrived at the school in 1938, said, "If you go way back, when you smoked, the students would throw you in the Red Cedar."

"Remembering Coral Gables: The 'Pioneer Land-Grant Tavern,'" was the title of a story by Bonnie J. Miller in the summer *MSU Alumni Association Magazine.* She told how Tom Johnson, who came to Michigan State in 1938 to play football, purchased Coral Gables in the mid-1940s, and later called it the "Pioneer Land-Grant Tavern." The Gables was "…a roadhouse named the Fleur de Lis Inn in the 1920s, a roller rink and square dance hall called Green Gables in the 1930s, then as Coral Gables Ballroom, a big band showcase in the 1940s, and finally the metamorphosis into the college beer and pizza bar of the 1950s, 1960s, and today." In 1969, Alex Vanis, a 1954 hotel ad grad, bought the Gables.

"Gruff Sparty" logo was saved by a student vote. Bob Perrin, vice president of university relations, questioned keeping the old "Gruff Sparty" logo, which featured the unshaven Spartan face. A Residence Halls Association poll of students resulted in 606 of 736 ballots voting for the Old Sparty logo. "Freshman Guy Swanson captured student sentiment, 'Sparty symbolizes the toughness, strength and spirit of athletics and our teams. He is and always will be popular with this student.'"

The 1976 university budget was $246,432,649. Enrollment was 43,749. During the year, 10,811 degrees were awarded.

1977

Dr. Edgar L. Harden Named MSU's Fifteenth President (served 1977-1979)—Dr. Clifton Wharton resigned as MSU's President to accept the position of Chancellor of the State University of New York on October 26, 1977. Dr. Edgar L. Harden (1906-1996), former President of Northern Michigan University and a former administrator and faculty member at MSU, was unanimously elected MSU's 15th president by the Trustees two days later. He was to take office January 1, 1978.

Harden was 70, and had been serving as President of Story, Inc., a conglomerate of five auto dealerships, two insurance companies, and real estate holdings in Lansing. He said "under no circumstances" would he seek a permanent position as MSU president. The appointment was immensely popular with faculty and students alike. Harden had a remarkably good relationship with the Michigan legislature and was very effective in selling MSU's needs to them.

Dr. Harden speaking at 1978 Commencement:

"May I commend to you an action agenda? Decide where you want to go; pick the road most likely to take you there; set out without delay. Bring your simmering to a boil, and honor your potential by achieving it."

Among outgoing president Wharton's achievements were his ability to maintain the quality of academic programs in spite of budget reductions, his commitment to the education of the economically and educationally disadvantaged, integration of the College of Osteopathic Medicine with the other medical colleges, and the creation of the College of Urban Development.

Major innovations implemented under Wharton included the Presidential Commission on Admissions and Student Body Composition and a Presidential Fellows Program. He also pushed the colleges to nurture students in competing for Rhodes Scholarships. MSU students won five Rhodes Scholarships during his tenure. He established an Anti-Discrimination Board, the Department of Human Relations, and an Office of Programs for Handicappers.

On the cultural side, President Wharton and his wife Dolores led the move to build the Center for Performing Arts, now named for them.

The world renowned Juilliard String Quartet became artists-in-residence at MSU for a minimum of three years, leaving their home base—the Juilliard School of Music in New York City—for the first time in 30 years. Robert Mann, a member of the Juilliard Quartet, said, "We've come to regard certain places as very strong islands of interest in the arts, and East Lansing is one."

Mary Norton, a 21-year old James Madison College senior, became MSU's first female Rhodes Scholar in the first year women were eligible to compete for the award. Only 13 women in the U.S. were selected out of 32 scholarships awarded to Americans. She was MSU's eighth Rhodes Scholar, and the fifth in six years. Norton also won a Danforth Fellowship and a National Science Foundation scholarship.

Dr. Edgar L. Harden, Fifteenth President

MSU students won a total of ten National Science Foundation scholarships during 1977, giving MSU 72 winners in five years, more than any other Big Ten school.

MSU led the nation in National Merit Scholar enrollment for the 1967-1977 decade.

MSU led all universities in the number of Peace Corps/Vista volunteers.

MSU's campus Volunteer Program—the nation's first—was the largest of any university.

Some 1,500 students worked as volunteers each term with more than 200 different service agencies.

MSU Provost Lawrence Boger was selected as the new President of Oklahoma State. Thus, he became the 42nd president of a four-year college to be selected from MSU faculty, alumni or administrators since 1940.

Professor George Hough, chair of the School of Journalism, published the book, *News Writing* (Houghton Mifflin), which was adopted by more than 200 journalism schools.

Michigan State's Volunteer Bureau "Adopt-A-Grandparent Program" reached out to older people without close friends or family.

Student demands for more healthful menus led to such items as wheat germ, yogurt, granola, spinach lasagna, quiche lorraine, and 100 other vegetarian selections at the Snyder-Phillips Hall cafeteria.

Student needs in the dorm were headed by a popcorn popper. Students used these appliances to heat soup, boil water for coffee, or fry donuts.

Donald W. Riegle, MBA '61, took office as a U.S. Senator from Michigan.

Bernard F. Sliger, '49, M.A. '50, and Ph.D., '55, was named president of Florida State University.

Patricia (Yaroch) Bario, '53, was assistant press secretary to U.S. President Jimmy Carter.

Martha "Bunny" Mitchell, '62, M.A. '68, was U.S. President Carter's liaison with the Washington, D.C. government and minority groups. According to the *MSU Alumni Association Magazine,* President Carter told a prominent Democrat, "Bunny Mitchell is one of three or four people who can come into my office without an appointment."

Gerald L. Hough, MSU graduate, was named director of the Michigan State Police.

Francis Ferguson, '47, was serving as president of Northwestern Mutual Life.

Richard D. Gibb, Ph.D. '59, was elected president of the University of Idaho.

Frank O. Anderson, III, MBA '71, appointed group vice president of Chrysler Corporation's U.S. automotive manufacturing.

Chuck Fairbanks, '55, New England Patriots head coach, was named National Football League Coach of the Year by the *Sporting News.*

Myra MacPherson, '56, *Washington Post* reporter, authored the book, *The Power Lovers,* a behind-the-scenes look at politics and marriage.

Lucy Jochen, '35, was named 1976-77 American Business Woman of the Year by the American Business Women's Association. She was director of special projects for the Michigan Chapter of the National Multiple Sclerosis Society.

Dr. W. Delano Meriwether, MSU pre-med 1961-1963, who became the first black to enroll in the Duke University Medical School, was featured on the cover of *Sports Illustrated* as "The Amazing Dr. Meriwether." He received his M.D. degree in 1967; did leukemia research at the Cancer Research Center in Baltimore, then continued at Boston City Hospital and Harvard Medical School. He then became a White House Fellow and joined the U.S. Dept. of Health, Education and Welfare as special assistant to the Assistant Secretary of Health. A natural sprinter, he became a track sensation at age 27, running the 100-yard dash in 9.0 seconds.

MSU women's teams won four Big Ten titles: volleyball, softball, track & field, and golf. And, they had second place finishes in basketball, gymnastics, and swimming & diving.

Earvin "Magic" Johnson, All-State, All-American basketball player with state champion Lansing Everett High School, who was recruited by 400 universities, finally **selected Michigan State**. He declared, "I've always wanted to go to Michigan State. Ever since 6th grade I've been going to their games. Once you get that Spartan in you, it's hard to get it out."

Kam Hunter, age 11, of Ionia, Michigan entered MSU in the Honors College. He scored in the top five percent on the freshmen entrance tests. Kam said, "MSU has good people, a fine program, and also has experience in handling kids like me." He was "referring to Michael Grost who entered MSU in 1964 at age 10, and had gone on to become a math professor at the University of Wisconsin."

The 1977 university budget was $263,845,105. Enrollment was 44,211. During the year, 10,537 degrees were granted.

1978

President Harden Takes Over; MSU Anti-Cancer Drug Approved by FDA—Dr. Edgar Harden took the reins as MSU's 15th president on January 1, 1978. He laid out the new building priorities: an $18.3 million Communication Arts Building, a Plant & Soil Sciences Building, a Science-Medical Library Building, and expansion of the existing Engineering, Veterinary Medical Buildings, and Eppley Center.

President Harden stated, "We need to make a two-way bridge to the legislature. Not only will we be asking for dollars, but we must let them know—in every way we can—how those dollars are being spent" to provide the return on investment the people of the state are seeking.

Cisplatin, a powerful anti-cancer drug, developed by MSU biophysicist Barnett Rosenberg, with help from his lab supervisor Loretta Van Camp, '48, and graduate student Thomas Krigas in the 1960s, was approved for use by the Federal Drug Administration in December, 1978. Cisplatin, it was stated, had the potential of saving 11,000 lives per year. Dr. Rosenberg offered to give his royalties from Cisplatin to MSU for a cancer institute if the university would match his contribution.

MSU's second cyclotron was being constructed with a $1 million grant from the National Science Foundation. The new atom-smasher was attracting worldwide attention in science circles. It featured the largest magnet ever built, weighing 100 tons and containing 25 miles of special wiring. The magnet was "capable of lifting 900 tons, or 40 railroad boxcars."

Jack Meyers, '51 and publisher of *Time Magazine*, right, greets Chinese leader Deng Xiaping.

While men still led women in total enrollment at MSU, 53 percent (23,346) to 47 percent (20,866), women were the majority in seven of the universities 17 colleges: Arts & Letters—58.7%, Communication Arts—55.4%, Education—67.3%, Human Ecology—94%, Justin Morrill—52%, Urban Development—64.5 %, and Veterinary Medicine—53.9 %.

Horticulture professor Stanley K. Ries reported that alcohol isolated from alfalfa hay could eventually increase world food production as much as 25 percent. In MSU field tests, the naturally occurring chemical—triacontanaol—increased yields on ten crops by an average of 12 percent. Included were navy beans, asparagus, cucumbers, lettuce, and wheat.

Jack Meyers, '51, was named publisher of *Time Magazine.*

Tom McGuane, '62, authored *Ninety-Two in the Shade* which was nominated for the National Book Award.

Carl M. Horn. '21, Ed. D. '51, retired professor of counseling and educational psychology, was named to the Michigan Education Hall of Fame.

Maxine Thome, '71, a psychotherapist, established a support group for battered women in Ingham County, Michigan, one of the first in the nation.

Judd Perkins, '44, M.A. '48, was general chairman of the 25th Annual Michigan Week. He was director of public affairs for General Telephone Co. of Michigan.

Dr. Suzanne Kennedy, D.V.M. '76, was the senior resident veterinarian at the National Zoo in Washington, D.C. She was the first woman doctor at the zoo.

A ten-minute, prime-time NBC-TV documentary praised the College of Human Medicine as "the most effective" of the few medical programs that emphasize family practice and primary care, rather than research and specialization.

The "Blizzard of '78" struck the campus before dawn on January 26. When it let up four days later, there was 20 inches of snow on the ground. It was the third time in the university's 123-year history that snow had shut the school down.

Michigan State named Dr. Gwen Norrell, associate director of the Counseling Center, as its faculty representative to the Big Ten conference. She was the first woman ever to be named to this prestigious body. The faculty representatives are responsible for establishing all legislation governing Big Ten athletics.

MSU was selected as a site for an official All-American Selections flower trial garden, as well as a test site for All-American rose selections.

The Board of Trustees approved corporate status for the MSU Alumni Association on July 28, 1978, to become effective July 1, 1979. Revised by-laws would create an organization that was to be run by the membership and yet serve as a partner with the university.

Beer keg parties, which had become popular in residence halls for students of age, **were outlawed**. Michigan law prohibited the sale of alcohol, which included barter, exchange or giving it away on state-owned land. The new policy, did, however, allow "bring your own" parties for students of age.

MSU's basketball team won the Big Ten title with a 15-3 record, and posted the school's finest overall record, with 25 wins and only five losses. **Sophomore Magic Johnson was on the cover of *Sports Illustrated's* annual college basketball issue** (November 20), at the opening of the 1978-1979 season. The Spartans just missed getting to the Final Four in the NCAA tournament, losing to the eventual champion, Kentucky, 52-49 in the quarter finals. **Earvin "Magic" Johnson was a unanimous All-Big Ten selection—the first freshman ever selected to the first team.** He also was selected a second team All-American. Greg Kelser was dubbed the "Sultan of Slam" for his 47 slam-dunks during the 1977-1978 basketball season. He had led the Spartans in scoring and rebounding, with 17.7 points, and 9.1 rebounds per game.

Head coach Jud Heathcote, who was named Big Ten Coach of the Year, stated, "Earvin is a winner and when it comes down to winning time, he'll come up with something." Illinois head coach Lou Henson said, "In Earvin Johnson, MSU has a 6-9 freshman who can do things like no other 6-9 freshman I've ever seen. He's ready for the pros now."

MSU's football team beat Michigan at Ann Arbor, 24-15. The Spartans gained 496 yards on the Wolverines—248 in the air and 248 on the ground—the second highest total ever gained against a Michigan team. *Sports Illustrated* named MSU quarterback Ed Smith, U.S. Player of the Week. The magazine reported the words from a Michigan official: "It's like the twerp next door dropping by the bully's house for his annual beating and the entire neighborhood coming out to watch. With the whole neighborhood watching, the twerps slugged the bullies, 24-15."

Darryl Rogers, head football coach, led the Spartans to a 8-3 record in 1978, and was named **Big Ten Coach of the Year.** MSU tied for first in the conference with a 7-1 record.

Steve Garvey, '72, L.A. Dodger All-Star first baseman, was named MVP of the Major League All-Star game, his second consecutive MVP honor.

Zeke—"The Wonder Dog"—entertained Spartan Stadium crowds with acrobatic frisbee catches. Senior Gary Eisenberg trained Zeke and led him to the runner-up position in the national frisbee competition in 1977.

The 1978 university budget was $289, 650,840. Enrollment was 43,744. During the year, 10,242 degrees were awarded.

Recruitment of Dr. Barnett Rosenberg

Leads to Discovery of Most-Prescribed Anti-Cancer Drugs and More Than $300 Million In Royalties for MSU

Dr. Barnett Rosenberg

President John A. Hannah, president from 1941 to 1969, was continually attracting young, high-achieving faculty to Michigan State by promising them great freedom to create innovative curriculums and research projects, and then delivering on the promise.

In 1960, he enticed Dr. Barnett Rosenberg, a young biophysicist, to leave New York University, and come to MSU to establish a Biophysics Department. Rosenberg states, "He offered me and others carte blanche to create the bio-physics program. We were given the money, space and freedom to set up a pure graduate department with emphasis on research, and to establish the terms of our Ph.D. program."

By 1968, the synergies developed by Rosenberg's team of scientists had discovered certain platinum compounds that inhibited the growth of cancer in experimental animals. Their creative research led to the development and approval of two monumental life-saving drugs. They became the most-prescribed anti-cancer drugs in the nation.

Cisplatin, a powerful anti-cancer drug which would become the world's best-selling cancer drug, was approved by the Federal Drug Administration in December 1978 for use in treating testicular, ovarian, and bladder cancers. The drug was based on certain platinum compounds. This landmark drug patent carried the names of Dr. Rosenberg, his laboratory supervisor Loretta Van Camp, '48, and graduate student Thomas Krigas. Later, Cisplatin proved highly effective against head, neck, prostate, cervical and some types of lung cancer.

Carboplatin, a second-generation anti-cancer drug, based on platinum compounds and a carbon ring, was developed next, and won FDA approval in the mid-1980s. Much more tolerable side effects proved major benefits of Carboplatin, which was highly effective against testicular, ovarian, bladder, head and neck, prostate and cervical cancers. Carboplatin also was more effective than Cisplatin against lung cancer. The patent for Carboplatin carried the names of Dr. Rosenberg, Michael Clear, James Hoeschele, and Loretta Van Camp, '48.

Lance Armstrong, U.S. cyclist who in 2003 won his fifth consecutive Tour de France race (tying the record), had his cancer arrested by cisplatin a few years prior to his win streak in what is considered the most grueling athletic event in the world.

More Than $300 Million in Royalties had flowed to Michigan State's Foundation from the Cisplatin and Carboplatin patents by 2004. These funds have provided support for other important MSU research and academic projects. This monetary engine is the result of allowing faculty, as Rosenberg puts it, **"the freedom to discover; to explore to the limits."**

1979

Dr. Cecil Mackey Named MSU's sixteenth President (served 1979-1985); Spartans Win NCAA Basketball Championship—Dr. Cecil Mackey (b.1929) was elected MSU's 16th president on June 8, 1979 by a unanimous 8-0 vote by the Trustees. Mackey, age 50, had been president of Texas Tech University, and the University of South Florida. Mackey had earned B.A. and M.A. degrees in economics from the University of Alabama in 1949 and 1953; a Doctor of Philsophy Degree from the University of Illinois in 1955; and a Bachelor of Law's degree from Alabama in 1958.

Dr. Cecil Mackey, Sixteenth President

Dr. Mackey, speaking on Higher Education at University of Michigan 1984 Winter Commencement:

"the university's mission is to search for truth, to know and nurture truth, to create new knowledge, and publish it freely."

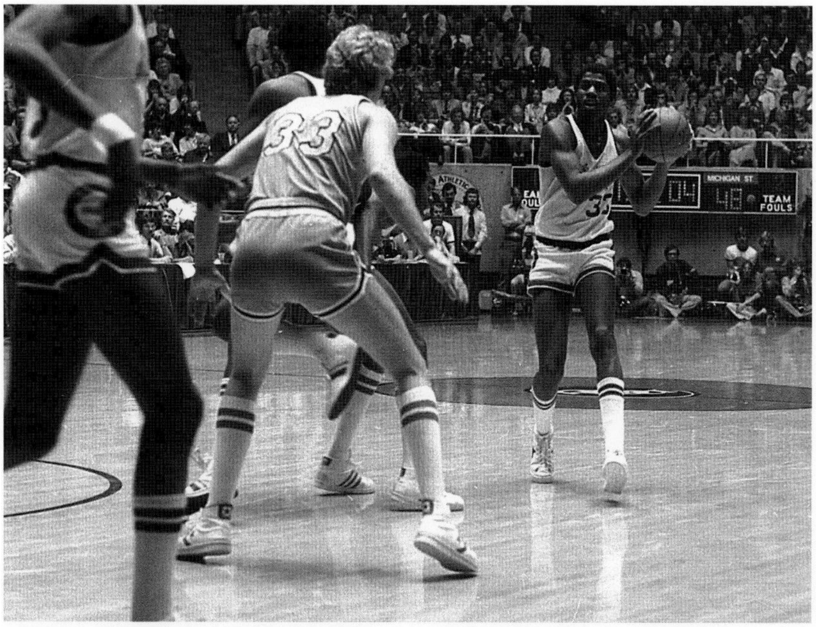

Magic Johnson, with ball, led MSU to its first NCAA basketball title, defeating unbeaten (33-0) # 1 Indiana State and Larry Bird (33), 75-64 in 1979.

Spartans Win First NCAA Basketball Title—In a magical season, the Michigan State family was thrilled and entertained by one of the most exciting basketball teams in college history. With Magic Johnson's sensational long passes to the 6-foot 7-inch leaping Greg Kelser for high-wire, floating slam dunks, it was show-time in East Lansing and on national TV. It was a new style of basketball and the country loved it. Early in the season, MSU was ranked No. 1 in the nation for the first time.

Then they stumbled, losing five games. Coach Jud Heathcote's adjustments righted the team, and they won 15 of their final 16 games to tie for the Big Ten title. Then they roared through the NCAA tournament to the National Championship, winning five consecutive games by an average margin of 21 points.

"The Game That Changed the Game"—The national championship game is considered the defining moment in college basketball. Played at the University of Utah's 15,500-seat arena in Salt Lake City, it drew the largest TV audience in the history of the NCAA finals. It featured Magic Johnson of MSU versus Larry Bird of Indiana State—arguably the finest basketball players in the country up to that time. Such fan interest erupted that it has been called "The Game That Changed the Game." Former UCLA center Bill Walton—winner of two NCAA titles—referred to the game as "the birth of basketball" and the "day basketball was invented."

Indiana State came into the game ranked No. 1 in the nation with a 33-0 record. MSU entered ranked No. 3, with a 25-6 record, which included an unprecedented three victories over Bob Knight's Indiana Hoosiers. MSU head coach Jud Heathcote devised a man-and-a-half defense to stop Larry Bird's awesome scoring average of 29 points per game. It worked. Bird was held to 19 points, shooting only 7 or 21 from the floor, and was forced into six turnovers.

Magic led both teams in scoring with 24 points. Kelser had 19 points and nine assists to Magic's five. MSU forward Terry Donnelly was key, hitting five out of five baseline shots and five of six free throws for 15 important points. Kelser led MSU in rebounding with eight. MSU led 37-28 at halftime, and won the game 75-64. Magic Johnson was named MVP of the Final Four.

Magic Johnson was again featured on the cover of *Sports Illustrated*, immediately after winning the NCAA title. Johnson became "the first college player to be featured on the *Sports Illustrated* cover both before and after the basketball season."

On May 11, 1979, Magic Johnson, age 19, announced he was turning professional. He was the No. 1 draft pick of the Los Angeles Lakers.

MSU Cheerleaders Won the National Championship—Hand-in-hand with the basketball team, MSU's cheerleaders also won a National Collegiate Championship in 1979. They brought home $10,000 for MSU's Development Fund. At the NCAA Final Four games in Salt Lake City, the Spartan cheerleaders unfurled a huge banner reading, "Welcome to the Magic Kingdom."

MSU's football, basketball and baseball teams won Big Ten titles in the 1978-1979 academic year. Only two other schools had won this triple crown: Illinois in 1914-1915 and 1951-1952; and Michigan in 1925-1926 and 1947-1948.

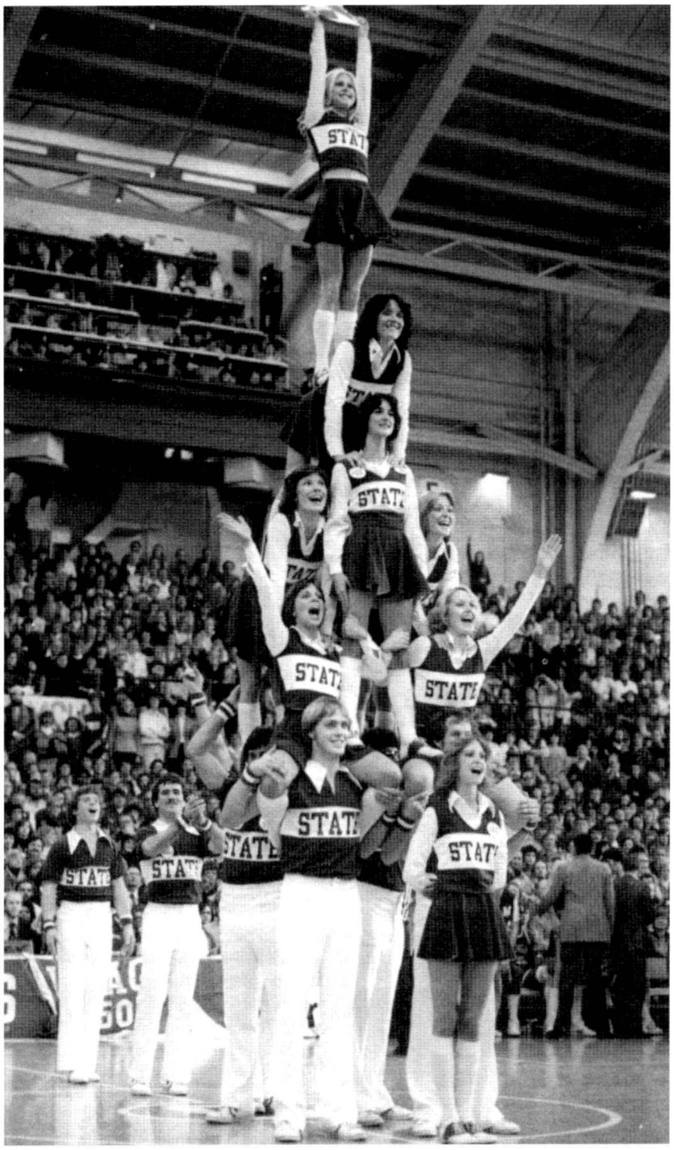

MSU's cheerleaders won the 1979 National Cheerleading title.

Sue Ertl, senior golfer, was named MSU Sportswoman of the Year. She had won Big Ten individual golf titles as a sophomore and junior. In Ertl's freshman, sophomore and junior years, MSU women won three of their five consecutive Big Ten team titles.

Dr. Sylvan Wittwer, Director of the MSU Agricultural Experiment Station, was elected to the Soviet Academy of Science, one of the highest scientific honors the Soviet Union ever conferred on an American.

Nancy Hayes Teeters, who had studied economics in graduate school at MSU, **became the first woman member of the Federal Reserve Bank.**

Nancy Dick, '51, became the first woman elected Lt. Governor of Colorado. She was one of only six women Lt. Governors in the nation.

Stanley O. Ikenberry, M.A. '57, Ph.D. '60, was elected president of the University of Illinois. **Later in his career, he served as president of the American Counsel on Education, the primary representative for all of education to the U.S. Congress.**

Carl G. Smith, '42, was elected president of Gerber Products.

Russ Mawby, '49, was president of the W.K. Kellogg Foundation.

Patricia McFate, '52, was named deputy director of the National Endowment for the Humanities.

Herb Haygood, '65, a successful builder of new homes in downtown Detroit, was called "Detroit's hottest real estate developer" by *Detroit Magazine.* In 1963, he was one of just 200 black students at MSU.

Craig Jones, '69, authored *Blood Secrets,* which won rave reviews and was selected as Book of the Month.

Ross E. Roeder, '60, was promoted to executive vice president of Denny's Inc., the restaurant company.

Frederick L. Halbert, '67, M.S. '68, chemical engineer and dairy farmer, was named chair of the State Toxic Substance Control Commission.

On July 1, 1979, the MSU Alumni Association became a Michigan Corporation and officially separated from the university. It thus became the ninth independent alumni association in the Big Ten.

In April, 1979, MSU named one of the proposed theaters in the newly planned performing arts center for Catherine Herrick Cobb in recognition of the major financial contributions by Mrs. Cobb and her family. Mrs. Cobb was the daughter of the late Ray W. Herrick, founder of Tecumseh Products in Tecumseh, Michigan. The Herrick family, including Mrs. Cobb and her brother Kenneth W. Herrick, chairman of Tecumseh Products, and the Herrick Foundation, had given MSU programs major financial support for the preceding 15 years.

Construction of the long-sought Performing Arts Center began in October, 1979.

Twenty new emergency telephones were installed in January at strategic locations around the campus. They were connected to the Department of Public Safety. It was called the "green light" system because of the green light burning above each phone location.

Under the leadership of Gene Kenney, Assistant Athletic Director, **MSU's summer Sports School** was thriving. It was **the nation's first and largest**—founded in 1972.

On January 18, 1979, a three-year NCAA probation of the football program ended.

Stanley O. Ikenberry, M.A. '57, Ph.D. '60, was elected President of the University of Illinois.

Ron Mason was named head ice hockey coach by athletic director Joe Kearney. At Bowling Green, Mason's teams won 160, lost 63 and tied 6, for a .710 winning percentage.

The Michigan drinking age was raised from 18 to 21 by a 57 percent plurality. Students now had to be 21 to possess or consume alcohol in their rooms.

Four MSU alumni and a former MSU English instructor were killed in an American Airlines DC-10 crash at Chicago's O'Hare Airport on May 25, 1969. It was the worst flight disaster in U.S. history, claiming 275 lives. Killed were: Gail Chariwal, '75, of East Lansing, 28; Marcia E. Platt, '75, of East Lansing, 26; John Robinson, former English instructor; Douglass Ruble, '71, of DeWitt Township, 29; and Margaret "Peggy" Stacks, '75, of East Lansing, 26.

President Emeritus John A. Hannah, age 77, delivered the June commencement address, "In 1999," before 20,000 in Spartan Stadium. He declared, **"one of the most pervasive of all human desires for people of all races…is an instinctive aspiration for recognition as a dignified human being—a hope for the maximum possible freedom for each person to determine the course and pattern of his own life…"**

The 1979 university budget was $320,175,608. Enrollment was 44,756. During the year, 9,847 degrees were awarded.

1980

MSU President and Alumni Battle Over Independence of Alumni Association; Department of Park & Recreation Resources Named # 1 in the Nation—A battle over the independence of the MSU Alumni Association (MSUAA), which started in 1979, spilled into 1980. The Alumni Association, with the blessing of the University Board of Trustees and President Harden, had received its independence in 1979 through incorporation as a Michigan corporation. The action became effective July 1, 1979, making the MSUAA the ninth such independent organization in the Big Ten.

When MSU's new president, Cecil Mackey, arrived on campus, he wanted the university to have greater control over alumni relations. He wanted more outreach to alumni through cultural and educational offerings, and less emphasis on athletic events as the primary way to engage the alumni.

Friction points between President Mackey and Alumni Director Jack Kinney and the Alumni Board, were: 1) The alumni director serve at the mutual pleasure of MSU's president, and 2) That alumni magazine content be approved by the university.

In an *MSU Alumni Association Magazine* story, alumni directors from the University of Michigan, University of Illinois, the University of Wisconsin, and the director of the Council for the Advancement and Support of Education (CASE), came down on the side of independent associations.

The Board of Trustees, which had supported alumni association independence, now turned to support President Mackey, who they had elected by a unanimous 8-0 vote. John Bruff, chairman of the Board of Trustees and an attorney, stated, "The constitution of the State of Michigan puts the authority for all the affairs of MSU with the Board of Trustees. That includes alumni relations. The Board of Trustees must maintain responsibility for alumni relations and we will. The Board has discussed this in individual sessions and we fully support President Mackey and the position he has taken, and, in fact, directed him to take that position. The acting officer of the alumni corporation has to be someone who can work with our president."

Bruff's statement pointed to a difference in philosophy about alumni relations that existed between Mackey and Kinney. The alumni board voted 12-4 to support Kinney and offer him a new contract. The MSU Board of Trustees backed Mackey. By November 30, 1979, Bruff introduced a resolution to the Board of Trustees "which declared the president's power over alumni relations whether he worked through the alumni association or not." The resolution was approved unanimously by the Board.

Thus, the die was cast for the eventual shutdown of the independent alumni association, and the re-institution of a university controlled alumni association. The battle for control would last for nearly two years.

President Mackey warned of tougher times in his "State of the University" address. He said, "Not every activity can be a first in our priorities. Some will be cut back, and some may have to be discontinued." He stressed that the highest priority would be given to retaining and attracting top faculty.

In response to projected major cuts in funding from the State Legislature, and the need to raise faculty salaries, the Board of Trustees increased student tuition by a hefty 13.5 to 14.5 percent and dorm rates by 10.7 percent.

MSU's Department of Park and Recreation Resources was named number one in the nation by a University of Maryland survey of 250 universities that had outdoor resources and park management programs.

Canoes "at-the-ready" for a favorite date activity—cruising the Red Cedar River. Refurbished canoe shelter and dock—called "The Red Cedar Yacht Club"—were gifts of the Class of 1988.

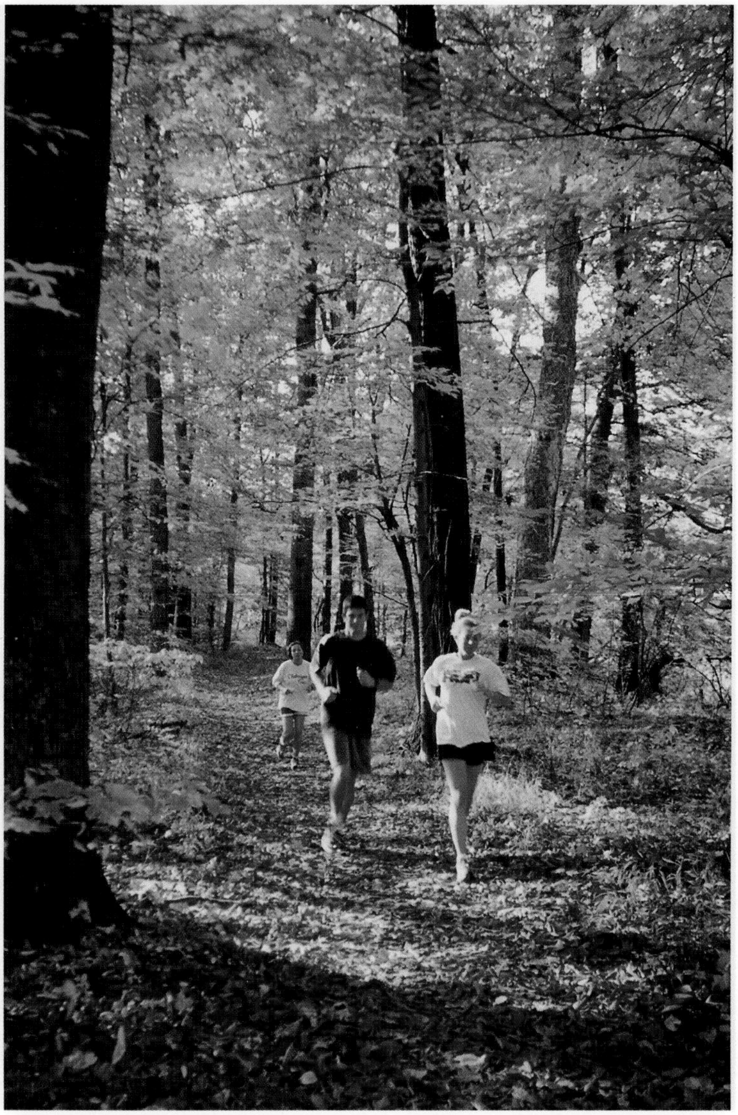

Fall jog through the canopy of trees in the 35-acre Sanford Natural Area—one of four unspoiled woodlots on the MSU campus. Sanford runs from the Bogue Street Bridge to Hagadorn Road on the south bank of the Red Cedar River.

The School of Nursing's excellence won for it the added status of being named the College of Nursing. Across the nation, there were 75 nursing programs that granted graduate and undergraduate degrees.

For the fourth time in six years, MSU students led the Big Ten in National Science Foundation fellowships.

Seven campus buildings—all on the eastern end of West Circle Drive—**were designated historical sites by the Michigan Historical Commission**. Included were Eustace Hall (now Eustace-Cole Hall), which was named a national historic site in 1971; Marshall Hall (now Marshall-Adams); Journalism (now Old Botany); Chittenden Hall; Cook Hall; and Agricultural Hall—all built between 1888 and 1909. Also included was Linton Hall, built in 1881.

President Emeritus John A. Hannah published his memoirs in 1980 and passed on his insights on several topics:

1. A "Tomorrow Vision,"—"The most important days are tomorrow and the days after that;"
2. What's Important in Life—"Only people are important;"
3. On Success—"the person who makes a mark in the world is the one who, as he approaches one goal, already has established another one beyond it, one much harder to reach;"
4. On the Legislature—"I learned early that one could deal much better with legislators by meeting them in their hometowns rather than in the halls of the State Capitol ;"
5. On Athletics—"Athletics unify a university probably more than any other feature of the institution."

Dial-A-Ride service was initiated on campus to aid student safety while traveling across campus at night.

Leonard Falcone, 81, MSU's Director of Bands for 40 years, received an award from the National Band Association's Academy of Wind and Percussion Arts, considered the "Oscar" of the band profession.

The new $1.6 million Football Building was named for Hugh "Duffy" Daugherty, who led MSU football teams to National Championships in 1965 and 1966.

Earl H. Hoekenga, '39, was serving as chairman & CEO of Ryder Truck Lines.

Nick Vista, '54, 25-year assistant sports information director, was named MSU's sports information director, replacing the legendary **Fred W. Stabley, Sr.**, who retired after 32 years service. **The university honored Stabley by naming the Spartan Stadium press box for him.** Both Stabley and Vista are members of the College Sports Information Directors Hall of Fame.

Dick Tamburo, former MSU All-American football player, was named Arizona State's athletic director.

Charles Engel, '60, was named executive vice president of Universal Television.

Ted J. Rakstis, '54, won the 1980 Mort Weisinger Award for the Best Magazine Article of 1979 by a member of the American Society of Journalists and Authors.

Jim Dunn, '67, won the U.S. House of Representatives seat for Michigan's sixth district.

Judy Forman, '69, opened her Big Kitchen Café restaurant in the Golden Hill section of San Diego, California. In the September 2002 issue of *Bon Appetite* magazine, her unique creation was rated "One of the Ten Best Breakfast Restaurants" in the nation.

Daniel D. McCrory, '53, was named senior editor of *Business Week* magazine.

Charles Renwick, '54, was named executive vice president of the NBC radio network.

Michelle Ackerman, '79, General Motors recruiter, pointed out that GM hired more MSU graduates—in all disciplines—than from any other university.

MSU's women gymnasts won their fourth consecutive Big Ten team title.

Sprinter Randy Smith won the Big Ten 60-yard dash for the fourth consecutive year.

Cheryl Gilliam won the women's Big Ten 200-yard dash title for the second consecutive year.

Jay Vincent, All-American basketball center, won the Big Ten scoring title. Overall in the 1979-1980 season, he averaged 21.6 points per game.

MSU left the Western Collegiate Hockey Association to join the Central Collegiate Hockey Association (CCHA), effective in the fall of 1981. The move was made to conserve on travel costs to western states. The CCHA, with MSU participation, would have seven schools in Michigan—MSU, Michigan, Michigan Tech, Northern Michigan, Western Michigan, Ferris State, and Lake Superior State.

Female students age 18 to 22 outnumbered male students in that age bracket for the first time. Overall, however, men still outnumbered women students, 23,202 to 21,154. Foreign students from 93 nations numbered 1,347.

The 1980 university budget was $353,150,624. Enrollment was an all-time record 44,940. During the year, 10,425 degrees were granted.

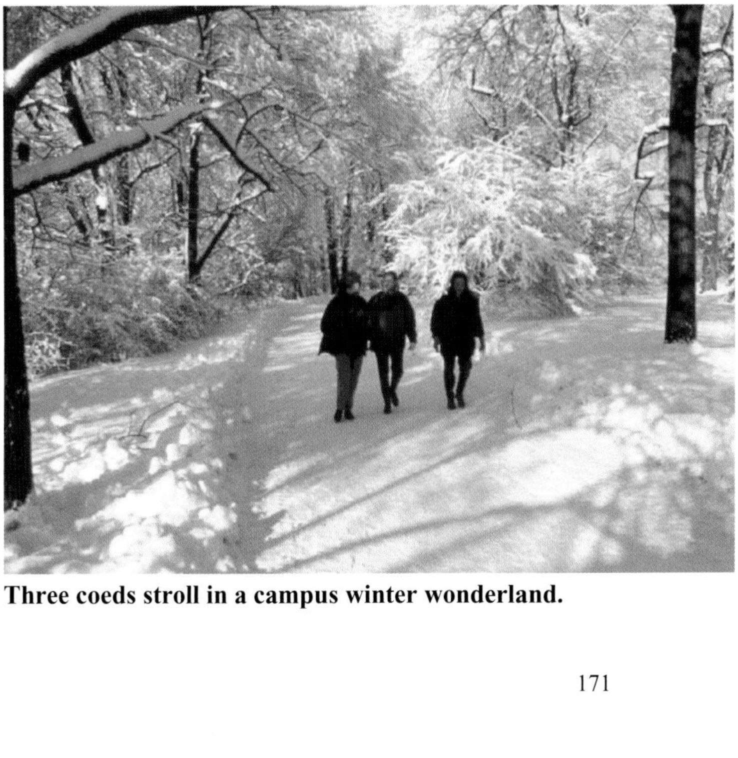

Three coeds stroll in a campus winter wonderland.

1981

Economic Recession Leads to State Appropriation Cuts—With the Michigan economy in recession, state appropriations for MSU were cut 3.6 percent or $7 million. The Board declared a "state of financial crisis." Deans recommended faculty reductions of between 400 and 500, including 150 tenured and tenure stream positions.

A faculty Select Advisory Committee appointed by President Mackey recommended the elimination of: the College of Nursing, James Madison College, Lyman Briggs College, the College of Urban Development, the School of Social Work, Justin Morrill College, and the School of Medical Technology. The committee also proposed putting all faculty on a 10-month basis instead of nine months.

Students and faculty reacted swiftly and with anger. Students from the endangered colleges protested in front of the Hannah Administration Building. Many faculty were upset and demoralized by the proposed actions.

Dean James Anderson, College of Agriculture and Natural Resources, said, "The faculty must have reassurance now. The most important thing is to retain faculty to insure that we have quality programs ten years from now." **Richard Lewis**, Dean of the College of Business, said the uncertainty at MSU was making it increasingly difficult to attract new faculty. Many professors warned that laying off tenured faculty would hurt MSU for decades.

While MSU's financial situation was being likened to the Great Depression by the Board and others, it wasn't even close. The 1981 budget cut was 3.6 percent. In 1932, during the depression, the state appropriation for Michigan State was cut 14 percent; and in 1933, it was chopped 28 percent from its 1931 level.

Under President Robert S. Shaw in the early 1930s, deans were asked to cut budgets as far as they could. And every faculty member who earned more than $1,000 per year, had his or her salary cut from four to 18 percent, depending on their pay level. As a result, no one was laid off.

In the spring of 1981, after strong protests by alumni, students and faculty, the College of Nursing, and James Madison College were saved from the axe.

By April 4, 1981, final Board budget decisions were announced, and they included the layoff of more than 100 tenured and tenure-stream faculty, 70 temporary faculty and 190 staff members. Eliminated were the Biophysics department, Justin Morrill College, Business Education and Office Administration curriculums; the School of Medical Technology, and the Education Institute for International Student Education.

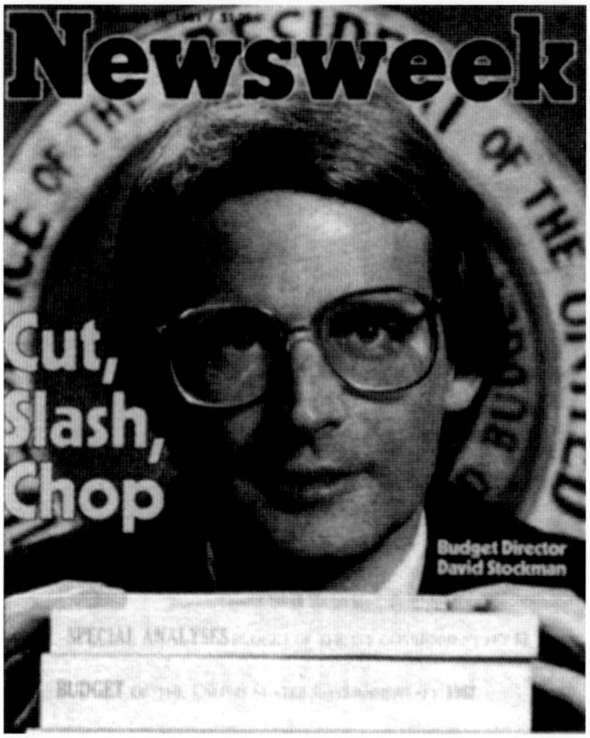

David Stockman, cum laude '68, was named director of the U.S. Office of Management & Budget by President Ronald Reagan in 1981.

The Chronicle of Higher Education called MSU's budget cuts "...one of the most sweeping actions ever taken at a single institution."

To make up for the budget cuts, the Board increased student tuition for the tenth time in 11 years. The increase was 11 percent, accompanied by a 13.5 percent hike in dorm rates.

In light of the fact that MSU's appropriations were cut only 3.6 percent, while the other 12 state-supported universities faced cuts averaging five percent, many people questioned the drastic action taken by the MSU Board of Trustees and the administration.

The University of Michigan also faced a similar downturn in appropriations, but cut no tenured faculty and did not make drastic cuts in programs. They took a longer view of the situation and found most of their savings from across-the-board six percent budget cuts.

Question of Elected vs. Appointed Trustees Raised—Because of decisions by a majority of the Board, the issue of how trustees are selected, was raised again. The question was, should trustees be selected by state-wide election, or appointed by the governor, working from a list of qualified candidates screened by select alumni committees?

A Penn State survey done for the Association of Governing Boards (AGB) that year, indicated that only seven public universities in the nation had governing boards that were popularly elected. Three of those boards were in Michigan: MSU, U-M, and Wayne State. President emeritus John A. Hannah stated on several occasions that the decision to make the MSU, U-M, and Wayne State board positions elective was a mistake made during the Michigan Constitutional Convention in 1962.

At Indiana and Purdue Universities, alumni voted on three of the nine board members from a slate screened by the alumni association boards. Other members were appointed by the governor.

At the University of Illinois, the alumni association executive board appointed autonomous Democrat and Republican screening committees. The committees recruited and interviewed candidates and presented their recommendations to the state party conventions, which by an 80-year tradition, at that time, were accepted in most instances. The MSU Alumni Association had executed a similar screening method for the 1970, 1972, and 1974 conventions, but were not as successful as the University of Illinois in getting candidates accepted.

Michigan Lt. Governor James Brickley called for the appointment of the governing boards of MSU, the University of Michigan, and Wayne State University. He noted "that Michigan elected more statewide officers (36) than any other state, and said 'the simple fact of political life is that 90 percent of these officials are unknown by 90 percent of the electorate.'" MSU Republican trustee Peter Fletcher called Brickley's proposal "an excellent idea that would be better than having the people vote in total ignorance." Ultimately, nothing materialized from Brickley's proposal.

The conflict over the alumni association came to an end in 1981. In December, the Board of Trustees voted 6-2 to disenfranchise the alumni association. Trustees Blanche Martin and Tom Reed cast the dissenting votes.

Jack Shingleton was named interim executive director of alumni programs.

"'Strip the Halls of All Their Ivy,' sung to the tune of 'Deck the Halls,' was an impromptu song by some 30 students protesting the removal of ivy from four campus buildings—Horticulture, Marshall (now Marshall-Adams), Giltner, and Anthony." The action by the Grounds department had been taken to save some $8,000 per year in ivy trimming, according to the *MSU Alumni Association Magazine.*

MSU alumnus Clare Fisher won a Grammy Award for the Best Latin Recording, and was nominated for three other Grammys.

David Stockman, cum laude '68 and elected to Congress in 1976, was President Ronald Reagan's new director of the Office of Management and Budget. Stockman was chosen as a stand-in for presidential candidates John Anderson and Jimmy Carter in practice debates with Reagan during the 1980 campaign. President Reagan later said, "I lost every debate with Stockman. After him, Anderson and Carter were a piece of cake."

M. Peter McPherson, '63, and future MSU president, was appointed director of the U.S. Agency for International Development, directing 5,400 employees in more than 60 nations.

Dean G. Gould, '58, was named senior vice president of Masonite Corp.

George G. Gargett, '40, was named senior executive vice president and director of marketing for the Mutual of Omaha Insurance Company.

The MSU Athletic Council approved the women's athletic department's decision to join the National Collegiate Athletic Association (NCAA) and leave the Association for Intercollegiate Athletics for Women (AIAW), effective in the fall of 1981. MSU was only the second Big Ten school to take this action, following Northwestern. The NCAA voted "to establish women's intercollegiate championships beginning with the 1981-1982 academic year."

Charles McCaffree, MSU swimming coach (1941-1969) and member of the International Swimming Hall of Fame, died in December, 1980. In 1981, **the Men's IM West indoor and outdoor swimming pools were named in his honor.**

Jay Vincent, All-American basketball center, won the Big Ten scoring title for the second consecutive year, averaging 24.1 points per game. Overall during the 1980-1981 season, he averaged 22.6 points per game. Vincent was MSU's sixth Big Ten scoring champion in ten years (Mike Robinson, 1973 and 1974; Terry Furlow, 1976 and 1977; and Vincent in 1980).

The 1981 university budget was $372,385,337. Enrollment was 42,094. During the year, 10,363 degrees were granted.

1982

National Superconducting Cyclotron and Performing Arts Center Dedicated; Jim Blanchard, '64, MBA '65, Elected Governor of Michigan—MSU dedicated two of its crown jewels on successive days in September: the National Superconducting Cyclotron Laboratory—the world's first—on the 26th, and the magnificent Performing Arts Center on the 27th. Dr. Henry G. Blosser, director of the laboratory, stated, **"This cyclotron and this laboratory will go on to be the leading center in the world for research in the present frontier of nuclear physics."**

K500 Superconducting Cyclotron—the world's first—made MSU a world leader in nuclear physics research. MSU's National Super-conducting Cyclotron Laboratory and the K500 were dedicated in 1982. Dr. Henry Blosser, cyclotron designer (gray sweater lower center), is shown with staff and students. MSU's nuclear science program today (2004) vies with MIT's as the finest in the U.S.

The Wharton Center for Performing Arts, with its 2,500-seat Great Hall and the 600-seat Shakespearean Theater, opened with the Chicago Symphony and Swedish soprano Birgit Nilsson. It was as classy an entertainment venue as any in America.

A new MSU Alumni Association was organized by the university administration and a select committee of alumni, faculty and students.

Dr. Charles Webb, Ph.D. '82, was selected as executive director of the alumni association in August, 1982. Webb had been assistant vice chancellor for development and alumni relations for the 64-campus State University of New York.

The first staff member Webb hired was Bob Bao, appointed editor of the new *MSU Alumni Magazine*.

MSU offered more undergraduate overseas studies programs than any other university. Twenty departments had programs in 18 nations, with 762 students participating.

Jim Blanchard, '64, MBA '65, was elected Governor of Michigan in the fall of 1982—the first MSU graduate to hold that position. He was elected on the Democratic ticket.

Blanchard joined two other MSU graduates who also were serving as governors. **George Ariyoshi, '49, was Governor of Hawaii; and Anthony Earl, '58, was Governor of Wisconsin. No other university in the nation had more state governors than MSU.**

President Cecil Mackey declared in his State of the University message, "We must look increasingly to private sources—corporate, foundation, and individual—for endowed chairs, other faculty support, capital improvements, student financial aid, and research."

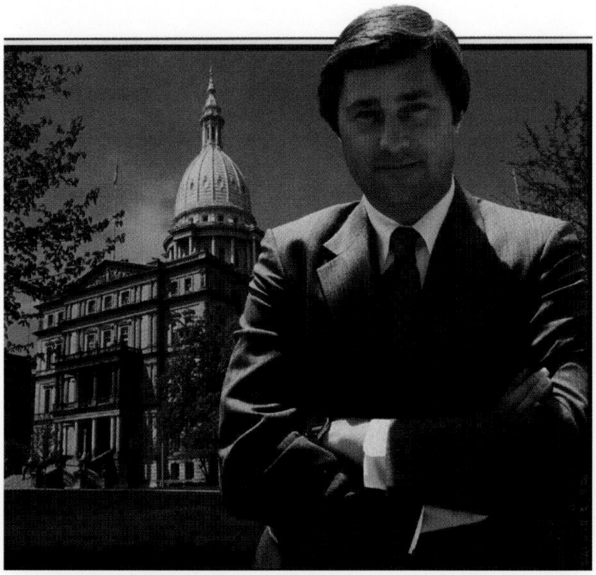

James Blanchard, '64, MBA '65, was elected Michigan's Governor in 1982–the first MSU graduate to hold that position.

Anthony Earl, '58, was serving as Governor of Wisconsin—1982.

He reported the remarkable fact that in the face of a depressed economy, the MSU Development Fund had passed the $20 million mark in private support in the 1980-81 academic year. Gifts to MSU increased 28 percent in 1981.

Dr. Barnett Rosenberg, biophysics professor, and Dewinder S. Gill, post doctoral fellow, announced a new anti-cancer drug developed in the MSU laboratory that had produced Cisplatin—the widely used, platinum based anti-cancer drug. At the national meeting of the American Chemical Society, they revealed a new anti-cancer drug based on palladium, a rare chemical cousin of platinum. They hypothesized the new compounds might work against intestinal cancers and tumors that Cisplatin did not touch.

MSU's African Studies Center was described as a model National Resource Center in African Studies at the National Advisory Board for International Programs.

A five-member MSU team won the National Invitational College Bowl Tournament, beating 15 of the nation's best universities. The competition was based on general knowledge, covering any subject—from ancient history and art to sports and zoology.

Molly Brennan, Waterford Township senior, became the second MSU coed to win a Rhodes Scholarship, and the only Michigan student to be so honored in 1982. She was MSU's ninth Rhodes Scholar, had a 3.83 grade point average, was captain of the MSU women's track & field team, was a member of the world record sprint medley team, and a member of the Big Ten championship mile relay team. She also played the piano and electronic synthesizer.

Wharton Center for the Performing Arts–a world-class venue–opened in 1982. It has attracted many first performances of major Broadway, musical, and dance shows in Michigan and among the nation's universities. In 1996, an eight-week visit by the *Phantom of the Opera* made Wharton the top Broadway Theater in the U.S., with weekly revenue of nearly $1 million. The Catherine Herrick Cobb Great Hall, shown above, seats 2,500.

Chris Bishop, senior mathematics major, won a Churchill Fellowship to study at Churchill College at Cambridge University in England. Bishop was among only ten students in the U.S. selected for the award.

Gary L. Jones, M.A. '68, Ph.D. '75, was named U.S. Under Secretary of Education.

MSU hired Robert Nelson, its first certified executive chef, to direct meal planning and execution for the residence halls. He had won the prestigious Escoffier Gold Medal and the Thomas Jefferson Gold Medal for Culinary Excellence. Ted Smith, food coordinator for the residence halls, pointed out that among the 276 different offerings in MSU's "Entree Planning Guide: were Eggs Florentine, Canadian cheese soup, California vegetable casserole, Spanish rice, Hungarian goulash, and French waffles.

The 1982 university budget was $400,020,994. Enrollment was 40,627. During the year, 10,712 degrees were awarded.

1983

Alumni Healing Begins; *MSU Alumni Magazine* Launched—Dr. Charles Webb, Ph.D. '82, new executive director of the new MSU Alumni Association, reached out to Michigan State alumni everywhere to heal the wounds from the battle between the old alumni association and the administration. In the newly created *MSU Alumni Magazine*, Webb wrote, "After my return to East Lansing last fall (1982), an alumnus wrote me urging all of us to bury the hatchet. 'Let bygones be bygones,' he said. "It reminded me of historian Madison Kuhn's observation that since MSU was founded in 1855, 'Mistakes have been made, false leads have been pursued, conflicts between persons and policies have torn the institution.' Yet despite setbacks, MSU has evolved into this nation's preeminent land-grant university."

MSU was chosen as the place for U.S. Secretary of Education Terrel H. Bell to make his first national response to the 65-page study titled, "A Nation at Risk: The Imperative For Educational Reform." MSU was selected because of its innovative leadership in educational research and training of future classroom teachers. Bell stated at the May 13, 1983 conference on campus, **"The**

MSU effort should be an example for the nation; the College of Education's Institute for Research on Teaching should draw the nation's close attention."

Secretary Bell's first act at the conference was to award the U.S. Department of Education's Certificate of Excellence to MSU's Institute for Research on teaching. It was described as a "one-of-a-kind" award by the Department of Education.

The College of Engineering opened its new Composite Materials and Structure Center to help promote the high-growth field.

The Kellogg Foundation gave MSU a $251,176 grant for establishing the nation's first coordinated network of adult continuing educational services.

The Michigan Biotechnology Institute (MBI) decided to locate permanently on the MSU campus on Collins Road.

MSU students won the National Invitational College Bowl Championship for the second consecutive year, defeating 17 other university teams, including five from the Big Ten. **MSU was the only university to have won the title more than once.** Ability to answer questions on virtually any subject, determined the winning team.

MSU students won ten National Science Foundation fellowships, leading the Big Ten for the fourth time in five years and placing second among all public universities in the nation.

Eric Carlson, senior physics major, **who had twice won the William Lowell Powell competition—the "Super Bowl" of mathematicians**—was called, "One of the smartest persons in his age group on the planet earth" by MSU mathematics coach Charles Maccluer.

Senior Dena Skran, a James Madison College international economics major, became MSU's tenth Rhodes Scholar and the third MSU woman to win the prestigious award.

Raymond D. McMurphy, '82, won the American Institute of Chemical Engineers annual competition.

Senior Christopher Bishop won a Churchill Scholarship to Cambridge University in England.

Russell E. Palmer, '56, CEO of Touche Ross International, was named dean of the Wharton School of Business at the University of Pennsylvania.

Dr. John McDougall, '69, M.D. '72, co-authored with his wife Mary, *The McDougall Plan*, which provided readers with a healthful eating and exercise regimen. It was a popular seller.

George Levitt, Ph.D. '57, was named a Distinguished Inventor of 1983 by the Intellectual Property Owners, Inc.

Paul M. Rothenberg, '63, was named general manager of the *Washington Times*, the nation's eighth largest newspaper.

Craig Jones, '67, released his second novel, *Fatal Attraction* (Crown Publishers, 1983), which had scenes set on the MSU campus.

Julee Rosso, '66, who opened the Silver Palate restaurant in Manhattan's Upper West Side, had grown it into a $5 million-a-year business whose premium products were sold by 600 retail stores. **She was selected "Business Woman of the Year"** by the U.S. Small Business Administration.

Michael Loukinen, '67, M.A. '72, Ph.D. '75, produced the PBS television drama *Finnish American Lives.* It **"won the equivalent of 'Oscars' for documentaries"**—the National Merit Award from the American Association for State and Local History, and Best Film by the National Endowment for the Arts.

Spencer Abraham, '74, future U.S. Senator and U.S. Secretary of Energy, was **elected chair of the Republican Party of Michigan.**

Katherine McCoy, '67, was elected president of the Industrial Designers Society of America. She was the youngest person and first woman to win the post.

Martha Smith, '74, appeared regularly in the TV series *Scarecrow and Mrs. King*. She had been a regular guest actress in such shows as *Dallas, Fantasy Island, Taxi,* and *Happy Days.*

Judi Brown won the NCAA title in the 400-meter hurdles in 56.44 seconds, the fastest time recorded in the U.S. She was selected the **Big Ten's Women Athlete of the Year**, and MSU's Sportswoman of the Year. She also won Big Ten titles in the quarter-mile run and 60-yard hurdles.

Steve Garvey, '72, San Diego Padres first baseman, set a new National League record, playing in 1,118 consecutive games. His streak finally ended at 1,207 games when he dislocated a thumb.

The women's track mile relay team won the Big Ten title, setting conference and school records. Team members were: Julie Boerman, Candy Burkett, Jacque Sedwick and Judi Brown.

The university budget for 1983 was $414,027,043. Enrollment was 40,122.

During the year, 10,058 degrees were granted.

Dr. Robert C. Trojanowicz

"Father" of Community Policing

Dr. Robert C. Trojanowicz

Dr. Robert C. Trojanowicz (1941-1994), late head of MSU's School of Criminal Justice, was the "father" of, and an international expert in, community policing. The innovative policing approach involved "a partnership between the formal control system—the police—and the informal system—the people," the late Trojanowicz explained. This system has now been adopted by police departments nationwide, and around the globe. To help spread the concept, Trojanowicz founded the National Center for Community Policing, which is located at Michigan State, in 1983.

Recognized as "Mr. Crime Stopper," Trojanowicz "redefined how police departments throughout the world could effectively serve their citizens," Gene Wriggelsworth wrote in the *Lansing State Journal* (March 22, 1994). Frank Hartmann, executive director of the criminal justice policy and management program at Harvard University's Kennedy School of Government, stated, "Bob was a very important figure to a great number of American police. Others would talk about things; Bob would do them. He did his homework. We learned from him." Trojanowicz served a fellowship at Harvard.

Trojanowicz wrote twelve books. Among them, *Community Policing: A Contemporary Perspective* and *Community Policing: How To Get Started* "are used by policy makers to plan, implement, and access community policing efforts." (*Town Courier*, East Lansing, February 19, 1994).

Honors won by Trojanowicz include: an FBI study citing him as one of the twelve top academicians in the police field; Criminal Justice Educator of the Year by the Michigan Association of Chiefs of Police; Outstanding Educator of the Year by the Michigan Corrections Association; and a Distinguished Faculty Award from Michigan State University.

Trojanowicz earned three degrees at Michigan State—bachelor's in police administration, '63; master's in social work, '65; and a doctorate in social science, '69.

1984

President Cecil Mackey announces retirement; Academic Excellence Flourishes—MSU women had won three consecutive Rhodes Scholarships—Molly Brennan, '82; Claudena Skran, '83; and Judith Stoddart, '84. This achievement was unmatched by any other public university in America. MSU students had won eight Rhodes Scholarships in 12 years, more than any other public institution in the nation in that time frame.

More National Merit Scholars attended MSU over the previous 15 years than any other public university in the country. For 1983-1984, MSU ranked first in the Big Ten and third in the nation among public institutions chosen by National Merit Scholars.

Michigan State led all public universities in the number of students who won or achieved honorable mention in the National Science Foundation Fellowship competition.

Lori Brown won the Truman Scholarship for the State of Michigan—the fifth time in eight years an MSU student won the honor.

MSU's computer science programming team finished sixth in the world, out of 22 finalists, in the International Scholastic Programming Contest. MSU had reached the finals five times in the previous eight years. Richard Reid, professor of computer science, was the dedicated coach.

On January 27, 1984, President Cecil Mackey said he would step down from the presidency at the end of the 1984-1985 academic year.

On November 15, 1984, the Board of Trustees selected Dr. John A. DiBiaggio as the 17th President of Michigan State University. He was to succeed Dr. Mackey on July 1, 1985.

Mackey Legacy: Important MSU Improvements

President Mackey, although surrounded with controversy early in his administration because of needed budget cuts and a battle over control of the alumni association, **was instrumental in initiating many important improvements at MSU.**

Three consecutive MSU female Rhodes Scholars– L to R: Judith Stoddart, '84; Claudena Skran, '83; and Molly Brennan, '82—unmatched by any other public university.

Fourteen endowed academic chairs were funded during Mackey's watch—MSU's first.

Annual fund-raising by the MSU Development Fund reached $18 million, a 240 percent increase from 1979, the year he became president.

The National Superconducting Cyclotron Laboratory, the Wharton Center for the Performing Arts, and the Communication Arts & Sciences Building all went up under his administration, and the Soil Sciences Building was started.

President Mackey Sells the Board on Major New Athletic Facilities—At a dinner meeting with the Board of Trustees at Cowles House in November 1984, President Mackey won trustee approval for a new $30-million All-Events Building (Breslin Student Events Center), a $6 million IM-East facility, a $3.8-million indoor football practice field, a $1.2-million indoor tennis building, and $3-million for renovating the 46-year-old Jenison Fieldhouse for intramural sports. **It was the most important action in the school's history for upgrading athletic facilities.**

Mackey also led the creation of the University's Corporate Research Park, and helped bring Neogen Corporation in as the first participant, and led the push to get the Michigan Biotechnology Institute located on campus. In the early 1980s, he led the opening of relations with Chinese universities.

MSU's department of music was elevated to the School of Music.

Biochemistry professor N. Edward Tolbert, became the fourth MSU scientist to be elected to the prestigious National Academy of Science, the third so honored in the previous two years.

Christopher R. Somerville, MSU associate professor of Botany and Plant Biology, **won a Presidential Young Investigator Award** worth $100,000 or more per year in unrestricted research funds for five years.

Alexander I. Popov, professor of Chemistry, was made a "chevalier" (a knight) in the prestigious French l'Ord re des Palmes Academiques. Under normal circumstances, only French academicians were so honored.

Robert G. Wetzel, professor of Botany and Zoology, was the first recipient of the Tage Erlander professorship established by the Swedish Parliament.

Leonard Falcone, MSU's director of bands for 40 years, was inducted into the National Hall of Fame of Distinguished Band Conductors.

The U.S. Agency for International Development selected MSU to head a $4.9 million, five-year project to assist the University of Zimbabwe (Africa) to expand and improve its agricultural programs.

For the first time in school history, commencement was conducted not as an all-university event, but rather by each college individually.

Judi Brown won an Olympic silver medal in the 400-meter hurdles at the 1984 Games in Los Angeles.

MSU's Kirk Gibson and Steve Garvey met in the 1984 World Series. Garvey played first base for the San Diego Padres. Gibson was the right fielder for the Detroit Tigers and hit game-winning home runs for the eventual World Champion Tigers. Both Garvey and Gibson had won most valuable player awards in their respective league playoffs.

Mary Fossum, MSU's first and only women's golf coach, was voted the **first ever Coach of the Year by the NCAA** Women's Golf Coaches Association.

Hockey coach Ron Mason led the Spartans to their first NCAA Final Four (now Frozen Four) **since 1967.** MSU lost 2-1 to eventual National Champion Bowling Green in the semifinals at Lake Placid, N.Y. Bowling Green athletic director Jack C. Gregory wrote MSU to thank Spartan fans for supporting BGSU, a fellow CCHA member, in their championship game versus Minnesota-Duluth.

MSU's cheerleaders were runners-up in the National Cheerleading Association's championship competition. Team co-captains were Dave Besemer and Sharon Ferguson. Tony Pizza was team coach.

Genevieve Gillette, '20, leader in founding the Michigan Parks Association and its first president, became **the first woman to be inducted into the Michigan Conservation Hall of Fame**. In the 1970s, she was instrumental in writing Michigan's Wilderness Bill, the first in the nation.

James H. Steele, DVM '41, former U.S. surgeon general and founder of the American College of Veterinary Preventive Medicine, was **awarded the Twelfth International Veterinary Congress Prize** by the American Veterinary Medical Association.

Lt. General James E. Light, Jr., '56, was named Commander of the U.S. 15th Air Force.

Kay Koplovitz, M.A. '68, was serving as president and CEO of the USA TV Network.

William J. Carr, '61, was elected president of Manufacturers Hanover Mortgage Corp.

Mary J. Layton, '64, was serving as U.S. Assistant Postmaster General.

Rick Inatome, '76, founder of Inacomp, Inc. which had 400 employees and 30 outlets nationwide, recalled seeking a job after graduation. He approached a computer firm run by "very technical University of Michigan graduates," who rejected him for lack of experience. "One year later," he said, "they wanted me to buy the company."

Luis Ramiro Beltran, M.A. '68, Ph.D. '77, won the first McLuhan-Teleglobe Canada Award—a preeminent award in the communications field.

Bill Skiles, '54, recounted his 28,000 hours of U.S. Secret Service protection of U.S. Presidents and world leaders in his biography, *Twelve Minutes to the White House.*

Clarence Underwood, '61, M.A., '65, Ph.D., '82, and future MSU athletic director (1998-2002), authored *The Student Athlete: Eligibility and Academic Integrity* (MSU Press, 1984).

Don Dinkmeyer, Ph.D. '58, saw his Systematic Training for Effective Parents program in use by 1.5 million parents in the U.S., and being picked up by Japanese, Spanish, and Greek parents.

Derrick Fries, '75, winner of two world and three national sailing championships in single-person boats, **authored the book, *Successful Sunfish Sailing*** (John de Graf, Inc., 1984). He was a former MSU sailing team captain.

Robert L. Hughes, '59, was elected president of the National Association of Life Underwriters.

MSU's Division of Housing and Food Services—which produced 12 million meals a year—won the grand prize for residence hall menus in the National Association of College and University Food Service Menu Contest.

In a marketing move to attract more students to the residence halls, Charles Gagliano, manager of University Housing, pointed to the availability of private rooms, having Case and Bryan Halls designated "quiet halls," turning 300 rooms in Mason and Abbot Halls over to Honors College students, and restricting Mayo, McDonel and Williams Halls to upper class students.

The 1984 university budget was $450,635,246. Enrollment was 40,272, including a record 1,747 students from 108 foreign nations. During the year 9,535 degrees were awarded.

1985

Dr. John A. DiBiaggio Takes Office As MSU's Seventeenth President (served 1985-1992)—Dr. John A. DiBiaggio (b. 1932) took office as MSU's seventeenth president on July 1, 1985. He had just served five years as president of the University of Connecticut, where he had successfully led a $25 million capital campaign.

DiBiaggio, a Detroit native and University of Detroit dental school graduate, migrated from dentistry to university administration. He attended Wayne State University, graduated from Eastern Michigan University in 1954, the University of Detroit Dental School in 1958, and earned an M.A. degree in administration from the University of Michigan in 1967.

DiBiaggio had two signs in his office: "Pace Yourself," and "Quie non piu da qui," Italian for "Here, I draw the line."

DiBiaggio interview with the *MSU News Bulletin*, July 18, 1985:

"I think it's my responsibility to make a case for more generous support of this University, and to increase the appreciation for the contributions of MSU to the economy of the state as well as to its cultural life."

John A. DiBiaggio, Seventeenth President

Daniel G. Nocera, age 27, assistant professor of chemistry, and **William G. Lynch**, age 34, assistant professor of physics, **each won 1985 Presidential Young Investigator Awards** which made each of them eligible for up to $500,000 in research funds over the ensuing five years.

Ron Tenpas, James Madison College, **and Rob Leland**, aerospace engineer, **won Rhodes Scholarships in 1985, providing MSU with as many of these scholarships** in four years as were given to all the rest of the Big Ten universities combined.

Sandra Pinnavaia, a bio-chemistry and political science major, won a prestigious Marshall Scholarship to Cambridge University in England. She was MSU's 1984 Homecoming Queen.

Harold Miller and Harold Sadoff, MSU professors and microbiologists, created a safer, quicker, less expensive method of checking developing fetuses for genetic abnormalities. It was an alternative to amniocentesis and simply involved drawing a blood sample.

In November, 1985, President DiBiaggio was elected chairman of the National Association of State Universities and Land-Grant Colleges by 1,500 representatives from 147 public research universities and colleges.

In a regrettable development, the MSU Yearbook—*Red Cedar Log* (formerly the *Wolverine*)—ceased publication after two years of financial losses. Students were offered a video yearbook. The video, however cost $41.95 versus $19.95 for the previous yearbook, and did not include any class or group pictures.

Carl G. Smith, '42, was serving as chairman and CEO of Gerber Products Co.

Harley Hotchkiss, '51, Calgary, Alberta gas, oil, and real estate businessman and part owner of the Calgary Flames National Hockey League franchise, **gave MSU $1.5 million**.

William Penn Mott, '31, age 75, was named Director of the National Park System by U.S. President Ronald Reagan.

Harry Moniba, Ph.D. '75, was elected vice president of Liberia, the tropical nation on Africa's western bulge.

Louis R. Ross, MBA '72, was named executive vice president of North American Automotive Operations for Ford Motor Company.

David R. Holls, '53, was named executive designer of North American passenger cars for the General Motors Design Staff.

Penny E. Harrington, '64, was named Portland, Oregon's chief of police—the first woman in the U.S. to head a major city police force.

Gregory J. Reed, '70, M.S. '71, published his third book, *The Business of Entertainment and Its Secrets* (New National Publishing Co., 1985). One of some twenty black tax attorneys in the U.S., Reed was a national expert in law, tax, and celebrity contract negotiation. He also was the producer of "the Pulitzer-winning *A Soldier's Play* in Detroit."

Spartan Stars—L to R: Mike Donnelly led MSU to the 1986 NCAA hockey title and scored 59 goals, breaking the NCAA record; halfback Lorenzo White led the nation in rushing, with 1,900 + yards in 1985; guard Scott Skiles was named Big Ten and National Player of the Year for 1985-86, and led the Big Ten in scoring, with a 29.1 points-per-game average.

MSU's Ice Hockey team set 18 team and 20 individual records in the 1984-1985 season. Its 38 wins were the most in NCAA history by one team. The Spartans won their first CCHA regular season title, their third consecutive Great Lakes Invitational title, their fourth consecutive CCHA play-off title, and made their fourth consecutive NCAA appearance. Unfortunately, the team ran into a red-hot Providence College goalie and lost 4-2 in NCAA regional competition, and lost a two-game, total goals series, 6-5.

Bruce Fossum, MSU men's golf coach, was **inducted into the Golf Association Coaches Association Hall of Fame.**

Lorenzo White, sophomore halfback, led the nation in rushing, with more than 1,900 yards. He finished fourth in the Heisman Trophy balloting.

$29.5-million Plant and Soil Sciences Building—world's finest plant science facility—opened in September, 1986.

Magic Johnson, former Spartan All-American basketball great, was featured on the cover of *Sports Illustrated* for the ninth time. He led the L.A. Lakers to their third NBA title in six years.

The 1985 university budget was $489,322,737. Enrollment was 41,032. Although college enrollment in Michigan declined 2.7 percent for the 1984-1985 academic year, MSUs freshman class was up 8.5 percent, rising from 6,020 the previous year to 6,531. Minority enrollment was a record 3,515, or 8.73 percent of the student body. During the year, 9,011 degrees were awarded.

1986

MSU Establishes National Center on Teacher Education; Spartans Win NCAA Ice Hockey Title—MSU was awarded a $6 million grant from the U.S. Department of Education to establish the National Center on Teacher Education in Erickson Hall. Combined with MSU's Institute for Research on Teaching, the College of Education expanded its reputation as a national powerhouse in teacher education and research.

NCAA Ice Hockey Champions—Coach Ron Mason's Spartan hockey team came from behind twice to beat Harvard University, 6-5 for the NCAA championship. The game was played March 29 in Providence, Rhode Island. **Mike Donnelly** fired the winning goal with 2:51 left to cap a super senior year, in which he **set MSU, CCHA, and NCAA-West single season records with 59 goals.**

In a great season, MSU, 34-9, also won the CCHA regular season title and their fourth consecutive Great Lakes Invitational tournament.

The new $29.5 million Plant and Soil Sciences Building was called "the world's finest plant science facility" by President DiBiaggio at the opening ceremonies in September.

MSU acquired a $500,000, 16,000-pound mass spectrometer, one of a few in the world. Jack Watson, professor of chemistry and director of the MSU Mass Spectometry Laboratory, said the equipment was funded by the National Institutes of Health because "MSU is a world-class institution in plant biology research."

MSU's new indoor tennis facility—with eight courts and seating for 1,000 spectators—was inaugurated on January 18, 1986.

President emeritus John A. Hannah won the singular U.S. Presidential End Hunger Award in the fall of 1986 for "Lifetime Achievement."

Amir U. Khan, M.S. '49, M.S. '52, Ph.D. '67, agricultural engineer with the International Rice Research Institute in the Philippines, **won the International Inventors Award**. It was presented to him by King Carl Gustaf of Sweden in Stockholm. Khan invented an axial flow thresher, heavily used in rice producing nations.

Morton B. Panish, M.S. '52, Ph.D. '54, senior scientist at Bell Laboratories, was **inducted into the National Academy of Engineering** and **won Japan's $61,000 Computer and Communication Award.** Panish's work on hetero-structure lasers with Japanese scientist Izuo Hayashi led to laser printers, bar code readers, digital signals in CD players, autofocus cameras, and fiber-optic communication. Panish held a dozen patents and had published 140 technical papers.

Luis Lopez Guerra, M.A. '75, was named to Spain's Supreme Court in 1986.

In recognition of a lifetime of service to Michigan State, **the Board of Trustees named the forthcoming Student Events Center for retired MSU executive vice president Jack Breslin—known fondly as "Mr. MSU."**

***Change* magazine ranked MSU's residence halls as "best in the nation"** with Yale University's. *Change* was published by The American Association of Higher Education.

Three MSU professors and one alum won Guggenheim Fellowships in 1986: **John A. Alford**, associate professor of English; **Cathy N. Davidson**, professor of English; and **David Sloan Wilson**, associate professor of zoology; and **Jan Radway, Ph. D. '77**, associate professor of American civilization, at the University of Pennsylvania.

John Eulenberg, director of MSU's Artificial Language Laboratory and his team of researchers, developed world-leading speech synthesis technology that allowed vocally impaired people to speak and sing in many languages.

Dr. Malcolm Trout, MSU dairy expert and the "father of homogenized milk," was honored on March 7, 1986 in a statewide "Malcolm Trout Day." He had joined the MSU faculty in 1928, and was a graduate of Iowa State and Cornell. He commented on the transfer of devotion from one's alma mater to Michigan State. He said it was a phenomenon he had witnessed many times in his 57 years on campus. **"This magnetic drawing power remains one of MSU's strongest if not fully appreciated assets."**

Jim Cash, '70, M.S., '72, and MSU professor, wrote two 1986 movie hits with Jack Epps, Jr., '72—*Top Gun* and *Legal Eagles*.

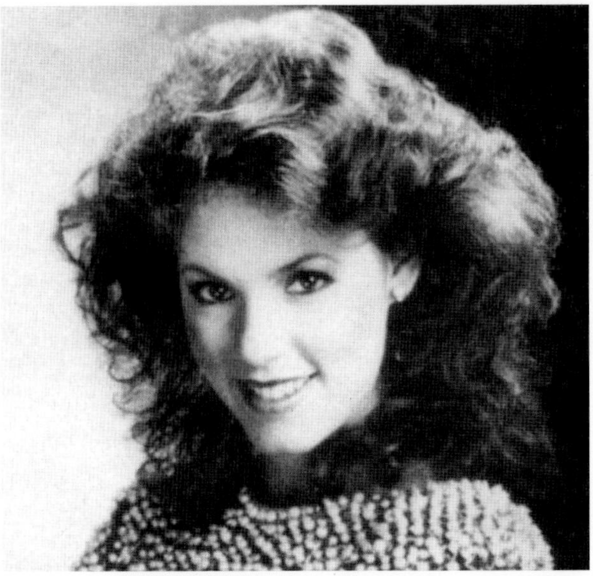

Kelly Lynn Garver, '86, won the 1986 Miss Michigan title. She was a National Honor Society member and Dean's List regular.

MSU researchers Gary Mills and James Malachowski perfected a method for growing Morel mushrooms year-around. Working under an agreement with Neogen Corporation, the growing process was patented, and considered a "landmark patent" because "no prior art" existed on Morel cultivation.

The movies "Top Gun" and "Legal Eagles" both smash hits during 1986, were written by MSU professor Jim Cash, '70, M.S. '72, and his former student Jack Epps, Jr. '72.

Gary Gildner, '60, M.A. '61, novelist and poet, won the 1986 National Magazine Award in fiction.

Spartan alum Jean Perron, age 39, Montreal Canadiens' head coach, led his team to the National Hockey League's highest honor—winning the Stanley Cup.

Ernestine Russell Weaver, Spartan gymnast from 1957-1961, was **inducted into the National Gymnastics Hall of Fame.** She was the women's gymnastics coach at the University of Florida, where she led the Gators to three national team titles, and posted a record of 140 dual meet victories versus just 8 losses.

Kelly Lynn Garver, '86, of Farmington Hills, Michigan, **won the 1986 Miss Michigan title**. Garver made the Dean's List for 13 consecutive terms, and was a member of the National Honor Society.

Robert Urich, M.A. '70, played Mike Hammer in ABC-TV's *Spenser: For Hire.*

"Stopped Clock" game ends great Spartan basketball season. MSU, 23-7, was facing the No. 2 Kansas Jayhawks, 33-3, in the "Sweet Sixteen" NCAA Mideast Regional game at Kemper Arena in Kansas City before

Sunraycer team members—1987 World Solar Car Race Champions–L to R: Terry Satchell, '68, driver; Bruce McCristal '54, PR director; Molly Brennan, '82, driver. The 1,950-mile race across the Australian Outback was won by a 2½ day margin.

16,800 fans—mostly Jayhawks. The Spartans were leading Kansas, 76-72 with 2:20 left in the game when the game clock unexplainably "froze" for 15 seconds. Coach Jud Heathcote protested the stopped clock with officials to no avail. With one minute to play, MSU led 80-74. Kansas then scored on two jump shots to cut the lead to 80-78. Finally, Kansas scored on a tip-in with 10 seconds left to play to tie the game at 80-80 and put it into overtime. It was the "extra 15 seconds" that let Kansas back into the game, which they eventually won 96-86. An NCAA rules expert called it "the most blatant error" seen in 20 years.

MSU, the only Big Ten team to make the NCAA "Sweet Sixteen," might have gone much further into the tournament as they matched up well with the remaining tournament teams.

Nonetheless, it was a great season, 23-8, and 12-6 in the Big Ten, good for third place. **Coach Heathcote was named Big Ten Coach of the Year.**

Basketball guard Scott Skiles was named to several All-American first teams and Big Ten Player of the Year. **He also was selected National Player of the Year by *CBS-TV* and *Basketball Times*.** He led the Big Ten in scoring with a 29.1 per game average.

Jim Morrissey, former MSU football captain and rookie linebacker with the Chicago Bears, intercepted a pass that **helped the Bears win Super Bowl XX**, 46-10 over the New England Patriots.

The campus was laced with 100 miles of sidewalks and nine miles of bike paths.

The 1986 university budget was $ 533,082,575. Enrollment was 41,897. During the year, 8,494 degrees were awarded.

1987

MSU Astronomer Discovers Largest Known Galaxy; MSU Wins Big Ten Football Title—MSU astronomer Susan Simkin, led a research team in discovering "Markarian 348," the largest known galaxy in the universe.

Head Coach George Perles led the Spartans to the Big Ten football championship, winning a trip to the 1988 Rose Bowl. MSU posted a regular season record of 8-2-1 as well as a 7-0-1 conference record—its first undefeated Big Ten season since 1966. The Spartans defeated Southern California, 27-13; Michigan, 17-11; and Ohio State, 13-7.

The Spartans' "Gang Green" defense held opponents to just 61.5 yards rushing per game; ranked first in the Big Ten in total defense (184.5 yards per game), and second in the nation (225.6 yards per game). Senior Halfback Lorenzo White won All-American honors and was voted Big Ten MVP. Greg Montgomery, junior All-American punter, averaged 49.7 yards per kick—a Big Ten record.

Coach Perles was voted *Football News'* National Coach of the Year, and Big Ten Coach of the Year.

"One Union Square," a new 7,800 square-foot food court was built into the space previously occupied by the old Union Grill. Five commercial food franchises moved

Norman A. Barkeley, '53, was elected chairman and CEO of Lear Siegler, Inc.

in. Seating was modernized and looked somewhat similar to the old grill.

To aid the state's developing wine industry, MSU established a Wine Research Center on campus in the fall of 1987. Professor of horticulture and wine expert Gordon "Stan" Howell, said the pilot winery was the first of its kind in the mid-west.

A computer laboratory for students was installed on the lower level of the Union Building, replacing the pool tables that had been there for years. They were moved elsewhere.

A former MSU economics professor and two MSU economics graduates were serving on the President's Council of Economic Advisors (CEA). Thomas Gale Moore, MSU professor, 1965-1974, advised President Reagan on key economic issues. **Carol A. Leisenring, M.S. '72, Ph.D. '78**, was one of CEA's senior economists. **Steven L. Husted, '71, M.A. '76, Ph.D. '80,** was a senior staff economist on trade issues.

Sylvan Wittwer, professor emeritus and former director of MSU's Agricultural Experiment Station, **co-authored** with two Chinese agricultural experts the book ***Feeding a Billion.***

Clare Fischer, '50, M.A. '55, jazz key boardist and composer, won his second Grammy Award in 1987 for Best Vocal Jazz Album, *Freefall.*

Dale W. Lick, '58, M.S. '59, president of Georgia Southern College, was elected president of the University of Maine.

Walter Adams, MSU president emeritus, walked in front of the MSU band at the 1988 Tournament of Roses Parade.

Norman A. Barkeley, '53, was elected chairman and CEO of Lear Siegler, Inc.

Jack Shingleton, '48, MSU's placement director, retired and was acknowledged as "the best placement director in the nation." Shingleton, who joined the MSU staff in 1949 and had served as head of placement since 1963, authored nine books. Among his titles were: *Which Niche* (1969), *College to Career* (co-authored with Bob Bao) in 1977, and *The Dynamics of Placement* (1985). He also wrote a chapter for the book *Business Today* (1984).

John B. Hoek, '54, was chief of flight training for American Airlines' Boeing 727 pilots.

Spartan Marching Band spells MSU at 1988 Rose Bowl game in Pasadena, California.

Three MSU graduates were part of General Motors' team that won the world's first transcontinental solar car race. The GM Sunraycer made a six-day, 1,950-mile dash across the Australian Outback in November, 1987, winning by a two and one-half day margin. Molly Brennan, '82 Rhodes Scholar and engineering manager at GM's Tech Center, was a driver; Terry Satchell, 68, suspension engineer at the Chevrolet-Pontiac-Canada Group, was a driver; and Bruce McCristal, '54, public affairs director for GM Hughes Electronics, was PR director for the Sunraycer team.

Grady Peninger, who coached Spartan wrestling teams to seven consecutive Big Ten titles—1966 through 1972—and an NCAA title in 1967, **was inducted into the National Wrestling Hall of Fame.**

Carl Banks, former MSU linebacker, made a game high ten tackles in Super Bowl XXI to help the New York Giants win the game 39-20 over the Denver Broncos.

Magic Johnson led the L.A. Lakers to the NBA title and became the first three-time winner of the NBA finals MVP award, and appeared on *Sports Illustrated's* cover for the tenth time.

The 1987 university budget was $581,759,024. Enrollment was 42,096. During the year, 8,979 degrees were granted.

1988

MSU Wins Rose Bowl—George Perles' Spartan football team beat the University of Southern California in an exciting Rose Bowl game 20-17. The victory broke the Big Ten's six-game losing streak at the "Grand Daddy of Bowl Games." It was MSU's third win in four appearances at the Pasadena stadium. This .750 Rose Bowl winning percentage tied MSU with Illinois as the most successful Big Ten teams at the big bowl.

Big Ten Commissioner Wayne Duke was brought to tears by the victory and vowed to fly the Spartan flag from his home in Barrington, Illinois for a month.

More than 265 million people in 40 nations watched the game telecast.

Spartan Champions, a 192-page book with more than 400 color pictures, captured MSU's 1987 Big Ten and 1988 Rose Bowl title achievements. It was written by award-winning *Lansing State Journal* sportswriter and MSU graduate Jack Ebling, and edited and produced by Bruce McCristal, '54.

The U.S. Department of Education selected MSU for a $2.5 million grant to fund a Center for Learning and Teaching of Elementary Subjects.

Lisa M. Gloss, a microbiology major, **won a Churchill Scholarship**.

Benjamin G. Dennis II, a sophomore, **won a Truman Scholarship**.

MSU's scholarship count stood at eight Churchill Scholarships in ten years; seven Truman Scholarships in 12 years; and five Rhodes Scholarships during the 1980s—more than any public university in the U.S.

Kevan Gosper, '55, left, chairman and CEO of Shell Oil-Australia, was elected to the Executive Committee of the International Olympic Committee in 1988. With him is Dr. Charles Webb, MSU Alumni Association executive director (now Vice President of MSU Development).

Myron S. Magen, D.O., dean of the College of Osteopathic Medicine, was named "Osteopathic Educator of the Year" by the National Osteopathic Foundation.

Three MSU faculty were elected fellows of the prestigious American Association for the Advancement of Science: James H. Anderson, vice provost and dean of the College of Agriculture and Natural Resources; Sam H. Austin, physicist and co-director of the National Superconducting Cyclotron Laboratory; and Denton E. Morrison, professor of sociology.

Under the leadership of E. James Potchen, M.D. and chairperson of the Department of Radiology, MSU had become a national leader in the use of magnetic resonance imaging (MRI). MSU's $8.5 million MRI facility was built with borrowed funds, cost the taxpayers nothing, and was totally self-supporting.

Dr. Harvey Sparks, professor of physiology and vice provost for human health programs at MSU, earned a National Institutes of Health Merit Award worth $1 million to fund MRI heart research.

Emanuel Hackel, MSU biochemist and national authority on genetic blood-typing, won the John Elliott Memorial Award—the top recognition given annually by the American Association of Blood Banks.

Horace A. Smith, MSU astronomer, won the American Astronomical Society's first Gaposchkin's Research Award.

President John A. DiBiaggio announced MSU's first comprehensive capital campaign, an effort to raise $160 million for buildings, professorship chairs, scholarships, and enhancement of many programs.

A custom-built Allen 9300 Concert Organ—the largest in the world—was selected for the Wharton Center for the Performing Arts.

Bruce Benson, director of MSU's Department of Public Safety, introduced community team policing—the first at any university—on the MSU campus.

Robert C. Stempel, MBA '70, was elected president and chief operating officer of General Motors Corporation.

James R. Kirk, M.A. '68, Ph.D. '71, was named president of research and development for the Campbell Soup Company.

In a national first, graduates from the same university were presidents of the two most visible press organizations in the nation's capital at the same time. Andy Mollison, '67, was president of the National Press Club, and James McCartney, '49, was president of the Gridiron Club—the organization that annually "roasts" the President of the United States.

Kevan Gosper, '55, an Australian and chairman and CEO of Shell Oil-Australia, was elected to the Executive Committee of the International Olympic Committee. He was the first Australian ever elected to the elite Committee of Ten. Gosper won an Olympic silver medal at the 1956 Melbourne games with the Australian 1,600-meter relay team. He captained the Australian track team at the 1960 Rome Olympics. At MSU he was a member of the Alpha Tau Omega fraternity.

George Weeks, *Detroit News* columnist, published the book, *Stewards of the State: The Governors of Michigan.*

Mary Fossum, MSU women's golf coach, was **inducted into the National Collegiate Golf Hall of Fame.** Fossum led the Spartans to five consecutive Big Ten titles in the 1970s, and to titles in 1982 and 1984.

Kirk Gibson, former Spartan great in baseball and football, inspired the L.A. Dodgers with a game-winning home run in the bottom of the ninth of the first game of the 1988 world series. The Dodgers went on to win the series over the Oakland Athletics.

Charles "Bubba" Smith, former MSU All-American tackle and former NFL All-Pro, was **inducted into the National Football Foundation's College Hall of Fame.**

Michelle Ingalls won three individual Big Ten gymnastics titles while setting conference records on the balance beam and in floor exercise.

The Spartan Marching Band won the John Philip Sousa Foundation's Intercollegiate Marching Band Trophy for 1988.

The 1988 university budget was $628,752,751. Enrollment was 42,695. During the year, 9,205 degrees were awarded.

Jacweir (Jack) Breslin, Class of 1946, *"Mr. MSU"*

The Breslin Student Events Center is Named in His Honor

"No Man Has Done More to Build MSU than Jack Breslin,"
—Dr. John A. Hannah, MSU President, 1941-1969

John Hannah recruited Jack Breslin for Michigan State in 1939. Hannah admired the fight that Breslin had demonstrated in overcoming polio as a teenager. At one point, it was thought he might never walk again. But Breslin fought back...first crawling...then walking. Then he became a star athlete at Battle Creek Lakeview High School.

Jack Breslin, "Mr. MSU"

At M.S.C. he won six varsity letters in football, baseball, and basketball. He captained the football and baseball teams in 1945. He played in the East-West Shrine football game in 1945 and 1946, and played in the College All-Star football game in 1946. He won the Governor's Award as MSC's most valuable football player in 1944. As a student he was elected president of the Union Board, president of his senior class, and vice president of the Varsity Club. He was a member of Alpha Tau Omega fraternity.

Jack Breslin, Most Valuable Player-1944; College All-Star 1946

John Hannah, first as secretary to the Board of Trustees, and later as President, mentored and molded Jack Breslin. "He was like a son to Hannah," according to Jack Shingleton, '48, director of placement emeritus and trustee emeritus.

Breslin served MSU for 38 years—Assistant alumni director (1950), director student placement (1953), assistant to the vice president for off-campus education (1958), assistant to the president (1959), secretary of the MSU Board of Trustees (1961), professor of administration (1961), executive vice president and vice president for administration (1975), vice president for administration and public affairs (1980), senior consultant to the president for state and public affairs (1985).

Breslin, '46, M.A. '56, Hon. Dr. '86 (1920-1988), was cited as the man "responsible for planning most of the buildings erected on the campus (1961-1988), and more importantly for procuring state funds to finance buildings," by MSU president John A. DiBiaggio in 1988.

Breslin evoked love and respect from his peers, faculty, students, alumni, legislators and government officials, the business community, and others. State Senator William Sederburg said of Breslin, "I have never seen anyone who had more respect from everybody in the legislature. He was always advocating for a cause that was bigger than himself. Jack was always doing things for other people...he was truly unique that way."

Blanche Martin, MSU graduate and trustee emeritus, said of Breslin, "Everyone that knew him loved him."

Marylee Davis, Ph.D. '74, former executive assistant to MSU's president and secretary of the Board of Trustees, and currently professor of education, said of Breslin, "He was approachable and accessible. He was admired and trusted in labor negotiations by the unions at MSU. He served MSU with a devotion, love, and loyalty as if he had been president of MSU, even though he didn't have the title. He will always be remembered as one of our great leaders. He had great ideas. Jack was a visionary for MSU. He loved it. His life signified what being a Spartan should be."

During his career, Breslin served on the boards of four corporations and several community service organizations. He won MSU's Distinguished Alumni Award, the Duffy Daugherty Award, and Distinguished Faculty Award. The Ingham County Medical Center's oncology center is named the Jack and Renee Breslin Cancer Center. A recognition that Breslin would have been most proud of was the naming of the MSU Distinguished Staff Awards Program in his honor.

Fortunately, before Jack Breslin died of cancer on August 2, 1988, MSU's new $43-million Student Events Center, was named in his honor. Students and the state legislators had petitioned the university to name the building for him. "When MSU President John A. DiBiaggio announced the facility would bear Breslin's name, tears welled in his eyes." (*Lansing State Journal,* story by Kimberly M. Gaudin). At the 1986 ground breaking ceremony, Breslin said, "Ladies and gentlemen you're looking at the proudest person in the whole world. Sometimes I wonder if this is a dream. It's hard to imagine a building bearing my name. To have this university that I love so much do this for me is really overwhelming."

1989

Communication Arts & Sciences Leads Nation in Scholarly Presentations; Breslin Center Opened—The College of Communication Arts & Sciences faculty led all U.S. universities in scholarly paper presentations at the annual convention of the Association for Education in Journalism and Mass Communications. It was the second time in three years, that these professors had won the distinction.

MSU's newest cyclotron was dedicated in May, 1989. John Moore, of the National Science Foundation stated, **"This cyclotron is the best of its kind in the world."** The National Superconducting Cyclotron Lab at MSU enabled nuclear scientists to conduct basic research on the fundamental nature of matter.

MSU's Julian Samora Research Institute, the first Hispanic Study Institute in the midwest, was dedicated

Jack Breslin Student Events Center, a $43-million, 15,000 seat arena, opened in the fall of 1989. MSU appropriately initiated the new facility by winning the 1990 Big Ten basketball title. First commencement held at Breslin—December 2, 1989.

in the fall. Dr. Richard Navarro said "the institute will study Hispanic problems in areas like student retention, employment, and civil rights."

Dr. Herbert J. Oyer, former dean of the College of Communication Arts and Sciences, was honored by having the MSU Speech-Language and Hearing Clinic named for him.

Joey Huston, assistant professor of physics, and **Mercouri Kanatzidis**, assistant professor of chemistry, each **won Presidential Young Investigators awards** worth up to $500,000 each in support of research over a five year period.

Glen Hatton, professor of psychology and director of the interdisciplinary neuroscience program, and **Stanley Chojnacki**, professor and associate chair of the history department, won 1989 Guggenheim Fellowship Awards.

James Dye, chair of the chemistry department, was elected to the National Academy of Sciences. Dye discovered two "impossible" compounds known as electrides.

Dr. Fred Honhart, director of MSU Archives and Historical Collections, won the C.F.W. Coker Prize—the top recognition from the Society of American Archivists—for pioneering a micro-based system that allowed archives nationwide to use the AMC (Archival Manuscript Control) format. **Anders Johanson**, MSU computer laboratory scientist, led the development of the applications program.

The U.S. Department of Agriculture (USDA) needed help in preserving 10,000 metric tons of pork being sent to Poland. **They turned to MSU's School of Packaging**—the world experts in packaging. The answer was: fibreboard boxes with polyethylene lining. At that time, MSU's School of Packaging and the USDA administered the packaging requirements for the world's largest

Engineering Building $35.5-million addition opened in the fall of 1989.

IM-East, a $6-million exercise "palace" featuring 68 different workout machines and basketball, squash and raquetball courts, opened in 1989 on E. Shaw Lane. It was the 3rd campus IM facility.

food distribution system: USDA's relief, sales, schools, and prison efforts.

The University Corporate Research Park, a 112.5-acre site between Collins Road and I-496, was approved by the MSU Trustees.

Senior Eric Hooper, an astrophysics, mathematics, and Russian major, was one of ten students in the nation to win a **Churchill Scholarship**.

Nicholas Milton, '88, graduate student and performance major in the School of Music, won the 1989 Louis Sudler Prize, and was named concertmaster of the Battle Creek, Michigan symphony. He came to MSU as a member of the Australian String Quartet.

The Jack Breslin Student Events Center was formally opened at a gala pre-football game luncheon, set on the arena floor. The 15,000-seat, $43 million center would give a big boost to MSU student events and the basketball program. The first commencement ceremonies were held in the Breslin Center on December 2, 1989.

A $35.5-million, 131,000 square-foot addition to the Engineering Building opened in the fall. The addition included teaching and research laboratories, and doubled the size of the engineering library.

The new $6 million, 55,000 square foot Intramural East facility opened. It provided a physical fitness outlet just a short walk from east campus residence halls, which housed 8,000 students. The new building included a running track, an air-conditioned weight room with 68 pieces of Nautilus equipment, four basketball courts, two squash, and eight raquetball courts, and a multi-purpose room for group exercise.

New graduation requirements were to include the equivalent of one college year of a foreign language.

The last of the Quonset Huts that housed so many students following World War II, were torn down to make way for the new Breslin Student Events Center parking lots.

Michigan State was the first university in the country to host the top musical of the year, *Les Miserables*.

Michigan State graduates held seven key positions in the executive branch of Michigan's state government, including that of governor. **In the Michigan legislature, MSU graduates held more than a quarter of all the positions**: nine seats (of 32) in the State Senate; and 29 (of 110) in the State House of Representatives .

Philip E. Austin, M.A. '68, Ph.D. '69, was elected chancellor of the University of Alabama.

Ed Feldman, '50, Hollywood Academy Award-winning producer (*Save the Tiger*, and *Witness*), produced *Wired*, based on Bob Woodward's story of John Belushi (star of *Animal House*, and a one-time MSU student). Feldman declared, "It is the single most important anti-drug movie ever made."

William R. Tiefel, '56, was elected president of Marriott Hotels and Resorts.

Carl T. Mottek, '51, was serving as president of the Hotels Division of Hilton Hotels.

Peter Secchia, '63, chairman of The Universal Companies, was named U.S. Ambassador to Italy.

Verghese Kurien, M.A. '48, was named the 1989 World Food Prize laureate. The $200,000 prize was given to the individual who has made an outstanding contribution toward improving the world food supply.

William R. Tiefel, '56, was elected president of Marriott Hotels & Resorts.

John D. Wilson, '53, Ph.D. '65 and Rhodes Scholar, was serving as president of Washington & Lee University, Lexington, VA.

Donald F. Keck, '62, M.S. '64, Ph.D. '67, Corning Glass Works scientist, developed, with two other researchers, a method for transmitting laser light through optical fiber.

Pete Gent, '64, former MSU basketball player and star receiver for the Dallas Cowboy football team, authored his fourth novel, *North Dallas After 40* (Village Books, 1989). His book *North Dallas 40,* introduced in 1972, sold 100,000 hard cover and two million paperback copies.

Tom McGuane, '62, authored his seventh novel, *Keep the Change* (Houghton Mifflin, 1989). The book quickly hit the best-seller lists.

Terry Van Der Tuuk, '63, CEO of Graphics Technology, Inc., was named Entrepreneur of the Year.

Bonnie Lauer, '73, winner of the national intercollegiate golf title in 1973 and successful golf pro, was elected president of the Ladies Professional Golf Association.

David Hirsch, '84, was selected by Dick Clark to take over as the host of TV's *American Bandstand,* after hosting the show for 33 years.

Magic Johnson, MSU and NBA basketball great, Joe Montana, and Wayne Gretzky were named the Athletes of the 1980s by *Sports Illustrated.*

Michelle Roper, '89, won her age bracket in the National Triathlon Federation championships. She swam 1.2 miles, biked 56 miles, and ran 13.1 miles in 4:44.2, an excellent time.

Percy Snow, Spartan All-American football linebacker, scored a first in college football, winning both The Butkus Award—given to the nation's best linebacker; and The Lombardi Award—given to the top linebacker or lineman in the country.

Julie Farrell won the women's NCAA one-meter diving title.

The 1989 university budget was $672,672,797. Enrollment was 42,866. During the year, 9,321 degrees were awarded.

Dr. Beatrice Paolucci

Nation's Leading Authority in Family Decision-Making

Dr. Beatrice Paolucci, (1924-1983), professor of family and child ecology, was acknowledged by many as the nation's leading authority in family decision-making and resource management. She joined the MSU Human Ecology faculty in 1951, and served as acting chair of her department, 1967-1969, and 1970-1973.

Paolucci was author or co-author of four books. Her 1961 book, *Teaching Home Economics,* was adopted as a text by the University of Illinois, Purdue University, and the Women's College of North Carolina.

Linda Nelson, professor of human ecology, remembering Dr. Paolucci, said, "I think the most outstanding thing about her was her commitment to students. She was available to them any day of the week, any hour of the day. Her books were always a little ahead of their time, always challenging people to think along new lines." (*Lansing State Journal*, Oct. 4, 1983).

Among her many awards were: the American Home Economics Foundation Distinguished Service Award; the Osborne Teaching Award from the National Council of Family Relations; and the MSU Distinguished Faculty Award. She served as vice chair of the 1970 White House Conference on Children.

In 1983, Dr. Paolucci became the first person to hold the Camilla Eyring Kimball Chair of Home and Family Life at Brigham Young University.

Dr. Beatrice Paolucci, the nation's leading authority in family decision-making, had the Home Management Building named in her honor in 1989.

MSU and the College of Human Ecology honored Dr. Paolucci by naming its Home Management Building for her in 1989. The college also established the Paolucci symposia in her memory in 1985 to attract national and international scholars to the campus periodically, and to provide intellectual leadership in the field.

World's first superconducting cyclotron for cancer therapy was designed by MSU's Dr. Henry Blosser, left, at MSU's National Superconducting Cyclotron Laboratory. Completed in 1990, it was installed at Harper Hospital in Detroit. Dr. William Powers, chief of radiation oncology at Harper, is shown standing.

1990

MSU Produces World's First Medical Cyclotron; Big Ten Football and Basketball Champions; Central Collegiate Hockey Champions—The world's first medical superconducting cyclotron—K100—was designed by MSU physicist Dr. Henry Blosser, and built at MSU's National Superconducting Cyclotron Laboratory. The new medical tool was delivered to Harper Hospital in Detroit to provide an efficient, inexpensive method of neutron therapy for the treatment of cancers that resist conventional radiation.

MSU's football team tied for the Big Ten football title with a 6-2 conference record, and an 8-3-1 overall season. Coach George Perles' gridders then defeated Southern California for the third time in three years, 17-16, in the John Hancock Sun Bowl in El Paso, Texas. Halfback Tico Duckett was named Big Ten player of the Year.

In one of the most exciting football games in Spartan history, MSU defeated #1 Michigan, 28-27 at Ann Arbor. In a wild finish, 27 points were scored in the final six minutes of the game.

The Spartan basketball team won the Big Ten title by running off ten consecutive conference wins to close the season with a 15-3 Big Ten record. It was an appropriate way to open the first season in the Breslin Center. Overall, coach Jud Heathcote's Spartans were 28-6, led by junior All-American Steve Smith.

Wrong Clock Call Costs Cagers—In the NCAA tournament, MSU beat Murray State and University of California-Santa Barbara to advance to the Sweet Sixteen. For the second time in four years, MSU lost the chance to get to the Elite Eight because of a wrong clock call. With less than six seconds left to play, MSU was leading Georgia Tech, 75-73. Tech guard Kenny Anderson raced down the court and launched a two-point shot with the game clock reading :00. The shot went in, tying the game, according to the umpire, who was wrong. Game photographs clearly showed that Anderson still had the ball in his hands when the clock ran out. His late shot tied the score 75-75, sending the game into an overtime that the Yellowjackets won 81-80. It was a wrong call by umpire Charles Range, and was deemed so by any objective observer of the game videotape.

Ron Mason's Spartan ice hockey team won the CCHA regular season title for the second consecutive year, and the CCHA playoff title for the seventh time in nine years. By February 23, MSU had stretched its CCHA-record unbeaten string to 27 games (24-0-3). MSU finished the season 26-3-3 in the CCHA, and 35-7-3 overall.

MSU's Kip Miller was named the Hobey Baker Award winner, college hockey's Heisman Trophy.

Sarah Shaw Hannah, '32, M.S. '33, MSU's first lady for 28 years, died on October 29, 1990 at the age of 79. Mrs. Hannah lived for 38 years in Cowles House—from 1928 to 1938 as the daughter of MSC president Robert S. Shaw, prior to marrying John A. Hannah, and from 1941 to 1969 as MSU's first lady. As a Michigan

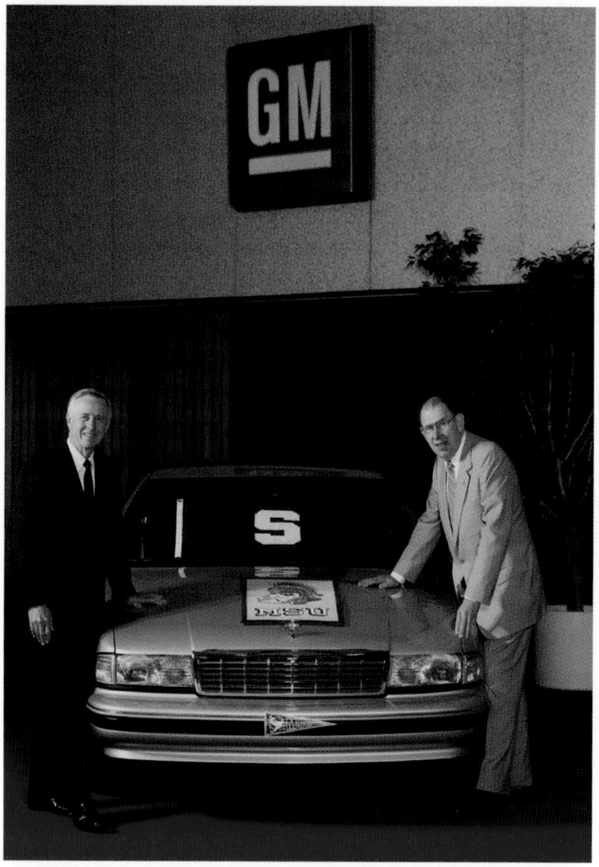

Spartans Lead GM—Robert J. Schultz, '53, MBA '69, left, was elected vice chairman, and Robert C. Stempel, MBA '70, was elected chairman and CEO of General Motors Corporation in 1990. MSU graduates also have served as CEO of Ford Motor Company, and presidents of Daimler-Chrysler, Mazda Motor-Japan, Porsche Cars-North America, and Toyota Motor Manufacturing-North America.

State student in the 1930s, she was the only woman of her day to be inducted into the Phi Sigma graduate honor society. She was survived by her husband and four children.

MSU astronomer Jeffrey R. Kuhn and colleagues discovered a super-giant cluster of stars more than six million light years in diameter. Before the discovery was revealed in an October 26, 1990 *Science* magazine cover story, the largest known galaxy had been Markarian 348, discovered by a team led by MSU's Susan Simkin in 1987.

Joseph Penicone, assistant professor of radiology, and James Siebert, chief engineer for MSU's Radiology Department, pioneered a method using superconducting magnets and radio waves to give physicians a picture of the body's blood flow from any angle.

Dr. Lisa Delpit, associate professor of teacher education, was awarded a MacArthur Fellowship. She was the first MSU faculty member to receive this "no-strings attached" award.

Donald M. Bott, mechanical engineering senior, won a Churchill Scholarship for a year of study at Cambridge University in England. He was the 11th MSU student in 12 years to win a "Churchill."

Wendy Fritzen, James Madison College sophomore in American public affairs, won a Harry S. Truman Scholarship providing up to $7,000 per year for four years.

MSU engineering students won the National Concrete Canoe competition, defeating 18 other universities.

James Dye, Department of Chemistry chair, won a second John Simon Guggenheim Foundation fellowship, and a "1990 Chemical Pioneers" Award form the American Institute of Chemists.

Daniel Nocera, associate professor of chemistry, won a Sloan Research Fellowship, a prestigious award for young scientists.

Dr. Charles Webb, executive director of the MSU Alumni Association, produced the *Handbook for Alumni Administration*, a 324-page book considered the "Bible" for alumni directors.

Stan Drobac, MSU men's tennis coach, 1958-1989, was inducted into the **Intercollegiate Tennis Hall of Fame.** Drobac was the Big Ten No. 1 doubles champion with Tom Belton in 1952 and 1953, and Big Ten No. 1 singles champion in 1953. He coached the Spartans to a Big Ten title in 1967. He produced 10 conference champions in singles, and four in doubles. His "Tenniscor" copyrighted scoreboard was used in 13 NCAA championships.

Michael Kasavana, MSU faculty representative to the Big Ten, was named by the conference as vice president of the NCAA. Kasavana was a professor and former chair of MSU's School of Hotel, Restaurant, and Institutional Management.

Alumni Lifelong Education, an academic division of the university, and MSU's Evening College, were placed

Richard Barkley, '54, right, was serving as U.S. Ambassador to the German Democratic Republic (East Germany) in 1990.

under the MSU Alumni Association. Chuck McKee, director of the program, said it was **the first such division in the Big Ten**, and possibly in the nation.

Two MSU graduates were elected to lead General Motors Corporation. Robert C. Stempel, MBA '70, was elected chairman and CEO of GM, and **Robert J. Schultz**, '53, MBA '69, was elected vice chairman.

Jack, '54, and Dortha Withrow, '55, established Endowed Teacher-Scholarship Awards, one each in the College of Business, and the College of Engineering, and made possible the Perennial Pond in the new MSU Horticultural Demonstration Gardens.

Richard Barkley, '54, U.S. Ambassador to the German Democratic Republic (East Germany), was key in keeping close watch on the emerging democratic and reunification efforts of the former communist country. The *New York Times* called Barkley "one of a handful of experts who are adequately prepared for the task."

Frank Price, '51, was elected chairman of Columbia Pictures.

Jack Epps, Jr., '72, and **Jim Cash, '70, M.S. '72,** wrote the screenplay for the smash movie hit *Dick Tracy*. This followed their successes with the screenplays for *Top Gun, Legal Eagles,* and *The Secret of My Success*.

Barbara Everitt Bryant, M.A. '67, Ph.D. '70, was nominated by President George H.W. Bush to be director of the U.S. Census Bureau.

Linda Draft, M.A. '77, associate athletic director and women's softball coach at the University of Wisconsin-Parkside, was named National Coach of the Year by the National Association of Intercollegiate Athletics.

Mary Alice Busby, '73, was named among the 100 "best and brightest" black women in corporate America by Ebony magazine. She was the senior legal counsel for Sun Refining and Marketing Company. At MSU, Busby earned a 3.75 grade point average and was a member of Phi Beta Kappa.

Dawn Riley, '87, led the 12-member female crew of "The Maiden" in the Whitbread Round-the-World Sailing Race in September, 1990. The first all-female crew finished second in their class.

Scott Skiles, former MSU basketball All-American guard, set the National Basketball Association record for assists in one game, executing 30 versus the Denver Nuggets in December.

Tom Narcy, MSU diving coach, was named **NCAA Diving Coach of the Year**.

David Tuttle, '71, who won the body-building World Cup, and Tournament of Champions titles in 1989, authored the book *Forever Natural: How to Excel in Sports Drug-Free* (Iron Books, 1990). His anti-steroid program was widely adopted in California's "drug-free" schools program.

Ann House Quinn, '83, was named executive director of the National Aquarium in Washington, D.C., the nation's oldest.

Peter Morris, M.A. '90, was the world's number one Scrabble player according to the computer ratings of the National Scrabble Association.

The 1990 university budget was $720,310,124. Enrollment was 42,785. During the year, 9,458 degrees were awarded.

1991

Eli Broad Gives $20 Million to College of Business; President Emeritus Hannah Dies; John Engler, '71, Elected Governor of Michigan—Eli Broad, '54, founder and CEO of Kaufman & Broad, Inc., gave $20 million to the MSU College of Business—the largest private gift to a public university up to that time. Broad stated, "Today, I believe it (MSU) is the ideal candidate to help America regain its industrial competitiveness. It will do so through an enlightened MBA curriculum that shifts the emphasis from 'business administration' to 'business management'—hence the name change to the Graduate School of Management."

President Emeritus John A. Hannah, considered by many the most visionary national university leader and builder of the 20th century, **died February 23, 1991**, at age 88. Hannah devoted 46 years of his life to Michigan State, 28 years as president. During his exemplary career, **he was selected by six U.S. Presidents (Roosevelt, Truman,**

Eli Broad, '54, founder and CEO of Kaufman & Broad, Inc., gave MSU's College of Business $20-million in 1991—the largest private gift to a public university up to that time.

John Engler, '71, took office as Michigan's 46th Governor in January, 1991. He was the second MSU graduate to become Michigan's CEO.

Eisenhower, Kennedy, Johnson, and Nixon) to serve the nation in various roles. He was the first chairman of the U.S. Commission on Civil Rights. **Hannah was honored with the USA Medal of Freedom—the nation's highest civilian award. His signature belief was, "Only people are important, especially poor people."**

John Engler, '71, took office in January 1991 as Michigan's 46th governor. Engler, a Republican, defeated fellow MSU alumnus and incumbent Democratic Governor James Blanchard, '64, by just 19,130 votes—less than one percent of the total cast.

MSU's College of Human Medicine was ranked No. 3 in the nation in teaching primary health care in a *U.S. News & World Report* survey for its cover story, "America's Best Graduate Schools (April 29, 1991). The nation's intern-residency directors, all of whom were surveyed, ranked MSU as "the best in the country."

The first occupant of the University Corporate Research Park was the North American Business and Technical Center of Himont Advanced Materials. The facility was dedicated in January of 1991.

A treasured mural, *Thomas Edison*, painted by Edgar Yaeger (circa 1935) as part of the federal government's Works Progress Administration economic uplift program in the depression, was installed in the main lounge of the Union Building. It was originally located in Detroit's Public Lighting Commission Museum Building. Yaeger restored the painting in 1988 and then donated it to MSU's Kresge Art Museum.

Dr. Henry G. Blosser, University distinguished professor and former director of the National Superconducting Cyclotron Laboratory at MSU, shared the top American award in nuclear physics.

Dr. Judith Lanier, dean of MSU's College of Education, was elected a member-at-large of the National Academy of Education, whose membership is limited to 75 individuals.

MSU honored its first black graduate—Myrtle Craig Mowbray, Class of 1907—with a scholarship named for her.

Michigan State advertising students won the American Advertising Federation's national competition in Chicago. The *Chicago Sun-Times* reported, "None of the other teams came close to MSU in executing the creative part of the assignment."

A $47 million, 72,000 square-foot expansion of the Veterinary Medicine Clinical Center opened in January, 1991. It included a high-tech, 132-seat lecture hall with computer terminals at every seat—one of the first in the nation.

Ronald Nelson, past chairman of MSU's Department of Animal Science, had his portrait hung in the Sirloin & Saddle Club gallery in Louisville, Kentucky. The $6,000 portrait is considered **the "Nobel Prize" of the world livestock industry**.

Renowned MSU economist Dr. Walter Adams was named one of the nation's ten best college professors by *Rolling Stone* Magazine. Adams stated, "(current students) consider me a Marine Corps sergeant in boot camp. But students who have gone through my class brag they made it."

MSU plant scientist Christopher Roland Somerville was named a member of the Royal Society of London for the Promotion of Natural Knowledge. The exclusive society was chartered in 1662 and includes such leaders as Isaac Newton, Christopher Wren, and James Cook.

MSU horticulture professor emeritus Robert F. Carlson received the Royal Horticultural Society's Gold Veitch Memorial Award—the highest honor bestowed on a non-British national. Carlson helped revolutionize fruit production worldwide with his root stock and dwarf tree developments.

Kathryn Book, professor of psychology, and **Charles Steinfield**, associate professor of telecommunication, won Fulbright Awards to conduct overseas research.

David Cohen, MSU Hannah distinguished professor of education and social policy, was elected to the prestigious National Academy of Education.

Richard Cohn, senior mechanical engineering major, won a Churchill Scholarship—the 12th in 13 years for MSU.

George Rowan, MSU professor of education, received the 1991 Peace Corps Black Educator of the Year Award.

Dale W. Lick, '58, M.S. '59, was elected president of Florida State University. He had been president of the University of Maine.

Julie Farrell-Ovenhouse scored a record-setting 576.8 points to win the 1991 NCAA 3-meter diving title.

Drayton McLane, Jr., MBA '59, president and CEO of McLane Co., Inc., was named vice chairman and director of Wal-Mart Stores.

Jerry Myers, '62, was elected president and CEO of Steelcase, Inc.

Richard H. Ruch, '52, was elected president of Herman Miller, Inc. He already held the CEO title.

Lt. General Gordon E. Fornell, '58, was serving as commander of the Electronic Systems Division of the Air Force Systems Command.

MSU junior Julie Farrell-Ovenhouse won the 1991 NCAA three-meter diving title with a record-setting 576.8-point performance. Ovenhouse, the 1990 NCAA Diver of the Year, won the NCAA one-meter diving title in 1990. She also was named **Big Ten-Jesse Owens Athlete of the Year**.

Eva Evans, M.A. '70, Ph. D. '77, deputy superintendent of the Lansing, Michigan School District, was elected vice president of Alpha Kappa Alpha, the world's oldest black sorority, which had 100,000 members worldwide and was a civic service organization. She would serve as vice president until 1994, and then rise to the presidency and serve until 1998.

Arthur Hills, '53, nationally recognized golf course architect, was selected to direct the renovation of MSU's Forest Akers-West Golf Course. The $1 million project, funded from the Forest Akers trust fund, involved adding more than 250 yards to the length of the course, new four-tier tee areas, new contours, and new United States Golf Association-specified grasses. Hills was a member of the golf team and ATO fraternity at Michigan State.

Wendy Fritzen, James Madison College junior and Truman Scholarship winner, was selected by *Glamour Magazine* as **one of the Top Ten College Women of 1991.** She served on MSU's Student Appeals Board and the All-University Judiciary Committee, ran a winning political campaign for county commissioner, and was a delegate to Michigan's Democratic convention. She spent fall term of 1991 as an intern at the U.S. Supreme Court, doing research for the Chief Justice.

Charles "Bubba" Smith, former MSU football All-American and three-time All-Pro defensive end, gave $150,000 to MSU to establish an endowment to finance scholarships for minority engineering students. Smith declared, "A lot of kids my size can get into school on a football scholarship, but kids with huge brains can't get in because their parents don't have the money."

Kelly Burke, '90, was the National Champion in dressage—the method of training a horse in obedience and precision movement.

Former MSU football greats Carl Banks and Mark Ingram helped lead the New York Giants to a 20-19 Super Bowl win over the Buffalo Bills.

The first step toward total computerization of the class registration process was taken during spring term, when some students selected their classes using 169 computer terminals located in four different campus buildings.

In 1991, MSU had land holdings in 21 of the state's 83 counties.

Wendy Fritzen receives her citation from Ruth Whitney, editor of Glamour *magazine.*

Wendy Fritzen, '92, R, Truman Scholarship winner, was named one of 1991's Top Ten College Women by *Glamour* magazine.

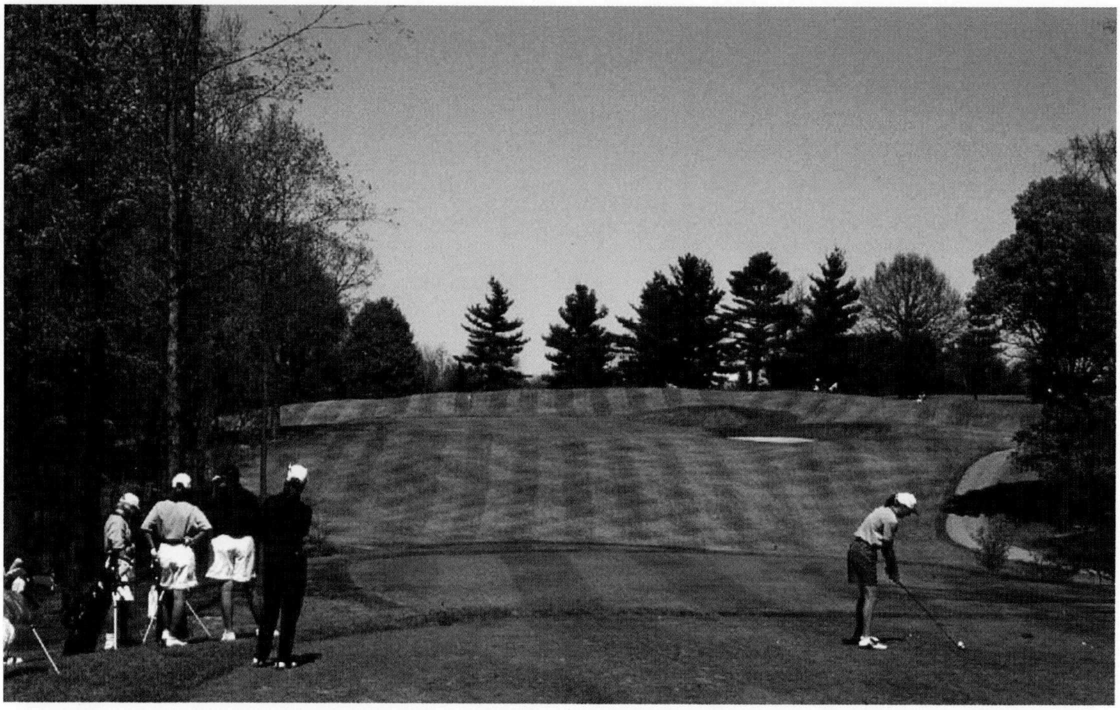

No. 9 Tee—the signature hole of Forest Akers West championship course at MSU—was part of the $1 million renovation directed by Arthur Hills, '53, nationally renowned golf course architect.

The 1991 university budget was $765,330,766. Enrollment was 42,088—spread almost evenly at 8,000-plus for each class—freshmen, sophomore, junior, and senior. There also were 8,000-plus graduate students. **MSU's minority enrollment reached a record level of 4,810, or 11.2 percent of the university's 42,785 students.** During the year, 9,621 degrees were awarded.

Dr. Henry G. Blosser

Winner of America's Top Award in Nuclear Physics
"Father" and Designer of the National Superconducting Cyclotron Lab

Dr. Henry Blosser, "Father" of the world's first Superconducting Cyclotron Laboratory.

Dr. Henry G. Blosser, University distinguished professor and former director of the National Superconducting Cyclotron Laboratory at MSU, shared **the top American award in nuclear physics in 1991**. He shared the Tom W. Bonner Prize, which is sponsored by the American Physical Society, with Indiana University professor Robert E. Pollock.

The two were cited "for their pioneering development of innovative accelerator configurations which have allowed new levels of precision and flexibility for nuclear physics research."

Blosser joined the faculty in 1958 specifically to design and build a research cyclotron, completed in 1965, which set new standards of precision in nuclear physics.

In the 1970s, he led the development of the K500 and K800 cyclotrons as the United States' principal effort in worldwide research on acceleration of heavy ions. The K500, completed in 1982, was the world's first superconducting cyclotron. The K800, which was completed in

1988, was the highest-energy cyclotron in the world. Both cyclotrons were located within MSU's National Superconducting Cyclotron Laboratory.

Blosser also designed the world's first medical superconducting cyclotron—K100—which was delivered in 1990 to Harper Hospital in Detroit. It was designed to provide an efficient, inexpensive neutron therapy for the treatment of cancers that resist conventional radiation.

Blosser's work helped MSU attain a ranking as the top program in nuclear physics studies, side-by-side with MIT. In 1991, he was one of only 21 MSU faculty to hold the title University Distinguished Professor.

Blosser has published 73 papers related to nuclear and accelerator physics.

Other awards and honors earned by Blosser include—National Science Foundation Predoctoral Fellow, 1953-1954, and Postdoctoral Fellow, 1966-1967; MSU Distinguished Faculty Award, 1972; Guggenheim Fellow, 1973-1974; and Michiganian of the Year, 1984 (*Michigan Magazine, Detroit News).*

Dr. Blosser earned a bachelor's degree in mathematics, '51, master's in physics, '52; and Ph.D. in physics, '54—all at the University of Virginia.

1992

Gordon Guyer Elected MSU's Eighteenth President (served 1992-1993); MSU Hosts Most-Watched U.S. Presidential Debate; MSU Moves to Semester System—Gordon Guyer, MSU vice president for government affairs, was elected the eighteenth President of Michigan State University by an 8-0 vote of the Board of Trustees on June 5, 1992. He took office on September 1, 1992.

Guyer, B.S. '50, M.S. '52, Ph.D. '53, (b.1926) had served MSU for 37 years and was an internationally recognized entomologist and author of more than 70 scientific papers. He was named chair of the Department of Entomology in 1963, and was instrumental in developing MSU's Pesticide Research Center. In 1973, he was named director of the Cooperative Extension Service and appointed assistant dean of the College of Agriculture and Natural Resources. In 1986, Guyer left MSU to serve two years as director of the Michigan Department of Natural Resources.

Dr. Gordon E. Guyer…

"The classroom, just as much as the laboratory, is where discovery begins. The blending of the classroom and the lab—the merging of teaching and research—have made MSU great."

"Students are our reason for being here."

"We are not only to transmit knowledge to the citizens of the 21st century, we are here to inspire those citizens."

President John DiBiaggio resigned as MSU president to become president of Tufts University, Medford, MA. During his seven year tenure, DiBiaggio injected new vigor and pride into Michigan State University and the MSU family. He was charismatic and one of the most persuasive and inspirational speakers to hold MSU's CEO position.

His major legacy was leading the university's MSU 2000 capital campaign—the school's first major fund drive—to a successful conclusion, raising $218 million. The original goal had been $160 million. DiBiaggio traveled the country to persuade well-to-do alumni to give generously, and they did.

He worked energetically with Provost David Scott on many reforms in the undergraduate and graduate education programs. They worked for a renaissance in lifelong education, and initiated "R-Cubed," a program to refocus, rebalance and refine educational operations for the 1990s.

Brought on stream during his tenure were the Breslin Student Events Center, the Himont Advanced Materials corporation in the University Corporate Park, and the annual Michigan Festival.

Dr. Gordon E. Guyer, Eighteenth President

The third and final debate of the 1992 Presidential campaign was held at MSU's Wharton Center. It featured, L to R—Ross Perot, President George H.W. Bush, and William J. Clinton. It drew a global TV audience of several hundred million—the largest in Presidential debate history. The debate poster, above, is displayed on the ground level of the Wharton Center.

DiBiaggio was embroiled for nearly two years in a controversy over whether one person should be head football coach and athletic director. This occurred toward the end of his administration. He said "no." The Board of Trustees ratified the dual position in 1989 in a 5-3 vote. The national experience favored DiBiaggio's position. Only four major universities vested the athletic director and head football coach positions in one person. In December of 1991, the Board reversed itself and voted 6-2 to abolish the dual position of head football coach and athletic director.

The third and final U.S. Presidential Debate of the 1992 campaign was held in MSU's Wharton Center on October 19, 1992. MSU President Gordon Guyer played hardball with the national political parties to maximize the number of students who could be present at the debate. As President George H.W. Bush, Bill Clinton, and Ross Perot debated, **the largest TV audience in presidential debate history**—hundreds of millions around the globe—watched. From a protocol standpoint, MSU had to host the leaders of three political parties, the U.S. Secret Service, and the global press corps.

When the event concluded, **the press corps and the National Debate Commission said MSU had provided the best-organized, smoothest running debate venue in their experience.** Nancy Leigh Brent, now MSU Alumni Association associate director (2004), was a key leader in directing the event.

Michigan State implemented the Semester System, replacing the long-standing quarterly academic system.

Hannah Recognized As the Twentieth Century's Premier Higher Education Leader—At the 1992 Association of Governing Boards (Universities) annual meeting, Dr. Ernest Boyer, President of the Carnegie Foundation for the Advancement in Teaching, identified Dr. John Hannah **"as a leader in this century who did more for higher education than any other person."**

Michigan State's International Studies and Programs curriculum was among the largest in the nation. There were 2,203 foreign students representing 108 countries on campus. Some 1,200 American students were participating in 70 overseas study programs in 24 nations. And, there were 450 visiting foreign scholars at MSU doing research and teaching in MSU classrooms.

MSU Campus: "One of the Botanical Wonders of Campusdom"—In the 1992 book, *The Campus As A Work of* Art, author Thomas A. Gaines ranked MSU among America's 25 most aesthetic campuses. He called the "Sacred Space" inside West Circle Drive "one of the botanical wonders of campusdom."

MSU students finished first among all colleges and universities in the Northern Hemisphere, and second in the world at the International Scholastic Computer Programming Competition at Kansas City. Stanford placed third; Harvard sixth.

Wendy Fritzen, '92, James Madison and Honors College student, won a Truman Scholarship worth $7,000 a year for four years.

William H. Cunningham, '66, M.A. '67, Ph. D. '71, president of the University of Texas-Austin, was elected chancellor of the entire University of Texas system.

Joan Sills, '75, president of Colony Hotels & Resorts, with 42 properties, was recognized by the *New York Times* as "the only woman to head a leading hotel company with worldwide operations."

Lynn C. Myers, '64, M.A. '67, was serving as general manager of the Pontiac and GMC Truck divisions of General Motors.

Richard E. Holmes, M.D. '77, had the Mississippi State University Office of Minority Affairs named in his honor—The Holmes Cultural Diversity Center.

Mel Buschman, '43, M.A. '47, Ph.D. '60, was inducted into the Senior Athletes Hall of Fame. At age 71, he won five of nine events at the Senior Olympics Indianapolis Classic.

Peter Morris, M.A. '90, won the 1992 World Scrabble Championship in London, England. While playing, he wore his Michigan State sweatshirt.

Stu Argo, Jr., '85, and Dawn Riley, '87, helped sail "America 3" to victory in the 1992 America's Cup competition.

The School of Music's Chamber Orchestra and Chorale were selected to participate in the Mozart Bicentennial at New York City's Lincoln Center.

The world's first endowed chef position at a university hospitality school was made possible by a one million dollar gift by Dr. Lewis J. and Ruth E. Minor to MSU's School of Hospitality Management.

Dr. Chris Somerville, MSU plant scientist, and colleagues discovered how to produce plastics from plants. *Time* magazine ranked their work among the top ten science stories of 1992, and reported, "Taking a cue from Rumpelstilskin, who spun straw into gold, botanists managed to coax a lowly potted plant into producing plastics."

Dr. Henry Blosser, director of MSU's National Superconducting Cyclotron, received the Tom W. Bonner Award—the top recognition in nuclear physics from the American Physical Society.

Dr. Keith Williams, associate director of the MSU Alumni Association, produced *The Handbook for Alumni Club Leaders*.

John Scott, MFA '65, distinguished professor of art at Xavier University, New Orleans, won the MacArthur Foundation's "Genius Grant" worth $315,000.

William H. Cunningham, '66, M.A. '67, Ph. D. '71, was elected chancellor of the entire University of Texas system.

Three MSU graduates won 1992 U.S. Presidential Teaching Professor Awards—all faculty members at Northern Illinois University: Jerry Johns, Mary Suzanne Schriber, and **John Niemi**.

Anita M. Clark, M.A. '72, M.A. '77, a mathematics teacher at Marshall, Michigan High School, received the **1992 Presidential Award for Excellence in Science and Mathematics Teaching**.

Martha Quentin, MSU Tanzanian graduate student, discovered a method of preventing weevils from destroying dry beans—a major source of protein in the Third World.

Hans Kende, a leading MSU plant researcher, was named to the National Academy of Sciences, the premier U.S. scientific society and advisor to Presidents and Congress.

Wolfgang Bauer, assistant professor of physics, received a $500,000 Presidential Faculty Award. He was named by President George H.W. Bush for the award, which was to help young scientists who demonstrated excellence in research and teaching.

Ron Mason, National Coach of the Year, led the MSU ice hockey team to the NCAA Frozen Four for the fourth time in seven years.

Dwayne Norris was named the **Central Collegiate Hockey Association's Player of the Year**.

Tom Smith, MSU baseball coach, was named Big Ten Coach of the Year. The Spartan team's record was 36-19.

Interim athletic director George Perles pushed for the establishment of an MSU Athletics Hall of Fame, an important contribution in preserving the history of the university's outstanding athletes and their accomplishments. The first class of the Hall of Fame—30 inductees—were inducted on September 11, 1992.

Merrily Dean Baker was named MSU athletic director on April 3, 1992, replacing interim athletic director George Perles. **She was the first female athletic director in the Big Ten,** and only the second in the entire nation in Division 1-A.

Misty Allison, junior cross country star, was named **Big Ten Athlete of the Year for 1991-1992.** She had won the 5,000-meter race at the Big Ten championships in the fall of 1991.

A "sack lunch" program was introduced at MSU residence halls, enabling a student to carry a lunch to practice teaching assignments, field trips, or other off-campus activities.

Animal rights terrorists set fire to 42 years of research work in Anthony Hall in February, 1992. Professor Richard Aulerich's work on mink and associated toxicology research was targeted. Ten years of research by Karen Chou also was destroyed. She was working on finding substitutes for animals in bio-medical research. President DiBiaggio declared, "This terrorist act did nothing to advance the cause of human treatment of animals on campus. In fact, it did the opposite."

Automatic Teller Machines (ATMs) were introduced in several residence halls.

The 1992 university budget was $820,176,721. Enrollment was 40,047. During the year, 10,267 degrees were granted.

1993

M. Peter McPherson Elected MSU's Nineteenth President (served 1993-); MSU 2000 Campaign Raises $218 Million; MSU Debate Team Wins National Title—M. Peter McPherson (b. 1941), Class of 1963, was elected Michigan State's nineteenth president by the Board of Trustees on August 19, 1993, succeeding President Gordon Guyer, who would retire on December 31, 1993. McPherson was serving as senior vice president for Bank of America, responsible for managing more than $50 billion. McPherson took over as MSU CEO on October 1, 1993. He stated, **"you must lead a university with ideas—vision."**

M. Peter McPherson, talking about MSU's role in society when he was appointed president...

"Land-grant universities in the 1990s must be centers of intellectual excellence combined with problem-solving. We must link university strengths with Michigan's problems more closely. We have been agents of change. We have never resided in the ivory tower."

Following graduation from MSU in 1963 with a B.A. in political science, McPherson joined the Peace Corps as a volunteer in Peru. He earned an MBA degree from Western Michigan University in 1967, and a J.D. degree from the American University Law School in 1969.

President Ronald Reagan named McPherson head of the Agency for International Development in 1981, an organization previously headed by MSU President Emeritus John A. Hannah. McPherson also served as deputy director of the U.S. Department of Treasury. Earlier in his career, McPherson served as a special assistant to U.S. President Gerald Ford.

McPherson's MSU roots ran deep. Both of his parents and seven brothers and sisters—all graduated from Michigan State.

Dr. Lou Anna K. Simon, Ph.D., '74, was named provost, the first woman to hold that position in the Big Ten.

Gordon Guyer, in his 16 months as MSU president, was a stabilizing influence in the transition from President DiBiaggio to President McPherson. Guyer was, and is, loved and respected by MSU faculty, students and alumni.

The conclusion of MSU 2000, the university's first major capital campaign, was celebrated in May of 1993. The campaign raised $217,854,609—36 percent more than the original $160 million goal set in 1988. The funds were earmarked for student and faculty endowments, building projects and program enhancements.

Michigan State's School of Hotel, Restaurant and Institutional Management was ranked # 2 in the nation in a survey by the Cornell University H.R.A. Quarterly (Hotel Restaurant Administration, Dec.,1993).

MSU's College of Education was cited as among the "Best of America" by *U.S. News & World Report* (Jan. 11, 1993) for its leadership in the reform of public

M. Peter McPherson, Nineteenth President

The Food Science & Human Nutrition Building was named for Dr. G. Malcolm Trout, "Father" of homogenized milk, world-renowned dairy scientist, and professor, 1928-1966.

schools. The magazine said MSU's teacher-training program at Holt, Michigan High School "sends a strong signal to beginning teachers that they are entering a profession with high standards."

Two MSU debating teams reached the finals of the National Junior Varsity Tournament, sponsored by the Cross Examination Debate Association. The two MSU teams were declared co-champions. The Michigan State sweep was remarkable since it was the university's first appearance as an official team. Will Repko of East Lansing was named the top debater.

MSU engineering students won five first place awards in Ford Motor Company's Hybrid Electric Vehicle Challenge.

Michigan State led all universities in the U.S. in 1993, with 46 student and alumni Peace Corps volunteers.

Rujuta Bhatt, a James Madison College student, won a Rhodes Scholarship—the eleventh for MSU in 20 years, the best record among all public universities in the U.S. Ms. Bhatt related why she chose MSU when she already had been accepted by Princeton, Duke and Cornell: **"What really stood out was the friendliness of the people. Everyone was very willing to show me around and to tell me about MSU. I was very impressed."**

Dr. Clifton Wharton, MSU President Emeritus, was appointed U.S. Deputy Secretary of State.

Dr. G. Malcolm Trout, the "Father of Homogenized Milk," was honored by having the Food Science and Human Nutrition building named for him. A world-renowned dairy scientist, Trout served on the MSU faculty from 1928 to 1966.

Theodore A. Bickert, dean of the College of Engineering, was awarded an honorary professorship from the Taganrog Radio Engineering Institute in Russia—only the second such award given by the Institute.

Clare Collins, professor of nursing, was inducted into the American Academy of Nursing.

Martin Crimp, assistant professor of materials science and mechanics, was named a Young Investigator by the National Science Foundation, winning research support of up to $500,000 over five years.

Roy T. Matthews and **F. DeWitt Platt**, both history professors, won first place in the college textbook division at the American Book Show of Bookbuilders West with their book, *Western Humanities*.

Darlene Clark Hine, Hannah professor of history, authored *Black Women in America*: An Historical Encyclopedia (Carlson Publishing, 1993). It was a two-volume, 1,530-page reference work.

MSU biochemist Jack Preiss developed a "super" potato that contained 60 percent more starch than normal. It was estimated the enhanced potato could reduce the cost of ethanol, high fructose corn syrup, and biodegradable plastics made from starch.

James J. Blanchard, '64, M.A. '65, former Governor of Michigan, was named U.S. Ambassador to Canada by President William Clinton.

William D. Brohn, '55, arranged the music for the musical *Miss Saigon*, which earned him a **Desk Drams Award**.

Barbara Ross-Lee, D.O. '73, dean of the Ohio University College of Osteopathic Medicine, became the first African-American woman to head a U.S. medical school.

Kristan Clark Taylor, '82, wrote *The First to Speak* in 1993. She had served as White House director of media relations—the first African-American woman to do so.

Barbara Ross-Lee, D.O. '73, was named dean of the Ohio University College of Osteopathic Medicine. She was **the first African-American women to head a medical school in the U.S.**

Kristin Clark Taylor, '82, authored the book *The First to Speak*. She had been the White House director of media relations for President George H.W. Bush, the first African-American women ever to occupy the post. She was communications director for the Bell South corporation.

MSU's magnificent new Horticultural Demonstration Gardens, set on 7.5 acres wrapped around the Plant and Soil Sciences Building, were dedicated on August 11, 1993. Five special areas were devoted to perennials, annuals, roses, an "idea" garden, and the 4-H Children's Garden. Antique roses in the garden trace their lineage back as far as the 16th century.

The "North Business Complex," a new $15-million, 6-story, 120,000 square-foot building was dedicated in October of 1993. It placed the Eli Broad College of Business facilities among the elite schools in the nation.

MSU's "Autumnfest" had its name changed to **"Taste of Michigan"** in the fall of 1993. The annual event, sponsored by the College of Agriculture and Natural Resources, showcased Michigan foods on a football Saturday, and was held in the sparkling new Agricultural Pavilion.

Magnificent New Horticultural Demonstration Gardens—7.5 acres wrapped around the Plant & Soil Sciences Building—were opened in 1993. The 4-H Children's Garden, above, was one of five areas, which also included gardens for perennials, annuals, roses, and an "idea" garden. The gardens have become one of Michigan's top tourist attractions.

MSU Ice Hockey Coach Ron Mason became the winningest coach in college hockey history, notching his 675th win in 27 years of coaching—a 5-2 victory over Kent State on March 12, 1993.

Heath Fell, Spartan golfer, was voted **Big Ten Player of the Year**.

MSU's Hancock Turf Research Center was selected to develop grass that would grow and survive indoors for the 1994 World Cup Soccer matches scheduled for the Pontiac, Michigan Silverdome. John "Trey" Rogers and Paul E. Ricke of Crop and Soil Sciences began developing the "indoor grass."

A Smoking Ban for all campus "enclosed spaces," except for designated private residential space was voted by the Board of Trustees, effective, January 1, 1994. The ban included tobacco-related sales on university grounds, and extended to all MSU facilities and vehicles.

The 1993 university budget was $850,246,503. Enrollment was 39,743. During the year, 9,652 degrees were granted.

1994

President M. Peter McPherson outlines Six Guiding Principles for MSU.

Shortly after assuming office, McPherson sought ideas and input from the faculty, administrators, students, and alumni to define what principles should guide Michigan State University.

Six Guiding Principles were developed by the MSU family, and explained by President McPherson:

1. Access to Quality—"We cannot allow ourselves to not be available to the traditional people we serve. Tuition affordability must be an important consideration. Between grants, loans and checks (paychecks to 19,000 students working part-time on campus), we provide about as much money to students, as students as a group pay us back in tuition."

2. People Matter—"We need to reinforce that concept." John Hannah used to emphasize: 'Only people are important, especially poor people.'"

3. Active Learning—"What we need to learn is how to learn, and how to keep learning. Virtually everything in our society keeps on changing so rapidly that unless you're a continuous learner, you'll soon be intellectually antiquated."

4. New Knowledge and Scholarship—"I think the best researchers are often the best teachers. Scholarly efforts will keep faculty excitement about their fields at high levels and that will be transmitted into their teaching."

5. Problem Solving—"How do we make sure our outreach programs address today's problems rather than yesterday's. Today's problems don't fall into narrow disciplines. They are going to be interdisciplinary problems because that's the way the world seems to be working."

6. Diversity Within Community—"Since coming here in the 1960s, I've always felt that has been one of MSU's strengths. We need a sustained effort to find qualified minorities for our (faculty and staff) positions. We must provide a positive and reinforcing environment for minority students—one that ensures their physical safety, and their emotional and intellectual growth."

Jim Mitzelfeld, '84, won the 1994 Pulitzer Prize for beat reporting with Eric Freeman, MSU adjunct professor.

Michigan State led the country with a tuition guarantee to students, approved by the Board of Trustees on December 14, 1994. The promise: MSU tuition would rise no more than the rate of inflation for the next three years, four years for freshmen.

MSU's African Studies Center, a national leader, was one of ten federally-designated National Resource Centers in African language and Area Studies.

Jim Mitzelfeld, '84, Detroit News reporter, and fellow reporter Eric Freeman, an adjunct professor in MSU's School of Journalism, won the 1994 Pulitzer Prize for beat reporting.

MSU students won a national environmental competition sponsored by the Waste-Management Education and Research Consortium.

MSU engineering students won Ford Motor Company's 1994 hybrid electric vehicle competition for excellence in safety engineering and best use of materials.

MSU student Elizabeth Repko became the school's first person to advance to the finals of the National Championship Debate Tournament.

Derek Haines, a senior packaging student, invented a packaging device while working as an intern at IBM that was estimated to save the corporation $1 million per year.

Dawn Riley, '87, was named to the crew of America 3, a women's team that would compete in the 1995 America's Cup sailing competition. She had been a member of the victorious America 3 in the 1992 America's Cup challenge.

MSU ranked No. 4 in the nation in dollars produced from research royalties. The university derived its

Alexander Trotman, MBA '72, was serving as chairman and CEO of Ford Motor Co.

$13,295,620 in royalty income from 25 licenses and 20 licensed patents. The bulk of the royalties came from cisplatin, the world's leading anti-cancer drug, developed by MSU biophysicist Dr. Barnett Rosenberg.

Community Policing, fathered by MSU's Robert C. Trojanowicz, '63, M.A. '65, Ph.D. '69, was being adopted by police departments across the nation.

MSU First Lady Joanne McPherson led the establishment of the MSU Domestic Violence Shelter—the first on-campus facility of its kind in the nation.

MSU's international travel/study program was named as one of the three best in the nation by the Association of Continuing Higher Education. MSU's annual Odyssey to Oxford University, England, originated by Dr. Charles McKee, was considered a national model.

The Crossroads Food Court was opened in the International Center in the fall of 1994 with five food franchises—Club Cappuccino, Panda Express, Subway, Taco Bell, and Wendy's.

J. Sutherland Frame, head of the mathematics department from 1943 to 1960, won the Yueh-Gin Gung and Dr. Charles Y. Hu **Award for Distinguished Service to Mathematics**—the highest award given by the Mathematical Association of America.

Barbara Given, professor of nursing, won the 1994 Distinguished Contribution in Nursing Science Award, presented by the American Nurses Foundation.

Kay Holekamp, assistant professor of zoology, won an unrestricted $500,000 fellowship from the David and Lucille Foundation.

Alexander Trotman, MBA '72, was chairman and CEO of Ford Motor Company.

Eljay Bowron, '73, was named the 18th director of the U.S. Secret Service.

Dan Darrow, MBA '61, Walt Disney World's manager of hotel relations, was named **Florida Hotelier of the Year**.

Ike McKinnon, Ph.D. '85, was serving as Chief of Police for the City of Detroit.

Drayton McLane, MBA '59, vice chairman of Wal-Mart stores, was owner of the Houston Astros baseball team.

Harley Hotchkiss, '51, was part owner of the Calgary Flames NHL hockey team. He was president and owner of Spartan Resources, Ltd., Calgary, Alberta—private investor in oil and gas, real estate, agriculture, and professional sports.

Magic Johnson, former MSU All-American and NBA All-Star and MVP, became a part owner of the Los Angeles Lakers basketball team.

Spartans Dixon Edwards, starting linebacker, and **Matt Vanderbeek**, special teams player, were members of the Super Bowl Champion Dallas Cowboys.

Ariya Chumsai (Sirisopha), '93 and journalism graduate, won the **1994 Miss Thailand** competition.

The 1994 university budget was $865,868,298. Enrollment was 40,254.

During the year, 9,088 degrees were awarded.

1995

Four Student Groups Win National Titles; Detroit College of Law Affiliates With MSU; President Clinton Delivers Commencement Address—Four different student organizations won national titles during 1995.

The Michigan State debate team won the national championship, defeating 227 two-person teams from 100 universities in a four-day event in San Diego. Biza Repko and John Sullivan were MSU team leaders. James Roper, associate professor of philosophy, was the MSU debate coach.

Eljay Bowron, '73, was named director of the U.S. Secret Service.

Sixty MSU finance students won the AT & T Collegiate Investment Challenge, outperforming all other universities. The runners-up were Harvard and the Wharton School of Business at the University of Pennsylvania.

MSU engineering students, for the second consecutive year, won the Waste-Management Education and Research Consortium National Design Competition. The competition included written and oral presentations.

The *State News* staff won the National Pacemaker Award for the outstanding college newspaper in America—an award won by MSU more times than any other university.

Adding a Law School to MSU's academic offerings—a long-sought goal—became a reality in 1995. MSU President Peter McPherson seized the opportunity and led a pro-active effort to bring the Detroit College of Law (DCL) to the MSU campus. McPherson and George Bashara, president of the DCL Board of Trustees, convinced a gathering of the Michigan House Higher Education Committee and the Appropriations Subcommittee on Higher Education that affiliation was a good idea. They repeatedly asserted that no taxpayer money would be involved in such a merger. The legislature approved.

Key to the deal was McPherson's insistence that DCL would remain private and require no State of Michigan or MSU funds. It was to be the first, and only affiliation of a private, independent law school on a public university campus in the United States.

After approval, MSU began the search for a law school dean and initiated plans for construction of a $28 million law building which would be financed by a bond issue to be repaid from the cash flow of the new institution.

DCL, founded in 1891, is the oldest continuously operating independent law school in the nation.

U.S. President William Clinton delivered the commencement address to 6,500 graduates in green gowns and 50,000 parents and friends gathered in Spartan Stadium on May 5, 1995.

U.S. President William J. Clinton, left, walks with MSU president M. Peter McPherson prior to delivering the 1995 commencement address at Spartan Stadium.

A $60-million campaign: "Continuing a Legacy of Leadership—The MSU Campaign for Endowment," was announced by President McPherson. He stated, "Endowed scholarships give us leverage in recruiting the most promising students. Endowed faculty positions make us competitive with other major universities and with industry in attracting top scholars to our faculty."

MSU's leadership in forensic science education was described by Jay Siegel, Ph.D. and Fellow of the American Academy of Forensic Sciences, in the *MSU Alumni Magazine*. He wrote, "Among the handful of colleges and universities that educate students in the forensic sciences, MSU has the oldest and largest program in the U.S."

H-Net, which supported more than 100 free electronic, interactive humanities and social science newsletters around the globe, was created at MSU to bring together the world's top scholars in those fields. It was housed in the College of Arts and Letters.

A Technology Exploration Center, an on-line laboratory to teach people how to use the World Wide Web, opened at the College of Education. It was funded by a $500,000 grant from Ameritech Corp.

American Sign Language interpreters for the deaf were featured at 14 performances at the Wharton Center for the Performing Arts. Wharton's "On &

Off Broadway" series included *Fiddler on the Roof*, *Crazy for You*, *Joseph & the Amazing Technicolor Dreamcoat*, *State Fair*, and *Phantom of the Opera*.

A team of MSU scientists and educators won the "Computer Software Innovation of the Year" Honor at the Discover Awards for Technological Innovations conference. They created the Personal Communicator, a hypermedia CD-ROM software program to enhance deaf students' communication with others. Team members included Carrie Heeter, director of MSU's Communication Technology Laboratory; David Stewart, associate professor for special education; and Patrick Dickson, professor of educational psychology; and a group of artists, computer programmers, musicians, and writers.

MSU scientists discovered how to clone a plant growth enzyme that would allow the creation of larger ears of corn, more fruitful soybean bushes, or taller oak trees. The researchers were MSU biochemist Robert Bandurski, and colleagues Jedrzej and Krzysztof Szczyglowski.

A College of Veterinary Medicine team won the $25,000 national Merck AgVet Award for Creativity. The team included Kent Ames, Jon Patterson, James Render, and James Cunningham.

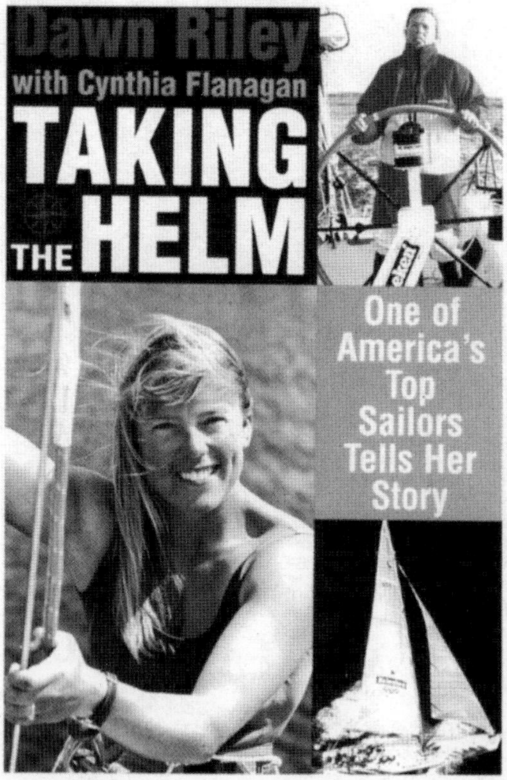

Dawn Riley, '87, the only woman to crew on a winning America's Cup team (1992), authored *Taking The Helm* in 1995. She also led the only women's team in the Whitbread Round-The-World race.

Bruce Vanden Burgh, chair of the advertising department, won the American Advertising Association's Aid to Advertising Award—one of only seven given nationally.

Restoration of the Michigan State Capitol gardens was led by Miriam Rutz, associate professor of geography and landscape historian. **Jennifer Hanna**, MSU graduate, assisted with research on Victorian flower beds to produce a design that "fit perfectly with the building."

President McPherson set an ambitious goal to have 40 percent of Michigan State students spend at last one semester in overseas study programs by the year 2006.

President McPherson sold Michigan Governor Engler and the legislature on adding $10.4 million annually to the MSU budget for learning technologies to keep the school at the cutting edge of the Information Age.

The fabulous Bay Harbor development on Lake Michigan near Petoskey—"The Pebble Beach of Michigan"—was being led by a number of Spartans. David V. Johnson, '71, president of Victor International, was the developer. Other MSU grads involved were: Mark Hubbard, '82, CEO of Victor International; Steve Kircher, '86, president of Boyne Resorts-Michigan Operations; Cameron Piggott, '71, of Dykema-Gossett and lead attorney; Arthur Hills, '53, renowned golf architect, was to design 27 golf holes; and Don Vidosh, who attended MSU, was one of the main contractors.

James Pentacost, '72, produced the Disney movie hit *Pocahontas*, which grossed $30.5 million in its first weekend.

Wilson "Bill" Livingood, '61, was named Sergeant of Arms for the U.S. House of Representatives. He was responsible for the security of the U.S. House and its members, and had the distinction of making the classic annual announcement introducing the Commander in Chief prior to his annual State of the Union message: **"Mr. Speaker, the President of the United States."**

Thomas Gale, '66, MBA '68, Chrysler's executive vice president for product design and international operations, was described by *Time* magazine as "the hottest automotive designer in history."

James E. Oesterricher, '64, was elected CEO and board member of the J.C. Penney Company.

Robert C. Lowes, '68, MBA '75, was named CEO of Burger King Corp.

Kenneth L. Way, '61, MBA '71, was serving as chairman and CEO of Lear Seating Corp.

Andree (Layton) Roaf, '62, was named to the Arkansas State Supreme Court.

Frank Kush, '53, All-American guard on MSU's 1951 and 1952 national champion football teams and highly successful Arizona State head coach, was inducted into the **National Football Foundation College Hall of Fame.**

Fred S. Wojtalik, '52, received the Presidential Rank of Distinguished Executive, given to only one percent of Senior Executive Service members. Wojtalik was manager of the Observatory Projects Office at NASA's Marshall Space Flight Center, Huntsville, Alabama.

Dawn Riley, '87, former MSU sailing captain and the only woman to be a crew member of a **winning America's Cup team (1992)**, authored the book *Taking The Helm* (Little Brown & Co., 1995).

MSU's Women's Volleyball team won the Big Ten title. Val Sterk, junior; Veronica Morales, sophomore; and Jeanna Wrobel, freshman, led the team with outstanding play.

Jud Heathcote, 19-year head basketball coach, retired in 1995 and was named **National Coach of the Year** by the *Sporting News*. He led MSU to the NCAA title in 1979, and to Big Ten titles in 1978, 1979, and 1990.

Tom Izzo, associate head basketball coach, was named head coach after serving as an assistant for 12 years. Izzo had earned a reputation as an outstanding coach, recruiter, and tireless worker.

Dr. Merritt Norvell was named MSU's 18th athletic director, succeeding Merrily Dean Baker, who resigned. He was the first African-American athletic director in the Big Ten. Norvell had been with IBM for 16 years, and had been a member of Wisconsin's 1963 Rose Bowl team.

Nick Saban, 43, was selected as MSU's new head football coach. He had coached at MSU from 1983 to 1988 as a successful defensive coordinator. He coached with the Cleveland Browns, producing the NFL's best defense in 1994. He also had coached at Kent State, West Virginia, Syracuse, Ohio State, Navy, Toledo, and the Houston Oilers.

MSU's football team defeated the 7th ranked Michigan Wolverines, 28-25, with an exciting 88-yard touchdown drive late in the fourth quarter at Spartan Stadium. MSU quarterback Tony Banks hit three key passes during the drive, the final one a 28-yard touchdown toss to Nigea Carter. Earlier, Derrick Mason returned a Michigan punt 70 yards for a telling score.

Michigan State's Marching Band was selected by ABC-TV to provide background music for the network's college football promotions.

The 1995 university budget was $ 896,472,900. Enrollment was 40,647. During the year, 8,260 degrees were awarded.

1996

Spartans Win Pulitzer Prize; National Debate and National Marketing Titles; and *USA Today* Honors; MSU Launches $70 Million Revitalization of Michigan Animal Agriculture.

Richard Ford, '66, won the 1996 Pulitzer Prize for fiction with his book, *Independence Day.*

MSU's debating team won its second consecutive national debate title. Elizabeth Repko was named the best debater at the tournament. John Sullivan placed fifth, and Jason Trice, eighth.

The debate team also won the National Invitational Round Robin. The two-person teams featured: juniors Erik Cornellier and John Sullivan; and junior Ian Klinkhamer and sophomore Geoff Wyatt. Sullivan won the best speaker award.

The MSU Business Marketing Association team won a national student competition by developing a complete marketing plan for Intel Corporation.

Jonathan E. Chudler, English major, was named to the All-USA College Academic Team by *USA Today*. He was one of 20 winners selected from 1,231 entries.

Dayne Walling, '96, James Madison College social relations major, won a Rhodes Scholarship, the only one awarded to a student from the State of Michigan.

MSU launched a $70 million initiative called the Revitalization of Michigan Animal Agriculture. Included in the plans were a new Swine Teaching & Research Center, a Poultry Building, a new facility for metabolism research on dairy cattle, and renovation of the Beef Cattle Research Center. Benefits from the undertaking by the College of Agriculture and Natural Resources were estimated at a $1 billion infusion into the Michigan agricultural economy and the creation of 22,000 jobs.

Jennifer Drayton, a senior in musical theater, won the **1996 Miss Michigan** Pageant. She intended to become a Lutheran minister.

Richard Ford, '66, won the 1996 Pulitzer Prize for fiction, authoring the novel *Independence Day*.

Jennifer Drayton, senior in musical theater, won the 1996 Miss Michigan title. She intended to become a Lutheran minister.

Kynda Kerr, sophomore elementary education major, won the world baton twirling championship in Brescia, Italy, winning over 32 other women from 11 nations.

Richard E. Lenski, Hannah professor of Microbial Ecology, won a $250,000, 5-year no-strings attached MacArthur Fellowship.

Verna Hildebrand, professor of Family and Child Ecology, received the **National Association of Early Childhood Teacher Educator's first award for meritorious leadership and professionalism.**

S. Tamer Cavusgil, executive director of MSU's International Business Center, was named **International Trade Educator of the Year** by the National Association of Small Business International Trade Educators.

Bruce G. Vanden Bergh, chair of the Advertising Department, was named the **Distinguished Advertising Educator for 1996** by the American Advertising Federation.

Howard Brody, professor of Family Practice, was elected to the Institute of Medicine of the National Academy of Sciences.

Dr. Michael Fossel, Ph.D., M.D., clinical professor of medicine, authored the book, *Reversing Human Aging.*

MSU's Graduate School of Education was ranked No. 1 in elementary education, and No. 1 in secondary education by *U.S. News & World Report* in its "America's Best Graduate Schools" issue of March 18, 1996.

President McPherson announced MSU's Technology Guarantee for students and alumni. "What we are guaranteeing is 'knowledge access' through use of cutting-edge technologies, now and in the future." Students would have an intensive, quality-based technological experience during their undergraduate years—from day of admission—when they automatically received e-mail access—to graduation. Alumni would have affordable lifelong technological access and two post-graduate years of free e-mail.

MSU initiated a campus-wide computer filing system which allowed the filing and grading of term papers electronically. It was part of MSU's Technology Guarantee. A fiber-optic communications system was completed campus-wide, linking 31 more buildings to the 16 already wired.

A $513,000 renovation of Beaumont Tower included 20 new upper bells and reconditioning of all 27 lower bells. A rededication ceremony of the tower was held on May 3, 1996.

Wharton Center became the top Broadway theater in the U.S. for eight weeks in the spring of 1996 by hosting *Phantom of the Opera*. *Variety* magazine reported Wharton's weekly income of nearly $1 million, exceeded every other show on Broadway.

Kamal Ahmed El-Ganzoury, Ph.D. '72, was named Egypt's prime minister by Egyptian President Hosni Mubarak.

William R. Tiefel, '56, president of Marriott Lodging, was named 1996 Corporate Hotelier of the World by the 60,000 readers of *Hotels,* the official journal of the International Hotel Association.

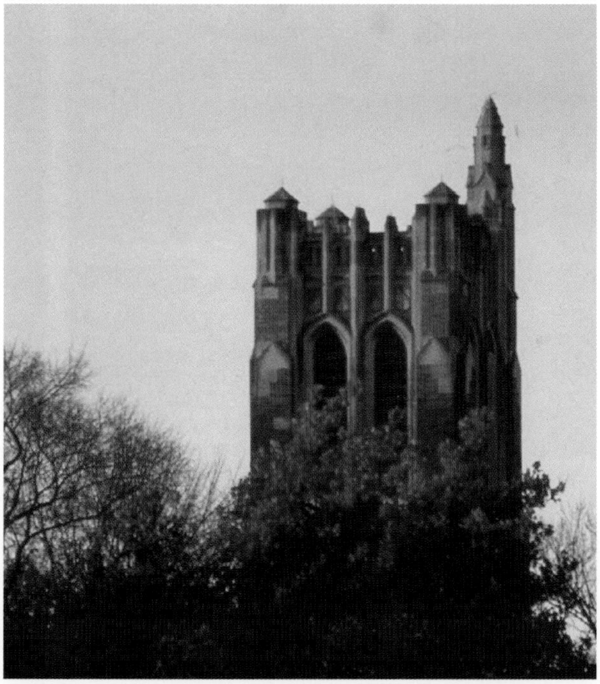

$513,000 Beaumont Tower renovation in 1996 included 20 new upper bells and reconditioning all 27 lower bells.

Arizona State University honored Frank Kush, '53, former MSU football All-American and Arizona State head football coach, by naming the football field in ASU's Sun Devil Stadium in his honor. Kush is a member of the Football Hall of Fame. At State, he was a member of Alpha Tau Omega fraternity.

David C. Broski, '69, M.A. '71, Ph.D. '74, was elected chancellor of the University of Illinois at Chicago.

Anthony Heald, '70, who portrayed Dr. Frederick Chilton in the movie *Silence of the Lambs* (1991), also was featured in *A Time to Kill* (1996), *The Client* (1994), and *The Pelican Brief* (1993).

Tyrone Willingham, '77, Stanford University football coach, was voted **PAC-10 Coach of the Year.**

Wendy Ingraham, '87, won nine international triathalon events in 1995 and 1996. *Women's Sports Fitness* featured her on the cover of their October 1996 issue. She was an All-American swimmer in 1985 and was a member of MSU's Big Ten champion 400-yard freestyle relay team in 1986.

MSU's Women's Volleyball team won its second consecutive Big Ten title, posted a 34-3 record, and advanced to the NCAA Final Four. **Head coach Chuck Erbe** was named **National Coach of the the Year** by the American Volleyball Coaches Association.

Stacy Slobodnik, assistant women's golf coach, won the **1996 Michigan Women's Amateur Golf Championship**.

Tom Minkel, MSU wrestling coach, was named **Big Ten Co-Coach of the Year**. Five MSU wrestlers were All-Americans: David Morgan, Eric Harvey, Brian Picklo, Joel Morissette, and Phil Judge.

Magic Johnson, MSU basketball All-American and NBA All-Pro, was featured on the covers of *Time, Newsweek*, and *U.S. News & World Report*, following his comeback with the L.A. Lakers pro basketball team, after testing HIV-positive in 1992.

MSU's Mascot Sparty was featured by ESPN-TV at the 1996 Atlanta Olympic Games, cradling U.S. gymnast Kerri Strug in its national advertising campaign for their program "SportsCenter."

The 1996 university budget was $925,605,689. Enrollment was 41,545. During the year, 8,766 degrees were granted.

1997

Students Earn Honors in Seven National and International Competitions; Steve Smith Gives $2.5 Million to MSU; MSU Joins SOAR Telescope Project.

An MSU student engineering team won the national title in the WERC Environmental Design Competition. Two hundred universities vied for the honor. Engineering faculty advisors were Susan Masten and Simon Davies.

Freshman Katy Hoffman won the National Junior Varsity Debate Tournament. Jim Roper, MSU's debate coach, said, "One of the guttiest performances I've seen."

Stephanie Palmer, a senior in chemical physics, became MSU's 16th Rhodes Scholar. The Walled Lake, Michigan Honors College student carried a 3.94 grade point average at MSU, and had been valedictorian of her high school senior class. She said, "At MSU everyone wants to help you do what you can. No one holds you back. There's a lot of opportunity to do a million things."

Steven Bevier, '97, a history major, defeated students from Harvard, Duke, Purdue and Boston University on his way to the finals of Jeopardy's College Week.

Sophomore Greg McNeilly, a social science/integrated studies major, was a winner in the Mont Pelerin Society's "Frederich Hayek Fellowship Contest" in Vienna, Austria. He was the only undergraduate student honored at the symposium.

Engineering students finished second in the national steel bridge-building competition. Two hundred teams were in the contest.

MSU engineering students finished second in the "Mini-Baja" competition which required building and racing 4-wheel drive dune buggies. They competed against 79 other universities.

Steve Smith, former MSU basketball All-American, Atlanta Hawks star, and U.S. Olympic Dream Team III member, announced on January 6, 1997 that he **would give $2.5 million to MSU for its new Student-Athlete Academic Center**. The center would be named for his mother, Clara Bell Smith. **The gift was the largest ever given to an American university by a professional athlete.**

MSU teamed with the University of North Carolina, the countries of Brazil and Chile, and the National

Steve Smith, MSU basketball All-American and Atlanta Hawks star, gave $2.5 million in 1997 to help build a Student-Athlete Academic Center. It was the largest gift ever given to an American university by a pro athlete. With Steve are wife Millie and young son.

Optical Astronomy Observatories to help build the first high-resolution telescope in the Southern Hemisphere. Images from the new Southern Observatory for Astronomical Research (SOAR), near La Serena at 9,000-feet in the Chilean Andes Mountains, were expected to rival those of the Hubble Space Telescope.

Dr. Milton Muelder, Honorary Alum '68, gave $1 million to MSU. The gift was to be allocated to the Department of History, Kresge Art Museum, the Russell Nye Lecture Series, Four Beaumont Carillon concerts per year, Intramural sports, and the Community Music Program. Dr. Muelder came to MSU in 1935 and served in a record number of high positions—Dean of the School of Science and Arts; Acting Dean, International Programs; Acting vice president of Student Affairs; and vice president for Research and Dean of the Graduate School.

MSU was named among the Top 20 Cyber-Universities in the nation by *Forbes* magazine in its June 16, 1997 issue. The rankings recognized leadership in the use of technology to provide quality education.

MSU added four internet courses to its offerings—Home Computing (CSS110, S 701), Nursing (NUR 591, S 701), Social Work (SW 830, S 701), and Telecommunications (TC 100, S 701). "Professor David Krauss taught nearly 1,300 students taking a home computing course, but never saw more than a few of them. To do so he would have had to travel to 46 countries around the world," according to a story by Charles Downs in the *MSU Alumni Magazine*.

The Detroit College of Law at MSU initiated a program where students could earn a law degree and an MBA in a four-year program.

Dr. Milton Muelder, Honorary Alum. '68, right, dean and professor emeritus, gave $1 million to MSU in 1997. Jack Shingleton, MSU trustee and placement director emeritus, congratulates Muelder.

The Wharton Center for the Performing Arts' Broadway series featured *Miss Saigon, Chicago, Smokey Joe's Café, Annie—the 20th Anniversary Production,* and *How to Succeed in Business Without Really Trying.* The center was the first theater in Michigan, outside of Detroit, to present *Miss Saigon.*

Dr. E. James Potchen, distinguished professor of radiology and chair of the department, **received the Gosta Forssell Medal, one of the highest honors awarded by the Swedish Academy of Medicine**.

Michael Kasavana, professor in the School of Hospitality Management, was inducted into the International Association of Hotel Administrators Technology Hall of Fame.

James Dye, university distinguished professor-emeritus of chemistry, was honored by the American Chemical Society for his discovery of two classes of materials with a range of practical applications.

Verna Hildebrand, professor emeritus of family and child ecology, updated her book, *Parenting: Rewards & Responsibilities* (McGraw-Hill, 1981, 1985, 1994, 1997), which was used as a high school text for child development courses.

Jeffrey Cole, '70, and his wife Kathryn (Kitty), MBA '90, gave $3 million for restoration of Eustace Hall (1888), home of the Honors College. Creation of endowed scholarships was another benefit of the gift.

Lynette and Richard Merillat gave MSU's College of Agriculture and Natural Resources their nationally recognized quarter horse farm. It was to be named the MSU Merillat Equine Center and serve as a teaching, research and outreach center. The farm, located near Adrian, Michigan, was **the largest in-kind gift ever received by MSU,** and included 43 horses, two premier stallions, an arena, storage buildings, and a breeding barn.

The new Pavilion for Agriculture and Livestock Education, an impressive $14.5 million, 200,000 square-foot facility, was dedicated in March 1997. It replaced the old livestock judging pavilion and features an arena seating 2,000, suitable for rodeos and concerts; a 350-seat auditorium; and a 77,000 square foot exhibit area. It is located on Farm Lane between Mt. Hope and Forest Roads.

A promenade and a beautiful mini-park were created on the site of the old livestock judging pavilion. The promenade runs north-south between Anthony Hall and Erickson Hall, linking North and South Shaw Lanes. Twelve limestone columns line the walkway—incorporate bricks from the old Judging Pavilion—and support the familiar copper lanterns that are found throughout the campus.

MSU solidified its position as a leader in keeping the nation's food supply safe with the dedication of the 115,000 square-foot National Food Safety and Toxicology Center in October, 1997. Robert Hollingsworth, director of the facility and entomology professor, declared,

Susan Packard, '77, M.A. '79, was serving as CEO of the Home & Garden TV Network.

"From what happens on the farm to food processing, packaging and distribution, we can examine it all right here."

The new, high-tech William C. Gast Business Library, located on the lower floor of the new Detroit College of Law-MSU building, was opened in the fall of 1997. The 25,717 square-foot library featured seating for 500, hard-wired computer stations for laptop computers, extensive Internet and CD-ROM resources and a large microfiche database.

James Quello, '35, who served as a commissioner and chair of the Federal Communications Commission, and as general manager for WJR radio in Detroit, was **inducted into the Radio Hall of Fame** in 1997.

Stanley Ikenberry, M.A. '57, Ph.D. '60, regent professor and president emeritus of the University of Illinois, was elected president of the American Council on Education.

Charles Fisher, '71, M.D. '73, was director of the Cleveland Clinic's Critical Care Research Unit, where he helped develop many drugs, such as Centoxin, which helped cut death rates from septic shock. He also served as a Lt. Colonel and Deputy Command Surgeon of U.S. Special Operations, and was sent around the world on missions known only by command officers and the President of the United States.

Susan Packard, '77, M.A. '79, was CEO of the Home and Garden TV Network.

John D. Hutson, '69, was nominated by U.S. President Bill Clinton to be Judge Advocate General of the U.S. Navy.

Lloyd V. Hackley, '65, was serving as president of the North Carolina Community College System.

Bill Foder, M.A. '78, won the National Hot Rod Association's World Championship.

Coach Karen Langeland led MSU's women's basketball team to the Big Ten title, tying Purdue and Illinois with a 12-4 record.

Junior Sevatheda Fynes won the women's NCAA titles in the 55-meter dash indoors, and the 100- and 200-meter events outdoors.

Reid Friedrichs, senior MSU soccer goalkeeper from Ann Arbor, was selected **Big Ten Player of the Year.**

Women's Crew (Rowing) was introduced as a varsity sport in the fall of 1997.

The Spartan Chariot was introduced at football pregame festivities. It was driven by a Spartan "warrior" and drawn by two handsome white horses. The idea began with a phone call from Jim Goodhart, director of the Michigan United Conservation Club to Gordon Guyer, MSU president emeritus. Guyer involved alum Russ Mawby, retired CEO of the W.K. Kellogg Foundation, who involved Jim Hall of Traverse City, who raced chariots. The chariot was seen at football games and at parades statewide.

The 1997 university budget was $960,732,606. Enrollment was 42,603. During the year, 8,328 degrees were awarded.

1998

President McPherson Focuses on Student Learning; MSU-Detroit College of Law Building Dedicated; MSU Wins Big Ten Basketball and CCHA Hockey Titles; MSU's First Billion Dollar Budget—President Peter McPherson emphasized the importance of taking learning seriously in his fifth State-of-the-University address on February 10, 1998. Although MSU had long been a leader in undergraduate education, the president called for "raising expectations regarding teaching and learning at MSU" and for strengthening the campus intellectual environment.

He cited several initiatives to improve learning. Tenured professors who made "demonstrable contributions to the undergraduate experience had risen to 94 percent. Freshmen seminars, living-learning residence hall experiences, and improved academic counseling were in place." Expanded Study Abroad opportunities, spending a work-study semester in Washington, D.C., and strengthening the freshman academic experience all were mentioned as efforts to enhance learning at MSU.

Former U.S. President Gerald Ford gave the keynote address at the dedication of the new Detroit College of Law (now MSU College of Law) at MSU building in April of 1998.

He declared, **"It's no exaggeration to say that at Michigan State University, breaking with tradition is a tradition. This new law school will combine the age-old pursuit of justice with some decidedly non-traditional fields."** The new $28 million DCL at MSU building featured internet ports at every seat in every classroom, amphitheater-style classrooms, and a distance learning classroom with closed-circuit TV. A magnificent Moot Court

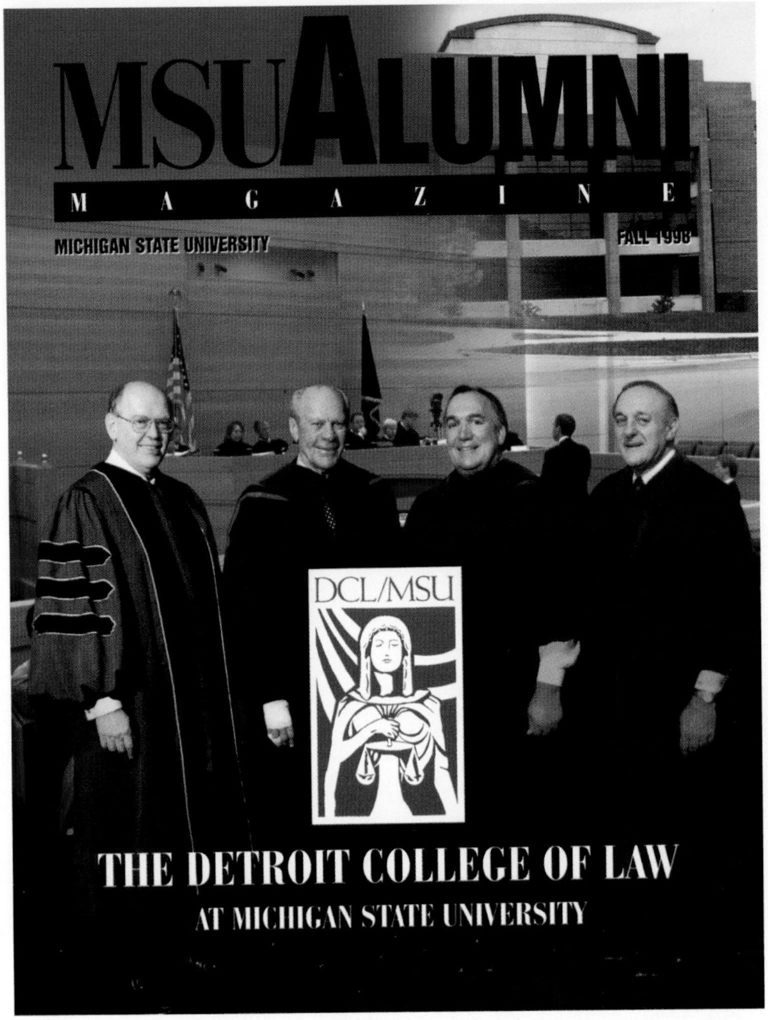

Former U.S. President Gerald Ford, second from left, keynoted the dedication of the Detroit College of Law at MSU. MSU President Peter McPherson, L; Michigan Governor John Engler, second from R, and DCL-MSU Board President George Bashara, Jr., right, participated in the ceremonies.

room featured video, audio and computer technology matching any courtroom in the nation.

Michigan State won its seventh Big Ten basketball championship in 1998 and advanced to the Sweet Sixteen round in the NCAA tournament. MSU was ranked No. 10 in the nation by the USA Today/ ESPN poll. Head coach Tom Izzo was named Big Ten and National Coach of the Year, and All-American guard Mateen Cleaves was named the Big Ten's most valuable player.

Ron Mason, the winningest hockey coach in the nation, led the Spartans to the Central Collegiate Hockey Association title, and notched the 800th win of his coaching career. MSU's hockey team was ranked No. 1 in the nation for most of the season, and beat arch-rival Michigan four times. Along the way the team also won the Team Cheerios Ice Breaker Invitational and the Great Lakes Invitational championships.

Twenty MSU scientists and their students were helping build the Large Hadron Collider, a particle accelerator in Geneva, Switzerland—the world's largest atom smasher. Joey Huston, professor of physics and astronomy, said, "You always want to be on the energy frontier. It's where new discoveries are made."

Eli Broad, '54, gave another $2 million to the College of Business and Graduate School of Management named in his honor. The gift was to expand the emphasis on information technology, and would create two new professorships related to information technology, and provide scholarships and support for MBA students with graduate assistantships and fellowships. Broad gave the school $20 million in 1991.

MSU opened one of the finest virtual radiology centers in the world in October 1998—a 30,000 square foot facility with computer rooms, laboratories, offices and meeting rooms. MSU is one of five General Electric Research Centers, aiding in magnetic resonance imaging (MRI) research and development. MSU MRI research started in 1984.

Virtual reality simulations were initiated at the College of Veterinary Medicine to teach repetitive surgical procedures that reduced the number of live animals used.

Jennifer Sykes, '99, a National Merit Scholar with a 3.95 grade point average, won a Truman Scholarship worth $30,000 for her graduate education. She was the seventh James Madison College student to win the award.

In a national competition, six MSU graduate students won twenty percent of the fellowships from the Social Science Research Council to do field research in Africa. Four other students won Fulbright-Hayes Scholarships from the Council.

Five Michigan State graduate students won $34,000 Environmental Protection Agency STAR (Science to Achieve Results) Fellowships for 1997-1998.

MSU's award-winning student-run newspaper, the *State News*, won top honors for the editorial content of its web page (www.statenews.com) at the annual Associated Collegiate Press convention.

Dr. Terrie Taylor, MSU associate professor of internal medicine, was co-director of the Malaria Research Project, funded by a National Institutes of Health grant of nearly $1 million. She was spending six months a year in Blantrye, Malawi, Africa researching and helping fight the disease.

Bill Mechanic, '73, CEO of Fox Filmed Entertainment, led his company in the production of the movie blockbuster *Titanic.*

Kris Berglund, professor of chemistry, chemical engineering and bio-systems engineering, and his research team developed a process for fermenting corn-starch into a salt substitute with no sodium or bitter taste: lysine. The lysine was then powdered into a crystal and sprinkled like salt.

Steve Hamilton, assistant professor of zoology based at MSU's Kellogg Biological Station, was awarded a $444,000 grant from the National Science Foundation's Faculty Early Career Development Program.

Gary Hoppenstand, associate professor of American Thought and Language and associate director of the department, was awarded the Ray and Pat Browne Award for Excellence in textbooks for his book, *Popular Fiction: An Anthology.*

Charles Ruggiero, professor of music and chair of music theory, was awarded the 1997-1998 American Society of Composers, Authors and Publishers Award—his 11th ASCAP honor.

Richard L. Witter, clinical professor of veterinary pathology, and **Jan A.D. Zeevaart**, professor with the Department of Energy Plant Research Laboratory at MSU, were elected to the National Academy of Sciences.

Richard Lenski, Hannah professor of microbiology, zoology, and crop and soil sciences, was named a Fellow of the American Academy of Arts and Sciences.

Student Aid at MSU totaled $231 million in 1997-1998. There were 18,525 students working part-time on the MSU payroll; 20,442 students received student loans; and 23,268 students received grants and scholarships.

The School of Criminal Justice offered an M.S. degree via the Internet and video-conferencing in January 1998. The first class for the two-year program consisted of 30 students.

MSU's popular Dairy Store re-opened in Anthony Hall on Farm Lane. Two long-time best sellers remained on the menu: Butter Pecan and Black Cherry. The store also sells low-fat flavors, gourmet coffee, cheese, many shakes and floats, and fresh Puffin pastries from MSU's bakery.

Jack Withrow, '54, MBA '71, and his wife Dottie, '55, provided funds for MSU to commission Pulitzer Prize-winning composer Ellen Taafee Zwilich to compose a symphony to glorify the beauty and inspiration of the MSU campus and gardens. Zwilich's forthcoming "Fourth Symphony" was to premier at the Wharton Center in the winter of 2000.

Spencer Abraham, '74, was serving the fourth year of his first term in the U.S. Senate in 1998.

John C. Kornblum, '64, was serving as U.S. Ambassador to the Federal Republic of Germany. A personal highlight of Kornblum's career was President Reagan's historic 1986 "Tear down this wall" speech in Berlin. Kornblum said, "That was a line that I wrote; it was very exciting."

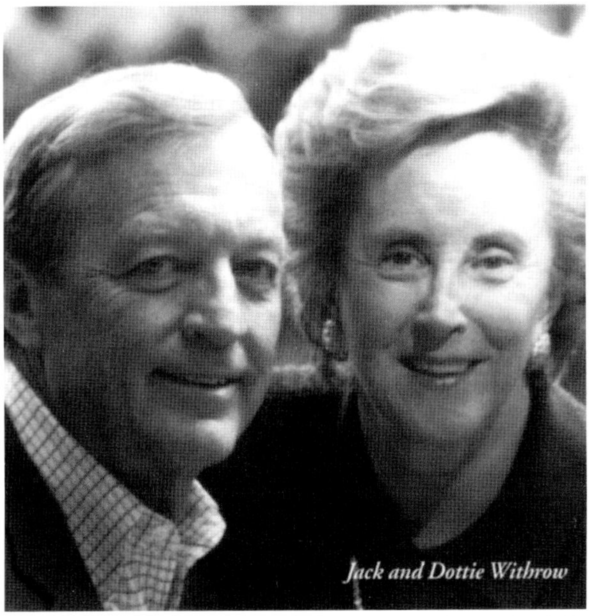

Jack Withrow '54, MBA '71, and his wife Dottie, '55, commissioned Pulitzer Prize-winning composer Ellen Taafee Zwilich to compose a symphony to glorify the beauty and inspiration of the MSU campus and gardens.

Clara Bell Smith Student-Athlete Academic Support Center was opened and named for the mother of Spartan basketball All-American Steve Smith, who gave $2.5-million towards its construction.

James P. Hoffa, Jr., '63, a Detroit lawyer, was elected president of the International Brotherhood of Teamsters in December 1998.

William D. Brohn, '55, music arranger and composer, won a Toni Award for his musical arrangement of *Ragtime*, a Broadway hit. He also was the arranger for *Miss Saigon*.

Soichiro "Sol" Yoshida, MBA '69, was credited by *Sports Illustrated* as the person most responsible for bringing the 1998 Winter Olympics to Nagano, Japan. Yoshida spent 200 days per year for several years campaigning for the Games. In Japan he built a chain of service stations and Kentucky Fried Chicken franchises.

Nancy Belck, Ph. D. '72, was elected president of the University of Nebraska-Omaha. She had been president of Southern Illinois University.

Bill Mechanic, '73, chairman and CEO of Fox Filmed Entertainment, led his company in the production of the smash movie hit *Titanic*.

Rear Admiral Joyce M. Johnson, D.O. '80, was Surgeon General of the U.S. Coast Guard. She was the first woman to hold that post, and the first woman to attain flag rank in the U.S.C.G.

James E. Miller, '71, MBA '73, was serving as president of Mazda Motor Corporation in Japan. He was the first American—and only non-Japanese—to head a major corporation in Japan.

Adnan Badran, M.S. '61, Ph.D. '63, was serving as the No. 2 executive of the 2,220-person United Nations UNESCO organization. UNESCO sponsors educational, scientific and cultural programs to help promote world peace.

John W. Porter, M.A. '59, Ph.D. '62, president emeritus of Eastern Michigan University, and superintendent of the Michigan Department of Education, was honored by having the the College of Education Building at EMU named in his honor.

Jack Ebling, '73, '75, *Lansing State Journal* sports columnist, and **John Farina,** MSU assistant sports information director, produced a beautiful 247-page book, *Magic Moments: A Century of Spartan Basketball* (Sleeping Bear Press, 1998).

The $8 million **Clara Bell Smith Student-Athlete Academic Support Center** was dedicated on September 12, 1998. It was named in honor of the mother of former Spartan All-American basketball player Steve Smith, who gave $2.5 million towards the facility.

The ***MSU Alumni Magazine*** debuted in a new all-color, glossy-paper format in the fall of 1998, providing a dramatic up-grade in appearance, making it a state-of-the-art publication. Content remained solid and substantive. Bob Bao, outstanding editor of the magazine, and Dr. Keith Williams, executive director of the MSU Alumni Association, led the well-received change.

MSU's football team, a 28-point underdog, stunned the No. 1 undefeated Ohio State Buckeyes, 28-24 in Columbus, Ohio on November 7, 1998. Paul Edinger kicked five field goals for MSU. It was the fourth major upset MSU had sprung on highly-ranked Ohio State football teams (1912, 1972, and 1974 were the others).

MSU cheerleaders had plenty to celebrate at the Breslin Center as the Spartan basketball team won its second consecutive Big Ten title in 1999, and set a conference record by winning 33 games during the season.

If there was any doubt that running a major university is big-time business, it was dispelled in 1998 with **MSU's first billion dollar budget: $1,020,842,907.**

Enrollment was 43,189. During the academic year, 8,888 degrees were granted.

1999

President McPherson Announces MSU's Role in Life Sciences Corridor and Introduces The MSU Promise; Basketball and Hockey Teams Win Big Ten and CCHA Titles—President Peter McPherson announced that MSU would "join colleagues from the University of Michigan, Wayne State University and the Van Andel Institute in Grand Rapids to embark on collaborative research through the State's new Life Sciences Corridor—making Michigan the global hub for world-class research in chronic diseases, genetics, neuroscience, aging, and biotechnology. Together, our world-renowned scientists will unlock important new discoveries in human health and well being."

The idea for the corridor was originated and promoted by McPherson and MSU with Michigan Governor Engler. The announcement was made at the National Press Club in Washington, D.C. in collaboration with Governor Engler, and the presidents of the other two universities.

Funding for the Life Sciences Corridor was approved in a bill signed by Governor Engler in July of 1999. It called for $1 billion to be invested over 20 years—at $50 million per year—to be taken from the tobacco settlement.

The MSU Promise, which included five goals, was presented by President McPherson in his annual State of the University address in February 1999. The stated goals **were: 1) Today's undergraduate education must deliver technological know-how** while preparing students to learn and to do; **2) We must promote and encourage outstanding research and graduate education**, especially in targeted initiative areas where Michigan State has great strength and great opportunity in the life sciences, environment, public policy, education, and food safety; **3) MSU will be a great global university, serving Michigan and the world**. MSU is known for its outstanding foreign studies research institutes and its current leadership in Study Abroad programs, and it will become a catalyst for a global Michigan, providing international linkages and training for Michigan business and industry; **4) MSU will be an exemplary "engaged university," transforming and strengthening outreach partnerships to address key Michigan needs; 5) MSU will be a more diverse and connected university.**

MSU's basketball team won its second consecutive Big Ten title in 1999, posting a 15-1 conference record, and **winning a Big Ten record 33 games overall**. The Spartans won the Big Ten tournament, and earned a No. 1

seed position in the NCAA tournament. They fought their way to the Final Four, coming back from a 13-point deficit to defeat defending National Champion Kentucky, 73-66. MSU lost in the semi-final game to Duke, 68-62. Coach Tom Izzo was named National Coach of the Year for the second consecutive year. Point guard Mateen Cleaves was selected Big Ten Player of the Year for the second straight year.

The Spartan hockey team won its second consecutive CCHA title, won the CCHA play-off title, and battled their way to the Frozen Four. It was the sixth time Ron Mason had led MSU to hockey's final four. **During one stretch, the icers set an all-time unbeaten string of 23 games, going undefeated for three months**. They were unbeaten at Munn Arena, and were the toughest defensive team in America, allowing just 1.44 goals per game. Mason was CCHA Coach of the Year; and Mike York, senior and captain, was named CCHA Player of the Year.

In NCAA history, only MSU and the University of Michigan had ever had their basketball and ice hockey teams in their respective Final Fours at the same time.

Four MSU graduate business students finished first in the annual Big Ten CASE (Council for the Advancement and Support of Education) Competition. They prepared a management strategy for a mythical company in just 24 hours. Amy Hill, management professor, was the team advisor.

Steve Donald and Aaron Monick, MSU debate team juniors, reached the finals of the National Debate Tournament, which featured 63 university teams.

Adam Wright, a James Madison College junior, won a Truman Scholarship.

Dr. Marie Dye, the longest-serving dean of the College of Human Ecology (1929-1956) and MSU's first female faculty member with a Ph.D., **was inducted posthumously into the Michigan Women's Hall of Fame.**

James V. Beck, mechanical engineering professor and national expert in heat transfer, won the Heat Transfer Memorial Award from the American Society of Mechanical Engineers.

Bradley S. Greenberg, distinguished professor of communication, won the Aubrey Fisher Mentor Award from the International Communication Association.

A *Science Watch* magazine national survey revealed MSU faculty publications were highly referenced. From 1993 through 1997, MSU ranked fourth in agricultural sciences with 460 references, and eighth in ecology/environment with 338 references. The survey covered the number of citations for the top 100 federally funded universities.

MSU's Center for International Business, Education and Research was selected as a national resource center by the U.S. Department of Education, thereby winning a $1 million grant.

Michigan State's participation in the Southern Astrophysical Research (SOAR) project was hailed by MSU astronomer Timothy Beers as "securing MSU's place in the worldwide astronomical community." SOAR was a consortium of MSU, the University of North Carolina, the National Optical Astronomy Observatories, and Brazilian astronomers. It was to place a 4.2 meter telescope on a 9,000 foot mountain top on the west side of the Chilean Andes.

MSU's Virtual University was advertised in the 1999 winter issue of the *MSU Alumni Magazine*, calling attention to internet computer courses in telecommunications, engineering, computer science, criminal justice, nursing, social work, computer-aided design, physics, and psychology. **Seven criminal justice students won master's degrees in December, 1999, becoming the university's first internet graduates.**

The new $2.3 million Lear Corporation Placement Services Center in the Eppley Building opened. It features 22 interview rooms, multimedia and teleconferencing, career resource center, and an employer's lounge. Ken Way, MBA '71, Lear chairman and CEO, stated, "This project aims to bring businesses and (business) graduates together in an atmosphere that is businesslike."

MSU had more students studying abroad than any other single campus in the U.S., according to an Institute of International Education 1998-1999 report. A total of

Spartan Spirit soared during the 1999 football season. MSU won 9 games for the first time in 33 years, beating rivals Notre Dame, Michigan, Ohio State and Penn State.

Ambassador Hrinak (left) and Bolivian President Hugo Banzer recently attended the inauguration of a bridge in Rurrenabaque, Bolivia. They are holding arrows used by an indigenous tribe.

Donna Hrinak, '72, was serving as U.S. Ambassador to Bolivia—the first female career foreign service officer to be named a U.S. ambassador.

1,565 MSU students were involved in 145 programs in 54 countries on six continents in the 1998-1999 academic year.

MSU's School of Journalism became the first in the nation to participate in Cable News Network's (CNN) pilot program to establish the CNN Student Bureau. Journalism students began reporting stories to CNN.

MSU's Campus Park and Planning unit initiated 2020 Vision to brainstorm and seek input from the MSU family on the future needs of the campus. Jeff Kacos, head of Campus Park and Planning, stated, "We want to 'green up' areas of the campus south of the river."

Michigan State University-Detroit College of Law was the new name of the law school. It had been Detroit College of Law at Michigan State University.

Featured during the year at the Wharton Center were four Broadway musicals—*Sunset Boulevard, Titanic: A New Musical*, *Rent*, and *Footloose*, as well as *Riverdance*. Other programming included the Smithsonian Jazz Orchestra, the Italian National Opera, the Tokyo String Quartet, the Moscow State Radio Symphony, the Boys Choir of Harlem, the Irish Rovers; and such stars as Bill Cosby, and comedian Mark Russell, Michael Feinstein, Leslie Nielson, and Mandy Patinkin.

Donna Hrinak, '72, was serving as U.S. Ambassador to Bolivia—the first female career foreign service officer to be named a U.S. ambassador.

Bob Campbell, '54, with Morris and Bev Anderson, guided the redesign of the Rose Garden section of the MSU Horticultural Demonstration Gardens. Campbell, a rosarian, researched and selected roses from the 16th, 17th, and 18th centuries, and all the way to the year 2000. Included is the first Tea Rose, "La France," from 1867. More than 1,500 plants, representing a variety of 350 different kinds of roses were chosen for the garden, including all the annual American Rose Society award-winning roses dating back to 1942.

Lynn C. Myers, '64, MBA '67, general manager of the Pontiac-GMC Division of General Motors, won an MSU distinguished alumni award. She had been named ***McCall's/Ward's Auto World's* first "Outstanding Woman in the Automotive Industry"** in 1994.

Barbara Ross-Lee, D.O. '73, dean of the Ohio University College of Osteopathic Medicine, was inducted into the Ohio Women's Hall of Fame. She was **the first African-American woman to head a medical school in the U.S.**

Shirley Weis, '75, was named chair of the Mayo Clinic's Department of Managed Care in Rochester, Minnesota.

Ercan Ozer, M.A. '72, was named the Ambassador of the Republic of Turkey to the United Arab Emirates.

San Oz-Alp, MBA '68, was elected president of Kocatepe University, Afyou, Turkey.

Kevin Rhodes, '87, was the principal ballet conductor for the Vienna, Austria State Opera and resident conductor for the Deutsche Oper am Rhein in Dusseldorf, Germany.

Heather Nabozny, '93, was named head groundskeeper for the Detroit Tigers.

Dawn Riley, '87, served as captain and syndicate CEO for "America True," one of the year's entries in the America's Cup sailing competition. She was the first woman to head an America's Cup syndicate.

Dr. Clarence Underwood was named interim athletic director, following the resignation of Dr. Merritt Norvell in April.

Spartans Beat No. 3 Michigan, 34-31, in Spartan Stadium. Both teams were 5-0. MSU staggered the Wolverines with a 400-yard passing attack by quarterback Bill Burke. It included ten receptions, two touchdowns and 255 yards by wide receiver Plaxico Burress.

The Spartan football team won nine games for the first time in 33 years, beat traditional powers Notre Dame, Michigan, Ohio State and Penn State, and won a berth in the January 1, 2000 Citrus Bowl. Head football coach Nick Saban resigned in early December to go to LSU. Bobby Williams, who had been associate head coach, was named head coach.

Landon Field was dedicated as Walter Adams Field on October 9, 1999, honoring MSU's 13th president and distinguished professor emeritus of economics. It was a perfect fall afternoon for the ceremony, which followed a 34-31 MSU football victory over Michigan.

MSU's men's track & field team won the Big Ten indoor championship.

MSU mascot Sparty was ranked No. 1 in the nation by *Muscle and Fitness* magazine.

Nobel laureate Elie Wiesel spoke at the 1999 undergraduate convocation, and stated, **"I have rarely been at a place where men and women speak about their alma mater with such glory, fervor, and pride."**

The 1999 university budget was $1,066,256,050. Enrollment was 43,038. During the year, 9,273 degrees were awarded.

2000

MSU Wins National Basketball Championship and Third Straight Big Ten Title—A talented, tough, fighting Spartan basketball team gave MSU fans a season-long thrilling ride—all the way to the 2000 NCAA championship. Along the road, they won their third consecutive Big Ten title and their second straight Big Ten tournament title, a conference first. They were **the first team in history to win all six of their NCAA tournament games by double digits.**

Mateen Cleaves was named the Final Four's Most Valuable Player. Four Spartans were named to the All-Final Four team: MSU seniors Cleaves (All-American and 1998 and 1999 Big Ten MVP), Morris Peterson (All-American and 2000 Big Ten MVP), A.J. Granger, and junior Charlie Bell.

Head coach Tom Izzo coached, cajoled, melded and inspired the team to a 32-7 overall record, the second consecutive 30-win season.

In the NCAA tournament, MSU defeated Valpariso, 65-38; Utah, 73-61; Syracuse, 75-58; Iowa State, 75-64; Wisconsin, 53-41; and Florida, 89-76. In the championship game, MSU's three senior starters led the way with 58 points: Morris Peterson–21, A.J. Granger–19, and Mateen Cleaves–18. MSU hit 55.9 percent of their shots from the field, including 11 of 22 from three-point range. They held Florida to a 40.7 shooting percentage.

Kellogg's Frosted Flakes featured a special edition box with MSU senior national champions Mateen Cleaves, Morris Peterson, and A.J. Granger as well as head coach Tom Izzo. It was a first in Kellogg's 94-year history.

Construction of a 128-suite Candlewood Hotel began in January 2000. It would be connected to the forthcoming MSU Executive Development Center, which would be connected to MSU's University Club. By December 2000, the $10 million hotel was to be donated to MSU by the Candlewood Hotel Company.

The new $2.5-million Mary Anne McPhail Equine Performance Center, unique in America, was opened in June 2000. The 18,000 square-foot facility was dedicated to expanding diagnosis and treatment of equine health problems as well as research. McPhail, '55, and her husband Walter, former CEO of Lectron Products of Troy, Michigan, funded a large part of the facility.

Sparty at the Spartan Statue. Sparty was ranked the No. 1 mascot in the nation by *Muscle & Fitness* magazine.

Debbie Stabenow, '72, MSW '75, was elected a U.S. Senator from Michigan in the fall of 2000. She defeated **Spencer Abraham, '74, who was named by newly elected U.S. President George W. Bush to the President's Cabinet as U.S. Secretary of Energy.**

The Partnership for the Advancement of CAD/CAM/CAE (computer-aided design, manufacturing, and engineering), comprised of General Motors, Unigraphics Solutions, Sun Microsystems, and Electronic Data Systems, **gave MSU's College of Engineering 110 sophisticated computer work stations, software, training and support valued at $30 million. It was the largest single gift in MSU history.**

The beautiful Brook Lodge and a 657-acre conference complex, valued at $6.7 million was given to MSU by Pharmacia & Upjohn Corporation. The property—formerly Upjohn's executive conference center—includes

Debbie Stabenow, '72, MSW '75, was elected a U.S. Senator from Michigan.

many buildings and cottages. It is located in Augusta, Michigan between Battle Creek and Kalamazoo, and is to be used as an educational conference center and public retreat.

The Smithsonian Institution gave its Computerworld Award, considered the most prestigious information technology recognition in the nation, to MSU. The award was for a joint School of Music and Artificial Language Laboratory project, which enables persons with physical disabilities to express themselves in music and singing.

MSU announced that all freshmen entering the university in 2001 would be required to have a computer. Critical to the new policy was the reality that Internet access opens thousands of information sources and databases to students.

MSU President Peter McPherson was named chair of the Big Ten Council of Presidents and Chancellors for 2000-2001.

MSU Provost Lou Anna Simon was named chair of the Committee on Institutional Cooperation, a consortium of Big Ten universities and the University of Chicago.

The Peter and Joanne M. McPherson Endowed Professorship for the Understanding of Science was created with a $2 million gift from an anonymous donor.

The Big Ten is the nation's only conference whose members all belong to the Association of American Universities, an organization of the nation's top research schools.

David Rohde, university distinguished professor political science, and **Anatoli Skorokhod**, professor of statistics and probability, were elected to the American Academy of Arts and Sciences.

Matthew Doumit, assistant professor animal science, was named Outstanding Teacher by the American Society of Animal Science and the American Dairy Science Association.

William M. Hartmann, professor and former Rhodes Scholar, developed "Local Performance Recording Reproduction." *The New York Times* reported a sense of "magic" prevailed at the fall meeting of the Acoustical Society of America when Hartmann played back Mozart's quartet in B flat. His recording system featured eight digital channels, isolating each instrument with direct sound pick-up microphones.

William S. Penn, professor of English and Native American writer, won the American Book Award for Literary Merit for his 2000 novel, *Killing Time With Strangers*.

Jason Fuller, a senior, won a Churchill Scholarship.

Kathleen Romig, a social science senior, won MSU's first George J. Mitchell Scholarship.

Carrie Preston, a senior, won the Andrew W. Mellon Fellowship in Humanistic Studies.

Brian Ngo, a junior, won the 2000-2001 Barry Goldwater Scholarship.

Anne Catherine Erickson, a senior in packaging with a 4.0 GPA won a Golden Key scholarship from the Golden Key National Honor Society.

Justin Bilicki, editorial cartoonist and graphics director for the *State News*, won the 2000 John Lochar Memorial Award for Editorial Cartooning from the Association of American Editorial Cartoonists.

MSU debaters Steve Donald and Aaron Monick reached the finals of the National Debate Tournament—the first time a duo from the same university had done so.

Harley Hotchkiss, '51, president of Spartan Resources, Ltd., Calgary, Alberta, gave $1 million for MSU's new Biomedical & Physical Sciences building (dedicated in 2002).

Beautiful Brook Lodge, a 657-acre conference complex with residence cottages and meeting halls, was given to MSU by Pharmacia & Upjohn Corp. The $6.7-million property is located in Augusta, Michigan, near Kalamazoo.

William Repko, MSU debate coach, was named Coach of the Year 2000. Repko, age 28, was the youngest coach to win the award since its inception in 1967.

James P. Holden, MBA '90, was named president of Daimler-Chrysler Corp.

Harley Hotchkiss, '51, president and owner of Spartan Resources, Ltd., Calgary, Alberta, was in his third term as chairman of the board of the Governors of the National Hockey League. He was part owner of the Calgary Flames NHL hockey team. In 2000, he gave $1 million for MSU's new Biomedical & Physical Sciences facility that would be dedicated in 2002. He previously had given MSU $1.5 million.

Thomas G. Weston, '66, M.A. '69, was named U.S. Ambassador to Cyprus.

William P. Weidner, '67, MBA '68, led the planning, development, financing and construction of the $1.4 billion Venetian hotel and casino in Las Vegas, Nevada. As president of Las Vegas Sands, Inc., he headed the 6,000-suite mega-resort.

Jay Johnson, M.A. '70, was named director of the U.S. Mint, which was founded in 1792. The mint produces 27 billion U.S. coins per year and generates $3.7 billion in annual revenues.

Robin Richards, '78, was president and founder of MP3.com.

Dave Kaiser, who kicked a 41-yard field goal to win the 1956 Rose Bowl, 17-14, over UCLA, became the first Spartan to be inducted into the **Rose Bowl Hall of Fame**.

Robin Stone, '86, was the new executive editor of *Essence,* a magazine for black women that had a circulation of one million.

MSU's student radio station—WDBM "Impact 89 FM"—was named **"College Radio Station of the Year"** by the Michigan Association of Broadcasters for 2000. The station also won the honor for the year 2001.

A $400,000 fire in Agricultural Hall was set by the Earth Liberation Front (ELF), a radical environmental group. ELF claimed to have damaged genetic engineering research on crops that was being conducted by Catherine Ives, associate professor of MSU's Institute of International Agriculture. An investigation was conducted by the U.S. Bureau of Alcohol, Tobacco, and Firearms.

Three Spartans won gold medals at the 2000 Olympic Games in Sydney, Australia. **Karen Dennis, '77, M.A. '79,** University of Nevada-Las Vegas track coach, was the U.S. women's team coach. The women's team won the most gold medals at the 2000 Olympics. **Steve Smith**, Spartan basketball All-American and NBA star, was a member of the gold medal winning U.S.A. basketball team—Dream Team III. **Sevatheda Fynes,** MSU track star, won a gold medal as a member of the Bahamas 4 x 100-meter relay team.

A last-second field goal by Spartan Floridian Paul Edinger gave the MSU football team an exciting 37-34 victory over the favored Florida Gators in the Citrus Bowl on New Year's Day at Orlando, Florida.

MSU won its ninth Central Collegiate Hockey Association play-off title at Joe Louis Arena in Detroit. State was the first team in history to shutout its opponents in the CCHA semifinals and finals.

Michigan State's Water Polo Club won its first Men's National Championship on November 19, 2000 in Seattle. In the tournament, they defeated the No.1, No. 2, and No. 5 teams in the nation. Earlier, they had defeated Michigan in Ann Arbor to win the Big Ten title.

Joanne McCallie was named MSU's women's basketball coach, replacing Karen Langeland who coached the Spartans for 24 years and led MSU to four NCAA appearances, and to the Big Ten title in 1997. McCallie had been head coach at the University of Maine, posting a 167-73 record, and leading her teams to six NCAA tournaments, and five North Atlantic Conference titles.

The 2000 university budget was $1,129,112,311. Enrollment was 43,366.

During the year, 9,568 degrees were awarded.

2001

Henry Center for Executive Development Opened; MSU Responds to 9-11 Tragedy; MSU Wins Fourth Consecutive Big Ten Basketball Title; Ice Hockey Team Wins Second Straight CCHA Playoff Title—The James B. Henry Center for Executive Development opened in September, 2001, and is named for the dean emeritus of the Eli Broad College of Business. The center, a national model for executive education, was made possible in large part because of an $8 million gift from James M. Cornelius, BS '65, MBA, '67, former chairman of Guidant Corp. Cornelius specified the center should be named for dean Henry.

The entire complex cost $25 million, and included the $10 million, 128-suite Candlewood Suites Hotel, a gift to MSU from that corporation.

Michigan State lost three alumni in the September 11, 2001 terrorist attacks—Kirsten Thompson Christophe, '83, age 39, vice president of Aon Corp., on the 104th floor of the World Trade Center's South Tower; Valerie Joan Hanna, MSU student 1962-1963, age 57, senior vice president Marsh & McLennan, offices in the World Trade Center; and Robert R. Ploger III, former MSU student, a passenger on American Airlines flight 77 that crashed into the Pentagon.

Henry Center for Executive Development opened in September, 2001. It is connected on the east to a 128-suite Candlewood Suites Hotel, and on the west to the University Club. The new $25-million complex includes a modern health club, golf pro shop, and is adjacent to the 1st tee of MSU's Forest Akers West championship course.

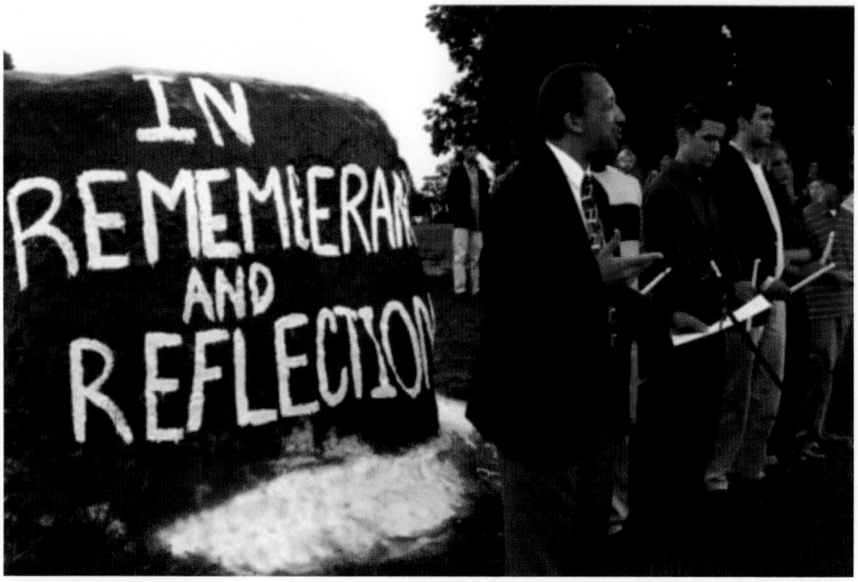

September 11th evening vigil at "The Rock" drew 1,200 students. Lee June, vice president for student affairs (left) led the "Remembrance & Reflection."

Michigan State responded to the terrorist attacks by establishing the "September 11 Scholarship Program." It provided full MSU scholarships to eleven young people whose parents were killed in the attacks.

A "Remembrance and Reflection" vigil drew 1,200 students to "The Rock" (Class of 1873 gift now at the northeast corner of the Farm Lane bridge) the evening of September 11. Some 4,000 students, faculty and staff attended an Interfaith Service of Remembrance at the Wharton Center on September 14. On the same day, hundreds gathered at Beaumont Tower to listen as carillonneur Sally Harwood played *Amazing Grace, America The Beautiful*, and the National Anthem.

A Michigan State basketball dynasty was solidified when the Spartans won their fourth consecutive Big Ten championship and earned their third straight trip to the NCAA Final Four in 2001. The Spartans became only the fourth Big Ten team to win four straight regular season titles. The other schools were: Chicago (1907-1910), Ohio State (1960-1963), and Indiana (1973-1976).

The basketball team ran their home winning streak at Breslin Center to a nation-leading 44 straight. **Seniors Charlie Bell and Andre Hutson established a Big Ten record by winning 115 games and losing only 25 in their four-year careers**. During Bell's career, he played in 140 games and started 136—both Big Ten and MSU records. In the NCAA tournament, **MSU stretched its double digit victories to nine—an NCAA tournament record.** The team finally lost in the NCAA semi-final game to Arizona, 80-61.

Head coach Tom Izzo was named NABC National Coach of the Year for 2001. He led all active coaches in the nation in NCAA tournament winning percentage at .842.

MSU's ice hockey team reaffirmed its position as a perennial national power by winning the Central Collegiate Hockey Association regular season title, its second consecutive CCHA playoff championship, its fourth straight Great Lakes Invitational title, and making it to the NCAA Frozen Four for the second time in three seasons. The Spartans posted a 23-game winning streak during the season, matching the school record. During the season, the Spartans defeated Michigan four times in five meetings.

Ryan Miller, sophomore goalie, won the 2001 Hobey Baker Memorial Award as hockey's best collegiate player (Hockey's Heisman). Miller broke the 70-year old NCAA record of 16 career shutouts, posting his 18th by season's end. He established a CCHA record for goals against average (1.32), and set new CCHA and NCAA records for saves percentage (.950). He also was named CCHA Player of the Year, CCHA Tournament MVP, and Great Lakes Invitational MVP.

For the second time, MSU had both its basketball and hockey teams advance to their respective NCAA Final Fours—becoming the only university to hold that distinction.

Michigan State displayed its traditional entrepreneurial leadership in staging the world's biggest ice hockey extravaganza in history on Saturday, October 6, 2001. **It was a happening that drew a world record 74,554 hockey and history fans to Spartan Stadium.** In a classic encounter—called the "Cold War"—Michigan State and Michigan battled to a 3-3 tie. The old hockey attendance record was 55,000, set in 1957, when Sweden beat Russia, 3-2 in the World Championships in Moscow Stadium.

A 252-foot long portable ice surface stretched between the 18-yard lines of the stadium. MSU's 300-member marching band, and a 90-piece Michigan band filled the air with fight songs. Karen Newman, National Anthem singer for Detroit Red Wing hockey games, did the same for this event. Gordy Howe, "Mr. Hockey" and Red Wing all-star legend, dropped a ceremonial puck just prior to the start of the game.

MSU's football team won the Silicon Valley Bowl game, defeating No. 20 Fresno State, 44-35 on December 31, 2001 in San Jose, California. State quarterback Jeff Smoker threw for a career-high 376 yards and three touchdowns. Wide receiver Charles Rogers—game offensive

World Record Hockey crowd of 74,554 watched MSU and Michigan fight to a 3-3 tie at Spartan Stadium on October 6, 2001 in a game dubbed the "Cold War."

MVP—caught ten passes for a school-record 270 yards, including scoring plays of 72 and 69 yards. Fullback T.J. Duckett gained a Spartan bowl record 184 yards on 27 carries.

U.S. President William Clinton made his fifth visit to MSU on January 9, 2001. Before an audience of 11,500 at the Breslin Center, the president reviewed the economic achievements of his administration, and honored MSU's 2000 NCAA championship basketball team.

MSU's nationally ranked academic programs, as reported by *U.S. News and World Report*, rose from five to 24 between 1994 and 2000.

MSU President Peter McPherson united the university's African connections and agricultural knowledge to focus on an international initiative called the "Partnership to Cut Hunger in Africa." He was co-chair of a coalition of international government leaders, humanitarian assistance organizations, religious relief groups, universities and the private sector. The goal was to cut hunger in Africa significantly by the year 2015. McPherson worked closely on this project with former U.S. Senator and Presidential Candidate Robert Dole.

Michigan State ranked No. 6 nationally in revenues earned from royalties among all universities and colleges in 2001 according to the *Chronicle for Higher Education*. MSU received $30 million from royalties, and payments from licenses on inventions by university researchers. Columbia University led all schools with $130 million in royalty revenues, followed by MIT, the University of California system, Florida State University, and Stanford University. Michigan State was the sole Big Ten institution listed in the top ten.

MSU seniors in biosystems engineering won first place in the national Waste-Management Education and Research Consortium 2001 competition. The student team was comprised of Megan Laird, Molly O'Flaherty, Nikki Ritchie, Kate Streams, and Maria Suparno.

MSU's Debate Team finished in the Final Four of both major national competitions in 2001—the Cross Examination Debates Association (CEDA) competition, and the National Debate Tournament (NDT). It was the second consecutive year the team had posted the highest cumulative score in the two top national tournaments.

Andrew Krepps, senior, won a 2001-2002 Carnegie Endowment for International Peace Award.

Dr. Michael F. Thomashow, professor of molecular biology, won the Alexander von Humboldt Foundation Award, considered the most prestigious honor for agricultural research in the United States.

Bruce R. Harte, director of MSU's School of Packaging, won the 2001 Institute of Food Technologists' Food

Lloyd Ward, '70, retired CEO of Maytag Corp., was elected CEO of the U.S. Olympic Committee—the first African-American to hold that position.

Packaging Division Riester-Davis Award for lifetime achievement.

Guy Bush, Hannah distinguished professor with appointments in zoology, entomology and the Kellogg Biological Station, was elected to the Academy of Arts and Sciences.

Anil K. Jain, distinguished professor of computer science and engineering, was named a 2001 Guggenheim Fellow.

The Eli Broad College of Business was ranked fourth in the nation in a listing of the top ten public business schools by the *Wall Street Journal* (April 30, 2001). The survey was based on the opinions of 1,600 MBA recruiters, using 27 criteria. In the same survey, MSU was ranked 12th among the top 50 business schools—both public and private. In this ranking, MSU was rated above the University of Pennsylvania's Wharton School, MIT's Sloan School, Duke University's Fuqua School, and Stanford University.

The College of Engineering received $60.7 million worth of software from Mechanical Dynamics, Inc. of Ann Arbor, Michigan. It was the largest software gift ever received by MSU.

The Delia Koo International Academic Center, a new 10,000 square-foot expansion on the top of the International Center, was to be completed in 2003. It would provide classrooms, an office for the Volunteer English Tutoring Program (VETP), and space for other programs. The new facility was named in honor of Dr. Koo, an MSU benefactor who founded the VETP program and taught English as a second language at MSU.

The Michigan State University-Detroit College of Law initiated a graduate level certificate program to be offered at Vytautas Magnus University School of Law in Kaunas, Lithuania.

MSU won a $5 million grant from the National Aeronautics and Space Administration to take the lead role in establishing the Center for Genomic and Evolutionary Studies on Microbial Life at Low Temperatures.

The first-ever virtual development program for estate and wealth planners, The Academy of Multi-Disciplinary Practice, Inc., was launched by MSU, working with wealth planning experts Robert Esperti and Renno Peterson. American General (AGC: NYSE), a leading financial services company, was the founding sponsor of the on-line program.

The College of Education's new Education Policy Center created the state's first non-partisan educational think-tank. Its research and outreach was to focus on K-12 issues.

Lloyd Ward, '70, former CEO of Maytag Corp, and former MSU basketball captain, was elected the chief executive officer of the U.S. Olympic Committee, the first African-American to serve in that position.

Marcellette G. Williams, '68, M.A. '70, Ph.D. '81, was named interim chancellor of the University of Massachusetts. She later was named chancellor. She was the first female and African-American to hold that position.

John Walters, '74, was nominated by President George W. Bush to be the U.S. Drug Czar. His title: Director of the White House Office of National Drug Control Policy.

Wallace Jefferson, '85, James Madison College graduate, was the first African-American to be named a Justice of the Supreme Court of Texas.

Larry Thompson, M.A. '69, was serving as U.S. Deputy Attorney General.

Julie Aigner-Clark, '88, who founded The Baby Einstein Company in 1997, sold the business to the Walt Disney Company in 2001. Julie explained that her company was aimed at "exposing them (children) to positive things like classical music, poetry, art and science, and do so in a stimulating way." (*MSU Alumni Magazine*, Fall 2002).

Mark A. Murray, '76, MLIR '79, was elected president of Grand Valley State University, Allendale, Michigan.

Judith L. Kuipers, '59, Ph.D. '69, was elected president of the Fielding Graduate Institute, Santa Barbara, California. She had been chancellor of the University of Wisconsin, La Crosse.

Col. Judith Fedder, '80, was commander of the 65th Air Base Wing at Lajes Field, Azores, Portugal. It was the first time a woman and non-aviator had commanded a U.S. Air Force base.

Lt. Col. DawnLee DeYoung, '83, was named the first woman commander of the Parks Reserve Forces Training Area in Dublin, California. Mission of the base: train the

Tyrone Willingham, '77, was named Notre Dame's head football coach—the first African-American to hold the position.

reserve forces of all the services—Army, Navy, Air Force, Marines, and Coast Guard.

Tyrone Willingham, '77, was named head football coach at the University of Notre Dame, the first African-American to attain that position.

Lou Schultz, '67, was chair and CEO of Initiative Media, America's leading communication strategy and advertising placement business. Company clients included Walt Disney, Unilever, Home Depot, and many others.

Gary Convis, '64, was named president of Toyota Motor Manufacturing Kentucky—the first non-Japanese to head the operation.

Gregory Josefowicz, '74, was serving as president and CEO of the Borders Group, Inc., the nation's second largest bookstore chain.

Bob Cook, '70, was elected president and CEO of Twentieth Television, the Century Fox syndication unit.

Wanda J. Herndon, '74, MA '79, was serving as Starbuck Coffee's senior vice president for worldwide public affairs.

Anita Covert, '72, M.A. '76 & '77, Ph.D. '89, president of Country Stitches, Ltd., was named **Michigan Small Business Person of the Year**. Her 12,000-square foot quilting shops in East Lansing and Jackson, Michigan are the largest in the nation. She founded her business in 1982, and is the author of 14 books on sewing and quilting.

Peter Marinos, '73, was playing twelve different characters in *The Producers*, the most highly awarded show in Broadway history.

Carl Johnson, '51, won the **American Society of Landscape Architects Medal** —their highest honor.

John C. Prost, '58, was inducted into the **Michigan Insurance Hall of Fame**.

Len Barnes, '43, former editor of *Michigan Living*—the Automobile Club of Michigan magazine—authored *Offbeat Cruises & Excursions* (Hour Publishing, 2001).

Eddie Davis, 2002, an MSU junior from Lake Orion, Michigan, became the first Westerner and second human to hike the 1,800 miles across the Great Wall of China.

MSU 26, Michigan 24—It was the final play of the game at Spartan Stadium. The clock was stopped. One second remained. Michigan led, 24-20. MSU quarterback **Jeff Smoker** took the snap at the U-M two yard line and lofted a soft pass over defenders to **T.J. Duckett** to win the game, 26-24.

Smoker had spiked the ball the previous play to stop the clock. UM thought time had run out. The officials said there was one second left.

MSU dominated the game, leading in time of possession, 36:57 to 23:03; first downs, 25 to 14; and total yards, 352 to 316. MSU's 252-pound back T.J. Duckett gained 211 yards on 27 carries.

MSU's women's golf team, coached by Stacy Slobodnik, won the Big Ten championship. The MSU team consisted of Allison Fouch, Stacy Snider, Emily Bastel, Kasey Gant, and Sarah Martin.

Michelle Carson won the 2002 women's Big Ten cross country championship, and was named the **Big Ten Cross Country Athlete of the Year**. She also won All-American honors and was named to the Verizon Academic All-America first team.

MSU's women's field hockey team won the Big Ten championship.

MSU All-American divers Carly Weiden and Summer Mitchell were named **Co-Big Ten Divers for 2001**.

John Narcy, MSU diving coach, won the Fred A. Cady Award recognizing coaching achievements and years of dedication from the Professional Diving Coaches Association.

Paul Terek was named Big Ten Men's Outdoor Track and Field Athlete of the Year for 2001. At the Big Ten meet he won the decathlon—setting an MSU and Big Ten record of 7,695 points—and won the pole vault, clearing 17' 5.5".

Magic Johnson, MSU All-American and NBA All-Star and entrepreneur, was honored by having a star with his name embedded in the Hollywood Walk of Fame on June 21, 2001.

MSU's athletic program was ranked second in the nation by the *Sporting News*, just behind Stanford. Four criteria were used in ranking the football and basketball programs of the 115 NCAA Division I universities—wins and losses, graduation rates, attendance and fan support, and compliance with NCAA rules.

The 2001 university budget was $1,277,533,579. Enrollment was 44,227.

During the year, 9,480 degrees were granted.

Dr. Michael F. Thomashow

Wins Top Agricultural Research Award

Dr. Michael Thomashow

Dr. Michael F. Thomashow, MSU plant molecular biologist, won the 2001 Alexander von Humboldt Foundation Award, considered the most prestigious recognition for agricultural research in America. The award is presented annually to the individual considered to have made the most significant contribution to American agriculture in the previous five years. Thomashow was the first MSU scientist to receive the award.

"The award committee judged Thomashow's research on environmental stress tolerance in plants to extreme temperature as having far-reaching impact for agriculture. The work holds promise to improve not only cold tolerance of plants but also tolerance to other stresses, such as salt and drought." (Francie Todd, *MSU News Bulletin*, Sept. 27, 2001). "Thomashow's research discovered the CBF cold-response pathway, which controls genes in plants that tolerate freezing and other stress conditions, such as salinity and drought." (Ryan Wallace, *State News*, Oct. 2, 2001).

Thomashow earned a bachelor's degree in bacteriology, '72; and a doctorate in microbiology, '78; both from UCLA.

2002

MSU Launches $1.2 Billion Capital Campaign; $93 Million Biomedical & Physical Sciences Center Dedicated; National Debate Champions—MSU President M. Peter McPherson announced on September 20, 2002 the launch of the largest capital campaign in MSU's history—a $1.2 billion fund raising drive to be completed by 2007.

At kick-off ceremonies in Wharton Center, McPherson indicated MSU already had raised $607 million of the total in the "silent phase" of the campaign. Called "The Campaign for MSU," its theme was *Advancing Knowledge* and *Transforming Lives*.

McPherson stated two objectives for the campaign: 1) Adding $450 million to MSU's total endowment, which stood at $810 million in September 2002; and 2) Raising $750 million to sustain MSU's excellence. These monies would go to support new research and teaching; support for students, faculty and staff; new facilities and infrastructure; and the enhancement of campus beauty, history and functionality.

MSU's $93-million Biomedical & Physical Sciences Center was dedicated on April 12, 2002. The 362,700-square foot building, which took three years to build, was the largest and most expensive academic facility ever constructed on campus. It matched or surpassed most university scientific research center capabilities worldwide.

The new center features a seven-story laboratory wing on the west side and a four-story classroom and office wing on the east. A spectacular four-story atrium corridor—128 feet by 27 feet—connects the two wings as well as the existing Chemistry and Biochemistry buildings, creating a major science complex.

The five departments and units headquartered in the building are: Microbiology & Molecular Genetics, Physiology, Physics/Astronomy, Laboratory Animal Care, and University Libraries.

President McPherson emphasized the new facility was critical to research findings that will be achieved by the Michigan Life Sciences Corridor—a statewide billion dollar research concept initiated by McPherson and MSU, which involves the University of Michigan, Wayne State University, and the Van Andel Institute in Grand Rapids.

MSU's debate team won the 2002 National Debate Championship, officially known as the Cross Examination Debate Association Seasonal National Championship. Harvard University finished 25th, and the University of Michigan 26th. It was MSU's third national debate title in seven years. MSU had finished among the top five debating teams in the nation for eight consecutive years.

Team members included Anjail Vats, Geoff Lundeen, Maggie Ryan, Jon Gillenwater, John Rood, Austin Carson, Calum Matheson, Greta Stahl, Suzanne Sobotka, John Green, Gabe Murillo, Amber Watkins, Aaron Hardy, and David Strauss. Coaching the team were: William Repko, head coach; Jason Trice, director of debate; and Alison Woidan and Michael Eber, both assistant coaches.

Eli Broad Graduate School of Management Team wins National Title—A team from MSU's graduate

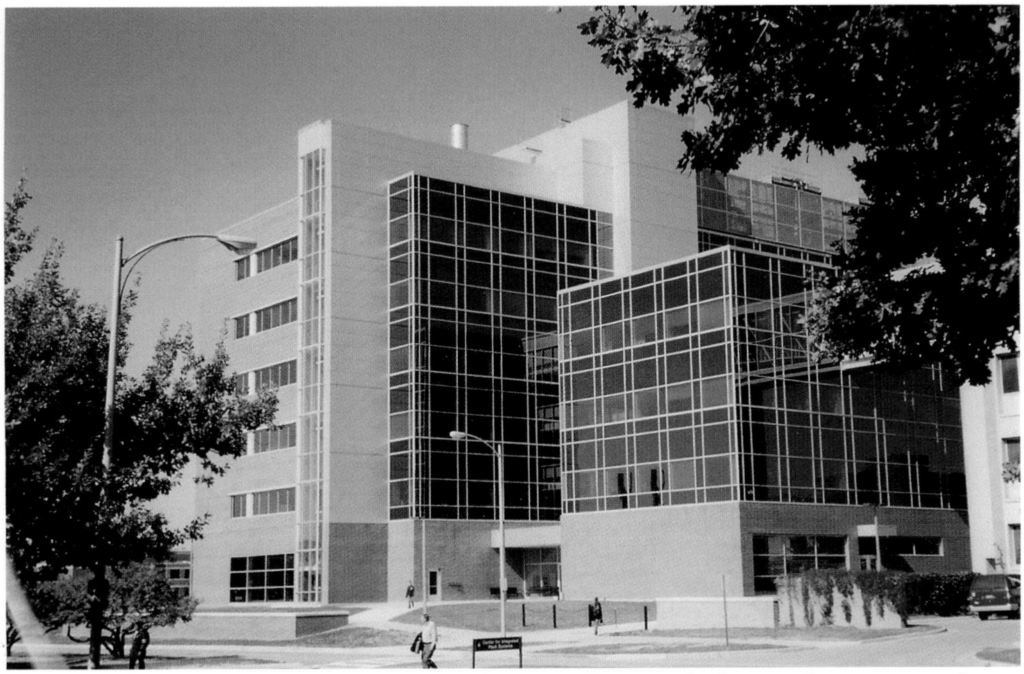

The $93-million Biomedical & Physical Sciences Center—the largest & most expensive academic facility on campus—was dedicated in April 2002. Its research capabilities matched or surpassed most university scientific centers worldwide.

business school took first-place honors at the National Black MBA Case Competition held in Nashville, Tennessee.

U.S. Vice President Richard B. Cheney addressed MSU's undergraduate convocation before 7,000 people on May 3 at the Breslin Student Events Center. In an eight-minute talk, he made the point, "There are some places where failure is final, but America is the land of second opportunity and most of us need it." He was the fifth U.S. vice president to visit MSU.

Dr. Ralph H. Smuckler, dean emeritus of MSU's International Studies and Programs, authored the book *A University Turns To The World* (MSU Press, 2002). It reviews the history of MSU's national leadership in international studies and programs, and can be purchased by members of the MSU Alumni Association from the MSU Press (msu-press.msu.edu) at a 25 percent discount. MSU President Peter McPherson described the book as "a fine story of the positive impact we can have on the world beyond our borders."

The Janice Thompson Granger Nursing Learning Center with labs, testing areas and other facilities was dedicated April 24 at the Life Sciences Building. The center was a gift from Alton and Janice Granger of Lansing, Michigan. Jan Granger is a 1980 graduate of the College of Nursing.

The Global Community Security Institute was launched by the School of Criminal Justice and MSU's Global Online Connection. The online education and training program was aimed at preparing and certifying security officials in Michigan and around the globe. MSU leadership disciplines involved included criminal justice, food and water quality safety, as well as hazardous materials management.

A new doctor's degree program in African American Studies was announced by **Curtis Stokes**, associate professor and director of African American and African Studies. Housed in the College of Arts & Letters, it was the sixth program of its kind in the nation and the first in the midwest.

The Department of Forestry celebrated its 100th anniversary. The department offers the oldest continuing undergraduate forestry program in the nation.

The Michigan State University-Detroit College of Law saw applications to the college jump by 32 percent, as compared with an 18 percent increase in law school applications nationally. There were 1,585 applications for the 2002-2003 academic year. The college has an enrollment of 820 students.

The $5.9 million Alfred Berkowitz Basketball Complex—a beautiful and functional addition to the Breslin Student Events Center—was dedicated in February 2002. The complex includes all-new, above ground offices, meeting rooms, and video rooms for the men's and women's basketball programs. It also includes a new 9,000 square-foot practice gym for the women's program (named for **Forest Akers**, former MSU Trustee), and a renovated gym for the men's program (named for **Jud Heathcote**, former head basketball coach). It is the finest facility of its kind in America.

Michigan State announced it would create the **Michigan Center for Structural Biology** to study the structure

Berkowitz Basketball Complex—a $5.9-million facility–houses new offices, meeting rooms, video rooms and practice gymnasiums for the men's and women's basketball programs. It's the finest of its kind in America.

and function of proteins as an aid to understanding diseases—their cause and their cure. The new center will be part of the Michigan Life Sciences Corridor and will be funded by a $17 million grant.

MSU's Museum was the first in Michigan designated a Smithsonian Institution affiliate. The affiliation creates an on-going exchange of research, programs, exhibitions and collections with the distinguished Smithsonian, the world's largest museum.

MSU Student Radio, WDBM—"The Impact," was named best college radio station of the year in 2002 by the Michigan Association of Broadcasters. The station also won the award in 2000.

MSU's Children's Choir, the only choir chosen by audition from the United States, performed at the Sixth World Symposium on Choral Music in Minneapolis.

Ron Mason, MSU head hockey coach for 23 years, was selected as MSU Athletics Director on January 28, 2002 to replace Dr. Clarence Underwood, who would retire on July 1, 2002. Underwood, who served from 1998 to 2002, generated a feeling of stability and a new spirit of cooperation in MSU's athletic community. Mason, who was the winningest college coach in history (924 victories), led MSU to the NCAA title in 1986, to 7 CCHA regular season titles, and to 10 CCHA playoff titles.

Rick Comley, former Northern Michigan athletics director and hockey coach, was named MSU's new hockey coach. Comley led Northern Michigan to an NCAA title in 1991, and played for Ron Mason at Lake Superior State.

The "MacCready Reserve," 408 acres of forest land six miles south of Jackson, Michigan was given to MSU by brothers **Lynn and Willis MacCready**, co-owners of the Michigan Seat Company. The gift was valued at $1.45 million.

Barbara Given, university distinguished professor of nursing, received the International Sigma Theta Tau Elizabeth McWilliams Miller Award, and the **Friends of the National Institute of Nursing Research Pathfinder Distinguished Researcher Award.**

MSU President M. Peter McPherson, '63, was named chair of the advisory board for the U.S. Secretary of Energy Spence Abraham, '74.

Mercouri G. Kanatzidis, chemistry professor and researcher, received a Guggenheim Foundation fellowship.

Jim Detjen, Eric Freedman, and **Charles Salmon**—all members of the College of Communication Arts & Sciences faculty—were named Fulbright Scholars for 2002.

Darlene Clark Hine, Hannah professor of history, was named **one of 12 "Michiganians of the Year"** by The *Detroit News*. Hine, author of a two-volume encyclopedia *Black Women in America* (1993), is considered a national pioneer in the field of comparative black history.

Camilla Smith won a Churchill Scholarship for study at Cambridge University in England, and a National Science Foundation fellowship.

Robin Stein was awarded a Gates Cambridge Scholarship—for study at Cambridge University in England, and a National Science Foundation fellowship.

Kathleen Romig, 2001, became the first MSU graduate to win a George J. Mitchell Scholarship, and studied at the University College of Cork in Ireland.

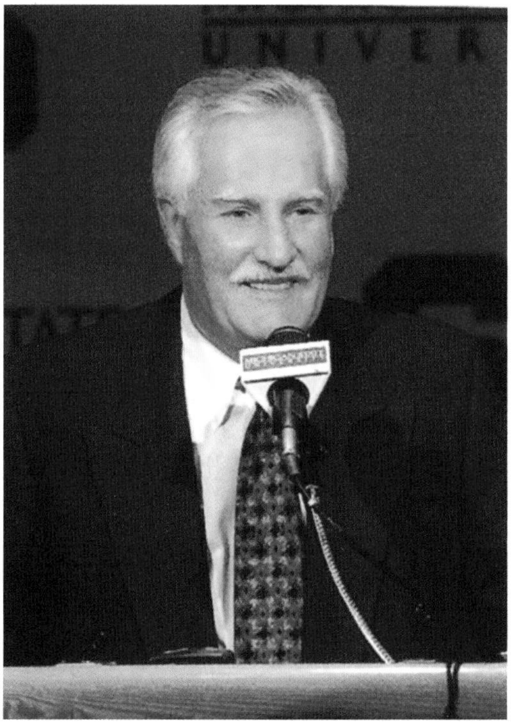

Ron Mason was named MSU Athletics Director in 2002. MSU Ice Hockey coach (1979-2002), Mason led the Spartans to an NCAA title in 1986, seven CCHA regular season titles, and ten CCHA playoff titles. His 924 wins at three universities make him the winningest hockey coach in history. He won national championships at MSU (1986) and Lake Superior State (1972). He led teams to 21 NCAA tournaments, a record.

Kwame Kilpatrick, 1999 graduate of the MSU College of Law, was elected the 60th mayor of Detroit. At age 31, he was the youngest mayor in the city's history.

Nicholas Perricone, M.D. '82, published *The Perricone Prescription* (Harper Collins, 2002), which was No. 1 on the *New York Times* best seller list. In his book, *The Wrinkle Cure* (Rodale, 2000), Perricone was credited with "the finest original thinking of the past 25 years in the fields of anti-aging and skin rejuvenation."

Perricone and his wife Madeleine gave $5 million to MSU to establish an endowment to generate funds for staff and program support of the College of Human Medicine, where he received his medical education.

Jim Popp, '86, general manager, director of football operations and player personnel for the Montreal Alouettes, led the team to the **Canadian Football League (CFL) Grey Cup championship**. In a decade with the CFL, including six with Montreal, Popp led his teams to divisional titles every year, and to four Grey Cup games, winning two.

Michael Budman, '68, and Donald Green, MSU graduate, were co-founders of Roots, the trendy Toronto-based clothing firm with some 200 stores worldwide, and annual sales of $300 million. They scored big at the 2002 Salt Lake City Olympic Games, providing the popular red, white and blue berets worn by the U.S. Olympic team. They became the hottest souvenir at the 2002 games. Budman declared, "Thanks in part to our exposure in the Olympics, we're the strongest brand name in the athletics lifestyle market today" (*MSU Alumni Magazine*, Spring, 2002).

Daniel N. Wenk, '75, was serving as director of the National Park Services headquarters in Denver.

Thomas C. Ryan, '79, M.S. '82, Ph.D. '85, was serving as McDonald's executive vice president and chief concept officer.

Carole Hutton, '78, was named managing editor of the *Detroit Free Press*. She was the first woman to attain the top editorial position at the 171-year old newspaper.

Donald G. Cook, '69, U.S. Air Force four-star general, was commander of the Air Education and Training Command at Randolph AFB, Texas.

Mark Hawkins, '81, was named vice president of finance for Dell Computer Corporation.

Judith A. Muhlberg, J.D., '86, was serving as The Boeing Company's vice president for communications.

Michael Phelps, M.A. '71, was appointed publisher of the *Quad-City Times*, Davenport, Iowa.

Bob Fish, '88, president and CEO; and **Mary Roszel, '88**, chief operating officer, were the founders of the Beaner's Gourmet Coffee house chain.

Nicholas Perricone, M.D. '82, was No. 1 on the *New York Times* bestseller list with his book, *The Perricone Prescription*. He and his wife gave MSU $5 million in 2002.

Donald G. Cook, '69, U.S. Air Force four-star general, was serving as commander of the Air Education & Training Command.

Kevin Brown, '77, was serving as president of Lettuce Entertain You Enterprises—a chain of creative restaurants in Chicago with annual revenues of $200 million.

Larry Pontius, '61, '66, authored a book on Walt Disney, titled *Waking Walt.* Pontius had served as marketing vice president for Walt Disney World and Disneyland, 1976-1980. He was the lyricist of more than 100 published songs, a writer, and published poet.

Cindy Brewer, M.A. '86, Ph.D. '91, Penn State associate professor of geography, won two **Blue Pencil Awards** for best government publications, which were covered in *Science* magazine, April 19, 2002. She co-authored *Mapping Census 2000: The Geography of U.S. Diversity*, and directed the color selection for the Center for Health Statistics' *Atlas of U.S. Mortality.*

Mary Marguerite Mathews, '70, was selected **New Hampshire Artist Laureate** for two years by Governor Jeanne Shaheen. Mathews founded Portsmouth's Pontine Movement Theatre, which over 25 years had produced more than 40 original productions. Mathews pointed out, "We're the only state that has an Artist Laureate." (*MSU Alumni Magazine*, Winter 2003).

James F. Linsell, '63, was named **Michigan's 2001-2002 Teacher of the Year**. He taught 6th grade at Eastern Elementary School in Traverse City, Michigan.

Robert Campbell, '54, sold the idea and led the planting of 300 rose plants, representing 57 varieties, on the west side of the Michigan State Capitol building. Red, white and blue annuals were favored. This "Cascade of Roses" lines both sides of the walkway leading from the Capitol's visitor entrance towards the state government buildings to the west. It was a timely project, conducted in 2002, declared by Congress as the National Year of the Rose. This was the third time in history that MSU alumni or faculty had volunteered to beautify the Capitol grounds.

John L. Smith was named MSU's head football coach on December 19, 2002, replacing Bobby Williams, who had been fired in early November. Smith had been the head coach at Louisville for five years where he produced a 41-21 record. He led Louisville to Conference titles in 2000 and 2001, and was named Coach of the Year for the conference in both seasons. Smith also was head coach at Utah State, and Idaho. With all three schools, he elevated the programs into winners. As Bob Bao reported in the *MSU Alumni Magazine* (Winter, 2003) edition, "In 14 years as head coach he's delivered six conference championships—two Big Sky, two Big West, and two Conference USA. His overall winning percentage of .740 in conference play is remarkable given the state of the programs he was hired to rebuild."

A New Bronze Spartan Statue replacement, preservation of the current ceramic statue, and relocation of the statue some ninety feet towards Demonstration Hall were announced. Dr. Keith Williams, executive director of the MSU Alumni Association, explained the $500,000 project in the *MSU Alumni Magazine* (fall, 2002): "Sparty is literally crumbling before our eyes as a result of Michigan weather and all its freeze-thaw cycles. Experts believe it may not last more than eight years where it now stands, exposed to the elements. A bronze statue would be easy to maintain and last eons." The original Spartan Statue would be preserved and displayed indoors. The original pedestal would be preserved, and moved toward Dem

Carl Angelo, '52, winningest pitcher in U.S. amateur baseball history——13 no-hitters, two perfect games, five world championships. Member Michigan Amateur Sports Hall of Fame, and Dutch Baseball Hall of Fame (2002).

Hall, integrating it into the eastern tip of the drill field. This would remove the triangular island on which the statue now stands, and improve the vehicular traffic pattern at that location. Plans called for unveiling the new Spartan Statue in 2005, the university's sesquicentennial year.

Steve Smith, MSU basketball All-American and San Antonio Spurs 2003 NBA Champion, and his wife Millie, were named honorary chair persons of the MSU Sparty Project in 2003. Working with the MSU Alumni Association, they will reach out to alumni worldwide for support.

MSU's Field Hockey Team won the Big Ten Tournament title. Coach Michele Madison's Spartans defeated defending national champion and No. 2 University of Michigan, 3-0 in the conference tournament. Sophomore midfielder Annebet Beerman was MSU's star, scoring on two penalty corner goals. **The team made its first appearance in the NCAA Final Four**, but lost in the semi-finals to eventual national champion Wake Forest.

Earvin "Magic" Johnson, NBA MVP three times and former MSU basketball All-American, was inducted into the **Basketball Hall of Fame** in Springfield, Massachusetts on September 27, 2002. Johnson led the Los Angeles Lakers to five NBA titles—1980, 1982, 1986, 1987, and 1988. He also led MSU to an NCAA title in 1979, and his Lansing Everett High School team to the Michigan state championship in 1977.

Carl Angelo, '52, the winningest amateur baseball pitcher in U.S. history, 353-69, became the first American inducted into the Dutch Baseball Hall of Fame in 2002. He already was in the Michigan Amateur Sports Hall of Fame, and the Grand Blanc (Michigan) High School Hall of Fame. During his pitching career with the Grand Rapids Sullivan's Baseball Club, Angelo led them to five world championships, threw 13 no-hitters as well as two perfect games.

MSU football wide receiver Charles Rogers set an NCAA record by catching a touchdown pass in a 39-24 win over Northwestern on September 28. It was his 13th consecutive regular-season game in which he caught a TD pass.

Mike York, former MSU All-American and New York Rangers forward, won an Olympic silver medal as a member of the U.S. hockey team at the 2002 Salt Lake City Winter Olympics.

Bob Malek, MSU baseball player, was named **Big Ten Player of the Year**. He led MSU with 16 home runs, became State's career leader with 162 runs batted in.

Michelle Carson won the individual Big Ten cross country title. She was named Big Ten Cross Country Athlete of the Year; an All-American; and a member of the Verizon Academic All-America first team.

An all-new grass field was installed in Spartan Stadium in June, 2002, replacing the artificial turf that had been used since 1968 (three sets of artificial grass had been used over 34 years). John N. "Trey" Rogers, III, professor of crop and soil sciences, led the MSU team in the project. The turf was installed in four-foot square modules—which can easily be replaced—and will have forced air heating capabilities from the sidelines, as well as in-ground irrigation.

The university budget for 2001-2002 was $1,241,000,000 (Current Fund Total Expenditures/Transfers). The expenditures drop from fiscal year 2000-2001 was due to adoption of an accounting change. Fall semester enrollment rose to a record 44,950. During the year 9,712 degrees were granted.

2003

President M. Peter McPherson was named by U.S. President George W. Bush to head the economic rebuilding of Iraq on April 17, 2003. McPherson was charged with the responsibility of coordinating the efforts of the U.S. Treasury Department and U.S. military officials on financial matters to bring Iraq back to economic health. *The Wall Street Journal* (April 18, 2003) reported McPherson "would coordinate a broad effort to get Iraq's banking system operational, to make sure civil servants are paid, and to decide how big a role the U.S. dollar should play in stabilizing the Iraqi economy…" He was to report to retired U.S. Army general Jay Garner, head of the U.S. Office of Reconstruction and Humanitarian Assistance for Iraq. McPherson described an objective of his task, "There is a close relationship between economic freedom and political freedom."

McPherson's experience and qualifications for the position were exemplary. He had served as Deputy Secretary of the U.S. Treasury where he oversaw Latin American debt re-structuring; as head of the U.S. Agency for International Development where he directed relief work for Third World nations; and as a senior vice president for Bank of America in charge of overseeing debt negotiations with troubled foreign borrowers.

In the tradition of the late, legendary MSU President John A. Hannah, fifty years before, McPherson took a leave of absence from MSU with plans to return to East Lansing. Hannah took a year's leave from MSU in 1953 to serve as U.S. Deputy Secretary of Defense.

President McPherson began his tenth year as MSU president in 2003. He already was the dean of all Big Ten Conference presidents. He also was the fifth-longest serving MSU CEO, behind Hannah—28 years, Abbot—22 years, Snyder—19 years, and Shaw—13 years. McPherson's decade leading MSU was remarkable because the average tenure of university presidents in the early 21st century, was four years.

Two MSU Professors elected to the prestigious National Academy of Sciences on April 30, 2003—On the same day, **Dr. James Tiedje**, University Distinguished Professor of crop and soil sciences and director of the National Science Foundation Technology Center for Microbial Ecology; and **Dr. Michael Thomashow**, professor of

MSU President McPherson was named by U.S. President George W. Bush to lead the economic re-building of Iraq in April, 2003. McPherson returned to MSU in September after having directed the re-establishment of the Iraqi banking system and re-constituting the currency from a Saddam to an Iraqi dinar.

crop and soil sciences and of microbiology and member of the MSU-Department of Energy Plant Research Laboratory, were elected members of the prestigious National Academy of Sciences.

Tiedje is internationally recognized for research on understanding the ecology, physiology and biochemistry of microbial processes important in nature and of value to industry.

Thomashow is internationally known for his work on the molecular mechanisms of cold acclimation in plants. His research on environmental stress tolerance in plants to extreme temperature holds promise to improve not only cold tolerance of plants, but also tolerance to other stressors such as salt and drought.

Douglas Schemske, Hannah Distinguished Professor of Plant Biology, was elected to the **American Academy of Arts and Sciences.** The elected class included three Nobel Prize laureates and four Pulitzer Prize winners.

Doug Cron, construction management professor, won the Outstanding Educator Award from the National Association of Home Builders.

Barbara Stridle, assistant provost for undergraduate education and academic services, was awarded the 2003 Distinguished Woman in Higher Education Leadership Award from the Michigan American Council on Education.

A new $58-million Diagnostic Center for Population and Animal Health opened early in 2004, replacing the first such center which "was established in the College of Veterinary Medicine in the mid-1970s." The first center was running over one million diagnostic tests per year and received more than 500 new requests daily to check on potential disease threats. Located on Farm Lane south of Forest Road, the new center's focus is on detecting "threats to animal and human populations." Linda Chadderdon, Pattie McNiel, and Kirsten Khire wrote about the old and new centers in the winter edition of the *MSU Alumni Magazine*.

Dr. Lonnie King, dean of the College of Veterinary Medicine, declared, "Over the past two decades, we have entered into an unprecedented era of infectious diseases. More than 30 emerging or re-emerging diseases have either produced epidemics or serious health problems. Of these 30 diseases, 75 percent are zoonotic—that is, they are transmitted to people either directly or indirectly through animals and their products. West Nile virus, tuberculosis, hanta virus, bovine spongiform encephlopathy ("mad cow" disease), and foodborne pathogens such as Salmonella Typhimurium DTD-104, and E. coli O157:H7 are examples of diseases or disease agents that occur in animals and have the potential to threaten human health."

Dr. King stated, "Today, millions travel worldwide, billions of people inhabit the planet, billions of animals are interacting, and trillions of tons of cargo are shipped globally. This phenomenon is creating a great melting pot of microbes and new hosts and the emergence of new pathogens that will impact societies…in ways we've never experienced."

Michigan State's Diagnostic Center for Population and Animal Health, and MSU's National Food Safety & Toxicology Center (built 1997) were both created to meet these challenges by "protecting animal and human health."

A new Center for Emerging Infectious Diseases at MSU was announced by Steve Bolin, professor of pathobiology and diagnostic investigation, and interim director of the center. He stated in the *MSU Alumni Magazine* (Winter, 2003), "(This) is in response to a national need to train people—the next generation, if you will—in infectious disease." Ned Walker, associate professor of microbiology and molecular genetics, and interim co-director of the center, said MSU is "putting a lot of emphasis on diseases that are zoonotic, which can affect both humans and animals."

The Structural Biology Center of the Michigan Life Sciences Corridor, a national facility for determining the atomic structure of biological macromolecules, was to be built and operated at MSU.

A gene responsible for the developmental disorder known as Smith-Magenis syndrome was identified by Michigan State researchers. "The discovery can lead to new therapies for the disorder…" Sarah Elsea, assistant

Spartan Marching Band Drumline warms up at Spartan Statue at 7 am on football Saturdays, a tradition started by Merritt Lutz, '65, M.A. '67. Photo: October 4, 2003 Homecoming Game vs. Indiana.

professor in pediatrics, human development, and zoology, stated, "Early diagnosis is beneficial because the child needs the most appropriate early interventions." (*MSU Alumni Magazine*, Spring 2003).

MSU's College of Natural Science's LON-CAPA project won the Computer World Honors 21st Century Achievement Award for "best IT (Information Technology) application in the world in education and academia." **Gerd Kortemeyer** was director of the project which "dramatically enhanced the delivery of virtual education." (*MSU Alumni Magazine*, Summer 2003).

MSU was awarded a $ 9 million grant by the National Institutes of Health to research new ways to fight high blood pressure. Dr. James Galligan, professor of pharmacology and toxicology, was selected as lead researcher on the project.

Major Gifts Flow to the $1.2 Billion *Campaign for MSU* (2002-2007)—Eli Broad, '54, and his wife Edythe, gave an additional $3,475,000 to the Eli Broad College of Business and the Eli Broad Graduate School of Business, bringing his total contributions to *The Campaign for MSU* to $16.6 million. These gifts were in addition to the $20 million pledged by Broad in 1991 to the College of Business now named for him.

The MSU Federal Credit Union gave $2.5 million to fund the MSUFCU Endowed Study Abroad Scholarship program which will offer student scholarships of $500 to $2,000 to offset study abroad costs.

MSU Faculty, Staff and Retirees committed some $5.7 million to *The Campaign for MSU.*

The Guidant Foundation gave $400,000 for annual support of an MBA student interested in pursuing a career in the life sciences industry. The gift was to honor James M. Cornelius, '65, MBA '67, founding chairman of Guidant Corporation. Cornelius and his wife Kathleen previously made a leadership gift that helped launch the James B. Henry Center for Executive Development.

The Detroit Area Development Council (DADC), an alumni organization initiated in 1996 to raise MSU's visibility in southeast Michigan, provide event assistance, and fund-raise, has provided $125,000 for MSU scholarships to metropolitan Detroit high school students. The DADC also gives funds to The President's Special Endowment Fund and the Athletic Director's Special Initiative Fund. The major fund-raiser for the group is the Annual Tom Izzo Spartan Golf Classic, held for the past seven years in late August. Gred Liposky, '85, was the first golf chair. Jack Withrow, '54, MBA '71, is the current golf chair. Michael R. Morrow, '72, served as chair of the DADC, 2001-2003. Tammy Moncrief, '85, was elected chair in 2003.

"Michigan State launched the online Horticulture Gardening Institute (*www.gardeninginstitute.com*). The Gardening Institute was an idea…to provide online courses for master gardeners and all gardening enthusiasts," according to Christine Geith, co-executive director of the Horticulture Gardening Institute and director of the MSU Global Institute. The Gardening Institute announced a partnership with the American Horticultural Society in May "to co-develop an innovative series of lifelong

Bill, '54, and Carol, '55, Brink, major MSU donors, and leaders in MSU Detroit Area Development Council scholarship fund-raising.

learning programs for master gardeners and gardening enthusiasts." (By Jill Sherman, *MSU Alumni Magazine,* Summer, 2003).

"MSU's College of Nursing offered several new degree programs completely online, a move to help address the national shortage of nurses and nurse educators." (*MSU Alumni Magazine,* Summer, 2003).

MSU's International Food Laws and Regulation Certificate Program won the 2003 National Award for Excellence in College and University Distance Education. The award was presented by the American Distance Education Consortium.

MSU Team Is First in U.S. to Win Jessep International Law Moot Court Competition—Five MSU-DCL students became the first U.S. team to win the Philip C. Jessep International Law Moot Court Competition. The 2003 victory was won by third-year law students Nic Camargo and Jina Han; and second-year students Joe Harte, David Pizzuti, and Camille Van Buren. The MSU team defeated five other regional winners—Georgetown, University of Michigan, Lewis & Clark, Columbia, and Harvard Law School.

Professor Deborah Skorupski, a seasoned judge, was the team's advisor.

MSU's saxophone quartet won the 2003 National Collegiate Chamber Music competition sponsored by the National Music Teachers' Association. Quartet members were Wilton Elder, Paul Forsyth, Bryan Jao, and Paul Nolen.

MSU's Children's Choir was selected to sing at the opening of the 2004 Ryder Cup international golf competition at the Oakland Hills Country Club in Birmingham, Michigan.

MSU's orchestra, wind symphony, top jazz band, and top chorale were selected to lead off the 2004 Midwest Music Conference at the University of Michigan's refurbished Hill Auditorium.

Jared S. English, a senior, won a $30,000 Truman Scholarship.

Megan Dennis, a junior, won a $7,500 per year Goldwater Scholarship.

Jason Evans, MSU College of Law graduate, earned the highest score in the Michigan Bar exam, becoming the second consecutive Spartan to take top honors.

Eugene N. Parker, '48, professor emeritus, University of Chicago, won the 2003 Kyoto Prize which includes $400,000, and a 20-karat gold medal. He first theorized the existence of a solar wind in solar space in 1958. By 1962, his theory was proven correct, "triggering a drastic change in space science and an entire new set of explanations of phenomena involving fixed stars, the interstellar medium, and the galaxy." (*MSU Alumni Magazine,* Fall, 2003). Parker authored *Cosmical Magnetic Fields—Their Origin and Activity* (1979), a leading text on the solar wind.

Jim Haveman, M.S. '68, was serving as senior advisor to Iraq's Ministry of Health, representing the Coalition Provisional Authority. He heads Haveman Group, Grand Rapids, Michigan, and formerly was the director of the Michigan Departments of Community Health, Public Health, and Mental Health.

James D. Spaniolo, '68, U-M M.P.A. and J.D. '75, dean of MSU's College of Communication Arts & Sciences, was elected president of the University of Texas-Arlington, a 25,000-student campus.

Richard Olstein, '64, MBA '66, was chairman and founder of the $1.4 billion Olstein Financial Alert Fund. From 1998 to 2003, his fund ranked in the top five percent of all equity funds.

Philip Hickey, '77, was serving as chairman and CEO of RARE Hospitality International, an Atlanta-based restaurant chain that includes 170 Longhorn Steak Houses, 23 Bugaboo Creek Steak Houses, and 15 Capital Grilles.

Paraj Mandrekar, '93, Promega Corporation genetic research scientist, helped develop two forensic DNA processing kits that were named among the year's top 100 technologies by *R&D Magazine*.

Ella Bully-Cummings, MSU-DCL, '98, was named Detroit's Chief of Police, in charge of 4,200 police officers. She was the first woman to hold the position.

Ted Peters, '63, was named interim president of Pacific Lutheran Theological Seminary, Berkeley, California.

Mark MacManus, Jr., '89, was owner, president and CEO of New Horizons, the world's largest independent information technology training company, specializing in courses for general users of computer programs.

Joellen Thompson, '79, Grand Rapids, Michigan assistant water system manager, became the first female "Engineer of the Year" named by the Michigan Society of Professional Engineers (MSPE). She also was the first woman elected president of MSPE, in 1999.

David C. George, '79, was elected president of Longhorn Steak Houses.

Kenneth E. Bow, '62, chief scientist at Dow Chemical Corp., was named a Fellow of the Institute of Electronic and Electrical Engineers.

Jeff Crilley, '85, Emmy award-winning anchor and reporter for KDFW-TV (Fox) in Dallas, authored the book *Free Publicity: TV Reporter Shares The Secrets To Getting Covered On The News.*

Jacqueline Woods, '70, was named executive director of the American Association of University Women, Washington, D.C. She was a founding member and past president of the Women Administrators in Higher Education.

Jeanne M. Huddleston, '90, MD '93, director of the Inpatient Internal Medicine Program at the Mayo Clinic, Rochester, MN, was selected as president-elect of the Society of Hospital Medicine.

Lynn C. Myers, '64, MBA '67, General Manager of Pontiac-GMC Division of General Motors, was the first woman honored with the John A. Hannah Outstanding Alumni Award. The presentation was made at halftime before the world-record 78,129 fans attending the MSU-Kentucky basketball game at Ford Field in Detroit on December 13, 2003. The award is to an alum embodying the spirit of former MSU President Hannah and for exceptional devotion to the growth and progress of MSU academics and athletics. Myers, shown with GMC Envoy XUVs, was named McCall's/Ward's Auto World's first "Outstanding Woman in the Automotive Industry" in 1994.

Elizabeth D. Boyd, '74, M.A. '90, was named press secretary to Michigan Governor Jennifer Granholm.

Amy Astley, '89, was named Editor-in-Chief of *Teen Vogue* magazine. She had been beauty director of *Vogue* magazine for a decade.

Susan Gutierrez, M.A. '92, TCRT '97, was named the 2002-2003 **"Michigan Teacher of the Year."** She was an 8th grade teacher at the Central Middle School in Grand Rapids, Michigan.

The Michigan Institute for Safe Schools and Communities was established at MSU. Its purpose was "to build stronger, safer and drug-free learning environments in Michigan," according to an *MSU Alumni Magazine* (Winter, 2003) story. MSU's Office of University Outreach and the College of Education's Office for K-12 Outreach Programs created the Institute through a $400,000 grant from the Michigan Department of Community Health's Office of Drug Control Policy. **Barbara Markle,** director of MSU's Office for K-12 Outreach Programs, and co-administrator of the project, said, "Safety is an essential element of an effective school." Hiram Fitzgerald, university distinguished professor of psychology and co-administrator of the project, stated, "Many of the resources that need to be tapped already are in place across campus..."

MSU led the nation in students studying abroad during the 2000-2001 academic year, according to the Institute of International Education. Some 1,835 students were engaged in academic efforts in foreign countries. MSU's stated goal was for 40 percent of the undergraduate student body to have a study abroad experience by 2006 while keeping costs at or near the cost of remaining in East Lansing.

A $5.3 million Red Cedar Greenway plan, featuring pedestrian and bike trails running along the Red Cedar River from Harrison to Hagadorn roads was announced. The plan called for separating walkers from bikers, and for connecting with Lansing's 8-mile River Trail as well as East Lansing to the north and Meridian Township to the east. Sharon Terlep reported in the *Lansing State Journal* that, "The new paths would be within 1,000 feet of 20 residence halls, four major classroom buildings, the main library and Spartan Stadium." Other features of the new trail system would be "twelve information kiosks with maps, and two new bridges over the Red Cedar River." Federal grants and local contributions were being sought for the project.

MSU's Basketball team advanced to the NCAA Elite Eight. Tom Izzo's Spartan cagers struggled during the regular season due to many injuries and a very young team, dominated by sophomores and freshmen. The regular season record was 18-11. In the Big Ten, MSU finished tied for third, with a 10-6 record.

However, by NCAA tournament time, Izzo had the Spartans clicking. They won three NCAA tournament games, advancing to the Elite Eight, farther than any other Big Ten team.

Two NCAA games were notable. At Tampa, Florida, MSU shocked a home-state crowd of 21,304, crushing the University of Florida Gators, 68-46. Coach Izzo called the game "a memory-maker." State shot 70 percent in the first half, and finished the game with a 55 percent shooting average. It was the first time in coach Billy Donovan's seven-year career that Florida scored fewer than 50 points. Freshman guard Maurice Ager led MSU scoring with 16 points, hitting on 6 of 9 shots. State held Florida freshman Anthony Roberson, former Saginaw, Michigan All-Stater, to zero points.

Next, Michigan State knocked off defending NCAA champion Maryland, 60-58, before 33,009 fans at San Antonio's Alamodome to advance to the Elite Eight. MSU was leading 54-40 with about six minutes to play, and appeared unbeatable. Then, in a 3 minute and 46 second stretch, Maryland turned up the defensive heat, causing seven turnovers, and outscored State, 15-0 to take a 55-54 lead.

Earvin "Magic" Johnson, who led Michigan State to its first NCAA basketball title in 1979, talks at the unveiling of the statue honoring him at the Breslin Center, November 1, 2003. Titled "Always A Champion," the statue's base lists Johnson's championships at the high school, college, NBA, and Olympic levels of competition.

Many teams would have folded after blowing a 14 point lead. But MSU responded. Freshman 6'11" center Paul Davis slammed home a tying basket with 50 seconds left. And with 4.7 seconds left, Davis made a remarkable leaning baseline drive and caromed the ball off the glass for a 60-58 lead. Maryland All-American Steve Blake launched a long three-pointer in the final second, but missed. Davis led the Spartans with 13 points. In their game to try to advance to the Final Four, the Spartans lost to the University of Texas, 85-76.

The win improved Spartan coach Tom Izzo's NCAA tournament record to 19-4 for a winning percentage of .826—the best among all coaches with at least ten wins.

Five Join MSU Athletic Hall of Fame— Lauren Brown, cross country All-American, 1928-1931; Joe DeLamielleure, All-American football center, 1970-1972, and member of the NFL Hall of Fame; Mary Fossum, MSU women's golf coach, 1973-1997, and winner of five consecutive Big Ten team titles, 1974-1978; Cheryl Gilliam, track All-American; and Tom Yewcic, All-American in football and baseball, who played for the Detroit Tigers and the New England Patriots.

A Statue Honoring Earvin "Magic" Johnson was unveiled outside the Breslin Center on November 1, 2003, prior to the MSU-Michigan football game. Sculptor Omri Amrany, creator of the Michael Jordan statue outside Chicago's United Center, sculpted the Johnson likeness. The marble base of the 12-foot statue carries the inscription: "Always A Champion," and lists Johnson's championships at four levels of competition—State Champion at Lansing Everett High School (1977), NCAA Champion at MSU (1979), Five-time National Basketball Association Champion with the Los Angeles Lakers (1980, 1982, 1985, 1987, and 1988), and Olympic Champion (1992). He was inducted into the Naismith Memorial Basketball Hall of Fame in 2002.

Contributors making the $250,000 statue possible were Mark and Regina Wickard, Dr. Steve and Samer Ajluni, Dr. Steve and Amy Almany, Dr. Bill Devlin and Molly K. Brennan, Gregory Eaton, Joel Ferguson, Bruce and Mary Jane Herrick, David Johnson, Steve and Brenda Ramsby, Jeff and Stephanie Wayne, Michigan Millers Mutual Insurance, and MSU Rebounders Club.

Steve Smith and **Kevin Willis**, former Spartan basketball stars, helped the San Antonio Spurs win the 2003 National Basketball Association championship.

Joe DeLamielleure, former MSU All-American offensive lineman and All-Big Ten for three seasons,

1970-1972, was inducted into **Pro Football's Hall of Fame** in August, 2003. DeLamielleure played in six straight Pro Bowls (1976-1981) during his 13 years with the Buffalo Bills, and was a key blocker helping O.J. Simpson set NFL rushing records. He was inducted into the Michigan State Athletic Hall of Fame in September, 2003.

Jamie Krzyminski won the Big Ten indoor track 5,000-meter title, and the outdoor 10,000-meter title. She was named an All-American, and elected a Verizon Academic All-America second team member.

MSU's Lindsay Bowen, guard, and Liz Shimek, forward, were named co-Big Ten basketball Freshmen of the Year. Bowen led all Big Ten freshmen in scoring with a 13.3 per game average. She hit 48 percent of her three-point shots, which led the conference and was second in the nation. Shimek was second in the conference among freshmen in scoring at 10.6 points per game, and second in rebounding at 9.3 per game.

Jason Richardson, member of MSU's 2000 National Basketball Championship team and Golden State Warrior player, won the National Basketball Association 2003 All-Star Slam Dunk competition. He wowed the judges with a between-the-legs, backward windmill slam.

MSU's Charles Rogers, All-American wide receiver, was picked second in the National Football League draft by the Detroit Lions on April 26. The *Detroit News and Free Press* front page banner headline on April 27, read: "MSU Pick To Elevate Lions."

Jacquie Joseph, MSU softball coach, was named Big Ten Coach of the Year. She led the Spartans to a 37-17 regular season record; 13-6 in the Big Ten; and into the NCAA Women's Softball Tournament for the third time in history. Six MSU players received All-Big Ten recognition: Jessica Beech, Tiffany Wallace, Sandy Lewis, Natalie Furrow, Elizabeth Peterson, and Margaret Schick.

John L. Smith, new head football coach, re-instituted two football uniform symbols—putting the Spartan helmet logo on the helmets, and the bold Michigan State on the front of the jerseys—both excellent identity and marketing moves. The Spartan helmet logo is far more distinctive than the block S, which appears on the helmets of a number of other universities. The bold *Michigan State* conveys the team's true identity and is superior to the miniature *State* that appeared on the 2002 jerseys. After all, there are at least one hundred universities that are known as "State." Smith also eliminated individual player names from the back of the jerseys, saying that the focus should be on the team, and not individuals. In the same vein, Smith eliminated use of the number "1" on any jersey.

John L. Smith led MSU to an 8-4 football season and was named Big Ten Coach of the Year.

Bebe Bryans, MSU women's crew coach, was named 2003 Big Ten Rowing Coach of the Year.

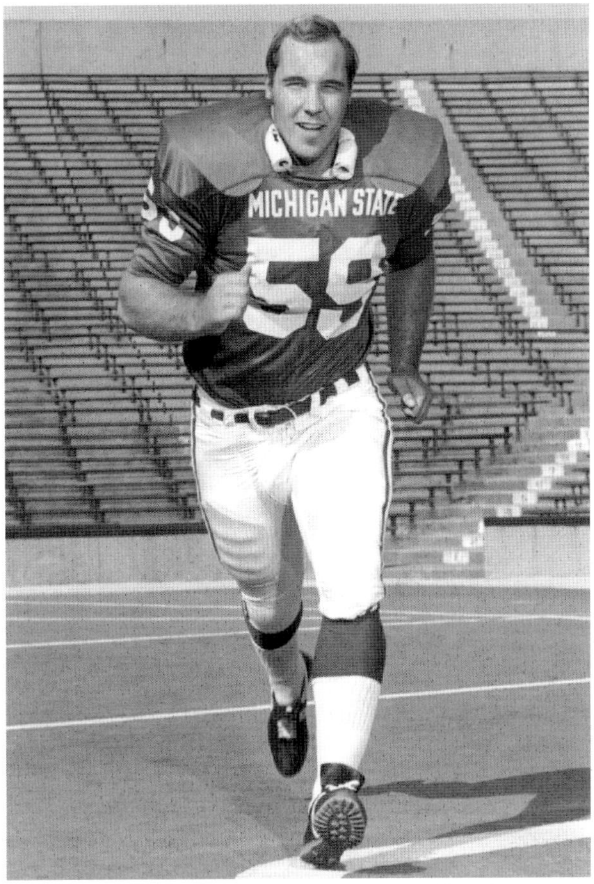

Joe DeLamielleure, MSU All-American offensive lineman and All-Big 10 for three years (1970-1972), was inducted into the Pro Football Hall of Fame in August, 2003. He played in 6 Pro Bowls (1976-1981) during 13 years with the Buffalo Bills. He was inducted into the MSU Athletic Hall of Fame in September, 2003, and the Michigan Sports Hall of Fame in 2004.

Denny Hill, MSU chemistry graduate and swimming coach at Ann Arbor's Pioneer High School, led his boys and girls swim teams to their second consecutive state championships in 2003. In 35 years as the Pioneer coach, Hill mentored the boys teams to 12 state titles, and the girls' teams to 10. His boys' teams had won 27 conference championships, and the girls teams, 25.

Andy Ruthkoski, junior on the MSU golf team, broke the Belvedere Golf Club course record in Charlevoix at the Michigan Amateur Golf Championship by shooting a six under par 64. His June 18th round beat the old course record set by Walter Hagen in the 1930s.

MSU's Football Team Defeated Notre Dame 22-16 at South Bend for their eleventh victory in Notre Dame Stadium, more than any other university. It also was the Spartans' fourth consecutive win in Notre Dame Stadium.

The Women's Field Hockey Team Tied for the Big Ten Regular Season Title and won the Big Ten tournament. Coach Michele Madison's Spartans posted a 17-5 record.

Three Spartans Among Those with the Most *Sports Illustrated* Covers—Spartans Magic Johnson, Steve Garvey, and Kirk Gibson were listed in the November 10, 2003 issue of *Sports Illustrated* as among the top MVPs (most visible players), appearing on the magazine's cover over its first 50 years. Magic Johnson was tied for third place with 22 covers, sharing that position with Kareem Abdul-Jabbar, and Jack Nicklaus. All-Star major league baseball players Steve Garvey and Kirk Gibson each had three covers. In all, 198 individuals were listed, and the number of covers ranged from 3 to 49. Michael Jordan was first with 49, and Muhammad Ali second with 37. Johnson also has appeared on the covers of *Time, Newsweek,* and *U.S. News & World Report.*

The World's Largest Basketball Crowd—78,129— saw Kentucky defeat MSU, 79-74, December 13, 2003 at the Detroit Lions' Ford Field in Detroit. Called the Basket-Bowl, the unique event sold more than 75,000 seats by mid-July, 2003. The original world record for basketball attendance was set in 1951 when the Harlem Globetrotters drew 75,000 to the Olympic Stadium in Berlin. The national attendance record was set on January 20, 1990 when LSU beat Notre Dame, 87-64, at the New Orleans' Superdome before 68,112 fans.

MSU head coach Tom Izzo declared, "Everything was awesome, except the biggest fact: we lost the game. We had the opportunity of a lifetime. This was an incredible setting. It'll be a good memory. It just won't be a good memory for a while," (*Detroit News,* December 14, 2003, story by Dave Dye).

By midway in the first half, Kentucky had raced to a 15-point lead on 66.7 percent shooting. Then MSU turned up its effort, and cut the lead at halftime to six points—Kentucky 49, MSU 43. In the second half, the Spartans made several runs at Kentucky, cutting the lead to two points on three occasions, and to one point once. However, every time MSU came close, Kentucky answered—particularly senior guard Gerald Fitch who hit four of six 3-pointers, and scored a game-high 25 points. Paul Davis led Spartan scoring with 24 points, including 14 of 14 from the free-throw line.

MSU put it all on the line, staging the largest basketball extravaganza in history. MSU was true to its risk-taking culture, and came out the winner, by securing a lasting historical memory.

This was the second world attendance record for Michigan State. The first was set in October of 2001, when MSU tied Michigan, 3-3 in an ice hockey game played before 74, 554 fans in Spartan Stadium.

MSU's football team was defeated at the Alamo Bowl by Nebraska, 17-3 on December 29.

Significant reductions in legislative appropriations resulted in a $31 million reduction in the university base budget by faculty, staff and top administrators.

The university budget for the 2002-2003 fiscal year was $1,397,283,080 (Current Fund Total Expenditures/Transfers). Student enrollment was 44,542 in the fall of 2003. The entering freshmen class of some 6,800 had a mean GPA of 3.58. During the 2002-2003 academic year, 10,154 degrees were granted.

2004

President McPherson Announced His Retirement at May 7 Graduation Ceremonies; Dr. Lou Anna K. Simon, MSU's provost elected MSU's 20th President; Trustees Voted 8-0, "In Principle," to Support Move of College of Human Medicine to Grand Rapids; President McPherson Speaks on MSU's New Opportunities; MSU Law Team Wins National Title; Debate Team Wins Four National Tournaments.

MSU President M. Peter McPherson announced he would retire effective December 31, 2004 at the May 7 graduation ceremonies at the Breslin Student Events Center. McPherson, whose tenure would reach 11 years by October 1, 2004, stunned the audience and surprised many in the MSU family. He told the *Detroit Free Press* (May 8, 2004), "I'd like to take on another big challenge. I don't ever want to retire." He added, "major institutions such as MSU need change 'every decade or so.'" McPherson, who was the "dean" of all Big Ten university presidents, more than doubled the average university president's tenure of about four years.

A May 9, 2004 *Detroit News* editorial mourned McPherson's announcement as "a major loss for both the college and the state." McPherson's accomplishments as president included, establishment of sound business practices, pioneering the idea of holding tuition to no more than the rate of inflation, doubling MSU's international studies program—making it the largest in the nation, bringing the Detroit College of Law to the MSU campus (now Michigan State University College of Law), expanding the Honors College from 1,000 to 2,400 students, leading the largest facility expansion program since the 1960s and 1970s, and launching The Campaign for MSU—a $1.2 billion fund-drive ($800 million already raised) scheduled for completion in 2007.

Facilities erected during McPherson's 11-year tenure included the Bio-Medical and Physical Sciences building, the James B. Henry Center for Executive Development, the College of Law building, the North Business Complex, the Clara Bell Smith Student-Athlete Academic Support Center, the Berkowitz Basketball Center, and the Mary Anne McPhail Equine Performance Center.

Dr. Lou Anna K. Simon, MSU provost for eleven years (1993-2004), was elected Michigan State University's 20th president on June 18, 2004 by an 8-0 vote of the MSU Board of Trustees.

Simon assumed the title of president designate and retained her title of provost for the remainder of President

McPherson's tenure. She was to become MSU's first woman president, and one of only nine women holding a university presidency among the Association of American Universities, the 62 leading research institutions in the U.S. When she became provost in 1993, Simon was the first woman to hold that position in the Big Ten.

Simon declared,

"This is an important point in our history, a time of transition and change, both intellectually and fiscally. It is also a time of unusual opportunity and possibility. 'Team MSU,' working tirelessly and passionately, will keep Michigan State University on the path of relevant and meaningful excellence."

Dr. Lou Anna K. Simon, Twentieth President (2005)

Dr. Simon earned her doctorate in administration and higher education at MSU in 1974, and then became a member of the MSU faculty and director of the Office of Institutional Research (now the Office of Planning and Budget). She has served as assistant provost and associate provost, and currently serves as provost of the Michigan State University College of Law. She earned a master's degree in student personnel and counseling as well as a bachelor's degree in mathematics, both from Indiana State University.

MSU Trustees Resolved "In Principle" to Move the MSU College of Human Medicine to Grand Rapids to provide West Michigan with a strong university medical school and add to the medical research nucleus already in that city. The May 7 resolution still needed faculty input and advice from the MSU Academic Council and the Faculty Senate. If approved by the faculty, the trustees and administrators would move to the transition phase of how to make the move and fund it.

National Security Adviser Dr. Condoleezza Rice delivered the graduation address at the Breslin Center on May 7. She made the following points to the graduates—1. Be optimistic; 2. Remember, others are not as fortunate as you; 3. Work to close the cultural gaps that divide our nation; 4. Do not let education lead you into false pride; and 5. Do not rest until you find your passion. Go out and better your world. Dr. Rice closed her talk with the line, "Welcome to the starting line."

MSU President M. Peter McPherson spoke of MSU's "New Opportunities for New Realities," in a February 10, 2004 Founder's Day message. He first told how MSU's exemplary Agricultural Experiment Station and MSU Extension programs were challenged and put on the budget-cutting chopping block by a State Government, unaware of the monumental contributions to the state, nation, and world by these organizations.

These agricultural research and outreach contributions have meant millions of dollars to the Michigan and U.S. economies, and have helped thousands of citizens solve problems. Fortunately, a spirited, substantive and successful defense of both programs was mounted by Dean Jeff Armstrong, College of Agriculture and Natural Resources; Margaret Bethel, director of MSU Extension; Ian Gray, acting vice provost and vice president of research and graduate studies; Steve Webster, vice president of governmental affairs; and Wayne Cass, chairman of the labor coalition.

The fact that these "gold standard" programs could even be called into question by the legislature, underscores the imperative that continual, effective communication on MSU programs is needed at the State Capitol.

Addressing the 2004-2005 fiscal year budget, McPherson reported on an agreement between the MSU Board of Trustees and Governor Jennifer Granholm. The agreement reduced state cuts to the MSU budget from five percent to two percent. In return, MSU agreed to limit the next fall's undergraduate tuition increase to 2.4 percent, the approximate rate of inflation.

McPherson emphasized, "There has been an alarming trend in Michigan toward disinvestment in public higher education during the past 35 years. **In the mid-1960s, the State of Michigan covered some 75 percent of the cost of a Michigan State University education. Today, state support for an MSU student is less than 50 percent of the cost.**

"This trend is not one the people of Michigan support. In a recent IPPSR (MSU's Institute for Public Policy & Social Research) survey, some 84 percent of those surveyed rate our universities as 'excellent' or 'good.' An even higher percentage—90 percent—judge the role of our universities in improving the state's economy as 'very important' or 'somewhat important.' Michigan's residents show strong support for universities when confronted with budget decisions. For example, they are twice as willing to support cuts in some other areas of the state budget than higher education."

"New Realities call for New Opportunities built upon our Guiding Principles," McPherson declared. Strengthening undergraduate education was one opportunity area cited, and he stated a number of goals:

- Higher admission standards require higher learning expectations with more research opportunities, more co-op placements, internships, and fuller integration of Study Abroad into the curriculum.
- Hybrid courses that include regular classroom work combined with interactive web learning. MSU had 7,000 students enrolled in web courses last year, including four master's degree programs.
- Reducing the time it takes to earn an undergraduate degree, which now averages 4.5 years. This would cut student costs for undergraduate education. Issues to be addressed include: the number of prerequisites to take courses, whether courses are available at proper times, and earning credits through examinations.
- Make global education more available through greater Study Abroad options.

McPherson said "research, in its many forms, is central to who we (MSU) are." He emphasized MSU's effort to "coordinate environmental and science policy," and pointed to a new PhD program in environmental science and policy.

President McPherson also said "MSU will provide the research and educational support needed" for Michigan Governor Granholm's concern for making state water quality a high priority.

Moreover, McPherson referred to a University-wide initiative, led by Provost Lou Anna K. Simon, to review and reinvigorate the liberal arts core academic area. Input came from the entire MSU academic community.

"Realizing the Vision: Liberal Arts and the 21st Century Land Grant University," a draft paper of the vision was sent by Provost Simon to members of the University Community on February 17, 2004, outlining four initiatives for review. She called it "an agenda designed to position MSU for the next 50 years."

The four initiatives, collectively, were called the most sweeping changes to the University since the Hannah era. Embedded in each of the initiatives were efforts to strengthen the international dimension of the University.

Initiative One: Strengthen the Organization and Coherence of Undergraduate Education.

- <u>Expand the role of the Assistant Provost for Undergraduate Education and add the title of Dean of Undergraduate Student</u>. The role of this person was to reduce fragmentation, excessive requirements, and other obstacles that impede a better undergraduate experience—including coordination of Integrative Studies, writing programs, career development, Undergraduate University Division, academic advising, new quantitative literacy initiatives, and international initiatives including Study Abroad.
- <u>Establish a single Center for Integrative Studies</u> to integrate the arts and humanities and the social and natural sciences into a curriculum focused on the complex and interrelated questions and challenges facing human beings.
- <u>Establish a broad-based faculty group on Integrative Studies</u> to provide intellectual leadership and foster a wide-ranging investment of time and resources in Integrative Studies.

Initiative Two: Continue to Strengthen Graduate Education.

- <u>Make a major revision of graduate handbooks</u> that will explicitly address research mentoring of students.
- <u>Improvement of the career advice and experiences for graduate students</u> to foster further connections between Career Services and Placement and the Graduate School.
- <u>Improvement of pedagogical training</u> for graduate students linked to the new undergraduate Integrative Studies and the Certification of College Teaching Program.
- <u>Continued focus on improving doctoral student completion rates</u>.

Initiative Three: Expand the University's Successful Living and Learning Options.

- <u>Create a new residential program in the liberal and creative arts and sciences</u>, using the Residential Option in Arts and Letters (ROIAL) as a basis for the new program.
- <u>Expand James Madison College and Lyman Briggs School.</u>
- <u>Develop new links between residential programs and professional programs, and between residential programs and other colleges</u>. Example: New efforts for pre-business students between James

Madison College and the Broad College of Business.

- Expand other residential options, particularly the Residential Initiative on the Study of the Environment (RISE), and the Residential Option for Science and Engineering Students (ROSES).

Initiative Four: Organize the Liberal Arts Core for the 21st Century

- Expand and rename the College of Social Science. The expanded "College of Social, Behavioral, and Economic Sciences" will bring together History, Philosophy, Religious Studies and the current programs of Social Science.
- Create a new "College of Communication, Arts, Languages and Media." This new college would bring together programs in communication, information and media, journalism, languages, linguistics, literature, music, telecommunication, theater, advertising, communication disorders, visual arts, and writing and rhetoric.
- Realign Human Ecology programs. Human Ecology programs would be linked to a set of new relationships and resources that afford greater intellectual possibilities and greater potential for developing distinction.

The above realignment would dissolve the colleges of Arts and Letters, Human Ecology, and Communication Arts and Sciences, while sustaining their respective legacies and strengthening their opportunities for distinction.

The realignment would result in three colleges: Natural Science; Social, Behavioral, and Economic Sciences; and Communication, Arts, Languages, and Media. These colleges would be of more equivalent size, with a better balance of majors and service enrollment, and with a better blend of opportunities for revenue generation.

MSU Law Students win the American Bar Association's 2004 Annual Law Student Tax Challenge—Melissa Bridges, third year law student, and **Matt Rockey-Hawley**, December 2003 law graduate, defeated teams from the University of Michigan, the University of Tennessee, Southern Methodist University, New York University, and others.

Michele Halloran, clinical professor of law and director of MSU's tax clinic, said the judges praised the MSU team "for their impeccable tax knowledge and outstanding verbal skills."

Debate Team Wins Four Consecutive National Tournaments—Two MSU seniors defeated top-ranked University of California-Berkeley to win the **2004 National Debate Tournament, the ultimate prize of intercollegiate debate,** held at Catholic University, Washington, D.C. Greta Stahl, history and international relations senior, and Dave Strauss, international relations senior, not only teamed to win the top honor, they also **won 22 consecutive debates in back-to-back tournaments at the University of Southern California and California State-Fullerton.** Mike Eber, interim director of debate, called the performance "nothing short of sensational." The Spartans won over teams from Harvard, California-Berkeley, University of Texas-Austin, Dartmouth, and others.

In addition, the Stahl-Strauss team also won the prestigious Dartmouth College Annual Herbert L. James Debates. Only the seven most-accomplished debate teams in the nation are invited. At Dartmouth, MSU defeated Harvard, California-Berkeley, Dartmouth, Northwestern, Georgia, and Emory universities. Will Repko was head coach of the MSU debate team.

MSU Eli Broad College of Business students won the Big Ten (Business) Case Competition. It was the second time in three years that MSU was victorious. The team of first-year MBA students included Corrie Brankatelli, Subhamoy Ganguly, Atul Suri, and Jon Wood. They made their winning presentation to Morgan Stanley Dean Witter, an investment banking firm. Team coach Frank Schultz, visiting professor, said, "This was truly an outstanding performance on a very challenging case."

Jared English and Greta Stahl, named Marshall Scholars for 2004—They both were members of the Honors College and were studying at James Madison College. The scholarships pay for graduate study at a British University. MSU has produced ten Marshall Scholars.

Jerilyn Church, a junior in social work, named a 2004 Udall Scholar. Church was one of 80 students selected nationwide to receive the Morris K. Udall Foundation award of up to $5,000 to juniors and seniors in environment-related fields and to American Indian and Alaska Natives in fields related to health care and tribal policy.

Four MSU students earned Fulbright Fellowships in 2004. Kristi Klomp was pursuing a doctorate in fisheries and wildlife and was to study the subject in Jamaica; Michelle Powell was to study cognitive impairment among HIV/AIDS patients in Lusaka, Zambia; Aaron Russell was to study the protection of fish breeding in Malawi, Africa; and Julie Baskin was to study history in Eastern Europe.

Carole Kuehl, senior in microbiology, won an American Society for Microbiology Undergraduate Research Fellowship, which included a $2,500 stipend to conduct full-time summer research at MSU.

Robin Stone, '86, executive editor of *Essence*—the nation's leading magazine for African-American women, authored the book, *No Secrets No Lies—How Black Families Heal From Sexual Abuse.*

Terry L. Grimm, a staff physicist at MSU's National Superconducting Cyclotron Laboratory, won the R.W. Boom Award an honor from the Cryogenic Society of America for work on a next-generation linear accelerator (LINAC). Grimm and an MSU scientific team developed the LINAC, which will be at the heart of the Rare Isotope Accelerator (RIA) project MSU is trying to bring to the university campus. The RIA project would bring 1,600 jobs and an annual $80-million federally funded budget as part of the $2 billion, 20-year endeavor.

MSU Education Experts were included in a $35 million National Science Foundation grant to improve science and math teaching and achievement in K-12 schools. The five-year project was to impact some 400,000 students and more than 5,000 teachers in some 70 Michigan and Ohio school districts.

A $25 Million Grant to Fight Hunger was received by MSU from the Bill and Melinda Gates Foundation. MSU, selected over several universities, will lead a team of researchers in HarvestPlus, which is to develop genetically modified crops to prevent malnutrition. Biochemistry professor Dean Della Penna, a researcher renowned for work in plant cellular, molecular and biochemical processes important to agriculture, was to coordinate the effort.

MSU's National Food Safety & Toxicology Center was awarded a $10.2 million research contract to study the genetics of microorganisms that cause food and waterborne infectious diseases by the National Institutes of Health. Hannah Distinguished Professor Thomas Whittam of the food science and human nutrition, and microbiology and molecular genetics departments, was to head the study.

MSU Joined the University of Chicago and Notre Dame to establish the Joint Institute for Nuclear Astrophysics (JINA). Funded by a five-year $10 million National Science Foundation grant, JINA was intended to foster an inter-disciplinary approach to nuclear astrophysics studies.

MSU Received $5 Million to Fund U.S.-China Center for Research on Educational Excellence—Hong Kong-based Sun Wah Education Foundation donated $5 million to create a joint center run by U.S. and Chinese scholars for the study of effective K-12 schools that will integrate strengths of Eastern and Western educational practices. It will be headquartered at Michigan State, and directed by Yong Zhao, associate professor of counseling, educational psychology and special education.

Zhao said the center will build on the strong international and research focus at MSU's College of Education. Goal of the center is research that will yield effective educational models that can be implemented in schools in China, and that inform educational reform efforts in the U.S., Zhao said. It was announced MSU was already building relationships with professors at Beijing Normal University.

The $1 Billion Rare Isotope Accelerator that MSU has been seeking to bring to Michigan moved a step closer to reality with the U.S. Department of Energy's approval of CD-O status—the Critical Decision Zero statement of mission need—for the new project. In the February 13, 2004 announcement, President McPherson stated that landing the federal project would create more than 1,600 new jobs, and have an annual operating budget of $80 million. When and if the project comes to MSU, it would take a decade to construct the high-tech facility.

McPherson related MSU's strengths for winning the project, "We are the home of the National Superconducting Cyclotron Laboratory, currently the top rare isotope research facility in the nation, and our nuclear scientists are recognized worldwide as leaders in the field." Moreover, MSU is ranked on a par with Massachusetts Institute of Technology as the nation's top nuclear physics graduate programs. And, MSU now awards ten percent of the nuclear science doctorates granted nationally each year, which ranks the university number one in the field.

The Michigan State University-Detroit College of Law's name was changed to the Michigan State University College of Law at the April, 2004 Board of Trustee's meeting.

Eli Broad, '54, pledged $6 million to fund a partnership between MSU and the Detroit Public Schools to recruit and train a new generation of urban teachers.

The Matilda R. Wilson Fund pledged $5 million to create the Matilda R. Wilson "Pegasus" Critical Care Center, an addition to the MSU Veterinary Clinical Center to provide critical care for horses.

Richard J. Metzler, '63, managing director of Trove Partners, L.L.C., funded a new $2 million Hoagland-Metzler Chair in Purchasing Supply Management in the Eli Broad College of Business. The chair honors Professor John H. Hoagland, who was Metzler's advising professor while at MSU.

Greg Bradbury made a $1 million charitable bequest—half for the Business Library, and half to the Eli Broad College of Business.

Kris Steensma made a $1 million charitable bequest to the College of Human Medicine—half to support the College of Human Medicine Endowed Fund for Innovation, and the remainder funding the Steensma Family Endowed Scholarship.

Fred and Katherine Arnold, who in 1998 pledged $1 million to establish the Frederick M. Arnold Wood Products Manufacturing and Marketing Program at MSU, added to their original pledge another generous gift.

Lisa L. Von Moltke, M.D. '87, won the 2004 William B. Abrams Award in Geriatric Clinical Pharmacology from the American Society for Clinical Pharmacology and Therapeutics. She was an associate research professor at Tufts University where she established a drug metabolism research program.

Robert Gustafson, Ph.D. '74, was elected president of the American Society of Agricultural Engineers. He was serving as associate dean for academic affairs and student services in the College of Engineering at Ohio State University.

Katy Barclay, **'78**, was serving as General Motors vice president for global human resources.

Dr. Susan Hendrix, MSU D.O., associate professor of obstetrics and gynecology, was named one of the 2003 Michiganians of the Year by the *Detroit News*. Dr. Hendrix was a key leader in ground-breaking work to find new ways to treat menopause and was Michigan's principal investigator in a national study involving 161,000 women.

James Haveman, M.A. '68, who led the re-building of Iraq's health care system in 2003 and 2004, was named one of the 2003 Michiganians of the Year by *The Detroit News*.

Kathryn Brown, '84, M.M. '86, voice and piano educator at the Cleveland Institute of Music, was performing with the Guarneri String Quartet and the Beau Arts Trio, had won several national competitions, such as the Pro Piano Competition, the San Antonio International Keyboard Competition, and the National Young Artists Competition.

Pamela K. Withrow, '79, was inducted into the Michigan Women's Hall of Fame. She was the first female warden of a male prison in Michigan.

Peggy S. Dunn, '75, M.A. '79, was selected the 2003 Elementary Science Teacher of the Year by the Michigan Science Teachers Association. She was a second grade teacher at Central Elementary School, Okemos, Michigan.

John K. Godfrey, III, '66, was elected mayor of Battle Creek, Michigan as well as to a third term as a city commissioner. He was CEO of Godfrey Jewelers.

Carolyn A. Clifford, 2001, was a co-news anchor at Detroit TV station WXYZ.

Glenda T. Lewis, '96, was a co-news anchor at Detroit TV station WXYZ.

MSU's WDBM-FM was named College Station of the Year by the Michigan Association of Broadcasters and Broadcast Music, Inc. in February, 2004. It was the fourth time in five years that WDBM-FM's staff dominated the awards competition.

Michigan State's University Club celebrated its 75th anniversary. The organization was founded in 1929 as the State College Club. Michigan State President Robert S. Shaw served as the first president of the club, which met regularly for years on the third floor of the Union building.

MSU's Softball Team won its first Big Ten tournament title and earned a trip to the NCAA tournament. Senior pitcher Jessica Beech led the Spartans to victories over Michigan, 5-1; Northwestern, 2-0; and Illinois, 7-5—three of the top four teams in the conference. Brittney Green, senior third baseman, hit a three-run homer to beat Michigan, and hit two four-baggers in the championship game with Illinois. Beech finished the tournament as MSU's career leader in victories (70), strikeouts (643), and shutouts (24).

In the first game of the NCAA tournament, MSU defeated Texas A & M, 5-1. Jessica Beech pitched a five-hitter. Elizabeth Peterson drove in four runs—three on a bases-loaded double in the first inning.

The Women's Water Polo Team (Club Sport) Won Its Fourth Consecutive Big Ten title. The team was to compete for the national championship, a title that MSU had won in 2001 and 2002.

Mateen Cleaves, All-American leader of MSU's 2000 NCAA Championship Basketball Team, was **named to ESPN's Big Ten Silver Anniversary Team.**

Greg Kelser, '79, named for NCAA Silver Anniversary Award, given to former student-athletes who have "distinguished themselves in the 25 years since graduation." Kelser was a TV broadcaster and color commentator for Fox Sports Net. Kelser, MSU's first Academic All-American, was a star performer on the Spartans' first NCAA championship basketball team in 1979.

Sparty, MSU's Mascot, was voted the nation's No. 1 mascot at the Universal Cheer Association/Universal Dance Association National Championships at Orlando, Florida. Sparty debuted in his current form in 1989. The mascot stands seven feet tall in a costume that weighs 30 pounds. Sparty is manned by anonymous students who are screened through interviews and auditions. They must stand 5'10" to 6'2" tall. Sparty was named the "Buffest Mascot" in the country by *Muscle & Fitness* Magazine in 1998.

Maurice Ager, Spartan sophomore basketball forward, scored an amazing 17 points in 5 minutes and 53 seconds against Northwestern on January 21, 2004 as MSU defeated the Wildcats 73-61 at Evanston, Illinois. The scoring included five for five from the three-point line, and a layup. Overall, Ager had 24 points, his career high, on six for six shooting from 3-point land. Two days before the game, coach Tom Izzo stated in a prescient moment that Ager "was poised to explode." The victory was MSU's first on the road, and gave the team an overall record of 8-7, and 3-1 in the Big Ten.

Miracle Win at Minnesota a hinge-point in the basketball season—After losing a heart-breaking overtime away game to Purdue, 79-74, MSU needed a victory to be a Big Ten title contender. The Gophers roared to a 23-point lead (37-14) late in the first half and they led at intermission by 16. In a remarkable resurgence, MSU tied the game at 53. With 2.8 seconds left in the game, Minnesota led 69-66. MSU took the ball out-of-bounds under the Gophers basket. A pass was fired to Paul Davis near the top of the key. He turned and rifled a pass to Maurice Ager who hit a 25-foot three-pointer to tie the game and put it into overtime. The Spartans prevailed in overtime for a miracle 78-77 win on January 28. The team record went to 9-8, and 4-2 in the Big Ten.

Spartans Shoot the Lights Out at Ohio State—In a rare shooting show, MSU hit 11 of its first 12 shots, and 21 of 26 in the first half for an unreal 81 percent. The lead was 48-30. For the entire game the Spartans shot 73 percent from the field, the second best shooting percentage in MSU history, and third best in Big Ten history. The Green and White won 84-70, running the team record to 12-8, and 7-2 in the Big Ten, putting the Spartans in undisputed first place on February 7.

MSU's Cagers Overcame a 12-Point Deficit to Beat Michigan 72-69 at Crisler Arena in Ann Arbor. Chris Hill hit a crucial 3-pointer inside the final minute to cement the win.

A 17-Foot Statue of MSU's Magic Johnson was unveiled in front of the Staples Center, home of the Los Angeles Lakers of the National Basketball Association in February. Johnson led the Lakers to five NBA titles during his career—1980, 1982, 1985, 1987, and 1988.

Women's Basketball Team Reaches a Historic High National Ranking—The Spartan women cagers were ranked No. 15 in one national poll, their highest ranking in history. Coach Joanne McCallie had the team playing high-energy defense, and aggressive offense. On February 12 at Ann Arbor, the Spartans overcame a 17-point deficit to beat Michigan 59-54, their second win over the Wolverines during the season and the fourth consecutive in the series. MSU fought back from a 13-point deficit at the half, and finished the game with an 11-0 run. State committed 14 turnovers in the first half, none in the second. Lindsey Bowen led State with 17 points. The game was played before 4,611, the largest women's basketball crowd in U-M history. The victory gave the Spartans a 19-4 overall record, and 9-3 in the Big Ten.

Women's Basketball Team Advanced to the NCAA tournament second round for the first time since 1997, defeating Arizona, 72-60. Sophomore Lindsay Bowen led the Spartans with 18 points, and sophomore Liz Shimek added 16. The tournament run ended with an 80-61 loss to Texas on their home court.

The Spartan Basketball Team earned its seventh consecutive NCAA tournament bid, the longest current string of NCAA appearances in the Big Ten. In their first game of the tournament, MSU led Nevada by ten points with some nine minutes to play. But then the Spartans failed to score for seven minutes and lost the game 72-66, ending the season with an 18-10 record.

Ice Hockey Team Makes NCAA Tournament for 10th Time in 11 Years. The Spartan hockey players earned a number three seed in the Midwest Region facing Minnesota-Duluth, as one of the "Sweet Sixteen." It was MSU's 23rd appearance in the NCAA tournament. The Spartans entered the tournament with a 23-16-2 record, including a 2-1-1 margin over Michigan. Freshman goalie Dominic Vicari went into the tournament with a nation-leading seven shutouts scored during the regular season.

Drew Neitzel of Wyoming Park High School (MI) Won Michigan's Mr. Basketball Award. Neitzel, an MSU commitment, was the fifth Mr. Basketball in six years to select Michigan State. The others were Paul Davis (2002), Kelvin Torbert (2001), Marcus Taylor (2000), and Jason Richardson (1999).

MSU's Synchronized Skating Team (Club sport) finished fourth in the 2004 U.S. Synchronized Skating Championships in San Diego on March 6.

The university budget for the 2003-2004 fiscal year was $1.4 billion (Current Fund Total Expenditures/Transfers).

Student enrollment was 44,542 in the fall of 2003. During the 2004 commencement, 8,465 degrees were granted.

MSU's Colleges and Study Programs

College of Agriculture & Natural Resources

Dr. Jeffrey D. Armstrong, Dean

www.canr.msu.edu

Michigan State University was founded as the nation's first agricultural college in 1855. America's first course in scientific agriculture was taught at Michigan State by Dr. Manly Miles, M.D. and zoologist (Manly Miles Building) in 1865.

Agricultural education at MSU has evolved into the College of Agriculture and Natural Resources (CANR), which is an international leader, ranked among the top five agricultural schools in the nation, and the leader in global outreach. In a 1994 survey by Penn State University, MSU was the only one of 15 premier agricultural colleges evaluated that had all 13 of its departments and one school ranked in the top ten nationally.

Among these departments, Animal Science, Crop and Soil Sciences, Park & Recreation Resources, and the School of Packaging are considered the best in the country.

The Departments of Agricultural Economics, Entomology and Horticulture are rated either # 1 or # 2 in the nation.

The Department of Forestry established the first professional forestry degree program in the country.

The first Ph.D. program in Agricultural Engineering was established at MSU.

The Construction Management program is recognized as one of the top programs in the United States.

Late in 2003, three departments were merged into one. Agriculture and Natural Resources Education & Communication; Park, Recreation & Tourism Resources; and Resource Development departments formed the new Community, Agriculture, Recreation & Resource Studies department.

The college ranked number one in international programs among 58 agricultural programs in the nation in a 1976 survey by the University of Minnesota, and has remained as the premier agricultural school in international programs and outreach since then. Dr. Sylvan Wittwer, professor emeritus and retired director of the MSU Agricultural Experiment Station, has pointed out that MSU sent the first U.S. university agricultural delegation to the Peoples Republic of China in 1980. Wittwer built an excellent relationship with the Chinese, and in 1987 co-authored

Ag Hall–Headquarters for the College of Agriculture & Natural Resources.

with three Chinese scholars the book *Feeding A Billion* (MSU Press, 1987).

Dr. Fred L. Poston, MSU vice president for finance & operations and former dean of agriculture and natural resources, has stated, "that the College of Agriculture and Natural Resources and MSU have more resources involved in environmental activities than any other university in the U.S."

From 70 to 80 percent of the college's students already have professional positions secured before their graduation.

MSU agricultural students and faculty observe vegetable harvesting by an international company in central England as part of the Study Abroad program.

Award Winning Faculty—College faculty members regularly win national awards and honors and lead national professional academic associations.

In September, 2001, Dr. Michael F. Thomashow, professor of molecular biology, won the Alexander von Humboldt Foundation Award, considered the most prestigious honor for agricultural research in the United States.

Six animal science faculty members have received the Borden Award, the highest honor in the American Dairy Science Association; four have received the American Society of Animal Sciences' highest research award, the Morrison Award; and three have won the Saddle and Sirloin Portrait Award, the cattleman's Nobel Prize.

More than a quarter of all past presidents of the American Society for Horticultural Science have been faculty of the MSU horticulture department. Nineteen faculty or former faculty are fellows of the American Society for Horticultural Science.

The Department of Crop and Soil Sciences has a lengthy list of fellows in scientific societies: The American Society of Agronomy (9), the Soil Science Society of America (6), the Crop Science Society of America (4), the American Academy for the Advancement of Sciences (3), and the Weed Science Society of America (1).

Three members of the Botany and Plant Pathology Department faculty have been selected fellows of the American Phytopathology Society. Professor Will Carlson has been responsible for the development and planting of bedding plants across the state.

Former MSU Dean of Agriculture and Natural Resources James Anderson stated, "I'd put our faculty against anyone. We have a can-do attitude. They are risk-takers and doers."

CANR's Centers, Institutes and Laboratories Make it an International Research Leader

The College of Agriculture and Natural Resources is home to eight centers, institutes, and laboratories:

1. Institute of Agricultural Technology;
2. Food Industry Institute;
3. Institute of International Agriculture;
4. W.K. Kellogg Biological Station, a 4,065-acre reserve, is world renowned for its contributions to ecological science and evolutionary biology (jointly administered with the College of Natural Science);
5. MSU-Department of Energy Plant Research Laboratory;
6. Michigan Travel, Tourism and Recreation Resource Center;
7. The Center for Integrated Plant Systems, a national research leader in pest control and pesticide safety, and the
8. Institute of Water Research coordinates research and educational programs on surface water and groundwater quality and quantity.

The Michigan Agricultural Experiment Station (MAES) provides research and development for agriculture, natural resources and rural communities in Michigan. It embraces the work of more than 330 scientists in five colleges at MSU: Agriculture and Natural Resources, Natural Science, Social Science, Human Ecology, and Veterinary Medicine. Fourteen field research stations located around the state also are part of MSUE.

Michigan State University Extension (MSUE), formerly the Cooperative Extension Service, helps Michigan citizens improve their lives through an educational process that applies knowledge to critical issues, needs, and opportunities. MSU county educators, supported by campus faculty, are serving in all 83 Michigan counties, providing programs focusing on agriculture, natural resources; children, youth and families; and community and economic development.

Animal Agriculture in Michigan Initiative—The Revitalization of Animal Agriculture in Michigan Initiative was launched with a $70 million state appropriation in

1994. The initiative is spearheaded by the MSU Colleges of Agriculture and Veterinary Medicine. The investment is aimed at helping to expand the $14 billion per year animal agriculture business in Michigan by $1 billion per year, and creating up to 22,000 new jobs in the state.

State funding was used to build a Food Safety/Toxicology Center Containment Building, an Agriculture and Livestock Education Center, an Equine Teaching and Research Center, new teaching facilities for the Poultry Teaching and Research Center, the Dairy Teaching and Research Center, a Swine Teaching and Research Center, and a Meats Laboratory and Dairy Plant Project Greeen.

Project GREEEN (Generating Research and Extension to meet Environmental and Economic Needs), the state's plant agriculture initiative at MSU, is a cooperative effort between plant-based commodities and businesses, the Michigan Agricultural Experiment Station, Michigan State University Extension and the Michigan Department of Agriculture to advance Michigan's economy through its plant-based agriculture. Its mission is to develop research and educational programs, ensure and improve food safety, and protect and preserve the quality of the environment.

The combination of agricultural production and food processing represents the second largest industry in Michigan, contributing more than $40 billion to Michigan's economy annually. Michigan leads the nation in the production of ten crops, and ranks fifth or higher in 32 crop categories. Plant-based agriculture—fruit, vegetables, turf, floriculture, woody ornamentals, and field crops—contributed more than $21 billion to the state's economy and generated nearly 75,000 jobs in 2000.

Project Greeen is aimed at decreasing growers' dependency on chemicals, increasing the value of crops through new market development and processing techniques, and improving food safety.

CANR Facilities Among Nation's Best—The college's $22.5 million Plant and Soil Sciences Building, which opened in 1986, is considered the world's finest plant science center.

The $19 million National Food Safety and Toxicology Center, a 124,000 square-foot building, opened in 1996 and solidified MSU as a national leader in keeping the nation's food supply safe. The center is under the direction of the Colleges of Agriculture and Natural Resources, Human Medicine, Osteopathic Medicine, Natural Science, and Veterinary Medicine (lead college for the center).

College Departments—There are eleven departments and one school in the college. All of these offer bachelor's, master's, and Ph.D. degrees. These educational units include: Agricultural Economics; Agricultural Engineering; Animal Science; Community, Agriculture, Recreation and Resources Studies Department; Crop and Soil Sciences; Entomology; Fisheries and Wildlife; Food Science and Human Nutrition; Forestry; Horticulture; School of Packaging; and Plant Pathology.

The Payoff From Agricultural Research and Outreach—There has been an immense payoff to the United States, its citizens and the economy from the investment in agricultural education, research and outreach. In the United States, 12 to 14 percent of the nation's disposable income is spent for food. In Europe it is 30 to 35 percent; in Russia, 50 percent; and in China, 75 to 80 percent.

This world agricultural leadership and expertise has enabled the United States to release vast numbers of people to other professional pursuits.

Distinguished Alumni

Graduates of the college and the positions they have attained include: John Engler, Governor of Michigan; Drayton McLane, former vice chairman, Wal-Mart Corporation; Russell Mawby, former chairman and CEO of the W.K. Kellogg Foundation; Gordon Guyer, president emeritus, Michigan State University; Ken Way, chairman and CEO, Lear Seating Co.; James Kirk, senior vice president, Campbell Soup Company; Dan Wyant, director of the Michigan Department of Agriculture; Mark Hollis, president and CEO of Publix Supermarkets; Salvadore Alemany, former president, University of Puerto Rico; O.D. Butler, retired chancellor for agriculture, Texas A & M University; Robert Helgeson, dean, College of Agriculture, University of Massachusetts; David Topel, dean, College of Agriculture, Iowa State University; the late Liberty Hyde Bailey, class of 1882, the "Father" of American Horticulture; and the late Genevieve Gillette, class of 1920, known as "Miss Michigan State Parks," founder and first president, Michigan Parks Association.

Feeding the Nation and the World; Agricultural Engineering Contributions; Eradicating Disease and Protecting Crops; Developing the Forestry Industry

Michigan State's contributions to feeding America and the world are exceptional. Its agricultural research results stand out and are matched by few other universities.

Dr. Manly Miles introduced the nation's first course in scientific agriculture at Michigan State in 1865. This educational thrust opened the avenues of research into greater food production and protection.

Through the years, MSU scientists have developed and released more than 240 varieties of grains, fruits, and vegetables adding greatly to the world's food supply.

MSU agricultural engineers have developed and designed dozens of automated machines and systems to enhance crop production and protection.

In addition, they have eradicated crop and animal diseases that formerly hurt food production. These breakthroughs have improved the production, quality, and disease- and insect-resistance of dozens of crops important to Michigan and the world.

Moreover, MSU's Forestry Department—the nation's first and national leader—for more than a century has developed silviculture (forestry) systems for major tree species to enhance tree production in Michigan and the Lakes States Region. This on-going research and outreach effort **has been key in sustaining Michigan's $9 billion-per year forest products industry, and literally restored the state's Christmas tree industry.**

Michigan State scientists have been the "Fathers" of hybrid corn; the Michigan sugar beet industry; homogenized milk; the herbicide 2 4-D which kills weeds, but not grass; and hybrid cucumbers.

Food Production

First Hybrid Corn—Dr. William J. Beal, botany professor and the "Father" of hybrid corn, was the first to demonstrate that crossing inbred lines of corn could result in hybrid vigor—thus opening the door to the development of hybrid corn, which almost immediately doubled the yield of corn plantings.

Creation of the Michigan Sugar Beet Industry—Dr. Robert C. Kedzie, chemistry professor and "Father" of the Michigan sugar beet industry, "...imported sugar beet seed from Germany, distributed it to farmers, and helped plan Michigan's first sugar beet factory in 1898." (*Michigan State—The First Hundred Years by* Madison Kuhn). He thus launched an entirely new and profitable industry to Michigan farmers.

Refrigerated Apple Storage and Apple Juice Clarification were advances developed by Roy E. Marshall who joined the faculty in 1920. Clarifying apple juice made the product much more desirable to consumers.

Development of Homogenized Milk—Dr. G. Malcolm Trout, dairy science researcher and professor, and the "Father" of homogenized milk, made the product possible by linking the processes of pasteurization and homogenization in the early 1930s. Homogenization made milk drinking much more palatable by eliminating the cream plugs that previously floated to the top of milk bottles.

Development of Hybrid Cucumbers—Dr. Clinton E. Peterson, crop & soil sciences professor, vegetable breeder, and "Father" of hybrid cucumbers, developed a new method of producing hybrids, thus improving cucumber production and variety.

World's Most Widely Grown Peach Helped Revive the Industry—Dr. Stanley Johnston, class of 1920, director of MSU's South Haven Experiment Station (1921-1969), developed the Redhaven Peach, which by the 1970s became the most widely grown variety in the world. It was introduced in 1940. Johnston's research helped revive the peach industry.

Making Michigan No. 1 in Blueberries—Dr. Stanley Johnston, class of 1920, director of MSU's South Haven Experiment Station (1921-1969), introduced two new varieties of blueberries in 1967. His 25-year research effort enabled Michigan fruit growers to become the nation's No. 1 producer of blueberries.

Michelite Beans Cover Michigan—Professor E.E. Down led the development of Michelite (Michigan elite) beans which were introduced to Michigan farmers in 1937. Within four years "they covered 40 percent of the state's navy bean acreage..." (*Michigan State—The First Hundred Years* by Madison Kuhn). "Michelite beans were estimated to have increased farm income by a sum greater than the entire cost of the Michigan Agricultural Experiment Station since its founding in 1888."

First Successful Apricot East of the Rockies—A new apricot variety called the "Goldcot," developed by MSU scientists and released in 1967, opened the first successful apricot production east of the Rocky Mountains.

Wheat Production Increased 50%—Two new soft, white winter wheat varieties—Frankenmuth and Augusta—introduced by MSU researchers in 1979 increased wheat yields by 50 percent.

First Radioactive Isotope Usage to Track Plant Nutrient Absorption—Dr. Harold B. Tukey, Dr. Sylvan H. Wittwer, and Dr. Martin J. Bukovac—MSU horticulturists—were the first in the world to use radioactive isotopes to follow the absorption of nutrients by plants. They also demonstrated the beneficial effects of CO2 enrichment on the growth of greenhouse vegetables.

Shorter, Faster-Growing Apple Trees Help Fruit Growers—Dr. Harold B. Tukey's research produced dwarf root stocks, enabling the apple industry to grow smaller trees whose fruit could be harvested from the ground, improving fruit growers' efficiency.

Ethephon Hastens Cherry Ripening; Aids Mechanical Harvesting—Dr. Martin J. Bukovac developed the use of ethephon (compound that releases ethylene gas) to hasten the "loosening" of sweet and sour cherries on tree branches to permit automatic harvesting by "catch and shake" machines.

MSU Horticulturists and Engineers Develop Mechanical Vegetable Harvesters—Dr. Stanley K. Ries worked with agricultural engineers to create mechanical harvesters for vegetable crops, including tomatoes and cucumbers.

Maleic Hydrazide Prevents Sprouting of Potatoes and Onions in Storage—Dr. Sylvan Wittwer's early work on the growth inhibitor maleic hydrazide led to commercial use of this chemical to prevent sprouting of potatoes and onions during storage, thus preserving these food products.

Self-Wrapping Cauliflower was introduced by Dr. Shigema Honma, vegetable breeder. His new variety eliminated the need to tie leaves over the cauliflower head to prevent greening.

Prolonging Storage Life of Apples—Dr. David R. Dilley developed new methods of controlling gas mixtures (low oxygen, high carbon dioxide) in enclosed spaces to prolong apple storage life and reduce the danger of explosions.

Pre-Packaging of Vegetables in Plastic was initiated by Dr. Robert L. Carolus.

Plant Cold-Temperature Stress Tolerance Understood Through MSU Research—Dr. Michael Thomashow, crop & soil sciences and microbiology professor, internationally acclaimed for his research on plant environmental stress tolerance to extreme temperatures, has opened the promise of improving not only cold tolerance of plants, but also tolerance to other stresses such as salt and drought.

MSU's Broad Program in Grape Production Research Spurs Michigan Wine Industry—Dr. G. Stanley Howell, Jr. established MSU's Research Winery and led the research program which is a significant stimulus in improving grape production in Michigan. For his contributions to the wine industry, Dr. Howell was presented the 2003 Wine Integrity Award by the Lodi-Woodbridge (California) Winegrape Commission.

Effect of Day-Night Temperature Differences Used to Program Plants for Specific Sales Dates—Dr. Royal Heins discovered that plant growth rate is a function of temperature, and by closely monitoring growth and adjusting temperature appropriately, plants such as Easter lilies can be programmed to be ready for sale on a given date. Dr. Heins developed a computer system for predicting when florist crops would flower, based upon temperature parameters. This research has helped plant growers to reduce costs and prevent losses.

Agricultural Engineering Contributions to Food Production and Protection

MSU's Agricultural Engineering Department has developed dozens of innovative systems and machines that have greatly enhanced agricultural crop production and protection, as well as inventions of useful products made from renewable resources. Many of these invention breakthroughs have become nationwide industry standards.

Ammonia Sod Knife, developed by Dr. Clarence Hansen, injects liquid ammonia into the soil and plant roots, resulting in superior fertilization with minimum disturbance to the soil. It is an industry standard.

Cucumber Harvester, developed by Dr. Bill Stout, chair of agricultural engineering; Dr. Stan Ries, chair of horticulture; and Max DeLong, graduate student, was the first practical once-over cucumber harvester to be commercially manufactured (1963). This system is used worldwide today.

Milking Sensor, developed by Dr. William Bickert and Dr. John Gerrish, detects when the flow of milk from a cow has stopped, and removes the milking machine connections automatically. This also prevents physical damage to the cows.

Potato Harvester and Potato Storage Systems, developed by Dr. Burt Cargill, have greatly improved harvesting efficiency as well as increasing the storage life of potatoes.

Cherry Pitting Machine, developed by Dr. C.M. Hansen, Dr. J. Harvey, and Dr. R. Ledebuhr, automated a previously tedious labor-intensive process.

Asparagus Harvester, developed by Dr. C. Hansen and R. Ledebuhr, allows harvesting and transplanting in one pass. This has boosted productivity in an industry in which Michigan is the second largest producer in the nation.

Sodium-Free Salt Substitute, developed and patented by Dr. Kris Berglund, has been commercialized and sold under the trademarks HalsoSalt and AlsoSalt.

Airport Runway De-icer, developed by Dr. Kris Berglund, is noncorrosive and biodegradable. It is patented, licensed, and in the process of commercialization (2003).

Finger Nail Polish Remover, developed by Dr. Kris Berglund, is safe, acetone-free, and made from renewable resources. It is patented.

Windshield Washer De-icer Fluid, developed by Dr. Kris Berglund, is patented and based on renewable resources.

Chemical Sprayers, developed by Agricultural Engineering, create an "air curtain" and control chemical droplet size to reach inside the canopy of a tree and provide optimal coverage of fruit to control diseases and pests.

Edible Bean Combine—A threshing machine that harvests beans without splitting them. It has been adopted as the industry standard, and also adapted as a peanut combine.

Ice Cream Softening—Introduction of a safe chemical additive, means ice cream can be frozen without becoming "rock hard," a huge benefit in the sale of ice cream.

Slow Moving Vehicle Symbol, developed by Dr. Richard Pfister, is the "triangle sign" that appears on the back of slow-moving farm equipment as well as horse-drawn carriages of certain religious sects. This safety symbol has been adopted nationwide.

Instrumented Sphere for Detecting Impact Brusing—Sphere with electronic circuitry and three accelerometers to detect pitch, roll, and yaw motions, detects shipping impacts on perishable crops, such as apples. Electronic readouts are then used to help design packaging that protects the fruit or vegetable product. This system has been used to develop packaging in the U.S., Australia, Israel and elsewhere. The work involved the Electrical Engineering Department and the School of Packaging as well as Agricultural Engineering—just one example of MSU's cross-disciplinary cooperation.

Onion Peeling Machine, developed by Dr. Ajit K. Srivastava, can peel 2,200 pounds of onions per hour with just two people in attendance. This system has added a value of 30 cents per pound of onions by peeling them prior to shipment for soup-making.

Leafy Green Vegetable Harvester and Buncher, developed by Dr. Don Peterson, greatly increases the efficiency of harvesting these vegetable crops.

Ammonia Injection into Corn Silage to increase protein content by four percent was developed by Dr. C.M. Hansen.

Fruit and Vegetable Decapping Machine, designed by Dr. C.M. Hansen, automatically removes caps from strawberries.

Mechanical Strawberry Harvester, developed by Dr. R.L. Ledebuhr and Dr. C.M. Hansen, cuts the plant off near the ground, separates the plant from the fruit, and places the fruit in a container.

Paristaultic Metering Pump for Air Chemical Application Systems, developed by Dr. R.L. Ledebuhr and Dr. G. VanEe, provides constant application of chemicals to crops at variable speeds.

Grape Mechanization provides grape combing, vine positioning, hedging, cleaning and handling, which adds to productivity, cuts costs, making this low-profit margin industry viable.

Tree Hedging with Double-Sickle Cutter Bar Design—Provides for summer-tipping of cherry trees, and contour-shaping of tree canopies for light penetration to enhance crop yield.

Development of a Michigan Fruit Brandy Industry—Support and assistance by Dr. Kris Berglund.

Articulated Tandem Tractor, developed by Dr. Fred Buchele, allows easy steering of heavy, high-powered tractors, and enables them to turn without losing traction.

Truss-Testing Facility, developed by Dr. Merle Esmay, Dr. Jim Boyd, and graduate student Robert Aldrich, optimizes the selection of the strongest truss designs for farm buildings.

Pickle Harvester, developed by Dr. G.R. Van Ee and Dr. R.L. Ledebuhr (1984); and a second one developed by the same professors, along with Dr. B.D. Wilde, and Dr. C.A. Rotz (1985).

Tomato Harvester, developed by Dr. Bill Stout, and graduate student Max Austin in 1959 and 1960, is used today in more than 4,000 harvesters in the U.S.

World's First Fork-Lift Bulk Fruit Handling, developed by Drs. Levin, Cargill, and H. Gaston, horticulture department (late 1940's). This allowed handling of 20-25 bushel pallet boxes, instead of a single bushel crate.

Tart Cherry Mechanical Harvesting and Handling Systems, developed by Drs. Levin, Hedden, Cargill, Tennis and Bukovack, horticulture department, and U.S. Department of Agriculture (USDA), are now commercially manufactured and used worldwide.

First Blueberry Mechanical Harvesting Methods, developed by Drs. Levin, Cargill, Hedden and Tennes, with the USDA, cut harvesting losses, and improved sorting and handling.

Bulk Handling of Apples in Water, developed by Drs. Levin and Tennes, with the USDA, detects and sorts apples with water cores, which are unsaleable.

First Mechanical Rhubarb Harvester, developed by Drs. Marshall and Dale, and the USDA.

Mechanical Pepper Harvester, developed by Dr. Marshall, with the USDA, made significant improvements in harvesting. About one-half of the mechanical pepper harvesters manufactured in the world use this design.

First Apple-Bagging Equipment which significantly reduced bruising, was developed by Drs. D.E. Marshall, G.K. Brown, R.J. Wolthuis, C.L. Burton, and P.V. Gilliland, with the USDA.

Controllable Amplitude, Frequency Direct Tree-Shaker for improved fruit harvesting was developed by Drs. T. Esch, and G.R. Van Ee.

Effect of Different Light Sources for improved fruit and vegetable sorting was developed by Drs. Brown, Marshall, and Timm, with the USDA.

Disease Eradication, Crop and Environmental Protection

Agricultural and other research efforts at MSU have produced major disease eradication and crop protection benefits for the nation.

Professor Albert J. Cook: Leader in Fungicide Development—Albert J. Cook **(Cook Hall)**, Class of 1862, was a nationally-known entomologist and developer of insect spraying. "Cook discovered that kerosene could be emulsified with soap to provide a cheap, effective spray to destroy plant-sucking insects without harming foliage. He was the first in the country to use a crude carbolic acid emulsion against bark lice, or carbon bi-sulfide as an insecticide." (*Michigan State—The First Hundred Years* by Madison Kuhn).

America's First Tree Fungicide Scientist—Professor Levi R. Taft published the first report on the successful control of an apple scab disease by orchard spraying with copper compounds in 1889. These experiments reduced the number of scab-infested trees from 88% (control) to 12% at an estimated cost of 25 to 30 cents per tree. His teaching and research at Michigan State spanned from 1888 to 1913.

Professor George Wallace: First to Demonstrate Problems With Pesticides affecting the environment. When robins were dying on the MSU campus in the mid-1950s, Wallace discovered the relationship of pesticides to robin mortality. Aerial DDT spraying of East Lansing to cut down on mosquitos turned out to be the culprit. His revelations were later used as the core of Rachel Carson's best-seller, *Silent Spring* in 1962.

Wallace and his family were honored in the early 1990s by MSU President Gordon Guyer, who presented them with an Honorary Degree.

Dr. Gordon Guyer: Instrumental in Developing MSU's Pesticide Research Center—Dr. Guyer, named chair of the Entomology Department in 1963, and future MSU President, led the multi-disciplinary cooperative effort involving 17 university departments to launch the Pesticide Research Center (now Center for Integrated Plant Systems) in 1969. It was another milestone in the University's nearly century-long involvement with successful agricultural pest control and quick reaction to the problems of pesticide contamination and amelioration.

The National Food Safety & Toxicology Center, a 115,000 square-foot scientific facility, was dedicated at MSU in October, 1997. It solidified MSU's national leadership position in keeping the country's food supply and environment safe.

Bang's Disease or Brucellosis (Undulant Fever) was attacked and conquered through research directed by Dr. I. Forest Huddleson in the animal pathology department in the 1920s and 1930s. He developed Brucellergen as a test for Bang's disease in cattle, and Brucellin as a treatment for undulant fever in humans. His work greatly cut farm cattle losses which had been running five million dollars per year in Michigan.

Swine Disease Parakeratosis was eliminated through 1956 research by an MSU research team comprised of an agricultural chemist, a veterinarian, and a swine nutritionist.

An Amoebic Dysentery Treatment—neoarasphenamin—was developed through animal pathology research in 1934.

Disease-Free Poultry resulted from research by Professor Henry J. Stafseth.

Mint Disease Was Attacked through research by Professor Ray Nelson, helping the chewing gum industry to survive.

Cherry Leaf Spot was controlled through the use of anti-biotic actidione. Professor Donald Cation led the research team that developed the process.

Disease-Resistant Wheat—Dr. Everett Everson identified some germ plasma from China and brought it to the U.S. to develop disease-resistant wheat. This work saved Michigan farmers millions of dollars.

2 4-D Herbicide Controls Broad Leaf Weeds Without Killing Grass—Dr. Harold B. Tukey was the developer and "father" of 2 4-D, a major aid in controlling broad leaf weeds.

A Method to Detect and Treat Fabry's Disease—a rare and fatal disease that caused kidney failure—was developed by an MSU research team of Richard L. Anderson, Carol Mapes, and Charles C. Seeley in 1970.

Marek's Disease, A Poultry Cancer, Eradicated—The disease was studied for years by the late scientist Dr. Lee Velicer and researchers at the U.S. Department of Agriculture poultry unit adjacent to the campus. They discovered "a contagious herpes virus was responsible for the disease"and developed a vaccine in 1977 that saved the U.S. poultry industry $200 million per year at that time. Ultimately, the vaccine was used worldwide. (*MSU Alumni Magazine,* 1977 by Jan Bryden and Bob Silber).

Weevils Prevented From Destroying Beans—By tumbling harvested beans in rotary containers twice a day, weevils were prevented from harming the product. The method was developed by MSU Tanzanian graduate student Martha Quentin in 1992.

Using Microbes to Degrade Toxic Wastes in Soil and Water—Led by Dr. James Tiedje, the National Science Foundation Science & Technology Center for Microbial Ecology at MSU has made outstanding progress in developing remediation schemes for pollutants, especially in the understanding of microbes that degrade toxic wastes in soil and water. Dr. Tiedje is a University Distinguished Professor of crop and soil sciences.

Developing the Forest Industry

Michigan's Christmas Tree Industry Restored—Dr. Mel Koelling led the research and outreach that restored Michigan's Christmas tree industry and brought it back to national prominence in the 1980s. Key to the transformation was the move to the Fraiser Fir and away from an over-commitment to the Scotch Pine.

Christmas Tree Industry Protected From Pine Shoot Beetle—Michigan's Christmas tree industry was protected from pine shoot needle damage by tree-growing management practices devised by forest entomologist Deborah McCullough and other MSU scientists in 1993.

MSU System Used Worldwide for Tree-Improvement and Breeding—Dr. Jonathan Wright developed a system of provanance (improved genotypes) testing that is used worldwide in tree-improvement and tree breeding.

MSU Developed "American Spruce" Planted at the White House—Dr. James Hanover developed a tri-hybrid spruce tree (red, white, and blue), named the "American Spruce" in 1976, America's Bi-Centennial. These trees have been planted on the White House grounds in Washington, D.C.

"Spartan Spruce," The First Patented Tree Species in the U.S.—Dr. James Hanover received a patent for a blue-white spruce called the "Spartan Spruce" in 1988. It was the first patented tree species in America.

College of Arts and Letters

Dr. Patrick McConeghy, Interim Dean

www.cal.msu.edu

Seven of Michigan State's 16 Rhodes Scholars have been graduates of the College of Arts and Letters. The college also has produced Marshall Scholars and Mellon Fellows as well as being the home to many National Merit Scholars.

Its **School of Music is known internationally** as a leading professional training ground for composers, music educators, music therapists, and performers. Its Music Therapy Program, initiated in 1944, is the oldest music therapy degree program in the world. The school's orchestra program, which includes four orchestras, is international in scope and the performance quality is the equal of any conservatory or university orchestras in the U.S.

MSU's saxophone quartet won the 2003 National Collegiate Chamber Music competition sponsored by the National Music Teachers Association.

Five U.S. Presidents have been entertained by the Spartan Marching Band—Theodore Roosevelt—1907, Herbert Hoover—1930, Franklin D. Roosevelt—1936, Lyndon Johnson—1965, and William Clinton—1996 and 2001.

The MSU Jazz Studies Program was initiated as an undergraduate degree offering in the 2001-2002 academic year, and is taught by one of the best faculties in the nation.

The Department of Linguistics and Germanic, Slavic, Asian and African Languages is home to the unique "on demand" African language program in which students can learn any one of more than 20 African languages. The MSU Center for Language Education and Research, based in the college, is recognized as a National Language Resource Center by the U.S. Department of Education.

MATRIX, the Center for Humane Arts, Letters, and Social Sciences Online, also is based in the College of Social Science. MATRIX is an international online resource center for humanities and social science teaching and research. It is the host for H-Net, which supports more than 100 free electronic, interactive humanities and social science newsletters that are edited by scholars in North America, Europe, Africa, and the Pacific.

The National Gallery of the Spoken Word recently was located at the college by the National Science Foundation, which is providing $3.6 million in funding. This national gallery revolutionizes audiotape repositories nationwide. It creates a fully searchable online database of spoken word collections spanning the 20th century—the first large-scale repository of its kind.

The Center for Great Lakes Culture, unique in America and one of 16 regional centers partially funded by the National Endowment for the Humanities, is housed within the college.

Arts & Letters: the Leader in Study Abroad Programs—The leader in study abroad programs at MSU, the college is sponsor to more than 50 educational options in more than 20 countries. All of the college's major academic units support one or more study abroad programs.

Liberal Education: Important in Life and Work— Arts and Letters is the center of liberal education at Michigan State. Skills taught by the faculty help students with the ability to think critically, to analyze complex issues, to quickly synthesize information and communicate it effectively in writing and speech. These skills, exemplified in intellectual creativity, are vital in life and work situations. In fact, many employers seek graduates with liberal arts degrees because of their ability to analyze and

Christiane Morel, a Fine Arts Master's student, performs in a 2002 Department of Theater production of the play "Oxygen" at the Pasant Theater in the Wharton Center for Performing Arts.

solve problems, communicate clearly, and to continue to learn and grow intellectually.

Strong Commitment to Undergraduate Teaching—Arts and Letters professors make a major commitment to undergraduate teaching and nurturing new students. They believe this commitment is the building block of education. And because of university requirements for liberal arts courses, every MSU student is taught by members of the college's faculty before they graduate.

Award Winning Faculty—Among many award-winning faculty in the history of the college are: **Russell B. Nye** (1913-1993), remembered as a founder of the academic study of popular culture. Nye was a distinguished English professor and a 1944 Pulitzer Prize winner for biography with his book, *George Bancroft, Brahmin Rebel*. Nye served at MSU for 38 years.

Darlene Clark Hine, Hannah professor of history, who was named one of 12 "Michiganians of the Year" by *The Detroit News* in 2002. Hine, author of a two-volume encyclopedia *Black Women in America* (1993), is considered a national pioneer in the field of comparative black history.

One School and Nine Departments—The College of Arts and Letters is comprised of one school and nine departments, all of which offer undergraduate and graduate degrees: The School of Music, and the departments of American Thought and Language, Art and Art History, English, History, Linguistics and Germanic, Slavic, Asian, and African Languages; Philosophy, Religious Studies, Romance and Classical Languages, and Theatre.

Other Research and Student Support Centers—College centers not mentioned above include the:

Center for Integrative Studies in the Arts & Humanities—Provides resources to the faculty, integrative studies courses to students, support for interdisciplinary arts and humanities teaching and research, and cross-disciplinary interaction among faculty in all areas of the arts and humanities.

English Language Center—Offers the Intensive English Program to all English learners, and English for Academic Purposes Program to MSU students.

Language Learning Center—Offers language-teaching laboratories equipped with computers, internet connections, DVD drives, audio and videotapes.

Residential Option in Arts and Letters—Offers College of Arts and Letters freshmen a residential study program housed in the newly renovated Abbot Hall.

Writing Center—Offers one-on-one consulting services for writers at all stages of the writing process. The service is available to undergraduate and graduate students.

Distinguished Alumni—Distinguished graduates of the college, and the positions that they have attained include: Richard Ford, '66, Pulitzer Prize winner for his novel *Independence Day*; Frank Price, '51, former chairman of Columbia Pictures, and former president of Universal Pictures; William Mechanic, '73, CEO of Fox Film Entertainment (20th Century Fox); Tom Gale, '66, M.A. '67, MBA '78, former Daimler-Chrysler executive vice president who led Chrysler's 1990s car and truck design revolution; William David Brohn, '55, who orchestrated music for *Miss Saigon, Crazy for You*, and *Ragtime*; John Kornblum, '64, U.S. Ambassador to the Federal Republic of Germany; Davidson Hepburn, who served as the Bahamas ambassador to the United Nations; Jim Cash, '70, M.S. '72, and Jack Epps, Jr., '72, who wrote the scripts for the movies *Top Gun*, *Legal Eagles*, and *The Secret of My Success*; Jim Harrison, author of *Legends of the Fall*, which was made into a movie, and author of *Dalva*, and *The Road House*; Dorothy Delay Newhouse, '36, the nation's foremost violin teacher and retired professor of the Juilliard School of Music; Julie Aigner-Clark, '88, founder of the Baby Einstein company, which was sold to The Walt Disney Company; and Peter Morris, M.A. '90, who won the World Scrabble Championship in 1991.

Arts and Letters Rhodes Scholars

Seven graduates of the college have been selected Rhodes Scholars—Douglas V. Steere, Philosophy, '26; John D. Wilson, English Literature,'53; Alan L. VerPlanck, English Literature, '72; Roy D. Pea, Philosophy,'74; Steven Holtzman, Philosophy, '76; Molly K. Brennan, Humanities,'82; and Judith A. Stoddart, English and French,'84. Rhodes Scholarships are awarded annually to only 32 students in the United States, making it one of the most coveted academic honors.

The Eli Broad College of Business and the Eli Broad Graduate School of Management

Dr. Robert B. Duncan, Dean

www.bus.msu.edu

The Eli Broad College of Business was ranked fifth in the nation in a listing of the top ten small business schools (less than 500 MBA enrollees) by the *Wall Street Journal* on September 9, 2002. The survey was based on the opinions of 2,221 M.B.A. recruiters, using 26 criteria. In the same survey, MSU was ranked 13th among the top 50 business schools—both public and private. In this ranking, MSU was rated above the University of California at Berkeley's Haas School, Duke University's Fuqua School, MIT's Sloan School, and Stanford University.

In *The Wall Street Journal's* 2001 survey story, Dwight James, a financial analyst at Delphi Corp. in Saginaw, Michigan, who has recruited at Northwestern, DePaul, and other private schools, stated, "Michigan State students are highly motivated and strong on communications and analytical skills. I don't see a big difference between them and higher-priced graduates at other schools."

Four Core Businesses

The Broad College focuses on four core businesses:

1. MBA Education—Three programs are offered. Recent *Wall Street Journal* rankings listed the Broad MBA as 13th in the nation and 5th among public universities. The MBA Placement Center is ranked as a national leader by Educational Benchmarking, Inc.

2. Undergraduate Education—The undergraduate program was ranked 19th in the nation in a recent *U.S. News & World Report* ranking.

3. Research & Doctoral Education—An interdisciplinary center for information technology research is being established in collaboration with the College of Communication Arts and Sciences, and the College of Engineering. Federal funding for MSU's Center of International Business Research has been renewed. And, a Center for Integrative Research is under consideration.

4. Executive Education—Executive Development Programs are being expanded in conjunction with the opening of the college's new, world-class, $25 million James B. Henry Center for Executive Development.

Broad College Programs Highly Ranked—In the College of Business, **the School of Hospitality Business** (Hotel, restaurant & institutional management) is consistently rated No. 1 or No. 2 in the nation. The school was ranked No. 2 in a survey by the *Cornell University H.R.A. Quarterly* (Hotel Restaurant Administration) of December 1993. The survey was conducted among 343 leaders in academia, and the hotel and restaurant industries. The school was the first to offer an MBA program in hotel, restaurant and institutional management and awarded its first master's degree in 1961.

Founded in 1927, the hospitality school was the second in America and has produced many national and international leaders in the hotel, resort and restaurant industry. The School of Hospitality Business is housed in MSU's Eppley Center and Kellogg Center for Continuing Education—a national leader as a hotel-restaurant training laboratory and as an adult education center.

The Department of Marketing and Supply Chain Management is widely acknowledged by academia and industry as the leader in creating, integrating, and disseminating knowledge in the fields of marketing, procurement, manufacturing, and logistics.

The Department of Accounting's undergraduate program ranks among the top five public programs in the

Financial Analysis Laboratory provides business students with real-time, hands-on training in financial modeling, valuation, and stock trading. Associate professor James Wiggins guides the student experience.

country and educates more Michigan CPAs than any other university.

The Department of Management's Ph.D. programs in organizational behavior/human resource management, and management/strategy and policy are ranked among the nation's finest.

The Department of Finance has been highly ranked in undergraduate education.

Broad College: Five Departments and One School—The Eli Broad College of Business is comprised of five departments and one school: the departments of Accounting, Finance, Management, Marketing and Supply Chain Management, Information Technology Management, and the School of Hospitality Business.

Broad Information Technology Center—The college opened its new Information Technology Center in the fall of 2001. The center includes a financial trading lab, as well as the technology to transmit financial information feeds to most offices and classrooms in the college. Purpose of the center is to permit Broad faculty to give students a state-of-the-art education in investments and to serve as an integrating force for all graduate courses in finance. The center is equipped with trading desks similar to those at financial institutions and investment banks.

International Business Center at MSU—The college's International Business Center (IBC) is home to the Center for International Business Education and Research (CIBER) and has been designated a national resource center by the U.S. Department of Education.

College of Business Has Built Two Overseas Schools—The first business school in Brazil was founded by the Broad College of Business. And, Africa's first North American-style business school also was established by the college.

Broad College Facilities: World-Class—The college's buildings and facilities are as fine as any in the nation. Most of the faculty offices and class rooms are housed in the North Business Complex—a modern, $106 million, high-tech building that connects to the Eppley Center wing.

The Lear Corporation Career Services Center, a new multi-million dollar unit housed in Eppley Center, provides the finest in placement facilities for visiting personnel executives to interview business college graduates. Across the street, in the MSU College of Law Building, is the **William C. Gast Business Library**, a new, state-of-the-art research center.

MSU's Management Education Center, a modern complex in Troy, Michigan, is the home of the Broad College's Executive MBA program which serves Greater Detroit and Southeast Michigan.

The James B. Henry Center for Executive Development, a new, magnificent $25 million facility was opened in 2001, and is connected to the $10 million, 128-suite Candlewood executive hotel, and MSU's University Club.

Distinguished Alumni—Graduates of the college include: Eli Broad, chairman and CEO of SunAmerica Corporation; Robert Stempel, retired chairman and CEO of General Motors; Alex Trotman, retired chairman and CEO of Ford Motor Company; Carl Mottek, retired president of Hilton Hotel Corporation; William Tiefel, retired president, The Marriott Corporation; Coy Eckland, retired president and CEO, Equitable Life Assurance Company; Drayton McLane, former vice chairman, Wal-Mart Corporation; Gary M. McCausland, former president, Domino's Pizza, Inc.; Carmine Guerro, vice chairman, Coopers & Lybrand; James Miller, president, Mazda Motor Corporation, Japan; Louis Ross, retired vice chairman, Ford Motor Co; Raymond Spinola, retired vice chairman, Deloitte & Touche; Frederick J. Schwab, president and CEO, Porsche Cars North America; Michael Ferrari, president Texas Christian University; Phillip E. Lippincott, former chairman and CEO, Scott Paper Company; James Oesterreicher, former chairman and CEO of the J.C. Penney Company; Jerry Myers, president and CEO, Steelcase, Inc.; Donald Riegle, retired United States Senator; Richard H. Ruch, president and CEO, Herman Miller Furniture; James N. Schmidt, former president, Doubletree Hotels; and Peter Secchia, former U.S. Ambassador to Italy.

College of Communication Arts & Sciences

Dr. Charles Salmon, Acting Dean

www.cas.msu.edu

MSU's College of Communication Arts & Sciences is recognized as No. 1 or No. 2 in the nation for its research and quality of educational programs. The college was the first of its kind in the country, founded in 1955.

Graduates of the college have won four Pulitzer Prizes and have been recognized as leaders in telecommunications, journalism, advertising, public relations, and higher education. **Thirteen alumni of the college are members of the Michigan Journalism Hall of Fame.**

The college is housed in a modern $23 million building, which includes the latest in telecommunications facilities and technologies, communication research laboratories as well as studios for MSU's public TV and radio stations—WKAR-TV, WKAR-AM, and WKAR-FM. There also is a studio for the university's campuswide closed-circuit television system.

Kevin Sullivan, telecommunications-information studies-media major, gains real-world TV production experience in fully-equipped TV studio laboratory.

A national innovator, the college's research and development efforts created one of the first interactive telecommunications systems in the U.S. in Rockford, Illinois in the 1970s. In the same decade, the college established a pioneering Telecommunications Department to address what today is called "convergence" of communication systems.

In the 1980s, the college established its leadership Information Technologies and Services Program and Laboratories.

The college is comprised of four departments and one school:

- **The Department of Advertising** was a pioneer in university-based programs in the United States. It has utilized advertising agencies as a real world model for its curriculum.
- **The Department of Audiology and Speech Sciences** is a national pioneer that began as the Speech and Hearing Clinic in 1937. The department's Anechoic Chamber and Reverberant Room qualify it as one of the highest technology research laboratories in the nation.
- **The Department of Communication** is consistently rated at the top across the key areas of interpersonal, organizational, mass communications, general theory and research. In terms of research productivity based on journal article output, several studies show the faculty number one in the nation in mainstream journals over the past three and one-half decades.
- **The Department of Telecommunication**, a leader in communication education, focuses students on the study of the systems, services and institutions that facilitate the telecommunications process, such as radio and television broadcasting, telephony, cable, digital media, the Internet, and virtual reality.

The School of Journalism began in 1909, and has been accredited continuously since 1949. It is **the only accredited journalism program in Michigan**. School alumni have gone on to careers in newspapers, magazines, broadcasting, online journalism, public relations, law, education, business and industry.

School of Journalism graduates have won four Pulitzer Prizes:

1. **Howard James**, Midwest bureau chief, *Christian Science Monitor*, for National Reporting, 1968.

2. **Richard Cooper**, Main Line bureau chief, *Philadelphia Inquirer*, for Spot News Reporting, 1972.

3. **Jim Mitzelfeld,** *Detroit News* reporter, for Beat Reporting, 1994.

4. **Ariel Melchoir, Jr.**, publisher, *The Daily News*, St. Thomas, Virgin Islands, for Public Service, 1995.

***The State News* Long-Time National Award Winner**—Many journalism and advertising majors have served on the staff of the nationally acclaimed *State News*, the university's student newspaper. The staff of this daily newspaper, with a circulation of more than 40,000, has won eight Pacemaker Awards for university newspaper excellence—more than any other university daily in the nation.

College Mass Media Ph.D. Program—The college's Mass Media Ph.D. Program, established in 1973, was unique in America, and is a national model today. It goes beyond the study of communication or media effects and includes public policy and economic elements. The program is run by a collaboration of the Departments of Journalism, Telecommunication, and Advertising.

Study Abroad Programs—The college offers summer as well as semester-long study abroad programs. Summer programs include: Audiology and Speech Science in England; Advertising in France and Italy; Journalism in Great Britain and Australia; and Telecommunications in England, Scotland and Europe. Semester-long programs are offered by the college in: Mexico, Jamaica, and Singapore.

College Home to Four Endowed Chairs

Four endowed professorial chairs are located in the college:

1. The Knight Chair in Environmental Journalism.

2. The Brandt Chair in Public Relations is in the Department of Advertising.

3. The Ameritech Chair in Telecommunication Technologies and Services, and

4. The James H. Quello Chair in Telecommunication Studies.

M.I.N.D. Research Laboratory

The Media Interface and Network Design (M.I.N.D.) Research Laboratory was underwritten by the Ameritech Chair endowment to the college, and is focused on the study of the application of technologies in communication.

Distinguished Alumni

Distinguished alumni and the professional positions they have attained include:

John A. Meyers, retired publisher of *Time* magazine; Gene Jankowski, former president of CBS Broadcasting; Kay Kopolovitz, founder, president and CEO of U.S.A. Networks; James Quello, former Commissioner and Acting Chair of the Federal Communications Commission; Anthony J. Hopp, chair and CEO, Campbell-Ewald Advertising; Clark Bunting, executive vice president and general manager, the Discovery Channel; Wanda Herndon, senior vice president, worldwide public affairs, Starbucks Coffee; Michael Vogel, chair and CEO of PentaMark, subsidiary of BBDO Advertising, in charge of Daimler-Chrysler global advertising for Chrysler, Jeep and Dodge brands; Byron Reeves, director of the Center for the Study of Language Information at Stanford University; Myra McPherson, former chief political reporter, *Washington Post*; Washington D.C. correspondents Tim O'Brien of ABC News, retired, and Susan Spencer of CBS News; James Sterba, *Wall Street Journal* reporter; William M. Fulkerson, president, The State Colleges of Colorado; Edmund C. Arnold, the developer of modern newspaper design; Brad Samuels, vice president, Comedy Central; Charles W. Larsen, president, MTM Television Distribution; Louis Gropp, retired editor-in-chief, *House Beautiful*; Ben Burns, former executive editor, *Detroit News*; Dan Ryan, publisher and editor, *Kalamazoo Gazette*; Dale Stafford, publisher, *Greenville Daily News*; Susan Goldberg, managing editor, *San Jose Mercury News*; Eileen Lehnert, editor, *Jackson Citizen Patriot*; Dale Petroskey, president, National Baseball Hall of Fame; Rex Thatcher, former publisher, *Saginaw News*; George Weeks, political columnist, *Detroit News*; Bill Kulsea, former Lansing bureau chief, *Booth Newspapers*; and Ken Winter, editor and publisher, *Petoskey News-Review*, and president, Michigan Press Association.

College of Education

Dr. Carole Ames, Dean

www.educ.msu.edu

The College of Education's graduate programs in elementary and secondary education were rated best in the nation for the tenth consecutive year in 2004 by *U.S. News & World Report*. Overall, the college had eight graduate programs ranked in the top nine.

A Century of Education Courses at MSU

The first formal course in education at Michigan State was offered in 1902. The subject was the history of education taught by Ms. Maude Gilchrist **(Gilchrist Hall)**, the first Dean of Women. The School of Education was established in 1952, and it became the College of Education in 1955, when Michigan State was designated a university. The oldest unit in the college is the Department of Kinesiology, whose predecessor—the Department of Physical Culture—was established in 1899.

Historical Leader in Research and Outreach

The College of Education's leadership in educational research and outreach is profound. The college has established signature institutes and centers which have developed advanced learning and teaching knowledge, then transferred it to the national and international educational community, and then moved on to other projects.

In 1976, the college won a national competition and established the Institute for Research on Teaching, which ran until 1986.

In 1985, the college established the National Center for Research on Teacher Education, which ran until 1990. In 1990, the college established the National Center for Research on Teacher Learning, which ran until 1996.

College Research

The College of Education's research work now totals more than $12 million annually. During the 2000-2001 academic year, more than half of the college's faculty had funded research projects. The college's 2000-2001 annual report listed 95 current research projects, with funding of $50.5 million.

College Research and Outreach Centers and Institutes

Center for the Improvement of Early Reading Achievement (CIERA)—This center's mission is to improve the reading achievement of America's children by generating and disseminating theoretical, empirical, and practical solutions to persistent problems in the learning and teaching of beginning reading CIERA is a collaborative center of Michigan State University and the University of Michigan.

Center for the Scholarship of Teaching—Has two primary goals. The first is to foster cross-university discussions about teaching and learning, and to engage in activities that will provide insight into improving teaching at Michigan State University. The second is to explore ways to support a scholarship of teaching and learning in local K-12 schools and the university.

The Education Policy Center—Provides timely, credible, and nonpartisan research and policy analysis to key audiences in Michigan's educational system and policy community. The center gives priority to activities that inform policy makers, educational leaders, and broader audiences such as business leaders and school board members about key educational issues and policy developments in Michigan and nationally.

Rudy Hobbs, education major, practice teaching at Spartan Village elementary school class.

Institute for Research on Teaching and Learning (IRTL)—This Institute is an umbrella organization designed to promote, encourage, and enhance research throughout the college.

Institute for the Study of Youth Sports (YSI)—Housed in the Department of Kinesiology, this Institute has been a respected leader in coaching education and research on youth sports for more than 20 years. It's primary goal is to help children and youth develop to their maximum potential through physical activity in the context of sport, including recreation, physical fitness, cultural and other productive activities.

Michigan Center for Career and Technical Education (MCCTE)—Conducts research, disseminates, and evaluates information and provides technical assistance in matters concerning adult education and training, applied academics, assessment, business services and technology, career development, and employment skills.

The Office of Teaching and Technology (OTT)—Provides leadership and support for technology integration in teacher education. It is responsible for the teacher education technology certification, professional development for faculty and teaching assistants in educational technology, and other initiatives involving technology in teacher education.

Third International Mathematics and Science Study (TIMSS)—The College of Education houses the National Research Center for the United States' participation in this effort. Operated in conjunction with the National Center for Education Statistics and the National Science Foundation, TIMSS is a ten-year survey of mathematics and science education in 51 countries.

Kids Learning in Computer Klubhouses (KLICK!)—This innovative after-school program now serves more than 5,000 Michigan students. The college provides the leadership in establishing and coordinating the computer clubhouses throughout Michigan.

Outstanding Faculty

College of Education faculty have held such positions as the presidency of the American Educational Research Association, the American Rehabilitation Counseling Association, the Association for the Study of Higher Education, and the National Association of Sport and Physical Education.

Faculty members also have had prominent roles with the National Council of Teachers of English, the National Council on Measurement in Education, the National Council of Teachers of Mathematics, the National Council of Teachers of Social Studies, and the American Psychological Association.

Prestigious awards such as the Fulbright Fellowship and the Spencer Foundation National Academy of Education Fellowship have been awarded to College of Education professors through the years.

College Departments

The College of Education has been a national leader in improving the education of teachers and students through research, teaching and service.

The college's five-year teacher preparation program has emerged as a national model.

Graduate education in the college provides the opportunity for advanced study and research in 11 Ph.D., three educational specialist, and 11 master's degree programs.

The four departments that make the College of Education a national leader in preparing students for careers in education, are:

The Department of Counseling, Educational Psychology and Special Education offers an undergraduate program in special education and graduate programs in counseling, counseling psychology, educational psychology, educational technology, measurement and quantitative methods, rehabilitation counseling, school psychology, and special education.

The Department of Educational Administration offers graduate programs in adult, lifelong, and higher education, student affairs administration, and elementary and secondary (K-12) educational administration.

The Department of Kinesiology offers cross-disciplinary programs at the undergraduate and graduate levels that relate physical activity to human well-being. Emphasis areas in the graduate program include athletic training, biomechanics, exercise physiology, motor behavior, psychosocial aspects of physical activity, and teaching.

The Department of Teacher Education offers students the opportunity to study teaching, learning, curriculum, and educational policy at all levels of school. This undergraduate program offers a post-baccalaureate certification program, and graduate programs in curriculum, teaching, and education policy.

Office of International Studies in Education

The goal of the Office of International Studies in Education is to find ways to enhance the learning of children, teachers, and other adults in the U.S. while contributing to the worldwide effort of educators to meet the economic, environmental, social, cultural and political challenges of our time.

The college also has collaborated to create educational conditions necessary to sustain development in other nations. A large body of research indicated that a more highly educated population throughout the world is necessary (though not sufficient) for reducing population growth, increasing democracy, fostering economic development, preserving the environment, and safeguarding other fundamental human values.

Moreover, the college has made a commitment to help U.S. educators become more internationally oriented. This includes a computer system linking all types of teachers to international cross-cultural education opportunities; specialized international education courses; study abroad; outreach to international schools; and support for international students.

Distinguished Alumni

Graduates of the college and the positions they have attained, include Dr. Norman A. Brown, former president and chief operating officer of the W.K. Kellogg Foundation; Dr. Stanley Ikenberry, M.A. '57, Ph.D. '60, former president of the University of Illinois, and past president of the American Council on Education; Surat Silpa-Anan, Ph.D. '72, senator, Thailand National Parliament's House of Senate, and chair of the Thailand Education Reform Committee; Dr.Kuk Bom Shin, president of the Korea National University of Education; Dr. James Votruba, president Northern Kentucky University; Panom Pongpaibool, M.A. '70, Ph.D. '74, permanent secretary of the Thailand Ministry of Education; Gerald Tirozzi, former assistant secretary of education for elementary and secondary education at the U.S. Department of Education, executive director of the National Association of Secondary School Principals; Sharif Shakrani, MA '69, Ph.D. '73, deputy executive director of the National Assessment Governing Board; and Lou Anna Simon, Ph.D. '74, Michigan State University Provost, elected MSU's 20th president, effective January 1, 2005.

College of Engineering

Dr. Janie M. Fouke, Dean

www.egr.msu.edu

MSU's College of Engineering is a national leader in automotive engineering, bioengineering, composite materials research and development, manufacturing and processing engineering, and environmental management and protection.

It also excels in the study of technologies that support the design, development, rehabilitation and security of critical infrastructure systems such as bridges, highways, airports, seaports, and spaceports.

Nation's Premier Composite Materials and Structure Center

The college is home to the nation's premier Composite Materials and Structure Center. This multi-disciplinary research, education, and characterization facility, is one of the nation's largest, located in a non-industrial setting.

Civil Infrastructure Laboratory Dedicated

A new Civil Infrastructure Laboratory, dedicated in the 2001-2002 academic year, is a leadership facility for the design and evaluation of large structures such as bridges.

Mission: To Foster Effective Learning; Provide Beneficial Public Service

The mission of the college is: "To foster effective learning and provide beneficial public service, both based upon the conduct of trend-setting scholarship." The college believes in the engineering dictum: "To wrest technology of matter, energy, and information to the end of improving the human condition." In keeping with this belief is the understanding that "Engineers are problem-solvers."

Six Engineering Departments: Education Rooted in Basic Mathematics & Science

The College of Engineering provides a professional engineering education rooted in basic mathematics and science, with an underpinning in engineering economics. The curriculum is well-rounded so as to produce a well-educated citizen as well as a professional engineer. Both undergraduate and graduate degrees are offered by the college in six departments.

1. Agricultural Engineering—Confronts the global issues of food safety and security, diminishing natural resources, declining environmental quality, and shrinking biological diversity. The education of professionals who can combine biology with engineering in a systems context to seek sustainable solutions that are economically feasible, socially acceptable and environmentally sound, is the mission of the Agricultural Engineering Department. Biosystems engineering majors can choose one of many options—agricultural engineering, natural resources/ environmental engineering, or food and process engineering. Students also may choose biomedical engineering, environmental science, or biotechnology.

2. Chemical Engineering and Materials Science—Chemical Engineering is a broad, versatile profession concerned with the development and application of processes in which chemical or physical changes of materials are involved. This branch of engineering is based on the sciences of chemistry, physics, mathematics, and the biosciences, and is guided by the principles of economics. Four academic options offered in chemical engineering are: biochemical engineering, environmental engineering, food science, and polymer science and engineering. Materials

Andy Fedewa, graduate student, uses Molecular Tagging Velocimetry (MTV), a breakthrough technology that will help automotive engineers develop more fuel efficient engines. MTV measures the velocity field of fluid contained in the Optical Engine (OE) at MSU's Engine Research Laboratory. The MTV/OE research equipment is unique in the world.

Science & Engineering—is the study of mechanical, physical, and chemical properties of engineering materials, such as metals, ceramics, polymers, and composites. The objective of a materials engineer is to predict and control material properties through an understanding of atomic, molecular, crystalline, and microscopic structures of engineering materials.

3. Civil and Environmental Engineering—The science and art of civil engineering helps adapt the needs of people and natural resources to the environment. Thus, the civil engineer is involved in the planning, design, and construction of many of the facilities that make modern life possible. Dams, tunnels, bridges, buildings, housing, highways, airports, water, and wastewater systems are all creations of the civil engineer. Academic specializations within the department include: construction engineering and materials, environmental engineering, geotechnical engineering, pavement engineering, structural engineering, transportation engineering, and water resources.

4. Computer Science and Engineering—Digital computers and digital information are revolutionizing our entire world. The disciplines of computer science and computer engineering are at the epicenter of this exciting revolution. While the core of computing still deals with the storage, processing, retrieval, and transmission of digital information, the fundamental nature of computing has changed dramatically. What were once rather narrow disciplines are now blossoming into a host of new disciplines, impacting medicine, biology, chemistry, music, and art, among others. Along with the traditional fields, computer science and engineering faculty at MSU are conducting world-class research in emerging fields, including biometrics, bio-informatics, evolutionary computing, machine learning, internet computing, wireless networking, and robotics.

5. Electrical and Computer Engineering—The field of electrical and computer engineering has had a significant impact on the life we enjoy today. The impact covers a wide spectrum of activities that range from communications, defense, medicine and transportation to simple household appliances. Recent years have seen this field become more inter-disciplinary with other science and engineering fields. Electrical and computer engineers could be working with a mechanical engineer on a new car design, or a biologist creating a micro-robot that can enter the human body to diagnose and fight disease. Academic specializations within the department include: biomedical engineering; circuits and systems; communications and signal processing; computer engineering and VLSI (very large scale integration); control systems and robotics; electromagnetics and electronic materials; and micro and nano engineering.

6. Mechanical Engineering—is a broad profession that combines design and communication skills with a science base to achieve benefits for society. A mechanical engineer might be involved in the design, building, and testing of power conversion devices like disk drives, washing machines, and automobiles; or medical devices like surgical instruments, prostheses, and heart pumps. Mechanical engineers work in virtually every industry.

Engineering Students Excel in Academics and National Competitions

Students at the college have distinguished themselves academically and in national competitions. MSU engineering majors have won two Rhodes Scholarships—Molly K. Brennan, computer science, 1982; and Robert W. Leland, electrical engineering, 1985; as well as Churchill Scholarships, Truman Scholarships, and National Science Foundation Fellowships.

In national and international competitions, engineering students have won:

1. The American Institute of Chemical Engineering national competition twelve times.
2. The Waste-Management Education & Research Consortium national design competition four times.
3. The World Computer Programming title once, and the national title once.
4. The National Concrete Canoe competition, and
5. Five first place awards in Ford Motor Company's 1993 Hybrid Electric Vehicle Challenge.

Outstanding Faculty

During the 2001-2002 academic year, the college faculty and staff partnered with Microsoft to become the first research institution in the nation providing students with a state-of-the art NET computing environment.

The engineering faculty also participated during the year in 31 invention disclosures and was issued 15 patents.

New books published in 2001-2002 by the faculty included the winner of the prestigious IFAC Control Engineering Textbook Prize, which is awarded every third year.

Distinguished Alumni

Graduates of the college and the positions they have attained, include: Lloyd Ward, '70, retired chairman & CEO, Maytag Corp., CEO of the U.S. Olympic Committee; Kenneth L. Way, '61, MBA '71, chairman and CEO, Lear Corp.; Dr. Richard M. Long, M.S. '67, Ph.D. '70, CEO, National Securities & Finance Corp., Taipei, Taiwan; Robert J. Schultz, '53, MBA '69, retired vice chairman, General Motors Corp.; John D. Withrow, '54, MBA '71, retired executive vice president, Chrysler Corp. and retired president, Lectron Corp.; Lud Koci, retired president, Detroit Diesel Corp.; Dana Squire, '54, Ph.D., retired group vice president, Upjohn Co.; and Charles Brady, '48, retired manufacturing vice president, General Motors Corp.

College of Human Ecology

Dr. William S. Abbett, Acting Dean

www.he.msu.edu

The College of Human Ecology is recognized nationally and globally for its world-class programs in Merchandising Management, Dietetics, Nutritional Science, Child Development, Family and Consumer Sciences, and Interior Design.

The Merchandising Management program is the only one in the nation with an international emphasis.

Trans-disciplinary research programs of the Institute for Children, Youth and Families have received national recognition for excellence.

The Interior Design program was among the first in the nation accredited by the Foundation of Interior Design Education Research.

The MSU Central School Child Development Laboratories are recognized as one of the top two child development labs in the nation, and are acclaimed as model early childhood teaching and research facilities.

MSU's Central School Child Development Laboratories in East Lansing are recognized as one of the two finest such laboratories in the nation, and as a model for early childhood teaching and research facilities.

The Dietetics program is ranked second in the nation, and the Nutritional Sciences program, third.

The college once provided the only program in the Human Ecology profession that was offered with the military—a master's degree program in Community Services at the Kadena Air Force Base in Okinawa.

As early as 1968, the college was first in the nation in producing master's degree graduates for the profession.

National and international recognition have come to the college's faculty for developing and implementing the human ecological perspective as exemplified in the work of Dr. Beatrice Paolucci, Dr. Margaret Bubolz, and Dr. Suzanne Sontag.

Dr. Julia Miller, dean; Dr. Lawrence Schiamberg, associate dean; and Dr. Richard Lerner, professor, published the first *Encyclopedia of Human Ecology* (2 volumes; 2002) ever written.

College History

The roots of the College of Human Ecology go back to 1896, when it was launched as one of the nation's first programs in home economics. It was the birthplace of programs for women at Michigan State University. Both the Colleges of Education and Nursing were first nurtured in the College of Human Ecology.

Two past deans of the college have residence halls on campus named for them—**Miss Maude Gilchrist (Gilchrist Hall),** the first dean, 1901-1913; and **Mrs. Louise Campbell (Campbell Hall)**, acting dean, 1922-1923.

Dr. Marie Dye, dean, 1929-1956, was the first Michigan State female faculty member to hold a Ph.D. degree. The student lounge on the first floor of the Human Ecology building is named for her and for Mrs. Lennah K. Backus, extension specialist in Child Development, 1946-1963.

Home Economics to Human Ecology—1970

In 1970, the college was the second in the U.S. (a year after Cornell) to change its name and its emphasis to Human Ecology from Home Economics. The shift was from "concern for the well-being of individuals and families to the interaction of humans with their environment, emphasizing in-depth study of the reciprocal effects that take place physically, socially, and aesthetically."

College Mission

The mission of the college is to create, extend and apply knowledge to solve critical problems facing individuals and families in their diverse and changing environments. Through the work of the college's three departments, this mission is accomplished.

Department of Family & Child Ecology

Child Development emphasizes the study of the young child, from infancy through the early elementary years. The major offers both teaching and non-teaching options.

Family Community Services focuses on the study of family and human development and on the community programs and services that assist families.

Family and Consumer Resources studies the financial well-being of families throughout the life cycle, including resource development and management, family dynamics and decision-making, family financial management, and basic business principles.

Family and Consumer Sciences integrates a broad range of home economics content with a human ecological perspective and education content for opportunities in teaching diverse audiences.

Department of Food Science & Human Nutrition

Dietetics is a science-based program that studies the relationship between nutritional care, foods, food service management, and human health. The major is approved by the American Dietetic Association. Graduates have career opportunities in nutritional care and counseling and food service operations in health care and wellness programs.

Nutritional Sciences studies the relationship between food nutrients and the physiology and biochemistry of the body. Students have the opportunity to meet admission requirements of professional schools of dentistry, allopathic, osteopathic or veterinary medicine while preparing for graduate study in nutrition.

Department of Human Environment & Design

Apparel Design and Textiles majors study the design, science, appropriate selection, and use of textile products and apparel. Students complete one of the following options: Entrepreneurship, Historic and Cultural Studies, Design Communications, Materials Science, or Applied Art.

Interior Design develops the knowledge and skills to design the functional and aesthetic solutions for commercial and residential interior spaces. Interior Design and Architecture in Europe has been offered as a six-week summer study opportunity each year since 1975.

Merchandising Management students apply business concepts to the study of consumer product distribution. This program is the only major in the nation that offers an emphasis on international merchandising.

Distinguished Alumni

Graduates of the college, and the positions they have attained, include: Nancy G. Belck, president of the University of Nebraska-Omaha; Thomas Miles, former general manager of the Somerset Collection complex of stores in Troy, Michigan—one of the top five upscale shopping centers in the U.S.; Judith Kuipers, chancellor, University of Wisconsin-LaCrosse; Hiroko Sho, first female vice governor of the Okinawa Prefecture; Rebecca Brevitz, founder of Pet Care Service, rated the No. 1 pet care franchise in the country by *Entrepreneur Magazine*; Regina Frisbie, director of home economics services department, Kellogg Company; Karen J. Morgan Elam, former director of consumer affairs for Nabisco Brands; Mildred W. Wahmhoff Johnson, merchandise manager, General Mills Corporation; Dr. Ronald Cichy, director of the School of Hospitality at Michigan State University; Dr. Gail L. Imig, former director of MSU Extension; Dr. Cecilia A. Florencio, dean of the College of Home Economics, University of the Philippines; Dr. Barbara S. Stowe, dean emeritus of the College of Human Ecology and Assistant Director, Agricultural Experiment Station, Kansas State University; and Dr. Bonita W. Wyse, dean emeritus of the College of Family Life, Utah State University.

College of Human Medicine

Dr. Glenn C. Davis, Dean

www.chm.msu.edu

Andrew Hunt, M.D., the founding dean of the College of Human Medicine (CHM), was attracted to MSU from Stanford University by **the opportunity to create a new kind of medical school that would produce a new kind of primary care physician.** The college was founded in 1964 in response to Michigan's need for more doctor's who were focused on primary care.

"Fundamentally Altering Medical Education"

"Dr. Hunt's vision for fundamentally altering medical education," according to Dr. Ruth Hoppe, Associate Dean of the CHM in 2002, was three-fold:

"First, make sure students understood the centrality of the doctor-patient relationship;

Second, expose students to more than the hard sciences by including the social sciences and humanities—the psycho-social aspects of medicine; and

Third, create a community-integrated educational system whereby students would receive their entire clinical training in 18 teaching hospitals, two Veterans Administration centers, and a number of community health care institutions in seven Michigan communities—Flint, Grand Rapids, Kalamazoo, Lansing, Marquette, Escanaba, and Saginaw. Students are taught by some 2,000 physicians who practice in these communities." This was a medical pioneering model.

Residency directors at the community hospital campuses have indicated that the MSU medical students are better able to relate to patients and have better clinical skills than students from other medical schools.

Another benefit from the community-integrated medical education system is the fact that graduates remain in Michigan, and many serve in small and rural communities where the need is great. A large number of the physicians in Michigan's Upper Peninsula are College of Human Medicine graduates.

Cost-Effective Medical Education

Michigan taxpayers have benefitted from the cost-effectiveness of the community-integrated medical education approach and the innovative use of resources. MSU was able to by-pass the need for an on-campus university hospital by integrating medical education with community hospitals throughout the state. Moreover, the College of Human Medicine uses existing MSU basic science departments, which have been augmented for medical education, to aid with the development of physicians.

In addition, the college is a leader in cross-collaboration with other colleges at MSU to efficiently teach relevant subjects. This multidisciplinary approach involves seven other colleges: Arts and Letters; Osteopathic Medicine; Engineering; Michigan State University College of Law; Natural Science, Nursing, Social Science, and Veterinary Medicine.

"The early faculty was excited about the possibility of doing something truly innovative in medical education," Dr. Hoppe recalls. Central to Dr. Hunt's mission was responding to the health professional needs of Michigan, specifically focused on direct community involvement in health care.

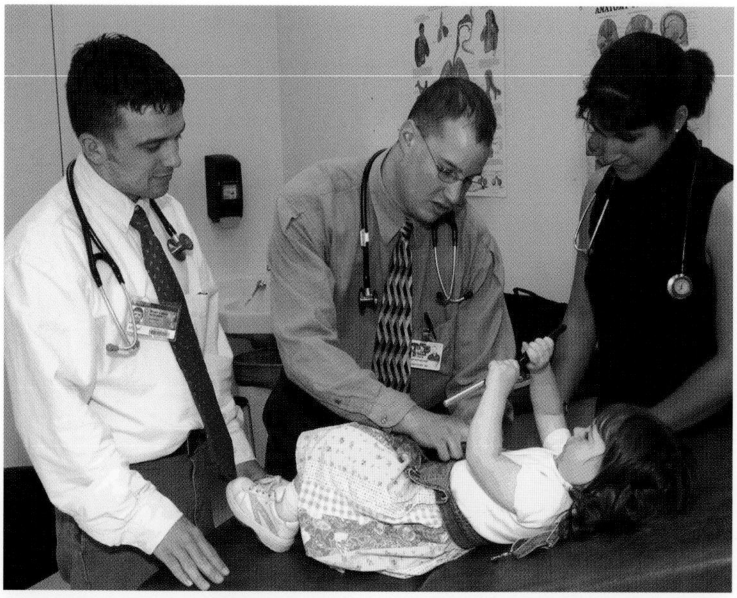

Simulated young child physical examination of Gillian Gaines is directed by Dr. Andrew J. DeHore, center. Medical students Brian Burnette, left, and Stacy Swistak, right, observe.

Revolutionary Curriculum

The college's revolutionary curriculum incorporated social science and the humanities, introducing students to the bio-psychosocial model of medical education. This approach gained a national reputation for a broader student orientation to patients and their care—producing "caring physicians." "Medical schools across the nation are now scrambling to make graduates humanistic, caring, and compassionate—with a scientifically competent background," Dr. Hoppe declares. This was a major contribution by MSU to medical education coast to coast.

MSU's College of Human Medicine also pioneered in the use of "Problem-Based Learning" (PBL)—small groups of students discussing cases from both biomedical and psychosocial perspectives. Instead of attending lectures, they gained their pre-clinical experience in small groups and in independent study. **Although considered radical when introduced, the PBL model gained greater acceptance when it was instituted at Harvard, following a visit to MSU by the Dean of the Harvard Medical School.**

Early faculty members were research leaders in how M.D.s solve clinical problems. This work led to a hypothetical deductive model of clinical problem-solving, which can make the difference between a good diagnostician and one not as skilled. The research was aimed at uncovering best practices, which can then be taught. This has been an historic contribution to medical education scholarship.

Another MSU medical education innovation was the pioneering use of "simulated patients" so students could learn communication skills before their first contact with real patients. This practice has now been adopted by medical schools across the U.S.

CHM Among the Best in the U.S.

Since its early days, the College of Human Medicine has consistently been ranked among the top ten of 144 medical schools in the U.S. in its main mission: the training and education of primary care physicians.

The college's Department of Family Practice, Department of Pediatrics and Human Development, and its internal medicine program are nationally known for their primary care education and research. **The Department of Family Practice is the most highly-funded family practice research department in the nation and is considered the national leader in primary care.** CHM is recognized in medical education circles for teaching professionalism, medical ethics, physician values, and enhancing the patient-physician relationship.

For three consecutive years, the American Academy of Family Physicians presented the college its highest recognition—the Gold Achievement Award—for graduating a high percentage of doctors who choose family practice residency as their specialty.

Some 70 percent of the college's graduates have gone into primary care specialties, about double the national average. A leader in community-integrated medical education, the college ranks in the top five of 25 medical schools that do a major part of their training in community hospitals.

The college's program is structured to emphasize medicine as a helping profession rather than an applied science. The goal is to produce caring doctors, sensitive to the needs of individuals. At the same time, the college provides practical education in cost containment, medical ethics, and preventive health care.

First Medical School With Entering Class of 50 Percent Women

The college was the first non-women's medical school to achieve an entering class of more than 50% women. Today, classes run about 50% men and 50% women. Committed to diversity, the college has a minority enrollment of approximately 20%, which compares with the national medical school average of 12%.

Distance Research and Teaching

Distance research and teaching are a daily reality in the college through the linkage of more than 3,000 physicians state-wide with the MSU computer system and the Internet.

College Departments and Divisions

Altogether the college has 13 departments and four divisions. Six departments are within the college: **Epidemiology; Family Practice; Medicine; Obstetrics, Gynecology and Reproductive Biology; Pediatrics and Human Development; and Surgery.** Two departments, in which the college is the lead, are: **Physiology** (with Osteopathic Medicine, Natural Science, Veterinary Medicine, and the Agricultural Experiment Station), and **Psychiatry** (with Osteopathic Medicine). Five affiliated departments in which another college is the lead are: **Biochemistry and Molecular Biology** (Natural Science-lead); **Microbiology and Molecular Genetics** (Natural Science-lead); **Neurology and Ophthalmology** (Osteopathic Medicine-lead); **Pharmacology and Toxicology** (Osteopathic Medicine-lead); and **Radiology** (Osteopathic Medicine-lead).

The college also has divisions of **Pathology** (joint with Osteopathic Medicine), **Medical Education Research and Development**, the **Center for Ethics and Humanities in Life Sciences, Institute for Health Care Studies, Office of Medical Education Research and Development (OMERAD),** and the **Great Lakes Cancer Institute.**

Distinguished Alumni

Graduates of the college and the positions they have attained, include John A. McDougall, developer of the McDougall Nutritional Program, author of *The McDougall Program* and *The New McDougall Cookbook.*

David Albala, associate professor of urology at Loyola Medical Center in Maywood, Illinois. He helped pioneer laparoscopic adrealectory with his medical research group. He also developed a fibrin-glue compound to halt complicated bleeding and to seal surgical wounds without sutures. He has authored two books, *Textbook of Endurology*, and *Atlas of Endurology.*

Charles J. Fisher, Jr., head of the Section of Critical Care Medicine and Director of the Critical Care Research Unit at the Cleveland Clinic Foundation.

Nicholas Perricone, M.D. '82, published *The Perricone Prescription* (Harper Collins, 2002), which was No. 1 on the *New York Times* best seller list. In his book, *The Wrinkle Cure* (Rodale, 2000), Perricone was credited with "the finest original thinking of the past 25 years in the fields of anti-aging and skin rejuvenation."

James Madison College

Dr. Sherman W. Garnett, Dean

www2.jmc.msu.edu

The James Madison College, one of MSU's academic crown jewels, has produced five Rhodes Scholars, six Marshall Scholars, eight Truman Scholars, ten Fulbright Scholars, five National Science Foundation Fellows, MSU's first George Mitchell Scholar, and the first Carnegie Junior Fellow.

James Madison students represented more than 38 percent of MSU's Phi Beta Kappa class for the 2000-2001 academic year. Phi Beta Kappa, founded in 1776, is a national honor society composed of college students and graduates of high academic distinction.

University of Chicago scholar Allan Bloom, author of *The Closing of the American Mind* and former visiting professor at James Madison, once noted that the brightest students he had ever taught "were not from Harvard or Yale, but from James Madison College."

Founded in 1967 as one of the nation's pioneer residential colleges on a large university campus, James Madison is a world-class pre-law and public policy school. The college offers an Ivy League education at a public university cost, one of the great bargains in American higher education today.

Its three fields of concentration are: International Relations, Political Theory and Constitutional Democracy, and Social Relations. The college also offers specializations in several disciplines.

Study Abroad Programs

James Madison College offers both summer and semester-long study abroad programs, and more than 50 percent of Madison students take advantage of this international enrichment opportunity.

Small College within a Large University

The 1,000 James Madison students have the dual advantage of being in a small college environment, while at the same time being surrounded by the rich academic, cultural and athletic offerings of a major university. The college is housed in the Case residential halls, where students live, and where faculty offices, classrooms, college seminar room, library, dining and recreational facilities are located. The Case Hall grill serves as a place to hang out and is a hub for coffee-house-style informal discussions.

Qualities that distinguish James Madison from residential colleges elsewhere in the nation, include: its own faculty, its own criteria regarding how faculty are hired and evaluated, and its own curriculum. The Madison faculty has won State of Michigan teaching awards, MSU teacher-scholar awards, as well as recognition by the MSU Senior Class Council for teaching excellence. Faculty members have authored dozens of books. Newspaper columnist and TV commentator George Will served on the faculty in the early 1970s.

The grade point average of Madison students is above 3.6. Dean Ken Waltzer said in 1992, "Our best students are as good as the best at Ivy League schools. We can't keep up with the demand for graduates from James Madison."

Writing Demanded in All Classes

Writing is demanded of students in all classes. Speaking and presentation skills are required in many classes. Critical thinking is taught in every class. **Business and government organizations that sponsor internships for Madison students report that "They write better and are better problem-solvers than other students we see."**

Madison Writing Consultancy

The college sponsors the Madison Writing Consultancy, which uses the disciplines taught by the MSU Writing Center to provide writing support to all Madison students free of charge. Peer consultants, who are upper division Madison students, are available to consult with students at any stage of their compositions—brainstorming, drafting, or revising. This is the only writing center located within a college at MSU.

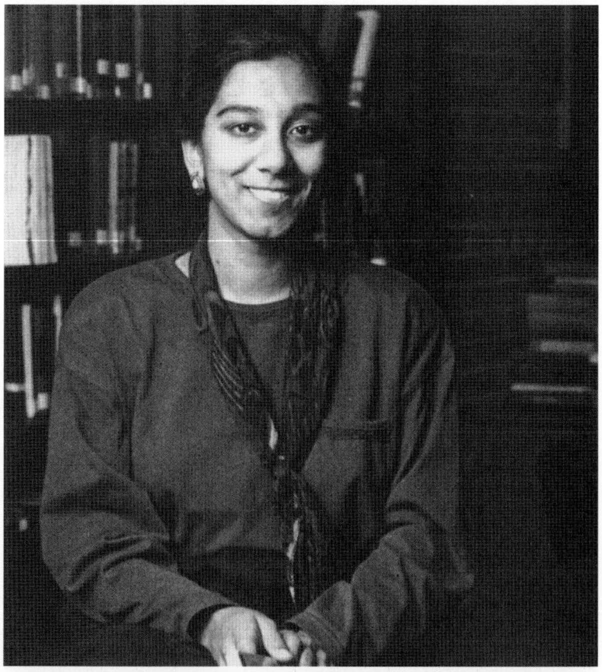

Rujuta M. Bhatt, '93 James Madison & Biochemistry graduate, won Rhodes, Marshall, and Truman scholarships. She is a graduate of the Harvard Medical School and was manager of business development for Millennium Pharmaceutical Industries in 2003. She is one of James Madison's five Rhodes Scholars.

Field Experience

Field experience is required of every Madison student. This enables students to apply what they have learned in the classroom by working for a business, government agency, law firm, or public sector organization related to their career goals. Field experience includes two courses taken during the junior and senior years.

More than 600 business and government organizations sponsor Madison students for internships during their junior and senior years, providing pre-professional experience and contacts that can prove invaluable after graduation.

Madison Curriculum

The James Madison curriculum is organized around three fields of concentration, and several specializations. Each concentration serves as excellent preparation for law school.

Concentrations

International Relations explores the problems of international society and the relations between nations. It deals with the making of foreign policy, the causes of war, conflict resolution, issues of international law and organizations, issues of international political economy, and the political and economic problems of developing nations.

Political Theory and Constitutional Democracy explores the powerful tradition of political thought that has developed in the West during the past 2,500 years. A major concern is the system of values that underlies our contemporary political life. It unites the study of political theory, sociology, politics, and history.

Social Relations focuses on the dynamics of individual and inter-group relations. It examines the relations among class, ethnic, racial, gender, and religious groups as these affect social problems and policies in the United States and internationally. It unites the study of social theory, sociology, politics, and history.

Specializations

Political Economy is a specialization that examines the interconnections between economic organization, social forces, economic power, and government policy—nationally and globally. It is a field of study in economic theory and applied economics and deals with issues of economic growth, industrial and technological change, and inequality.

Other specializations include: African-American history and culture, Asian studies, environmental studies, film studies, Jewish studies, Latin and Caribbean studies, Latino studies, and Russian and European studies.

Graduates have earned positions as the administrative assistant to the Chief Justice of the United States Supreme Court, as staff members in foreign embassies, the U.S. State Department, the U.S. Congress, local Congressional offices, and the State Legislature.

Distinguished Alumni

Among the college's graduates and the positions they have attained, are: Teresa Sullivan, former chancellor, University of Texas-Austin; Randall Smith, '73, president and chief operating officer of NFO WorldGroup, the marketing research arm of the Interpublic Group of Companies, Inc.; John Walters, '74, U.S. Drug Czar or national drug control policy director; Wallace Jefferson, '85, Texas Supreme Court Justice; Rogers Smith, '73, Christopher H. Browne, Distinguished Professor of Political Science at the University of Pennsylvania; Steven Webster, vice president for Governmental Affairs at Michigan State University; Lawrence Pobuda, '82, senior vice president, United Properties Corp., Minneapolis-St. Paul; Susan Shafer, '94, director of communications and press secretary for Michigan Governor John Engler; and Lawrence (Scott) Sheets, '90, National Public Radio's Moscow, Russia bureau chief.

James Madison's Rhodes Scholars

James Madison College has produced five Rhodes Scholars—Mary Norton, International Relations, '77; Claudena Skran, International Relations, '83; Ronald J. Tenpas, International Relations, '85; Rujuta M. Bhatt, International Relations, '93; and Dayne A. Walling, Social Relations, '96.

Michigan State University College of Law

Terence Blackburn, J.D., Dean

www.law.msu.edu

The Michigan State University College of Law was created by moving the Detroit College of Law (DCL) to the MSU campus in 1996. DCL, founded in 1891, was the nation's oldest continuously operating independent law school. The new school is a national leader in offering 15 dual degree programs. **It also is home to America's first Trial Practice Institute located at any law school, and home to the National Trial Advocacy Competition.**

Dual Degree Programs

The new school has enabled the creation of multi-disciplinary programs that combine a DCL legal education with the offerings of four different MSU colleges, and Grand Valley State University.

These are combination JD and Masters degree programs, and two JD-PhD programs. The integrated approach provides for a more comprehensive education in a four-year curriculum.

Certificate Programs

The MSU College of Law offers two certificate programs—Trial Practice, and Child & Family Advocacy.

Trial Practice—This program is covered below under the Trial Practice Institute.

The Child & Family Advocacy Certificate Program provides an effective way to develop the advocacy skills needed to work with abused, neglected, and at-risk children and families. This program is offered jointly with the MSU Graduate School of Social Work. In a volunteer "Chance at Childhood" program, students work in the community to help children and families that have difficult problems.

Nation's First Law School Trial Practice Institute

The college is well-known for producing outstanding trial attorneys and judges. Bolstering this tradition is the new Trial Practice Certificate Institute and Trial Practice Program for students who have a strong desire to be trial practitioners.

With a generous $4 million gift from alumnus Geoffrey N. Fieger, '79, MSU-DCL established the first trial practice institute at any law school in the nation in November, 2001. The Geoffrey N. Fieger Trial Practice Institute is designed specifically to train law students as successful trial lawyers and to establish a set of programs aimed at bridging the law school experience with the practice of trial law in real-world settings.

Moot Court & Advocacy Board

Moot court is the practical and competitive application of legal skills learned in the classroom. Students put these skills to the test in a world-class Moot Courtroom located in the new law building.

The MSU College of Law's Moot Court and Advocacy Board has a national reputation as one of the leading appellate advocacy programs in the nation and is home to the National Trial Advocacy Competition, which is directed by law students.

MSU's Moot Court is a national model, unsurpassed in technological innovation. It is home to the annual National Trial Advocacy Competition, run by MSU students.

Students Win International & National Competitions

In 2003, five law students became the first U.S. team to win the Philip C. Jessep International Law Moot Court Competition. The 2003 victory was won by third-year law students Nic Camargo and Jina Han; and second-year students Joe Harte, David Pizzuti, and Camille Van Buren. The MSU team defeated five other regional winners—Georgetown, University of Michigan, Lewis & Clark, Columbia, and Harvard Law School. Professor Deborah Skorupski, a seasoned judge, was the team advisor.

Law students also won 2003 Best Brief awards at the American Bar Association National Appellate Advocacy Competition, Northeast Regional, New York; New York

New $28-million Law building, a high technology model for legal education in America, was built at no expense to taxpayers.

Young Lawyers Bar Association Advocacy Competition, Region Six; Fordham Securities Law Competition, New York; and Irving R. Kaufmann, Memorial Securities Law Moot Court Competition.

Five Law Concentrations

Students may select one of five concentrations to focus their legal education on an area that interests them the most. Concentrations include: **Corporate Law, Environmental and Natural Resource Law, Health Law, International and Comparative Law, and Taxation.**

Pro Bono Clinics Serve the Community

The College of Law operates two law clinics—the Rental Housing Clinic, and the Tax Clinic—to benefit low-income citizens and give law students an opportunity to put their legal knowledge into practice. This part of the college's mission is to provide service to the community and instill in students the desire to use their legal education for the betterment of society.

Externships Offer First-Hand Experience

With externships—field placements—students gain practical legal training under the supervision of a practicing attorney and a faculty member. Externships include Judicial, Legal Aid, and Government Attorney experiences.

In Judicial Externships, for example, students have been placed with federal, state, local and Canadian courts, including the Michigan Supreme Court, the U.S. Court of Appeals for the Sixth Circuit, the U.S. District Court, and the Ontario Provincial Court.

MSU also sponsors a summer externship program in Washington, D.C., and international externships in Canada and Mexico.

Independent Law School Run at No Cost to the Taxpayer

In an arrangement unique in American legal education, the College of Law retains its independence as a private school—with its own board of trustees—while being affiliated with a large, international research university.

The College of Law is run entirely with private funding. All costs—including faculty and staff salaries—are covered by fees, tuition, and private gifts, which means no cost to Michigan taxpayers.

The college is housed in a new $28 million building which is considered a model of excellence in layout, built-in technologies, and facilities. With its ubiquitous broadband and computer connections, the college is one of the 15 "most-wired" law schools in the U.S. This educational complex is being paid off at the rate of $1.7 million per year at no cost to the taxpayer.

Founded in Detroit in 1891, the Detroit College of Law has produced more than 8,000 graduates who have become attorneys, judges, public officials, and business executives.

Distinguished Faculty

Distinguished faculty in the history of the college have included Frank Murphy and Harold Norris.

Frank Murphy, who taught at the college from 1920 to 1925, served as Mayor of Detroit from 1930 to 1933, and as Governor of Michigan in the mid-1930s. He was appointed Attorney General of the U.S. by President Franklin Roosevelt in 1939, and a year later appointed to the U.S. Supreme Court.

Harold Norris, professor emeritus of the college, first joined the faculty in 1961. He was a delegate to Michigan's Constitutional Convention in 1962. He helped write Michigan's Bill of Rights; and also wrote the provisions prohibiting racial and religious discrimination. Norris was one of the authors of Article V, Section 5, which created the Michigan Civil Rights Commission.

Faculty Experience Spans the Nation

The full-time faculty brings a wide spectrum of legal experience to the classroom. Staff members have law degrees from Harvard, Yale, Columbia, Duke, University of California-Berkeley, University of Chicago, Georgetown, North Carolina, Michigan, Wisconsin, Indiana, Notre Dame, Brown University, San Francisco, William and Mary, Vanderbilt, Wayne State, Detroit, Detroit College of Law, and several others.

The Michigan State University-Detroit College of Law is accredited by the American Bar Association, and is a member of the Association of American Law Schools.

Distinguished Alumni

Graduates and the positions they have attained, include: Clifton E. Haley, retired CEO of Budget Rent-A-Car Corp., and former chairman of Air South Airlines; Kwame Kilpatrick, elected Detroit's Mayor in 2002; Dennis Archer, retired Detroit Mayor and former Justice of the Michigan Supreme Court; Geoffrey N. Fieger, noted Detroit trial attorney; Robert Traxler, retired member of the U.S. House of Representatives; Richard F. Suhrheinrich, Judge, United States Court of Appeals, Sixth Circuit; Philip G. Tannian, former Chief of Police, City of Detroit, member of Tannian & Macuga PC, Detroit law firm; Michael G. Morris, executive vice president, CMS Energy Corp. and president and CEO for Consumers Energy; Honorable Robert L. Templin, retired judge of the Sixth Judicial Circuit; Donald B. Lifton, CEO, Phoenix Steel Corp.; Elliott B. Oppenheim, M.D., author of *The Baseline: Detecting the Doctored Medical Record*, and *A Trial Lawyer's Guide to the Medical Record*; and Ella Bully-Cummings, Chief of Police, City of Detroit.

College of Natural Science

Dr. George Leroi, Dean

www.ns.msu.edu

The College of Natural Science is a world leader in the basic and applied sciences—from astronomy through zoology.

Eminent programs include the plant sciences, structural biology and chemistry, nuclear and high-energy physics, and materials and environmental sciences.

Nationally acclaimed interdepartmental graduate programs include genetics, ecology, evolutionary biology and behavior, cellular and molecular biology, and neuroscience.

Among the college's distinguished alumni are: Nobel Prize winner Dr. Alfred Day Hershey, B.S. '30, Ph. D. '34, for physiology or medicine; and four Rhodes Scholars—Calvin J. Overmyer, '19, chemistry; Paul Hunt, '74, chemistry; Rujuta M. Bhatt, '93, biochemistry; and Stephanie Palmer, '97, chemical-physics.

Dr. Barnett Rosenberg, formerly professor of biophysics and chemistry, and his research team of **Loretta Van Camp, '48, and Tom Krigas**, developed first cisplatin, and then carboplatin. These have been the most-prescribed anti-cancer drugs in the U.S., and among the largest royalty producers for any university in America. As of 2004, these drugs had produced royalties of $300 million for Michigan State University—one of the all-time highest returns from a university research development.

The college's **National Super/ Conducting Cyclotron Laboratory (NSCL)—the world's first**—has earned international recognition for its active program of basic research in nuclear physics and for its innovation in cyclotron design. At the dedication of the K-500 cyclotron facility in 1982, **Dr. Henry Blosser**, director of the super/ conducting cyclotron laboratory, stated, **"This cyclotron and this laboratory will go on to be the leading center in the world for research in the present frontier of nuclear physics."**

At the 1989 dedication of MSU's second and newest cyclotron—the K1200, John Moore of the National Science Foundation stated, **"This cyclotron is the best of its kind in the world.** It's a wonderful example of U.S. leadership—with government and a university working together."

Dr. Wolfgang Bauer, chair of the department of physics and astronomy, stated in 2001, "It (NSCL) has produced many results at the leading edge of the worldwide nuclear science effort and helped us gain a thorough understanding of the nuclear structure and the reactions of nuclei. **The research conducted here has been widely recognized and led to the current ranking of MSU's nuclear science group as number two in the entire nation, only slightly behind MIT."**

By 2004, MSU's nuclear science research and curriculum was vying with MIT as the top program in America, producing one of every ten nuclear physics Ph.D.s in the U.S.

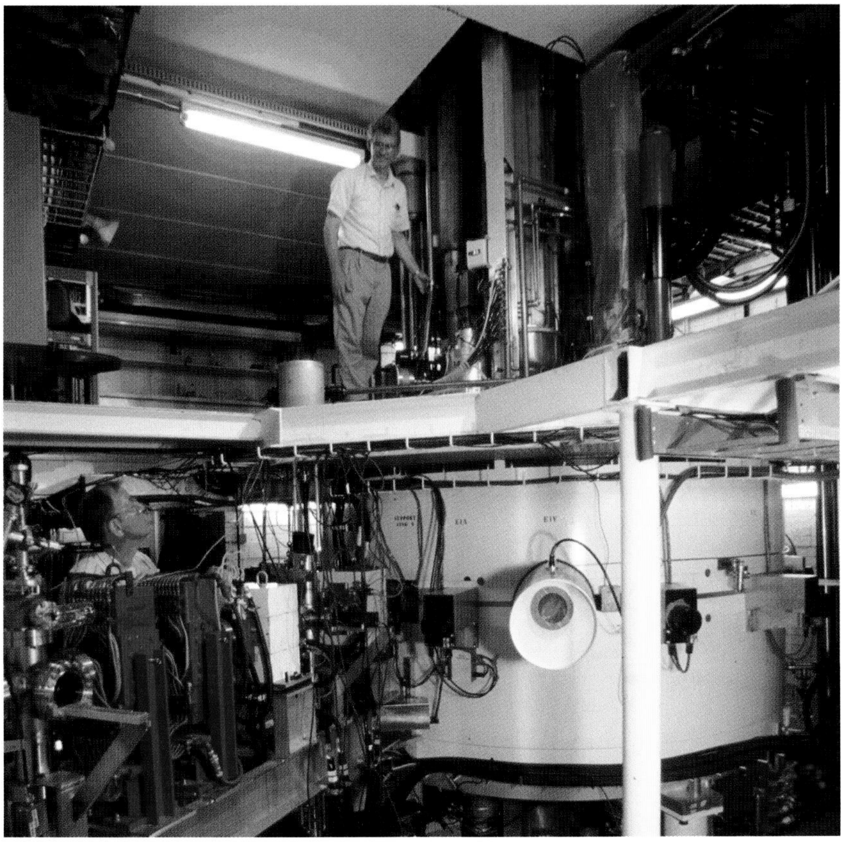

K500 Superconducting Cyclotron—the world's first—which is connected to the K1200 cyclotron at MSU's National Superconducting Cyclotron Laboratory (NSCL), makes Michigan State a world leader in nuclear physics research. MSU's nuclear science program vies with MIT as tops in America. Peter Miller, standing, head of NSCL operations dept. and Harold Hilbert, retired head of fabrication & assembly dept. check the K500. Some 80% of the NSCL staff also are faculty of the College of Natural Science.

"The nuclear science program annual budget of more than $15 million is mainly financed by the U.S. National Science Foundation."

New Coupled Cyclotron Facility

Between 1998 and 2001, MSU scientists worked on a $20-million project to overhaul and couple the K500 cyclotron with the K1200 cyclotron to greatly expand research capabilities. "The purpose of the Coupled Cyclotron Facility," according to Dr. David Morrissey of the NSCL, "is to provide intense beams of nuclear material of any chemical element at energies high enough to create new isotopes across the periodic table. In nature, these isotopes are only created in the explosions (supernova) of stars and haven't been seen in our region of the universe for billions of years." The NSCL is now ready to study the origin of the elements in our Universe. This powerful new system—with its new capability—was dedicated July 27, 2001.

Dr. Bauer, stated, "Teams of scientists from many countries around the world come here to take part in experiments and make use of the world-leading research opportunities provided at the NSCL."

The world's first medical super/conducting cyclotron—K100—was designed by Dr. Henry Blosser at MSU's National Super-conducting Cyclotron Laboratory, and then delivered to Harper Hospital in Detroit in 1990. The new medical tool provided an efficient, inexpensive method of neutron therapy for the treatment of cancers that resist conventional radiation.

At the **MSU-Department of Energy Plant Research Laboratories**, MSU scientists have produced biodegradable plastics in plants. *Time* magazine reported this development as one of the top ten scientific advances of the year in the early 1990s. The college was selected by the Atomic Energy Commission (now the U.S. Department of Energy) in 1964 as the site for a major facility to study intensively the effect of radiation on plant life.

In the **Physics and Astronomy Department**, 40 high-energy physicists are part of an international team of 400 scientists that discovered the top Qwark, while working at the Fermi Laboratory. This discovery advances the understanding of the universe.

Other MSU scientists are working with an international consortium of high-energy physicists in Cern, Switzerland to understand the basic building blocks of matter. MSU physicists are building some of the instruments that will be used in this research.

Major breakthroughs were made in the department in 1991, when MSU astronomer Jeff Kuhn and two associates discovered a galaxy that was considered the largest known object in the universe—a cluster of galaxies called Abell 2029 that was six million light years in diameter. Kuhn, working with a colleague, also took the first infrared color photographs of the sun, using a computerized camera built at MSU.

MSU is a partner in the Southern Astrophysical Research telescope in the Chilean Andes, providing an unparalleled view of the universe.

In the same year, Timothy Beers, physics and astronomy professor, led a scientific team that identified one thousand stars believed to be 15 billion years old—four times older than the sun and as old as the universe itself. In 2001, Beers was "part of a team that discovered gold in an ancient star in the halo of the Milky Way, the first time the existence of the element has been discovered in a star other than the earth's own sun," according to a story by Tom Oswald of MSU's media relations office.

MSU A Partner in Southern Astrophysical Research (SOAR)

MSU astronomers were working in 2002 to build the $43 million Southern Astrophysical Research telescope—a new generation, light-weight, computer-controlled 14-foot diameter optical instrument in the Chilean Andes, which promises to provide an unparalleled view of the Universe. There, on top of Cerro Pachon mountain, the view of the southern sky is scientifically important because the nights are dry and clear all year long. The elegant new telescope will be controlled in part from the atrium of MSU's new $93 million Biomedical and Physical Sciences Building, which opened in 2002.

MSU is a major partner ($8 million) in the SOAR telescope with the University of North Carolina, the National Optical Astronomical Observatories, and the governments of Brazil and Chile.

New Biomedical and Physical Sciences Center—A National Resource

MSU's new $93 million Biomedical and Physical Sciences Center is among the nation's scientific crown jewels.

It was dedicated in April, 2002. It matches or exceeds the best in the nation, and will attract top researchers, faculty and students. At 360,000 square feet, it is the largest and most expensive academic building ever constructed at MSU. It makes the university a national leader in scientific facilities, and is home to the departments of physics and astronomy, physiology, and microbiology. More than a dozen science related departments with 400 researchers have laboratories in the building.

The giant building is connected by skywalks and underground tunnels to MSU's Chemistry and Biochemistry buildings. As part of MSU's science campus, it is in close proximity to facilities for nuclear physics, engineering, food safety and toxicology, and plant and soil sciences.

Two National Science Foundation Centers are located in the college—the **Center for Microbial Ecology** and the **Center for Sensor Materials**.

The W.K. Kellogg Biological Station is a 4,000-acre world-renowned ecological research center which includes the Kellogg Bird Sanctuary, Kellogg Experimental Forest, Kellogg Farm, Kellogg Education Center and Laboratories and Lux Arbor Reserve. This center is located 63 miles southwest of MSU's East Lansing campus. This complex is under the direction of the Colleges of Natural Science, and Agriculture and Natural Resources.

The **Lyman Briggs School** within the college is a popular, stimulating residential science program which attracts top students in pursuit of a basic education in mathematics and science. The School celebrated its 35th anniversary in 2002. The grade point average of entering freshmen is 3.8. Approximately 35 percent of the freshmen in MSU's Honors College are Lyman Briggs students.

Some 1,200 Briggs' students are housed in Holmes Residential Hall, where the school's classrooms, laboratories and offices are located. This living-learning environment provides for small, intimate classes with a rich personal intellectual interaction.

Two other residential living-learning options in the college are: the **Residential Option for Science and Engineering (ROSES)**, and the **Residential Initiative on the Study of the Environment (RISE).**

Major academic areas in the college are:

BIOLOGICAL SCIENCES

Biochemistry and Molecular Biology, Plant Biology (College of Natural Science leads) and **Plant Pathology** (College of Agriculture & Natural Resources leads), —**Entomology** (jointly administered with College of Agriculture & Natural Resources), **Medical Technology and Clinical Laboratory Sciences**, **Microbiology and Molecular Genetics**, **Physiology**, and **Zoology.**

MATHEMATICAL SCIENCES

Mathematics, and Statistics and Probability.

PHYSICAL SCIENCES

Chemistry, Geological Sciences, and Physics and Astronomy.

The college is housed in the Natural Science building, which was the largest of its kind in the world when it was completed in 1949.

Distinguished Alumni

Graduates and the honors and positions they have attained include: Dr. Alfred D. Hershey, 1969 Nobel Prize Winner for Physiology or Medicine; Dr. Gordon Guyer, president emeritus, Michigan State University; Harley Hotchkiss, former president, Alcon Petroleums, Ltd., and of Sabre Petroleums, Ltd., and owner of the Calgary Flames hockey team; Ron Rogowski, vice president of research and development for Quaker Oats; Paul O. P. Ts'o, chair of the Central Laboratory of Molecular Biology in Taiwan, and a world renowned researcher in nuclear magnetic resonance, chemical and viral carcinogenesis, aging and differentiation and the application of computerized microscopic imaging in cell biology; Lorenz Kull, retired president and CEO, Science Application International; B.L.S. Prakasa Rao, director of the internationally acclaimed Indian Statistical Institute of Calcutta, India; Michael Bryman, president, Microsmart, Inc.; and Roger Kolasinski, president, Kol Biomedical Instruments.

College of Nursing

Dr. Marilyn L. Rothert, Dean

www.nursing.msu.edu

The College of Nursing pioneered primary care graduate education in Michigan and is a leader in faculty practice.

A Master of Science degree in nursing was first offered by the college in 1977, and a Ph.D. program focusing on community-based research was initiated in 2000.

Faculty practice leadership has been demonstrated at the MSU Nursing Healthcare Center in Lansing, Michigan. The center is managed by MSU faculty nurses. The center provides a unique, holistic approach to healthcare, is self-sustaining, and has received high ratings and accreditation from the Joint Commission on Accreditation of Healthcare Organizations. The center serves 1,300 veteran patients and more than 500 Ingham Health Plan patients, who are underinsured Ingham County residents.

The college also heads up the Health Care for the Aging: South Washington Clinic for low income elderly citizens living in the South Washington Senior Apartment complex in Lansing, Michigan.

Courses Offered

The College of Nursing offers degree programs leading to the Bachelor of Science in Nursing (BSN), RN to BSN (this program allows RNs with an associate degree to continue working and obtain a BSN), Masters of Science in Nursing (MSN), Post Master's Certificate and Doctor of Philosophy in Nursing (PhD).

Students Taught in 150 Health Care Facilities Statewide

In addition to the education program offered on campus, the college has productive partnerships with 150 health care facilities throughout the state, where 300 clinical instructors and adjunct faculty train students in community hospitals, clinics, physician's offices, and local health departments. This community-based education system provides real-world training for nursing students.

Study Abroad Programs

International education for nursing students is provided through two study-abroad programs.

The nursing in Great Britain program, operating since 1979, is a five credit summer course offered by MSU College of Nursing in collaboration with the Florence Nightingale School of Nursing and Midwifery at King's College London. The course compares nursing education, practice, and health care policy in the United Kingdom and the United States.

The second program is located in the cities of Guanajuato and Celaya, in Mexico. The semester-length program is offered in collaboration with the University of Guanajuato and is open to senior-level MSU nursing students. Students who participate in this program are immersed in the Spanish language and culture and gain a unique perspective on nursing and health care in Mexico.

High-Achieving Students and Faculty

Students who enter the nursing program are strong academically. The mean grade point average of entering students is 3.5, and there are three applicants for each student accepted into the college. Most MSU nursing students have secured positions in the profession prior to graduation.

Four College of Nursing faculty members have been elected Fellows of the American Academy of Nursing. This is an elite national group of 1300 registered nurses who are distinguished leaders in nursing and have been recognized for their outstanding contributions to the nursing profession and to health care.

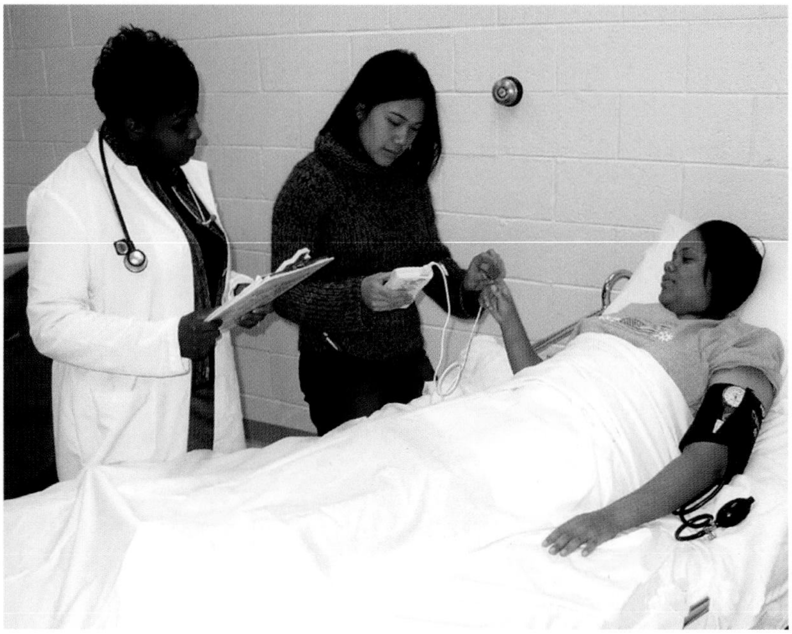

Nursing student learns vital signs procedures under direction of Regina Traylor, RN, MSM, left, assistant director of student counseling at the College of Nursing.

Research

MSU Nursing is recognized for its research in primary care, as well as its research focus on the management of chronic disease and the promotion of healthy families and communities. MSU ranks among the top 50 nursing programs in the nation in funding received from the National Institutes of Health.

The management of chronic disease includes evaluating the needs of family caregivers, developing home care nursing interventions for cancer patients, and assessing the impact of complementary therapies on patient and caregiver outcomes.

The Center of Excellence focuses on research in end-of-life care. And, faculty members working with the Institute of Healthcare Studies focus on cancer screening and other cost effective strategies for management of vulnerable populations. Other major areas of research include decision-making and depression.

Research on the promotion of health in families and communities evaluates Early Head Start Programs. In this study, faculty members examine the importance of communication and role modeling healthful eating behaviors on child development. There also is a study that researches the role of animals in maintaining the health of chronically ill children.

Distance Learning

The College of Nursing was the first college at MSU to use two-way interactive television for distance learning. Students in off-campus and on-campus sites attend classes together using an interactive compressed video system (CODEC).

The college also was one of the MSU campus pioneers with the use of the Web-based courses offered through the Virtual University. Currently the College offers four graduate courses via the World Wide Web.

At this time, the college is developing 27 on-line credit courses and six on-line non-credit professional education courses. The credit courses will offer the core masters level courses on the online and enable students to complete the RN to BSN program through the web.

College of Nursing History

In the summer of 1950, the MSC trustees authorized a Department of Nursing based in the Division of Biological Sciences in the College of Science and Arts. Miss Florence Kempf was the first director of the department.

The department's first graduating class was in 1954. The ten graduates received the highest scores in Michigan on the State Board Licensure Examination. The class consisted of: Barbara Anderson, Patricia Bakke, Joyce Carlson, Marilyn Grigg, Mildred Heslip, Sarea Johnson, Betty Klingelsmith, Margaret Morgan, Mildred Small, and Patricia Watkins.

The nursing education program became the School of Nursing in 1957, and was elevated to the College of Nursing in 1980.

Distinguished Faculty

Barbara A. Given, RN, PhD, FAAN
University Distinguished Professor

Dr. Barbara Given has made outstanding contributions to nursing science with 23 years of continuous NINR funding totaling over $6.8 million. She is the longest funded nurse researcher in National Institute of Health history, and has mentored future Nursing Researchers into the 21st Century. She has received many national awards, some of which included Sigma Theta Tau's Elizabeth McWilliams Miller Award for Excellence in Research, FNINR Pathfinder Award, Oncology Nursing Society's Excellence in Cancer Nursing Research Award and Michigan State University's University Distinguished Professor.

Patricia L. Peek, R.N., C.S., M.S., P.N.P.
MSU Presidential Outstanding Community Service Award Recipient

Patricia Peek has provided volunteer health care, helped to establish health care services for the underserved in her local community as well as her global community. She is a hospice volunteer, volunteer nurse practitioner in the Petoskey Free Clinic, and a team leader for medical missions to Siberia, Jamaica, Romania, and Ukraine.

Louise C. Selanders, RN, EdD
Florence Nightingale Historian

Louise Selanders is internationally recognized as one of the few Nightingale historians. She has published and presented extensively on the topic. Florence Nightingale (1820-1910), English nurse and hospital reformer, was a leader in the development of modern nursing. Selanders teaches a course in England which emphasizes the historical origins of modern, western nursing as applicable to modern practice. She is currently working to define the links between the current profession and its historical past.

Distinguished Alumni

Shirley Weis, Vice Chair of Administration Mayo Clinic-Scottsdale, BSN '75 *Michigan State University Distinguished Alumni Award*

Janice Thompson Granger, Nursing Board of Visitors, BSN '80 *Michigan State University Outstanding Philanthropist Award*

Nance Kline Leidy, Vice President for MEDTAP International, Inc., BSN '75 *Michigan State University Distinguished Alumni Award*

Kathleen Schwartz, President Of Nursing Alumni Association & Board of Visitors, BSN '75
Michigan State University Alumni Service Award

College of Osteopathic Medicine

Dr. William Strampel, Dean

www.com.msu.edu

MSU's College of Osteopathic Medicine (COM) is a flagship osteopathic school in the United States. The only osteopathic medical college in Michigan, it is the first university-based, and first state-assisted osteopathic college in the nation. The college was the first osteopathic school approved by the American Osteopathic Association to administer both residency and internship programs.

COM was ranked fourth in the nation, out of 144 medical schools, for its primary care education in April, 2003 by *U.S. News & World Report*. It is the only osteopathic college in the U.S. that has been ranked in the top ten in primary care by *U.S. News & World Report*.

COM was the first osteopathic college where a person could earn a Doctor of Osteopathic Medicine degree (D.O.) and a Ph. D. All students who graduate in this pioneering six-year medical program earn their D.O. degree as well as a Ph. D. in basic biological sciences. It is the first college to offer joint D.O./Ph.D. degrees in a Medical Scientist Training Program.

COM is the only osteopathic college in the world that is co-located with an Allopathic (M.D.) college—MSU's College of Human Medicine (CHM). CHM students attend certain basic science classes with COM students beginning with their first year of study.

COM was established by the Michigan State Legislature in 1969 to help remedy the state's shortage of primary care physicians. Ninety percent of the college's students are from Michigan. Two-thirds of them are practicing primary care medicine, and two-thirds of them have remained in the state—many working in medically underserved areas.

Dr. Myron S. Magen, D.O., was the founding dean of the college and served in that vital leadership position for 22 years. Commenting on the early years of the college, Magen declared, "The surprise for us was that we quickly became the template for other osteopathic educational institutions that received state support. The formation of this college thrust osteopathic education into the eye of the public…"

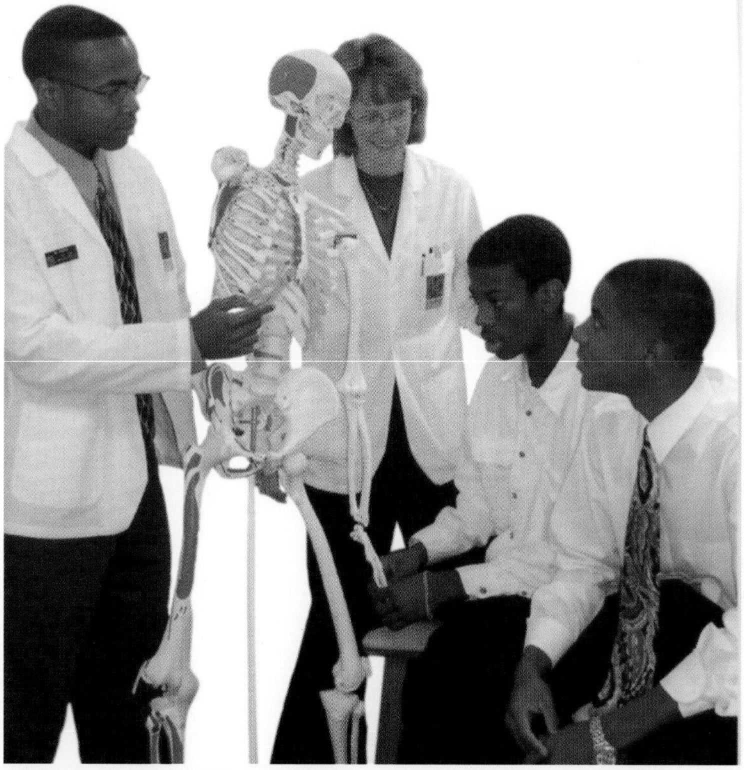

Eric Hawkins, L, and Kristin Gaumer, 2nd from L, osteopathic medicine students, explain human skeleton to Crockett Technical High School (Detroit, MI) students Rondy Goins, R, and Marcus Askew, 2nd from R. This "Osteo Champs" educational outreach program helps in recruiting minority and underserved students, and is part of the College of Osteopathic Medicine culture.

COM's Educational System: A National Model

The college's education system is a national leader, with the final two years of training offered state-wide in 20 different osteopathic hospitals—a Statewide Campus System that has been adopted as a national model. COM pioneered this innovative Consortium for Osteopathic Graduate Medical Education and Training—pooling community hospital and college resources to develop high quality residency training.

This training system has become a national model, and today the osteopathic profession requires each osteopathic hospital to be affiliated with a college in order to be accredited. This requirement has elevated training standards throughout the profession. Besides aiding osteopathic medical services in communities, the statewide training program has eliminated the need for a costly central campus hospital.

The faculty at COM recruits a different kind of student to produce a kind and caring physician. Students with a strong commitment to community service—based upon past volunteer efforts—are actively sought.

Many enrollees are second career people, who tend to be older, and who bring more life experience to the classroom. Dean Strampel states, "We are looking for people who are motivated to become primary care physicians."

The college receives 2,000 student applications annually for 125 educational openings.

Volunteerism: Part of the COM Culture

Volunteerism is part of the culture at MSUCOM. Faculty and students sponsor community health screenings and immunization programs for people who have limited access to good health care.

COM alumni who have provided medical care to the under-served in the state, nation and world, include:

Sister Anne Brooks, D.O., provided care for people in one of the nation's poorest communities, Tutwiler, Mississippi. Her work was featured on CBS's 60 Minutes, ABC's "Good Morning America," and in *People* magazine.

Julie Dixon, D.O. and **Tim Lambert, D.O.**, provided medical care to Native Americans living in the six county area surrounding the Peshawbestown reservation in Northern Michigan.

Joyce Foster-Hartsfield, D.O., provided comprehensive care to members of the large Medicaid population living in Detroit's inner city.

Harry Hernandez, D.O. and **Linda Welch, D.O.**, have traveled to Romania to bring desperately needed medical expertise and supplies to that nation's many orphaned children.

Margaret Pramstallar, D.O., worked with Chippewa Indians in Michigan's Upper Peninsula on a pilot program to attract more Native Americans to osteopathic medicine, so they can return home to serve their people.

The college is a leader in medical research among American osteopathic colleges. COM's first dean, and now dean emeritus, Dr. Myron S. Magen was a missionary-pioneer in introducing medical research into the osteopathic discipline.

Research Units

The MSU Department of Neurology and Ophthalmology, chaired by David Kaufman, D.O., is dedicated to clinical care and research of visual disorders due to brain disease.

The Carcinogenesis Laboratory, directed by distinguished faculty members J. Justin McCormick, Ph.D., and Veronica M. Maher, Ph.D., is one of the nation's premier research facilities using human cells to investigate the genetic changes involved in the development of cancer. This laboratory has achieved international recognition for its basic research of the mechanisms that transform normal cells into cancer cells.

Tropical Infection Disease Research is led by Terrie Taylor, D.O. in the Department of Internal Medicine. Malaria kills one million children under the age of five every year in sub-Saharan Africa. Professor Taylor spends six months of each year in Malawi, South Africa treating children who develop malaria and has conducted internationally recognized research on the disease, and created a unique educational opportunity for students of the college.

Vertical MRI Technology: First at a University

Dr. Malcolm Pope, an internationally recognized and highly regarded spine researcher joined the COM faculty in 2002 as the Patenge Endowed Chair professor. To support Pope's research, COM is acquiring a vertical Magnetic Resonance Imaging (MRI) machine, the first at a U.S. university, and only the second in the nation. Dr. Pope is a pure researcher who holds three doctorates.

Osteopathic Medicine: A Holistic Approach

Osteopathic physicians (DOs) are one of only two types of physicians licensed for unlimited practice of medicine in all 50 states. DOs perform surgery, deliver babies, and prescribe medicine. Like their MD counterparts, they work in hospitals, medical centers, rural clinics, and private offices across the nation. Whether they are family doctors or specialists, DOs use all the tools of modern medicine.

Osteopathic medicine emphasizes a holistic approach to health care. DOs help patients develop attitudes and lifestyles that don't just fight illness, but prevent it. They give special attention to how the body's nerves, muscles, bone and organs work together to influence health. Through osteopathic manipulative medicine, DOs use their hands to diagnose and treat illness and injury, and to facilitate the body's natural ability to heal itself. This whole-person philosophy is the hallmark of osteopathic medicine. It is a century-old tradition of caring for people, not just treating symptoms. Because of this, osteopathic physicians are the most successful alternative to traditional medicine in history.

Dr. Philip Greenman, D.O., emeritus professor and emeritus senior associate dean of the college, is world renowned in manipulative medicine, and has written the classic textbook on the osteopathic approach to patients. The book has been translated into several languages, including German and Japanese.

College Departments

The College of Osteopathic Medicine has 13 departments. Six are within the college: **Family and Community Medicine, Internal Medicine, Osteopathic Manipulative Medicine, Osteopathic Surgical Specialties, Pediatrics, and Physical Medicine & Rehabilitation.** Three departments, in which the college is the lead, are: **Neurology and Ophthalmology** (with Human Medicine), **Pharmacology and Toxicology** (with Human Medicine), and **Radiology** (with Human Medicine). Four affiliated departments in which another college is the lead, are: **Biochemistry and Molecular Biology** (Natural Science-lead), **Microbiology**

and Molecular Genetics (Natural Science-lead), **Physiology** (Human Medicine-lead), and **Psychiatry** (Human Medicine-lead).

Distinguished Alumni

Graduates of COM and the positions they have attained, include: Barbara Ross-Lee, D.O., former dean of the Ohio University College of Osteopathic Medicine; Matthew Terry, D.O., former dean of the Nova Southeast College of Osteopathic Medicine in Florida; Rear Admiral Joyce Johnson, D.O., surgeon general of the U.S. Coast Guard; Eric Deal, D.O., emergency medical doctor in Atlanta, served as director of Emergency Medical Services at the 1996 Atlanta Olympic Village; L. Bing Liem, chief of experimental cardiac electro-physiology in the Stanford University medical system; and Larry Nasser, D.O. and sports medicine professor at MSU, was team physician for the U.S. women's gymnastics team at the 2000 Sydney Olympic Games.

College of Social Science

Dr. Marietta L. Baba, Dean

www.ssc.msu.edu

The College of Social Science is nationally known for its leadership programs in Anthropology, Criminal Justice, Economics, Geography, Labor and Industrial Relations, Political Science, Psychology, Social Work, and Sociology.

The School of Criminal Justice is the nation's oldest continuous degree-granting criminal justice program, established in 1935. It ranks as the national leader in its field and was named one of seven centers of excellence for studies in criminal justice in 1973 by the U.S. Department of Justice. The school's faculty has produced dozens of textbooks and hundreds of articles on every aspect of law enforcement.

The School faculty has led the nation with many "firsts," including: 1. The concept of police-community relations (community policing), 2. The study of highway safety, and 3. The development of the field of industrial security.

MSU's criminal justice curriculum includes forensic science, in which MSU is a national leader. The school is the home of Community Policing, a discipline fathered by MSU's Robert C. Trojanowicz, '63, MSW '65, Ph.D. '69, and adopted by police departments across the nation. The late Trojanowicz explained that the new policing approach involved "a partnership between the formal control system, the police, and the informal system, the people."

In 2002, the Identity Theft University-Business Partnership at the School of Criminal Justice was announced. Unique in America, it works in collaboration with business and industry to prevent thefts of information, including identities.

The Department of Anthropology's research-oriented Medical Anthropology program is internationally known. Its Great Lakes studies program has a strong reputation for its research, teaching and outreach, and is a key participant in the development of the new MSU Center for Great Lakes Culture. **The Department of Economics** has earned global recognition as an international center for the study of applied and theoretical econometrics, and is home to one of the highest ranked Ph.D. programs in the country.

The Department of Geography is ranked among the best in North America and is a research leader on global change studies. It is a national leader in the use and teaching of geographic information science, remote sensing, cartography, and related geographic technologies.

The School of Labor and Industrial Relations is recognized as one of the top four of its kind in the U.S. Its Master's and Ph.D. programs consistently rate among the top offerings in the nation. In 2002, this school established the nation's first and only certificate training program for workers' compensation professionals.

The Department of Political Science has earned global recognition as an international center for the study of compelling policy and philosophy issues, and is home of the renowned LeFrak Forum and Modern Democracy Symposium series. Its Public Law program is rated among the top three in the nation. The department is a pioneer in the behavioral revolution in Political Science, noted for its research on American politics and public policy and political institutions. It is nationally known in the study of policy issues facing state and local governments.

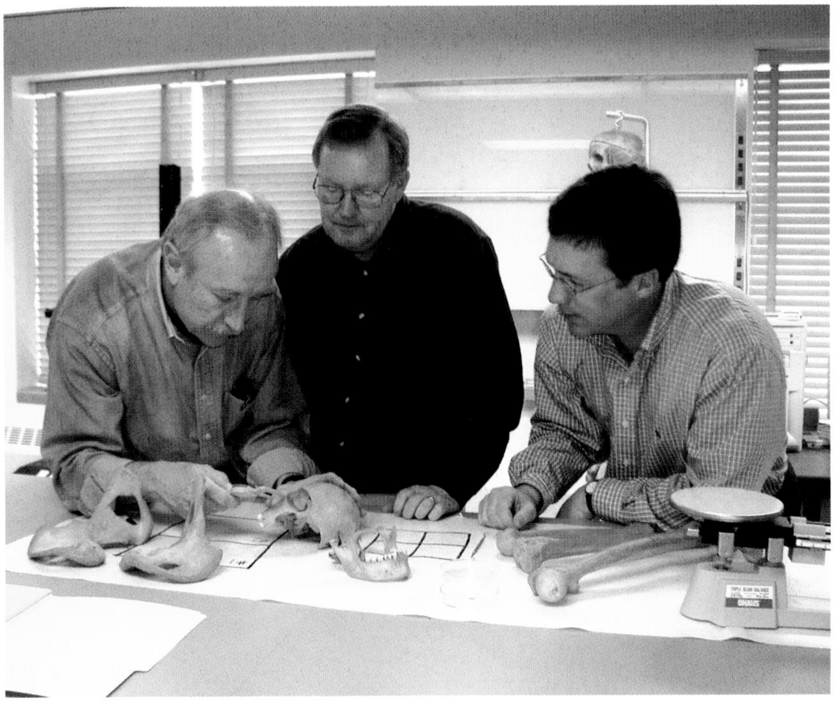

Forensic Anthropology Laboratory–L-R: Professors Norman Sauer, Roger Hunt, and Todd Fenton examine a skull. The lab specializes in human remains cases and is an important resource for local, state, and national law enforcement agencies, including the FBI. Faculty and students using the lab perform DNA testing and laser fingerprint analysis.

The Department of Psychology's Industrial/Organizational Psychology Program is ranked # 1 in the nation by *U.S. News & World Report.* The department's unique Juvenile Diversion project is renowned nationwide for its effectiveness in addressing school violence and juvenile crime. Its neuroscience program is one of the best in the country, addressing research into parental behavior, Parkinson's disease, and the relationship between dementia and stroke.

The School of Social Work's Bachelor of Social Work program is ranked seventh nationally out of more than 400 programs. The graduate program leading to a Master's in Social Work, is ranked in the top third nationally. The school offers a unique child welfare cross-training program for law students, children's attorneys, and health care providers.

The Department of Sociology is a recognized world leader in international migration research, and has one of the top two programs nationally in scholarly resources dedicated to race and ethnicity issues. It is a national leader in family issues, rural and environmental sociology, and interdisciplinary teaching and the use of technology in society. **The Social Research Council has awarded more International Pre-dissertation Fellowships to MSU sociology graduate students than at any other university in the U.S.** The department also is home to the Julian Samora Research Institute—one of the top Latino Studies Centers in the country.

Schools, Departments, Centers & Institutes

The college encompasses three schools, six departments, two programs, and five centers and institutes.

Schools include: **The School of Criminal Justice, The School of Labor & Industrial Relations, and The School of Social Work.**

Departments include **Anthropology, Economics, Geography—which includes the nationally recognized Landscape Architecture**, and **Urban & Regional Planning** programs; **Political Science, Psychology, and Sociology**.

Centers & Institutes

The Center for Advanced Study of International Development (CASID) is a national leader in conceptualizing and acting on key transformations in international development, including globalization of trade, and financial, communications and other networks. Since 1981, **the center has been recognized as a Comprehensive National Resource Center for Foreign Language by the U.S. Department of Education.**

The Center for Integrative Studies in Social Science curriculum provides an interdisciplinary introduction to the body of knowledge, theory, practice, and methods that the social sciences bring to an understanding of the human condition.

Center for Remote Sensing and Geographic Information Science is a cutting-edge leader in geo-spatial technologies applied to human-environmental issues for the MSU campus, the State of Michigan, and other public and private agencies. The center is the state leader in Geographic Information Science applications, remote sensing, cartography, and related geographic technologies.

The Institute for Public Policy & Social Research is the nonpartisan public policy network at Michigan State University. The Institute applies research to pressing public policy issues and builds problem-solving relationships between the academic and policy-maker communities.

The Julian Samora Research Institute is a national leader in multidisciplinary approaches to furthering knowledge, understanding, and social policy on emerging Latino social issues and concerns. Samora, an MSU and Notre Dame professor emeritus in sociology and anthropology, was a pioneer in advancing scientific understanding of immigration, migration, and various social issues confronting the development and advancement of Latinos in the U.S.

Distinguished Alumni

Graduates of the college and the positions they have attained, include: James Blanchard, former Governor of Michigan and U.S. Ambassador to Canada; Debbie Stabenow, U.S. Senator from Michigan and former member of the U.S. House of Representatives, Michigan 8th District; James P. Hoffa, president, International Teamsters Union; Ernest G. Green, one of the group known as the "Little Rock Nine," the first nine black children to integrate Little Rock High School in Arkansas in the 1950s, and a Managing Director with Lehman Brothers investment banking; Schun Hagiwara, president Schun Hagiwara & Urban Matrix, Inc., Tokyo, Japan, a nationally known architect and urban planner; David Lyon, president and CEO, Public Policy Institute of California, and former vice president of the RAND Corporation; Harvey Carey Dzodin, vice president, Capital Cities/ ABC Television Network Group; Kate Pew Wolters, executive director of the Steelcase Foundation; and Martha Bibbs, personnel director, the State of Michigan.

College of Veterinary Medicine

Dr. Lonnie J. King, Dean

www.cvm.msu.edu

The College of Veterinary Medicine ranks among the top five veterinary medicine schools (of 28) in the nation. Recognized as a premier veterinary educational center, the college has produced disease-eradicating, surgical, and clinical research; developed nationally recognized leaders in the profession; and pioneered in the use of electronic education techniques.

John Wesler, dean of the college in 1977, said "the college had a distinguished reputation in companion animal medicine and declared, **'It's the Mayo Clinic for people who bring their animals here.'"**

Leadership by the college is exemplified in:

- **Its world-renowned Large-Animal and Small-Animal Clinical** faculty.
- **Its world-class Containment Center** which studies diseases that have a very high bio-safety level to protect animals and humans.
- **Its nationally known genetics researchers**—who have discovered several genes that cause diseases—"Drs. Vilma Yuzbasiyan-Gurkan and Patrick Venta cracked the puzzle surrounding von Willebrand's disease in Scottish and Manchester terriers, Shetland sheepdogs, and Doberman pinschers; and they also tracked the gene responsible for copper toxicosis in Bedlington terriers," as reported by David Weinstock in the Winter 2000 *Vet Med Alumni News*. Currently they are charting the canine genome—the sum of all the hereditary factors of the dog—in effect, a map of the species' genetic heritage.

  Once completed, it will make it considerably easier for veterinary medical scientists to predict which animals will produce offspring affected by various hereditary diseases and conditions.
- **Its Laboratory for Comparative Orthopadic Research**, a national leader in the basic science investigation of musculoskeletal tissues in all species. The laboratory is directed by Steven P. Arnoczky, DVM. Just one example of its work is the research titled, "Use of Small Intestine Submcosal (SIS) Implants for the Regeneration of Rotator Cuff Defects in a Canine Model."
- **Its Small Animal** orthopedics expertise ranks among the best in the nation. Surgical techniques developed for use on animals have been refined and applied to human surgery.
- **The Mary Anne McPhail Dressage Chair in Equine Sports Medicine**—held by Dr. Hilary Mary Clayton, veterinarian and world authority on dressage—is unique in the world. "Clayton was the first investigator to quantify the biomedical stresses placed on the horse when performing dressage maneuvers and when jumping." According to an article by Tom Oswald and Linda Chadderdon in the Summer 1997 *Vet Med Alumni News*. "Dressage, derived from the French word dresser which means 'to train,' has come to denote both a training method and a competitive sport." The new Mary Anne McPhail Equine Performance Center, a new $2.5 million, 19,000 square-foot facility, opened in 2000, and is the finest in the country.

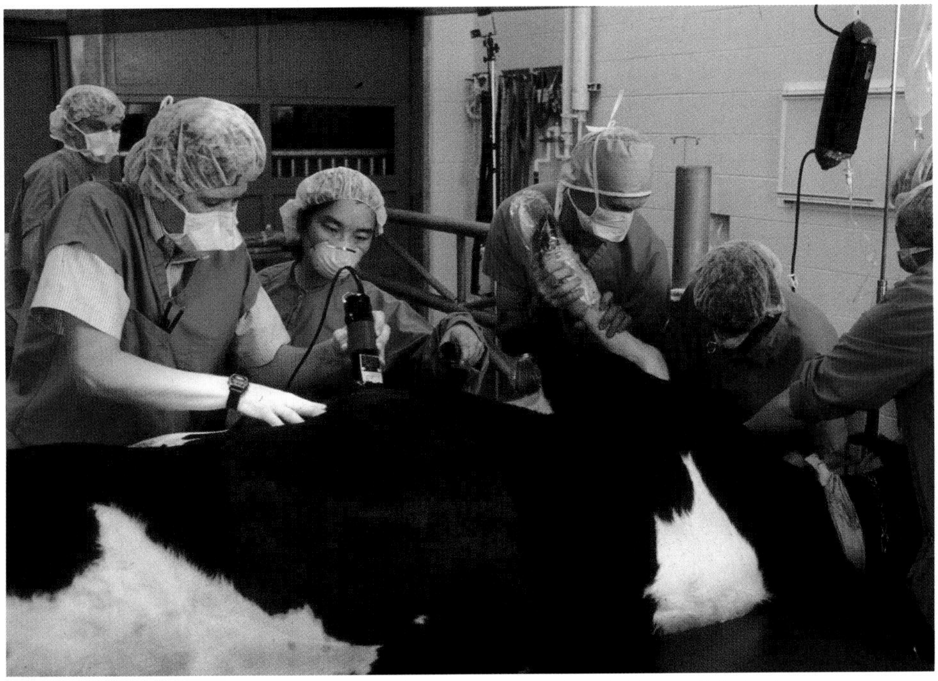

Veterinary students prepare a cow for surgery at the College of Veterinary Medicine's premier Large Animal Clinic.

- **Its Respiratory Research**—Dr. Jack Harkema leads research on the health effects of urban air pollution; and Dr. Ed Robinson leads equine airway research. A 53-foot mobile air research laboratory with the best air quality measuring equipment available, has been used "to analyze the air in urban Detroit and observe how animals with some of the characteristics of human asthmatics respond to the particulate-polluted air," according to a story by Janet Rohler and Tom Oswald in the Fall 1998 *Vet Med Alumni News.*
- **Its new Diagnostic Center for Population and Animal Health**—completed early in 2004—is a world-class facility, and the only one in Michigan. The first center was established in the College of Veterinary Medicine in the mid-1970s, and in 2002 was running more than one million diagnostic tests a year and received more than 500 requests for service per day. Dean Lonnie King said, "Over the past two decades, we have entered into an unprecedented era of infectious diseases. More than 30 emerging or re-emerging diseases have either produced epidemics or serious health problems." "Of these 30 diseases, 75 percent are zoonotic—that is, they are transmitted to people either directly or indirectly through animals and their products." (*MSU Alumni Magazine*, Winter 2003, by Linda Chadderdon, Pattie McNiel and Kirsten Khire).
- The college also has a leadership role in the **National Food Safety and Toxicology Center**, located on the MSU campus. The mission of the center is to conduct research to understand the chemical and microbial hazards in foods, and to use that knowledge to develop a safer food supply for the nation, well-founded public policy, and a greater public understanding of food safety issues.
- **The college is a national leader in computer use.**
- Another leadership example was winning the **Merck Award for innovative veterinary education**.

Academic Departments

Academic departments in the college include: **Large Animal Clinical Sciences**, **Small Animal Clinical Sciences**, **Pathobiology and Diagnostic Investigation**, **Microbiology and Molecular Genetics**, **Pharmacology and Toxicology**, and **Physiology**.

College Professorial Chairs

The College of Veterinary Medicine has six endowed professorial chairs:

- The Wade Brinker Chair of Veterinary Surgery.
- The Matilda Wilson Chair of Large Animal Clinical Sciences.
- The Mary Anne McPhail Dressage Chair in Equine Sports Medicine.
- The Pat Carrigan Chair in Feline Health—to be funded by a bequest.
- The Meadowbrook Farm Animal Chair.
- The Dr. Edward C. Liebler Chair in Veterinary Practice Management and Law at MSU—to be funded by a bequest.

Disease Eradication

The concept of disease eradication was pioneered by the veterinary profession, and MSU researchers have made notable contributions in this activity.

Dr. I. Forest Huddleson established the Central Brucella Laboratory at MSU in the 1920s. His team's research included the development of the rapid aglutination test for the diagnosis of the disease—the key to the eradication of brucellosis, also known as Bang's disease or undulant fever, which was transmitted from animals to humans.

Dr. C.E. Marshall, in 1899, wrote papers on "Killing the Tubercle Bacillus in Milk," and "Pasteurization of Milk." His informational alert helped stop the transfer of tuberculosis through tainted milk. Pasteurization was not common before 1920, and was not mandated in Michigan until 1948.

MSU also is credited with development of the first vaccine for Marek's Disease, a major leukemia-like ailment in poultry.

Disease eradication and control and food safety still are prime objectives of the college. Parasitology research at MSU has national stature and investigates the problems of the parasitical transfer of disease from animals to humans, and from parasites to animals.

Orthopedic Surgical Leader

Dr. Wade O. Brinker, who first joined the faculty in 1939, established an international reputation in repairing fractured bones in dogs, and devised unique surgical materials and procedures.

Comparative Medical Studies

As the only university in the nation with three colleges of medicine (Human, Osteopathic and Veterinary), Michigan State has a unique opportunity to conduct comparative medical studies—bridging the gap between animal disease research and human disease research. This knowledge coordination and synthesis may prove fruitful in combating some major diseases. Cats, for example, have viruses related to chronic diseases that have a similarity with AIDS. Viral research in this area could prove to be highly productive.

College History

Animal physiology and "veterinary" courses were offered at Michigan State from its first year of actual classes—1857. It was not until 1883, however, that a veterinarian—Dr. Edward A.A. Grange—was added to the faculty to teach a full-year course designed to enlighten prospective stockmen, not to train practitioners.

In 1910, the State Board of Agriculture (now MSU Board of Trustees) created the Veterinary Division and hired Dr. Richard P. Lyman as its first dean. Lyman was a graduate of the Massachusetts Agricultural College and Harvard Veterinary School. He had practiced for 17 years, and taught for several years at the Kansas City Veterinary College.

Leader in Electronic Education

In 1961, the college pioneered the use of closed-circuit TV for teaching, and won an American Veterinary Medical Association award. In 1965, a "Telecture" program for the continuing education of veterinarians that reached ten cities won the Creativity Award of the Year by the National University Extension Association's Division of Conferences and Institutes.

In 1968, auto tutorial carrels to teach histology were installed in two campus animal labs.

Leader in Computer Use

In the use of computers, the college is a leader among veterinary schools in the nation. Reaching back to 1987, former Dean Waldo F. Keller was using electronic mail to communicate with colleagues. He led the profession in encouraging faculty and students to use computers to deliver information, and promote interactive discussions and problem-solving. To facilitate computer understanding, the **Keller Education Center** was established in the college.

First Computerized Lecture Hall; World-Class Facilities

The first computerized veterinary medicine lecture hall in the United States was opened at MSU in 1991. It was located in the brand new $28 million Veterinary Medical Center wing that added 157,344 square feet of educational space to create a 353,700 square foot facility.

Distinguished Faculty

Every faculty member holds a doctor of veterinary medicine degree, and/or a doctor of philosophy degree. Seventeen of the 20 specialty boards recognized by the American Veterinary Medical Association have MSU veterinary medicine faculty on them. Many of the faculty members are national or international leaders in their specialties.

Distinguished Alumni

Graduates of the college and the positions they have attained, include: Dr. James H. Steele, DVM '41, former Assistant Surgeon General for Veterinary Affairs, U.S. Public Health Service—the highest ranking veterinary officer in the federal government, and considered the "Father" of American veterinary public health; Dr. William Ray, former chief of staff of the Animal Medical Center, New York—the largest veterinary medical hospital in the world, and considered the "Mayo Clinic for Animals;" Dr. Arthur Hurvitz, head of Pathology Dept., Animal Medical Center, New York, and a leading animal cancer researcher; Dr. Myron "Max" Essex, a department head at the Harvard School of Public Health, and a leading AIDS researcher; Dr. John Welser, '59, DVM, 61, M.S.,'62, dean emeritus, MSU's College of Veterinary Medicine; Dr. Mike Marder, DVM '61, past president, the American Board of Veterinary Practitioners; Dr. H. Michael Chaddock, DVM '73, past State Veterinarian for Michigan, and past director of the Animal Industry Division of the Michigan Department of Agriculture; Dr. John H. Richardson, DVM '57, M.S. '60, past president of the Michigan Veterinary Medical Association, and recipient of the American Animal Hospital Association's Practitioner of the Year Award in 2000; Dr. Brian Gerloff, recipient of the National Award for Excellence in Dairy Preventive Medicine from the American Association of Bovine Practitioners; Dr. Don Dykhouse, DVM '66, past president, the Wisconsin Veterinary Medical Association; Dr. Vic Eggleston, DVM '66, past president, Wisconsin Veterinary Medical Association; Dr. Dean Peterson, DVM '71, past president, Wisconsin Veterinary Medical Association; Dr. Richard Witter, DVM '60, veterinary medical officer at the Avian Disease and Oncology Laboratory of the U.S.D.A.'a Agricultural Research Service on campus, member of the National Academy of Sciences; and Dr. Z.A. Hashmi, served as first Vice Chancellor of West Pakistan's Agricultural University. He also was a leader in establishing a land-grant-like university in Pakistan.

The Honors College

Dr. Ronald C. Fisher, Director

www.msu.edu/unit/honcoll/

Michigan State was the first of America's 74 land-grant universities to establish an honors college as a major part of its undergraduate programs. A 1994 *Money Magazine* report ranked MSU's Honors College among the finest in the nation.

Since its inception in 1958, the Honors College has helped in the development of thirteen Rhodes Scholars, ten Truman Scholars, seven Marshall Scholars, eleven Churchill Scholars, and a Mitchell Scholar. "It's presence and success (The Honors College) surely aided in acquiring a Phi Beta Kappa chapter (at Michigan State)," Paul Dressel declared in his book, *College to University—The Hannah Years at Michigan State—1935-1969.*

In 1962, Michigan State became the first public university to sponsor a program of Merit Scholarships to attract National Merit Scholars, many of whom were Honors College students. By 1969, with 684 National Merit Scholars enrolled, MSU led the nation in this category for the sixth consecutive year, and led the nation for the 1967-1977 decade.

Don Lammers, director of the Honors College in 1992, said, **"Unless you attract excellence, the whole academic process suffers. The honors students are role models and an energizer."**

Unparalleled Flexibility in Creating a Study Program

Honors College students at MSU enjoy unparalleled flexibility in enriching their university studies. They are freed of many specific university requirements. They have enrollment priority in registering for classes. And, they have the opportunity to create their own highly personalized course of study with the guidance of an academic advisor. This freedom allows them to build a study curriculum of unusual breadth. They must earn the required credits in their major field of study, but at the same time, the wide spectrum of courses they can pursue differentiates the MSU Honors College program from others.

First year Honors College students have to meet rigorous requirements to enter the honors program. They have to stand in the top five percent of their high school class, have an SAT score of at least 1,360 or an ACT composite of at least 30. Others, who don't meet the initial criteria, but have strong, promising academic records may be invited to enroll on the basis of letters of recommendation from teachers, as well as personal statements explaining why they wish to participate in the honors program.

A major objective of the honors program is to serve and assist talented students in achieving academic excellence. This concept is attractive to high-achieving students

Eustace-Cole Hall, first horticultural laboratory in the nation, was designed by Liberty Hyde Bailey, class of 1882 and the "Father" of American Horticulture. It was built in 1888 for $7,000, and restored in 1998 for $1.3 million. It is home to the Honors College.

who are offered the opportunity of highly flexible, challenging, and individually tailored study programs. A good number of these students choose to live on one of the honors floors available in the residence hall system.

MSU: A Leader in Offering Research Options

MSU is a leader in offering research options for academically talented students in every discipline. The Honors College targets the top one percent of students in the nation to be involved in MSU's most selective undergraduate research program.

Each year, students who meet eligibility requirements are appointed as Professorial Assistants (PAs). They work with the teaching faculty on tasks related to research or innovative teaching. This student-mentor relationship is aimed at developing the student's knowledge and academic skills. PAs work eight to ten hours per week and are paid a stipend of about $1,700 per academic year. Eligibility for PA selection requires a minimum SAT total of 1,500, ACT composite of 33, or National Merit Index of 216, or selection as a National Merit Scholar.

Many honors students are recipients of scholarships. For example, 15 applicants each year are eligible to win Alumni Distinguished Scholarships, which provide for board, room, tuition and books for four years. Another 20 students win Distinguished Freshmen Scholarships, which are four-year, full-tuition grants. There also are 15 Distinguished Freshman Achievement Scholarships which pay full tuition for minorities for four years.

Moreover, there are Mowbray Scholarships—named for Myrtle Mowbray, Michigan State's first African-American graduate, class of 1907. These minority scholarships provide for faculty mentors, financial support for educational travel or research during two summers, and a monthly dinner with university faculty or staff leaders.

In addition, a number of grants are awarded to out-of-state honors students with exceptional academic records. At least two students planning to produce a senior thesis or equivalent project, are awarded Genevieve Gillette Fellowships of $2,200 to cover living expenses during the summer prior to the senior year. Genevieve Gillette, class of 1920, was founder and first president of the Michigan Parks Association, and was inducted into the Michigan Women's Hall of Fame in 1984.

Fall 2003 enrollment in The Honors College reached a record 2,575, more than double the number of students in the program in the early 1990s.

Distinguished Alumni

The Honors College has produced many outstanding alumni, including more than 50 who serve as MSU faculty and staff.

Jeffrey Cole, 1970 Honors College graduate, CEO and owner, Ferrous Processing, Detroit, and his wife Kathryn, MBA 1990, gave $3 million in 1997 to support the Honors College, and to provide scholarships and renovate Eustace Hall, home of the college. Building restoration cost $1.3 million. It was the first major restoration of an historic campus building on West Circle Drive. The hall was rededicated and renamed Eustace-Cole Hall in 1999.

International Studies and Programs

Dr. John K. Hudzik, Dean

www.isp.msu.edu

Michigan State is among the top centers of international education in the nation, with 193 study abroad programs reaching into more than 60 countries on all seven continents. In addition, there are more than 500 on-campus courses with international content. MSU was the first university in the U.S. to establish an Office of the Dean of International Programs—in 1956.

Peter McGrath, past president of the National Association of State Universities and Land-Grant Colleges, stated, **"Michigan State is a model and inspiration for the international public service role of our nation's universities."**

In a study of leading international programs, conducted in 1988 and reported in the *Educational Researcher*, Michigan State ranked number one.

MSU: National Leader in Students Studying Abroad

MSU is a national leader in the number of students studying abroad—more than 2,000—according to the Institute of International Education. Michigan State is a national leader in the number of international students, with approximately 3,000 foreign students from 126 countries, studying on campus. In addition, there are some 750 visiting foreign scholars at MSU doing research and sharing their knowledge and findings in MSU classrooms.

MSU #5 in Peace Corps Volunteers

From its inception in 1961, the U.S. Peace Corps has attracted nearly 1,900 MSU graduates. That ranked MSU fifth among all universities in Peace Corps volunteers.

National Resource Centers

Michigan State's international reputation is reflected by the fact that seven internationally focused centers at MSU are currently designated national resource and language resource centers by the U.S. Department of Education Title VI program.

The African Studies Center, established in 1960, has continuously been ranked among the best in the country. It is designated a U.S. National Resource Center for African Language and Areas Studies. For more than a decade, MSU graduate students produced more Ph.D. dissertations on Africa than any other North American university.

Asian Studies Center—was named a National Undergraduate Resource Center in 2000 by the U.S. Department of Education. The center directs one of the most diverse programs of Asian education in the Midwest. It is distinguished by its comprehensive attention to East, South, and Southeast Asia in its curriculum, faculty research, and scope of outreach.

Center for Latin American and Caribbean Studies (CLACS)—founded in 1963, has become one of the leading programs in the country. It has been a U.S. Department of Education National Undergraduate Resource Center since 1991. CLACS generates and disseminates knowledge about Latin America and the Caribbean at the national, state, and local levels.

Center for Advanced Study of International Development (CASID)—has been designated a National Resource Center in International Studies since its founding in 1981. CASID's program activities, organized within the College of Social Science in cooperation with the Dean of International Studies and Programs, promote the study of international development in the areas of teaching, research, and outreach.

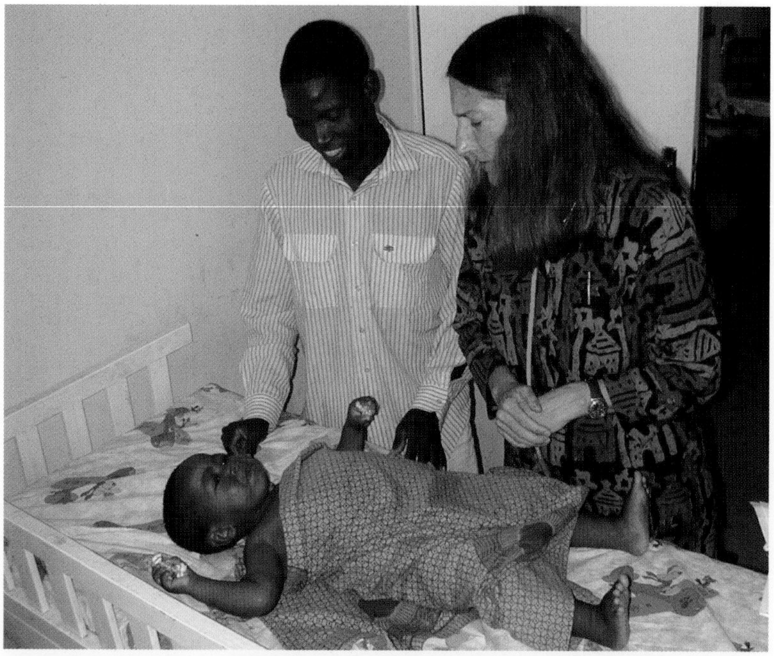

Dr. Terrie Taylor, professor of internal medicine, College of Osteopathic Medicine, attends to a malaria patient in Africa while the father looks on. Taylor spends months each year treating patients and conducting research in the Malaria Project, Queen Elizabeth Memorial Hospital, Blantyre, Malawi.

Center for International Business Education and Research (MSU-CIBER)—was designated a National Resource Center in 1990. It is a unit of The Eli Broad College of Business and The Eli Broad Graduate School of Management, collaborating with MSU International Studies and Programs, the core colleges of the university, and the language departments to promote interdisciplinary education. The center's mission is to enhance international management education and research and to assist businesses as they address the challenges of global market competition.

Women and International Development Program (WID)—was established in 1978, and is recognized nationally and internationally for its publications, teaching, research and outreach programs. It was designated a National Resource Center in 1994. The program's primary focus is the Southern Hemisphere, but recognizes that international development is a global process. The program fosters recognition that international development and globalization bring costs as well as benefits—and that these are not shared equally by women and men of different nations, races, classes, and ethnicities.

Center for Language Education and Research (CLEAR)—was created in 1996 and is recognized as a national Language Resource Center by the U.S. Department of Education. Its primary objective is to promote the teaching and learning of foreign languages in the U.S. through collaborative efforts across departmental, college, and institutional boundaries.

Other Centers and Institutes

Canadian Studies Centre—founded in 1957 is the senior international studies center at MSU, and is one of the oldest in the nation. Goals of the center are to promote the study of Canada at the national, regional, and local levels, and to educate our citizenry about the impact of U.S.-Canadian issues on their lives.

Center for European and Russian Studies—was established in 1992, consolidating existing programs in Russian and Eastern European Studies, and Western European Studies, which were established in 1964 and 1978, respectively. More than 200 courses, including more than 70 non-language courses, are offered in Western European Studies. The Russian and Eastern European Studies program offers a full range of Russian language courses and more than 40 non-language courses.

Institute of International Agriculture—founded in 1964, promotes, facilitates, and coordinates international agricultural and natural resources programs and activities on campus, in Michigan and abroad.

Institute of International Health—was established in 1987. It marshals university resources to address problems of world health by facilitating faculty and student research and academic interest in international health, undertaking collaborative international health projects abroad, and serving as a center for information exchange and dissemination on world health problems.

Japan Center for Michigan Universities—was established in 1989, is a study-abroad experience featuring intensive Japanese language instruction, courses in various academic disciplines, and a variety of experiential activities designed to acquaint students with Japan and its people. MSU operates the center on behalf of the JCMU Consortium (Michigan's public universities) and other universities. The JCMU facility is located on the shore of Lake Biwa in the City of Hikone, Shiga Prefecture, Japan, and is supported by the state governments of Michigan and Shiga as part of their strong sister-state relationship, and the University of Shiga Prefecture in Hikone, Japan.

Volunteer English Tutoring Program (VETP)—was created in 1983 by Dr. Delia Koo, M.A. and Ph.D., Radcliffe College, M.S. '54, MSU. It is an informal and highly personalized program to help newly arrived international students, spouses, and visitors adapt to life in an unfamiliar country. Staffed by volunteer tutors, the program is free of charge.

Delia Koo International Academic Center

A major endowment from Dr. Delia Koo, the largest single gift by an international alumna to MSU, has made possible a 10,000 square-foot addition to MSU's International Center. It has been named the Delia Koo International Academic Center and was completed in the spring of 2003. It is home to new classrooms, visiting international scholars, an office for the VETP, the Asian Studies Center, and the Center for Latin American and Caribbean Studies.

MSU Founded and Developed Three Overseas Universities and Helped Establish Many Others

Michigan State's international outreach has included key roles in the founding and development of three overseas universities, and significant contributions in establishing 19 others.

- In 1951, MSU sent teams of teachers and advisors to establish the University of Ryukus on Okinawa.
- In 1960, Michigan State professors and administrators went to Africa to help establish the University of Nigeria. In the years following these early outreach efforts, MSU has led or participated in more than 200 overseas development, research and assistance projects.
- In the 1990s, MSU played a key role in the creation of the National University of Science & Technology in Pakistan.
- MSU also has been a major partner in establishing universities, colleges, schools, and departments in 19 other nations: Argentina, Bangladesh, Brazil,

Colombia, Costa Rica, Guatemala, India, Indonesia, Iran, Malaysia, Mexico, Nepal, Peru, Philippines, Taiwan, Tanzania, Thailand, Turkey, and Vietnam.

International Studies Began in 1943

Michigan State's international programs began in 1943, when President Hannah brought Shao Chang Lee to the campus as professor of foreign studies and director of the Foreign Studies Institute. Professor Lee was instrumental in developing MSU's Center for International Programs.

Hannah's International Vision: "Citizens of the World"

As an international educator and visionary, President John Hannah was without peer. He declared, "We feel that we really have no acceptable alternative to being active in the international field, nor can any university with traditions such as those by which we live. We cannot plan to educate only citizens of Michigan or of the United States. We must prepare our students to be citizens of the world." Michigan State is firmly committed to incorporating a strong international dimension in all of its teaching, research, and outreach programs. The mission of International Studies and Programs is to stimulate such an international culture in all units of the university.

President McPherson: Study Abroad for 40 Percent of MSU Students

Peter McPherson, MSU's 19th president, also is a strong internationalist. In fact, when he graduated in 1963, he was one of the first of MSU's Peace Corps volunteers. He later served as the head of the U.S. Agency for International Development. One of his Guiding Principles for MSU is to offer a semester of study abroad to 40 percent of all MSU students by the year 2006, at no greater cost than traditional study on the East Lansing campus.

Michigan State's international alumni numbered more than 30,000 in 2002. They have included: a past prime minister of Egypt and former minister of education for Thailand.

International Leader in Outreach

Michigan State pioneered in extending the mission of higher education beyond teaching and research. Energetic faculty have done this by reaching out to share existing and new found knowledge with the people of the state, nation, and world to help them solve problems.

Peter McGrath, past president of the National Association of State Universities and Land-Grant Colleges, stated,

"Michigan State is a model and inspiration for the international public service role of our nation's universities."

Faculty outreach began in 1872, when professors formed a class in chemical manipulations to help public school teachers be more effective in chemistry education. The class was free.

The First Farmers' Institutes to share the latest scientific agricultural knowledge were held at six locations in Michigan in 1876. Subjects focused on crops, fertilizers, even lightning rods.

By 1895, Farmers' Institutes featuring specialized agricultural education, reached into all 67 Michigan counties (now 83).

"Railroad Institutes" were inaugurated in 1905. Three, 3-car railroad trains with agricultural faculty and exhibits traveled throughout the state to reach local farmers. Seventy-three two-day, and 200 one-day institutes were conducted.

Food Production was developed and promoted during World War I (1917) by the college's Agricultural Extension Service, which worked with the State's Food Preparedness Committee.

Extension Schools were established in Every Michigan County in 1918 to bring the latest scientific agricultural knowledge more directly to farmers. County (Agricultural) Agents already were located in virtually every county. The county agent had local knowledge of farming conditions, and could combine this with the research findings provided by Extension scientists at the college.

Gordon Guyer, B.S. '50, M.S. '52, Ph. D. '53, MSU's 18th President, has pointed out that the Extension Agents, who maintain regular contact with citizens, county commissioners, and legislators, in every Michigan county greatly enhance MSU's visibility and opportunities to serve, as well as extend the classroom to the real world.

First Radio Outreach in America—1922—Professor Howard C. Rather (Rather Hall) broadcast agricultural information over the air waves in March, 1922 from radio station WWJ in Detroit. It was the first recorded use of radio to extend agricultural knowledge to citizens in the state or nation.

Michigan State helped boost food production during the depths of the Depression (1932), when there was 25 percent unemployment in the state. To help feed families, the college promoted extensive gardening projects and shared knowledge on poultry raising, and the use of farm produce.

Low-cost meal lectures were conducted statewide by the Home Economics Division in 1933. Welfare agencies appealed to the college for help in planning minimum-cost meals, and the bulletin "Low-Cost Meals for the Family," was produced and distributed.

Food production was vital to victory during World War II. Michigan State research on food preservation by drying was passed on to Michigan citizens in 1943. The Home Economics Division helped Michigan housewives with canning larger and larger quantities of homegrown vegetables.

Professor directs Victory Gardens for Michigan (1943)—The Michigan State Defense Council requested that MSC loan the services of P.R. Krone, assistant professor of floriculture, to direct the operation of Victory Gardens in Michigan.

The major launch point for International Outreach was in 1951—MSC was selected by the American Council on Education, at the insistence of the U.S. Department of Defense, to foster and develop the newly created University of Ryukus on the Island of Okinawa. Michigan State was chosen among all of the land-grant colleges in the nation.

Since then MSU's educational mission has reached around the globe. Faculty and administrative know-how have helped create three overseas and one domestic university—Ryukus University, Okinawa (1951); University of Nigeria, Africa (1960); the National University of Science & Technology, Pakistan (1990s); and Oakland University, Rochester, Michigan (1957).

Moreover, MSU was a major partner in establishing universities, colleges, schools and departments in nineteen other nations—Argentina, Bangladesh, Brazil, Colombia, Costa Rica, Guatemala, India, Indonesia, Iran, Malaysia, Mexico, Nepal, Peru, Philippines, Taiwan, Tanzania, Thailand, Turkey, and Vietnam.

MSU has had more faculty working overseas than any other American university for 50 years or more. Their objective: help other nations with agricultural development and problems.

MSU's Institute of International Agriculture, sponsored by the College of Agriculture and Natural Resources, regularly transmits agricultural knowledge to countries around the world.

Alumni Achievement & Leadership: A True Measure of University Success

A true measure of a university's success lies in the achievements of its alumni. Michigan State University's heritage in producing graduates who make a difference in the world is notable.

Michigan State alumni have won the Nobel Prize, Pulitzer Prizes, the Congressional Medal of Honor, Distinguished Flying Crosses, Academy Awards for movie production, Emmy Awards, Grammy Awards, a Toni Award, and a Peabody Award.

Three U.S. Presidential cabinet members, four state governors, three U.S. senators, a dozen members of the U.S. House of Representatives have been MSU graduates. Seven graduates have been U.S. ambassadors to foreign countries.

MSU alumni have served as the White House physician, the White House press secretary, and presidential speech writer. Two alumni have headed the U.S. Secret Service, and one has been the domestic chief of INTERPOL. Another graduate was the administrator of the National Highway Traffic Safety Administration. Still another alum served as chairman and a member of the Federal Communications Commission. An MSU graduate was named director of the U.S. Mint in 2000. In 2001, an MSU alum was named the nation's drug czar: national drug control policy director.

Federal Reserve Bank board members—including the first woman—and state supreme court justices are among the graduates of Michigan State. One MSU graduate was the Judge Advocate General for the U.S. Navy and another was the Director of the U.S. Census. An MSU graduate has been the Director of the National Park System. Still another alum was the Sergeant of Arms for the U.S. House of Representatives.

At one time, up to one quarter of the entire Michigan Legislature and the Michigan Congressional delegation was comprised of MSU graduates.

Two MSU graduates have been elected Mayor of Detroit.

A prime minister of Egypt was a graduate of MSU.

On 107 occasions alumni have been elected university or college presidents or chancellors.

Among the universities they have led are: Illinois, Wisconsin, Texas, Nebraska, Missouri, Alabama, Florida State, Colorado State, Idaho, Maine, Massachusetts, Bradley, New Mexico State and Washington & Lee. Hundreds of graduates have become deans or department heads at universities across the nation, including the dean of the Wharton School of Business at the University of Pennsylvania and the chairman of the Nutrition Department at the Harvard School of Public Health.

Hundreds of graduates have been corporate chairmen, CEOs, presidents, or executive vice presidents and several have been named to business Halls of Fame.

MSU alumni have headed many major hotel and restaurant corporations.

Seven TV networks and three motion picture studios have been led by Michigan State graduates. MSU graduates have written several movie scripts that have been box office winners. Spartan alumni also have had successful acting careers.

A retired publisher of *Time* magazine was an MSU graduate.

Major advertising companies have been headed by Spartans.

Two major labor unions have had MSU graduates as their presidents.

Michigan State alumni have commanded the U.S. 15th Air Force, the U.S. Air Force Education and Training Command, and the National Women's Land Army.

Dozens of Spartans have been elected presidents of national and state professional and business associations.

Spartans have been members of Super Bowl, NBA, World Series, Stanley Cup and America's Cup championship teams.

Three alumni are owners or part owners of professional sports teams—the Houston Astros baseball team, the Los Angeles Lakers basketball team, and the Calgary Flames hockey team.

Twenty-three graduates have won Olympic medals—ten of them gold.

One alum was chief executive of the U.S. Olympic Committee. Another has been a member of the International Olympic Executive Committee.

Thirteen graduates are in international or national Sports Halls of Fame.

Spencer Abraham, '74, left, with MSU President Peter McPherson. Abraham was named U.S. Secretary of Energy in President George W. Bush's cabinet in 2001.

MSU alumna have won the Miss America, Miss Michigan, Miss Arkansas, Miss Alaska, Miss Hawaii, and Miss Thailand crowns.

The achievements of MSU alumni and the positions that they have attained are detailed by category on the following pages.

Presidential Cabinet Members

Frederick H. Mueller, class of 1914, was appointed U.S. Secretary of Commerce by President Dwight D. Eisenhower in 1959.

David Stockman, '68, Director of the U.S. Office of Management and Budget in the Ronald Reagan administration, and at age 39, was the youngest Presidential Cabinet member in the 20th century.

Spencer Abraham, '74, was named U.S. Secretary of Energy in President George W. Bush's cabinet in 2001.

State Governors and Lt. Governors

Four MSU graduates have been elected state governors.

George R. Ariyoshi, '49, was elected governor of Hawaii.

Jim Blanchard, '64, M.A. '65, was the first graduate elected governor of Michigan.

Anthony Earl, '58, was elected governor of Wisconsin.

John Engler, '71, served three terms as Michigan's governor.

F. Fernando Fontana, MBA '66, served as the administrator of Brazil's State of Parana.

Nancy Dick, '51, was elected Lt. Governor of Colorado.

Dick Posthumus, '72, was elected Lt. Governor of Michigan.

U.S. Senators

Donald W. Riegle, MBA '61, elected U.S. Senator from Michigan.

Spencer Abraham, '74, elected U.S. Senator from Michigan.

Debbie Stabenow, '72, MSW '75, elected U.S. Senator from Michigan.

U.S. House of Representatives

James Blanchard, '64, MBA '65; 4 terms—1975-1983.

William S. Broomfield, attended MSC; 18 terms—1957-1993.

Albert J. Campbell, attended M.A.C.; 1 term—1899-1901.

M. Robert Carr, graduate studies at MSU; 3 terms—1975-1981.

James W. Dunn, '67; 1 term—1981-1983.

Melbourne H. Ford, attended M.A.C.; served from March, 1891 until his death in April, 1891.

John C. Mackie, '42, LL.D '65; 1 term—1965-1967.

Robert J. McIntosh, attended MSC '40-'42; 1 term—1957-1959.

Nick H. Smith, '57, 6 terms—1993-to present (2003).

Debbie Stabenow, '72, MSW '75; 2 terms— 1997-2001.

David A. Stockman, '68, 2 terms—1977-1981.

J. Robert Traxler, '53, 10 terms—1974-1993.

George Ariyoshi, '49, served as Governor of Hawaii—the first Asian-American, and first MSU graduate elected a state governor.

International Government Leaders

Kalmal Ahmed El-Ganzoury, Ph.D. '72, served as Egypt's prime minister. He was named to that position in 1996 by Egyptian president Hosni Mubarak.

Harry Moniba, Ph.D. '75, served as vice president of Liberia, the tropical nation on Africa's western bulge.

Adnan Badran, M.S. '61, Ph.D. '63, served as the No. 2 executive of the 2,220-person United Nations UNESCO organization. He previously served as Jordan's Minister of Education and Agriculture, and as president of two universities—Yarmouk University and Jordan University of Science and Technology.

Luis Lopez Guerra, M.A. '75, was named to Spain's Supreme Court in 1986.

Tom David-West, '60, served as minister of education for Nigeria, and as minister of mines, power, and steel.

U.S. and Foreign Ambassadors

Nine alumni have served as Ambassadors to foreign countries. They include:

Clarence A. Boonstra, 1936, U.S. Ambassador to Costa Rica.

Richard Barkley, '54, U.S. Ambassador to the German Democratic Republic (East Germany).

Peter F. Secchia, '63, U.S. Ambassador to Italy.

James J. Blanchard, '64, M.A. '65, U.S. Ambassador to Canada.

John Kornblum, '64, U.S. Ambassador to the Federal Republic of Germany.

Donna Hrinak, '72, named U.S. Ambassador to Brazil in 2002. Previously was U.S. Ambassador to Bolivia—the first female career foreign service officer to be named a U.S. ambassador.

Thomas G. Weston, '66, M.A. '69, U.S. Ambassador to Cyprus.

Lawrence D. Owen, '67, U.S. Consul General in Bermuda.

Ercan Ozer, M.A. '72, served as the Republic of Turkey's Ambassador to the United Arab Emirates.

John Walters, '74, U.S. "Drug Czar." Director, White House Office of National Drug Control Policy—2001.

John Kornblum, '64, served as U.S. Ambassador to the Federal Republic of Germany. He wrote the famous Ronald Reagan line: "Mr. Gorbachev, tear down this wall."

Federal Government & Washington, D.C. Leaders

Kenyon L. Butterfield, class of 1891, and Michigan State president 1924-1928, served as Commissioner in charge of Agricultural Education for the American Expeditionary Forces in World War I; Advisor to U.S. President Woodrow Wilson on rural credit; Advisor to the Chinese government on agricultural techniques.

Harry J. Eustace, class of 1901, Master's 1911, (Eustace-Cole Hall) was Associate in Charge of the Perishable Food Division under U.S. Food Administrator Herbert Hoover during World War I.

Ray Stannard Baker (Baker Hall), class of 1889, was appointed by U.S. President Woodrow Wilson as a special commissioner of the U.S. Department of State in 1918; and as director of the press bureau of the U.S. contingent to the Paris Peace Conference in 1919.

Lyman Briggs (MSU's Lyman Briggs School, specializing in mathematics & science), Class of 1893 and a top U.S. physicist, was named director of the National Bureau of Standards in 1933. In *Lyman Briggs-A Biography*, author Tony Lush reported, "U.S. President Franklin Roosevelt appointed Briggs in October, 1939 to head the original Uranium Committee to lead a top-secret investigation to study the possibility of using atomic energy in warfare. **This advisory committee, chaired by Briggs, reported back to President Roosevelt in November, 1939 that both atomic power and an atomic bomb were possible.** Just prior to the Japanese attack on Pearl Harbor in December, 1941, the committee, now designated S-1, recommended a strong effort to produce an atomic weapon. The effort was soon transferred to the Office of Scientific

Research and Development, and then became the Manhattan Project in the summer of 1942, which led to the development of the first atomic bomb."

Clarence Beaman Smith, class of 1894, was named Chief of Agricultural Extension Work in the United States in 1921. He authored, with E.W. Wiel, two encyclopedias —*The Farmer's Cyclopedia of Agriculture* (1907), and *The Farmer's Cyclopedia of Livestock* (1907).

C.M. Granger, class of 1907, headed the national reforestation program in 1934, and was later in charge of all National Forests for the U.S. Forest Service.

Charles Dwight Curtis, 1911, served as Deputy Commissioner for the U.S. Bureau of Public Roads.

John A. Hannah, '23, served as Deputy Secretary of Defense in the Eisenhower Administration in 1953-1954. In 1969, he was named head of the U.S. Agency for International Development in the Nixon Administration.

James D. Hittle, '37, served as Assistant Secretary of the Navy.

Dr. William Lukash, '52, Navy Rear Admiral, Chief White House Physician, as well as President Gerald Ford's personal doctor.

Jerald F. ter Horst, '45, White House Press Secretary under President Gerald Ford. He wrote a book about Air Force One—the President's aircraft—titled *Flying Whitehouse*. ter Horst was an assistant editor of the *State News* when he was on campus.

John Walters, '74, was named the U.S. Drug Czar—Director of the White House Office of National Drug Control Policy in December of 2001.

Robert Siegrist, '40, was a speech writer for President Ronald Reagan.

Nancy Hays Teeters, graduate study in economics at MSU, became the first women member of the Federal Reserve Board. She also served as the chief economist for the U.S. House Budget Committee.

James H. Quello, '35, chairman and member of the Federal Communications Commission for 24 years.

Douglas W. Toms, M.A. '59, administrator of the National Highway Traffic Safety Administration.

M. Peter McPherson, '63, served as head of the Agency for International Development. He also served as Deputy Secretary of the U.S. Treasury Department. In 2003, McPherson was selected by U.S. President George W. Bush to head the financial reconstruction of Iraq.

Barbara Everitt Bryant, M.A. '67, Ph.D. '70, director of the U.S. Census Bureau, nominated by President George Herbert Walker Bush.

William Penn Mott, '31, director of the National Park System.

Daniel N. Wenk, '75, director of the National Park System headquarters.

Jay Johnson, M.A. '70, Director of the U.S. Mint

Gary M. Stolz, '80, M.A. '82, Chief Naturalist for the U.S. Fish and Wildlife Service, and the nation's outdoor recreation planner.

William "Bill" Livingood, '61, Sergeant of Arms for the U.S. House of Representatives. He was responsible for the security of the U.S. House of Representatives, and prior to each State of the Union address, announced to the joint session of Congress, **"Mr. Speaker, the President of the United States."** He served 30 years in the U.S. Secret Service.

Rex Scouten, '47, Secret Service agent assigned to the White House in 1957, served as Chief Usher at the president's home from 1969 to 1986, in charge of "the official entertainment, all the ceremonies, even the conservation of the fine arts collection."

James H. Steele, DVM '41, U.S. Assistant Surgeon General. He was the founder of the American College of Veterinary Preventive Medicine and a professor emeritus at the University of Texas.

Larry D. Thompson, M.A. '69, was nominated U.S. Deputy Attorney General by President George W. Bush, and approved by the U.S. Senate in 2001.

John Weigett, '69, DVM '70, one of he nation's top trauma surgeons, accompanied the U.S. President during visits to high-risk countries.

Jay Johnson, M.A. '70, was named director of the U.S. Mint in 2000. Founded in 1792, the Mint produces 27 billion U.S. coins per year.

Donald A. Jones, '33, Navy Rear Admiral, served as director of the National Ocean Survey for the National Oceanic and Atmospheric Administration.

Frederick C. Belen, '37, served as Assistant U.S. Postmaster General.

Kwame Kilpatrick, elected Mayor of Detroit in 2002, is a 1999 graduate of the MSU College of Law.

Mary J. Layton, '64, served as Assistant U.S. Postmaster General.

Gary L. Jones, M.A. '68, Ph.D. '75, served as U.S. Under Secretary of Education.

Patricia McFate, '52, served as deputy director of the National Endowment for the Humanities.

In a national "first," graduates from the same university were presidents of the two most visible press organizations in the nation's capital at the same time: 1988. Andrew Mollison, '67, was president of the **National Press Club**; and **James McCartney, '49,** was president of the **Washington, D.C. Gridiron Club**, that annually "roasts" the President of the United States.

State & County Government Leaders

Frank F. Rogers, class of 1883, was appointed Michigan State Highway Commissioner in 1913, and led the development of a superior highway system in the state.

Dr. Howard Tanner, MSU graduate, was the first director of Natural Resources for the State of Michigan.

Spencer Abraham, '74, was elected state chairman of the Republican Party of Michigan in 1983. At age 30, he was the youngest state GOP party head in the nation.

Genevieve Gillette, '20, founder and first president of the Michigan Parks Association, in 1994 was the subject of a children's book titled, *Genevieve Gillette: Nature's Guardian Angel*."

Linda Chapin, '63, served as chairperson of Orange County, California—one of the largest counties in America. She was the first chairperson of the county, and won her second term in 1994, with 61 percent of the vote.

Dr. Gordon Guyer, '50, M.S. '52, Ph.D. '53, director of the Michigan Department of Agriculture.

Dan Wyant, '82, director of the Michigan Department of Agriculture.

Judicial Leaders

John Fitzgerald, '47, Chief Justice, Michigan Supreme Court. He was a founding director and professor of law at the Thomas M. Cooley Law School in Lansing, Michigan.

Andree (Layton) Roaf, '62, member of the Arkansas Supreme Court. She also served in a Little Rock, Arkansas law firm.

Luis Lopez Guerra, M.A. '75, named a member of Spain's Supreme Court in 1986. He taught at the Universidad de Extramadura in Caceres, where his wife founded an MSU study program in 1980.

Wallace Jefferson, '85, became the first African-American to be named a Supreme Court Justice in Texas in 2001.

Detroit Mayors

Dennis Archer, MSU-Detroit College of Law alum, served as Mayor of Detroit and as a Justice of the Michigan Supreme Court.

Kwame Kilpatrick, 1999 graduate of the MSU College of Law, was elected the 60th Mayor of Detroit in 2002. At age 31, he was the youngest mayor in the city's history.

Major Award Winners

Dr. Alfred Day Hershey, B.S.'30, Ph.D. '34, won the 1969 Nobel Prize for physiology or medicine.

President emeritus John A. Hannah, '23, won the singular U.S. Presidential End Hunger Award in the fall of 1986 for "Lifetime Achievement." He also was given the **USA Medal of Freedom—the nation's highest civilian award.**

Wallace Jefferson, '85, right, with wife & sons, the first African-American to be named a Texas Supreme Court Justice—May, 2001.

1st Lt. Harry L. Martin, '36, Congressional Medal of Honor Winner.

Harold Furlong, class of 1918, won the Congressional Medal of Honor for his service to the nation in World War I. This is the highest recognition the nation can pay to a soldier. Fewer than 50 of these awards were made during World War I.

First Lt. Harry L. Martin, '36, was posthumously awarded the Congressional Medal of Honor—the nation's highest military decoration—in 1948 for his bravery in World War II in the U.S. Marine Corps.

Dr. I. Forest Huddleson, class of 1925, research professor in bacteriology, won the **International Veterinary Congress prize for 1940** for his work to eliminate undulant fever. Dr. Harry W. Jakeman, chair of the executive board of the American Veterinary Medical Association stated in the citation, "You have contributed liberally and practically not only to the livestock industry of the world, but also to the protection of human health."

Lt. Douglas MacDonald, '42, won the **Distinguished Flying Cross** for aerial rescue of Army pilots on a Greenland ice cap.

Captain James Gibb, Jr., '38, won the **Distinguished Flying Cross** for assisting in the rescue mission to bring General Douglas MacArthur out of the Philippines.

Robert Zant, '39, won the **Distinguished Flying Cross** for aerial flight against the enemy.

Captain Leon Williamson, '39, won the **Distinguished Flying Cross** for meritorious achievement with the Marine Air Corps.

Daniel E. Hester, '50, won the **Distinguished Flying Cross** for combat in World War II.

Lt. General James E. Light, Jr., '56, former commander of the U.S. 15th Air Force, flew 220 combat missions and was awarded the **Distinguished Flying Cross and the Bronze Star**.

USAF Major Monte L. Smith, '59, won the Distinguished Flying Cross in 1970 for heroic aerial achievement in Southeast Asia.

Michael L. Thompson, '70, won two Distinguished Flying Crosses for aerial achievement in Southeast Asia.

Ed Feldman, '50, won **Academy Awards** for the movie "Save The Tiger," and the 1983 smash hit "Witness," starring Harrison Ford.

Bob Leonard, '63, won a special scientific **Academy Award** for the invention of Sensurround, a low-frequency sound system that "surrounds your senses."

Brian Vallee, '67, was researcher and associate producer of **John Zaritsky's** *Just Another Missing Kid,* which won an **Academy Award** in 1983.

Ray Stannard Baker, class of 1889, won a 1940 **Pulitzer Prize** for his eight-volume biography—*Woodrow Wilson: Life and Letters*—which was published sequentially from 1927 to 1939.

Howard James, Midwest bureau chief, *Christian Science Monitor,* won the **Pulitzer Prize** for national reporting in 1968.

Dick Cooper, '69, Main Line bureau chief, *Philadelphia Inquirer,* teamed with John Machacek to win a 1972 **Pulitzer Prize** for reporting on the Attica Prison riot of September 14, 1971.

Jim Mitzelfeld, '84, *Detroit News* reporter, won the 1994 **Pulitzer Prize** for beat reporting.

Ariel Melchoir, Jr., publisher, *The Daily News,* St. Thomas, Virgin Islands, won the **Pulitzer Prize** for public service, 1995.

Richard Ford, '66, won the 1996 **Pulitzer Prize** for fiction, authoring the book, *Independence Day.*

Clare Fischer, '50, M.A. '55, has won two **Grammy Awards**—one for the Best Latin Recording in 1981, and a second in 1987 for the Best Vocal Jazz Album, "Freefall."

Jay Schadler, '74, Emmy award winning anchor for ABC News' 20/20 program.

Dennis Lewin, '65, won **three successive Emmy Awards** as director of production coordination for ABC-TV's *Wide World of Sports* program.

Jim Dunbar, '61, won **Emmys** and **AP Newscaster of the Year** honors at KGO radio station San Francisco.

Jay Schadler, '74, won an **Emmy** as a correspondent and anchor for ABC News 20/20 and host of National Geographic Presents.

Jeff Crilley, '85, won an **Emmy** as a KDFW-TV (Fox) anchor and reporter in Dallas, Texas.

William D. Brohn, '55, won two **Desk Drams Awards** in 1993—**the Oscar equivalent in musical arrangement**—for arranging the music for *Miss Saigon* and *Secret Garden.* In 1998 he won a **Toni Award** for his musical arrangement for *Ragtime*, a Broadway hit.

Dr. Edward R. Garrett, '41, also M.S. and Ph.D. from MSU, won the **1963 Ebert Prize—the nation's highest pharmaceutical research award—for** "the best published research in all the pharmaceutical sciences" by the American Pharmaceutical Association.

Dr. William F. Jackson, DVM '47, M.S. '49, was presented the **National Gamma Award as "the most outstanding veterinarian in the U.S." in 1968.**

E. Genevieve Gillette, class of 1920, won the **Park and Conservationist of the Year Award from the National Wildlife Federation.** She is known as "Miss Michigan State Parks."

Cathe Ishino, '74, who was art director for the MacNeil/Lehrer News Hour, won **Emmy and Peabody awards** for her work.

Verghese Kurien, M.A. '48, chairman of India's National Development Board, was named the **1989 World Food Prize Laureate**. This annual $200,000 prize goes to the individual who has made an outstanding contribution toward improving the world food supply.

Morton B. Panish, M.S. '52, Ph.D. '54, senior scientist at Bell Laboratories, **won Japan's $61,000 Computer and Communication Award**, and was inducted into the National Academy of Engineering in 1986. In collaboration with Japanese scientist Iquo Hayashi, Panish developed hetero-structure lasers.

Amir U. Khan, M.S. '49, M.S. '52, Ph.D. '67, an agricultural engineer with the International Rice Research Institute in the Philippines, won the **International Inventors Award,** presented by H.M. King Carl Gustaf of Sweden in Stockholm in 1986. The $36,500 award was considered the **equivalent of the Nobel Prize for invention.** Kahn's invention—an axial flow thresher—is an implement widely used by farmers in tropical rice producing nations.

Automotive Industry Leaders

MSU graduates have led all three of America's major automobile corporations.

Robert C. Stempel, MBA '70, served as chairman and CEO and president of General Motors Corporation.

Alexander Trotman, MBA '72, served as chairman and CEO of Ford Motor Company.

James P. Holden, MBA '90, served as president of Daimler-Chrysler, A.G.

Robert J. Schultz, '53, MBA '69, served as vice chairman of General Motors.

Edward Hagenlocker, MBA '82, served as vice chairman of Ford Motor Company.

Ronald K. Evans, 1912, served as executive vice president of General Motors. During his career he also served as managing director of GM's Adam Opel automotive subsidiary in Germany.

John D. Withrow, '54, MBA '71, served as Chrysler's executive vice president for engineering and product development.

Thomas Gale, '66, M.A. '67, MBA '78, served as Chrysler's executive vice president for design and international operations.

Gary C. Valade, '66, MBA '68, served as Chrysler's executive vice president for finance.

Lewis R. Ross, MBA '72, served as an executive vice president at Ford Motor Company.

Bob McCurry, '50, served as executive vice president of Toyota Motor Sales, U.S.A. He also served as vice president for sales for Chrysler Corporation.

John Middlebrook, MBA '67, served as vice president and general manager of vehicle brand marketing for General Motors.

Charles Brady, '48, served as manufacturing vice president for General Motors.

James P. Holden, MBA '90, served as president of Daimler-Chrysler, A.G. He was the third MSU graduate to head one of America's Big Three car companies.

Joseph F. Kerigan, MBA '66, served as vice president and group executive of Chrysler Corporation's car assembly and stamping group.

Frank O. Anderson, III, MBA '71, served as group vice president for Chrysler Corporation's U.S. automotive manufacturing.

Lynn C. Myers, '64, MBA '67, served as general manager of the Pontiac-GMC Division of General Motors. She was named McCall's/Ward's Auto World's first **"Outstanding Woman in the Automotive Industry"** in 1994.

Gary Convis, '64, was named president of Toyota Motor Manufacturing of North America in 2001. He was the first non-Japanese to head the Georgetown, Kentucky operation—the largest auto plant in North America, with annual production of 500,000 vehicles.

James E. Miller, '71, MBA '73, served as president of Mazda Motor Corporation in Japan.

Frederick J. Schwab, '60, served as president and CEO of Porsche Cars-North America.

Steven J. Landry, MBA 2000, served as president of Chrysler Jeep Automotive in Europe.

Susan Unger, '72, was senior vice president and chief information officer, Daimler-Chrysler, A.G. in 2003.

Karen L. Healy, '76, was vice president corporate affairs, marketing communications & facilities, Delphi Corporation—world's largest automotive components supplier—in 2003.

Harold C. MacDonald, '40, served as vice president for car engineering and product development for Ford Motor Company.

Stanley A. Zdeb, '67, served as vice president of engineering for Nissan Motor Manufacturing Corporation.

Pat Carrigan, '50, served as the first female manager of a General Motors domestic assembly plant. She also served as chair of the MSU Board of Trustees.

Frank Johnson, class of 1895, was named chief engineer for Ford Motor Company's Lincoln Division in 1926. He had been chief engineer of the Lincoln Motor Company prior to its purchase by Ford. Johnson was key in the design of the famous Ford model "A," and Lincoln cars. Earlier in his career, he was with the Cadillac Motor Car Company and helped design some of the historic Cadillacs.

University and College Presidents and Deans

MSU graduates have been named university or college presidents or chancellors on 107 occasions, serving in 38 different states, as well as Brazil, Japan, Jordan, Liberia, Turkey, and the District of Columbia.

Six graduates have served as the president of Michigan State: Oscar Clute, class of 1862—fifth president (1889-1893); **Frank S. Kedzie, class of 1877**—eighth president (1915-1924); **Kenyon L. Butterfield, class of 1891**—tenth president (1924-1928); **John A. Hannah, class of 1923**—twelfth president (1941-1969); **Gordon Guyer, class of 1950, M.S. 1952, Ph.D. 1953**—eighteenth president (1992-1994); and **M. Peter McPherson, class of 1963**—nineteenth president (1994-).

Philip E. Austin, M.A. '68, Ph.D. '69, served as president of the University of Alabama, and Colorado State.

Other alumni who have been university presidents or chancellors include:

Edgar A. Burnett, class of 1887, elected chancellor of the University of Nebraska in 1928.

Dr. Hiroshi Naito, class of 1920, president of Tokyo University of Agriculture, Japan.

Dr. William H. Sewell, B.A. 1933, M.A. 1934, Chancellor, University of Wisconsin-Madison.

Donald V. Bennett, MSC student 1933-35, Superintendent, U.S. Military Academy, West Point; Major General, U.S. Army.

Edward Q. Moulton, 1947, University of North Dakota.

Philip E. Austin, M.A. '68, Ph.D. '69, University of Alabama; Colorado State University.

William H. Cunningham, '66, M.A.'67, Ph.D. '71, president University of Texas-Austin, and chancellor of the entire University of Texas system.

Charles A. Kiesler, '58, M.A. '60, University of Missouri.

Stanley Ikenberry, M.A. '57, Ph.D. '60, University of Illinois.

Bernard F. Sliger, '49, Florida State University.

Dale W. Lick, '58, M.S. '59, Florida State University; University of Maine.

Richard D. Gibb, Ph.D. '59, University of Idaho.

Adrian R. Chamberlain, '51, Colorado State University.

David C. Broski, '62, M.A. '63, Ph.D. '74, has served as president of University of Illinois-Chicago and Bradley University.

Michael R. Ferrari, '62, M.A. '63, MBA '68, Drake University.

David C. Broski, '69, M.A. '71, Ph. D. '74, Bradley University; University of Illinois-Chicago.

John D. Wilson, '53, Ph.D. '65, Washington & Lee University.

James D. Spaniolo, '68, U-M M.P.A. & J.D., '75, University of Texas-Arlington.

Marcellette G. Williams, '68, M.A. '70, Ph.D. '81, University of Massachusetts.

Jay Gogue, Ph.D. '73, New Mexico State University.

Adnan Badran, M.S. '61, Ph.D. '63, president of Jordan University of Science and Technology in the nation of Jordan.

Michigan State graduates have served as the presidents of the following Michigan universities—Central Michigan, Detroit College of Law, Calvin College, Eastern Michigan, Ferris State, Michigan Tech, and Grand Valley State.

Dr. Charles McKenney, class of 1881, was president of Michigan State Normal College (now Eastern Michigan University) in 1931.

Harold E. Sponberg, Ph. D. '52, was elected president of Eastern Michigan U. in 1965.

John W. Porter, M.A. '57, Ph.D. '62, was serving as president of Eastern Michigan U. in 1985.

Leonard E. Plachta, Ph.D. '64, was elected president of Central Michigan U. in 1994.

Grover C. Dillman, class of 1913, was elected president of Michigan College of Mining & Technology (now Michigan Technological University) in 1935.

Dr. Robert L. Ewigleben, B.S. '52, M.A. '56, Ed.D. '59, was elected president of Ferris State University (Big Rapids, MI) in 1971.

Anthony J. Diekema, M.A. '58, Ph.D. '65, was elected president of Calvin College (Grand Rapids, MI) in 1976.

Richard W. Heiss, '52, was elected president of the Detroit College of Law in 1984.

University and Medical Deans & Department Heads

Hundreds of alumni have served as university deans or department heads. Notable among them are:

Russell E. Palmer, '66, dean of the Wharton School of Business at the University of Pennsylvania.

Major General David S. Trump, '55, dean of the Military Medicine Education Institute and vice president of the Uniformed Services University of Health & Sciences, the Defense Department's military medical school.

Barbara Ross-Lee, D.O. '73, dean of the Ohio University College of Osteopathic Medicine, was the first African American woman to head a medical school in the U.S. She also served as chair of the Ohio Council of Medical School Deans, and was inducted into the Ohio Women's Hall of Fame. She also was the first black woman to chair a department at Michigan State University: Family Practice in the College of Osteopathic Medicine.

Charles Fisher, '71, M.D. '73, director of the Cleveland Clinic's Critical Care Research Unit, where he helped develop many drugs like Centoxin, which helped cut death rates from septic shock.

Walter Willett, '66, chair of the Nutrition Department at the Harvard School for Public Health. He was considered the world expert in nutritional epidemiology—the study of the impact of diet on health. He authored the 396-page book, *Nutritional Epidemiology* in 1990. **He**

Barbara Ross-Lee, D.O. '73, served as Dean of Ohio University's Osteopathic Medicine College. She was the first African-American to head a medical school in the U.S.

helped persuade the U.S. Food and Drug Administration that the national food supply be fortified with folic acid because evidence showed it helped prevent birth defects.

Steven Leibel, B.S. & M.D. '70, chair and physician, department of Radiation Oncology, Memorial Sloan-Kettering Cancer Center, New York.

Martha L. Gray, '78, co-director of the Harvard-MIT Division of Health Science and Technology at MIT. She was elected to the board of directors of the National Space Biomedical Research Institute.

Corporate CEOs, Presidents, Vice Chairmen & Top Officers

Hundreds of alumni have led corporations as CEOs, presidents, vice chairmen, and executive vice presidents. Corporate leadership positions attained by MSU alumni include:

Francis Ferguson, '47, president of Northwestern Mutual Life insurance company.

William Kostecke, '51, president of Miller Brewing Company.

Coy G. Ecklund, '38, president of the Equitable Life Assurance Society of New York.

Gary S. Grimes, MBA '60, president of Spaulding U.S.

John R. Hamann, '37, president of Detroit Edison.

Earl Hoekenga, '39, chairman of Ryder Truck.

Jack Meyers, '51, publisher of *Time* magazine.

Carl G. Smith, '42, chairman and CEO of Gerber Products.

Raymond S. Colladay, '65, M.S. '66, Ph.D. '69, president of Lockheed Martin Astronautics.

Dr. Russell G. Mawby, '49, Ph.D. '59, chairman of the Kellogg Foundation.

Frank Paganini, M.S. '58, president and general manager of Speed Queen corporation.

Tom Grimes, '60, chairman and CEO Gimbel's department stores.

A.J. "Tony" Pasant, president of Jackson National Life Insurance Co.

Rick Inatome, '76, president and CEO of Inacomp corporation.

John F. Reynolds, '42, president of Transamerica Insurance company.

Harold G. Bernthal, '55, president of American Hospital Supply Corporation.

Warren J. Carr, '61, president of Manufacturer's Hanover Mortgage Corporation.

Ray Stamp, '53, president and CEO, Blaikie, Miller & Hines, Inc.—the "Cadillac" of business and industry food service organizations.

Norm Barkeley, '53, chairman and CEO of Lear Siegler, Inc.

hoto courtesy of Borders, Inc.

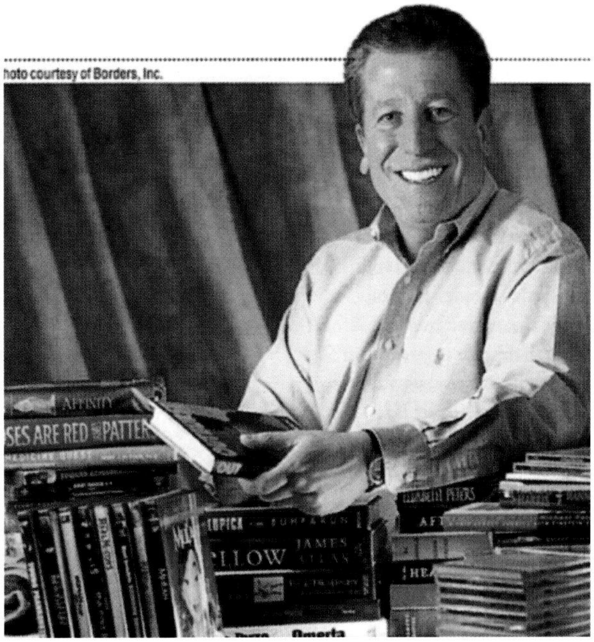

Gregory Josefowicz, '74, president & CEO, Borders Group, Inc.—nation's second largest retail bookstore chain.

Ken Way,'61, MBA '71, chairman and CEO, Lear Seating Corporation.

William H. Bricker, '53, M.S. '54, chairman and CEO of Diamond Shamrock, Corporation.

Surinder Kapur, '64, M.A. '65, Ph.D. '72, chair of the Confederation of Indian Industry, Northern Region of India. He was chairman and managing director of Soma Steering Systems, Ltd., New Delhi, India.

Robert A. Burgess, '66, president and CEO, Pulte Homes, Inc.

Randall Pittman, '76, MBA '78, chairman and CEO, Chatham Capital Corp. and Forest Health Services Corp.

Jim Cornelius, '65, MBA '67, CEO, Guidant Corporation.

Darryl Allen, '65, CEO of Libbey-Owen Ford.

Lawrence T. Wong, Ph.D. '70, CEO of the Hong Kong Jockey Club, Hong Kong, Peoples Republic of China.

Drayton McLane, Jr., MBA '59, vice chairman of Wal-Mart Corporation.

John McConnell, '49, founder, chairman and CEO of Worthington Industries.

Gene McKay, '51, president and owner of Archway Cookies.

Howard Stevens, '64, president of Penn Mutual Fire Insurance Co.

William H. Ames, '66, MBA '69, president SCM Allied Paper Co.

Robert D. Rowan, '47, chairman of Fruehauf Corporation.

Dean Richardson, '50, CEO of Manufacturers National Bank.

Tom Bailey, '61, president, CEO and chairman of the Janus Fund.

John Costello, MBA '70, president and CEO of MVP.com.

Richard A. Benson, Ph.D. '70, president of Caterpillar Industrial, Inc.

Douglas F. St. John, '62, president of Owen-Illinois-Nippon Electric Glass Company, Ltd.

Brian Walker, '71, '84, president of Herman Miller, Inc. North America.

Myron A. Roedeer, MBA '61, president of Tropical Products International Division.

Nicholas J. DeGrazia, Ph.D. '74, president of Lionel Trains.

Richard H. Ruch, '52, president and CEO of Herman Miller, Inc.

William Alldredge, '61, MBA '62, president, international development for Newell Rubbermaid.

Susan M. Schaffer, M.A. '69, vice president of United Airlines in-flight services.

Sally Macut, '72, M.A. '79, vice president of operations for Northwest Airlines.

Ingrid Saunders Jones, '69, vice president, corporate affairs, Coca Cola Company.

James R. Jensen, '69, president of Gray & Company—nation's largest producer of maraschino and glace cherries.

James R. Kirk, M.A. '67, Ph.D. '71, president of research and development, Campbell Soup Company.

Russell E. Palmer, '66, Managing Partner and CEO of Touche Ross & Co.

Toichi Takenada, MBA '80, CEO of Takenada Corp.—Japan's premier construction company.

James E. Oesterricher, '64, CEO, J.C. Penny Co.

SPARTAN PROFILES

Robin Richards, '78, president of mp3.com, No. 1 music service provider on the Internet.

Roots clothing company founders Michael Budman, '68, left, and Donald Green, fraternity brother of Budman, won the competition to outfit the 2002 and 2004 U.S. Olympic teams. Their U.S. team berets became the hottest selling item at the 2002 Winter Olympics in Salt Lake City.

Robert C. Lowes, '68, MBA '75, CEO, Burger King.

Randall Smith, '73, president and COO of NFO WorldGroup, a marketing research group that is part of the Interpublic Group of Companies, Inc.

Paul H. Woodruff, '59, M.S. '61, founder and CEO of the Environmental Resources Management Group. He was named 1995 CEO of the Year by the Franklin Institute in Philadelphia.

Lloyd E. Ward, '70, CEO of Maytag Appliances; CEO United States Olympic Committee.

Steve Akers, '80, founded Sprint Tide Networks which he sold to Lucent Technologies for $1.3 billion. He was serving as chief technology officer of Lucent's Inter-Networking systems Division in 2001.

Gregory Josefowicz, '74, president and CEO of Borders Group, Inc., the nation's second largest retail bookstore chain.

John Costello, MBA '70, president and CEO of MBP. com, the leading online company for outdoor and sporting goods.

Kenneth B. Yerrick, '59, M.A. '62, executive vice president of Dow Corning.

Julie Aigner-Clark, '88, founder of the Baby Einstein Co., producer of cultural multimedia educational materials for babies and toddlers. The company was sold to Disney in 2001.

Dale A. Petroskey, '78, senior vice president, National Geographic Society; president Baseball Hall of Fame.

Michael Budman, '68, and Donald Green, MSU graduate, co-founded Roots, the $300-million Toronto apparel company with some 200 stores worldwide. Their company was selected as the official outfitter for the U.S. Olympic teams in 2002 and 2004. The Roots' berets worn by the U.S. team became the hottest sales item at the 2002 Winter Olympics.

David L. Witte, '64, chairman and CEO of Ward Howell International.

Thomas E. Evans, MBA '81, president of Tenneco Automotive.

Jerry K. Myers, '62, executive vice president and CFO of TRW, Inc.

Michael Lawton, '80, president of Gerber Products Baby Care Division.

William C. Van Fassen, MBA '81, president and CEO of Blue Cross-Blue Shield of Massachusetts.

Robin Richards, '78, president of MP3.Com, that has become the No. 1 music site on the Internet. Richards was named Ernst & Young "Entrepreneur of the Year."

Don Marsh, '61, president, CEO and owner of Marsh Supermarkets in Indianapolis, Indiana, a chain with 14,000 employees and 78 supermarkets.

Julie Aigner-Clark, '88, founded the Baby Einstein Company, producer of cultural multimedia educational material for babies and toddlers. Baby Einstein videos are popular sellers nationwide. Aigner-Clark, and her husband Bill, sold the company to Disney in 2001.

Ted D. Wasson, '61, president and CEO of Beaumont Hospital, Royal Oak, Michigan, major regional health care center.

C. Lee Jones, '78, vice president of pharmaceutical development for Abbott Laboratories.

Randy M. Whaley, '77, vice president of sales for PepsiCo worldwide.

Robert N. Cooper, MBA '82, president of Ameritech Michigan.

Frederick S. Addy, '53, M.A. '58, executive vice president of Amoco Oil Company.

Martin J. Allen, Jr., MBA '62, senior vice president of Old Kent Financial Corp.

Hospitality Industry Leaders

Michigan State's School of Hospitality Business, for years has ranked among the top two schools in America, and has produced many leaders in the hotel, restaurant, resort, and institutional management industry.

Their service has spanned the globe. Examples of this leadership and the positions they have attained include:

William R. Tiefel, '56, president of Marriott Hotels and Resorts, was named **1996 Corporate Hotelier of the World** by the 60,000 readers of *Hotels*, official journal of the International Hotel Association.

Carl T. Motteck, '51, president of Hilton Hotels.

John Brogan, '55, president of Sheraton Hotels-North America. Also served as senior vice president ITT Sheraton Corporation and president of Sheraton Hotels in Hawaii.

Jack Barksdale, '50, president of Holiday Inn's food and lodging division.

Joan Sills, '75, president of Colony Hotels and Resorts. The *New York Times* described her as "the only woman to head a leading hotel company with worldwide operations."

Thomas C. Ryan, '79, M.S. '82, Ph.D., '85, McDonald's Corporation executive vice president and chief concept officer.

Ross E. Roeder, '60, executive vice president of Denny's Restaurants.

Carl T. Motteck, '51, served as president of Hilton Hotels.

Joan Sills, '75, served as president of Colony Hotels & Resorts—the first woman to head a worldwide hotel corporation.

Robert E. Dirks, '69, MBA '72, senior vice president hotel operations marketing for the Hilton Corporation.

Sebastian DiMeglio, '57, vice president and general manager of Colonial Williamsburg in Virginia.

William P. Weidner, '67, MBA '68, president and chief operating officer of Las Vegas Sands, Inc.; led the planning, development, financing and construction of the $1.4 billion Venetian Hotel in Las Vegas and is general manager of the 6,000-suite mega-resort.

Karl Eitel, '51, general manager of the world-renowned Broadmoor Hotel in Colorado Springs, Colorado.

Robert H. Burns, '58, founder and president of Regent International Hotels.

Richard Brooks, MSU graduate and vice president of Bridge Street Accommodations, was inducted into the International Association of Hotel Administrators Technology Hall of Fame.

Dan Darrow, MBA '61, Walt Disney World's manager of hotel relations, was selected **Florida's Hotelier of the Year in 1994.** His operations hosted 30 million visitors a year in 18,000 hotel rooms.

Richard Kolasa, '66, manager of the Skyline Country Club in Tucson, Arizona, was named **1995 Club Manager of the Year** by Club Management magazine.

R. Scott Morrison, '61, president and managing director of the world-famous Boca Raton Hotel and Club in Florida.

Bernard Seiler, MBA '73, president of the Seiler Hotel Neues Schloss in Zurich, Switzerland and five family hotels in Zermatt.

Frank Arthur Banks, '61, M.A. '62, general manager, RIHGA Royal Hotel, New York. He also managed the Waldorf Astoria and St. Regis hotels in New York.

Thomas W. Glasgow, Jr., '68, senior vice president, McDonald's Corporation.

Louis Elias, '38, president of Elias Bros. Big Boy Restaurants.

Gary McCausland, '73, president of Domino's Pizza.

David V. Johnson, '71, developer of Bay Harbor Resort in Petoskey, Michigan ("Pebblebeach of the Midwest), was named **1997 Michigan Entrepreneur of the Year.**

Jerry Best, '59, president and CEO of Omni Hotels in America.

David C. George, '79, president of Long Horn Steakhouses.

Bob Fish, '88, president and CEO, and **Mary Roszel, '88**, chief operating officer, are the founders of Beaner's Gourmet Coffee houses.

Lou Weckstein, '58, senior vice president-operations, Windsor Capital Group, headed operations for a series of hotels in the U.S. He helped pioneer the residential-style Embassy Suite concept.

Kevin Brown, '77, president of Lettuce Entertain You Enterprises—a Chicago-based restaurant chain with revenues of $200-million annually.

Susan Smith,'59, M.S. '77, president of Denver-based Food Technologies, Inc.

Robert Johnson, '74, president of Club Corp International.

Hans Schuler, '59, CEO, Schuler's, Inc., chain of up-scale Michigan restaurants.

Richard Helfer, '72, president and CEO of Raffles International Hotel, Singapore.

Donald Jankura, '51, owner of the Waverly Hospitality Associates and past chairman of the American Hotel and Motel Association.

David Kenney, '57, owner of Kenney Enterprises, and past chairman of the American Hotel and Motel Association.

Philip Hickey, Jr., '77, chair and CEO of Rare Hospitality International—an Atlanta-based restaurant company that includes 170 Long Horn Steakhouses, 23 Bugaboo Creek Steak Houses, and 15 Capital Grilles.

Dr. Lewis J. Minor, holder of two MSU degrees, is one of a few chefs in the **American Academy of Chefs Hall of Fame.** He and his wife Ruth gave MSU's School of Hospitality $1 million to create the first endowed chef position at such a school.

Gene F. Jankowski, M.A. '69, served as president of CBS Broadcasting Group.

Richard Cregar, '58, founder of Cregar Enterprises in Rochester, Michigan, and past president of the National Restaurant Owners Association.

Harris O. Machus, '32, past president of Machus Restaurants, and past president of the National Restaurant Association.

Mike Getto, '56, senior vice president of Friden Hotel Co. in California.

Bill Zehnder, '71, president of Bavarian Inn Restaurant, Frankenmuth, Michigan.

Herman Berghoff, '58, owner of Berghoff Restaurant in Chicago.

Michael Hurst, '53, owner of the 15th Street Fisheries and past president of the National Restaurant Association.

Paul Smith, '66, owner-operator of the regionally famous Hitching Post restaurant in Cheyenne, Wyoming.

Daniel J. Corrigan, MBA '74, president of Charley's Steakery, headquartered in Columbus, Ohio.

Dawn Kuchar, '87, was selected Ambassador for Walt Disney World out of a cast of 35,000 employees.

Television Network Leaders

Gene F. Jankowski, M.A. '69, president of CBS Broadcasting Group.

Frank Price, '51, president of Universal Television.

Kay (Smith) Koplovitz, M.A. '68, president and CEO of USA Network.

Bob Cook, '70, president and CEO of Twentieth Television, the Twentieth Century Fox syndication unit.

Susan Packard, '77, M.A. '79, CEO of the Home and Garden Television Network (HGTV). She also headed the Food Network and the Do-It-Yourself Network. She was named **Cable TV's "Woman of the Year" in 1998**.

Charles Engel, '61, executive in charge of the ABC Mystery Movie series, which included *Columbo* with Peter Falk, *B.L. Stryker* with Burt Reynolds, and *Gideon Oliver* with Louis Gossett, Jr. In 1968, he developed the hit TV series *It Takes a Thief*.

Robert A. Chapek, MBA '84, president of Buena Vista Home Entertainment (BVHE). He was responsible for domestic distribution of Disney's home video and DVD products, including Touchstone, Miramax and Dimension labels.

Clifford M. Kirtland, '45, president of Cox Broadcasting.

Edward L. Palmer, M.A. '62, Ph.D. '64, was co-founder of the Children's Television Workshop.

Charles W. Larsen, '67, M.A. '70, president of Domestic TV distribution for Republic Pictures Corp.

Rob G. Tapert, '78, and **Sam Raimi, '78**, co-produced the hit TV syndicated shows: *Xena: Warrior Princess* and *Hercules: The Legendary Journeys*.

Neil Rosen, '62, was writer-producer for the following TV series: *The Dick Van Dyke Show*, *Too Close for Comfort*, *Welcome Back Kotter*, *The Loveboat*, and *Silver Spoons*.

Tom Patchett, '62, served as the creative director for the *Dick Van Dyke*, *Carol Burnett*, and *Bob Newhart* shows.

Yale Udoff, '57, wrote for episodic TV, including *The Man from U.N.C.L.E.* and *Baretta & Batman*.

Dennis Lewin, '65, senior vice president of ABC-TV broadcast planning for National Football League games.

Jennifer Purtan, '83, senior vice president of sales at the ABC Radio Networks, New York.

David Hirsch, '84, was selected by Dick Clark to host *American Bandstand*, after Clark's 33-year career leading the show. It was the longest running variety show in TV history.

Suzanne Sena, '85, host of the *Celebrity Homes* show on the E! Entertainment Television network.

Hollywood Executives, Producers, Writers and Actors

Frank Price, '51, chairman of Columbia Pictures; president of Universal Pictures. He was involved in the production of *Kramer vs. Kramer*, *Tootsie*, *The Big Chill*, *Out of Africa*, and *Back to the Future*.

Sam Raimi, '78, directed *Spider-Man*, which set an all-time box office record $114 million in sales in its first weekend, May 3-5, 2002.

Bill Mechanic, '73, CEO of Fox Film Entertainment (Twentieth Century Fox). He helped produce *Mrs. Doubtfire*, the *Star Wars Trilogy*, *The X-Files*, *There's Something About Mary*, and the blockbuster *Titanic*.

Dan Romanelli, '64, president of Warner Bros. Worldwide Consumer Products.

Ed Feldman, '50, was an **Academy Award-winning movie producer**—*Save The Tiger*, and the 1983 hit *Witness*, starring Harrison Ford.

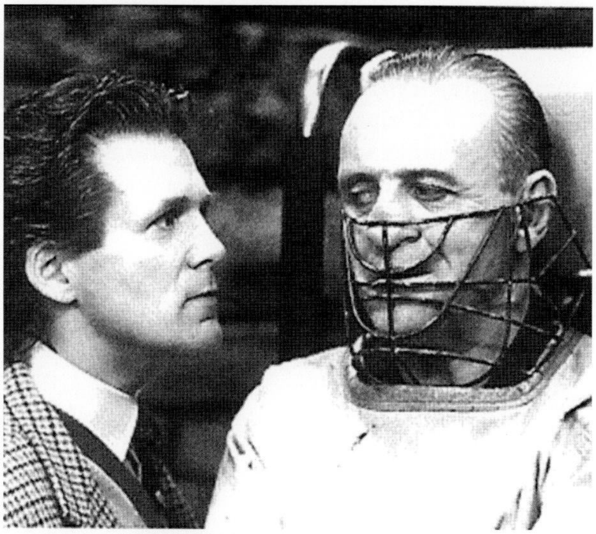

Anthony Heald, '71, left, playing Dr. Frederick Chilton in movie *Silence of the Lambs*, stares down Anthony Hopkins

Walter Hill, '62, has produced dozens of films, including *Extreme Prejudice, The Last Man Standing, Southern Comfort, and Streets of Fire.*

Sam Raimi and Bob Tapert, '78, teamed to produce the films *Evil Dead, Evil Dead II*, and the *Army of Darkness*. Raimi also produced *Darkman*, and *The Quick and the Dead*.

Dana Precious, '85, executive vice president for Sony Pictures Entertainment, has run the advertising campaigns for more than 30 movie hits, including *Charlie's Angels, The Wedding Planner, Men in Black, Stuart Little, The Patriot*, and *Godzilla*.

James Pentecost, '72, produced the Disney hit movie *Pocahontas*.

Mike Lobell, '62, has produced the following movies: *Striptease, It Could Happen To You, Honeymoon in Vegas*, and *The Freshman*.

Michael Cimino, '59, directed the movies: *Thunderbolt and Lightning, The Deer Hunter*, which starred Meryl Streep, Robert de Niro and Christopher Walken in 1978, and *The Sunchaser* starring Woody Harrelson and Anne Bancroft in 1996.

Yale Udoff, '57, wrote screenplays for the films *Third Degree Burn* in 1989, and *Eve of Destruction* in 1991.

Tom McGuane, '62, wrote scripts for the movies *Rancho Deluxe*, and *Missouri Breaks*. In 1975, he directed *92 In The Shade*.

Jim Harrison, '60, M.A. '64, wrote the novel on which the movie *Legend of the Fall*, was based. He teamed with Tom McGuane to write *Cold Feet*. Harrison also scripted *Revenge*, and *Wolf*.

Walt Lockwood, '63, wrote the screenplay for the movie *Finnegan Begin Again*.

James Zatolokin, '67, co-produced the Stallone film *Cliffhanger*.

Jim Cash, '70, M.S. '72, and Jack Epps, Jr. '72, teamed as screenwriters to help create the following movies: *Top Gun, Legal Eagles, The Secret of My Success, Dick Tracy*, and *Anaconda*.

Joe Vecchio, '65, was executive producer for the movie *Oscar*. As an actor, he appeared in the TV series *The Fall Guy*, and *Police Story*.

Maureen McElheron, '73, won an Oscar nomination for the best short animated feature in 1988, composing the music for *Your Face*, teaming with MTV animator Bill Plympton.

Robert Urich, M.A. '70, starred in the TV series *Vega$*, and *Gavilon*. He also was the captain in the new *Love Boat* series.

Anthony Heald, '71, appeared in *Silkwood* and played Dr. Frederick Chilton *in Silence of the Lambs*. He also had roles in three John Grisham movies, *The Pelican Brief, The Client*, and *A Time to Kill*.

Joel Higgins, '66, starred in *Silver Spoons*.

Martha Smith, '74, played Babs, the sorority blonde in *Animal House*. She also starred in the TV series *Scarecrow and Mrs. King*.

Charles "Bubba" Smith, '67, former All-American tackle at MSU and NFL All-Pro tackle, appeared in the popular *Police Academy* movie series.

Bob Apisa, '69, All-American fullback at MSU, appeared in many Hollywood action movies and such TV series as *Hawaii 50*.

Jon Erik-Hexum, '84, appeared opposite Joan Collins in Male Model, and starred in NBC's Voyagers as Phineas Bogg. He died in an accident on a movie set in 1984.

Steve Van Wormer, '92, appeared in Disney's *Meet the Deedles*.

Stage Entertainment Leaders

Sherrie Payne, '66, joined the famous Motown trio "The Supremes" in 1975. She composed 250 songs. The religious singer said, "He's guiding my hands and making my fingers move." She was a medical technology graduate and also taught school.

Kevin Rhodes, '87, was the principal ballet conductor for the Vienna, Austria State Opera and resident conductor for the Deutsche Oper am Rhein in Dusseldorf, Germany.

Peter Marinos, '73, was playing 12 different characters in *The Producers* in 2001. It was the most highly awarded show in Broadway history. Marinos also has appeared in *Evita, Zorba*, and *The Secret Garden*.

James P. Hoffa, '63, president of the International Brotherhood of Teamsters.

Labor Union Leaders

James P. Hoffa, '63, president of the International Brotherhood of Teamsters.

Linda (Peterson) Puchala, '69, president of the National Association of Flight Attendants. She was the only woman to lead an AFL-CIO affiliate.

Mark Bathurst, '72, President of the Master Executive Council for United Airlines in the Airline Pilots' Association.

Advertising Leaders

Don Johnston, '51, president and CEO of J. Walter Thompson Co., then the world's largest advertising agency.

Louis T. Hagopian, '47, chairman and CEO of N.W. Ayer ABH, International, the oldest advertising agency in the U.S.

Anthony Hopp, '67, M.A. '68, vice chairman and CEO, Campbell-Ewald Advertising.

Dick O'Connor, MSU, chairman, Campbell-Ewald.

Frank Hoag, MSU, president and chief operating officer, Campbell-Ewald.

Lou Schultz, MSU, president and CEO of Campbell-Ewald's sister company, C-E Communications. Campbell-Ewald is the advertising agency for the Chevrolet Division of General Motors.

D. Stan Fields III, executive vice president of D'Arcy, Masius, Benton & Bowles Worldwide.

Dick Beals, '49, was the voice of Speedy Alka-Seltzer ads, and had done voices for commercials and characters on network shows such as *Gunsmoke, Fibber McGee & Molly, One Man's Family, The Cisco Kid*, and *The Flintstones*. Beals, a former MSU cheerleader, owned an advertising firm in Escondido, California.

Military Leaders

Florence Hall, Class of 1909, headed the National Women's Land Army during World War II. This program involved 60,000 women farm workers. It was a descendent of the "Farmerette" organization of World War I, and part of the new "Crop Corps," designed to beat the food shortage threat.

Ernest H. Burt, 1914, Brigadier General, U.S. Army.

William H. Kasten, 1915, Major General, U.S. Army.

Donald A. Stroh, 1915, Major General, U.S. Army.

Omer O. Niergarth, 1917, Brigadier General, U.S. Air Force.

Lawrence G. Fritz, 1920, Major General, U.S. Air Force.

George F. Shulgren, 1922, Brigadier General, U.S. Army.

Herbert A. Hall, 1927, Brigadier General, U.S. Army.

Thomas L. Sherburne, 1927, Major General, U.S. Army.

Melvin D. Losey, 1929, Brigadier General, U.S. Army.

Don A. Jones, 1933, Rear Admiral, U.S. Navy; Director, National Ocean Survey for the National Oceanic and Atmospheric Administration.

Ronald D. McDonald, 1933, Major General, National Guard.

L.W. VanAntwerp, 1936, Rear Admiral, U.S. Navy.

John D. Hutson, '69, 3rd from right, with family, served as Judge Advocate General of the U.S. Navy.

James D. Hittle, 1937, Brigadier General, U.S. Marine Corps.

Thomas R. Ford, 1938, Brigadier General, U.S. Air Force.

Emil P. Eschenburg, 1939, Brigadier General, U.S. Army.

Collins H. Ferris, 1941, Brigadier General, Air National Guard.

Russell F. Gustke, 1941, Brigadier General, U.S. Air Force.

Lt. General James E. Light, Jr., '56, Commander of the U.S. 15th Air Force. He was a command pilot with 8,700 flying hours and 220 combat missions. He was awarded the **Distinguished Flying Cross and the Bronze Star.**

Lt. General E. Fornell, '58, Commander of Electronic Systems Division, U.S. Air Force Systems Command. He was a highly decorated command pilot with more than 6,000 flying hours in 40 different aircraft. He was a member of the 1957 MSU Big Ten champion swimming team.

Eleftherios S. Kanellakis, M.A. '62, Brigadier General, Royal Hellenic Air Force Chief Justice, Athens, Greece.

Charles Metcalf, M.A. '64, retired U.S. Air Force Major General, director of the U.S. Air Force Museum at Wright-Patterson Air Force Base in Dayton, Ohio.

Four-Star General Donald G. Cook, '69, Commander of the U.S. Air Force Education and Training Command at Randolph Air Force Base, Texas.

John D. Hutson, '69, Judge Advocate General of the U.S. Navy.

Rear Admiral Joyce M. Johnson, D.O. '80, Surgeon General of the U.S. Coast Guard. She was the first woman to hold the post, and the first woman to attain flag rank in the U.S.C.G.

Law Enforcement & Security Leaders

H. Stuart Knight, '48, director of the U.S. Secret Service.

Eljay Brown, '73, director of the U.S. Secret Service. He joined the Secret Service when Stuart Knight was the director.

Kenneth Gianoules, '58, domestic chief of INTERPOL, the international police organization.

Gerald A. Behn, '39, U.S. Secret Service, was named Chief of the White House Detail, in charge of guarding the U.S. President, in 1961.

Colonel John R. Plants, '57, director of the Michigan State Police.

Gerald L. Hough, Police Administration graduate, director of the Michigan State Police.

E. Wilson Purdy, '42, public safety director for Dade County, Florida.

Rod Puffer, '59, chief of security for the National Aeronautics and Space Administration Center in Houston, Texas.

Gordon W. Kettler, B.S. '63, M.A. '64, General Motors' director of global security.

Isaiah "Ike" McKinnon, Ph.D. '85, Chief of Police for Detroit, Michigan.

Penny Harrington, '64, Chief of Police for Portland, Oregon—**the first woman to head a major U.S. city police force.**

Richard Arthur, '51, director of the National Training Center for Lie Detection.

MSU Criminal Justice graduates have been and are chiefs of police in dozens of U.S. cities, including Flint, Jackson, Benton Harbor and East Lansing, Michigan.

News Media Leaders

Jack Meyers, '51, publisher of *Time* Magazine.

Paul M. Rothenberg, '63, general manager of the *Washington Times*, the nation's eighth largest daily newspaper.

Carole Leigh Hutton, '78, publisher and editor, *Detroit Free Press*.

Joan Lee Faust, '50, garden editor for the *New York Times*. She authored three best-selling books: *The New York Times Book of House Plants*, *The New York Times Book of Vegetable Gardening*, and *The New York Times Book of Flower Gardening*. She was named **National Garden Writer of the Year in 1972**, and taught at the Brooklyn Botanical Garden.

Paul Cox, '80, assistant managing editor of the Wall Street Journal Online.

Robin Stone, '86, executive editor of *Essence*, a magazine for black women with a circulation of one million.

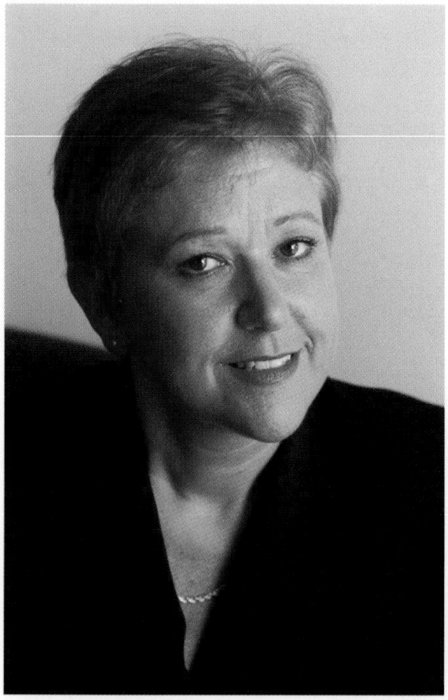

Carole Leigh Hutton, '78,
publisher and editor, *Detroit Free Press.*

Roger C. Palms, M.A. '71, editor of *Decision Magazine*, a publication of the Billy Graham Evangelic Association. He has written 14 books and became editor of *Decision* in 1976 at Billy Graham's request.

Presidents of Professional Organizations & Associations

Stephen A. Bransdorfer, '51, president of the State Bar of Michigan.

Katherine McCoy, '62, was the youngest and first woman elected president of the Industrial Designers Society of America. She authored the book *Design in Michigan* in 1977.

Barbara Stonewater, Ph.D. '77, president of the National Association for Women Deans, Administrators and Counselors.

Dawn Riley, '87, president, Women's Sports Foundation. Riley, former MSU sailing team captain, was the first woman to crew on a winning America's Cup team (1992).

William F. Huey, Jr., M.S. '54, Ph.D. '59, president of the Council for Agricultural Science and Technology.

Harris O. Machus, '32, president of the National Restaurant Association.

James W. Timmerman, '64, M.S. '68, president of the Golf Course Superintendent's Association of America.

Robert L. Hughes, '59, president of the National Association of Life Underwriters.

Janice Newman, M.S.N. '83, president of the Michigan Society of Hospital Nursing Administrators.

Alfred R. Bransdorfer, '50, president of the Michigan Press Association.

Paul Scott, '60, president of the Michigan Association of Realtors.

Crystal Lange, Ph.D. '72, president of the Michigan Association of Colleges of Nursing.

Andy Mollison, '67, president of the National Press Club, Washington, D.C.

James M. McCartney, '49, president of the Washington D.C. Gridiron Club.

Len Barnes, '43, president of the Society of American Travel Writers.

Eugene Bonofito, '52, president of the Michigan Dental Association.

Barry Grant, '57, president of the Michigan Probate Judges Association.

Wesley H. Maurer, Jr., '73, president of the Michigan Press Association.

Terrell R. Oetzel, M.S. '64, president of the American Institute of Real Estate Appraisers.

M. Rupert Cutler, Ph.D. '72, president of the Defenders of Wildlife, a national conservation group.

Bonnie Lauer, '73, president of the Ladies Professional Golf Association. At MSU, she won the 1973 NCAA women's golf championship. She was a professional golfer and won the Patty Berg Classic in 1977, and the Uniden International in 1985.

Linda M. Gobler, '77, president of the Michigan Grocers Association.

Hugh M. Jarvis, '60, M.A. '64, president of the Michigan Federation of Teachers.

Thomas R. Castle, '83, president of the Ohio Hospital Association.

Michael E. Hurst, '53, M.A. '54, chairman of the board, the National Restaurant Association.

Nola J. Pender, '64, M.A. '65, president of the American Academy of Nursing.

Theodore J. Lowi, '54, president of the American Political Science Association.

Don McIntosh, '57, president of the International Food Service Executives Association.

Richard J. Lewis, Ph.D. '64, president of the American Assembly of Collegiate Schools of Business.

Robert P. McBain, '64, president of the American Association of Attorney-Certified Public Accountants, Inc.

James Barret, '70, chairman of the American Chamber of Commerce Executives. He was CEO of the Michigan Chamber of Commerce.

Cynthia S. Johns, '75, chair of the 48,000 member American Society of Clinical Pathologists Associate Member Section.

Arthur Hills, '53, president of the American Society of Golf Course Architects.

Jerry Matthews, '56, '60, M.A. '64, president of the American Society of Golf Course Architects, succeeding Arthur Hills.

Alan C. Harnish, '66, president of the Federal Bar Association. He was elected by the largest margin in history.

R. Stephen Radcliffe, '67, president of the Society of Actuaries.

Kun Mo Chung, Ph.D. '63, president of the Institute for Advanced Engineering in South Korea. He served as provost of the Korea Advanced Institute of Science and Technology; as president of the International Atomic Energy Agency; and as chair of the International Nuclear Energy Academy.

Dominic A. Palazzolo, '64, M.A. '68, president of the National Association of Elementary School Principals.

Matthew A. Terry, D.O. '75, M.A. '80, chair of the Council of Deans of the American Association of Colleges of Osteopathic Medicine.

Elton D. Aberle, M.S. '65, Ph. D. '67, president of the American Society of Animal Science.

Stan Ikenberry, M.A. '57, Ph.D. '60, president of the American Council on Education, the primary representative for all of education to the U.S. Congress. He was a past president of the University of Illinois.

Paul M. Oliaro, M.A. '71, Ph.D. '83, president of the American College Personnel Association.

William Mottel, '51, chair of the National Safety Council.

William F. Jackson, DVM '47, president of the World Small Animal Veterinary Association.

Ronnie Barnes, M.S. '79, president of the Professional Football Athletic Trainers Society. He was the head athletic trainer for the New York Giants football team.

Gregory Hauser, '75, M.A. '77, president of the National Inter-fraternity Conference.

Jerry L. Johns, M.A. '66, Ph.D. '70, president of the International Reading Association. He was a distinguished professor at Northern Illinois University.

Michael Williams, '82, president of the American Association of Critical Care Nurses.

David H. Gibbs, '62, president of the Construction Financial Management Association.

William H. Mayes, '69, MA '74, president of the Michigan Association of School Administrators.

John K. Everett, D.O. '87, president of the Michigan Osteopathic Association.

Honors and Award Winners, Inventors, Discoverers, National-International Recognition

Edmund C. Arnold, '54, was "father" of the easier-to-read six-column newspaper format that has been adopted nationwide. He served as chairman and professor of the graphic arts and publishing departments at Syracuse University's School of Public Communication.

Carl M. Horn, '21, '51, was inducted into the Michigan Education Hall of Fame. He was an MSU professor of counseling, personnel services and educational counseling.

Dr. Michael Schulz, '64, won a $10,000 achievement award from the Aerospace Corp. of Los Angeles for his theory on the structure of the interplanetary magnetic field—considered one of the great advances of the decade in 1983.

David Slowinski, '76, MBA '80, in 1983, discovered the largest known prime number, a 25, 962-digit monster that filled six computer printout pages. He was a senior systems analyst at Cray Research.

George Levitt, Ph.D. '57, was named a "Distinguished Inventor of 1983" by the Intellectual Property Owners, Inc. He was cited for the discovery of sulfonglurea herbicides, a class of highly active materials that were believed to be safe to human health and the environment.

Michael Loukinen, '67, won the National Merit Award from the American Association for State and Local History, and "Best Film" by the National Endowment for the Arts for his PBS TV documentary, "Finnish American Lives."

Genevieve Gillette, '20, in 1984, became the first women and eighth person to be inducted into the Michigan Conservation Hall of Fame. She was a leader in establishing the Michigan State Park system, and led the drive to found the Michigan State Parks Association, and became its first president.

James H. Steele, DVM '41, was awarded the XII International Veterinary Congress Prize by the American Veterinary Medical Association in 1984. He was a former U.S. Assistant Surgeon General, founder of the American College of Veterinary Preventive Medicine, and a professor emeritus at the University of Texas.

Loretta L. VanCamp, '48, was a major collaborator in the discovery of Cisplatin (FDA approval 1978) and Carboplatin (FDA approval mid-1980s), which became the most-prescribed anti-cancer drugs in the nation. She was laboratory supervisor for Dr. Barnett Rosenberg, MSU Biophysics department head, who led the development of the two platinum-based drugs. Her name appears with Dr. Rosenberg's on both drug patents.

Marvelle J. Vannest, M.A. '82, was named Michigan Teacher of the Year in 1984. She taught English and Language Arts and coached two high school quiz teams to international championships.

Luis Ramiro Beltran, M.A. '68, Ph.D. '77, won the first McLuhan-Teleglobe Canada Award in 1984. Beltran beat 40 candidates from 28 nations to win the $50,000 prize, which is awarded every two years.

Rick Inatome, MSU graduate and president of Inacomp Computer Centers, Inc. was named a Michiganian of the Year for 1985 by the *Detroit News.*

Amir U. Khan, M.S. '49, M.S. '52, Ph.D. '67, won the International Inventors Award in 1986, which was presented by H.M. King Carl Gustaf of Sweden in Stockholm. The award worth $36,500, was considered the equivalent of the Nobel Prize for invention. Khan's invention was an axial flow thresher, an implement widely used by farmers in tropical rice producing nations. He was an agricultural engineer with the International Rice Institute in the Philippines.

Gary Gildner, '60, M.A. '61, won the 1986 National Magazine Award in Fiction, the highest honor in the magazine world. He was a poet, novelist and English professor. His first novel was *The Second Bridge.*

Morton B. Panish, M.S. '52, Ph.D. '54, won Japan's $61,000 Computer and Communication Award and was inducted into the National Academy of Engineering in 1986. He was a senior scientist at Bell Laboratories. In collaboration with Japanese scientist Iguo Hayashi, Panish helped develop hetero-structure lasers. **Their work enabled the use of digital signals in CD players, laser printers, barcode readers, autofocus cameras, and fiber-optic communication.**

Three MSU graduates were part of General Motors' world championship team which won the first transcontinental solar car race ever staged, in November, 1987. The GM Sunraycer team won the first World Solar Challenge by racing 1,950 miles through the outback, from the top of Australia to the bottom, and won the race by a two and one-half day margin over 25 other vehicles. MSU alums on the winning team were driver **Molly Brennan, '82**, Rhodes Scholar and track star at MSU and production engineering manager at GM's Tech Center; **Terry Satchell, '68**, driver and suspension engineer for GM's Chevrolet-Pontiac-Canada Group; and **Bruce McCristal, '54**, public affairs director for the Sunraycer team and GM Hughes Electronics.

Clyde P. Davenport, '51, was named Physician of the Year for 1987 by the Michigan Chapter of the American Academy of Family Physicians.

Nancy Corbin Bray, '62, was named Michigan Teacher of the Year for 1987. She was a music teacher for the Jenison public schools.

G.D. Hsiung, M.S. '48, Ph.D. '51, won the 1988 Welcome Diagnostics Award for Achievement in Viral Diagnostics. Hsiung was a Yale medical school professor and director of the Veterans Administration Medical Center's Virology Reference Laboratory.

Karen Falkentstein, '72, M.A. '73, was named Michigan's Outstanding Principal for 1988. She was principal of Buchanan's Ottawa Elementary School.

Ronald J. Patten, '57, M.A. '59, CPA, named Honorary Fellow and Dean of the Year in 1988 by the Academy of International Business. He was dean of the School of Business at the University of Connecticut.

Edward Brayton, '74, M.A. '84, won the 1988 John C. Timmer Award as the nation's leading construction educator, selected from a field of 100. He was an assistant professor of building construction technology at Ferris State University, Big Rapids, Michigan.

R. Paul Singh, Ph.D. '74, won the 1988 International Award from the Institute of Food Technology. He was a professor of food engineering at the University of California-Davis.

David E.S. Marvin, '72, was named Michigan's Outstanding Young Lawyer of the Year for 1988 by the Michigan Bar Association.

Cathy Jaros, '71, was featured on the cover of *Fortune* Magazine (April 10, 1989). From the number two position at Tappan Capital Partners, she specialized in leveraged buyouts of food companies.

Terry Van Der Tuuk, '63, was named Entrepreneur of the Year for 1989. He was chairman of Graphics Technology, Inc., a bar code label manufacturer.

Donald F. Keck, '62, M.S. '64, Ph.D. '67, working with two other researches at Corning Glass Works in 1989, **discovered a way to transmit laser light across miles of optical fiber.** He was elected a Fellow of The Institute of Electrical and Electronics Engineers.

Peter Morris, M.A. '90, won the North American Scrabble Open in December, 1998, which was considered the world championship.

Philip Von Voightlander, '68, D.V.M. '69, M.S. '71 and Ph.D., was named Distinguished Scientist V (the highest level) at the Upjohn Co in 1989. His discoveries have led to potential products for the treatment of schizophrenia, pain, depression and epilepsy and for protection of the nervous system.

Mary Joy Haywood, Ph.D. '75, received the 1991 President's Award for Excellence in Teaching. She also authored the book *Wildflowers of Pennsylvania*.

Jaw-Kai Wang, M.C. '56, Ph.D. '58, won the 1991 American Society of Agricultural Engineers' Kishida International Award, given for professional efforts that improve food production, living conditions, and/or educational levels outside the U.S.A. He was director of the Aquaculture Program at the University of Hawaii. He was inducted into the National Academy of Engineering in 1995.

Ivan Lahaie, '79, was named the Outstanding Radar Engineer of 1991 by the Institute of Electrical & Electronics Engineers. He developed the "passive sensor" which did not use any beams, such as microwaves or infrared light which could alert an enemy that they were being watched. Lahaie was a research scientist at the Environmental Research Institute of Michigan.

Three MSU alums were honored as 1992 Presidential Teaching Professors. They were **Jerry Johns, Mary Suzanne Schriber**, and **John Niemi**—all faculty members at Northern Illinois University.

Anita M. Clark, M.A. '72, M.A. '77, won the 1992 Presidential Award for Excellence in Science and Mathematics Teaching and the 1992 Milken Family Foundation Educator Award. She was a mathematics teacher at Marshall, Michigan High School.

Judy Ferris, M.A. '67, was presented the 1992 Presidential Award for Excellence in Science Teaching by President George Herbert Walker Bush at the White House. She also was awarded $7,500 by the National Science Foundation.

John Scott, MFA, '65 won the 1992 MacArthur Foundation's "Genius Grant," a $315,000 award that could be spent in any way. He was a distinguished professor of art at Xavier University, New Orleans.

Shelby Hunt, Ph.D. '68, received the American Marketing Association-Irwin Distinguished Marketing Education Award for 1992. He was the Paul Whitfield Horn professor of marketing at Texas Tech University.

George Levitt, Ph.D. '57, won the National Medal of Technology in 1993—the highest award bestowed by the President of the United States for extraordinary achievements in technology. Levitt discovered a family of herbicides that were environmentally friendly, less toxic than salt. He was a retired DuPont agricultural chemist.

Dorothy Delay, '36, master violin teacher at the Juilliard School in New York, was honored at the 1993 Aspen Music Festival where her former pupils played five original works for her. She had taught the world's leading violinists—Itzak Perlman, Cho-Liang Lin, Shlomo Mintz, Nadza Salermo-Sonnenberg, Nigel Kennedy, and Midori and Sarah Chang.

Hugh A. Andrews, '71, M.A. '72, was named to Puerto Rico's Hall of Fame of Top Businessmen. Andrews managed the San Juan Hotel and Casino and the Condado Plaza Hotel.

Donald A. Opila, M.D. '75, was named Young Internist of the Year in 1993 by the American Society of Internal Medicine. He was coordinator of Medical Education-Primary Care Track at the State University of New York-Buffalo.

Charles Dare, Sr., '56, was named by *Town & Country* magazine as one of America's Top Ten Brokers. He was a vice president and financial consultant with Merrill Lynch.

Richard Kolasa, '66, named 1995 Club Manager of the Year by *Club Management* magazine. He was the manager of the Skyline Country Club, Tucson, Arizona.

Fred S. Wojtalik, '52, received the Presidential Rank of Distinguished Executive. The rank, granted by the President of the U.S., is given to only one percent of Senior Executive Service members. Wojtalik was manager of the Observatory Projects Office at NASA's Marshall Space Flight Center, Huntsville, Alabama.

Herbert S. Eleuterio, Ph.D. '53, received the DuPont Company's Lavoisier Medal for Technical Achievement. He made two major discoveries in polymer chemistry in his 38-year career.

Paul H. Woodruff, '59, M.S. '61, was named 1995 CEO of the Year at the Enterprise Awards event at the Franklin Institute in Philadelphia. He was founder and CEO of the Environmental Resources Management Group.

Jack Ebling, '73 and '75, was named the 1995 Sports Writer of the Year by the National Sportscaster and Sportwriters Association. He was a sports writer for the *Lansing State Journal*, Lansing, Michigan.

George Weeks, '55, was inducted into the Michigan Journalism Hall of Fame in 1996. He was a political columnist with the *Detroit News.*

James Quello, '35, was inducted into the Radio Hall of Fame in 1997. Quello was chairman and a member of the Federal Communications Commission, serving 24 years. Earlier in his career he had been general manager of WJR radio in Detroit; president of the Michigan Association of Broadcasters and received its lifetime achievement award. He also received the Distinguished Service Award from the National Association of Broadcasters, its highest honor.

JoAnn Burkholder, Ph.D. '86, discovered the "cell from hell," or Pfiesteria piscicida, a toxic algae found in the eastern waterways of North Carolina in 1997. It had killed hundreds of millions of fish in the Albermarle-Pamlico Estuary and the Neuse River. A hundred humans had been victimized by the organism. Burkholder received a $250,000 grant to study the "cell from hell."

Martin J. Allen, MBA '62, was inducted into the Bank Marketing Association's Hall of Fame in 1997. He had served as senior vice president of the Old Kent Financial Corporation in Grand Rapids, Michigan.

John R. Short, '67, M.S. '68, Ph.D. '71, was presented the Presidential Rank Award by the U.S. Secretary of the Navy, one of the highest honors a public employee can receive. Short was the director of Submarine Combat Systems at the Naval Underseas Warfare Division, Newport, Rhode Island.

Francis C. Byrnes, Ph.D. '63, received the 1997 Outstanding Service Award from the Association for International Agricultural Education and Extension. He was a senior associate at Winrock International Institute for Agricultural Development.

Alden "Denny" Townsend, Ph.D. '69, plant geneticist with the U.S. Department of Agriculture's Agricultural Research Service, worked twenty years with a research team to clone two disease-tolerant elm strains named "New Harmony" and "Valley Forge." They were to go on sale in 2000. The long research effort was in part an answer to Dutch Elm Disease.

Jim Adams, MSU alum who broadcast MSU football and basketball games for 45 years on WKAR radio, was elected to the Michigan Journalism Hall of Fame in 1998.

Ted B. Martonen, M.S. '71, received 1998 *Computerworld* Smithsonian Award in Medicine for his supercomputer simulations on the human being. He was a research physicist with the Environmental Protection Agency's Research Laboratory, Triangle Park, NC.

Theda L. Rudd, '71, M.A. '74, owner/operator of six Lansing, Michigan-area McDonald's restaurants, won a 1998 McDonald's Golden Arch Award. She was president of the Michigan McDonald's Operators Association.

John Hall, Ph.D. '74, received the Merck Sharp and Dohme International Award for Research in Hypertension in Amsterdam, Holland. He had accomplished breakthrough research on the mechanism of obesity leading to hypertension and kidney disease. He was chairman of physiology and bio-physics at the University of Mississippi Medical Center.

Patricia Martin, '79, was named 1999 Influential Woman in Business by the National Association of Women Business Owners. She was president of the Martin Resource Group, Inc., Elmhurst, Illinois.

John Bamberger, MSU alum and president of Panurgy Co., was named Michigan Entrepreneur of the Year for 1999.

Steven Briggs, M.A. '80, Ph.D. '83, was elected to the National Academy of Sciences. He was president of Novartis Agricultural Discovery Institute, Inc.

Don Nugent, '65, was named Michigan Manufacturer of the Year. He was CEO of Graceland Fruit, and a member of the MSU Board of Trustees.

William C. Van Fassen, MBA '81, named "New Englander of the Year," in 2001. He was president and CEO of Blue Cross/Blue Shield of Massachusetts.

Carl Johnson, '51, won the American Society of Landscape Architects Medal in 2001, the society's highest honor. Johnson is co-founder of Johnson, Johnson & Roy, Inc., Ann Arbor—the largest landscape architectural firm in Michigan.

Kathleen Smiler, '68, D.V.M. '70, received the Garvey Award presented by the American Association for Laboratory Animal Science in 2001. She was senior director of Bio-resources & Administration, Drug Safety Evaluation at WyethAyerst Research.

Pam Withrow, '75, was named Warden of the Year by the North American Association of Wardens and Superintendents in 2001. She was the retiring warden of the Michigan Reformatory in Ionia, Michigan.

Anita Covert, '72, M.A. '76 & '77, Ph.D. '89, was named 2001 "Michigan Small Business Person of the Year" by the U.S. Small Business Administration. She was president of Country Stitches, Ltd., America's largest quilt shops.

Shelly (Ling) Blanchard, '77, was named "Woman of the Year 2001" by the California Legislature. She was editor of the award-winning *Rancho Cordova Grapevine Independent*, Cordova, California.

Medical Leaders

Charles Fisher, '71, M.D. '73, director of the Cleveland Clinic Critical Care Research Unit.

Steven Leibel, chairman and physician, Department of Radiation Oncology, Memorial Sloan-Kettering Cancer Center.

Dr. William Lukash, '52, Navy Rear Admiral, served as White House Physician as well as President Gerald Ford's personal doctor.

Barbara Ross-Lee, D.O. '73, was the first African American woman to head a medical school in the U.S. She served as dean of the Ohio University College of Osteopathic Medicine, and was inducted into the Ohio Women's Hall of Fame.

Shirley Weis, '75 Nursing, served as chairperson of the Mayo Clinic's Department of Managed Care in Rochester, Minnesota.

Jeanne M. Huddleston, '90, MD '93, director of the Inpatient Internal Medicine Program at the Mayo Clinic, Rochester, MN, was selected as president-elect of the Society of Hospital Medicine in 2003.

Mary G. Nash, MBA '89, chief operating officer at the University of Alabama Hospital in Birmingham, Alabama.

Martha L. Gray, '78, co-director of the Harvard-Massachusetts Institute of Technology Division of Health Science and Technology at MIT.

Athletic Leaders

MSU athletes have won 23 Olympic medals—ten gold, eleven silver and two bronze. In all, 73 Spartans have participated in 17 different Olympic Games events.

Lloyd Ward, '70, former CEO of the Maytag Corp., was elected CEO of the U.S. Olympic Committee in October, 2001, the first African -American to serve in that position.

Names and details of MSU excellence in the Olympics are covered in the chapter titled, "Spartan's Splendid Sports Success."

Former Spartan football players have helped win eight Super Bowl games: Herb Adderley, won two Super Bowl rings with the Green Bay Packers in the late 1960s, and one with the Dallas Cowboys in the early 1970s, as a defensive halfback. **Earl Morrall** quarterbacked the Baltimore Colts to a 1971 Super Bowl victory, and the Miami Dolphins to a 1972 win; **Jim Morrisey**, linebacker, Chicago Bears, 1986; **Carl Banks**, linebacker and **Mark Ingram**, wide receiver, New York Giants,1987.

Magic Johnson led the Los Angeles Lakers to five National Basketball Association titles. He also was the first three-time MVP in the NBA finals.

Spartans have helped professional baseball teams to three World Series championships: Herb Washingon, a designated runner with the Oakland Athletics, in 1975; **Kirk Gibson**, right fielder with the Detroit Tigers in 1984, and again with the Los Angeles Dodgers in 1988. **Steve Garvey,** first baseman and **Mike Marshall**, relief pitcher, played for the L.A. Dodgers in the 1975 World Series; and Garvey played for the San Diego Padres in the 1984 World Series.

Mike Marshall of the L.A. Dodgers, became the first relief pitcher in pro baseball history to win the coveted Cy Young Award. He did this in 1975.

Jean Perron, MSU graduate, as head coach, led the Montreal Canadiens to the 1986 Stanley Cup title.

Two Spartans have won the Hobey Baker Award, college hockey's "Heisman Award." Kip Miller won this prestigious award in 1990, and his cousin **Ryan Miller** won the trophy in 2001.

Spartans Stu Argo, '85, and Dawn Riley, '87, helped crew the victorious U.S. team in the 1992 America's Cup sailing competition.

Three Spartans have owned or had part ownership of professional athletic teams: Drayton McLane, the

Houston Astros baseball team; **Harley Hotchkiss**, the Calgary Flames hockey team; and **Earvin "Magic" Johnson**, the Los Angeles Lakers basketball team.

Pat Peppler, '47, served as general manager of the Atlanta Falcon NFL team.

Thirty-eight MSU coaches, athletes, and staff have been named to international and national sports halls of fame.

Twenty-eight Spartan coaches and athletes have been named to the Michigan Sports Hall of Fame. **Eighteen MSU coaches have been named national coach of the year, and twelve named Big Ten coach of the year**. Names and details of these achievements are covered in the chapter on sports.

National, State and Big Ten Beauty Pageant Winners

Nancy Ann Fleming, '65, won the **Miss America** Pageant of 1961. She also won the **Miss Michigan** title for 1961. She later hosted a morning TV talk show in San Francisco. She graduated from MSU in 1965 with honors and a 3.8 grade point average.

Barbara Tanner, '49, was named the **"Ideal American Coed,"** in a *Ladies Home Journal* poll in her junior year, 1947-48. In 1948, as a senior, she was selected the **National "Sweetheart of Sigma Chi."** The title included a Hollywood screen test.

Mary Lonn Trapp, '54, was selected **National Cherry Queen**, and was MSC's 1951 Homecoming Queen.

Dee Means '54, was selected **Miss Big Ten** as well as **Miss MSC**.

Janice Somers, '56, won the 1954 **Miss Michigan** title. She also was elected **Miss MSU**, and **Miss Big Ten.**

Diane Lee, freshman liberal arts major, entered Michigan State University-Oakland's first class in 1959 as **Miss Alaska**. She won the honor in America's Junior Miss Pageant.

Patricia Visser, freshman business major, entered MSU at East Lansing as **Miss Hawaii**, an honor won in the 1959 Miss Universe competition.

Sally Jane Noble, MSU gymnast, won the 1964 **Miss Michigan** title.

Robin Fields, '78, won the 1975 **Miss Arkansas** title.

Kelly Lynn Garver, '86, won the 1986 **Miss Michigan** title. She was a member of the National Honor Society and made the Dean's List for 13 consecutive terms.

Ariya Chumsai (Sirisopha), '93, won the 1994 **Miss Thailand** title.

Jennifer Drayton, '96, won the 1996 **Miss Michigan** Pageant. She intended to become a Lutheran minister.

MSU Students Win National and International Championships In Many Disciplines

High-achieving Michigan State students have won national and international team championships in 19 different disciplines:

- Mathematics
- Chemical engineering
- Chamber music
- Computer programming
- Journalism
- Culinary Arts
- Advertising
- Engineering
- Debate
- Oratory
- Business
- Business marketing
- Economics
- Investing
- Waste management
- International moot court competition
- National law student tax challenge
- Dairy judging
- College bowl

From a victory in the sheep-shearing competition at the 1904 St. Louis Exposition (World's Fair) by freshman E.S. Bartlett, to national titles in debate and law in 2004, international moot court competition, and chamber music in 2003, MSU students have an impressive record in competitions with other universities and colleges.

MSU Law Team Wins National Title—2004—Melissa Bridges, third year law student, and Matt Rockey-Hawley, December 2003 law graduate, won the American Bar Association's Annual Law Student Tax Challenge. They defeated teams from the University of Michigan, University of Tennessee, Southern Methodist University, New York University, and others.

Michele Halloran, clinical professor of law and director of MSU's tax clinic, said the judges praised the MSU team "for their impeccable tax knowledge and outstanding verbal skills."

Debate Team Wins Four National Tournaments—2004—Two MSU seniors defeated top-ranked University of California-Berkeley to win the 2004 National Debate Tournament, the ultimate prize of intercollegiate debate, held at Catholic University in Washington, D.C. Greta Stahl, history and international relations senior, and Dave Strauss, international relations senior, not only teamed to win the top honor, they also **won 22 consecutive debates at back-to-back tournaments at the University of Southern California and California State-Fullerton.** Mike Eber, interim director of debate, called the performance "nothing short of sensational." The Spartans won over teams from Harvard, California-Berkeley, University of Texas-Austin, Dartmouth, and others.

The Stahl-Strauss team also won the prestigious **Dartmouth College Annual Herbert L. James Debates.** Only the seven most-accomplished debate teams in the nation are invited. At Dartmouth, MSU defeated Harvard, California-Berkeley, Dartmouth, Northwestern, Georgia, and Emory universities. Will Repko was head coach of the MSU debate team.

Student journalists at MSU's *State News* won the school's eighth National Pacemaker Award in 1995 for outstanding college journalism. No other university had won as many of these prestigious awards. The *State News* won top honors for the editorial content of its Web page at the 1998 Associated Collegiate Press convention. It is the biggest college newspaper in the nation in terms of budget, number of pages, amount of news carried, and advertising. It also is the third largest morning daily newspaper in the state, trailing only the *Detroit Free Press* and the *Detroit News*.

Chemical engineering students led all universities—public or private—six times in the American Institute of Chemical Engineering national competition: 1969, 1971, 1974, 1979, 1980 and 1982. MSU students had finished in the top three in the U.S. twelve times.

Mathematics students won the National Putnam Mathematical Competition in 1961, 1963, and 1967. The 1967 champions finished ahead of Caltech, Harvard, the Massachusetts Institute of Technology, and the University of Michigan. Professor Fritz Herzog coached the title winning team.

In 2002, the MSU debate team won the Cross Examination Debate Association Seasonal National Championship. Harvard finished 25th and the University of Michigan, 26th. With this title, MSU had finished among the top five debating teams in the nation for eight consecutive years.

Team members included Anjail Vats, Geoff Lundeen, Maggie Ryan, Jon Gillenwater, John Rood, Austin Carson, Calum Matheson, Greta Stahl, Suzanne Sobotka, John Green, Gabe Murillo, Amber Watkins, Aaron Hardy, and David Strauss. Coaching the team were: William Repko, head coach; Jason Trice, director of debate; and Alison Woidan and Michael Eber, both assistant coaches.

In 2001, MSU's Debate Team finished in the Final Four of both major national competitions. It was the second consecutive year the team had posted the highest cumulative score in the two top national tournaments—CEDA and NDT.

In 2000, MSU's Debate Team was the first university team in history to reach the final round of both national debate tournaments—the Cross Examination Debate Association (CEDA) and the National Debate Tournament (NDT).

In 1995, MSU's debate team defeated 227 two-person teams from some 100 universities. Elizabeth Repko and John Sullivan were team leaders. MSU repeated as national team debate champion in 1996, winning nine of 15 debate tournaments and recording a record 182 points in cross examination competition. Elizabeth Repko was named the best debater at the University of California-Long Beach tournament. John Sullivan, Repko's partner finished fifth in individual awards, and Jason Trice placed eighth. MSU debate coach James Roper, stated, "Having three of the top ten debaters in the nation is really quite an accomplishment." In 1994, Elizabeth Repko became the first MSU student to advance to the finals of the National Championship Debate Tournament.

In 1993, MSU debate teams won the National Junior Varsity Tournament sponsored by the Cross Examination Debate Association—the nation's largest intercollegiate debate organization. Two MSU teams were declared co-champions. Will Repko was named the top debater. In 1997, freshman Katy Hoffman won the National Junior Varsity Debate Tournament. Debate coach Jim Roper called it "One of the guttiest performances I've seen."

MSU Team Was First From U.S. to Win Jessep International Law Moot Court Competition—2003— Five MSU-DCL students became the first U.S. team to win the Philip C. Jessep International Law Moot Court Competition. The 2003 victory was won by third-year law students Nic Camargo and Jina Han; and second-year students Joe Harte, David Pizzuti, and Camille Van Buren. The MSU team defeated five other regional winners—Georgetown, University of Michigan, Lewis & Clark, Columbia, and Harvard Law School. Professor Deborah Skorupski, a seasoned judge, was the team's advisor

MSU's saxophone chamber music quartet won the National Collegiate Chamber Music competition—2003—The quartet included Wilton Elder, Paul Forsyth, Bryan Jao, and Paul Nolen.

In 1942, Glen Wagner won first place in the National Oratorical Pi Kappa Delta tournament in competition with students from 50 other colleges.

MSU engineering students have won the Waste-Management Education & Research Consortium National Design Competition four times. In 1994, they defeated 29 other universities in cleaning up soil contamination by pesticides, metals and organic material. They won the $10,000 first prize and another $1,000 for the best oral presentation. In 1995, MSU repeated as the national champion, winning $14,500 in prize money for devising the best plan to create a waste retrieval system to clean up pond sludge. The prize money went to MSU's Environmental Engineering Society. In 1997, the MSU team defeated 199 other universities to win the national title. Susan Masten and Simon Davies were the engineering faculty advisors for the team. In 2001, the MSU team of Megan Laird, Molly O'Flaherty, Nikki Ritchie, Kate Streams, and Maria Suparno—all seniors in bio-systems engineering—won the national competition held at Las Cruces, New Mexico.

A team from MSU's Eli Broad Graduate School took first-place honors at the 2002 National Black MBA Case Competition held in Nashville, Tennessee.

In 1938, Donald C. McSorley, Class of 1938, won the American Society of Mechanical Engineers Undergraduate Student Award for the best technical paper of the year for any mechanical engineering student in the U.S.

A five-member MSU student team won the National Invitational College Bowl Tournament in 1982, competing against 15 of the nation's best teams. The competition was based on general knowledge, covering any subject—from ancient history and art to sports and zoology. In 1983, MSU repeated as national champions, defeating 17 other university teams, including five from the Big Ten. **MSU was the only school to have won the title more than once**. The MSU team included senior captain Cliff Fox; graduate student John Filipus; seniors Mike Nawrocki, Larry Given and Ron Ellis; and freshman Gavin Borchert.

In 1983, Eric Carlson, senior physics major, who had twice won the William Lowell Powell competition—the "Super Bowl" of mathematicians—was called, "One of the smartest persons in his age group on the planet earth," by MSU mathematics coach Charles Maccluer.

MSU students won the world computer programming title in 1977, and finished second in 1979. In 1992, MSU won the national computer programming competition, finishing first among all colleges and universities in the Northern hemisphere, and second in the world at the International Scholastic Computer Programming Competition. Stanford finished third; Harvard sixth. Six hundred three-person teams competed in the world event. The MSU team included Jacob Lorch, David Thaler, and Steven Klocek. Richard Reid and William Punch coached the championship team. The Spartan team won $5,000 and a new lap-top computer.

Engineering students won the 1990 National Concrete Canoe Competition, defeating 18 other universities. *Sports Illustrated* reported the victory as the Spartans "Concrete Achievement" in their July 9, 1990 issue. The 109-pound canoe was named "Rowing Stone." The students won four of five races to win the $5,000 first prize.

Advertising students won the 1991 American Advertising Federation's national competition. "None of the other teams came close to MSU in executing the creative part of the assignment," the *Chicago Sun-Times* reported. The Spartans won a $3,500 award with a 50-page, multimedia presentation designed to win a $40-million account. Jim Gilmore was the team's faculty advisor.

Bonnie Atwell, a journalism senior, was one of three first place winners in a **1948 National Advertising competition** conducted by Gamma Alpha Chi, national advertising sorority.

Sixty finance students won the 1995 AT&T Collegiate Investment Challenge, outperforming all other universities. The runners-up were Harvard and the Wharton School of Business at the University of Pennsylvania.

The MSU Business Marketing Association team won a 1996 national student competition by developing a complete marketing plan for Intel Corporation.

Graduate students from MSU's Eli Broad Graduate School of Management won **2002 first place honors from the National Black MBA Case Competition held in Nashville, Tennessee.**

MSU's Culinary Arts Club won two top awards in the 1984 National Restaurant Association's competition in Chicago. Senior Mary Woehrle won a "Best of Show" victory with an unprecedented perfect score. The club included many students from the School of Hospitality Business (Hotel, Restaurant and Institutional Management).

Engineering students won five first place awards in Ford Motors Company's 1993 Hybrid Electric Vehicle Challenge. The awards included "best use of electronics." The vehicle was named "Spartan Charge" and was the award winner at the 1994 Detroit Auto Show. John Gerrish, professor of agricultural engineering, mentored the students. In 1994, the MSU engineers won Ford Motor Company's Hybrid Electric Vehicle competition for excellence in safety engineering and best use of materials.

Peter Morris, MSU M.A. '90, won the 1992 World Scrabble Championship in London, England. While playing, he wore his Michigan State sweat shirt.

Jonathan E. Chudler, English major from Bloomfield Hills, was named to the **1996 All-USA College Academic Team** by *USA Today*. He received a $2,500 award for intellectual achievement and leadership. He was one of 20 winners selected from 1,231 entries from 49 states.

Steven Bevier, a history major, defeated students from Harvard, Duke, Purdue and Boston University on his way to the 1997 finals of Jeopardy's College Week.

Greg McNeilly, a social science/integrated studies major, won the 1997 Mont Pelerin Society's "Frederich Hayek Fellowship Contest" in Vienna, Austria. He was the only undergraduate student honored at the symposium.

Dairy Husbandry students won the 1925 National Students' Judging Contest at the National Dairy Show over 23 other colleges. Their scores were tops in all classes of cattle judged. Frank Williamson won the sweepstakes prize and was awarded a $400 scholarship. Other team members were E.S. Weisner and R.P. Britsman.

Robert Miller was chosen as one of ten college students out of 50,000 nationwide to compete in the final auditions of the 1933 Atwater-Kent Radio Contests in New York City.

Mary Norton, '77, James Madison College graduate, shown working as a waitress during her student days. She was MSU's first female Rhodes Scholar and one of the first 13 women in America to win a "Rhodes." She also won a Danforth Fellowship and a National Science Foundation Fellowship. Norton graduated with a 3.99 GPA.

Academic Excellence a Way of Life

Rhodes Scholars, National Merit Scholars, 3.60 Freshman Classes

From its inception as a college open to "the poorest and the proudest," Michigan State has challenged students with intellectually stimulating courses.

In 1858—the school's second academic year—course work included analytical chemistry, trigonometry, surveying, ancient history, rhetoric, mechanics and engineering, biology, geology, physics, astronomy, ethics, psychology, geography and constitutional law.

The course in analytical chemistry preceded by one year the teaching of similar courses at Harvard and the University of Michigan.

In 1886, President Edwin Willits, commenting on a proposal to raise the college admission standards, declared, "I'm clearly of the opinion there should be no change. **The standard is practically the same as that at the Military Academy at West Point and the Naval Academy at Annapolis."**

Today, MSU is a top producer of Rhodes, Churchill, Truman, Marshall and National Science Foundation Scholarship winners, and annually attracts a large number of National Merit Scholars.

MSU's nationally ranked academic programs rose from five in 1994 to 24 in 2000, according to *U.S. News and World Report* in 2001. The magazine also rated MSU as the "best value" among public Big Ten universities.

MSU students won 13 Rhodes Scholarships between 1972 and 1997—more than any other public university in America—bringing MSU's Rhodes total to 16. Spartans also have won 15 Churchill Scholarships, 13 Truman Scholarships, ten Marshall Scholarships, four Woodrow Wilson Scholarships, two Danforth Scholarships, several Mellon Fellowships, a Mitchell Scholarship, and a Goldwater Scholarship.

Michigan State led all universities in attracting National Merit Scholars, starting in 1963, with a total of 195. By 1974, MSU had 462 National Merit Scholars on campus, leading all public universities, and second only to America's oldest private university: Harvard. From that time forward, Michigan State has continued to attract large numbers of National Merit Scholars, usually ranking among the top three universities in these gifted students.

MSU has been a leader in producing National Science Foundation (NSF) fellowship winners for many years. These awards provide tuition and fees plus an annual stipend for graduate study for three years at a university of the student's choice. As an example, in 1983 ten MSU students won NSF fellowships and 14 honorable mentions—tops in the Big Ten for the fifth time in six years, and second among all public universities in the nation. Today, MSU continues as a leader in producing NSF fellowship winners

The academic quality of MSU's overall student body has improved year by year. In the fall of 2003, the entering freshman class had a mean 3.58 grade point average. For more than 25 consecutive years, the grade point average of the freshman class has been at 3.0 or above. The Lyman Briggs School, a unit specializing in science and mathematics within MSU's College of Natural Science, for years has had entering freshman classes with a 3.8 grade point average.

MSU Rhodes Scholars

The Rhodes Scholarship is one of the most prestigious academic awards in the world. Each year 32 of these scholarships are awarded to university students in the United States. The scholarship provides for two years of study at Oxford University in England.

- ▼ 1919—Calvin J. Overmyer—Chemistry
- ▼ 1926—Douglas V. Steere—Philosophy
- ▼ 1953—John D. Wilson—English Literature
- ▼ 1972—Alan L. VerPlanck—English Literature
- ▼ 1974—Roy D. Pea—Philosophy
- ▼ 1975—Paul Hunt—Chemistry
- ▼ 1976—Steven Holtzman—Philosophy
- ▼ 1977—Mary Norton—James Madison College
- ▼ 1982—Molly K. Brennan—Computer Science, and Humanities
- ▼ 1983—Claudena Skran—James Madison College
- ▼ 1984—Judith A. Stoddart—English and French
- ▼ 1985—Robert W. Leland—Electrical Engineering
- ▼ 1985—Ronald J. Tenpas—James Madison College
- ▼ 1993—Rujuta M. Bhatt—Biochemistry, and James Madison College
- ▼ 1996—Dayne A. Walling—James Madison College
- ▼ 1997—Stephanie Palmer—Natural Science

MSU Churchill Scholars

Churchill Scholarships provide for one year of graduate study in engineering, mathematics, or sciences at Cambridge University in England.

- ▼ 1964—Thomas R. Stoeckley
- ▼ 1969—Larry K. Benninger
- ▼ 1978—T. Kevin Murphy
- ▼ 1979—Thomas J. Pence
- ▼ 1980—Stephen J. Scherr
- ▼ 1982—Christopher J. Bishop
- ▼ 1983—Ronald E. Ellis
- ▼ 1985—Frank J. Sottile
- ▼ 1986—Rebecca L. Ellis
- ▼ 1988—Lisa M. Gloss
- ▼ 1989—Eric J. Hooper
- ▼ 1990—Donald M. Bott
- ▼ 1991—Richard K. Cohn
- ▼ 2000—Jason E. Fuller
- ▼ 2002—Camilla Smith

Gates Cambridge Scholar

Gates Cambridge Scholars win tuition to Cambridge University in England.

- ▼ 2002—Robin Stein

MSU Truman Scholars

The Truman Scholarship is a $30,000 merit-based grant awarded to undergraduate students to attend graduate or professional schools in preparation for careers in government, the non-profit sector, or elsewhere in public service. Candidates must attend an accredited U.S. college or university and be nominated by the institution's Truman Faculty Representative. Students must be U.S. citizens or U.S. nationals. About 75-80 scholarships are awarded annually.

- ▼ 1978—Steven J. Kautz
- ▼ 1979—Donna J. Pickrell
- ▼ 1980—Linda K. Ewing
- ▼ 1982—Thomas M. Young
- ▼ 1984—Lori K. Brown
- ▼ 1985—Connel R. Fullenkamp
- ▼ 1987—Benjamin N. Dennis
- ▼ 1989—Wendy M. Fritzen
- ▼ 1991—Rujuta M. Bhatt
- ▼ 1994—Dayne A. Walling
- ▼ 1997—Jennifer E. Sykes
- ▼ 1999—Adam L. Wright
- ▼ 2003—Jared S. English

MSU Marshall Scholars

Marshall Scholarships finance young Americans of high ability to study for a degree in the United Kingdom. Up to 40 scholars are selected each year to study at a United Kingdom institution in any field of study. Each scholarship is held for two years.

- ▼ 1974—Katharine L. Clarke
- ▼ 1977—Ian H. Redmount
- ▼ 1978—Robert D. Koons
- ▼ 1978—Stuart P. Rosenthal
- ▼ 1980—Richard A. Cordray
- ▼ 1984—Sandra M. Pinnavaia
- ▼ 1993—Rujuta M. Bhatt
- ▼ 1998—Jennifer E. Sykes
- ▼ 2004—Jared English
- ▼ 2004—Greta Stahl

MSU Mitchell Scholar

George G. Mitchell Scholarships allow Americans to pursue one year of post-graduate study at institutions of higher learning in Ireland and Northern Ireland. At least nine scholarships are provided annually.

- ▼ 2000—Kathleen C. Romig

Kathleen Romig, Class of 2001, and Mitchell Scholar, is congratulated by Ireland's Prime Minister Bertie Ahern in Dublin. Mitchell Scholars win a year of post-graduate study at Ireland and Northern Ireland universities.

MSU Goldwater Scholar

Goldwater Scholarships provide for academic support of $7,500 per year.

- ▼ 2003—Megan Dennis

Udall Scholar

The Morris K. Udall Foundation annually awards 80 undergraduate scholarships of up to $5,000 to juniors and seniors in environmental-related fields and to American Indian and Alaska Natives in fields related to health care and tribal policy.

- ▼ 2004—Jerilyn Church

Fulbright Scholars

Fulbright Fellowships are aimed at increasing mutual understanding between the people of the United States and other countries through the exchange of people, knowledge and skills. The fellowships generally provide transportation, language and/or orientation courses, tuition, book allowance, living expenses, research allowance, and health and accident insurance.

Since the 1973-1974 academic year, Michigan State students have won 103 Fulbright Scholarships.

1973-1974–Patricia Whittier
1975-1976–James Seroka
1976-1977–Carolyn Sargent
1977-1978–Ronald Hurt
1980-1981–Marie Grosz-Ngate
–Gary Carkin
–James McCann
1981-1982–Walter Hoops
–William Howard
1983-1984–Chris Sutherland
–Timothy Wilt
–Paul Malling
–Edith Dolnikowski
–Andrew Davidson
–Andrew Clark
–Jeffrey Redmond
–Kenneth Walicki
–David Sterling-Decker
1984-1985–Rita Laker-Ojok
–John Hanson
–Anthony Woods, Jr.
–Roy Cole
1985-1986–Nancy Horn
–Laird Jones
–Stephen Burges
–Nancy Westrate
–Mary Bivins
–Jonathon Landeck
–Mary Cameron
1986-1987–Catherine Pelissier
–Jeffrey Redmond
–Paula Spencer
–James Teft
–Mark Blackmore
1987-1988–Heidi Applegate
–Julie Fischer
–Joan Wolf
1988-1989–Donna Randall
–Vicky Scott
1990-1991–Mark Pires
1992-1993–Nadine Pullar
–Jack Glascock
–Bradley Deacon
–Corey Alguire
–Robert Glew
1993-1994–Corey Alguire
–Douglas Wilson
1994-1995–Nancy Mezey
–George Menz
1995-1996–Ghislaine Lydon
–Tim Carmichael
–Janice Harper
–Sheryl Welte
1996-1997–Teresa Swezey
1997-1998–Erika Dirkse
–Shari Anderson
–Dean Fealk
–Elizabeth MacGonagle
–Mariaelena Jefferds
–Janice Sipple
1998-1999–Edward Paulino
–Jeremy McClane
–Sonja Magdevski
–Ellen Foley
1999-2000–Annelise Carleton
–Carmela Garritano
–Megan Plyler
–Heather Holtzclaw
–Kiel Christianson
–Michelle Kuenzi
2000-2001–Pam Galbraith
–Tom Smucker
–Kimberly Butler
–Gina Lambright
–Mark Holbert
–Kimberly Smiddy
–Hilary Jones
–Mark-Andre Timinsky
–Shannon Vance
2001-2002–Daniel Nappo
–Denise Mainville
–Sarah Kraus
–Dawne Curry
–Keri Brondo
–Gregory Wolynec
2002-2003–Hamada Hamid
–Lisa Molloy
–John Waytena
–Suzanne Schneider
–Stephen Cameron
–Solomon Getahun
–Teresa Heinie
–Kirsten Johnson
2003-2004–Kristi Klomp
–Erik Houle
–Holly Dygert
–Jennifer Brewer
–Aaron Russell
–Natalie Bourdon
–Julie Bashkin
–Michelle Powell
–Jessica Vernieri
–Kari Bergstrom

MSU: National Leader In Minority Opportunity

For more than a century, Michigan State University has been a champion of equal rights and opportunity for minorities and the disadvantaged. MSU has continuously demonstrated a warm heart, a helpful hand, and an openness to blacks, Hispanics, Asians, Native Americans, women, and the handicapped. It is a proud heritage, totally in keeping with Michigan State's mission to provide access and opportunity for all citizens in a friendly and non-elitist atmosphere.

Of course, there have been campus protests and conflicts regarding recognition of minority and disadvantaged rights and access to opportunity. But, MSU has a history of listening to criticism and resolving conflicts with sweeping policies and actions to make sure everything has been done so that minorities and the disadvantaged have equal opportunities and access to every kind of help to enhance their educational and social success at Michigan State University. This comprehensive policy and program effort includes not only minority and disadvantaged students but faculty and staff as well.

Equal Opportunity Leadership An MSU Tradition

Michigan State's leadership in producing an equal opportunity culture is punctuated with substantive examples:

- ▼ **The first major university in the United States to elect an African-American as president**—Dr. Clifton R. Wharton, Jr. was elected MSU's 14th president in 1970.
- ▼ **The first university in the Big Ten to select a woman as provost**—Dr. Lou Anna K. Simon, Ph.D. '74, was named MSU provost—chief academic officer—in 1993, first in the Big Ten.
- ▼ **The first university in the nation to accept American-born Japanese as students during World War II**, when the Federal Government was herding American-born Japanese into internment camps. President John Hannah put Michigan State on record as willing to accept American-born Japanese who had been employed for six months in Michigan as students. The Board of Trustees approved this action.
- ▼ **The first university in the nation to create an on-campus shelter for victims of domestic violence**, who are primarily women—MSU's First Lady Joanne McPherson led the establishment of the MSU Domestic Violence Shelter on campus, now called Safe Place. It was the first of its kind on any U.S. campus.
- ▼ **The first university medical school (co-educational) in the nation with more than 50 percent women**—The 106-member class of 1985, which entered the College of Human Medicine in the fall of 1981, included 55 women.
- ▼ **The first university in the nation to select an African-American as head of its Jazz Studies Program**—Rodney Whittaker.
- ▼ **The first university in the Big Ten to select a black athletics director**—Dr. Merritt Norvell was named MSU's 18th athletics director in 1995, the first African American ever named to that position in the Big Ten.
- ▼ **The first university in the Big Ten and the second in the nation to select a woman athletics director**—Merrily Dean Baker was named MSU's athletic director in 1992. She was the first female to hold that position in the Big Ten, and only the second in the nation.
- ▼ **The first university in the Big Ten to select a woman as the faculty representative to the conference's governing board**—MSU named Dr. Gwen Norrell as its faculty representative to the Big Ten in 1978, the first woman to be so named.
- ▼ **The second university in the Big Ten to hire an African-American as head football coach**—Bobby Williams became MSU's first African American head football coach in 1999, and was only the second black named to that position in the Big Ten.
- ▼ **The first university in the State of Michigan to enroll women**—Ten women students enrolled at Michigan State in 1870, the first females admitted to any college in Michigan.
- ▼ **The first university in the State of Michigan to create a women's curriculum**—1870. The women's course included English, mathematics, history, literature, French, German, botany, chemistry, entomology, natural philosophy, and homemaking. The frosting on the cake was two years free instruction on the piano.

- **The first university in the State of Michigan to have a woman as a member of the Board of Trustees**—Mrs. Dora Stockman of Lansing, Michigan was elected the first woman member of the State Board of Agriculture (Board of Trustees) in 1920.
- **One of the first universities in the nation to open its doors to the sons and daughters of migrant workers**—In 1972, MSU trustees made sons and daughters of migrant workers in Michigan eligible for "in-state" tuition, provided their parents were employed for a minimum of two months each year for three of the past five years.
- **An international leader in educating and helping the handicapped**—MSU was a national pioneer by establishing its Office of Handicapped Students in 1972. MSU was chosen in 1976 as the home of an international center for research, information and training in the rehabilitation of handicapped individuals. The Rehabilitation Services Administration of the U.S. Department of Health, Education and Welfare provided a $1.5 million grant for the center's support. MSU won the center as the result of 15 years work in handicapped research and rehabilitation.

MSU Women and Minorities Have Broken Employment Barriers

MSU women and minority graduates who have broken employment and recognition barriers include:

- **The first Asian-American to be elected a state governor**—George R. Ariyoshi, '49, Japanese-American, became the first Asian-American governor in the nation when he was elected Hawaii's chief executive officer in 1975.
- **The first black to be elected CEO of the U.S. Olympic Committee**—Lloyd Ward, '70, became the first African-American elected CEO of the U.S. Olympic Committee in 2001. Ward, former CEO of Maytag Corp., was captain of MSU's basketball team in 1970.
- **The first woman to be selected a member of the Federal Reserve Bank Board**—Nancy Hays Teeters, who studied graduate economics at MSU, became the first woman member of the Federal Reserve Bank Board in 1978.
- **The first woman career foreign service officer to be named a U.S. Ambassador to a foreign country**—Donna Hrinak, '72, was named U.S. Ambassador to Bolivia in 1997—the first woman career foreign service officer to be appointed an ambassador. In 2002, she was named U.S. Ambassador to Brazil.
- **The first woman to head a major U.S. automotive vehicle division**—Lynn C. Myers, '64, MBA '67, as general manager of the Pontiac-GMC Division of General Motors became the top woman operating officer in the U.S. auto industry. She was selected the first "Outstanding Woman in the Automotive Industry" in 1994 by *McCall's/Ward's Auto World* magazine.
- **The first African-American woman to head a medical school in the U.S.**—Barbara Ross-Lee, D.O. '73, was appointed Dean of the Ohio University College of Osteopathic Medicine in 1993, the first African-American to lead a U.S. medical school.
- **The first woman to head a leading hotel company with worldwide operations**—Joan Sills, '75, was elected president of Colony Hotels & Resorts in 1991. *The New York Times* described her as "the only woman to head a leading hotel company with worldwide operations."
- **The first woman to rise to flag rank and to become surgeon general in the U.S. Coast Guard**—Rear Admiral Joyce M. Johnson, D.O. '80, Surgeon General of the U.S. Coast Guard.
- **The first woman to be named publisher and editor of the *Detroit Free Press***—Carole Lee Hutton, '78, in 2003.
- **The first woman to head an America's Cup sailing syndicate**, and the first woman to serve as a crew member on an America's Cup championship team—Dawn Riley, '87, served as captain and syndicate CEO for "America True," one of the 1999 entries in the America's Cup sailing competition—the first woman ever to do so. In 1992, Riley helped crew "America 3" to victory in the America's Cup sailing competition—the first woman crew member in history.
- **The first African-American to be named a Supreme Court Justice in Texas**—Wallace Jefferson, '85, became the first African-American to be named to the Texas Supreme Court.
- **The first African-American to be elected to the Mississippi legislature since Reconstruction** following the Civil War—Robert C. Clark, Jr. '59, elected in 1968. He championed laws to make junior college education available to every young person in Mississippi.
- **The first person and first woman to be elected chairperson of Orange County, California**—Linda Chapin, '63, was elected the first chairperson of Orange County, California—one of the largest counties in America.

- **The first woman commander of the Parks Reserve Forces Training Area in Dublin, California**—U.S. Army Lt. Col. Dawnlee DeYoung, '83, became the first woman commander of the Parks Reserve Forces Training Area—in charge of training Army, Navy, Air Force, Marine and Coast Guard reservists.
- **The first woman commander of the U.S. Air Force 65th Air Base Wing,** Lajes Field, Azores, Portugal. U.S. Air Force Col. Judith Fedder, '80, became the first woman commander of the 65th Air Base Wing, which is home to 2,500 American service people.
- **The first woman elected Lt. Governor of Colorado**—In 1979, Nancy Dick, '51, was the first woman elected Lt. Governor of Colorado. She was one of only six women Lt. Governors in the U.S.
- **The first African-American woman to be elected chancellor of the University of Massachusetts**—In 2001, Dr. Marcellette G. Williams, '68, M.A. '70, Ph.D. '81, became the first African-American woman elected chancellor of the University of Massachusetts.
- **The first black female to serve as director of media relations for the President of the United States**—Kristin Clark Taylor, '82, was serving as the White House director of media relations for President George H.W. Bush in 1992, the first African American ever to occupy the post.
- **The first woman to join the "Caterpillar Club"**—Fay Gillis Wells, graduated in the winter term of 1929. She would become a White House correspondent for Storer Broadcasting. She was one of the first female pilots in the U.S., and with Amelia Earhart, founded the Ninety-Nine Club, an association of women pilots. **Wells became the first women member of the "Caterpillar Club," bailing out of an airplane and being saved by the silk parachute.**
- **The first woman to serve as press secretary for the Governor of Michigan**—Roberta Applegate, '40, was named press secretary to Michigan Governor Kim Sigler in 1947.
- **The first woman inducted into the Michigan Conservation Hall of Fame**—Genevieve Gillette, '20, was a prime leader in the development of Michigan's State Park system, and was known as "Miss Michigan State Parks." She was inducted into the Michigan Conservation Hall of Fame in 1984.
- **The first woman manager of a domestic General Motors assembly plant**—Patricia Carrigan, '50, was the first woman to head a General Motors domestic assembly plant. In 1977, she became the first woman to be elected chair of the MSU Board of Trustees.
- **The first woman chief of police of a major U.S. city**—Penny E. Harrington, '64, was named Chief of Police for the City of Portland, Oregon in 1985.
- **The first woman chief of police of the City of Detroit**—Ella Bully-Cummings, MSU-DCL, '98, was named Detroit's Chief of Police, in charge of 4,200 police officers, in 2003. She was the first woman to hold the position.
- **The first woman elected president of an AFL-CIO affiliate union**—Linda (Peterson) Puchala, '69, president of the National Association of Flight Attendants.
- **The first woman elected president of the Industrial Designers Society of America**—In 1983, Katherine McCoy, '67, became the first woman and the youngest person, elected president of the Industrial Designers Society of America.
- **The first black to become head football coach at the University of Notre Dame**—Tyrone Willingham, '77. He was the first African-American to be head coach of any sport at Notre Dame.
- **The first black quarterback to play in the National Football League**—Willie Thrower, former MSU quarterback, became the first African-American quarterback in National Football League history in 1953. On October 8, 1953, he played his only game with the Chicago Bears, completing three of eight passes.

Other Female Faculty & Officer Firsts at MSU

- **Connie W. Stewart**, vice president of university relations, was named MSU's first female vice president in 1980.
- **Judith E. Lanier, Ph.D.**, was the first woman dean of the College of Education—1981.
- **Barbara Ross-Lee, D.O.**, chair of family medicine, College of Osteopathic Medicine, was the first woman department head of any of MSU's three medical schools—1983.
- **Mary Elizabeth Kurz**, was named MSU's first woman general counsel in 1987.
- **Marylee Davis, Ph.D.** '74, secretary of the Board of Trustees and executive assistant to the President, was the first woman to hold these positions—1988.
- **Harriet B. Rigas, Ph.D.**, chair of electrical engineering, was the first woman department head in the College of Engineering.

Buildings and Places Named for MSU People

Buildings, Facilities, and Places Off Campus

Great recognition has been paid to many Michigan State trustees, administrators, faculty, coaches and alumni through the naming of buildings and facilities in their honor. Their achievements have earned them long-lasting visibility. (Source for photos and information on 19th century graduates and buildings named for them—*MSC Record, April 15, 1951*—by Madison Kuhn and Joseph G. Duncan).

Liberty Hyde Bailey

Dr. Liberty Hyde Bailey, class of 1882, has a building on the **Cornell University** campus named for him: **Bailey Hall**. Bailey served as a distinguished professor of horticulture at Cornell from 1888 to 1903 and then as dean of agriculture from 1903 to 1913. Bailey was the "Father of American Horticulture" in the U.S. and the designer of the first building and laboratory in the nation devoted wholly to horticulture in 1888. It is still standing as Eustace-Cole Hall on the east end of MSU's West Circle Drive and is home to the Honors College. Bailey was the most prolific agricultural author in U.S. history, producing 75 books, editing 117 others, and writing and editing 700 scientific papers.

Bailey Hall at Cornell University—named for Liberty Hyde Bailey, class of 1882.

The Liberty Hyde Bailey Museum in Bailey's hometown of South Haven, Michigan was dedicated as a National Historic Site in 1984.

Dr. Charles E. Bessey, Class of 1869, served as professor of botany and then dean of agriculture at the **University of Nebraska. Bessey Hall** stands in his honor on the Nebraska campus. Bessey's son, Ernest A. Bessey, became a world-famous botanist at MSU, served as the first dean of the Graduate School, and had Bessey Hall on the Michigan State campus named for him in 1961.

Charles E. Bessey

Bessey Hall at the University of Nebraska—named for Charles E. Bessey, class of 1869.

A.L. Bibbins, Class of 1915, was considered America's outstanding seedsman and agricultural industrialist, and rose to be president of G.L.F. Mills, Inc., the largest manufacturer of dairy and poultry feeds in the world. In his honor, the auditorium at the G.L.F. School of Cooperative Administration was named **Bibbins Hall** on October 15, 1940. This school is located opposite the Cornell University campus in Ithaca, New York.

Burnett Hall at the University of Nebraska—named for Edgar A. Burnett, class of 1887.

Dr. Edgar A. Burnett, Class of 1887, served as dean of agriculture and later, chancellor of the **University of Nebraska. Burnett Hall** on the Nebraska campus is named in his honor.

Dr. Eugene Davenport, Class of 1878 and professor of agriculture, left the M.A.C. faculty in 1891, to serve as president of the first agricultural school in South America, the Escola Agricola de Sao Paulo. He later served as dean of agriculture at the **University of Illinois** (1895-1922), and had a building named for him in 1901: **Davenport Hall**, which was the home of the College of Agriculture at Illinois for years, and still stands. His campus home at Illinois was Davenport House, which no longer exists.

Edgar A. Burnett

Eugene Davenport

Davenport Hall at the University of Illinois—named for Eugene Davenport, class of 1878.

Herbert W. Mumford

Frederick B. Mumford

Mumford Hall at the University of Illinois—named for Herbert W. Mumford, class of 1891, brother of Frederick B. Mumford. The brothers were known as "The Siamese Twins of Agriculture."

Dr. Herbert W. Mumford, **Class of 1891,** who pioneered in livestock management economics at M.A.C., succeeded Eugene Davenport as dean of agriculture at the **University of Illinois** (1922-1938), and had a building named for him in 1922: **Mumford Hall**, which is the main building for the College of Agriculture at Illinois today. His campus home at Illinois was Mumford House, a demonstration farm house, which stills stands.

Dr. Frederick B. Mumford, Class of 1891 and professor of agriculture at M.A.C., served as dean of agriculture at the **University of Missouri** (1909-1938). He had a building named for him there in 1930: **Mumford Hall**, which still stands. It was completed in 1923.

Frederick and Herbert Mumford were brothers, graduates of the class of 1891, and for years were known as **"the Siamese twins of agriculture."**

Dr. Harold A. Iddles, Class of 1918, had the **Lecture-Library Wing of the Chemistry Building at the University of New Hampshire** named for him. He served in the university's chemistry department from 1929 to 1961.

J. Frank Witter, DVM '32, had the **Animal Science Center at the University of Maine** named for him. Witter served for many years teaching animal husbandry at Maine, and was head of the department of animal pathology for 15 years.

Percy J. Hoffmaster, **Class of 1918**, Horticulture, had the beautiful state park located five miles north of Grand Haven on Lake Michigan, named for him: **P.J. Hoffmaster State Park**. Hoffmaster had a distinguished 29-year career with the Michigan Department of Natural Resources. In 1922 he was named Superintendent of State Parks for Michigan. In 1934, he was promoted to Director of Conservation for the State of Michigan (equivalent to Director of the Department of Natural Resources today).

From 1933 to 1942, during the great economic depression, Hoffmaster was involved with the hiring of 10,000 Civilian Conservation Corps workers who built many of the State Parks in Michigan. With great vision, he was instrumental in establishing numerous wilderness and recreation areas in southeast Michigan.

Mumford Hall at the University of Missouri—named for Frederick B. Mumford, class of 1891, brother of Herbert W. Mumford.

Genevieve Gillette, Class of 1920, the first woman graduate in Landscape Architecture, had the **Nature Center at P.J. Hoffmaster State Park** near Grand Haven, Michigan named for her in 1967. There also is a **Genevieve Gillette Park in Washtenau County, Michigan.** Gillette was known as "Miss Michigan State Parks." She was the founder, and first president of the Michigan Parks Association, and was **instrumental in the creation of the Sleeping Bear National Lakeshore, Porcupine Mountain State Park, Hartwick Pines State Park, Wilderness State Park, and the Detroit Area Metroparks.**

She was named to the Michigan Women's Hall of Fame in 1984. She worked a decade to win voter approval in 1969 of a $100 million Michigan recreation bond issue.

George Gauthier, class of 1914, had the **football field and stadium at Rutherford B. Hayes High School in Delaware, Ohio** named in his honor. Gauthier was Michigan State's first alumnus to serve as head basketball coach (1917, 1918, 1919 and 1920), and as head football coach (1918). He left East Lansing to become head football coach and athletic director at Ohio Wesleyan University in Delaware, Ohio, where he served for 34 years. In his single year as M.A.C. football coach, he led the Aggies to a memorable 13-7 victory over Notre Dame, defeating first year Irish coach Knute Rockne and his star halfback George Gipp.

Bill Maskill, Michigan State football and track letter winner, 1944-46, had the **Galesburg-Augusta, Michigan High School football field** named for him. Maskill was the winningest Michigan high school football coach in history.

William Haithco, '50, had **a park in Saginaw County, Michigan** named in his honor. He was president of the Saginaw Medical Credit Union, and in 1969 founded the Saginaw County Parks & Recreation Commission, which created five parks. In 1950, Haithco co-founded Alpha Phi Alpha, MSU's first black fraternity.

Dr. John A. Hannah, '23, President Emeritus, builder of the modern, international MSU, has three buildings named for him that are off-campus. **The Hannah Community Center,** which was East Lansing High School from 1926 to 1955, located on north Abbott Road; **The Hannah Technology Center,** located on south Hagadorn Road across from the campus; and **The John Hannah Building** in Lansing, Michigan, which appropriately houses the Michigan Department of Education (formerly called the South Ottawa Tower). There also is **Hannah Boulevard**, located just east of Hagadorn Road near the Hannah Technology Center.

Pete Newell, Michigan State basketball coach, 1950-1954, had the **basketball arena at the University of California-Berkeley** named for him: the **Newell Center**. After leaving MSU, Newell coached the California Golden Bears, where he led them to an NCAA basketball title in 1959.

The late Durward B. "Woody" Varner and his wife Paula have buildings at Oakland University and University of Nebraska named in their honor. Varner was MSU's 1st VP; and was chancellor at MSU-Oakland and Nebraska.

Robert Devaney, former assistant football coach at MSU, had the basketball arena at the University of Nebraska named for him: **the Devaney Center**. Devaney, after leaving Michigan State was head football coach at the University of Wyoming and finally the University of Nebraska, where he led the Cornhuskers to national championships in 1970 and 1971.

Durward B. "Woody" Varner, served as the first officer at Michigan State to have the title of vice president. In 1957, he was selected by President John Hannah to create a new university—Michigan State University-Oakland—on the 1,600-acre Meadow Brook Farms and Estate in Rochester, Michigan, which had been given to MSU by Mr. And Mrs. Alfred G. Wilson. Woody Varner and his wife Paula, the first chancellor and first first lady of MSU-O, by 1970 had built an educational treasure for Oakland County, Michigan residents. Today it is **Oakland University**, with 16,000 students. On the campus stands the **Paula and Woody Varner Hall, the Performing Arts Center**, named in their honor.

Woody and Paula Varner moved to Lincoln, Nebraska in 1970, where Woody was named chancellor of the **University of Nebraska**. After years of service to the university, the **Woody and Paula Varner Administrative Center** was built, a tribute to their contributions.

Dr. Edgar L. Harden, MSU's 15th president, and past president of Northern Michigan University (NMU), had **a building at NMU** named in his honor.

Richard E. Holmes, M.D. '77, emergency room physician at Decatur General Hospital in Decatur, Alabama, and the first black graduate of Mississippi State University (prior to earning his medical degree at Michigan State), was honored by having the Mississippi State Office of Minority Affairs renamed the **Holmes Cultural Diversity Center**.

Frank Kush, '53, former MSU All-American football guard, had **the football field in Arizona State's Sun Devil Stadium,** named in his honor. Kush was head football coach at Arizona State from 1958 through 1979, and established a .764 winning percentage. He is a member of the Football Hall of Fame. Two national championship football games (Bowl Championship Series) have been played on Frank Kush Field—the 1998 Tennessee victory over Florida State, and the 2003 Ohio State win over the University of Miami.

Natalie Kreeger, M.A. '64, Ph.D. '96, had the **Fowlerville, Michigan elementary school** from which she retired in 1990, named in her honor. She earned her Ph.D. degree at MSU when she was 73.

Dr. Karl G. Merrill, M.A. 1938, had a **dormitory named for him at Ferris State University**, Big Rapids, Michigan in 1961. Merrill was a vice president emeritus at the school.

Jack E. Morgan, '58, retired assistant to the director of the Michigan Department of Transportation, had the northbound **U.S. 127 Lansing Rest Area** named in his honor. He served the department for 36 years.

John W. Porter, M.A. '59, Ph.D. '62, president emeritus of Eastern Michigan University (EMU), had the **EMU College of Education Building** named in his honor. He had served as director of the Michigan Higher Education Assistance Authority, superintendent of the Michigan Department of Education, interim superintendent for the Detroit Public Schools, and president and CEO of the Urban Education Alliance.

Earvin "Magic" Johnson, MSU basketball All-American and National Basketball Association All-Star and MVP, had the **Lansing Everett High School gymnasium** named in his honor. It was in that gymnasium, that Johnson earned the nickname "Magic." In his senior year, he led Everett to the 1977 Michigan Class A state championship. Johnson also led MSU to the NCAA title in 1979, and the Los Angeles Lakers to five NBA titles, starting in 1980.

Frank F. Rogers, class of 1883, Michigan Highway Commissioner (1905-1929), was honored with the placement of a monument on June 4, 1930 at the intersection of highways US 2 and US 31, near St. Ignace, Michigan.

Buildings & Facilities On Campus

Theophilus C. Abbot Hall was named in honor of Michigan State's third president, 1862-1884. It was built in 1938 ($525,000), and renovated in 1997. An earlier dormitory named for Abbot was built in 1888 at a cost of $10,000. It housed 60 students and was located where the present Music Practice Building stands. In the mid-1890s, the dorm was turned over to 40 women students and was affectionately called "The Abbey," according to Madison Kuhn's book on MSU. Old Abbot Hall was razed in 1968. Of course, the main north-south street in East Lansing is named for Abbot, although misspelled on road signs with two t's as Abbott Road.

Talbert and Leota Abrams Planetarium was built in 1963 ($297,957) and named for the founder of the Abrams Aerial Survey Corp. He built the world's first purely photographic aircraft and in 1938 began manufacturing cameras and aerial mapping devices. The National Geographic Society named a mountain for him in Antarctica, and his first pilot's license was signed by Orville Wright. The planetarium was made possible by a $250,000 gift from Mr. and Mrs. Abrams.

Forest H. Akers Hall, built in 1964 ($4,780,121), was named for the MSU alum who served on the MSU board of trustees from 1940-1958 and was a vice president of Chrysler Corp. Akers also provided the gift to underwrite the construction of MSU's Forest Akers Golf Courses, the first of which was opened in 1958. He also left money that was used to help build the MSU University Club in 1970.

Forest H. Akers, MSU alum, has two campus golf courses, a residence hall, and a gymnasium named in his honor.

Forest Akers Gymnasium in the Alfred Berkowitz Basketball Complex was dedicated on January 12, 2002.

The Forest Akers Trust gave $1 million towards the construction of the facility.

Robert D. Angell University Services Building, built in 1988 ($3,641,879), honors the man who joined the MSU purchasing department in 1935, and served the university for 46 years.

Anthony Hall honors Ernest L. Anthony who served for two decades as the dean of agriculture. It was constructed in 1955 ($3,870,380), expanded in 1964 ($9,477) and in 1997 ($ 8,812,379). In the 1930s, Anthony promoted teaching, research and outreach that lowered farming costs during the great depression. Following World War II, he and his staff were integral in the conversion of agriculture from a war-time to a peace-time basis.

W. G. Armstrong Hall, built in 1955 ($1,586,470), honors a former member of the MSU board of trustees who was a former student, a farmer, former master of the State Grange and treasurer of the National Grange.

Liberty Hyde Bailey Hall, built in 1955 ($1,509,607), honors the "Father of American Horticulture," who was a member of the class of 1882, professor of horticulture at M.A.C., and then professor and dean at Cornell University. He authored 75 books, was a leader in agricultural education, and had a building named for him at Cornell. Bailey also had Bailey Street and Bailey Elementary School in East Lansing named after him.

Bailey was honored with a U.S. postage stamp in 1958, issued on the 100th anniversary of his birth.

Ray Stannard Baker Hall, built in 1967 ($1,647,464), honors an 1889 alumnus who wrote a Pulitzer-prize winning biography of U.S. President Woodrow Wilson. Baker wrote for *McClure's* Magazine early in the 20th century. His 1908 book, *Following the Color Line*, protested injustices against blacks. He also authored many *Adventures in Contentment* books. The hall named for him houses the Schools of Criminal Justice, the School of Social Work, and the Department of Anthropology. Baker married William J. Beal's daughter (Beal Botanical Garden).

William J. Beal Botanical Garden, started by Beal in 1873 and the oldest of its kind in the U.S., was named for the nationally renowned professor of botany who served on the Michigan State faculty for 40 years—1870-1910. Beal was the "Father" of hybrid corn and the "Father of seed-testing in America." He was a leader—along with Dr. Robert C. Kedzie in promoting tree-planting and forestry science in Michigan.

He also served as the first president of the American Association for the Advancement of the Science of Agriculture, being elected in 1880. Beal Street in East Lansing is named for him, as is the Beal Street Entrance to the MSU campus. The Beal-Darlington Herbarium at MSU dates back to 1863, and contained 200,000 plant specimens in 1973, some collected as early as 1815.

Beaumont Tower, constructed in 1928 ($110,437), was a gift from John Beaumont, class of 1882 and member of the Eclectic Society, (now ATO). He was a Detroit attorney, and, at one time, taught at the Detroit College of Law, which is now on the MSU campus as the Michigan State University College of Law. The tower stands on the highest ground on the MSU campus on the site of Old College Hall (1857-1918), the first building in America devoted to the teaching of scientific agriculture. The tower is Michigan State's signature architectural landmark.

William H. Berkey Hall, built in 1947 ($1,177,019), and renovated in 1994, honors a former member and chairperson of the MSU board of trustees. Built as one of the largest classroom structures in the U.S. to help accommodate the post-World War II flood of veterans, it was affectionately called "Berkey High School" by many students. The hall houses the offices of the College of Social Science.

Alfred Berkowitz Basketball Complex connected to the east side of the Jack Breslin Student Events Center was named in honor of Alfred Berkowitz, whose trust, through chairman David Levine, gave $2 million toward the $7 million building. Levine stated at the dedication of the complex on January 12, 2002, "His gift to you is my gift to him."

The late Berkowitz made a fortune in the steel industry in Detroit, and maintained that he "was happiest when helping others." The building, which includes basketball practice gymnasiums named for **Forest Akers** and former MSU head basketball coach **George "Jud" Heathcote**, houses beautiful offices, small auditoriums, and video editing rooms for the coaching staffs of the MSU men's and women's basketball programs. The Forest Akers Trust gave $1 million towards the new complex.

Ernest A. Bessey Hall, built in 1961 ($2,201,200), honors a world-famous botanist who was the first dean of the Graduate School. He also served as a professor and head of the botany department. He was an educator at MSU from 1910 to 1946. The building, located on the site of the former the band shell—a gift of the class of 1937—was expanded and renovated in 1994 ($3,039,255).

Jack Breslin Student Events Center, constructed in 1989 ($37,475,716), is named in honor of the man known as "Mr. MSU," who devoted nearly 50 years of his life to the school. Breslin, class of 1946, rose to become an MSU executive vice president and served as a special counselor to the university's presidents.

During his administrative tenure, some 60 buildings and additions to the campus were completed. In 2002, MSU Provost Lou Anna Simon, referred to Breslin as a "dream builder." As an MSU student he starred in football, basketball and baseball and was student council and senior class president. He was a member of Alpha Tau Omega fraternity.

The "Bricks," eleven faculty apartment buildings, are **named for MSU alumni who gave their lives in World War II—Joseph L. Bale, III, '46; H. Thane**

"The Bricks," eleven faculty apartment buildings, are named for MSU alumni who gave their lives in World War II.

Bauman, '43; Edwin B. Crowe, '40; Royce A. Drake, '27; Carl N. Frang, '42; Robert L. French, '42; Arthur J. Howland, '41; Robert Parker, '43; Joseph H. Pelton, '36; William T. Rafferty, '41; and **Arthur K. Ungren, '32.** Built in 1946, these buildings were critical in attracting new and distinguished faculty following World War II.

Eli Broad College of Business & the Eli Broad Graduate School of Management were named for Eli Broad, '54, founder and CEO of Kaufman & Broad, Inc., who gave $20 million to the MSU College of Business in 1991. It was the largest private gift to a public university up to that time. The $14.4 million North Business Complex, built in 1993 on Bogue Street, was partially funded by the Broad gift.

Clark L. Brody Hall honors a man who served for a third of a century on the MSU board of trustees, half of that time as chairperson. A member of the class of 1904, Brody was a one-time county agricultural agent and executive manager of the Michigan Farm Bureau from its founding. The hall, built in 1954 ($1,619,099) and expanded in 1955 ($1,479,636) and 1979 ($384,820), serves as the dining and recreation facility for the Brody complex of six residence halls.

Claude S. Bryan Hall is named for the former dean of the College of Veterinary Medicine, who was a distinguished research scholar in dairy hygiene. The hall was built in 1954 ($1,652,730).

Kenyon S. Butterfield Hall, built in 1954 ($1,537,421), honors Michigan State's tenth president (1924-1928). Butterfield, Class of 1891 and a member of the Eclectic Society (now ATO). He also served as president of Rhode Island State College, and the University of Massachusetts. He was a leader in expanding Michigan State's outreach education

programs for farmers, and was a pioneer in introducing the concept of "Continuing Education."

Louise H. Campbell Hall, built in 1939 ($474,628), honors the lady who headed MSU's home economics outreach in the 1920s. She developed a "relay" system in which rural women were trained to teach groups of their neighbors. Campbell introduced the annual Farm Women's Week, which brought women to the campus each July for cultural and technical education. The hall was expanded in 1969 ($32,000).

Albert H. and Sarah A. Case Halls, built in 1961 ($3,862,279), honor the Cases who gave MSU more than one million dollars for scholarships and other projects. Albert H. Case was a 1902 graduate of M.A.C. and captain of the 1901 football team. He later became a vice president with the Tennessee Corporation. His wife Sarah, also an M.A.C. graduate, taught physical training after graduation to women students in the new (1900) Women's Building (now Morrill Hall), which had its own gymnasium. Case Halls were built on the site where post-World War II temporary married student apartments once stood. The hall was expanded in 1969 ($674,662).

Alfred K. Chittenden Hall, built in 1901 ($15,000), honors the professor who directed the academic work in forestry at MSU from 1914 to 1930. He led reforestation and maple sugar production research, and developed a campus nursery that supplied millions of seedlings planted throughout the state of Michigan.

Elisabeth W. Conrad Hall, built in 1964 ($455,510), honors the woman who served as dean of women and as a professor of French from 1928 to 1945. The building houses the University Archives and Historical Collections, the Digital Information Group, and a classroom auditorium.

Albert J. Cook Hall, built in 1889 ($7,500) as the Entomology Building, was the first agricultural laboratory in the nation. It honors the professor who was recognized as one of the top three "leading economic entomologists in the nation, when insects were beginning to threaten the future of fruit-growing in Michigan," according to Madison Kuhn's book *Michigan State—The First Hundred Years.* He was a member of the class of 1862 and a leader in the development of insecticides. Kuhn reported, "Cook discovered that kerosene could be emulsified with soap to provide a cheap, effective spray to destroy plant-sucking insects without harming foliage. He was the first in the country to use a crude carbolic acid emulsion against bark lice, or carbon bi-sulphide as an insecticide."

Alice B. Cowles House, the MSU president's home, was built in 1857 and is the oldest structure on campus. It was named for the mother of Frederick Cowles Jenison (Jenison Fieldhouse), whose bequest helped finance enlargement of the home in 1950 ($112,577) and the construction of the fieldhouse and gymnasium in 1940. Alice Cowles father, Albert E. Cowles, was a student in 1857, a member of the first class at the college. He helped make bricks dug from clay out of "Sleepy Hollow"—the beautifully landscaped depression just southeast of the Music Practice Building—for the construction of what is now the president's home.

Duffy Daugherty Football Building, built in 1980 ($1,429,925), honors Hugh "Duffy" Daugherty, MSU football coach from 1954 through 1972. Daugherty led MSU to national championships and Big Ten titles in 1965 and 1966. He was named national football "Coach of the Year" in 1955 and 1965. The building was expanded in 1985 ($2,807,141), and 1997 ($4,597,172).

Lloyd C. Emmons Hall, built in 1955 ($ 1,475,787), honors the former dean of Liberal Arts and then Science and Arts at MSU. Emmons was a professor of mathematics and statistics and served as an advisor to the president on academic matters. As chairperson of the MSU Athletic Council, he was a leader in earning the university membership in the Big Ten.

Eppley Wing of the College of Business, built in 1961 ($1,381,866), honors Eugene C. Eppley whose Eppley Foundation contributed $1,500,000 to construct the building. He was an Omaha hotel chain owner and pioneer in hotel education. The Eppley building was connected to the new College of Business building in 1993, when that structure was completed.

Erickson Hall, built in 1957 ($3,563,610), honors Clifford E. Erickson, who had served MSU as dean of the College of Education, dean of the University College, and as university provost. The hall houses the College of Education. It was expanded in 1964 ($33,508), and 1974 ($770,000).

Eustace-Cole Hall, built in 1888 ($7,000), honors Harry J. Eustace, class of 1901, Masters' 1911, chaired the Horticulture Department from 1908 to 1919, and Jeffrey Cole, class of 1970, and his wife Kathryn, MBA 1990, who gave $3 million in 1997 to the Honors College for enhancing programs and for renovation of the building. The building was restored in 1998 at a cost of $1,339,353.

Eustace was in charge of the perishable food division under Herbert Hoover during World War I.

Cole, chairperson and CEO of Ferrous Processing and Trading Company, Detroit, was an Honors College graduate.

When originally constructed in 1888, it was the first building and laboratory in the nation devoted wholly to horticultural research and education. It is listed on the National Register of Historic Places (1971) and was designed by M.A.C. graduate Liberty Hyde Bailey.

Fairchild Theatre, built in 1940 as part of the Auditorium ($1,025,000), honors George T. Fairchild who was a professor of English and political economy in the 1870s, and the school's first librarian. He served as acting president of M.A.C. from May 1873 to May 1874, when president Abbot was granted a leave of absence for his health. In 1879, Fairchild left M.A.C. to become president of Kansas Agricultural College, now Kansas State University.

Arthur W. Farrall Agricultural Engineering Hall, constructed in 1948 ($681,542), honors a pioneer in the agricultural engineering profession, who was named chairperson of Agricultural Engineering in 1945. Under Farrall's leadership, the department established the first agricultural engineering doctorate program in the nation. A 1999 addition to the building cost $937,562.

Harry A. and Jessie T. Fee Halls, built in 1964 ($4,780,121), were named for Harry A. Fee and his sister Jessie T. Fee. Harry Fee and his wife Harriet Kimball Fee established the elegant Hidden Lake Gardens in the scenic Irish Hills near Tipton, Michigan in 1926, and gave the 226-acre treasure to Michigan State in 1945. Jessie T. Fee has since contributed generously to the development of the gardens which have expanded to 670 acres. Fee Halls were converted from residence halls to use by the College of Human Medicine in the 1971-75 period, and later also used to house the College of Osteopathic Medicine.

Maude Gilchrist Hall, built in 1948 ($584,239), honors a graduate of M.A.C. who was the first dean of the Women's Department, serving 1901-1913. She insisted that music, art, and literature were as essential as domestic science in training the homemaker.

Ward Giltner Hall, honors the former dean of the College of Veterinary Medicine (1923 to 1947). Giltner, a bacteriologist, led the introduction of medical technologist training at Michigan State, and added the fifth year to the veterinary medicine program to increase the scientific and liberal education of its graduates. The hall for years housed the College of Veterinary Medicine. Built in 1913 for $33,000, the building was enlarged in 1931 ($110,165), 1938 ($120,938), 1940 ($59,874), 1952 ($2, 287,483), and 1968 ($118,168).

Hancock Turfgrass Field Laboratory, built in 1980 ($106,504), honors Robert Hancock, who left part of his estate to MSU to expand research on turfgrass. He attended the turfgrass educational programs at MSU, was an avid golfer and successful businessman. A field laboratory and cold storage building were added to the complex in 1996 at a cost of $113,434.

John A. Hannah Administration Building, built in 1968 ($5,215,167) honors MSU's twelfth president, who served as CEO for 28 years. He was the architect of MSU's spectacular growth from a small college to an internationally recognized university. The building houses the offices of the president and many other university officers as well as the University Admissions Office.

Jud Heathcote Gymnasium at the Alfred Berkowitz Basketball Complex is connected to the east side of the Jack Breslin Student Events Center. It is the MSU men's basketball practice gymnasium and was named and dedicated in 2002 in honor of the legendary MSU head basketball coach, 1976-1995. Heathcote coached MSU to an NCAA title in 1979, and Big Ten titles in 1978, 1979, and 1990. He was named National Coach of the Year in 1995 by the *Sporting News*, and Big Ten Coach of the Year in 1978, and 1986. He was inducted into the Michigan Sports Hall of Fame in 2001.

James B. Henry Center for Executive Education, opened in September, 2001, is named in honor of James B. Henry, dean emeritus of the Eli Broad College of Business. The center, a national model for executive education facilities, was made possible in large part because of an $8 million gift from James M. Cornelius, BS '65; MBS '67, former chairman of Guidant Corp. and former vice president and Chief Financial Officer of Eli Lilly and Company. Cornelius specified the center should be named for dean emeritus Henry. The entire center complex, including the Candlewood Suites Hotel, cost $25 million.

James and Lynelle Holden Halls, built in 1967 ($5,993,441), honor James Holden and his wife Lynelle, who were generous contributors to Michigan State. Holden, class of 1892, was a successful Detroit realtor who served 38 years on the Detroit Zoological Commission and gave that institution nearly $2 million.

John C. Holmes Halls, built in 1965 ($5,524,798), honors the man who was the chief advocate for an agricultural college in Michigan, separate from the University of Michigan and the Normal School (Eastern Michigan University). Holmes, who organized the Michigan Agricultural Society, signed a society petition to the state legislature that called for the establishment of an agricultural college. This was also circulated statewide to build momentum for the passage of such an act, which ultimately led to the founding of MSU.

Holmes also was key in selecting the land that would become the MSU campus. He served M.A.C. as a professor of horticulture and directed the landscaping of the original campus.

Landon Hall viewed through spring blossoms.

Bela Hubbard Halls, built in 1966 ($5,785,328), honors the man who wrote the first resolution calling for an agricultural college in Michigan. It was passed by the executive committee of the Michigan Agricultural Society on December 19, 1849. On January 1, 1850, Hubbard wrote a memorandum to the state legislature calling for the scientific and liberal education of farmers and their sons. He, thus, was a leading pioneer in selling the idea of establishing the school that would become Michigan State University.

Frederick Cowles Jenison Gymnasium and Fieldhouse, built in 1940 ($1,025,000), honors the man who bequeathed his $408,481.49 estate to Michigan State. The bulk of the estate was used to help build the gymnasium and fieldhouse. In 1950, the remainder of his estate ($126,900) was used to remodel and expand the president's home, which is named after Jenison's mother, Alice B. Cowles. Jenison, an engineering student at M.A.C. from 1902 to 1907 and a member of the Eclectic Society (now ATO), was a successful real estate investor in Lansing, Michigan, died in 1939.

North Kedzie and South Kedzie Halls honor Dr. Robert C. Kedzie, the school's first chemistry professor, who began his career in 1863 and served M.A.C. for nearly four decades. His son, Dr. Frank S. Kedzie, Michigan State's eighth president, 1915 to 1924, had a 47-year tenure at the school. North Kedzie Hall was built in 1927 at a cost of $113,800.

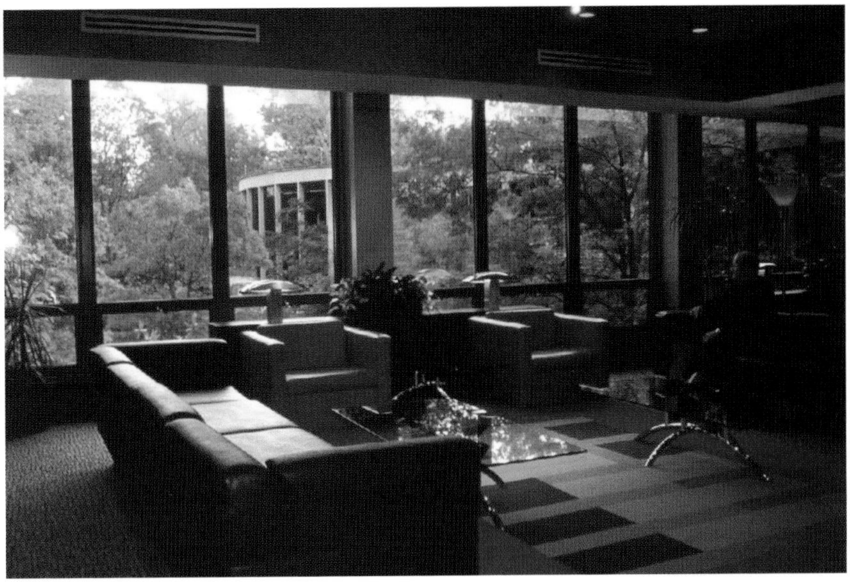

Kellogg Center lounge brings campus scenery indoors. The hotel conference center serves as a premier Hospitality Business laboratory,

South Kedzie Hall was built in 1966 at a cost of $2,035,768. Robert Kedzie was a pioneer in public health and consumer protection. In the mid-1870s, he warned the legislature and the public of the dangers of volatile illuminating oils, poor ventilation in buildings, the use of Paris green—which contained arsenic—as a coloring agent, and digging drinking wells too close to outhouses and graveyards. He was asked by the Michigan legislature to become the first Director of Public Health for Michigan. In 1875, he proposed the Farmers' Institutes to share new-found agricultural knowledge with the farmers of the state. This was the beginning of the school's extension and outreach programs. Kedzie, with Dr. Beal, led the reforestation of Michigan in the 1870s and was the first director of the State Forestry Commission in 1888.

Kellogg Center for Continuing Education, built in 1951 ($1,768,052); honors W.K. Kellogg, the pioneer cereal producer, whose foundation underwrote cost of the building. Kellogg Center is recognized as the finest hotel-restaurant hospitality training laboratory and the finest adult education center in the nation. The facility was a pioneer in the movement towards continuing education buildings around the nation. It was expanded in 1955 ($413,430), 1959 ($381,650), and 1988 ($3,320,759).

IM-West 50-meter Olympic-sized pool, named for Charles McCaffree, Jr., MSU swimming coach 1941-1969.

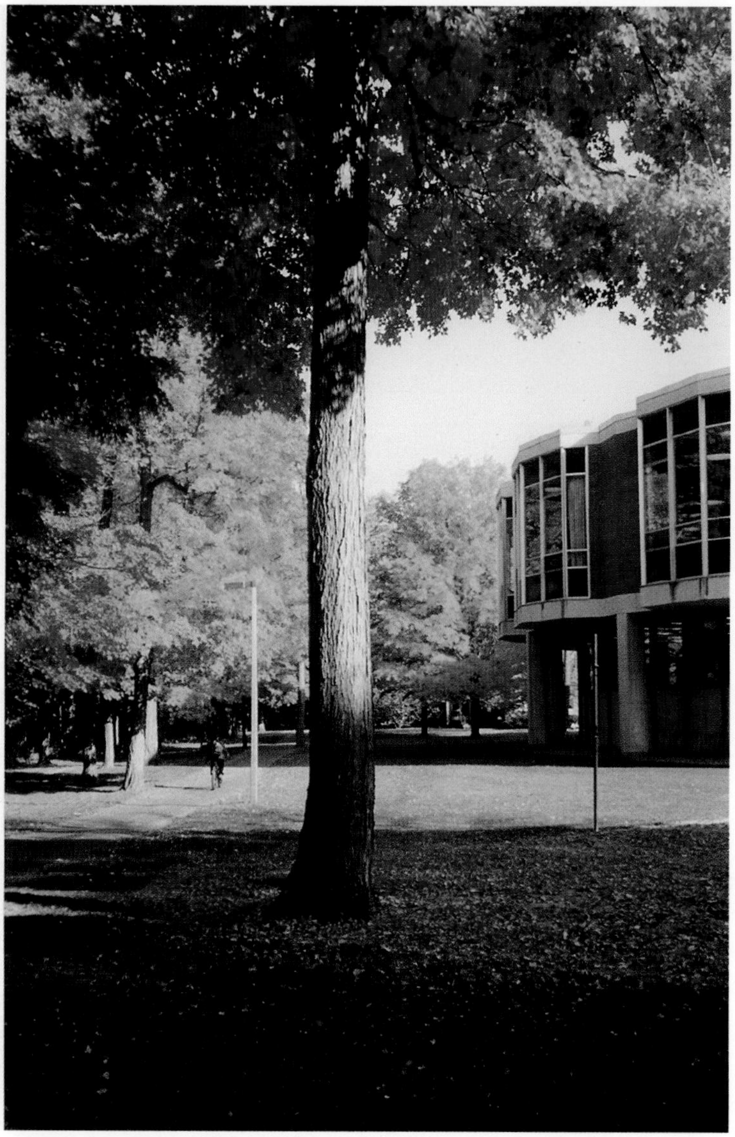

Autumn splendor along walkway behind McDonel Halls.

John H. Kobs, MSU baseball coach for 39 years, had the varsity diamond and grounds named in his honor as John H. Kobs Field on May 10, 1969. The bronze plaque at the field reads: "Dedicated to a man who coached baseball at Michigan State for 39 years, 1925 to 1963. His love for the game and players was the hallmark of his great success as a coach and a teacher."

Dr. Delia Koo, M.A. and Ph.D., Radcliffe College, M.S. '54, MSU, had MSU's new 10,000 square foot International Academic Center named for her. It opened in the spring of 2003. A major endowment from Dr. Koo made possible this addition to the MSU International Center, which will be home to new classrooms, visiting faculty programs, and such academic programs as the Delia Koo Global Faculty, and the Delia Koo Global Scholars. It also will house the Volunteer English Tutoring Program, which was created in 1983 by Dr. Koo, to help newly arrived international students, spouses, and visitors adapt to life in an unfamiliar country.

Kresge Art Center was a gift of the S.S. Kresge Foundation. It houses Kresge Art Museum, studios, classrooms, and offices. It was built in 1958 ($1,480,160), and expanded in 1966 ($320,720) and 1973 ($40,000).

Linda E. Landon Hall, built in 1947 ($1,346,256) and expanded in 1969 ($37,000), honors the lady who served Michigan State as librarian from 1891 to 1932. She developed the first cataloging system for classifying books and had "a deep interest in students."

Robert S. Linton Hall, built in 1881 ($22,000) and expanded in 1947 ($368,550), and in 1996 ($348,741), honors education professor Robert S. Linton, long-time university registrar, who streamlined the registration process by introducing IBM enrollment cards in 1939. Built originally as the library-museum-president's office, it now is home to the College of Arts and Letters and the Graduate School.

Marshall-Adams Hall, built in 1902 ($27,000), honors Dr. Charles E. Marshall, the university's first bacteriology department head, and the late Dr. Walter Adams, MSU's 13th president and distinguished emeritus professor of economics. Marshall moved his bacteriology department into the new building—the nation's first Bacteriology Building for research and teaching—in 1903.

Later the economics department took over the building. Walter Adams had his office in the building for many years. The structure was remodeled and renovated in 1991 ($196,423). In 2002, MSU Trustee Randall and his wife Mary, gave $6 million to renovate Marshall Hall and rename it Marshall-Adams Hall to honor the late MSU president.

Stevens T. Mason Hall, built in 1938 ($525,000), honors the State's first (1837) and youngest governor (age 21). He led Michigan's fight for statehood and undertook a railroad and canal building program to link Michigan's frontier farms and towns with the East Coast.

Mary Mayo Hall, built in 1931 ($425,000), honors Mary A. Bryant Mayo, who was the leader of the Michigan Grange women (farmers' organization for social and cultural purposes) in the 1890s. She mobilized the organization to demand for its daughters an education equivalent to that offered to its sons. Her efforts were rewarded when the Women's Course was inaugurated on the East Lansing campus in 1896.

Charles "Mac" McCaffree—MSU's varsity swimming pools—indoor and out—at the IM-West Building (1958–$3,212,508)— are named for the man who coached MSU swimming from 1941 to 1969. McCaffree was elected to the International Swimming Hall of Fame in 1976. He coached MSU swimmers who won 22 individual NCAA titles, 34 individual Big Ten titles, and a National AAU team title. In his 28-year career, he led MSU to 24 consecutive winning seasons, and an all-time dual meet record of 191 wins, 58 losses and two ties. He coached the U.S. Pan American team in 1959 and was past president of the College Swimming Coaches Association of America.

Karl H. and Irma N. McDonel Halls, built in 1963 ($4,020,925), honors Karl McDonel, who served as Secretary of the MSU Board of Trustees from 1941 to 1960, and his wife Irma. He was key in planning, financing and erecting MSU buildings for nearly two decades.

Mary Anne McPhail Equine Performance Center—A new $2.5 million, 19,000 square-foot facility, which opened in 2000, houses MSU's Equine Sports Medicine program. A 1997 gift of $1.5 million from Mary Anne McPhail, '55, and her husband Walter, created the Mary Anne McPhail Dressage Chair in Equine Sports Medicine—the first of its kind in the world.

Manly Miles Building, built in 1959 ($749,325), honors the first professor of scientific agriculture in the U.S., who served at M.A.C. from 1860 to 1875. When Miles left for the University of Illinois in 1875, the *Michigan Farmer* said of him, "We doubt very much if his place could be filled, in every way, by any two men picked out of any collegiate institution in or out of our country."

Morrill Hall, built in 1900 ($91,000), honors Justin S. Morrill, Vermont Congressman, who authored the bill—signed by President Lincoln in 1862—that created the land-grant colleges and universities in America. MSU, by virtue of having been founded in 1855, is considered the pioneer land-grant university in the nation. Originally built as the Women's Building at M.A.C., the building now is home to several programs of the College of Arts and Letters.

Clarence L. Munn Ice Arena, built in 1974 ($3,581,700) honors "Biggie" Munn, MSU's most successful football coach with an .857 winning percentage during the 1947-1953 seasons; and highly successful athletic director from 1954 until his retirement in 1971. In his 17 years as athletic director, he guided MSU to six Big Ten all-sports titles and eleven seconds. He was inducted into the National Association of Collegiate Athletic Directors United Savings Helms Hall of Fame in 1972, and the Citizens Savings College Football Hall of Fame in 1975. Munn was an All-American football player for the University of Minnesota in the early 1930s.

The 6,470-seat Munn Arena is home to MSU ice hockey. VIP suites were added to the arena in 1999 ($3,306,057). Record crowd: 7,121, March 1, 2001 vs. Michigan.

Stelphen S. Nisbet Office Building, built in 1973 ($1,587,019), honors an alumnus who also served on the MSU Board of Trustees.

R.E. Olds Hall, built in 1916 ($202,000), honors the founder of the Oldsmobile and REO Motor automobile companies, who gave $100,000 to help rebuild M.A.C.'s nine year old engineering building which had burned to the ground. President Frank Kedzie wired Olds the day after the March 5, 1916 fire with an appeal for help. Olds remembered that Kedzie's father—Dr. Robert Kedzie—had loaned Olds money when he was struggling to launch their motor car business. Today, the building houses MSU's University Relations offices, the Campus Park & Planning Department and other offices and classrooms.

Olin Memorial Health Center, built in 1939 ($250,000), honors Richard M. Olin, director of the MSU Health Service, 1925 to 1938. He was the first full-time campus physician. The hospital, which cost $250,000, was expanded in 1956 ($1,318,900), and 1969 ($343,062).

Owen Graduate Center, built in 1960 ($2,347,266), honors Floyd W. Owen, class of 1902 and 1930, who gave MSU a $420,000 bequest. The residence hall, which houses graduate students was expanded in 1965 ($2,266,047). Owen Graduate Center is the home of MSU's Urban Affairs Programs. A $600,000 contribution from Owen and Forest Akers was key in building MSU's University Club in 1970.

Herbert J. Oyer Speech & Hearing Center, built in 1963 ($649,811), honors Herbert J. Oyer, dean emeritus of the College of Communication Arts and Sciences (1971-1975), dean emeritus of the MSU Graduate School, and former head of the Department of Audiology and Speech Sciences. Oyer, who came to MSU in 1960 from Ohio State, was a leader in developing the graduate and research programs in speech, language and hearing. He was instrumental in obtaining a federal grant to help finance the Speech and Hearing Center named for him.

The Paolucci Building, built in 1947 ($253,601), honors Beatrice Paolucci, a 30-year veteran with the Department of Family and Child Ecology, and leading authority on family decision-making and resource management. The facility was used for home management training.

T. Glen Phillips Hall, built in 1947 ($1,080,765), honors the Detroit landscape architect, class of 1902, who was Michigan State's long-time campus planner. Phillips produced a "General Campus Plan" in 1926, which was praised by Harold Lautner, who succeeded Phillips in 1946. Lautner said in his book *From an Oak Opening*, that Phillips "reserved ample space for dormitories, academic buildings, athletics and agriculture and the most saleable aspects of Phillips plan was his informal spacious placement of buildings and groups of buildings, all with 'studied

Wharton Center for Performing Arts.

random effect.'" Phillips also kept the "sacred space" inside West Circle Drive sacrosanct.

Howard C. Rather Hall, built in 1954 ($1,572,656), honors the first dean of the Basic College (1944), who served as an extension specialist, professor and department head. A member of the class of 1917, Rather chaired the committee that planned the Basic College, which re-introduced the concept of liberal education at MSU following World War II. This men's residence hall was expanded in 1962 ($26,138).

Robert S. Shaw Hall, built in 1950 ($3,482,153), honors the eleventh president of Michigan State, who served as CEO from 1928 to 1941. When it opened in 1950, the new structure was the largest residence hall in the United States.

Shaw introduced innovative bond financing in 1931 to build Mary Mayo Hall, which would be repaid from the fees earned from the student residents. This successful private financing led Michigan State to build many more residence halls at no cost to the taxpayers. He also initiated the practice of buying up farm land adjacent to Michigan State to add to the campus acreage. Three times prior to being elected president, Shaw had served the school as interim president. He came to the college in 1902 as a professor of agriculture and was later named dean of agriculture. Shaw Lane on campus and Shaw Estates in East Lansing are named for him.

Theodore B. Simon Power Plant, built in 1965 ($7,961,135), honors the long-time MSU assistant vice president for physical facilities. The plant has been added to and expanded ten times between 1965 and 1998 at a total additional cost of $76 million.

Clara Bell Smith Student-Athlete Academic Center, built in 1998 ($5,669,343), was named by former MSU basketball All-American and current NBA star Steve Smith, in honor of his mother. Smith gave MSU $2.5 million towards the construction of the facility, the largest gift ever given by any professional athlete to a university.

Jonathan L. Snyder Hall, built in 1947 ($1,096,285), honors Michigan State's seventh president, who served from 1896 to 1915. Snyder implemented ten recommendations from an 1896 faculty study to improve the attractiveness of the college. This action resulted in a jump in new student enrollment from 135 in 1897 to a record 244 in 1898. Snyder was brilliant in leading the planning and execution of the school's semi-centennial celebration in 1907 (50 years from the opening of classes in 1857), which brought U.S. President Teddy Roosevelt to campus to speak and attend the commencement exercises. Under Snyder's leadership, some 25 different academic departments were added between 1901 and 1911.

Fred W. Stabley, Sr. Press Box—In 1980, the press box at Spartan Stadium was named in honor of Fred Stabley, Sr., who served as MSU's Sports Information Director from 1948 to 1980. Stabley was a leader in his field, winning many awards for sports publicity. He was inducted into the College Sports Information Directors' Hall of Fame in 1969.

"The Weav"—MSU's indoor football practice facility was built in 1985 ($2,807,141). It has been dubbed "The Weav," for Douglas W. Weaver, '53, who served as MSU athletic director from 1980 to 1990. Weaver was a starting linebacker for MSU's national championship football teams of 1951 and 1952. In his 1950-1952 playing career the Spartans won 26 of 27 games.

During his tenure as athletic director, Weaver oversaw the construction of several major athletic facilities, including the Duffy Daugherty Football Building, the indoor football practice building, the indoor tennis pavilion, and the Breslin Student Events Center.

G. Malcolm Trout Food Science and Human Nutrition Building, built in 1966 ($3,442,532), honors a pioneer in dairy science research who was the "Father of Homogenized Milk." Trout was a distinguished faculty member from 1928 through 1966.

Van Hoosen Hall, built in 1957 ($447,781), honors Dr. Sarah VanHoosen Jones, a Ph.D. in science, "Master Farmer," leading raiser of purebred Holsteins, and a former member of the MSU Board of Trustees. She gave the university her home and farm. Van Hoosen Hall, a cooperative housing project for women, contained 32 apartments, each housing six students.

Hezekiah G. Wells Hall, built in 1967 ($4,659,834), honors the lawyer and county judge who was a founder of the college through his efforts in the Michigan Agricultural Society and at the 1850 Michigan constitutional convention. Wells remarkable service as the first chairman of the school's board of trustees, from 1861 to 1883, helped sustain the life and growth of the college. The current Wells Hall is the third building to bear his name. The first was a dormitory that burned in 1905; the second was razed in 1966 to make way for an addition to the MSU library. The building was expanded in 1970 ($826,500).

Clifton and Dolores Wharton Center for Performing Arts, built in 1982 ($16,583,483), honors the 14th president of MSU and his first lady. Wharton, who served from 1970 to 1977, was the first black president of a major university in the United States. He and his wife, an ardent patron of the arts, together inspired the work that led to the building of this magnificent building. Wharton resigned in 1977 to become chancellor of the State University of New York, which had 64 campuses and 345,000 students.

Sarah Langdon Williams Hall, built in 1937 ($500,000) honors the wife of Joseph K. Williams, the first president of Michigan State. In 1858, when the college was broke, the college steward and staff left. Sarah Williams, the school's first lady, stepped in to help keep the dormitory kitchen going, working with students to cook and serve meals. During the Civil War, she served as a nurse behind the front lines. Williams is a residence hall.

H. Merrill Wills House, built in 1927 ($37,500), honors the man who ran the U.S. Weather Bureau on the university campus in the 1930s and 1940s. He continued a tradition, begun in 1863 by chemistry professor Dr. Robert C. Kedzie, of publishing daily the weather observations. **Thus, the oldest series of continuous weather reports in the state go on**.

Matilda R. and Alfred G. Wilson Halls, built in 1962 ($4,583,085), honor Matilda R. Wilson, a member of the university Board of Trustees from 1932 to 1937, and Alfred G. Wilson, a Detroit philanthropist. The Wilsons gave MSU their 1,600-acre Meadowbrook Farms in Rochester, Michigan, and $2 million to establish MSU-Oakland in 1957. In 1970, it became Oakland University. MSU bestowed an honorary LL.D. degree on Mrs. Wilson in 1955, and made Mr. Wilson an honorary alumnus in 1959.

Wallace K. and Grace Wonders Halls, built in 1963 ($4,429,982), honor Wallace K. Wonders, class of 1902, and his wife Grace Wonders, who were generous contributors to Michigan State.

Elida Yakeley Hall, built in 1948 ($1,439,000), honors the lady who was secretary to President Snyder from 1903 to 1908, and became the college's first registrar in 1908, a position she held for thirty years.

Ralph H. Young Track & Field is named in honor of the late MSU athletic director who served from 1923 to 1954. He was elected to the National Association of College Directors of Athletics Hall of Fame in 1979. Young was instrumental in hiring and inspiring head coaches of every sport Michigan State competed in for three decades. The late MSU sports information director Fred W. Stabley, Sr., stated, "Without Young and his exuberant public relations work, it is a safe bet MSU would not be in the Big Ten today."

The Campus Beautiful

The most pleasant memory of Michigan State by its family members—other than people—is the stunning beauty of the campus. It is a prime reason for students selecting MSU. The random layout of the campus with its elegant lawns, trees, flower beds and walkways is a vision embedded in the minds of Spartans. A casual stroll within the "Sacred Space" of West Circle Drive—punctuated by Beaumont Tower, the towering oak trees and spacious lawns is a feast for the eyes. The picturesque and peaceful Beal Botanical Garden, the appealing footpaths along the Red Cedar River corridor, which pass by the rapids and miniature parks bring nostalgic feelings to MSU alumni, faculty, and students. Many other vistas throughout the campus contribute to this love of Michigan State.

Many Spartans rhapsodize about the calming effect and peacefulness that a stroll across the campus gives them. Deans and professors have told the author that the tensions of the day can be erased by the uplift they get from taking in the beautiful ambiance of the picturesque arboretum that surrounds them. Dr. Ken Corey, dean of the College of Social Science in 1992, commented, "Walking the campus is a refreshment…I love it."

Duane Vernon, '53, voiced a sentiment felt by many Spartans…

"Every time I drive or walk on the campus…I get a special feeling… like I'm home."

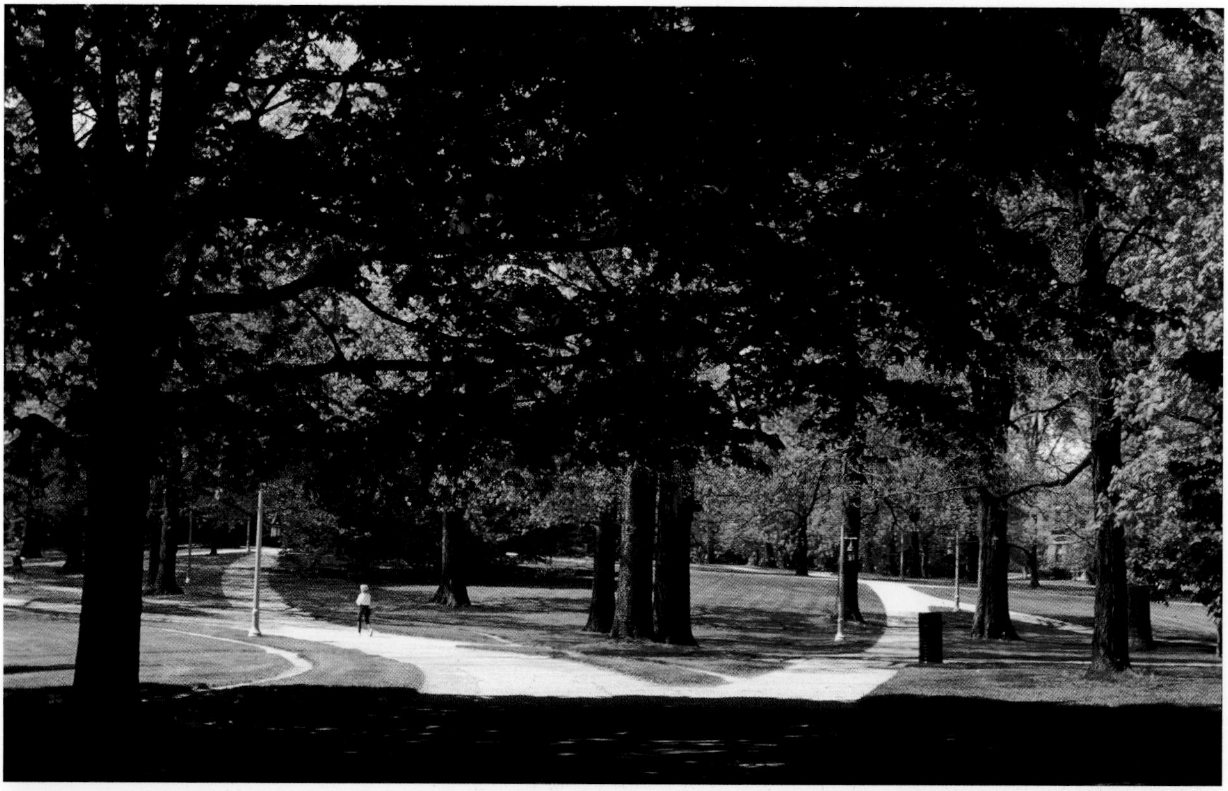

The central campus within West Circle Drive was first called "Sacred Space" in 1906 by O.C. Simonds, noted Chicago landscape architect, who recommended that these beautiful grounds be protected forever from any new buildings. After his pronouncement, four buildings within Circle Drive eventually came down. They would be replaced by four new structures. Old College Hall (1857-1918) was replaced by Beaumont Tower (1928); first Williams Hall (1869-1919) replaced by a new Library (now Museum, 1924); the Armory (1885-1939) replaced by the Music Building (1940); and the first Abbot Hall (1888-1967) replaced by Music Practice Building (1968).

Coeds jog along Red Cedar River corridor.

After 149 years of nurturing (as of 2004), the campus park features more than 7,800 varieties of trees, shrubs, plants and flowers, and is one of he world's great arboretums. One example of the extent of plantings: there are 300 varieties of crab apple trees on campus. To keep the campus park robust, some one hundred diseased or broken trees are removed each year, and an additional 300 to 400 added. The Beaumont Nursery, with two greenhouses and a propagation house, is constantly growing new plants, shrubs and trees for planting on the campus.

Unique at MSU are the natural areas—the Sanford Natural Area (35 acres), **the Red Cedar Natural Area** (76 acres), and **the Baker Woodlot** (78 acres). On the south part of the campus, adjacent to Hagadorn Road, MSU owns **the 24-acre Toumey Forest**, which is listed in the National Park Service Register of Natural Landmarks. It is an example of protected beech and maple forest land.

MSU off-campus crown jewels include:

- ▼ **Brook Lodge**, beautiful 657-acre conference center near Augusta, Michigan;
- ▼ **Kellogg Biological Station,** a 1,996-acre spread which includes the **Kellogg Bird Sanctuary**,
- ▼ the 756-acre **Kellogg Experimental Forest,** all located at or near Hickory Corners, Michigan, and
- ▼ **W.K. Kellogg's summer mansion** overlooking Gull Lake, given to MSU in 1951. It was valued at $1,000,000.
- ▼ **Hidden Lake Gardens,** a magnificent 755-acre horticultural layout at Tipton, Michigan; and
- ▼ **Camp Wa Wa Sum**—MSU's 251-acre rustic camp overlooking a stretch of the pristine Au Sable River a few miles east of Grayling, Michigan.
- ▼ **MSU's Tollgate Education Center**—A 160-acre facility with a beautiful homestead, rolling land with a pond, woodlot, an orchard, and several farm buildings, located in Novi, Michigan.

Overall, the MSU campus—a 2-mile by 3.5-mile contiguous land mass—incorporates 5,198 acres, making it one of the largest in the nation. Added to the 17,000 acres of land owned by MSU elsewhere in the state, the university holdings total more than 22,000 acres.

1855—"A judicious and admirable location"

Starting as an agricultural, horticultural and botanical leader, the school's care and beautification of the campus was virtually ordained. Selected in 1855 from ten different sites, the original campus included 676 and 57/100ths acres. The price was $15 per acre. The executive committee of the State Agricultural Society picked the location and described the site: "It lies on both sides of the Cedar River (not yet called the Red Cedar), and is regarded as a judicious and admirable location, although it was nearly in a state of nature."

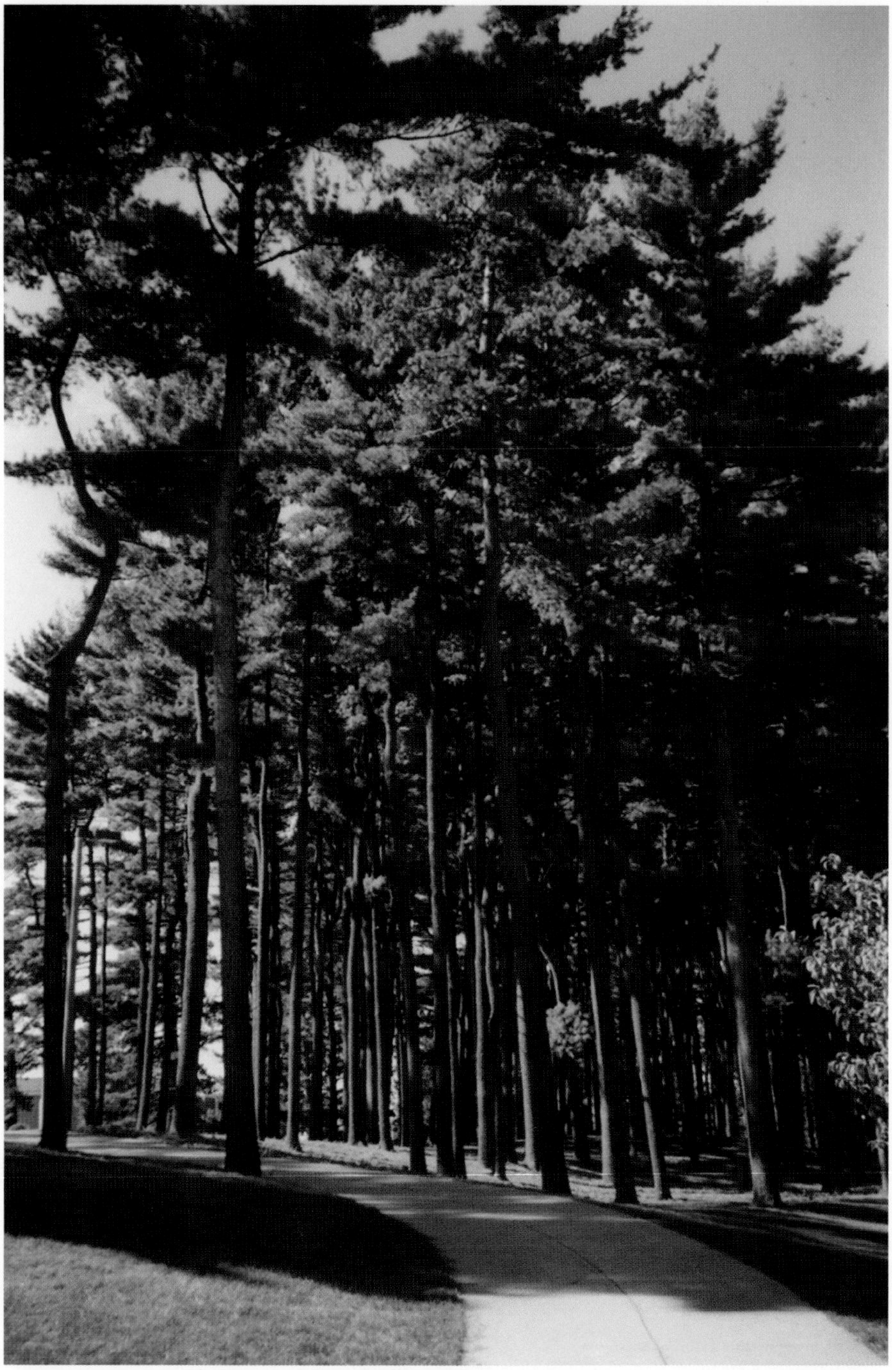

Pine grove between Dem Hall and Munn Arena was planted in 1914 by Forestry Professor Frank Sanford. The 35-acre Sanford Natural Area, located between Bogue Street and Hagadorn Road, is named for him.

"Properly Laid Out and Tastefully Arranged"

In Harold Lautner's book, *From An Oak Opening*, he wrote, "Even before its dedication (1857), the college had established a policy, recorded in the board minutes, 'that the college premises shall be properly laid out and tastefully arranged.'"

"Second, there was imagination used in locating the first two buildings in an oak opening"on a central dominant elevation. (site of Beaumont Tower and the Museum).

"Third, from the very beginning there is a record of continuous thought and effort by the college administrators and professors of horticulture and landscape gardening on the planning and care of its roads and walks and its beautiful trees, shrubs and lawn areas. The attention and effort

Pristine fall day—Union Memorial Building south entrance.

resulted in an environment of landscape beauty, repose, dignity and a certain elegance."

1857—"A Most Desolate Scene"—Today's campus—one of the most beautiful in the world—did not start that way. In 1857, when the school opened, the campus grounds were not pretty. Charles Jay Monroe, who was a student at the 1857 dedication of the school, described the campus in a 1907 speech: "On every hand were old stubs and partially burned trees. The fire had scorched the timber next to the clearing, so that at every point of the compass to which you turned, you beheld dead and blackened trees which presented **a most desolate scene."** (*History of the Michigan Agricultural College* by Dr. William J. Beal, 1915).

1861—2,000 Trees and Shrubs Planted

Beautification of the campus began with the planting of 2,000 trees and shrubs by students in 1861.

1869—Care For The Campus: An Early Priority

Early respect for campus beauty was evident in President Abbot's 1869 report: "The grounds around the new Boarding Hall and the farmhouse will be graded and put in order in the coming season. Improvements have progressed in the getting out of stumps, the building of fences, the eradication of bushes, cleaning fields of rubbish, and bringing the land into grass as rapidly as the character of the season will allow."

1871—President Abbot Proposes "Proper Layout of the College Grounds."

President Abbot proposed that the board "Take steps to provide for the proper layout of the college grounds, planting of trees, location of buildings, etc., by a competent landscape gardener, as soon as the means can be spared." (*From an Oak Opening* by Harold Lautner).

1873—Dr. Beal Starts His Botanical Garden

Dr. William J. Beal, the botany professor who would become internationally renowned, started planting a botanical garden in the ravine next to the Red Cedar River, and across from today's Music Building, in 1873. This living laboratory, with more than 5,000 species and varieties of plantings (today), is a delight to the eye. It has grown since 1873, and is the oldest, continuous botanical garden of its kind in the United States.

Beal Creates Miniature Arboretums on Campus

Beal was ubiquitous with his plantings, which he started in the 1870s. He created miniature arboretums around the campus, including the trees standing to the

Old Horticulture Gardens once located behind the Natural Science Building. This beautiful location became a favorite campus wedding site. The pool was rebuilt in 1978, a gift of the Class of 1978.

north of Campbell Hall and just east of Mary Mayo Hall; and "Pinetum," the pine forest east of Hagadorn Road along the Red Cedar River.

Beal Initiates Plant and Tree Labeling—First in Nation

Beal labeled and catalogued hundreds of trees and plants to aid his botany students in their studies. It is believed this was the first tree and plant labeling program on any college campus in the nation. To this day, the plant and tree identification effort is the most extensive in America.

Royal Gardens of England Donate Seeds to College

International plant additions to the campus began in 1873, when the Royal Gardens of Kew, England donated 200 varieties of tree seeds and 70 varieties of grass seeds to the college. Thus began a continuing practice of trading seeds and plantings with garden horticulturists around the globe.

1878—Beal: "...make the college grounds the most beautiful...in our state"

Professor Beal emphasized in 1878, "I am trying to make the college grounds the most beautiful and attractive of any in our state."

1894—10,000 Plants for "Sleepy Hollow"

Ten thousand plants were laid out in beds in the hollow ("Sleepy Hollow") between Old College Hall (site of Beaumont Tower) and Abbot Hall (first Abbot Hall, now the site of the Music Practice Building) in 1894. Today this hollow is one of the visual gems of the campus.

1905—8,000 Trees Planted

The incredible focus on campus beautification continued in 1905, with the planting of 8,000 trees on campus.

Lyrics from Michigan State's first Alma Mater (1907-1949) describe this photo: "Close beside the winding Cedar's sloping banks of green; spreads thy campus Alma Mater, fairest ever seen."

1906—O.C. Simonds: Inner Campus "Sacred Space" Should be Protected

O.C. Simonds, noted Chicago landscape architect, was hired briefly to look over the campus to suggest a plan for the placement of future buildings. His major recommendation—which is still honored—was that no new buildings be placed on the inner campus (inside West Circle Drive). Simonds wrote, "...I would regard all the ground within the areas marked by a dotted red line on the accompanying map (inside West Circle Drive) as sacred space from which all buildings must be forever excluded. This area contains beautifully rolling land with a pleasing arrangement of groups of trees...I am sure that feature of the college (is the one) which is most pleasantly and affectionately remembered by students after they leave their Alma Mater." Four buildings located inside the sacred space in 1906, eventually would come down. They would be replaced by four new structures. Old College Hall (1857-1918) was replaced by Beaumont Tower (1928); the first Williams Hall (1869-1919) was replaced by a new Library (now Museum, 1924); the Armory (1885-1939) was replaced by the Music Building (1940); and the first Abbot Hall (1888-1967) was replaced by the Music Practice Building (1968).

1923—T. Glen Phillips Hired as Campus Planner

In a far-sighted move, T. Glen Phillips **(Phillips Hall)**, class of 1902, and landscape architect and city planner for Detroit, was hired as a consultant on campus planning. For a salary of $1,000, he was to visit the campus monthly to confer with college board members on where to locate new buildings and on the layout and design of the college grounds. His impact on the look of the campus over the next 22 years was significant.

1926—Phillips Produces a General Campus Plan

A "General Campus Plan" was produced by campus planner T. Glen Phillips in 1926. He took a large overview of existing college land and buildings. His vision was to use all of the campus property from Bogue Street on the east to Harrison Road on the west, and included land south of the Red Cedar for athletic and agricultural use.

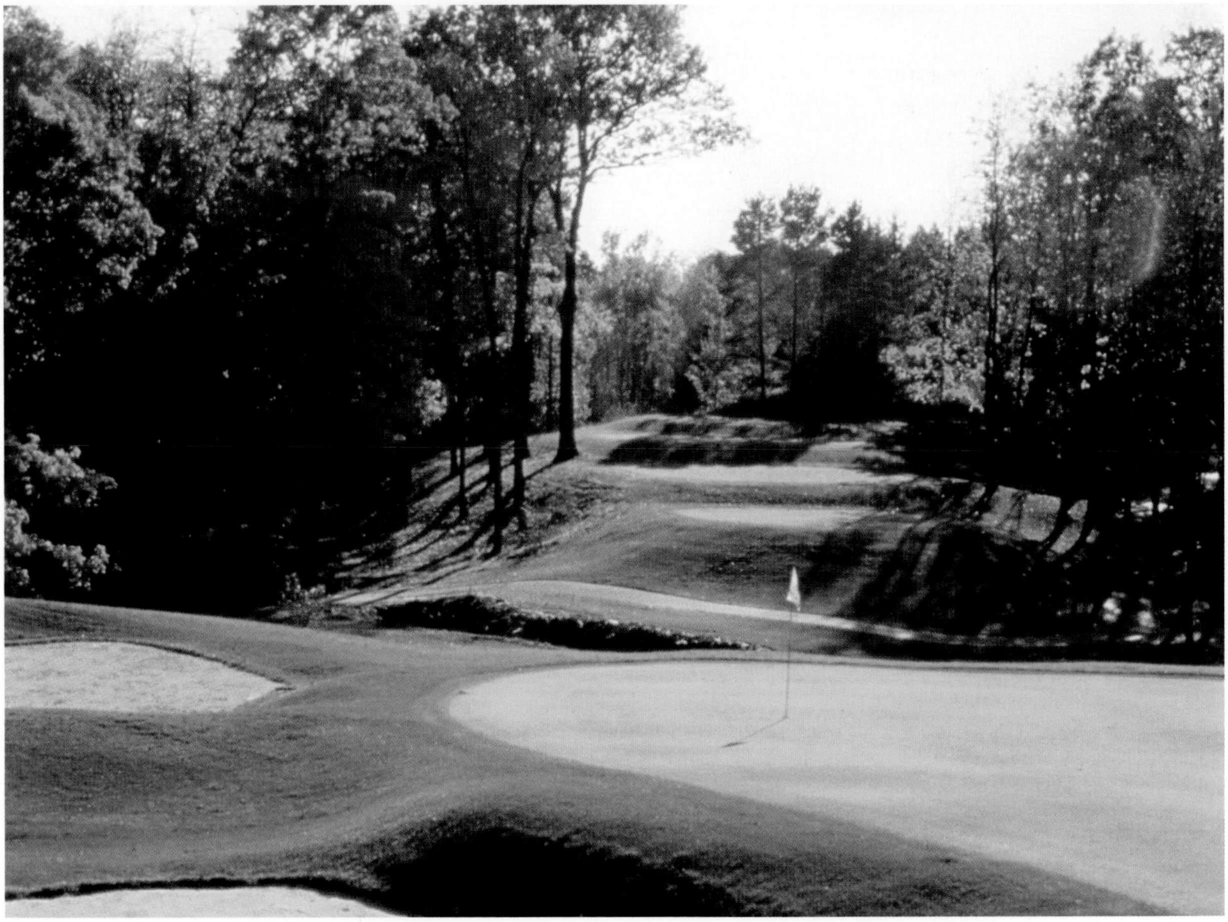

Signature hole–No. 9—at Forest Akers West championship course.

"Studied Random Effect" Key to Campus Beauty

In a remarkably visionary plan, Phillips "reserved space for dormitories, academic buildings, athletics and agriculture." The planning insight was described in Harold Lautner's book *From an Oak Opening:* "...the most saleable aspect of Phillips plan was his informal spacious placement of buildings and groups of buildings all with 'studied random effect.'"

Phillips kept the "sacred space" inside West Circle Drive sacrosanct. "He tied blocks and super-blocks of buildings together with a curving road system." Phillips' plan retained the charm of the old while providing a layout that would give Michigan State the beauty and free-flowing, informality of the future campus.

1946—Michigan State: The Leader in Campus Planning

President Hannah brought Harold W. Lautner, class of 1925, aboard in 1946 to direct all campus planning. Lautner, who succeeded T. Glen Phillips, had been in Washington, D.C. during World War II and had invaluable experience in planning war housing in the Division of Defense Housing. It was another case of Hannah selecting people with superior expertise. He surrounded himself with the best.

Lautner wrote in his book, "No other university is known to me that equals Michigan State for its foresight immediately after the war, in creating its own permanent campus planning office with clear responsibility to answer the daily and long-term needs for expanding its physical plant. This was entirely due to a president who understood the building process and the professions that could make and carry out plans."

Creation of the Red Cedar Corridor

One of the finest contributions to the beauty of the Michigan State campus started in 1946 with discussions between Harold Lautner and President Hannah. Lautner wanted to clean and landscape "the entire flood-plain of the Red Cedar River from Harrison Road to Bogue Street as a first step in exploiting the natural beauty of the stream in every way...incorporating it into the campus scene to the north. One way was face new buildings toward the river." Hannah was impressed with the idea. Because of the need to move the power plant, giant coal piles, and

Winding walkways criss-cross the central campus "Sacred Space."

service facilities (from behind Olds Hall) elsewhere, and tear down the old railroad bridge that spanned the Red Cedar, it took Lautner and Hannah 20 years to accomplish the creation of this ribbon of beauty through the heart of the campus. Today, one of the most pleasant walks on campus is through this "Red Cedar Corridor," with its beautiful landscaping, lawns, park-like vistas, and walkways.

1964—New "Science Campus" Started

A new Chemistry Building, to supplement the Kedzie Chemical Laboratories, was completed on South Shaw Lane east of Farm Lane. It was built next to the Cyclotron building (1963), the second of four buildings to occupy an area designated as the new "Science Campus," south of Shaw Lane. A new Bio-Chemistry Building also was completed in 1964. It was located on Wilson Road, east of Farm Lane. In 2002, the $93-million Bio-Medical and Physical Sciences Building was completed, and was connected with the Chemistry and Bio-Chemistry Buildings, creating a giant, world-class science center.

1968—Campus Zoning Regulations were established.

Zones were set in which buildings would have the same use. The area a building would cover on a given site was restricted to 30 percent of the land. According to Harold Lautner, building setbacks from adjacent roads were specified, and the height of buildings was limited— "all for preserving the campus environment of spaciousness and landscape beauty, promoting order and unity, minimizing the number of people per acre and therefore avoiding congestion."

1992—MSU Campus Among America's Most Aesthetic; "One of the Botanical Wonders of Campusdom"

MSU's campus was ranked among America's 25 most aesthetic campuses by Thomas A. Gaines in his 1992 book *The Campus As A Work of Art.* He called the sacred space inside MSU's West Circle Drive **"one of the botanical wonders of campusdom."**

1993—Spectacular Horticultural Demonstration Gardens Open

MSU's magnificent new Horticultural Demonstration Gardens, set on 7.5-acres wrapped around the Plant and Soil Sciences Building, were dedicated on August 11, 1993. Five different gardens included—the Judith A. DeLapa Perennial Garden; Frank's Nursery & Crafts Rose Garden; Amien A. & Florence M. Carter Annual Trial Garden; the Samuel Synge Cater and Dorothy Cater Mayhew Garden,

Linton Hall—built in 1881—is MSU's oldest academic building. It's home to the College of Arts & Letters, and the university's Graduate School.

featuring flowering trees and plants; and the 4-H Children's Garden, a one-half acre section packed with mini-gardens and whimsical features designed to entertain and educate.

2000—MSU Campus Wins National Awards

The American Society of Landscape Architects awarded bronze centennial medallions to the entire MSU campus, and MSU's Michigan 4-H Children's Garden in 2000.

2001—"MSU 2020 Vision" New Campus Master Plan

A new Campus Master Plan was revealed on December 7, 2001 by Jeffrey R. Kacos, Director of Department of Campus Park and Planning. The work, another collaborative initiative by President Peter McPherson, had been underway since 1999. In the process, McPherson had involved leaders from across the spectrum of university academic and administrative units, as well as alumni.

The Greening of South Campus

Highlights of the plan included special emphasis on extending "the park-like qualities of the campus to academic and research areas south of the river to enhance the scenic beauty of the campus."

"The area immediately south of the river at Farm Lane is (to be) transformed from parking lots to open space and three major tree planting corridors are proposed along Bogue Street, Red Cedar Road, and Birch Road."

"A large south campus commons and park is proposed immediately south of the Red Cedar River at Farm Lane."

On the north side of the campus, "The historic horticulture gardens (behind the Student Services and Natural Science Buildings) will be expanded west of the new (pedestrian) mall (between Farm Lane and Berkey Hall) and will include a contemplation greenhouse."

Campus Living—Yesterday and Today

Campus Living Through the Decades

Living on campus in 2004 was pure luxury when compared with conditions that existed in Michigan State's early history.

Yesterday—Life Without Amenities—1857

When the college opened in May, 1857, each room in the single dormitory, known as the Boarding Hall, or "Saints Rest," was heated by a pot-bellied stove. There was no running water, no electric lights, no telephones, no indoor toilets or bath facilities. The school had no gymnasium or athletic program. There were no local restaurants or theatres. And, there were no coeds.

The first students were to live by certain rules: "There will be chapel exercises every morning and religious services every Sunday..." "Spiritous liquors will not be allowed upon the premises. The use of tobacco will be discouraged. Exact conformity to the hours of study and labor will be required."

Board Called Exorbitant at $2.50 Per Term

In the college's 1857 annual report, it was noted "board will be charged at cost, not exceeding, however, $2.50 per term. It is a subject of regret, that the exorbitant ruling prices of all articles of consumption will make the board high during the first term of the Institution."

50 Mile Trip to Campus Took 11 Hours

A freshman described his trip to East Lansing in 1862. He took a horse and carriage from Jackson, Michigan—50 miles south of the campus—and had to get out several times to help push the buggy through heavy mud. The trip took 11 hours and the student arrived on the campus after dark. He finally found President Abbot's home and knocked on the door. The president warmly welcomed him to the Agricultural College of Michigan.

Four Hours of Class; Three Hours of Labor

In 1870, students ate breakfast shortly after six (a.m.) and were out of chapel by seven, where the president called roll. Academic classes ran for four hours, followed by dinner (lunch). In the afternoon, all students performed manual labor for three hours on the campus or the farm. A new Boarding Hall was completed in the fall of 1870 and accommodated 132 students.

Today (2004)—
Plush Living Compared With the Past

Today, living on campus is plush when compared with previous generations' life styles, and is considered just that by many foreign students. Each MSU residence hall room has a private telephone line, and a computer Internet connection. Students can get free computer training in their own hall. Every student is assigned his or her own e-mail address. Clean bed clothing is provided weekly.

Roller-Blading to Class While Talking on a Cell Phone

Necessities for most students include: a laptop computer, a cell phone, a portable CD player, a backpack, and a bicycle or roller blades. For some, even a Palm Pilot is obligatory. High-tech has arrived on campus. It's not unusual to see a student with backpack, roller-blading across the campus while talking on a cell phone, or listening to a CD.

MSU Hired Its First Certified Executive Chef in 1982

MSU hired Robert Nelson, its first certified executive chef, in 1982 to direct meal planning and execution for the residence halls. Nelson had worked as an executive chef at hotels, restaurants, country clubs and banquet centers, and had won the prestigious Escoffier Gold Medal and the Thomas Jefferson Gold Medal for Culinary Excellence.

Dining Halls Cater to Students' Tastes

The dining halls are carpeted, provide attractive outdoor views through giant window walls, and offer up to 276 different dinner entrees, salads, side dishes, drinks and desserts. If students want to prepare their own low-fat or vegetarian meals, the food and cooking utensils are available. If a student is going off-campus during the day for a field trip or practice teaching, the dining hall staff will pack a nutritious box lunch for them.

Moreover, students can eat at any of the 35 residence hall cafeterias at any time. Regularly through the year, the students meet to plan special "Night On The Town" meals with their favorite foods on the menu. These once-a-semester affairs are held in a separate dining room, with linen table cloths, floral arrangements and themed decorations.

The golden glow of campus autumns lives fondly in the memory of Spartans.

The MSU residence hall dining rooms have won many awards for creating high quality meals at a low cost. Students also have a cafeteria in each hall that is open for snacks after regular dining hours.

On the closed-circuit TV system at Owen Graduate Center, cafeteria menus for the day are shown with the calories and grams of fat listed for each entrée.

Popular movies also are shown on a regular basis in the residence halls.

World-Class Intramural Facilities for Physical Fitness

Michigan State boasts three intramural buildings for student recreation and physical fitness.

The newest building is the 55,000 square-foot Intramural East opened in 1989. It provides a physical fitness outlet just a short walk from east campus residence halls where 8,000 students live. The new building housed a running track, an air-conditioned weight room with 68 pieces of Nautilus equipment, four courts for basketball and volleyball, two squash and eight racquetball courts, and a multi-purpose room for group exercise.

The new fitness center complements the IM Circle (former Women's Gym), and IM West sports and health facilities, which met the needs of students living near the center and west end of campus.

Union Building Provides Many Student Services

At MSU's Union Building there is a 24-hour Computer Lab featuring 80 new computers—both MACs and IBMs—available to students free of charge.

There are quiet study lounges for students on the third floor, in the Union Station Cafeteria, the Main Lounge, and in the Women's Lounge. These are open from 7 a.m. to midnight, Monday through Friday, and from 7 a.m. to 1 a.m. on weekends.

Food service is available at four franchises in One Union Square (old Union Grill): Wendy's, Blimpies, Little Caesers, and Beaners. Good cafeteria luncheon and dinner meals are available at the Union Station Cafeteria on the lower level.

Recreation offerings at the Union include: Spartan Lanes—16 bowling alleys, and U-Cue Billiard Room—8 tables.

T-Styles Barbershop is on the lower level of the Union.

Free Newspapers Available

Free daily newspapers are available at several campus locations. At the Owen Graduate Center (graduate student residence hall), *USA Today* and the *Lansing State Journal* are available. At the North Business Complex, the *Financial Times* of London can be picked up. At the Union Station Cafeteria, the *New York Times* and *Wall Street Journal* are offered.

Student Affairs and Services

An incredible array of services and activities are available to Michigan State students. Services as comprehensive as any in the nation are provided through the MSU Student Affairs and Services Division.

"Services & Activities Designed for Positive Student Growth"

With 44,950 students (2002)—a "City of Youth," most of them age 18 to 22 and living away from home for the first time—helpful student services and recreation are vital on a university campus.

Dr. Lee June, vice president of student services, pointed out in 2002 the student services staff recognizes that there are many human developmental issues that need addressing as these young people transition from late adolescence to adulthood. Among the issues are career development, ethics, separation from family, and exploring life options. June stated, "Our staff designs services and activities to provide an environment for positive student growth."

500-Plus Student Organizations

Virtually any interest can be pursued through more than 500 registered student organizations, including some 50 that are community-service oriented.

The range of organizations includes honorary academic societies, professional organizations and professional fraternities and sororities, recreational and athletic groups, international, racial/ethnic, religious, political, social service, volunteer, and media organizations.

The following sampling of 61 organizations provides an insight into the variety of interests served:

The Academic Competition Club, Aerospace Club, African-American Film Association, Alliance of MSU Composers, Alpine Ski Team, American Advertising Association, American Medical Women's Association, Amnesty International, Archery Club, Badminton Club, Ballroom Dance Club, Baptist Student Union-Christian Challenge, Black Poets Society, Block & Bridle Club, Bowling Club, Campus Crusade for Christ, Chess Club, Chinese Students Coalition, Coalition of Indian Undergraduate Students, College Republicans, Democrats-MSU, European Club, Fencing Team, Folksong Society, Food Science Club, French Club, Gospel Chorale, Graduate Theatre Showcase, Hillel Jewish Student Organization, Hospitality Association, International Relations Organization, Investment Club, Karate Club, Les Gourmets, MBA Association, Men's Glee Club, Men's Lacrosse Club, Minority Pre-Law Student Association, Model United Nations, Mortar Board National Honor Society, MSU Motion Dance Team, Multi-Racial Unity Living Experience, National Society of Collegiate Scholars, Owen Graduate Association, Pediatric Interest Group, Phi Sigma Theta National Honor Society, Ping Pong Club, Polish Club, Psychology Scholars Association, Rodeo Club, Scuba Club, Snowboard Club, Society of Engineering, Solar Racing Team, Student Cancer Support Network, Student Filmmakers Group, Student Parents on a Mission, Turkish Student Association, Water Ski Club, Women's Club Soccer, Yoga Club, and Zoological Students Association.

Students Develop the Standards and Rules for Campus Living

New students at Michigan State are mentored by upperclassmen who help them adjust to college life. Students meet in small living unit groups to discuss and develop the standards and rules they want to live by on their residence hall floor. A key consideration in these rules is enhancing the academic-study environment. The student discussions focus on activities they won't allow, holding others accountable for their behavior, and self-regulation. At MSU, there is a Residence Hall Bill of Rights as well as Residence Hall Regulations.

Discipline is Educational Rather Than Punitive

When rules are broken and behavior unacceptable, discipline at MSU is imposed as education, not as punishment. Disciplinary action includes writing papers and community service projects. The spectrum of discipline ranges from a warning to suspension.

Thirteen Categories of Services Offered Students

A spectrum of 13 categories of service are available to MSU students. These include Academic Affairs, Activities, Career Services and Placement, Student Employment Office, Financial Aid, Food, Governance at MSU, Health Services, Housing, Personal Security, Recreation, Services for Special Groups, and Transportation.

The MSU Family's Favorite Things

Lifetime friendships, gorgeous campus, meeting your soulmate, gaining a university education—all flood the memories of Michigan State alumni as they recall with fondness their days spent close beside the Red Cedar River.

Favorite people, places, activities, and events rise nostalgically in remembrances as MSU graduates think back to their days on campus. As one alum put it, "I had a dream; I dreamt I never left the campus."

Duane Vernon, class of 1953, stated in 2002, "Every time I walk or drive through the campus, I get a special feeling...Like I'm Home!"

He captured a sentiment shared by thousands who have listened to the Beaumont Tower chimes as they walked through the cathedral of trees in the "Sacred Space," surrounded by West Circle Drive. The incomparable beauty of the campus park—one of the world's great arboretums—stands tall in memory, yet is just one of dozens of things treasured by the Michigan State family. Here, then, is a round-up of "Favorite Things" compiled from alumni memories. It is not complete, but then, it never could be.

Fond Memories Past and Present

"Family feeling on campus." (Blanche MacNoughton Coryell, Class of 1916).

"My college family—I really felt a part of it. Many great instructors and good friends." (Jennie Day Bruffy, Class of 1938).

"Forming lifetime friendships." (Jeane Beukema Visscher, Class of 1938).

"The Friendliness of the MSC Administration and staff really inspired me." (Freeman "Pete" Lehman, '50).

The Water Carnival, which was inaugurated in 1923, featured themed floats created by fraternities, sororities, and residence halls. The floats streamed down the Red Cedar River at night, and were described with timely commentary and music as thousands watched from bleachers. The event was enormously popular, and held during graduation week. In the late 1940s, the Red Cedar River was dyed red for a *Life* magazine photo-feature on the Water Carnival. Unfortunately, a breaking news story precluded use of the pictures.

"The old Smoke Shop (Grand River Ave.) was a favorite gathering place." (J. Carlton Perry, Class of 1921). Meeting at the Smoke Shop was a "man-thing" for years at Michigan State. Pool, bowling, and smoking were the recreations. Women not allowed.

The College Christmas tree which stood at the Abbot Street entrance to the campus.

The Big Barbecue and large Bonfires in Sleepy Hollow in front of Wells Hall (first two decades of the 20th century) on Friday evenings before home football games. This was the second Wells Hall and stood on the site of the present Library. The hollow is right next to the Music Building across from the Library (Robert W. Gerdel, class of 1923, Alfred E. Howell, class of 1924, and Ray A. Bailey, class of 1926).

"Weekly Dances at Peoples Church—met my wife there." (John B. Burns, Class of 1926).

"Forbidden midnight canoe rides—My girlfriend jumped out of the first floor window of the 'Coop' (the Women's Building; now Morrill Hall)." (Paul A. Piper, Class of 1928).

Floats for 1950 Water Carnival are readied prior to their night-time parade down the Red Cedar River. The carnival, launched in 1923, was a popular commencement week event.

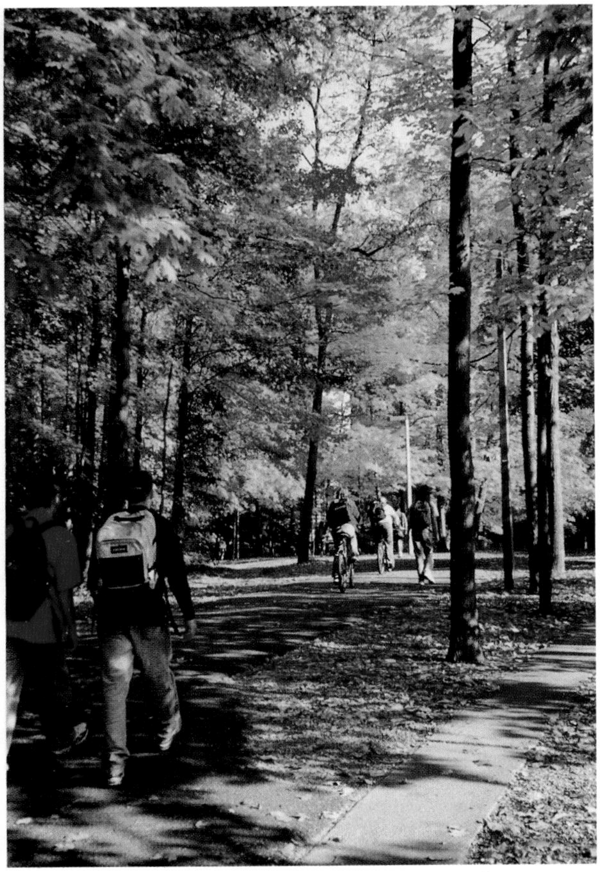
Campus fall colors invigorate the senses and are a universal favorite with students, faculty & alumni.

"Fixing breakfast on Sunday mornings over an open fire at Pinetum." (Dorothy Robinson Ross, Class of 1928). Pinetum is a pine wooded area planted by William J. Beal in 1896 along the Red Cedar River east of Hagadorn Road.

"Skating under the lights on the flooded tennis courts." (Irma Coswell McCandlish, Class of 1929).

"Sitting on the Stone Bench With your Fiance planning for the future." (Mary Ladd Simpson, Class of 1929). This was called the "Engagement Bench" by many. Ted Haskell, '49, recalled, "It was sheltered next to a large slab of rough stone ("The Rock"—gift of the class of 1873)." Both were located just north of Beaumont Tower.

"Dances at the driveway of the Union (West entrance); rice was sprinkled on the pavement so couples could dance on the pavement." (Maxwell A. Goodwin, Class of 1929).

"Saying hello to instructors and students on the way to class—everyone was so friendly." (Lucile Schnackenberg, Class of 1931.)

"Barrel of apples at the dairy building with a sign that said 'Help Yourself.'" (Marion Lee Aylesworth, Class of 1932).

"Ice Skating on the Red Cedar River for a mile east of the dam." (Florence M. Findlay, Class of 1934).

Tearing Down the Goal Posts at Michigan Stadium in Ann Arbor—John N. Calkins, Class of 1937, remembered, that in 1934, when MSC beat Michigan in football for the first time in years, students were unsuccessful in bringing the U-M steel goal posts down. Calkins wrote, "The following year, 'some wise and optimistic students snuck down (to Ann Arbor) the night before, and using a hacksaw, cut almost through them.'" MSC won the 1935 game, and Calkins recalled, "One push, and over they went."

"Listening to the band play the Alma Mater under the direction of Leonard Falcone." (Paul E. Kindig, Class of 1935).

Forestry Club's Paul Bunyan Dances at the Gymnasium (now IM Circle). The gymnasium was turned into a forest. The men wore lumberjack clothing. (Edward C. Carpenter, Class of 1937).

Campus Colors in the Fall; Football Games—Alice Scott, Class of 1938, wrote, "I'm forever grateful to Charlie Bachman (MSC head football coach) for explaining the game at our freshman orientation."

Sunset Suppers held in the Union at commencement time for returning classes.

"The Tug-O-War Between the Frosh & Sophs across the Red Cedar River," (James Steele, '41).

"The Concert Series at MSC was wonderful and was included in our tuition." (Mary L. Vary, '43).

"The Beauty of the North Campus especially in the spring with the flowering trees." (Sally Roberts, '49).

"The Bright Yellow Maple Tree across from the Union Building as it stood against a bright blue autumn sky." (Martha Robinson Van Patten, '49).

"Ice Cream at the Dairy Store behind Ag Hall." (James O. Trew, '49). "Stopping to get a Peppermint Stick ice cream at the Dairy Building." (Martha Robinson Van Patten, '49).

The Forestry Cabin (Site of Erickson Hall) was a popular party location for many student group parties and meetings. The cabin was built in the woods near the south bank of the Red Cedar in 1918. The College of Education's Erickson Hall (1958) now stands on the site.

Homecoming Displays in front of fraternity and sorority houses, and residence halls. These elaborate themed statements took weeks, sometimes months to design and build.

"A Huge Pecan Roll and Glass of Orange Juice at Byrnes Drug Store after attending People's Church." (Muriel Read McGuire, '49). McGuire added, "We should have had stock in Kewpie's hamburgers."

"The Activities Fair under the stadium concourse each fall to acquaint students with MSC activities and events—sponsored by the Associated Women's Students." (Rose Mary (Nahra) Wells, '49).

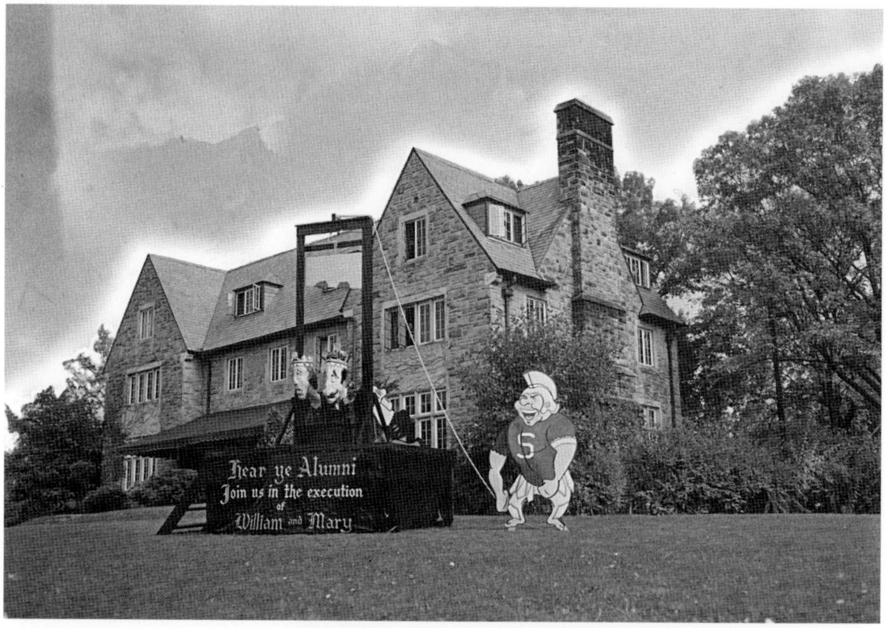

Phi Delta Theta fraternity 1950 Homecoming display proclaims "Hear ye alumni, join us in the execution of William & Mary," the football opponent.

"The First Snowfall on the Pines with the cardinals on their branches is a picture I will always remember." (Elizabeth J. Wright Mutch, '49).

"The Evening-Long Discussions over coffee in the eating places on Grand River." (Peter Blake, '50).

"The Smell of Lilac Bushes outside the Union was wonderful." (Alfred R. Bransdorfer, '50).

"Helen O'Connell singing *Green Eyes* with the Jimmy Dorsey Orchestra at a local bistro just east of East Lansing (probably Coral Gables). (John F. Faulkes, '50).

"Concerts in the Band Shell"—(Louis F. Hekhuis, '50). The band shell was a Class of 1937 gift. It was on the banks of the Red Cedar and faced north up a sweeping lawn that is now the site of Bessey Hall (1961).

"Performing in the Fraternity Sing in the outdoor bandshell." (Don Leatherman,'50).

J-Hops and Other Big Dances at the Auditorium featuring famous big bands such as Ray Anthony, Tommy Dorsey, Duke Ellington, Skitch Henderson, Glen Grey, Gene Krupa, and Stan Kenton and others. This was the big band era of the 1940s and 1950s.

"Dancing to 'I'm in the Mood for Love.'" (Mary Lou Straith Duncan, Class of 1951).

"The many random acts of kindness and generosity displayed by faculty, school administrators, and fellow students" (Harold E. "Hal" Nord, Jr. '50).

"A Last Lingering Embrace in the dorm coat room before curfew." (Mary Lou Straith Duncan, Class of 1951).

"My Favorite Hangout—Kewpies on Grand River." (Sid Stein, Class of 1951).

MAC-MSC Landmark Smokestack—"My favorite landmark was the old smokestack which had MAC on one side and MSC on the other." Today, the stack has MSC and MSU on opposite sides.

Fraternity Serenades in front of the women's dorms and sorority houses when a girlfriend had been

"Contemplating the Red Cedar River scene from a pedestrian bridge".

"A walk through the Red Cedar River corridor"—a visual delight.

"pinned" by a fraternity member. Coeds hung from every window to watch and listen.

Kissing in the Shadow of Beaumont Tower. It's a tradition.

Movies at the State Theatre or the Lucon. They're both gone.

Contemplating the Red Cedar River scene from a pedestrian bridge.

Trips to the Rose Bowl—The 1954 and 1956 trips featured transcontinental chartered trains and planes, where there was little sleep and much partying. Michigan State fans brought record Big Ten crowds to the "Granddaddy of Bowl Games." In 1988, more than 50,000 MSU fans were in the big bowl, which seated 103,000.

Visiting Coral Gables, Dagwood's, Paul Revere's, Mac's or the Deerhead Inn for social hour.

The Turkey Trot—Student cross-country run with a Thanksgiving turkey as first prize.

Junior 500 Pushcart Derby—Fraternity and men's residence hall raced in homemade pushcarts around West Circle Drive.

Ugliest Man on Campus Contest—Iconoclastic competitors campaigned to be voted the ugliest on campus.

The Spinster's Spin—Coeds asked their favorite man to the dance.

The Delta Street Shuffle—An outdoor, all-campus social gathering in front of two fraternity houses on Delta Street.

Spartacade—Student talent from residence halls, fraternities and sororities competed in separate booths in this annual all-campus show that once was held in Jenison Fieldhouse.

Union Building "Mixers"—Get acquainted dances for freshman students.

Zeke "The Wonder Dog" caught Frisbies at halftime in Spartan Stadium in the 1970s. A "new" Zeke was back in 2002 and 2003.

Freaks-Pigs Football Game between students and the East Lansing police drew 25,000 to Spartan Stadium in 1971.

The Lecture-Concert Series—Was first held in the sanctuary of People's Church

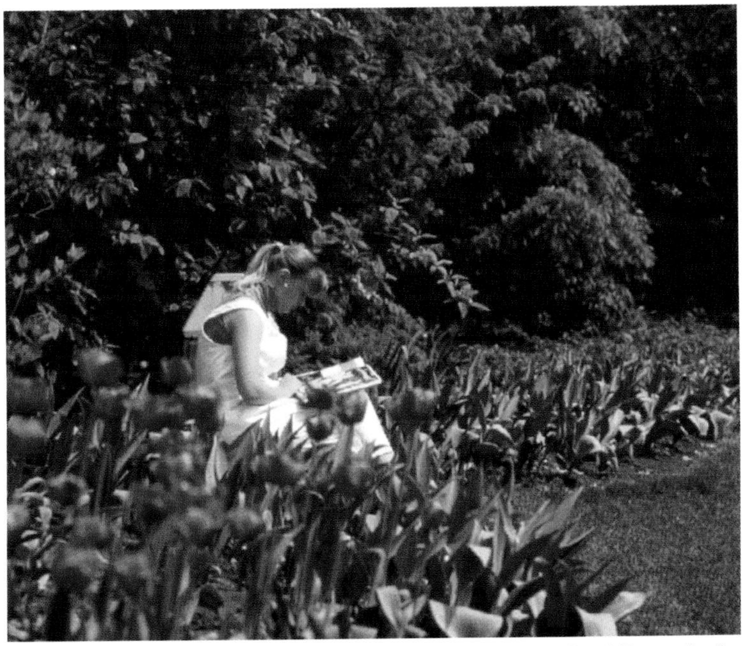

"Finding a hidden, quiet place to study"...like the Beal Botanical Garden.

and later moved to the Auditorium. This series was particularly popular as a diversion during WWII.

A Walk Through the "Sacred Space"—The beautiful lawns, trees and plantings that create the picturesque park inside West Circle Drive. Richard W. Hutchinson, Class of 1939, wrote, "Walking from class to class among buildings on the very pretty campus."

A Walk Through the Red Cedar River Corridor—From the Kalamazoo Street Bridge to the Bogue Street Bridge, and back. This linear, landscaped journey is a visual delight, and refreshing to the spirit in any season.

A Wedding at the Alumni Memorial Chapel—The beginning of an "MSU merger."

Finding a Hidden Quiet Place to Study—Beal Botanical Gardens, a riverside lawn, or the upper floors of the Union Building which are now available as study refuges.

Spartan Marching Band practice on Friday afternoons" gets the blood and spirits stirring. Come face-to-face with a 300-piece concert band and "be blown away."

Listening to the Beaumont Tower Chimes or a concert from the carillon bells.

A Stroll Through the Peaceful Beal Botanical Gardens to view the array of 5,000 plants.

Tower Guard's May Morning (Now April Morning) Sing—A memorable annual event held at the foot of Beaumont Tower with the scent of spring blossoms in the air. When MSU went to the semester system, the May Sing was moved into April.

MSU Marching Band Practice on Friday Afternoon—Prior to a home football game. Band members dress very casually, many making statements with signs on their apparel. These practices have become so popular that a set of bleachers has been erected for the "Band Fans" on the Demonstration Hall field. These practices used to take place on Walter Adams Field (formerly Landon Field).

MSU Marching Band Rehearsal on Walter Adams Field—Immediately prior to a home football game. Band Fans, alumni, students and faculty gather to hear the power and precision of a 300-piece concert band "blow them away" from just a few feet. When the rehearsal is over the crowd turns and marches with the band to Spartan Stadium. Walking next to the percussion section, you can feel your chest vibrate from the drum beat. During the march, you will see "Band Nuts" perched on the Spartan Statue holding a banner that reads: "Spartan Band Fans."

The MSU Band Marching Around the Spartan Statue—This occurs following the final home football game. Returning from the stadium, the band circles the statue three times before returning to Walter Adams Field.

MSU Marching Band on Halloween Day—the band shows up for practice dressed in costumes.

Tailgating at Spartan Stadium and around campus before a home football game. The grills are cooking; the flags are flying; the tables are set—some with candelabra; and the conversations are upbeat. It's a special time at MSU.

Spartan Marching Band tradition—circling the Spartan Statue three times following the last home game of each football season.

"Feeding the ducks at the Red Cedar rapids." Photo: 1955.

Walking with the Football Team from Kellogg Center to Spartan Stadium two and one-half hours before kickoff. The players are dressed in suits and ties. The team stays at Kellogg Center the night before home games.

Singing the MSU Fight Song—"Victory for MSU!"

Feeding the Ducks at the Red Cedar Rapids behind the Hannah Administration Building.

The Homecoming Parade passing through East Lansing on the Friday evening before the game, with the MSU Marching Band, cheerleaders, coaches, floats, antique cars, and Spartan celebrities.

Observing the World's Night Skies and Stars at the Abrams Planetarium.

Viewing the magnificent Horticultural Demonstration Gardens located behind the Soil Sciences Building. This is becoming one of Michigan's top tourist attractions. The 4-H Children's Garden is nationally recognized as a creative gem.

Attending the popular Spartan Spectacular—The annual fall MSU band, orchestra and choral show at the Breslin Center on Saturday evening following the Homecoming football game.

Small Animals' Day at the Agricultural Pavilion.

A Quiet Visit to Sleepy Hollow—The picturesque hollow next to the Music Building—with its carpet of lawn surrounded with eye-pleasing flowers and shrubs. This was the setting for the barbecues and bonfires on Friday evenings in the early part of the 20th century.

Viewing the Changing Historical and Cultural Exhibits at the MSU Museum.

A Slow Drive Around Campus to absorb the visual beauty. It's good for the spirit.

Listening to the Geriatric Six Plus One Dixieland band before home football games.

Attending a Wharton Center Performance—A Broadway show, a symphony orchestra, a professional dance group, musical groups or solo artists. It's the cultural mecca of central Michigan.

The MSU Milton Muelder Summer Carillon Concert Series—Four special Beaumont Tower concerts are staged during the summer. The MSU family and public are invited to bring lawn chairs and a picnic lunch, kick back and enjoy superb carillon concerts.

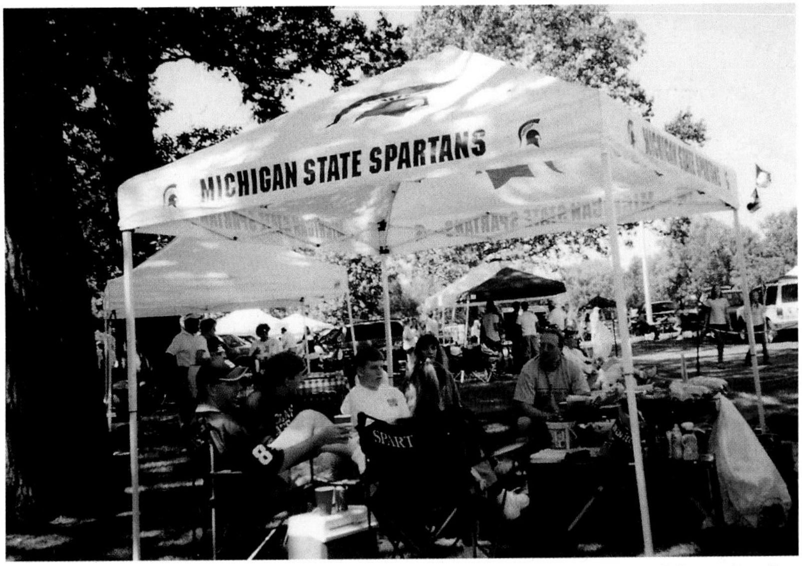

"Tailgating before a home football game…the grills are cooking, the flags are flying, the tables are set, the conversations are upbeat."

Visit to Beaumont Tower—Sitting on a bench, quietly reading or contemplating the beauty of the "Oak Opening" which brackets the tower.

Viewing Colorful Butterflies at MSU's Butterfly House.

"Taste of Michigan" Event at the new Agricultural Pavilion sponsored each fall by the College of Agriculture and Natural Resources. This is a memorable culinary food-fest featuring Michigan-grown products, held on the Saturday morning of a home football game.

Former Michigan Governor John Engler, class of 1971, with wife Michelle and their triplet daughters in the MSU Homecoming parade through East Lansing. Parade is an MSU favorite staged on the Friday evening before the Homecoming game.

Veta-Visit—An all-day open house sponsored by the College of Veterinary Medicine, which features a range of live animals from pocket pets to draft horses. Animal lovers young and old enjoy this event. It's an informal entry door to the veterinary profession for many young visitors.

Guarding the Spartan Statue the week prior to a home football game with the University of Michigan. Ever since the statue went up in 1945, members of the Spartan Marching Band have voluntarily guarded the Spartan. All-night vigils are customary throughout game week.

Getting Your Picture Taken with Sparty—The most-recognized school mascot in the U.S.

The MSU Jazz Train—A train trip to Chicago with MSU alumni and the jazz faculty of the School of Music. World renowned jazz artists of the faculty play a lively concert on the way to "Chi Town." The weekend includes a visit to a jazz venue on Friday night; and a jazz concert by the faculty group on Saturday night, which is better than anything else in town. This five-year old event (in 2004) is sponsored by the College of Arts and Letters.

Cars on Campus—MSU's own Concours d'Elegance display of antique automobiles.

Attending MSU Athletic Booster Club Luncheons, Dinners and Events—The Downtown Coaches Club (football); the Rebounders (men's basketball); the Blue Line Club (ice hockey); and the Fastbreak Club (women's basketball). Here's where dedicated Spartan fans learn first hand from the head coaches the status of the MSU teams and the opponents.

MSU's Cheerleaders—Annually they are among the best in the nation. In 1979, they won the national cheerleading championship.

MSU Dance Team—The female Spartan dance team that has been ranked as high as third in the nation.

Attending Twilight in the Garden, a premier Kresge Art Museum event.

The Spartan Brass—a high-energy pep band which performs with vigor at basketball and ice hockey games.

Weekend First-Run Movies at no cost at the International Center and Wells Hall.

Tip-Off Cafe Luncheons or Dinners prior to home basketball games at the Breslin Center. Events include a message from head basketball coach Tom Izzo and a great buffet.

Coffee at the Union Grill or Crossroads Cafe at the International Center.

Finding a Parking Place on Campus.

A Walk Through the Sanford Natural Area along the Red Cedar River behind Holmes, McDonel, and Owen Halls.

Canoeing on the Red Cedar River—Dr. Robert S. Shaw, who joined the agricultural faculty in 1902, became dean of agriculture in 1908, and would become president in 1928, is said to have put the first canoe into the Red Cedar in 1903.

"Canoeing on the Red Cedar." Coeds paddling near "Pinetum" woods, east of Hagadorn Road—circa 1925. Dr. Beal planted Pinetum in 1896.

Reading on a Sun-Drenched Campus Lawn in the spring, summer or fall.

Attending Athletic Events—All Sports. The electric atmosphere at Spartan Stadium, Breslin Arena, and Munn Arena are memorable.

A Fall Color Walk through the campus.

A Tasty Meal at the State Room or River Cafe in the Kellogg Center.

Annual Alumni Association Homecoming Luncheon at Kellogg Center. Featured are appearances by the MSU Marching Band, the cheerleaders, and talks from the head football coach and the president.

School of Music Jazz Concerts.

Sibling Weekends on campus.

Guiding a campus tour for your parents.

Watching an away football or basketball game at Trippers Sports Bar in the Frandor Shopping Center between East Lansing and Lansing.

Alumni Association International Educational trips—These exquisitely planned trips are great educational experiences and always provide the opportunity of making great new friends.

Viewing the 6,500+ Works of Art at the Kresge Art Museum.

GRADUATION!

Savoring the Delectable Menu at the annual Les Gourmet banquet staged by students of the School of Hospitality Business.

MSU University Club—meals, events, and facilities. One of MSU's crown jewels, the University Club will match the excellence of major country clubs anywhere in the nation.

"Kissing in the shadow of Beaumont Tower." It's a tradition. (Photo: *Wolverine*, 1962)

"The drum beat when the Spartan Marching Band enters the football stadium." Merritt Lutz, '65, M.A. '67, and Joel Leach, both former Spartan drummers, wrote "The Series," the drum cadence used each football Saturday by the band in its march from Adams Field to Spartan Stadium. Lutz is a Morgan Stanley executive.

Campus Camaraderie—The friendly student body and faculty—a smile and hello across the campus.

Parties and Dances at residence halls, fraternities and sororities.

Away Football or Basketball Trip—Learning the culture, the traditions, and the favorite spots at other Big Ten schools.

Dinner and Discussions with Faculty in their homes. This tradition started with Michigan State's third President, Theophilus Abbot, who read Milton at the students' request in his home.

Decorating your Dorm Room when first arriving on campus.

Pre-Game Pep Rallies.

Visits to MSU's Crown Jewel Off-Campus Facilities—The beautiful **Brook Lodge** conference center near Augusta, Michigan; the elegant **Kellogg Summer Mansion** and the **Kellogg Biological Station** at Hickory Corners, Michigan;

"Spring blossoms on campus, the wind blows the petals...you can smell the fragrance." Scene—Landon Hall, built 1947.

and the magnificent **Hidden Lake Gardens** at Tipton, Michigan.

Current Student Favorites

MSU students Jenny Doepker, Adam Raak and Chris Ripple supplied several favorite things during a winter 2002 semester interview. Jenny Doepker, president of the MSU Student Alumni Foundation, provided these favorite memories:

The September 11, 2001 Memorial Carillon Concert held September 14 at the foot of Beaumont Tower. "There was 15 minutes of silence and peaceful reflection. This was followed by a concert of songs, including *Amazing Grace, America The Beautiful,* and *The National Anthem*. Students and faculty were standing and sitting everywhere. People riding bikes or walking, stopped and listened."

Spring Blossoms on Campus—"The wind blows the petals…you can smell the fragrance."

Saturday Mornings Prior to a Home Football Game—"The cars streaming by, the banners flying, people grilling their lunch all over campus."

Adam Raak and Chris Ripple mentioned the following as favorites:

Cooking Breakfast on a Grill in the Munn Parking lot before a home football game.

The150-Member Traveling Izzone (Student Basketball Cheering Section) bus trips to away basketball games. Walking around the concourse of the opposition's arena, carrying the State flag, and singing the Fight Song.

Following the MSU Marching Band out of Notre Dame Stadium after a victory over the Fighting Irish.

Studying Beside the Red Cedar Rapids near Wells Hall.

Walking to the dorm from the Library during a silent snowfall.

Painting the Rock—The Class of 1873 gift, which now stands at the northeast corner of the Farm Lane Bridge. "You have to paint your message at 2 a.m., but you can't leave. You have to protect your work, or someone else will paint over it."

Sending the Basketball Team Off to the Final Four—This happened for three consecutive years (1999, 2000, and 2001). More than a thousand students gathered to cheer the team as they boarded their bus for the airport.

Knowing Half the People in a Huge Lecture Hall.

Walking in the Homecoming Parade with the MSU Student Alumni Foundation float.

NCAA Basketball Championship Parade in 2000—From the State Capitol steps to Spartan Stadium.

The Drum Beat When the Spartan Marching Band enters the football stadium.

MSU Cheerleaders are among Spartan fans' favorite memories.

Band Fans line both sides of Kalamazoo Street bridge "getting pumped" and cheering on the 300-piece Spartan Marching Band in its traditional pre-game march to Spartan Stadium. During the march, the game-day opponent's flag is flown upside-down.

Returning to Campus the First Week of School—The crisp fall air; seeing old friends; the exhilaration of a new school year.

The Spartan Chariot leading the MSU Marching Band to Spartan Stadium before a football game.

The Izzone Taking Over U-M's Crisler Arena when MSU played U-M in basketball in 2000. Spartan fans bought more than 4,000 seats in the Michigan arena and dominated the cheering to the surprise of the Wolverine fans and administration. The Izzone chanted, "Breslin East. We Own Crisler." This experience changed the U of M's basketball ticket sales policy, greatly limiting outside access to tickets.

December 2000 Winter Storm—Hundreds of students walking on campus streets through two-feet of snow on a Monday evening during finals week. It was beautiful, fun, unusual.

Other current favorites include:

Enjoying the Camaraderie at The Peanut Barrel, Mac's Bar, P.T. O'Malleys, The Rivera, Crunchy's, or Harper's, which used to be Dooley's.

Midnight Madness at Breslin Center—The official kick-off of basketball season, with spectacular entries into the arena by head coaches Tom Izzo, Joanne McCallie and the men's and women's basketball teams.

Leaving A Living Legacy

"We make a living by what we earn—we make a life by what we give."

—Winston Churchill

"Nobody makes a greater mistake than he who did nothing because he could only do a little."

—Edmund Burke

"He gives twice who gives promptly."

—Publius Syrus

There is no better way to leave a living legacy than to contribute to the improvement of the education of future generations. Many opportunities for this kind of giving are available at Michigan State University.

The late Herman B. Wells, Indiana University president, 1938-1962, stated, **"The support of great universities is the most lasting of all investments."**

Dr. John A. DiBiaggio, MSU president, 1985-1992, speaking at the September 20, 2002 kick-off of the $1.2 billion *Campaign for MSU*, stated, **"With finite resources, the only way to maintain and enhance excellence is through private support."**

Dr. Pauline Adams, wife of the late MSU president Dr. Walter Adams, and former MSU first lady, told the audience at the *Campaign for MSU* kickoff, **"There are endless ways to gratify your passion for MSU."**

Private Gifts: $9 Million in 1975 to $211 Million in 2002

The acceleration of private-giving to Michigan State has been remarkable—from a total of $9,029,884 in 1975 to $211.6 million for the 2001-2002 fiscal year.

While large gifts capture the most attention, it is the broad giving by many thousands of people that is vital to university fund-raising success. All gifts, no matter their size, are important.

MSU Began As a State-Supported School

Michigan State began its existence as a state-supported school. Heavy reliance on legislative appropriations to run the university was prevalent up into the 1960s. At that point state support started to erode. Instead of the state providing two-thirds of the funds needed to maintain the university, legislative funding began to decline until today it represents some 46 percent of the annual budget.

Artist's concept of proposed $80-million Music Complex. New facility is part of the $1.2-billion fund-raising *Campaign for MSU* (2002-2007). Byron and Dee Cook, both Class of '54, pledged $1 million toward the complex, which will include a concert hall and live music café. It will be located near the Kresge Art Center.

Thus, the school can realistically be called state-assisted, not state-supported.

President's Club: First Formal Donor Group—1963

As a result of this history, MSU was late to the game of serious private fund-raising. In 1963, the MSU President's Club was established, with membership set at a contribution of $10,000 to the university. It was the first formal donor group in the school's history. At the start of 1973, there were 153 members in the club. In that same year, the university began a full-fledged professional program to raise private money, moving the responsibility for fund-raising from the MSU Alumni Association to the University Development offices. As a major first step, University Development established The Michigan State University Foundation in 1973 as an independent non-profit corporation for the purpose of supporting the advancement of MSU.

Over the next quarter century, four additional donor groups were added to enhance the fund-raising effort: the **Beaumont Tower Society**—$25,000 to $49,999; the **Hannah Society**—$50,000 to $99,999; **Benefactors**—$100,000 to $999,999; and the **Kedzie Society**—$1,000,000 and above.

During the year 2000, University Development restructured the club levels and added three new donor groups: Abbot Society—$250,000 to $499,999; **Shaw Society**—$500,000 to $999,999; and the **Williams Society**—$5,000,000 or more. The former Benefactors group was renamed the **Snyder Society** with a donor range of $100,000 to $249,999. The **Kedzie Society was given a new donor range** of $1,000,000 to $4,999,999.

MSU's Eight Donor Societies Had 5,826 Members in 2001

Membership in the eight MSU Donor Societies at the end of the 2000-2001 fiscal year was as follows: President's Club ($10,000)—3,315; Beaumont Tower Society ($25,000 to $49,999)—1,010; Hannah Society ($50,000 to $99,999)—486; Snyder Society ($100,000 to $249,999)—763; Abbot Society ($250,000 to $499,999)—82; Shaw Society ($500,000 to $999,999)—49; Kedzie Society ($1,000,000 to $4,999,999)—113; Williams Society ($5,000,000 and above)—8. Six of the donor groups are named in honor of past Michigan State presidents.

Lifetime Giving By Eight Donor Societies Reached $530 Million by 2001

During the 2000-2001 fiscal year the 5,826 members of the eight MSU donor societies gave MSU a total of $46.8 million, and their lifetime giving to the university totaled more than $530 million.

Private Giving Built MSU Endowment to $810 Million in 2002

MSU endowment funds—preserved in perpetuity—rose to $810 million in 2002. These private gifts—to create a scholarship, fund a professorship, or endow a department chair—are never spent. Only the investment income from the endowment is used for the endowment's purpose.

Andre Blay, '59, MBA '70, Gave New Focus to MSU Foundation

Andre Blay, '59, MBA '70, was recruited in 1986 by MSU President John DiBiaggio to serve on the MSU Foundation Board. Blay became chair of the foundation board in 1991. His leadership led to a focus on long-range planning, growing the endowment, investing in future patents or intellectual property, and capitalizing on under-utilized intellectual property.

Under Blay's leadership, the assets of the MSU Foundation grew from $20 million to $100 million in four years. Today, the foundation's assets total $291 million.

Endowment Levels Identified

MSU's Development Fund leaders have stated, "An endowed scholarship can be established with a minimum gift of $30,000. A scholar can be named for $500,000. A total of $1.5 million is required to name an existing chair, and $2.5 million is required to create a new position."

Although MSU's endowments have been increasing each year, the university—because of its late start in private fund-raising—lags behind other Big Ten schools in total dollar endowment size.

History of Giving to MSU

The history of private giving to Michigan State began in 1858 with small gifts, primarily publications. Representative highlights of giving to MSU are traced in this chapter from 1858 to 2002.

First Gifts to the School: 1858

One thousand books and publications that President Joseph Williams solicited in 1858 from members of Congress, government agencies, book publishers and others, were the first recorded gifts to the college. The publications included scientific and agricultural textbooks and works of literature.

Herbarium Given in 1863

In **1863**, a herbarium of some 20,000 specimens was donated to the school by the widow of the late D. Cooley, M.D.

Fifty-Five Gifts Received in 1864

The first pronounced private giving to the Agricultural College of Michigan occurred in 1864, when 55 gifts were received. Among the items mentioned in the 1864 annual report were: publications for the library from Congressmen Chandler, Howard, and Longyear; a Sanborn's turn-wrist plough from the Ames Plough Co., Boston; a Harrington's convertible seed-dropper & hand-cultivator (not yet tried) from S.E. Harrington of Greenfield, Massachusetts; the right to use Hayne's portable fence, from William Chamberlain of Oberlin, Ohio; and a Harxthal & Lee's self-opening gate from J.H. Hawley & Co., Pontiac, Michigan.

Founder of Cornell University Makes a Gift to the College—1865

The Honorable Ezra Cornell of Ithaca, New York, co-founder of Cornell University, gave the college a South Down ram in 1865. It was described in the 1865 annual report as "bred from stock imported by that gentleman from the noted flock of the late Jonas Webb of Babraham, England." Cornell was a farmer and gave his farm land to create the Cornell University campus.

Other gifts, among 52 received in 1865, were a Suffolk boar from the Honorable John Wentworth of Chicago, Illinois; a Farmer's Root-Cutter (improved) from T.H. Flower, Pontiac, Michigan; a Reynolds Horse-Fork from M.S. Baker, Lansing, Michigan; and a Brinkerhooff's Patent Corn-Husker from F.F. Fowler & Co., Upper Sandusky, Ohio.

Royal Gardens of Kew, England Donate to College—1873

The Royal Gardens at Kew, England donated 200 varieties of trees and 70 varieties of grass seeds to the college in 1873.

Ilgenfritz Nursery Donates Trees to College—1874

In 1874, the Ilgenfritz Nursery Company of Monroe, Michigan gave the college 35 apple trees, five peach trees, 20 plum trees, 13 ornamental trees, and 200 apple stocks.

Harvard Makes Donation—1879

Harvard University donated many greenhouse plants from its botanic garden to the college in 1879.

Harvard Donates Plant Species to College—1884

Harvard University's Botanic Garden donated 2,500 European plant species to the college herbarium in 1884. This gift, as with others from the Cambridge, Massachusetts institution, was undoubtedly due to Professor Beal being a Harvard graduate who maintained contact with his educational mentors, and because he was a leader in the botanical field.

First Foreign Gift From A Student—1886

A student from England, who spent two years at the college and was amazed at the "wonderful facilities for scientific study (that were) free of charge," sent the school a gift of $150 in 1886. President Willits said, "the money would be used, with the student's approval, for the erection of a 100-foot flag pole in front of the Armory." The student requested anonymity.

Land Donated to College in 1891

The College Agricultural Experiment Station received three gift parcels of land in 1891: 80 acres at Grayling, Michigan worth $1,850; ten acres at Harrison, Michigan, valued at $300; and five acres at South Haven, Michigan, worth $500.

Another Gift From the Royal Gardens—1899

The Royal Gardens at Kew, England sent the college 103 different kinds of seeds in 1899. These were for planting in the growing campus arboretum.

First Great Private Gift From R.E. Olds—1916

Out of a disaster came the first great private gift to M.A.C. On Sunday morning, March 5, 1916, fire roared through the Engineering Building, destroying a proud structure and shops, just nine years old. On Monday afternoon—the day after the fire—President Frank Kedzie wired Ransom E. Olds, founder of Oldsmobile and the REO Motor Company, who was vacationing in Florida, with an appeal for help in rebuilding the engineering facility. Previously, Kedzie had talked with Olds about giving a building to M.A.C. And, Olds remembered that Kedzie's father had loaned the Olds family money when they were struggling to launch their motor car business.

On April 29, 1916, President Kedzie received a letter from R.E. Olds, declaring he "would give $100,000 towards the reconstruction of the Engineering Building at the Michigan Agricultural College."

Olds wrote, "I have great faith in the college and see no reason why it should not become one of the foremost colleges in the United States."

It was the largest private gift the college had ever received.

Beaumont Gives Signature Landmark to Michigan State—1927

John Beaumont, class of 1882, Detroit attorney and former member of the college board, gave Michigan State the funds to build the beautiful carillon tower that bears his name in 1927. The tower was erected in 1928 on the site of Old College Hall (1857-1918), the first building on the campus and the first place where scientific agriculture was taught in America. It commands the highest ground on campus and is the most-photographed structure at MSU.

Kellogg Gives MSC Its Experimental Farm and Bird Sanctuary—1928

The Kellogg Company gave Michigan State its W.K. Kellogg Experimental Farm and Bird Sanctuary on December l, 1928. This magnificent gift consisted of 860 acres, including the 90-acre Bird Sanctuary with its Wintergreen Lake. The land value was estimated at $300,000. In addition, a $265,000 endowment was donated for the upkeep of the properties.

Rackham Foundation Gives to MSC—1938

A 1938 gift of $500,000 to create the Horace H. Rackham Research Endowment of the Michigan State College of Agriculture and Applied Science was to be held in perpetuity by the board.

An additional $6,000 from the Horace H. Rackham and Mary A. Rackham Fund was given to the college for brucellosis study under Dr. Ward Giltner and Dr. I.F. Huddleson.

Frederick C. Jenison Bequeaths $408,581.49 to MSC—1939

Frederick Cowles Jenison, who died in 1939, bequeathed his estate of $408,581.49 to Michigan State. This generous gift helped underwrite the construction of Jenison Gymnasium and Fieldhouse in 1940.

Harry A. Fee Gives MSU the Hidden Lake Gardens—1945

Harry A. Fee gave MSU his spectacular Hidden Lake Gardens in 1945. The 755-acre beauty spot is located 8 miles west of Tecumseh, Michigan on highway 50 in the scenic Irish Hills.

Michigan State College Fund Established—1949

To encourage more private gifts to the school, the Michigan State College Fund was established in 1949, with William L. Davidson, class of 1913, as its director. Early gifts enabled the addition of bells to Beaumont Tower's carillon, strengthened the Library, stimulated research and funded an annual "Distinguished Teacher" award to recognize outstanding faculty.

MSC Receives Two Half-Million Dollar Gifts in 1951

Although private giving was still in its infancy at Michigan State, the school received two half-million dollar gifts in 1951.

Harry Fee **(Fee Halls)** created a trust for MSC with stocks amounting to $525,000.

The Edward K. Warren Foundation Museum, located in Three Oaks, Michigan, gave MSC $500,000.

Kellogg Manor Given to MSC in 1951

After W.K. Kellogg's death in 1951, Kellogg Manor, his summer home on the highest land overlooking Gull Lake, near Kalamazoo, was given to Michigan State. It was valued at $1 million.

MSU Fund to MSU Development Fund—1956

The MSU Fund was renamed the MSU Development Fund in February, 1956. A pledge card system was initiated to make giving easier for alumni.

Wilsons Give Meadowbrook Farms and $2 Million to MSU—1957

One of the premier gifts ever received by MSU was given to the university in 1957 by Mr. and Mrs. Alfred G. Wilson of Rochester, Michigan. They gave their magnificent 1,600-acre Meadowbrook Farms and Estate and $2 million with which to establish a university in Oakland County near Rochester. The estate included the classic 110-room Meadowbrook Hall, built in 1927, and an 18-hole golf course, which had been built by one of the founders of the Dodge Motor Company, later a part of the Chrysler Corporation.

Michigan State launched MSU-Oakland in 1957, with Durward B. Varner, vice president of Off-Campus education, as the first chancellor. In 1970, MSU gave up its administration of MSU-Oakland and it became Oakland University.

Van Hoosen's Stony Creek Farm Given to MSU—1957

Dr. Sarah Van Hoosen Jones (Van Hoosen Hall), former college board member, gave the university her home and the 300-acre Stony Creek Farm, which had been in her family for more than 100 years. This property was located two miles outside Rochester, Michigan.

Floyd Owen Gift Builds New Dorm—1960

A gift of $420,000 from Floyd Owen, class of 1902, made possible the construction of the Owen Graduate Center in 1960. It is a residence hall dedicated specifically to graduate students.

Eppley Gift For Hospitality Training—1960

The Eugene C. Eppley Foundation of Omaha, Nebraska granted $1,500,000 to MSU in 1960 "For Graduate Training in the Fields of Hotel, Restaurant & Institutional Management." A plaque in the Eppley Building reads: "Eugene C. Eppley—1884-1958; Hotel Man-Philanthropist-Patron of Education."

Albert H. and Sarah A. Case Halls Recognize Giving—1961

The Albert H. and Sarah A. Case Halls were completed in 1961. The Cases were recognized for their many gifts to MSU, totaling more than a million dollars. Albert H. Case was a 1902 graduate of M.A.C. and captain of the

1901 football team. He became a vice president of the Tennessee Corporation. Sarah Avery Case, also an M.A.C. graduate, taught physical training to women students in the newly completed (1900) Women's Building gymnasium (now Morrill Hall).

Abrams Gift Builds Planetarium—1964

The Abrams Planetarium was dedicated in 1964. It was made possible by a $250,000 gift from Mr. & Mrs. Talbert Abrams of Lansing, Michigan, as well as other alumni contributions.

Ray Herrick Gives Activities Center at Hidden Lake Gardens—1966

Ray Herrick and his family of Tecumseh, Michigan, gave MSU a substantial gift to build an Activities Center at MSU's beautiful Hidden Lake Gardens in Lenawee County in 1966. The new center was to serve the 200,000 visitors that annually come to the gardens.

First Major Capital Drive Announced—1977

Dr. Patricia Carrigan, '50, and board of trustees chairperson, announced in 1977, "For the first time, MSU is conducting a major capital drive—the recently launched $17 million 'Enrichment Program.'" The drive was focused on the proposed Performing Arts Center, the first phase of new museum construction, library books and microfilm holdings, and money to endow faculty chairs and professorships.

Wallace K. Wonders, Benefactor and Class of 1902 Graduate, Dies—1977

Wallace K. Wonders, class of 1902, one of MSU's oldest graduates and benefactors, died at the age of 96 in Detroit on January 6, 1977. He and his wife Grace were major contributors to Michigan State. **Wonders Hall,** completed in 1963, was named in their honor.

Performing Arts Theatre Named for Catherine Herrick Cobb—1979

In April, 1979, MSU named one of the proposed theatres in the newly planned performing arts center for Catherine Herrick Cobb, in recognition of the major financial contributions by Mrs. Cobb and her family. Mrs. Cobb was the daughter of the late Ray W. Herrick, founder of Tecumseh Products in Tecumseh, Michigan. The Herrick family, including Mrs. Cobb and her brother Kenneth W. Herrick, chairman of Tecumseh Products, and the Herrick Foundation had given MSU major financial support for the preceding 15 years.

Kellogg Foundation Gives $11 Million to Upgrade Kellogg Center—1985

The W.K. Kellogg Foundation gave MSU $11 million in 1985 to upgrade Kellogg Center, built in 1951. Improvements included new energy-saving windows, upgraded guest rooms, expanded conference facilities—including restaurant space, renovated food service operations, and a new demonstration kitchen/food laboratory for the School of Hospitality Business.

MSU Launches $160 Million Capital Campaign—Largest in History—1988

President John A. DiBiaggio officially announced MSU's first comprehensive capital campaign, an effort to raise $160 million for buildings, professorship chairs, scholarships and enhancement of many programs. It was called "MSU 2000: Access to Opportunity."

GM Gives $5 Million to "MSU 2000" Campaign—1988

Robert J. Schultz,'53, MBA '69, General Motors vice president and group executive, announced a $5 million gift from GM to the "MSU 2000" capital campaign—the largest corporate gift received.

MSU Adds Beaumont Tower Society to Donor Groups—1989

The Beaumont Tower Society, a new MSU donor recognition group, was created in 1989 for those giving between $25,000 and $49,999 to the university, Bruce McCristal, '54, chair of MSU's Development Fund, said, "We expect more than 200 gifts in this category for MSU's $160 million capital campaign."

Richard & Cherrill Cregar Sponsor Hospitality Scholarship—1989

Richard Cregar, '58, and CEO of Cregar Enterprises, a large restaurant and catering business in Detroit, and his wife Cherrill, established a $30,000 fund in 1989 to support an Outstanding Hospitality Student Scholarship.

McConnell, Rowan and Withrows Make Major Gifts to MSU—1990

Three leaders of the MSU 2000 capital campaign made major gifts to the MSU 2000 capital campaign in 1990.

John McConnell, MSU graduate, founder and CEO of Worthington Industries and campaign co-chair for the mid-western states, gave $1.5 million to MSU. One million dollars was to fund an endowed chair in the College of Business, and $500,000 was to help with the construction of a new business building.

Robert Rowan, '47, retired CEO of Fruehauf Corporation—the world's largest truck-trailer manufacturer, gave $260,000 to the College of Business, where he earned his degree. He was national campaign chair for MSU 2000.

Jack, '54, MBA '71, and Dortha, '55, Withrow became Benefactors (gifts of $100,000 to $1 million), by establishing the John D. and Dortha J. Withrow Endowed Teacher-Scholarship Awards—one each for the College of Business and the College of Engineering, and also funded the

Perennial Pond in the new Horticultural Demonstration Gardens. Jack, former executive vice president with Chrysler Corporation, and president of Lectron Products, was campaign co-chair for the state of Michigan.

Eli Broad, '54, Gives $20 Million to College of Business—1991

Eli Broad, '54, founder and CEO of Kaufman & Broad, Inc., gave $20 million to the MSU College of Business in 1991—the largest private gift to a public university up to that time. Broad stated, "my gift will go to fund scholarships worldwide to recruit exceptional young minds for MSU's MBA program. It will endow professorships to attract internationally eminent MBA faculty. It will fund a new associate dean, exclusively for the MBA program. It will create a full-time director of MBA placement. And, it will fund some modest enhancements to the major business school building program already underway." He concluded, "I believe the MBA program at MSU will become a model for the 'New Breed' of Top Ten business schools in America."

Richard & Irmgard Light Give 1,232-Acre Lux Arbor Farms to MSU—1991

Dr. Richard and Irmgard Light gave their 1,232-acre Lux Arbor Farms to MSU's Kellogg Biological Station (KBS) near Gull Lake, increasing its size by 50 percent. The 1991 land gift was worth $1 million and was located six miles north of KBS in South Barry County and was to be used for research. Dr. Light, an adventurer, flew across Africa in 1927.

Herbert H. and Grace A. Dow Foundation Gives $5 Million to MSU—1992

The Herbert H. and Grace A. Dow Foundation gave $5 million to MSU in 1992 to establish a Composite Materials & Structures Center. It was the largest gift ever received by the College of Engineering. The grant assured MSU's position among the nation's leaders in composite materials research. The contribution made possible a new wing on the Engineering Building to house the Herbert H. and Grace A. Dow Institute for Materials Research.

MSU 2000 Raises $218 Million—1993

MSU 2000, the university's first major capital campaign, raised $217,854,609—36 percent more than the original goal of $160 million set in 1988. The funds were earmarked for student and faculty endowments, building projects and program enhancements.

Thirty-four thousand donors and hundreds of volunteers made it happen. A total of $36 million was raised for bricks and mortar. MSU Development Fund vice president Richard Meyer declared, "Most heartening is the increase in our total endowment level. We went from a $32 million endowment in 1987 to $83.9 million in 1992." Annual private support to the university rose from $23 million in 1988 to $50 million in 1992.

The campaign made possible:

- ▼ A 325,400 square-foot business building.
- ▼ A new seven-acre Horticulture Demonstration Garden.
- ▼ Major renovations at the College of Engineering and the Kellogg Center.
- ▼ A dozen new professorships.
- ▼ 240 new scholarships and fellowships.
- ▼ New laboratories.
- ▼ Expanded research opportunities, and
- ▼ Strong programs.

Of the 34,000 contributors to the campaign, 27,309 were alumni, and 3,106 were faculty and staff. The largest gift was $20 million from Eli Broad, '54; the smallest was $1, of which there were several.

Campus Arboretum Fund Established—1993

MSU's Campus Park & Planning Department launched a Campus Arboretum Fund in 1993 to add to the beauty of the university's grounds. Commemorative tree plantings were key to the program, and commemorative benches would be added later. For a contribution of $2,500 the department will plant a commemorative tree with a plaque listing the honoree. Replacement of the tree was guaranteed for ten years, and the tree would be maintained for its lifetime.

Commemorative benches were added later as a giving option. Benches cost $5,000 and are styled according to the surrounding architecture and location on campus. Each includes an inlaid metal plaque honoring the donor. Four benches to be located around Beaumont Tower were being offered as giving opportunities in 2001, at a donation of $10,000.

MSU Announces Endowment Campaign—1995

President McPherson announced a $60 million fund-raising campaign in 1995: "Continuing a Legacy of Leadership: The MSU Campaign for Endowment." He stated, "Endowed scholarships give us leverage in recruiting the most promising students. Endowed faculty positions make us competitive with other major universities and with industry in attracting top scholars to our campus. And, special endowed funds for specific government programs provide the extra measure needed to make good programs great."

Barbara Sawyer-Koch Makes Bequest to Cancer Center—1995

Trustee emeritus Barbara Sawyer-Koch, M.A. '90, made a $125,000 bequest to the MSU Cancer Center in 1995 to create an endowed fund. And, she also made a deferred gift annuity to the university.

Steve Smith Gives MSU $2.5 Million: The Largest Gift Ever By A Professional Athlete to a University—1997

Steve Smith, former MSU basketball All-American, Atlanta Hawk's star and U.S. Olympic Dream Team III member, announced on January 6, 1997 that he would give $2.5 million to MSU for its new Student-Athlete Academic Center. The center would be named for his mother, Clara Bell Smith. His gift put the $6 million campaign for the center over the top. Co-chairs for the campaign were Peter Secchia, '63, and Kirk Gibson, former Spartan star football and baseball player and professional star with the Detroit Tigers and Los Angeles Dodgers.

Milton Muelder, Retired Dean & Officer, Gives MSU $1 Million—1997

Milton Muelder, 88 year-old retired dean, officer and professor, gave MSU $1 million in 1997 to benefit the department of history, the Kresge Art Museum, the Russell Nye lecture series, to create the Beaumont Tower carillon concerts, intramural sports, and the Community Music Program. Muelder came to Michigan State in 1935 and served MSU for 41 years. He served as dean of the School of Science & Arts, chair of Political Science and Public Administration, acting dean of International Programs, acting vice president of Student Affairs, executive director of the MSU Foundation, vice president for Research and Development, and dean of the Graduate School.

W.K. Kellogg Gives $3.5 Million for Biological Station—1998

The W.K. Kellogg Foundation gave a $3.5 million grant in 1998 to renovate and expand the historic Manor House at MSU's W.K. Kellogg Biological Station at Hickory Corners, near Kalamazoo. The gift included expansion of teaching and computer facilities.

Withrows Give the Gift of Music to MSU and the World—1998

Jack Withrow, '54, MBA '71, and his wife Dottie, '55, provided funds in 1998 for MSU to commission Pulitzer Prize-winning composer Ellen Taafee Zwilich to compose a symphony to glorify the beauty and inspiration of the Michigan State campus and gardens. Zwilich's forthcoming "Fourth Symphony" was to premier at the Wharton Center in the winter of 2000. The composition was to be performed by the MSU Symphony under the direction of Leon Gregorian, MSU director of orchestras.

Ford Motor Company Gives $5 Million for New Labs—1999

Ford Motor Company pledged $5 million to MSU, in 1999, to be paid over five years to build two laboratories in MSU's new Biomedical and Physical Sciences Building, and another in the College of Engineering.

Ford Motor Company employed some 2,300 MSU graduates in 1999.

Lear Corporation $1 Million Gift Funds Career Services Center—1999

A $1 million gift from the Lear Corporation, in 1999, was key to funding a new $2.3 million Lear Corporation Services Center located in the Eppley Building at the Eli Broad College of Business. In the new 9,500 square-foot center were an elegant lobby, 22 interview rooms, multimedia and teleconferencing technology, a comprehensive career resource center and an employer's lounge.

Ken Way, MBA '71, Lear Corp. chair and CEO, stated, "This project aims to bring businesses and graduates together in an atmosphere that is businesslike." Jim Henry, dean of the Eli Broad College of Business, said the new center was the finest in the nation.

Patricia M. Carrigan, '50, Gives $1 Million for Endowed Chair—1999

Patricia M. Carrigan, '50, made a bequest of more than $1 million in 1999 to endow a professor's chair for feline health—the first of its kind in the U.S.—in the College of Veterinary Medicine. Carrigan also established the Pat Carrigan Endowed Woodwind Scholarship in the School of Music, and, in addition, donated her extensive collection of feline memorabilia to the MSU Museum.

Carrigan was the first woman to manage a General Motors assembly plant, and the first woman to serve as chair of the MSU Board of Trustees.

MSU Annual Private Support Tops $100 Million For First Time in 1999

MSU raised $104.1 million in private gifts in the 1998-1998 academic year—topping the $100 million mark for the first time, and surpassing the $92.3 million raised the previous year. The number of donors increased to more than 70,000, up four percent.

The Council for Advancement and Support of Education (CASE) awarded MSU its Circle of Excellence Award for overall fund-raising improvement at a public research/doctoral institution for the second consecutive year.

MSU Receives $30 Million Industry Gift for Computer Aided Education—2000

The Partnership for the Advancement of CAD/CAM/CAE (computer aided design, manufacturing and engineering) (PACE), comprised of General Motors, Unigraphics Solutions, Sun Microsystems, and Electronic Data Systems, gave Michigan State's College of Engineering 110 sophisticated computer work stations, software, and training and support valued at $30 million in 2000. MSU received the first and largest of $190-million in such grants that were being given by PACE to 40 universities.

Jay Wetzel, General Motors vice president with responsibility for GM's Technical Center, pointed out that 3-D solid modeling was the future of automotive design. The PACE gift would enable students to generate drawings along the X, Y and Z axes, and view how a design would look in three dimensions.

$10 Million Hotel Given to MSU by Candlewood Hotel Co.—2000

Candlewood Hotel Company donated a $10-million, 128-suite hotel to MSU in 2000 to serve the new Michigan State Executive Development Center (EDC). Both the hotel and EDC were under construction on Forest Road. The new hotel would be connected to the EDC, which was to be connected to the MSU University Club.

James M. Cornelius, BS '65; MBA '67, Gives $8 Million for James B. Henry Executive Development Center—2000

James M. Cornelius, BS '65; MBA '67, former chairman of Guidant Corp., and former Chief Financial Officer of Eli Lilly and Company, gave $8 million to MSU and the Eli Broad College of Business to help build the James B. Henry Executive Development Center, which opened in 2001. Cornelius specified that the new center be named for Jim Henry, dean emeritus of the Eli Broad College of Business and Eli Broad Graduate School of Management.

Pharmacia & Upjohn Gives $6.7 Million Brook Lodge Property to MSU—2000

Pharmacia & Upjohn Corporation gave MSU a gift of 657 acres and the beautiful Brook Lodge conference center in 2000. The property was valued at $6.7 million, included residence cottages, several handsome colonial-style buildings and was located in Augusta, Michigan near MSU's Kellogg Biological Station. It was to be used as a regional educational conference center and public retreat.

College of Engineering Receives Record $60.7 Million Gift—2001

Mechanical Dynamics, Inc., of Ann Arbor, Michigan gave the College of Engineering $60.7 million worth of software in 2001. It was the **largest software gift ever received by MSU, and it was the company's largest gift in history to an academic institution.**

Michael E. Korybalski, Mechanical Dynamics chairman and CEO, stated, "This will give current and future MSU engineering students a competitive advantage when they enter the workforce.

Marriott Foundation Gives MSU $550,000 for Scholarships—2001

The J. Willard and Alice S. Marriott Foundation gave $550,000 in scholarship support to MSU's School of Hospitality Business, a unit of the Eli Broad College of Business. The grant provided an endowment of $475,000 to make scholarships available to students interested in pursuing a career in the hospitality industry, and $75,000 to launch the program.

PepsiCo Gives $500,000 for Minority Scholarships—2001

PepsiCo, Inc., through its subsidiary Tropicana Products, Inc., gave MSU $500,000 in 2001 to fund full-tuition scholarships for six minority students over the next five years, and provide financial support for the College of Agriculture and Natural Resources career center in the Department of Food Science and Human Nutrition. It was the largest gift toward minority recruitment ever received by the college, and was called the Tropicana Diversity Scholarship program.

MSU Kicks Off "The Campaign for MSU" to Raise $1.2 Billion for Advancing Knowledge and Transforming Lives—2002

MSU President M. Peter McPherson announced on September 20, 2002 the launch of the largest capital campaign in MSU's history—a $1.2 billion fund raising drive to be completed by 2007. At the kick-off ceremonies in Wharton Center, McPherson indicated, MSU already had raised $607 million of the total in the "silent phase" of the campaign.

McPherson stated two objectives for the campaign—1) Add $450 million to MSU's total endowment, which stood at $810 million in September 2002; and 2) Raise $750 million to sustain MSU's excellence. These monies would go to support new research and teaching; support for students, faculty and staff; new facilities and infrastructure; and the enhancement of campus beauty, history and functionality.

Pittmans Give $6 Million to Renovate Marshall Hall—2002

MSU Trustee Randall Pittman, and his wife Mary, gave $6 million for the renovation of Marshall Hall and the renaming of the building to Marshall-Adams Hall to honor the late MSU president and economics professor emeritus, Dr. Walter Adams. For years, Adams office was in Marshall Hall.

Nicholas and Madeleine Perricone Give $5 Million for Endowment—2002

Dr. Nicholas Perricone, and his wife Madeleine, gave $5 million to establish an endowment in his name to generate funds for staff and program support in the College of Human Medicine. Perricone, a graduate of the college, was the author of two books that were on the New York Times Best-Seller Lists at the time of the gift (September, 2002)—*The Wrinkle Cure* and *The Perricone Prescription.*

Michigan State & Notre Dame: A Special Relationship

At a critical time in Michigan State's quest for Big Ten membership in the 1940s, the University of Notre Dame aided the Spartans by re-instituting a football rivalry between the schools. Michigan State had played Notre Dame in football 15 times between 1897 and 1921, but then the series died.

Hannah's Vision for Big Ten Membership

When John A. Hannah was elected president of Michigan State at age 38 in 1941, he already had a vision of Michigan State becoming a member of the Big Ten. The University of Chicago, then a Big Ten member, had partially opened the door by withdrawing from conference football competition in 1939. But a stumbling block to membership was the fact that Michigan State did not have a Big Ten-caliber football program or stadium. Macklin Stadium (now Spartan Stadium) seated just 25,000, and most games drew crowds considerably under that capacity.

1943 Luncheon Seals the Modern MSU-Notre Dame Series

With his uncommon forward vision, President Hannah took the first step toward football respectability in the World War II year of 1943. He approached Michigan Governor Harry F. Kelly, Sr., who was a Notre Dame alumnus and a past president of the N.D. alumni association, about holding a meeting with Notre Dame's vice president and chairman of the faculty athletic board, Rev. John J. Cavanaugh (N.D. President 1946-1952). Hannah wanted to establish a new football series with Notre Dame, which had one of the most storied

Three of MSC's four football coaches in 1932 were former Notre Dame stars—Jim Crowley, head coach (2nd from L), Glenn "Judge" Carberry, line coach (2nd from R), and Frank Leahy, assistant line coach (R). Miles "Mike" Casteel was backfield coach (L). Crowley was one of Notre Dame's legendary "Four Horsemen" and a member of the 1924 National Championship team. Leahy played on the 1929 National Championship team. He coached ND to 4 national titles in the 1940s.

football programs in the nation, to elevate Michigan State football.

Mrs. Anne Kelly, Michigan's first lady 1942-1944, recalled the circumstances in a 1992 interview with the author when she was 84. She said that Governor Kelly invited Father Cavanaugh to a luncheon at the Governor's home in Lansing to meet with John Hannah. "Father Cavanaugh arrived in a limousine, which was hidden behind our home so the press wouldn't know what was going on. I went to our freezer and pulled out some precious steaks, which were rationed during the war. I cooked the steaks and served them to Father Cavanaugh, John Hannah and my husband in our dining room.

"Over a two-hour luncheon, Father Cavanaugh agreed to play Michigan State in football again." When Vice President Cavanaugh returned to South Bend he put things in motion to add Michigan State to Notre Dame's football schedule, starting in 1948. Meanwhile, in 1946, the University of Chicago withdrew entirely from the Big Ten. This really opened the opportunity for conference membership. But it wasn't a slam-dunk. Pittsburgh and Syracuse also were strong contenders for the tenth position in the Big Ten.

Hannah Sets the Stage for Big Ten Entry

At this point John Hannah took aggressive action. In 1947, he hired Clarence L."Biggie" Munn, head coach at Syracuse and former Michigan assistant, to head Michigan State's football program. Munn had been an All-American on a national championship Minnesota team in the early 1930s. Hannah then launched a construction project to double the size of the stadium from 25,000 to 51,000 by the fall of 1948.

With the Notre Dame football series scheduled to start in 1948, and the University of Michigan agreeing to play Michigan State in East Lansing in 1948—the first time since 1924 and only the fifth time in history—the school would prove that it could attract football crowds of 50,000 plus and play at a Big Ten level.

The Hannah strategy worked. In December of 1948, the Big Ten university presidents voted Michigan State into membership.

Michigan State's modern football series with Notre Dame did elevate the program and almost immediately gained national visibility for the Spartans. In the 1949 game at East Lansing, a capacity crowd of 50,965 watched as Michigan State played very competitively against the national champion Fighting Irish, losing 34-21. It was Notre Dame's first visit to East Lansing since 1920.

In 1950, the Spartans played the Irish at South Bend in their first-ever televised game. The regional TV audience saw Michigan State win a thrilling 36-33 game. The Spartans finished the season 8-1 and were ranked No. 7 in the nation, their highest ranking in history.

The Game That Put Michigan State Into National Prominence

In 1951, playing in East Lansing before its first national TV audience, the Spartans crushed Notre Dame 35-0. They handed head coach Frank Leahy—winner of four national championships—the worst defeat of his career. On Michigan State's first play from scrimmage, fullback Dick Panin raced through a wide hole in the Notre Dame line and sprinted 88 yards to a touchdown. That set the tone for the entire game, the game that launched Michigan State into national football prominence. Michigan State closed the season undefeated at 9-0 and was voted the national champion.

"Game of the Century"—1966: 10-10 Tie

In what many people call the "Game of the Century," Michigan State and Notre Dame—both undefeated—met on November 19, 1966 before 80,011 fans at Spartan Stadium. MSU was ranked No. 1 in the polls and Notre Dame, No. 2.

ABC-TV was scheduled to telecast the game on a regional basis only. The network received 50,000 letters from football fans requesting the game be nationally televised, which was done. MSU Sports Information Director Fred Stabley, Sr., squeezed 754 sports writers and broadcasters into the Spartan Stadium press box, now named in Stabley's honor. It was the largest press turnout in the history of college football and would be the largest even when compared with Super Bowls for years to come. Even the *Wall Street Journal* had a front-page story on the game the day before it was played.

320-Page Book Written on The Game

Mike Celizic, a 1970 Notre Dame graduate and sports columnist for *The Record* of Bergen County, New Jersey, wrote a 320-page book on the game in 1992. It's titled, *The Biggest Game of Them All.*

Amazing! 25 All-Americans on the Field

Twenty-five of the players who took the field that day were or would become All-Americans. Ten of them would be first-round draft picks in the National Football League, and 33 of those that saw action that day would play in the NFL. In a titanic struggle, MSU and ND fought to a 10-10 tie. Following the season they shared the national championship.

Knute Rockne Accepted Michigan State Job; Then Stayed at N.D.

But the relationship between Notre Dame and Michigan State goes deeper than the modern series. Following the 1917 football season, Knute Rockne, then a highly successful assistant football coach at Notre Dame, verbally accepted the head football coaching job at Michigan State (then Michigan Agricultural College). M.A.C. offered him a salary of $4,500. However, early in 1918, Jesse Harper quit as Notre Dame's head football coach and athletic director. The Notre Dame fathers didn't want Rockne to leave and prevailed upon him to stay. For years afterward, Lyman Frimodig, Michigan State's athletic business manager, kept the signed contract with the $4,500 offer to Rockne in one of his desk drawers in East Lansing.

M.A.C. Defeats Rockne's First Team and "The Gipper"

On Saturday, November 16, 1918, Rockne brought his first Notre Dame team to play M.A.C. at East Lansing on Old College Field. His star was George Gipp. Playing in a sea of mud, M.A.C. beat Notre Dame and the "Gipper," 13-7. It was Notre Dame's only loss that season and for the next two. George E. Gauthier, who coached his only football season at M.A.C. in 1918, was the first M.A.C. alumnus to head the football program.

M.A.C. Draws Record Crowds at Notre Dame

In 1919, M.A.C. played at Notre Dame's Cartier Field in South Bend and drew a record crowd of 6,000 fans, but lost 13-0.

In 1921, M.A.C. again drew a record Notre Dame crowd at Cartier Field, this time 15,000 people. Notre Dame won the game 48-0.

Notre Dame Supplies Michigan State With Coaches

Michigan State turned to Notre Dame in 1929 for a new head football coach: Jim Crowley, one of Notre Dame's famous Four Horsemen backfield of the mid-20s. Crowley led the Spartans to a 22-8-3 record in the 1929-1932 period and brought the program into national prominence.

Former Notre Dame All-American Glenn "Judge" Carberry was Crowley's assistant, coaching the line and ends for four years.

Frank Leahy Wanted the Michigan State Head Coaching Job

Frank Leahy, another Notre Dame graduate, was a Michigan State assistant coach in 1932 under Crowley. Crowley had been impressed with Leahy's coaching when he lost to Leahy's Georgetown team, 14-13, in 1930, and brought him aboard as line coach in 1932.

Crowley left MSC in 1933 to coach Fordham University, where he helped create the "Seven Blocks of Granite," which included Vince Lombardi. Leahy expressed interest in the Michigan State head job. At that time, however, MSC President Robert S. Shaw thought Leahy was too young and inexperienced for the position. Leahy went on to coach Boston College, and then Notre Dame where he won four national championships and posted six undefeated seasons during the 1940s.

Another Notre Dame alumnus and All-American, Charlie Bachman, was hired away from the University of Florida, and coached Michigan State from 1933 through 1946. Bachman hired Tom King, a former Notre Dame teammate, to assist him. Later, King would become dean of students at MSC, and serve as the head of the Police Administration School. Bachman was an All-American guard at Notre Dame, playing from 1914-1916. At South Bend, Bachman was coached by Knute Rockne, who was an assistant. Bachman captained the Fighting Irish in 1916.

In 1918, during World War I, Bachman was an assistant coach and the star center on the undefeated, national champion Great Lakes Naval Training Station team, which

Charlie Bachman, MSC coach, 1933-1946, was a Notre Dame All-American in 1916 and was coached by Knute Rockne, then an N.D. assistant. He is a member of the College Football Hall of Fame. Photo: Spring, 1933.

won the title over the Mare Island Marines in the 1919 Rose Bowl. A Bachman teammate at Great Lakes was George Halas, who would go on to establish the Decatur, Illinois Staleys, which became the Chicago Bears in 1921—one of the four original National Football League teams (others: Detroit Lions, Green Bay Packers, and New York Giants).

Bachman was named head coach at Northwestern University in 1919, thus being tagged, "Boy Coach of the Big Ten." He was 26. In 1920, Bachman became head football coach at Depauw University in Indiana. On Sundays, he would drive to Decatur, Illinois, where he played under an assumed name for the Decatur Staleys professional football team—owned and coached by George Halas.

During Bachman's 14-year career at Michigan State, the Spartans defeated Michigan four consecutive years—1934 through 1937—took MSC to its first bowl game—the 1938 Orange Bowl, and posted an excellent record of 70-34-10. Bachman, who died in 1985 at 93, is a member of the College Football Hall of Fame.

Notre Dame Went After Duffy Daugherty in 1964

In 1964, Notre Dame approached MSU head football coach Duffy Daugherty about taking over the coaching reigns at South Bend. Duffy was so rooted at East Lansing, however, that he turned the Notre Dame fathers down. That decision opened the door for Ara Parseghian to become the Fighting Irish head football coach.

MSU Supplies Notre Dame With Its First African-American Head Coach

In the year 2002, the unique Michigan State-Notre Dame relationship took another twist, as Notre Dame hired Tyrone Willingham, an MSU graduate, as its head football coach. Willingham, the first black head coach of any sport at Notre Dame, had been Stanford University's head football coach for seven years and had been named PAC-10 Coach of the Year twice.

MSU: 22-30-1 in Modern Series With Notre Dame

Through the 2003 season, Notre Dame led Michigan State with 43 wins, 24 losses, and one tie. The single tie was the storied 1966 game. In the modern series, dating back to 1948, and running through 2003, there were 53 games. The Spartans have won 22, lost 30 and tied one.

Holds Longest Win Streak Over Notre Dame

From 1955 through 1963, Michigan State beat Notre Dame in football eight consecutive times, the only team in history to do so. From 1997 through 2003, MSU again established dominance in the series, winning six of seven games.

MSU: More Wins at Notre Dame Stadium Than Any Other School

Michigan State's 22-16 victory over the Fighting Irish at Notre Dame Stadium in 2003, was the Spartans' eleventh win at South Bend—more than any other university. The win also was MSU's fourth consecutive on Notre Dame's home field, second only to Purdue's five straight wins between 1954 and 1962. No other team has more than two consecutive football victories at Notre Dame.

In the 2003 win over Notre Dame, MSU's Jeff Smoker became only the second quarterback to lead his team to three victories over the Fighting Irish. Mike Phipps of Purdue is the other quarterback to hold that distinction.

MSU One of Three Universities With 20 or More Football Wins Over Notre Dame

Only three university football teams have beaten Notre Dame more than twenty times: University of Southern California—27, Michigan State—24, and Purdue—24.

Since 1950, MSU is Tied With USC for the Most Football Wins Over Notre Dame

Since 1950, when MSU began staking out a position among the nation's top football programs, the Spartans are tied with USC for the most football victories over Notre Dame—22. Purdue is second with 20 wins.

Michigan State will always be grateful to Notre Dame for helping it get into the Big Ten and big-time football competition.

The Big Ten Conference: Important In MSU's Development

The most significant event in the transition of Michigan State from a small land-grant college to a world-class university was its election to membership in the Big Ten Conference in December, 1948.

Joining the premier conference in the nation put the seal of approval on Michigan State's emergence as a true university and placed the school in the inner circle of academic excellence and big-time athletics. The Big Ten is the only conference in which all member universities are members of the Association of American Universities, a prestigious association of major academic and research institutions.

More than 320,000 students are enrolled annually in Big Ten universities, representing 17 percent of all students attending research universities in the U.S. Academically, 41 percent of Big Ten students have graduated in the top ten percent of their high school class, and 74 percent have graduated in the top quarter of their high school class. The Big Ten also has more than 3,500,000 living alumni, twice as many as any other conference in the nation. **One in 64 Americans is a Big Ten graduate.**

More than 70 Nobel laureates have been faculty, students or researchers at Big Ten universities. The conference also produces more graduates heading Fortune 500 companies than any other collegiate conference in the country.

Big Ten universities are involved in more than \$2.8 billion of funded scientific and engineering research annually, which amounts to 14 percent of the total funds expended on research by U.S. universities.

Eight of the country's 20 largest academic libraries are housed on Big Ten campuses. All of the conference libraries are inter-connected through an on-line library system (the Virtual Electronic Library). The Big Ten is the only conference in the U.S. in which all of the schools have a university press.

Big Ten Athletics

Big Ten athletic teams have won 189 national team titles and 1,250 individual national titles. The conference has produced more than 900 Olympic Games participants. From 1999 to 2002, Big Ten universities won 16 national championships.

The Big Ten not only has the largest television market of all conferences in the nation, it also has led the nation in the largest average football and basketball attendance for years. Moreover, it is a national attendance leader in women's basketball, women's volleyball, and wrestling.

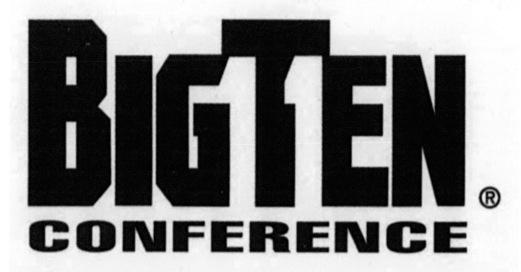

Big Ten logo incorporates a subtle number "11"—tucked under the arms of the letter "T"–which recognizes the eleven universities in the conference. Penn State became the eleventh member in 1990.

In the 2000-2001 academic year, Big Ten athletic events were showcased 250 times on national, regional or local television, representing more than 550 hours of programming.

The eleven Big Ten schools compete for 25 conference championships—12 for men, and 13 for women. **Men's sports include**: baseball, basketball, cross country, football, golf, gymnastics, soccer, swimming & diving, tennis, indoor track & field, outdoor track and field, and wrestling. **Women's sports include**: basketball, cross country, field hockey, golf, gymnastics, rowing, soccer, softball, swimming & diving, tennis, indoor track & field, outdoor track & field, and volleyball.

Big Ten History

On January 11, 1895, under the leadership of James H. Smart, president of Purdue University, the presidents of seven mid-western universities met at the Palmer House in Chicago, Illinois to found the Intercollegiate Conference of Faculty Representatives, known as the Western Conference, and later the Big Ten Conference. Eleven months later, one faculty member from each of the seven universities met at the Palmer House to establish the mechanics of the conference.

The founding universities were: the University of Chicago, University of Illinois, University of Michigan, University of Minnesota, Northwestern University, Purdue University and the University of Wisconsin. Indiana University and the State University of Iowa were admitted in 1899. Ohio State became a member in 1912. Chicago withdrew from the conference in 1946, and Michigan State College, now Michigan State University was voted into membership in late 1948, and officially admitted in 1949. On June 4, 1990, the Council of Presidents voted Pennsylvania State University into membership.

Big Ten Logo Recognizes Eleven Members

Although the entry of Penn State enlarged the conference to eleven schools, the brand name Big Ten was so strong, it was retained. In deference to the eleventh member, the Big Ten logo incorporates the number 11. Two numerals one appear subtly on either side of the capital T in Big Ten. If you look closely, you'll see the number 11.

Big Ten Principles

The Big Ten was the first conference in the nation to establish the control and administration of college athletics under the direction of appointed faculty representatives. The first action of the founders was to enforce "restricted eligibility for athletics to bona-fide, full-time students who were not delinquent in their studies." This prevented the participation of professional athletes and non-students in collegiate athletics. This proved to be a landmark foundation for amateur intercollegiate athletics.

In 1906, the faculty representatives approved pioneering rules that required eligible athletes to meet entrance requirements and to have completed a full year's work, along with having one year of residence. Freshmen and graduate students were not permitted to compete. Training tables or quarters were forbidden, and coaches were to be appointed by university bodies "at modest salaries."

The first conference commissioner—Major John L. Griffith—was appointed in 1922 "to study athletic problems of the various conference universities and assist in enforcing eligibility rules which govern conference athletics." Griffith died in 1944 and was succeeded as commissioner by Kenneth L. "Tug" Wilson, former Northwestern athletic director. He retired in 1961, and was succeeded by Bill Reed, an assistant commissioner since 1951. Reed died in 1971 and was succeeded by Wayne Duke, who served until June 30, 1989. James F. Delany succeeded Duke on July 1, 1989. He came to the Big Ten after ten years as commissioner of the Ohio Valley Conference.

The Big Ten headquarters are located at 1500 West Higgins Road, Park Ridge, Illinois 60068, just ten minutes from O'Hare Airport.

U.S. Presidential Visits to MSU

Nine U.S. Presidents have visited Michigan State University on 14 different occasions. Five U.S. Vice Presidents also have come to events on the East Lansing campus.

President Theodore Roosevelt—1907—The first Commander & Chief to grace the campus was President Theodore Roosevelt in 1907. He came to East Lansing on May 31, 1907 to deliver an address at the 50th anniversary of the opening of the school in 1857. (Michigan State was founded in 1855). The president addressed a crowd of 20,000 from an elevated platform at the top of the hill sloping down to the drill field (Walter Adams Field in front of Landon and Gilchrist-Yakeley Halls). There was no public address system. Following his address, the president personally handed diplomas to the 96 graduating seniors in the Class of 1907, including Myrtle Mowbray, the school's first African-American graduate.

Former President William Howard Taft—1919—Former president William Howard Taft delivered a lecture on the League of Nations before the assembled student body and faculty in the new college Gymnasium (Now IM-Circle Drive) on April 6, 1919. The Gymnasium building had been completed in 1918 at a cost of $220,000.

Future President Richard M. Nixon—1957—Vice President Richard M. Nixon gave the 1957 commencement address to the graduating class at Spartan Stadium. Nixon received an Honorary Doctor of Law Degree from MSU. A total of 2,929 bachelor's degrees were awarded to the Class of 1957.

Future President John F. Kennedy—1960—In October of 1960, three weeks prior to his election as president, John F. Kennedy campaigned on campus, and was welcomed by 12,000 enthusiastic students.

Former President Harry S. Truman—1960—Former president Harry S. Truman delivered the commencement address to the Class of 1960. He stated, "I may be talking now to the person who will be the leader of the next generation."

President George H.W. Bush, center; future president William J. Clinton, right; and Ross Perot; met in the third Presidential Debate of the 1992 campaign on October 19 at the Wharton Center. It was history's most-watched TV debate.

PREZ AT THE BRES—(l to r) Tom Izzo acknowledges a rousing cheer at Breslin Center on Jan. 9, as Mateen Cleaves presents a No. 1 MSU jersey to President Clinton as Charlie Bell looks on. "There's no quit in this team," Clinton said of the Spartan cagers, whom he honored after having cancelled their July visit to the White House.
CLINTON
1

President William Clinton congratulates MSU's 2000 NCAA basketball champions at Breslin Center in January 2001. MSU All-American Mateen Cleaves presents No. 1 MSU jersey to the president as Charlie Bell, R, looks on. Coach Tom Izzo celebrates with raised fist.

Former President Dwight D. Eisenhower—1961—Although President Eisenhower couldn't appear as the keynote speaker at MSU's Centennial Celebration on February 12, 1955 due to a heart attack, MSU President John A. Hannah invited him to visit Michigan State in 1961 after he had left office. Hannah gave Eisenhower a one-of-a-kind, inspirational tour of the campus.

Future President Gerald Ford—1965—Future president Gerald Ford was the winter term commencement speaker at MSU on March 14, 1965. He was then a member of the U.S. House of Representatives and U.S. House minority leader.

Future President Gerald Ford—1974—U.S. Vice President Gerald Ford spoke at Kellogg Center on May 24, 1974. He was presented a Distinguished Citizen Award by MSU. Outside, some 300 demonstrators protested the Watergate issue.

Future President William Clinton—1992—William Clinton brought his presidential campaign to the MSU campus in the fall of 1992.

President George H.W. Bush and Future President William J. Clinton—1992—President George Herbert Walker Bush and Future President William Jefferson Clinton met with H. Ross Perot in the most-watched U.S. Presidential debate in history on October 19, 1992. The debate, held in the Wharton Center, was viewed on television worldwide by hundreds of millions of people.

President William J. Clinton—1995—President William J. Clinton addressed 6,500 MSU graduates in green gowns and 50,000 parents and friends gathered in Spartan Stadium on May 5, 1995 for the commencement ceremonies. The president told the graduates, "You who graduate today will have the chance to live in the most exciting, the most prosperous, the most diverse and interesting world in the entire history of humanity."

President William J. Clinton—1996—President William J. Clinton campaigned for a second term on the MSU campus in the fall of 1996. It was his fourth visit to Michigan State.

Former President Gerald Ford—1998—Former president Gerald Ford gave the keynote address for the dedication of the new Detroit College of Law at MSU building in April. Former President Ford stated, **"It's no exaggeration to say that at Michigan State University, breaking with tradition is a tradition.** The new law school will combine the age-old pursuit of justice with some decidedly nontraditional fields." Following the formal ceremonies at the Wharton Center, most of the 2,500 people attending, walked to inspect the new $28 million law building.

President William Clinton—2001—President William Clinton made his fifth visit to the MSU campus on January 9, 2001 to belatedly honor MSU's 2000 NCAA championship basketball team, and to review the economic achievements of his administration. He spoke to a crowd of 11,500 at the Breslin Center. The team's scheduled visit to the White House in July, 2000 had been cancelled due to a peace summit the president was attending.

First Lady Eleanor Roosevelt—1940—First Lady Eleanor Roosevelt visited the Michigan State campus on the occasion of the dedication of the school's new Auditorium Building in 1940. She was welcomed and introduced by future MSC President John A. Hannah, who was then Secretary of the State Board of Agriculture (Board of Trustees).

Vice Presidential Visits

Vice President Alben Barkley visited the MSU campus in 1950.

Vice President Richard M. Nixon gave the MSU commencement address in 1957.

Vice President Hubert H. Humphrey visited the MSU campus in 1966.

Vice President Gerald Ford spoke at Kellogg Center on May 24, 1974.

Vice President Richard B. Cheney addressed the University Convocation on May 3, 2002.

East Lansing: Home of Michigan State University

Grand River Avenue, looking west, divides East Lansing. To the north, or right, is the city; to the south, or left, is the Michigan State campus.

East Lansing should be on everyone's list of the "Best Places to Live in America." It is the home of Michigan State University and owes its existence to the founding of the University at that location in 1855.

The picturesque location is two cities in one. On the north side of Grand River and Michigan Avenues is the City of East Lansing with its tree-shrouded streets and many historic and elegant residential neighborhoods. South of these avenues lies the magnificent 5,198-acre campus of Michigan State University—often called one of the most beautiful in the world.

East Lansing is located in the lower center of Michigan's "mitten," the Lower Peninsula, at **42 degrees, 44 minutes north latitude; and 84 degrees, 26 minutes west longitude**. The city is 819.13 feet above sea level.

East Lansing's population in the 2000 census was 46,525. Some 70 percent of the people over age 25 hold either a university bachelor's or graduate degree. Michigan State's enrollment was 44,542 in the fall of 2003. Making the greater East Lansing area especially attractive is the mixture of the University family, State government officials and employees in Lansing—the State Capital (three miles to the west), and leaders and workers from General Motors and other industries and businesses in Lansing. Population of the greater Lansing metropolitan region is more than 500,000.

The "just right" size of the East Lansing metropolitan area affords uncrowded living combined with the world-class cultural, educational and athletic offerings of an internationally prominent university. The city's educational system—elementary and secondary—is outstanding, as would be expected in an environment where the sons and daughters of many university faculty members are attending school.

In his *History of the City of East Lansing*, J.E. Towar, an 1885 graduate of Michigan Agricultural College and an agriculturist at the M.A.C. Experiment Station, wrote, **"Indeed, had there been no Michigan Agricultural College in this place, there would have been no City of East Lansing."** Towar took an active part in organizing the City of East Lansing.

Until the college was founded in 1855, about the only home in the area was the log cabin of B. Robert Burcham **(Burcham Drive)** which was located on the site of the present MSU Music Building. The three acres of land Burcham had cleared for farming later became the college drill and athletic field. This is now the Walter Adams Memorial Field (formerly called Landon Field), named in honor of the late MSU president emeritus, world renowned economics professor, and loyal advocate for the MSU Marching Band. Adams Field is where the band stages its pre-game warm-ups and post-game concerts on football Saturdays.

The town's first housing consisted of four homes built on campus for faculty members in 1857. This was the genesis of "Faculty Row." Today, the only surviving residence from that storied string of houses is Cowles House—the president's home—at One Abbot Road.

As the faculty grew, professors built homes just north of the campus. In 1887, professors William Beal **(Beal Botanical Garden & Beal Street)** and R.C. Carpenter laid out the first subdivision near the campus, just north of Michigan Avenue, where Beal Street is located. It was called Collegeville, an apt name. This was the first of several housing subdivisions developed by entrepreneurial faculty members. It well could have been their retirement plan or "19th century 401-K," as there were no faculty pensions in those days.

Dr. Manly Miles **(Manly Miles Building)**, the first professor of scientific agriculture in the United States, bought the plot of land on which People's Church now stands in 1866. This acreage later became the Oakwood subdivision, where Miles planted many Norway spruce, triggering the name **Evergreen Street**, which runs behind the church.

Later faculty subdivision developers included President Robert S. Shaw **(Shaw Estates, Shaw Hall, Shaw Lane)**, and Veterinary Medicine Dean Ward Giltner **(Giltner Hall)**, who even named a street after his daughter—**Dorothy Lane**.

The interweaving of city and university—'Town & Gown,' runs deep. **Charles S. Collingwood (Collingwood Drive),** class of 1885, postmaster, and later an Ingham County circuit judge, first proposed the idea of incorporating the town as a city in 1907. There were 800 people in the area and only two of them owned automobiles. A committee comprised of Collingwood, Addison M. Brown, then secretary of the college board of directors, and C.C. Wood, drafted the original charter and a bill for the legislature. The bill creating the city was accepted unanimously by both houses and was signed by Governor Fred M. Warner on May 8, 1907.

Popular "College Park" Name Ignored by Legislature

Prior to passage of the bill, the question of the city's name was debated. In a straw vote, the most popular name was College Park. Other names offered were Collegeville, Agricultural College, Oakwood, Montrose, and East Lansing. The legislature, with little feel for tying the name of the town to the college, ignored popular opinion and the very appropriate College Park name. Instead, they opted for East Lansing because they felt it was practical and described the community's proximity to Lansing.

The city's Common Council met on campus in Old College Hall from 1907 to 1911. Six of the first seven mayors of East Lansing were college faculty or staff members, and 17 of the 26 people who have served as mayor from 1907 to the present (2004) have been MSU alumni, faculty or staff.

Professor Clinton D. Smith was the first mayor in 1907. **Professor Warren Babcock** was the second in 1908. **Thomas Gunson (Gunson Street)**, the college green house manager for more than 40 years, served as the third mayor from 1909 to 1913. **Jacob Schepers**, college treasurer was the fourth mayor, serving from 1914 to 1917. **Professor E.H. Ryder** was elected the fifth mayor in 1918, and served for seven years. **Professor H.B. Dirks** was the seventh mayor, serving 1929-1930. **Luther H. Baker,** class of 1893, was elected mayor in 1932. **Lyman Frimodig**, MSU's only sports ten-letter winner, and 40-year business manager of MSU athletics, was the tenth mayor, serving 1933-1937. **Professor C.G. Card** was the eleventh mayor, serving 1938-1947.

Alumnus Harold F. Pletz was the 16th mayor, 1959-1961. **Professor Gordon L. Thomas**, the 17th mayor, served from 1961 to 1971. **Professor Wilbur B. Brookover** was the18th mayor, serving 1971-1973. Alumnus **Larry Owen**, the 20th mayor, served 1979-1983. Alumnus **John Czarnecki**, the 21st mayor, served 1983-1987. Alumnus **Joan Hunault**, the 22nd mayor, served 1987-1989. Alumnus **Liz Schweitzer**, the 23rd mayor, served 1989-1993. Alumnus **Mark S. Meadows**, MSU College of Law, is the 26th mayor. He was first elected in 1997. Re-elected in 2003, his term runs until 2007.

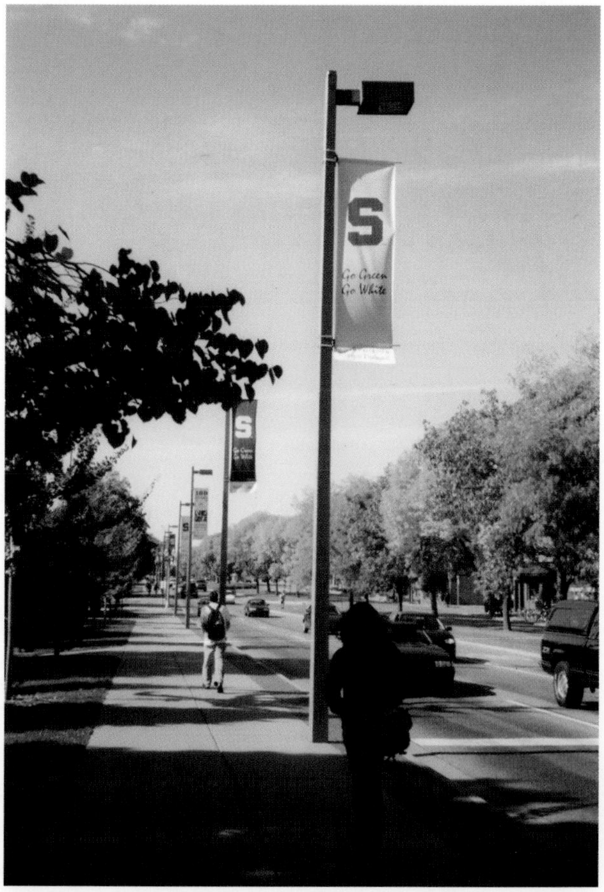

"S" banners give East Lansing that "collegiate look." West view from the south side of Grand River Avenue.

Several city streets are named after Michigan State presidents, faculty, and alumni. **Abbott Road**, inexplicably spelled with two "t's," was named for **Theophilus Capen Abbot** (one "t"), L.L.D. **(Abbot Hall),** president from 1862 to 1884. **Snyder Road** was named for **Jonathon LaMoyne Snyder**, L.L.D. **(Snyder Hall),** president from 1896 to 1915. **Hannah Boulevard** was named for **Dr. John A. Hannah (Hannah Administration Building)**, president from 1941 to 1969.

Butterfield Drive was named in honor of **Kenyon Leach Butterfield, L.L.D. (Butterfield Hall)**, president from 1925 to 1928. **Kedzie Street** honors **Dr. Robert Clark Kedzie (Kedzie Laboratories)**, professor of chemistry for nearly 40 years and the father of Frank S. Kedzie, president of the college from 1915 to 1924. **Beal Street** is named for the "Father of Hybrid Corn," **Dr. William James Beal (Beal Botanical Garden)**, professor of botany for 40 years. **Marshall Street** honors **Dr. Charles Edward Marshall (Marshall-Adams Hall)**, professor of bacteriology for 16 years. **Durand Street** remembers William Frederick Durand, professor of mechanics for four years.

Bailey Street is named for alumnus **Liberty Hyde Bailey (Bailey School and Bailey Hall),** class of 1882. Bailey is considered the "Father of American Horticulture," and was the founder of the 4-H movement. After leaving the East Lansing campus, he became a renowned professor and dean of Agriculture at Cornell University, where a building is named for him. **Gunnisonville Road** was named for the **Gunnison** family, which provided three of the first students of the college.

East Lansing's street numbering system was devised in 1911 by professor Chace Newman.

The city's school system and Peoples Church also were the product of initiatives by college faculty and alumni. First school classes were held in the YMCA rooms of Williams Hall on campus in the fall of 1900. In 1901, a one story, one room brick school house was built for $1,364.03 on the site of the future Central School (now MSU's Central School Child Development Laboratories), located at Grand River and Hillcrest Avenues. To accommodate a rapidly growing student population, a second story was added to the school in 1905. In March of 1916, the school burned to the ground on the same night the college engineering building was destroyed by fire.

A larger, two story brick school building was erected on the same site in 1916 and became East Lansing's High School. It remained the high school until 1926, when it became Central School for elementary students. The high school moved to a new building erected on Abbott Road (now the East Lansing Hannah Community Center).

In 1987, MSU purchased and renovated the old Central School for the College of Human Ecology's Child Development Laboratories.

The genesis of People's Church—a national model for inter-denominational churches—began in the brand new one-room school house (Central School) at Grand River and Hillcrest on January 5, 1902. Adults and children of the district were there to enroll in a new Sunday School. By the fall of 1902, **Professor Ernest E. Bogue (Bogue Street)**, Forestry Department head, was superintendent of the school and Mrs. Bogue was a teacher. The Sunday School flourished at the schoolhouse until 1908, when People's Church was organized and moved to the college chapel located in Old College Hall.

A campaign to raise funds for a church site and building was initiated in 1910. It was led by **Professors T.C. Blaisdell, Chace Newman, and E.H. Ryder.** The new church was dedicated on October 23, 1911. It cost $17,000 and was located on East Grand River at the site of the present People's Church. In 1917, **Rev. Newell A. McCune, M.A.C. class of 1901**, was called to the pulpit. He served the church as senior pastor for several decades.

On November 24, 1923, the cornerstone was laid for the present People's Church on East Grand River, and would cost some $400,000. The new structure was dedicated in a week of ceremonies, May 11-18, 1926.

Modern East Lansing

Today, East Lansing is a thriving, up-scale community. The $7 million redesign and renovation of the old East Lansing High School building into the world-class Hannah Community Center **(Honoring the late MSU President Emeritus John A. Hannah)** in 2001 provides citizens with remarkable facilities. Located on Abbott Road, the center includes an elegant 520-seat Performing Arts Theater, a Children's Theater and Recital Hall, a Dance/Aerobics Studio, a Fitness Center, a Seniors Lounge and meeting rooms, the Abbott Cafe, the Hot Spot Teen Club, a 25-yard heated indoor swimming pool, locker room facilities, two gymnasiums, an Executive Conference Room that holds 160, banquet facilities for 150, and an on-site, short-term child care center.

A new $3.5 million Water Park, located off Abbott Road north of Lake Lansing Road opened in 2001. This magnificent facility provides swimming, diving, three water slides, and changing facilities. It has become a favorite place for school and birthday parties, and other social events.

Downtown East Lansing cultural events include the Great Lakes Folk Festival (August), the Summer Solstice Jazz Festival (June 21st), Live! At Ann Street Plaza Concerts held under the clock tower, the annual Winter Festival and Chili Cook-Off, and the annual Art Festival (May).

Spartans Sports Success

24 Team National Championships in 10 Sports

"When the young men of ancient Sparta went off to war, they were told to come home with their shield on high, or come home carried on it."

—**George S. Alderton**, long-time sports editor of the *Lansing State Journal*, who gave Michigan State athletes the name Spartans in 1926.

Michigan State's proud athletic heritage stands on a foundation of:

- ▼ 24 team national championships in ten different sports
- ▼ 104 individual NCAA titles
- ▼ 58 Big Ten men's team titles in 13 sports (men's teams started competition in 1951)
- ▼ 31 Big Ten women's team titles in 10 sports (women's teams started competition in 1971)
- ▼ 343 Big Ten men's individual titles in nine sports
- ▼ 147 Big Ten women's individual titles in six sports
- ▼ 7 Central Collegiate Hockey Association regular season team titles
- ▼ 10 Central Collegiate Hockey Association playoff team titles
- ▼ Ten Olympic Gold Medal winners and a total of 23 Olympic medals
- ▼ University and professional Hall of Fame Inductees
- ▼ World Series, Super Bowl, NBA, Stanley Cup, and America's Cup champions
- ▼ Pro baseball and pro basketball MVPs, and
- ▼ Individual world, NCAA and Big Ten record setters.

A detailed listing of individual Olympic, National and Big Ten champions as well as all other categories appears later in this chapter under the heading "Great Spartan Individual and Team Performances."

MSU: Only University With Multiple NCAA Titles In Football, Basketball and Ice Hockey

Only five universities in America have won both football and basketball national championships: Michigan State, Michigan, Ohio State, Maryland, and UCLA. Only two universities have won football, basketball and ice hockey national titles: Michigan State and Michigan. But just one school has won multiple national championships in football, basketball and ice hockey: Michigan State.

National Team Titles in Eight Sports

MSU has won men's national team championships in eight different sports, ranking it in a tie for third in the nation with Ohio State. Stanford and UCLA are tied for first place with national team titles in 10 sports. Michigan and Southern California are tied for second with team titles in 9 sports.

MSU National Team Titles

MSU's national championships were won in **basketball–2** (1979 and 2000), **boxing–2** (1951 and 1955), **cross country–8** (1939, 1948, 1949, 1952, 1955, 1956, 1958 and 1959), **football–4** (1951, 1952, 1965 and 1966), **gymnastics–1** (1958), **ice hockey–2** (1966 and 1986), **soccer–2** (1967 and 1968), and **wrestling–1** (1967).

Spartan teams have won two other national titles: the **men's National Amateur Athletic Union (NAAU) outdoor swimming crown in 1945**, and the **Association of Intercollegiate Athletics for Women (AIAW) women's Softball World Series in 1976.**

MSU One of Ten Schools With Four or More National Football Titles

Michigan State is one of ten universities to have been selected as football national champion four or more times. The ten leaders and number of titles won are: Notre Dame—11, Michigan—11, Oklahoma—7, Alabama—6, Minnesota—5, Ohio State—5, Southern California—5, Nebraska—5, Miami (FL)—5, Michigan State—4.

MSU went undefeated in regular season play in all four years in which it was selected national champion—1951 (9-0, 2 selectors), 1952 (9-0, 11 selectors), 1965 (10-0, 11 selectors), and 1966 (9-0-1, 4 selectors). MSU also was selected national champion in 1955 (9-1,one selector), and 1957 (8-1, 3 selectors), but was not undefeated.

MSU One of 13 Schools With Two or More NCAA Basketball Titles

MSU is one of thirteen universities to have won two or more NCAA basketball championships. The leaders and the number of titles won are: UCLA—11, Kentucky—7, Indiana—5, North Carolina—3, Duke—3, Michigan State—2, Oklahoma State—2, Kansas—2, San Francisco—2, Cincinnati—2, North Carolina State—2, Louisville—2, and Connecticut—2.

Spartan Stadium $61-million improvement project includes two-story glassed-in box above the west second deck, which will house the press box (1st level), and 24 VIP suites (2nd level); 862-seat Club Level (between 1st and 2nd decks, center); and new offices for University Development, the MSU Alumni Association, MSU Foundation, and the 4-H Foundation. Stadium seating capacity will rise to 75,000 from 72,000. No tax-payer money will be used. Funding will be from athletics and elimination of off-campus office rentals. Project completion: 2005.

Since 1950, MSU is a Leader in Football Wins vs. Michigan and Notre Dame, The Two Winningest Football Programs in the Nation.

Beginning in 1950, when Michigan State first emerged as a top ten football team, the Spartans have faired very well against the two winningest football programs in the nation. MSU and USC lead all other universities in wins over Notre Dame since 1950—22. Versus Michigan, MSU has 22 wins since 1950, second only to Ohio State's 25 victories over the Wolverines in that time frame.

MSU also holds the distinction of having beaten the Fighting Irish eleven times at Notre Dame Stadium—more wins in South Bend than any other university.

104 NCAA Individual Championships

Spartan athletes have won 104 individual NCAA titles in seven different sports. A listing of these national champions appears later in this chapter under the section titled "Great Individual and Spartan Team Performances."

MSU First to Win Titles in All 12 Big Ten Sports

In view of the fact MSU only started championship play in the Big Ten in 1951—fifty-five years after the conference was organized—its athletic performance has been remarkable. Playing "catch-up" beginning in 1951, when the Spartans started Big Ten competition, MSU raced to Big Ten titles in all 12 men's sports by 1969, becoming the first conference member ever to attain that distinction.

The twelve sports and the years in which the first Big Ten titles were won are as follows: **Tennis–1951, Football–1953, Cross Country–1956, Basketball–1957, Swimming–1957, Ice Hockey–1959, Wrestling–1961, Fencing–1963, Outdoor Track–1965, Indoor Track–1966, Gymnastics–1968, and Golf–1969.**

MSU: Center Stage in The Greatest Games In Football, Basketball, and Hockey

Michigan State stands alone in the U.S., having been at center stage in history-making games in football, basketball and hockey.

1966—Football Game of the Century "Changed the Game Forever": MSU 10, Notre Dame 10—"It was the first nationally televised mega-game of the modern era," according to Mike Celizic's 320-page book *The Biggest Game of Them* All (Simon & Schuster, 1992). Celizic wrote, "Few games have ever captured the public's imagination or had such a long-lasting effect as Notre Dame-Michigan State. Nationwide interest was so intense that **it demonstrated to ABC and the NCAA just how much money there was to be made in televising college football—a development that would change the game forever. Notre Dame-Michigan State was the Super Bowl before the Super Bowl became what it is today."**

New York Times writer Allen Barra wrote in 2001, **"The 1966 Spartans-Irish clash remains a seminal moment in college football. In nearly every respect, the game fit the definition of a classic: It summed up everything in college sports that came before it, and changed everything that came after it.** The NCAA had allowed no more than one (nationally) televised home game a season, but caved in to public pressure and permitted the game to be televised. The bending of broadcast limitations started the flood of televised games that has resulted in a full menu of TV games every week."

Quarterback Jimmy Raye sprints against Notre Dame in classic 1966 10-10 tie. Irish defenders in pursuit—Pete Duranko (64), Tom Rhoads (87), and Alan Page (81), who became a Minnesota Supreme Court Justice. MSU and Notre Dame both were voted National Champions for 1966.

Prior to this titanic struggle on November 19, 1966, as mentioned above, ABC was planning only regional TV coverage. But they received an unprecedented 50,000 letters from fans nationwide, pleading that the game be televised nationally. ABC complied, even changing the NCAA rule that allowed only so many nationally televised games per school.

The television ratings for the game were higher than those of the first Super Bowl between Green Bay and Kansas City, two months later.

MSU and Notre Dame entered the game with identical 9-0 records, and were respectively ranked No. 2 and No. 1 in the nation. The talent on the two teams was remarkable—25 players who were or would become All-Americans; 33 players who would play in the NFL, including ten first-round draft picks.

The sports writing corps, hundreds strong, landed on the MSU campus on Monday of game week, four days earlier than normal. Fred Stabley, Sr. MSU's sports information director, led daily news conferences on the game all week, and then packed 754 newsmen into the Spartan Stadium press box now named for him. It was the largest news media crowd in college football history up to that time, and remained the biggest sports journalist turn-out for years, even surpassing those of Super Bowl games.

Michigan State and Notre Dame each were voted National Champions at the end of the season.

1979—"The Game That Changed Basketball"; MSU 75, Indiana State 64—The game was for the national championship, and is considered the defining moment in college basketball. The largest television audience in NCAA history (a 24.1 rating and 38 share; 24.1 percent of the nation's TVs were tuned to the game, 38 percent of all viewers saw it) watched MSU's Magic Johnson and Indiana State's Larry Bird—the two finest players in the country—battle it out. Indiana State went into the game ranked No. 1 with a 33-0 record. It has been called, "The Game That Changed the Game." **Former UCLA center Bill Walton—winner of two NCAA titles under legendary coach Johnny Wooden—referred to the game as "the birth of basketball," and the "day basketball was invented."**

Famous sportscaster Dick Vitale stated, **"That game, pitting Magic vs. Bird...kicked off the unbelievable interest in March Madness. It set the tempo for the biggest growth in college basketball."** (*MSU Alumni Magazine,* Fall, 2003).

Magic Johnson dunks to help defeat Indiana State, 75-64, and win the 1979 NCAA basketball title at Salt Lake City. Magic led both teams with 24 points. ISU's Larry Bird (above # 23), was held to 19, ten below his season average.

2001—World's Largest Hockey Crowd—74,554; MSU 3, Michigan 3 in "The Cold War"—The Spartans and the Wolverines battled to a 3-3 tie before 74,554 hockey fans in Spartan Stadium. The October 6th game was billed as "The Cold War." The attendance broke the former ice hockey world record of 55,000 fans set in 1957 when Sweden defeated Russia, 3-2, in the World Championships in Moscow's Lenin Stadium. It also broke the all-time U.S., NHL, and college hockey attendance records—28,183 set during the 1996 Stanley Cup playoffs in the St. Petersburg, Florida Thunderdome when Philadelphia beat Tampa Bay, 4-1; and 21,576 set in 1984, when MSU beat Michigan Tech, 7-0 in the Great Lakes Invitational at Joe Louis Arena in Detroit. (A new NHL attendance record was set in 2003, drawing 55,000 fans to an Edmonton Oilers vs. Montreal Canadiens Heritage Classic game at Commonwealth Stadium in Edmonton, Alberta).

World Record Hockey Crowd of 74,554 saw MSU and U of M skate to a 3-3 tie in the "Cold War" at Spartan Stadium, 2001.

2003—The World's Largest Basketball Crowd—78,129—saw Kentucky defeat MSU, 79-74, December 13, 2003 at the Detroit Lions' Ford Field in Detroit. Called the BasketBowl, the unique event sold more than 75,000 seats by mid-July, 2003. The original world record for basketball attendance was set in 1951 when the Harlem Globetrotters drew 75,000 to the Olympic Stadium in Berlin. The national attendance record was set on January 20, 1990 when LSU beat Notre Dame, 87-64, at the New Orleans' Superdome before 68,112 fans.

1956—Rose Bowl: MSU 17, UCLA 14—Largest Bowl TV Audience in History—Dave Kaiser kicked a 41-yard field goal with seven seconds left in the 1956 Rose Bowl game to defeat UCLA 17-14. The game was television's all-time top-rated college football bowl game, with a 67 percent share of the TV audience. In 2000, Kaiser was inducted into the Rose Bowl Hall of Fame.

MSU: Only School With Four-Time Individual National Champions in Boxing and Wrestling

Charles "Chuck" Davey, who became the youngest NCAA boxing champion in history at age 17 in 1943 (127 pounds), went on to win three additional NCAA titles following his WWII service. He won in 1947 (135 pounds), 1948 (136 pounds), and 1949 (145 pounds). In the history of NCAA boxing, he was the only four-time champion. He was a member of the 1948 U.S. Olympic boxing team, and was elected Michigan State's boxing team captain in 1947, 1948, and 1949. Davey won the LaRowe Trophy as the outstanding boxer of the NCAA tournament three times—the only boxer ever to win it more than one time.

Walter Jacobs won four individual national championships in wrestling. He won the NCAA title his senior year at 158 pounds in 1936, and the National AAU 160-pound title in 1937, 1938, and 1939 as a graduate student at Cornell. In his honor, the Walter C. Jacobs Award, instituted in 1940, is presented each year to the MSU wrestler with the highest point total for the season.

MSU: Only School With 17-Year-Old National Champions in Boxing and Wrestling

Charles "Chuck" Davey won the NCAA 127-pound boxing title in 1943 at age 17.

Gale Mikles won the 145-pound National AAU wrestling title in 1945 at age 17.

MSU: Only School to Twice Have Its Basketball and Ice Hockey Teams in NCAA Final Fours Simultaneously

MSU's basketball and ice hockey teams first earned their way to Final Four and Frozen Four simultaneously in 1998. Again, in 2001, both the basketball and hockey teams fought their way to the prestigious Final Fours at the same time. It was a distinction achieved by no other university sports program.

MSU Big Ten All-Sports Record: Six Firsts; 11 Seconds

By 1971, Michigan State had won six Big Ten all-sports competitions; finished second eleven times, third three times, and fifth once. MSU's first place finishes were in 1954, 1959, 1960, 1966, 1967, and 1971. In its first 20 years in Big Ten competition, MSU had finished either first or second in the all-sports competition 17 times.

This remarkable start in Big Ten sports was the result of the selection of excellent coaches by Athletic Directors Ralph Young (1923-1954) and Biggie Munn (1954-1971), and Munn's high expectations of excellence and extraordinary motivation of coaches and athletes. MSU head football coach Hugh "Duffy" Daugherty once proclaimed Munn as "The greatest motivator I ever knew."

During Munn's administration, MSU athletes won individual NCAA titles in seven sports, a record matched only by Navy; and NCAA team titles in six different sports, an achievement bettered by no other institution, and matched by just a few.

Spartans Have Won 23 Olympic Medals; 10 Gold

In Olympic competition, 73 Spartan athletes have participated in 16 sports and won 23 medals: ten gold, eleven silver, and two bronze.

Lloyd Ward, '70, retired CEO of Maytag Corp., was elected CEO of the U.S. Olympic Committee in October of 2001. Ward was the first African-American to serve in this position.

Eleven MSU staff members have served as U.S. Olympic Committee physicians, athletic trainers, coaches, or news media liaisons.

Ralph H. Young, MSU athletic director, 1923-1954, served as assistant treasurer of the U.S. Olympic Committee in 1952, and **Dr. Roy T. Bergman** served on the U.S. Olympic Committee for a period of years through 1984. **Dr. Eric Deal**, '77, D.O. '81, served as the emergency medical director for the 1996 Olympic Games in Atlanta, Georgia. **Tom Minkel**, MSU wrestling coach, was named head coach of the U.S. Olympic Greco-Wrestling team for the 1992 Games. Minkel had won a position on the U.S. 1980 Olympic team, but didn't compete because the U.S. boycotted the games which were held in Moscow, Russia.

Spartans in 18 Consecutive Olympic Summer Games and Nine Winter Olympic Games

In all, MSU athletes and staff members have represented the United States and other nations in 18 consecutive Summer Olympic Games—1924 through 2000—and in nine Winter Olympic Games—1956, 1960, 1968, 1984, 1988, 1992, 1994,1998, and 2002.

MSU Olympic Participants by Year

1924—Col. William D. Frazer—pistol.
1928—Frederick P. Alderman—track—**gold medal winner** in the 1600-meter relay; world record—3:41.1.
1932—Ernest Crosbie—track.
1932—Thomas C. Ottey—track.
1932—Ralph H. Young, MSC athletic director—associate track coach.
1936—Ernest Crosbie—track.
1936—Albert J. Mangan—track.
1940 and 1944—Olympic Games not held due to World War II.
1948—Ernest Crosbie—track.
1948—Charles P. Davey—boxing.
1948—Lyle E. Garbe—10,000-meter walk, Team Canada.
1948—John G. "Jack" Heppinstall—MSC trainer—trainer.
1948—George A. Hoogerhyde—swimming.
1948—Robert G. Maldegan—wrestling.
1948—Leland G. Merrill—wrestling—**bronze medal winner** at 160.5 pounds.
1948—Howard F. Patterson—swimming.
1948—Charles W. Speiser—boxing.
1948—Dale O. Thomas, MSU physical education staff—wrestling.
1948—Adolph G. Weinacker—track.
1952—Warren O. Druetzler—track.

1952—Allen S. Kwartler—fencing.
1952—C. Clarke Scholes—swimming—**gold medal winner** in the **100-meter freestyle, setting an Olympic record.**
1952—Charles W. Speiser—boxing.
1952—Adolph F. Weinacker—track.
1952—Ralph H. Young, MSC athletic director—assistant treasurer for the U.S. Olympic team.
1956—Virginia D. Baxter—figure skating.
1956—Judy K. Goodrich—fencing.
1956—Kevan Gosper—track—**silver medal winner** on Australian 1,600-meter relay team.
1956—David Lean—track—**silver medal winner** on Australian 1,600-meter relay team.
1956—Allen S. Kwartler—fencing.
1956—Pearce A. Lane—boxing.
1956—Choken Maekawa—boxing.
1956—Weldon N. Olson—ice hockey—**silver medal winner**.
1956—Ernestine Russell (Weaver)—gymnastics—Canada.
1956—William Steuart—swimming—South Africa.
1956—Adolph F. Weinacker—track.
1960—Virginia D. Baxter—figure skating.
1960—Judy K. Goodrich—fencing.
1960—Kevan Gosper—track—captain of the Australian Olympic track team.
1960—Eugene W. Grazia—ice hockey—**gold medal winner** on U.S. championship team that defeated Russia.
1960—Allen S. Kwartler—fencing.
1960—Weldon N. Olson—ice hockey—**gold medal winner** on U.S. championship team that defeated Russia.
1960—Ernestine Russell (Weaver)—gymnastics—Canada.
1964—Solomon Akpata—track—Nigeria.
1964—Fendley Collins—MSU wrestling coach—manager, wrestling team.
1964—Gary J. Dilley—swimming—**silver medal winner**, 200-meter backstroke.
1964—Marcia I. Jones—canoeing.
1964—William A. Smoke—canoeing.
1968—Donald R. Behn—wrestling—**silver medal winner**, bantamweight.
1968—George Gonzalez—swimming—Puerto Rico.
1968—Fred Lowe—weightlifting.
1968—David B. Thor—gymnastics.
1968—Ernie Tuchscherer—soccer.
1968—Douglas Volmer—ice hockey.
1968—Kenneth M. Walsh—swimming—**gold medal winner**, 400-meter freestyle; **gold medal winner**, 400-meter relay; **silver medal winner**, 100-meter freestyle.
1968—Peter E. Williams—swimming.
1968—Marcia Jones Smoke—singles kayaking—**bronze medal winner**.
1972—Art "Buzz" Demling—soccer.
1972—Fred Lowe—weightlifting.
1972—Roger Young—cycling.
1976—Fred Lowe—weightlifting.
1980—Dave Burgering—diving.
1980—Fred W. Stabley, Sr.—MSU sports information director—press liaison.
1980—Diane Williams—track.
1984—Dr. Roy T. Bergman, MSU staff member—concluded many years of service on the U.S. Olympic Committee in 1984.
1984—Judi Brown—track—**silver medal winner**, 400-meter hurdles.
1984—Gary Haight—ice hockey.
1984—Nick Vista, MSU sports information director—press liaison.
1988—Dave Carrier—trainer, ice hockey.
1988—Geir Hoff—ice hockey, Norwegian team.
1988—Kevin Miller—ice hockey.

1988—Sally Nogle—trainer.
1992—Dave Carrier—trainer, ice hockey.
1992—Jason Woolley—ice hockey—Team Canada.
1992—Julie Farrell-Ovenhouse—diving.
1992—Earvin "Magic" Johnson—basketball—**gold medal winner** on championship U.S. "Dream Team."
1994—Jason Dungjen—figure skating.
1994—Dwayne Norris—ice hockey, Team Canada.
1994—Geir Hoff—ice hockey, Norwegian team.
1996—Pam Bustin—field hockey.
1996—Dr. Eric Deal—emergency medical director for the Olympic Games.
1996—Sevatheda Fynes—track—**silver medal winner** in the sprints, representing the Bahamas.
1996—Michele Madison—assistant coach, field hockey.
1996—Ken Hoffman—MSU sports information director—press room manager, main press center.
1998—Rod Brind'amour—ice hockey, Team Canada.
2000—Karen Dennis—U.S. women's Olympic track coach, **gold medal winner**.
2000—Sevatheda Fynes—track—**gold medal winner** on the Bahamian 400-meter relay team.
2000—Steve Smith—basketball—**gold medal winner** on U.S. championship team.
2002—Mike York—ice hockey—**silver medal winner** as a member of the U.S. hockey team.

Ralph H. Young and Clarence "Biggie" Munn: Builders of MSU's Winning Athletic Tradition

Under Ralph H. Young, athletic director (1923-1954), MSU became a national sports power. Between 1950 and 1954, MSU had no fewer than five sports teams ranked in the top ten nationally every year. He hired and inspired nine coaches who were ultimately inducted into National Halls of Fame. He initiated the annual NCAA cross country championship meet.

Ralph H. Young, (1889-1962), Director of Athletics 1923-1954, established the foundation of Michigan State's winning athletic tradition. In his 31-year career leading MSU athletics, **he hired and inspired nine coaches who ultimately were inducted into National Halls of Fame**—Fendley Collins, wrestling; Ben VanAlstyne, basketball; John H. Kobs, baseball; Clarence "Biggie" Munn, football; Charles McCaffree, swimming; Charles Bachman, football; Pete Newell, basketball; Amo Bessone, ice hockey; and George Szypula, gymnastics. Moreover, during Young's tenure, three assistant football coaches, hired by "Biggie" Munn, also went into National Halls of Fame: Duffy Daugherty, Bob Devaney, and Dan Devine.

By the end of Young's career, Michigan State was a national power in many sports. **From 1950 through 1954, the Spartans had no fewer than five teams in the top ten nationally every year**.

1950—five teams—cross country #2, boxing #3, gymnastics # 5, swimming #5, and football #7.

1951—seven teams—football #1, boxing #1, swimming #2, track #4, wrestling #6, fencing #7, and gymnastics #7.

1952—six teams—football #1, cross country #1, boxing #2, fencing #4, swimming #4, and gymnastics #6.

1953—six teams—football #3, boxing #4, swimming #5, cross country #6, gymnastics #7, and wrestling #8.

1954—five teams—baseball #3, gymnastics #5, boxing #6, wrestling #6, and swimming #8.

Young initiated the annual NCAA cross country meet in 1938, an event that was held on the MSU campus every year from 1938 through 1964.

He served the U.S. Olympic Committee as associate track coach in 1932, and assistant treasurer in 1952.

Young's amiable personality and salesmanship were key in helping win over Big Ten athletic directors on supporting Michigan State's quest for Big Ten membership.

In addition to being athletic director, Young coached Spartan cross country (1924), football (1923-1927), and track (1924-1940). The rotund Young weighed more than 300 pounds, and used to end track practices by telling the team, **"Take three laps around me before you hit the showers."**

Young holds the distinction of being the only person to play football under two legendary coaches—Amos Alonzo Stagg at the University of Chicago in 1911, and Fielding H. Yost at the University of Michigan in 1918 where he was in Army training for WWI. He graduated from Washington & Jefferson University in 1915, where he played football (1912-1914) on teams that won 28, lost 3, and tied 2.

Young served as athletic director at Depauw University and Kalamazoo College prior to his career at Michigan State.

Named in his honor are the **Ralph Young Track and Field at MSU, and the Ralph Young Fund for MSU athletics.**

Ralph Young's exceptional career was recognized in 1979 when he was inducted into the National Association of College Directors of Athletics Hall of Fame. Young died in 1962 at age 72.

Clarence L. "Biggie" Munn, (1908-1975), Athletic Director, 1954-1971, built upon the athletic excellence established under Ralph Young's tenure. Munn was an exceptional leader of coaches, continually setting high expectations of excellence. Duffy Daugherty said Munn was the **"greatest motivator of men"** he ever knew.

During Munn's 17-year tenure as A.D., MSU athletes won NCAA titles in seven different sports, an all-time record, matched only by Navy in the NCAA's 100-year history. In addition, MSU teams won NCAA titles in six different sports, an achievement bettered by no other school during that period.

Under Munn, Spartan men's teams won 16 Big Ten team titles and MSU became the first university in the conference to win titles in all 12 men's sports.

In seven seasons as head football coach (1947-1953), Munn led the Spartans to two National Championships (1951 and 1952), MSU's first Big Ten title (1953), and the school's first Rose Bowl title (1954). His teams won 54, lost 9, and tied 2, for a .857 winning percentage—the best in MSU history.

Munn told his players, **"The difference between good and great is a little extra effort."** That work philosophy is inscribed on a ceiling beam in the main dining room of the flagship restaurant of the Schuler chain in Marshall, Michigan, run by CEO Hans Schuler, class of 1959.

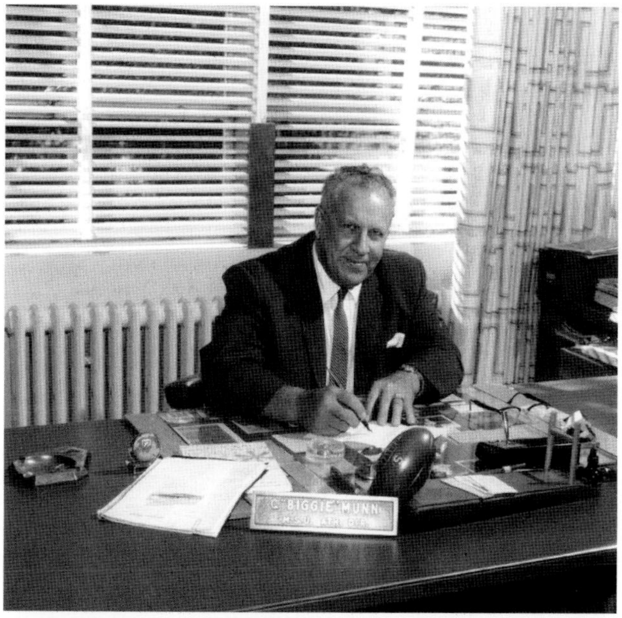

Under Biggie Munn, athletic director (1954-1971), MSU teams won NCAA titles in 6 sports, and MSU athletes won NCAA titles in 7 sports—a record surpassed by no other university during his tenure. As head football coach, Munn led the Spartans to National Championships in 1951 and 1952, and a 54-9-2 record in seven seasons (1947-1953). His .857 winning percentage stands as the best in MSU history.

At the University of Minnesota, Munn was a two-time All-American in football, playing fullback and guard, and was named the Big Ten's most valuable player in 1931 by the *Chicago Tribune*. He also set a Big Ten record in the shot put.

Following graduation, Munn served as an assistant football coach and track coach at Minnesota (1932-1934). Next, he became Albright College's athletic director and all-sports coach (1935-1936). He served as line coach at Syracuse in 1937, and then at Michigan (1938-1946). Syracuse named him head football coach in 1946.

Munn Arena, home of MSU's ice hockey team, is named in his honor.

In 1975, Biggie Munn was named to the Citizens Savings College Football Hall of Fame. Munn died of a stroke on March 18, 1975 at age 66.

Fred Stabley and Nick Vista, Members, College Sports Information Directors of America Hall of Fame Set National Standards for Sports Information Integrity and Service

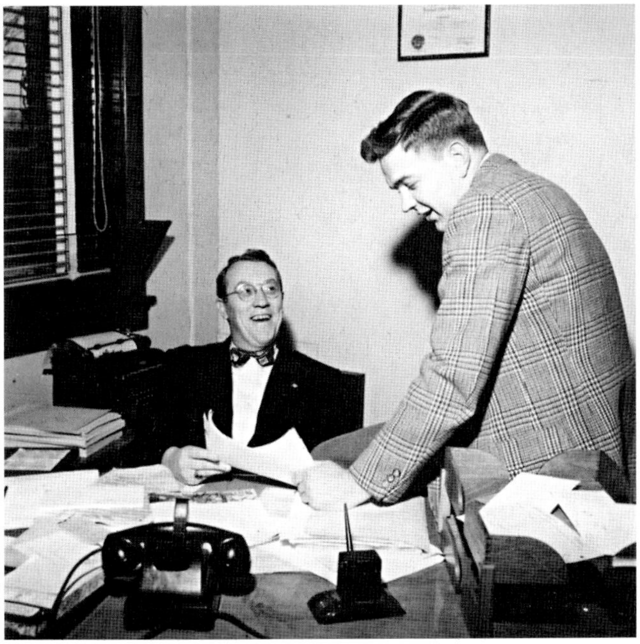

Fred Stabley, Sr., left, Sports Information Director, 1948-1980, chats with Edward "Bud" Erickson, Assistant SID, and former MSU baseball captain. Photo: 1951.

Michigan State's rise to national prominence in athletics was aided greatly by the professional communications and human relations skills of **Fred W. Stabley, Sr.,** (1915-1996), sports information director (SID) from 1948 to 1980; and **Nick Vista, '54,** assistant SID from 1955 to 1980, and SID 1980 to 1988.

For 40 years, these two popular communicators told the Michigan State sports story with eminent success nationwide. They had the reputation of running the best sports information program in the country. They established the highest standards of sports information integrity and service. They made friends for MSU from coast to coast, enhancing the university's reputation with sports journalists everywhere. And, their timely sports publicity thrusts and comprehensive news coverage helped elevate many MSU athletes to All-American status, and coaches to national honors. They deserve the appellation "Poets in the Press Box," which they truly were.

Former ***Detroit News*** **sports columnist Joe Falls said of Stabley, "He did more than anyone else to put Michigan State on the sports map.** When the networks first started televising college football in the 1950s, he recognized the impact this would create and made Michigan State the most desirable campus in the country to visit. He offered a kind of warm hospitality unknown anywhere else. And, with Duffy Daugherty there to serve as the perfect host with his Irish wit and wisdom, MSU became the most popular stop in the land."

Writing about Stabley in 2004, Vista said, "The Spartan Stadium press box, enlarged in 1957, was built to specifics Stabley encouraged. It turned out to be one of the nation's finest facilities. It featured superb camera angles for television and close proximity to the field seating for the working press. A press lounge served pre-game lunches that once a year featured turkey provided by the MSU poultry department. Choice Michigan apples were placed at every seat. Famed New York sports writer Red Smith was so impressed with the box that he dubbed it, 'The Stabley Hilton.'" The Spartan Stadium press box, fittingly, was named in Stabley's honor in 1980 when he retired.

Vista wrote, "Fred was a pioneer with the College Sports Information Directors of America (CoSIDA) formed in 1955, and was its fourth president in 1958-1959." He won CoSIDA's top honor, the Arch Ward award in 1962. He was in the original class of the CoSIDA Hall of Fame in 1969. He was among the first inductees into the MSU Athletics Hall of Fame in 1992, and is a member of the Michigan Journalism Hall of Fame as well as the Lansing Sports Hall of Fame. He was inducted into the Michigan Sports Hall of Fame in 2004.

Stabley co-authored *Spartan Saga,* a history of Spartan athletics, with Lyman Frimodig in 1971. In 1975 he wrote *The Spartans—Michigan State Football,* and produced a second edition in 1988.

One of his lasting contributions was launching the communications careers of dozens of MSU students whom he mentored as Spartan Sports aides while they were on campus, including Nick Vista and the author.

Nick Vista, Stabley's assistant for 25 years, was the first assistant SID in America to be voted into the CoSIDA Hall of Fame. He served eight years as SID.

Terry Denbow, MSU's vice president of university relations, stated, "Nick was the consummate professional—committed to the integrity of the public relations profession which he loved. He had an appreciation for Michigan State University, recognizing that athletics were a part of the university...and not apart from it. He was concerned about the reputation of MSU and the athletic program. He had the ability to bring the needs of the news media to the university, and the needs of the university to the media."

Nick's commitment to serving the sports news media was remarkable. He helped newsmen meet tough deadlines with critical information at all hours of the day. Nick was ever the goodwill ambassador for MSU. His friendly demeanor was welcomed by stressed-out writers. And, Nick won over many sports journalists for Michigan State with his objectivity. He made it a practice not to hold ill-will towards writers who on some occasions produced negative stories. This demeanor paid dividends in the long run, creating friends for MSU as well as favorable news coverage.

Nick Vista, left, Sports Information Director, 1980-1988, with Mike Pearson, Assistant SID, at Jenison Fieldhouse. Photo: 1984.

Thirty-Eight Spartans in National or International Halls of Fame

Fourteen MSU coaches, sixteen former athletes, three athletic directors, one athletic trainer, and three retired staff members are in national or international Halls of Fame.

Fendley Collins, MSU wrestling coach from 1929 through 1961, was elected to the Helms Foundation Wrestling Hall of Fame in 1956. His teams finished as NCAA runnersup in 1941, 1942, and 1948. He coached 20 wrestlers who won NCAA and national AAU titles. His 1961 team won MSU's first Big Ten wrestling title.

Ben VanAlstyne, MSU basketball coach, 1926-1949, who posted a 231-163 winning record, was inducted into the Helms Foundation Hall of Fame for basketball achievement in 1959.

Jack Heppinstall, MSU athletic trainer for 45 years (1914-1959), was inducted into the National Athletic Trainers Association Hall of Fame in 1962.

John H. Kobs, MSU baseball coach from 1925 to 1963, was inducted into the American Association of College Baseball Coaches Hall of Fame in 1966. His 39-year record was 576-377-16. His teams had winning records in 35 seasons, including the 1954 Big Ten title and a third place finish in the NCAA tournament.

Burl Jennings (Bo), Merle Jennings (Cut), and William "Billy" Martin—were elected to the Helms Foundation Amateur Wrestling Hall of Fame in 1966. The Jennings twins won NCAA wrestling titles in 1941 and 1942. Merle Jennings also won a National AAU title in 1943. Martin, who had a 19-4 record as an MSU wrestler in 1939 and 1940, was the first high school wrestling coach ever to be elected to the Hall of Fame. His Granby High School (Norfolk, VA) teams produced 75 college wrestlers, five of whom became NCAA champions.

Biggie Munn (Munn Arena), MSU's winningest football coach (.857 winning percentage, 1947-1954), and most successful athletic director, guiding MSU to six Big Ten all-sports titles and 11 seconds (1954-1971), was selected by the National Association of Collegiate Athletic Directors for the United Savings Helms Hall of Fame in 1972. In 1975, Munn, who had been an All-American fullback and guard at the University of Minnesota in 1931, was named to the Citizens Savings College Football Hall of Fame.

Charles "Mac" McCaffree, Jr. (McCaffree IM West indoor and outdoor pools), retired swimming coach, was elected to the International Swimming Hall of Fame in 1976. He coached MSU swimmers who won 22 individual NCAA titles, 34 individual Big Ten titles, and a National AAU team title. In his 28 year career (1941-1969) he led MSU to 24 consecutive winning seasons and an all-time dual meet record of 191 wins, 58 losses and two ties. He coached the U.S. Pan American team in 1959 and was past president of the College Swimming Coaches Association of America.

Weldon Olson, MSU ice hockey MVP in 1953, leading scorer in 1954, and co-captain 1955 won Olympic gold and silver medals as a member of the U.S. Olympic hockey championship team in 1960, and the U.S. Olympic hockey runners-up in 1956. He has been inducted in the Olympic Hall of Fame.

Charles Bachman, who was head football coach at Michigan State from 1933 through 1946, was named to the National Football Hall of Fame in 1978. Bachman led the Spartans to a 70-34-10 record in 13 years (no football played in 1943 due to WWII). He was an All-American at Notre Dame in 1916 and was coached by assistant coach Knute Rockne. He played center for the national champion Great Lakes Naval Training Station in 1919. He then coached at Northwestern, Kansas State, Florida, Michigan State and Hillsdale.

Ralph H. Young (Ralph Young Track and Field; Ralph Young Fund), MSU athletic director, 1923-1954, was elected to the National Association of College Directors of Athletics Hall of Fame in 1979. Young was instrumental in hiring and inspiring head coaches of every sport Michigan State competed in for three decades. Sports information director Fred Stabley, Sr. commented, "Without Young and his exuberant public relations work, it is a safe bet MSU would not be in the Big Ten today.

Pete Newell, who coached Michigan State basketball for the Spartans first four seasons in the Big Ten—1950-51 through 1953-54—was selected for the Basketball Hall of Fame in 1979. Newell, who went on to coach the University of California at Berkeley, led the Golden Bears to the NCAA championship in 1959.

Herb Adderley, All-American halfback who played in four Super Bowls and won three championship rings, was inducted into the Pro Football Hall of Fame in 1980. Adderley played for Green Bay, 1961-1969, winning in two Super Bowls, and with the Dallas Cowboys, 1970-1972, winning in one of two Super Bowl appearances.

Bob Devaney, an assistant MSU coach under Biggie Munn, who went on to coach Nebraska to two national championships, was inducted into the College Football Hall of Fame in 1981.

Duffy Daugherty (Daugherty Football Building), MSU's head football coach from 1954 through 1972, was inducted into the College Football Hall of Fame by the National Football Foundation in 1984. Daugherty led the Spartans to two consecutive undefeated regular seasons, national championships and Big Ten titles in 1965 and 1966. Daugherty was named college "Coach of the Year" for his 1955 and 1965 teams. His Spartans won the 1956 Rose Bowl, and he coached 27 All-Americans.

Dan Devine, an assistant coach under Biggie Munn who went on to coach Notre Dame to a national championship, and coach the Green Bay Packers, was inducted into the College Football Hall of Fame in 1985.

Bruce Fossum, MSU men's golf coach, was elected to the NCAA Golf Coaches Hall of Fame in 1985.

Ernestine Russell Weaver, Spartan gymnast, 1957-1961, was inducted into the National Gymnastics Hall of Fame in 1987. She was head women's gymnastic coach at the University of Florida, and led the Gators to three national titles. In her coaching career at Florida, her teams had a 140-win, 8-loss dual meet record. She produced 80 All-Americans and ten individual national champions.

Mary Fossum, MSU women's golf coach for 16 years, was inducted into the National Collegiate Golf Hall of Fame in 1989. In the 1970s, she led MSU to five consecutive Big Ten titles. She also coached the Spartans to Big Ten championships in 1982 and 1984. She was voted NCAA Midwest Region "Coach of the Year" in 1984.

Grady Peninger, head wrestling coach for 24 years, retired in 1986 and was inducted into the Helms Hall of Fame. He also served as president of the National Wrestling Coaches Association. Peninger led the Spartans to the NCAA team wrestling title in 1967, and to seven consecutive Big Ten team titles—1966 through 1972. He coached wrestlers to eleven individual NCAA titles and 43 individual Big Ten titles.

He was the first Big Ten coach to produce a three-time NCAA champion (Greg Johnson), and a four-time NCAA finalist (Pat Milkovich). Peninger was a National freestyle wrestling champion in 1945.

Stan Drobac, MSU tennis coach from 1958 to 1989 and 1953 MSU Big Ten singles and doubles tennis champion, was inducted into the Intercollegiate Tennis Hall of Fame in 1991. He coached the Spartans to a Big Ten title in 1967 and produced ten league singles champions and four doubles champions.

Amo Bessone, Spartan hockey coach from 1951 to 1979, was inducted into the U.S. Hockey Hall of Fame in 1992. Bessone led MSU to its first NCAA hockey championship in 1966. His 1959 team was NCAA runner-up. And, his 1967 team placed third in the NCAA tournament.

George Szypula, MSU's first gymnastic coach, who served for 38 years, was named to the Polish Hall of Fame in 1985. He led the Spartan gymnasts to an NCAA team title in 1958.

Tish Loveless, Ph.D. '77, was named to the National Association of Collegiate Directors of Athletics Hall of Fame in 1989. Loveless coached 28 Michigan Intercollegiate Athletic Association women's championship teams in

31 years at Kalamazoo College, where she also served as director of athletics. Her tennis teams won 25 league titles. She also coached two champion teams in archery and one in field hockey.

Nell Jackson, former MSU women's athletics director, was inducted into the International Women's Sports Hall of Fame in 1993. She served as women's track coach and assistant athletics director from 1973 to 1981.

Fred W. Stabley, Sr., MSU sports information director, 1948-1980, was inducted into the College Sports Information Directors Association Hall of Fame in 1969.

Nick Vista, MSU sports information director, 1980-1988, and assistant director, 1956-1980, was inducted into the College Sports Information Directors Association Hall of Fame in 1975. Vista was the first assistant sports information director ever to be voted into the hall.

Johnny Pingel, '39, All-American halfback, was elected to the National Football Foundation Hall of Fame in 1968.

Don Coleman, '52, M.A. '58, Ph.D. 1971, was named to the National Football Foundation Hall of Fame in 1975. He was MSU's first unanimous All-American, playing tackle on the great 1950 and 1951 teams that won 17 of 18 games. The 1951 team won the national championship. Coleman was the first MSU football player to have his jersey, No. 78, retired.

George Webster, consensus All-American linebacker on MSU's 1965 and 1966 national champion football teams, was named to the Citizens Savings College Football Hall of Fame in Los Angeles.

Robin Roberts, '47, was elected to the Baseball Hall of Fame in 1976. Roberts won 20 or more games for six consecutive seasons—1950 through 1955—with the Philadelphia Phillies, and compiled a 19-year record of 286 wins. He was named to the National League's All-Star team seven times, and started five All-Star games. Roberts pitched no-hitters for John Kobs' Spartans in 1946 and 1947. His college roommate was Jack Breslin (Breslin Center), MSU's first baseman.

Clarke Scholes, 1952 Olympic 100-meter freestyle swimming champion and record setter, was elected to the International Swimming Hall of Fame in 1980. Scholes was NCAA 100-yard freestyle champion for three consecutive years (1950-1952). He also was the NCAA 50-yard freestyle champion in 1951, and was a member of the NCAA champion 4 x 100-yard relay team.

Charles "Bubba" Smith, All-American defensive end on MSU's 1965 and 1966 national championship teams, and an All-Pro end, was inducted into the National Football Foundation's College Hall of Fame in 1988.

John Wilson, '53, Ph.D. '65, president of Washington & Lee University and Rhodes Scholar, was inducted into the GTE Academic All-America Hall of Fame. Wilson played on MSU's 1951 and 1952 national championship football teams. He was named to the first Academic All-American Football team in 1952. He won the Western Conference (Big Ten) Medal for Scholarship and Athletic Prowess and the John A. Hannah Award for Distinction in Academic and Athletic Activity. As a Rhodes Scholar, Wilson received an M.A. degree from Oxford University in England.

Mel Buschman, '43, M.A. '47, Ph.D. '60, was inducted into the Senior Athletes Hall of Fame in 1992. At age 71, he won five of nine events at the Senior Olympics Indy Classic in Indianapolis. He won the 5,000-meter race walk, the 100-meter dash, the javelin throw, the long jump and the softball throw. Buschman was a retired MSU Extension director and volunteer track coach.

Frank Kush, '53, All-American guard on MSU's 1951 and 1952 national champion football teams, was named to the National Football Foundation College Hall of Game in 1995. He was head football coach at Arizona State and built the Sun Devils program into one of the best in the nation. He led ASU to a 12-0 season in 1975 and a No. 2 national ranking. He was among the top ten winningest coaches at one university, with 176 victories at ASU. And, he was among the top twenty coaches of all time in winning percentage: .764.

Brad Van Pelt, former Spartan football All-American and five-time All-Pro in the National Football League, was inducted into the College Football Hall of Fame in South Bend, Indiana in 2001. In his 1970-1972 MSU career, he made 256 tackles and 14 interceptions. In 1972, he became the first defensive back to win the Maxwell Award as the nation's top collegiate player. He played for 14 years in the NFL.

Sue Ertl, Big Ten golf champion and medalist in 1977 and 1978, was inducted into the National Collegiate Golf Hall of Fame.

Earvin "Magic" Johnson, NBA MVP three times and former MSU basketball All-American, was inducted into the Basketball Hall of Fame in Springfield, Massachusetts on September 27, 2002. Johnson led the Los Angeles Lakers to five NBA titles—1980, 1982, 1986, 1987, and 1988. He also led MSU to an NCAA title in 1979, and his Lansing Everett High School team to the Michigan state championship in 1977. Magic was voted the NBA's most valuable player in 1987, 1989, and 1990. He was voted NBA All-Star MVP twice, and was voted to the all-NBA first team nine times. Johnson also won an Olympic gold medal in 1992, playing on the U.S. "Dream Team," which won the championship.

Institutional, State, or City Halls of Fame

Nine other Spartans have been voted into institutional, state, or City Halls of Fame:

Abe Eliowitz, fullback and halfback, 1930-1932, later was a star in the Canadian Football League, playing for the Ottawa Roughriders and the Montreal Alouettes. Following his pro football career, he was inducted into the Canadian Football Hall of Fame. He also is a member of the Michigan Jewish Sports Hall of Fame.

Edward Klewicki, star end at Michigan State from 1932 through 1934, was inducted into the Polish-American Sports Hall of Fame in 1982. Klewicki was MSC's most valuable player in 1934. He played four years for the Detroit Lions and was a member of their 1935 World Championship team,

Bob Monnett, speedy halfback on the 1930-1932 teams and an honorable mention All-American, played for the Green Bay Packers from 1933-1938. He was inducted into the Packers Hall of Fame in 1973.

Glenn H. Johnson, football letterman in 1941 and 1945, won five Michigan Amateur golf titles—1954, 1955, 1956, 1958, and 1961; and four Michigan Senior Amateur golf titles—1980, 1982, 1983, and 1986. He was inducted into the Michigan Golf Hall of Fame in 1981.

Charles Frankel, MSC basketball and baseball player in 1944-1945, is a member of the Michigan Jewish Sports Hall of Fame.

Leonard Brose, Big Ten tennis singles champion in 1951, is a member of the Michigan Jewish Sports Hall of Fame.

Herb Washington, four-time All-American sprinter who set world records in the 50-yard dash (5.1 seconds), and in the 60-yard dash (5.8 seconds), has been inducted into the Flint, Michigan Hall of Fame.

Ron Perranoski, of the Los Angeles Dodgers, was one of baseball's all-time greatest relief pitchers was inducted into the Polish-American Sports Hall of Fame in 1983.

Joe DeLamielleure, MSU All-American offensive lineman in 1972, was inducted into the Pro Football Hall of Fame in 2003, and into the Buffalo Bills Hall of Fame in 1997. A 13-year National Football League veteran, he was named All-Pro six straight seasons—1975 through 1980. At MSU he was a three-time All-Big Ten selection.

Dave Kaiser, who kicked the 41-yard field goal to win the 1956 Rose Bowl, 17-14 over UCLA, was the first Spartan to be inducted into the Rose Bowl Hall of Fame in 2000. His Rose Bowl kick was made with seven seconds remaining in the game. Earl Morrall, All-American quarterback and twice a Super Bowl winner, was holder for the kick.

Richie Jordan,'67, who lettered in basketball, was inducted into the National High School Hall of Fame in 2001. At Fennville High School (Michigan), he posted a 44.4 scoring average in basketball, which is still a record.

Ed Rutherford, MSU football administrative assistant, was inducted into the Michigan High School Football Coaches Association and the Wayne State University Sports Hall of Fame in 1985.

Paula Saunders, who helped lead MSU's women's basketball team to a Big Ten co-championship in 1997, was inducted into the Detroit Catholic League Hall of Fame. She led MSU in scoring (12.6 points per game), and in rebounding (9 per game), and was voted to the All-Big Ten first team. At Harper Woods Regina High School, she led her team to two Detroit Catholic League titles, in 1990 and 1991.

Chet Aubuchon, MSU's first basketball All-American (played 1938-1942), was inducted into the Indiana Basketball Hall of Fame in 1998.

28 Spartans in the Michigan Sports Hall of Fame

Twenty-eight Spartan coaches, players and athletic directors have been inducted into the Michigan Sports Hall of Fame.

They include: Athletic director and football coach **Clarence L. "Biggie" Munn**, 1961; athletic director **Ralph H. Young**, 1962; baseball coach **John H. Kobs**, 1968; All-American halfback **Johnny Pingel**, 1973; football coach **Hugh "Duffy" Daugherty**, 1975; associate athletic director **Lyman L. Frimodig,** 1976; All-American and Super Bowl quarterback **Earl Morrall**, 1979; four-time NCAA boxing champion **Chuck Davey**, 1980; **Don L. Ridler**, football tackle 1928-1930, who coached all sports at Lawrence Tech and was 198-75 in basketball, taking Tech to the NAIA tournament seven times, the NIT once, 1981; MSU sports information director **Nick Kerbawy**, who later was general manager of the Detroit Lions and the Detroit Pistons, 1985; **Glenn Johnson**, won Michigan Amateur golf title fives times and the Michigan Senior Amateur title four times, 1988; All-American halfback **Lynn Chandnois**, 1988; All-American and pro end **Bob Carey**, 1990; MSU, Hillsdale and Saginaw Valley head football coach **Frank "Muddy" Waters**, 1992; All-American and All-Pro defensive end **Charles "Bubba" Smith**, 1993; MSU alumnus **Carl Angelo** pitched the Grand Rapids Sullivans to five world championships in 1963, 1968, 1969, 1988 and 1990, pitched 13 no-hit games and two perfect games, 1994; MSU hockey coach **Ron Mason**, the winningest coach in college hockey, 1994; All-American and All-Pro halfback **Herb Adderley**, 1996; All-American guard **Don Coleman**, 1997; All-American and All-Pro linebacker **George Webster**, 1998; All-American, All-Pro basketball player **Magic Johnson**, helped MSU win its first national title and led the Los Angeles Lakers to five NBA titles, 1998; former MSU quarterback and head coach of Brother Rice High School in Birmingham, Michigan, **Al Fracassa**, 1999; star end at MSU and twice World Series champion **Kirk Gibson**, 1999; **Robin Roberts**, Baseball Hall of Fame pitcher who started five All-Star games for the National League, 1999; **Jud Heathcote**, MSU basketball coach 1976-1995, who led the Spartans to the NCAA title in 1979, 2000; **Brad Van Pelt,** All-American football player and winner of the 1973 Maxwell Trophy as the nation's outstanding football player, and member of the College Football Hall of Fame, 2002; **Fred W. Stabley, Sr.**, MSU sports information director, 1948-1980, and member of the College Sports Information Director's Hall of Fame, 2004; and **Joe DeLamielleure,** All-American offensive lineman, All-Pro six times, Buffalo Bills Hall of Fame—1997, and Pro Football Hall of Fame—2003, 2004.

Five Spartans in Michigan Amateur Sports Hall of Fame

Glenn H. Johnson, football letterman 1941 and 1945, won five Michigan Amateur golf titles—1954, 1955, 1956, 1958, and 1961; and four Michigan Senior Amateur titles—1980, 1982, 1983, and 1986. He was inducted into the Hall of Fame in 1972.

Carl Angelo, the winningest amateur baseball pitcher in history—353 wins, 69 losses. He threw 13 no-hitters, and two perfect games while leading the Grand Rapids Sullivan's Baseball team to five world championships.

Jim Bibbs, MSU assistant track coach, was inducted into the State of Michigan Amateur Sports Hall of Fame in 1974. He joined two other Spartans already so honored: Olympic figure skater **Virginia Baxter McKendrick**, and two-time Olympic ice hockey forward **Weldon Olson**.

MSU Coaches Named National Coach of the Year 18 Times; Twelve Named Big Ten Coach of the Year; Mason Named CCHA Coach of the Year Seven Times—4 at MSU

Spartan coaches have won 18 national Coach of the Year Awards in nine different sports. It began with head football coach **Biggie Munn (Munn Arena)** being named National Football Coach of the Year in 1952 when Michigan State won its second national football championship.

Duffy Daugherty (Daugherty Football Building), head football coach, was named National Football Coach of the Year twice: in 1955 and 1965. His '55 team was 9-1, winning the 1956 Rose Bowl over UCLA, 17-14, and his 1965 team won MSU's third national championship.

Amo Bessone, hockey coach, was named National Coach of the Year in 1966, when MSU won the NCAA championship.

Gene Kenney, men's soccer coach, was named U.S. Coach of the Year in 1966 by *Pro Soccer Magazine*. At that time Kenney's coaching record for 11 seasons was 90-10-5. MSU had been NCAA team runner-up in 1964 and 1965, and lost in the NCAA semi-finals in 1966. His MSU teams would win the NCAA title in 1967 and 1968. He also was named coach of the year for the 1964-65 season by the MSU student body, who presented him with a trophy.

George Szypula, gymnastics coach, was named National Coach of the Year in 1966.

John Bennington, basketball coach, was runner-up in the voting for National Basketball Coach of Year in 1966.

Frank Kush, (Kush Field in Sun Devil Stadium)'52, former MSU All-American football guard and head football coach at Arizona State University, was named College Coach of the Year for 1975. He led the Sun Devils to a 12-0 season and a No. 2 national ranking in 1975.

Danny Litwhiler, baseball coach, was named College Coach of the Year in 1976.

Chuck Fairbanks, '55, New England Patriots head football coach, was named National Football League Coach of the Year by a vote of the NFL coaches in 1977. Prior to going "pro," Fairbanks was head football coach at the University of Oklahoma, leading them to a 52-15-1 record in seven years.

Darryl Rogers, head football coach, 1976-1979, was named Coach of the Year in 1978 by *The Sporting News.*

Mary Fossum, MSU's first women's golf coach, was named the first woman NCAA Coach of the Year by her peers in the NCAA Women's Golf Association in 1984. At the time of her election, Fossum had led MSU to six Big Ten titles, five of them consecutively.

George Perles, head football coach, was voted National and Big Ten Coach of the Year by Football News in 1987. The Spartans posted a 9-2-1 record, won the Big Ten title, won the 1988 Rose Bowl, and were ranked No. 8 in the nation.

Ron Mason, the winningest hockey coach in America, was named National Coach of the Year in 1992. He led the Spartans to the NCAA Frozen Four for the fourth time in seven years. Mason was named CCHA Coach of the Year four times at MSU: 1985, 1989, 1990, and 1999; and three times at other schools: 1976, 1978, and 1979.

Jud Heathcote, head basketball coach, was named National Coach of the Year by *Sporting News* in 1995. He led the Spartans to a 22-6 season, a No. 9 national ranking, and to second place in the Big Ten.

Chuck Erbe, head volleyball coach, was named the American Volleyball Coaches Association Tachikara National Coach of the Year in 1996. He led the MSU women's volleyball team to a 34-3 record, won the Big Ten title and went to the Final Four, losing in the semi-finals to eventual NCAA champion Nebraska.

Tom Izzo, head basketball coach, was named national and Big Ten Coach of the Year for 1998. He led the 22-8 Spartans to Big Ten title and to the Sweet Sixteen in the NCAA tournament. In 1999, Izzo was again named National Coach of the Year, leading the Spartans to a second consecutive Big Ten title and to the Final Four in the NCAA tournament. In 2001, Izzo was named NABC National Coach of the Year.

Big Ten Coach of the Year

Thirteen Spartan coaches have won Big Ten Coach of the Year honors in eight different sports.

Denny Stolz, head football coach, was named Big Ten Coach of the Year in 1974. His 7-3-1 Spartans finished third in the Big Ten with a 6-1-1 record.

Darryl Rogers, head football coach, was named Big Ten Coach of the Year in 1978. His Spartans tied Michigan for the Big Ten championship with a 7-1 conference record. Overall, the team was 8-3. The 1978 team averaged 481.3 yards and 41 points per game, both Big Ten records at the time.

Jud Heathcote, head basketball coach, was named Big Ten Coach of the Year in 1978 when the Spartans won the Big Ten title and fell one game short of reaching the Final Four. Again in 1986 he was named Big Ten Coach of the Year. His Spartans posted a 23-8 record, finished third in the Big Ten and reached the Sweet Sixteen in the NCAA tournament. The Spartans beat Big Ten champion Michigan twice.

George Perles, head football coach, named Big Ten Coach of the Year for 1987, when the Spartans won the Big Ten title.

Karen Langeland, women's basketball coach, was named Big Ten Coach of the Year for 1989.

John Narcy, diving coach, was voted Big Ten diving Coach of the Year for 1989.

Tom Smith, baseball coach, was named Big Ten Coach of the Year for 1992. His Spartan team was 36-19.

Tom Minkel, MSU wrestling coach, was voted Big Ten Co-Coach of the Year for 1996.

Tom Izzo, head basketball coach, named Big Ten Coach of the Year for 1998.

Bebe Bryans, MSU women's crew head coach, was named co-Big Ten Rowing Coach of the Year in 2001.

Michele Madison, MSU women's field hockey coach, was named Big Ten Coach of the Year in 2001.

Jacquie Joseph, MSU softball coach, was named Big Ten Coach of the Year in 2003.

John L. Smith, in his first year as MSU's head football coach, was named Big Ten Coach of the Year for 2003. He led the Spartans from a 4-8 season in 2002 to an 8-4 regular season record in 2003.

MSU Alumnus Named PAC-10 Coach of the Year

Tyrone Willingham, '77, head football coach of Stanford University, was named PAC-10 (Pacific Athletic Conference) Coach of the Year for 1996. He led his team to a 7-3-1 record in his first year as head coach. In 2001, he was named head football coach at the University of Notre Dame.

Great Spartan Individual and Team Performances

Michigan State sports fans can luxuriate in the number of outstanding performances by Spartan athletes and teams. These achievements are sprinkled through many sports and throughout the school's athletic history.

1901-1903

M.A.C. basketball teams were undefeated for three straight years. The records: 1900-1901—3-0; 1901-1902—5-0; and 1902-1903—6-0. Opponents included Eastern Michigan, Olivet, Alma, Hillsdale, the Governor's Guard, Detroit YMCA, and the Grand Rapids YMCA.

1904

M.A.C. won Michigan Intercollegiate Athletic Association (MIAA) championships in four sports: football, basketball, baseball and track. The football team went 8-1, losing only to Albion, 4-0. Madison Kuhn wrote in *Michigan State—The First Hundred Years*, that basketball players were skilled at arching shots over the steel beams in the Armory for baskets.

Brewer reported that the athletic field (Old College Field and Kobs Field) was now equipped with movable bleachers, which added to the grandstand, gave the field a seating capacity of over 1,000.

1904

M.A.C.'s Harry Moon was runner-up in the 100- and 200-meter races at the World's Collegiate Championships held in St. Louis, Missouri. He was one of the first sprinters in the nation to run the 100-yard dash in ten seconds. This time was not beaten by anyone in the Michigan Intercollegiate Athletic Association (MIAA) until 1934. During his collegiate career—1902-1905—Moon won nine MIAA sprint titles.

1905

M.A.C. wins State titles in tumbling and track. The track team won all of its meets, including a victory over Notre Dame. The relay team broke a state record that had stood for 17 years. The football team won 9 of 11 games; the baseball team, 12 of 16.

1908

M.A.C.'s first undefeated football team won six games and tied two. Both ties were 0-0 games, one with the University of Michigan and one with DePaul. The Michigan game was played on Old College Field and drew the largest athletic crowd in school history—more than 1,000.

1909

The basketball team won the MIAA championship.

1910

The basketball team repeated as MIAA champions. In athletic director Chester L. Brewer's annual report, he pointed out that the bath house receipts from 900 young men totaled $1,500.

1913

M.A.C.'s football team was undefeated and untied for the first time. Head coach John Macklin led M.A.C. to a 7-0 season record, that included the school's first win over the University of Michigan, 12-7, the Wolverines only loss that season. The Aggies also beat defending Big Ten champion Wisconsin, 12-7.

1914

M.A.C. Rifle Team Wins International Intercollegiate Gallery Championship. In 13 matches, the team shot a series of 12 perfect scores of 1,000 points each. In their first match they shot 998 out of 1,000. Team members were: R.D. Kean, R.A. Pennington, R.R. Clark, S.W. Harman, R.W. Shane, M.R. Freeman, A.J. Patch, E.H. Pate, M.M. Harman, and R.W. Berridge.

1915

M.A.C. Football Team Defeated Michigan, 24-0. Fullback Jerry DaPrato scored all three M.A.C. touchdowns and drop-kicked a 23-yard field goal. He had 153 yards rushing and receiving. Captain Blake Miller, an end and half-back, gained 115 yards. The team won five and lost one during 1915, outscoring opponents 259-38. Daprato and Miller were named the school's first All-Americans.

1916-1920

George Gauthier, Class of 1914, was the first alumnus to coach the basketball team. In four seasons he led M.A.C. to a 4-0 record vs. Notre Dame, and a 3-2 record vs. Michigan. In 1918, he had the distinction of coaching the football and basketball teams to victories over Notre Dame, the only coach ever to do so.

His football team defeated Knute Rockne's first team, 13-7, and in basketball, defeated the Irish 27-12. Over all, his four basketball teams won 47 and lost 39 during the 1916-17, 1917-18, 1918-19, and 1919-20 seasons. Gauthier also served as track coach for M.A.C. in 1918, and as assistant athletic director. At M.A.C., Gauthier played four basketball seasons and was captain his senior year. He went on to become head football coach and athletic director at Ohio Wesleyan for 34 years.

1922

DeGay Ernst set a world record in the 40-yard dash—:04.56 seconds. Ernst was captain of the track team in 1922-1923. He held eight M.A.C. track records in dash and hurdle events.

1925

Fred P. Alderman, '27, set a 220-yard dash record of :21.12 seconds at the Big Ten meet. At that time, other schools were allowed to compete in the Big Ten track meet.

1927

Fred Alderman("S" center) wins 1927 NCAA 100-yard dash title at Chicago's Soldiers' Field. Bohn Grim ("S" right) finished 4th. Alderman also won the 1927 NCAA 220-yard title, becoming the 1st Spartan to win individual NCAA titles. At another track meet, Alderman and Grim, ran with Forrest Lang and Henry Henson on MSC's 440-yard relay team to tie the World Record in 1927.

Fred P. Alderman, '27 and 1927 team captain, won the NCAA 100-yard and the 220-yard dash titles—the first NCAA individual titles for any Michigan State athlete.

MSC 440-Yard Relay Team Ties World Record—Sprinters Forrest Lang, Henry Henson, Bohn Grim, and Fred Alderman tied the 440-yard relay world record.

1928

Fred P. Alderman became the school's first Olympic Gold medal winner as a member of the world record-setting U.S. 1,600-meter relay team (3:41.1) at the 1928 Olympics in Amsterdam.

1931

Clark Chamberlain won the NCAA two-mile run title.

1932

Head football coach Jim Crowley, one of Notre Dame's legendary Four Horsemen, resigned after four successful seasons. His 1929, 1930, 1931 and 1932 Spartan teams won 22, lost 8, and tied 3. His coaching brought Michigan State into national prominence. In 1930 and 1931, the Spartans fought the University of Michigan to scoreless ties.

His 1932 team won seven games, including back-to-back wins in New York state against eastern powers Fordham, 19-13, and Syracuse, 27-13. This caught the attention of the east coast sports writers.

Walter Jacobs, four-time National Wrestling Champion.

1936

Walter Jacobs won the NCAA 158-pound wrestling title as a senior at MSC. The next three seasons, he won National AAU titles while a graduate student at Cornell.

1937

Walter Jacobs won the National Amateur Athletic Union (NAAU) wrestling title at 160 pounds.

1938

Walter Jacobs won the National AAU wrestling title at 160 pounds.

1938

Harvey Woodstra tied world's records in the 60-yard high hurdles in 7.4 seconds and the 70-yard high hurdles in 8.6 seconds.

1939

The Cross Country team won the NCAA championship—Michigan State's first national title in any sport. Roy Fehr of Royal Oak and Dick Frey of New York paced the team.

Walter Jacobs won his fourth consecutive National Wrestling Championship—the National AAU wrestling title at 160 pounds.

The Walter C. Jacobs Wrestling Award is now presented annually to the Spartan wrestler with the highest point total for the season.

1940

Roy Fehr won the NCAA outdoor two-mile run championship.

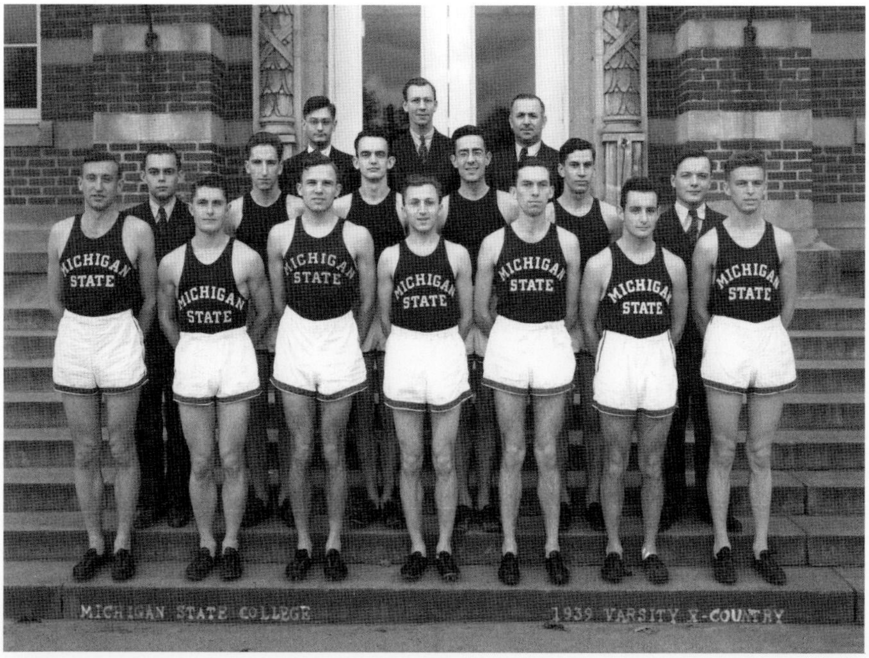

1939 NCAA Cross Country Champions—the first Spartan team to win a National Championship in any sport. Front Row—Warren Anderson, George Keller, Roy Fehr, Capt. Dick Frey, Bill Mansfield, Ed Mills, and Alfred Mangan; 2nd Row—D. Smith, assistant manager, W. Beardsley, D. Cowden, W. Scales, A. Wetzel, and G. Campbell, assistant manager; Top Row—Lauren Brown, coach, W. Christman, manager, and Jack Heppinstall, trainer.

1941

The Jennings twins—Merle (Cut), and Burl (Bo) won NCAA wrestling titles at 121- and 128-pounds, respectively. They had been AAU Junior Champions in 1940, and Oklahoma high school state champions in 1939.

MSC's Wrestling Team was runner-up in the NCAA tournament.

1942

Merle (Cut) Jennings, Burl (Bo) Jennings, and William Maxwell won NCAA wrestling titles at 121, 128, and 136 pounds, respectively. Michigan State hosted the NCAA championships at Jenison Fieldhouse. The remarkable Jennings twins were featured in a multi-page spread in *Life* magazine.

MSC's Wrestling Team was runner-up in the 1942 NCAA tournament.

Chet Aubuchon, MSU's first basketball All-American (played 1938-1942), was inducted into the Indiana Basketball Hall of Fame in 1998.

1943

Merle (Cut) Jennings won his third national wrestling crown, a National AAU title, this time at 134 pounds. J. William Maxwell won his second national wrestling crown, a National AAU title, at 145 pounds.

Bill Zurakowski won the NCAA 120-pound boxing title.

Chuck Davey, a 17-year old freshman, won his first NCAA boxing title at 127 pounds. He was the **youngest boxer in NCAA history to win a championship**.

Chet Aubuchon, MSC's first basketball All-American was nicknamed "The Houdini of the Hardwoods."

1945

Coach Charles McCaffree's MSC swimming team won the National Amateur Athletic Union outdoor swimming championship. Dave Seibold led the team, winning the 200-meter breaststroke, the 300-meter individual medley, and helped win the 300-meter medley relay with Howard Patterson and Jim Quigley.

Gale Mikles won the National Amateur Athletic Union 145-pound wrestling title as a 17-year old freshman.

Swimming Seibold Brothers of Jackson, Michigan—L to R: Paul, Dave (uniform), and Jack, with MSC Coach Charles McCaffree—1946. Dave led MSC to 1945 Outdoor National AAU Team Title, winning the 200-meter breaststroke, the 300-meter individual medley, and the 300-meter medley relay with Howard Patterson and Jim Quigley. Dave, above, had just returned from the Army.

1946

MSC swimmers won the NCAA 400-yard relay title in 3:27.2. The team included: Zigmund Indyke, John DeMond, Jim Quigley, and Robert Alwardt.

Spartan pitching ace Robin Roberts threw a no-hitter to defeat Great Lakes Naval Training Station, 8-0. Great Lakes was loaded with big league baseball players and had been expected to win easily.

1947

Gale Mikles won the NCAA 155-pound wrestling title. He placed second in the NCAA championships in 1948, when he captained the Spartan team. Legendary head wrestling coach Fendley Collins described Mikles as having "the speed of a sprinter, the agility and suppleness of a dancer, and the athletic poise of a champion."

Robin Roberts, star pitcher, signed with the Philadelphia Phillies for $25,000 in 1947. He would win 286 major league games and be inducted into the Baseball Hall of Fame in 1976. An MSC forward, he was named Michigan's College Basketball Player of the Year in 1946 by the *Detroit Free Press.*

Chuck Davey, returning from WWII, **won his second NCAA boxing title**, this time at 135 pounds.

George Hoogerhyde won the NCAA swimming 1,500-meter freestyle title.

Most Exciting Track Meet in Michigan State History—On January 25, 1947 at Jenison Fieldhouse, it came down to the final event between Michigan State and Ohio State. Whoever won the mile relay would win the meet. The final 440-yard leg was a duel between OSU's Mal Whitfield (1948 NCAA 880-yard champion and U.S. Olympian), and MSU's Jack Dianetti, an 18-year old freshman speedster.

Whitfield took the baton ahead of Dianetti as they started their two 220-yard laps around the Jenison clay track. At the end of the first 220, Whitfield had a six-yard lead and maintained it as he disappeared behind the bleachers on the south side of the Jenison track. Both runners were out of view for a few seconds...then as they reappeared from behind the bleachers, with less than 100 yards to go, Dianetti had pulled even with Whitfield. The 1,700 spectators exploded with a roar (including the author). At the top of the final curve of the track, with 65 yards to go, Dianetti put on a sensational kick, and flew by Whitfield. He hit the tape five yards ahead of the future Olympian, and Michigan State had the victory—66 7/12 to 66 5/12.

MSC Coach Karl Schlademan said it was "the most dramatic" moment he had experienced in 30 years of coaching (*Spartan Sports Encyclopedia* by Jack Seibold, Sports Publishing LLC, 2003).

1948

MSC's Cross Country Team won three National Titles. Coach Karl Schlademan's cross-country team won an unprecedented three national titles: the NCAA, IC4A and Senior AAU competitions.

MSC's 400-yard freestyle relay team swam to the NCAA title in 3:31. Team members were: Abel Gilbert, George Hoogerhyde, Robert Allwardt, and Jim Duke.

Chuck Davey won his third NCAA boxing crown, this time at 136 pounds. He also was a member of the U.S. Olympic boxing team at the Games held in London.

Ernie Charboneau won the NCAA boxing title at 112 pounds.

Richard Dickenson won the NCAA 136—pound wrestling title.

Leland G. Merrill won an Olympic wrestling bronze medal at the London Olympic Games at 160.5 pounds, and won the National AAU Senior wrestling title at 160 pounds.

MSC's Wrestling Team placed second in the NCAA championships. Coach Fendley Collins' wrestlers won every dual meet of the season.

All-American Fred Johnson tied the World Record in the 65-yard low hurdles and won the NCAA outdoor long jump title in 1949. His championship leap was 25'2".

1949

Chuck Davey won an unprecedented fourth NCAA boxing title at the NCAA Boxing Tournament held at Michigan State's Jenison Fieldhouse. He won at 145 pounds. Davey is the only boxer in college history to win four NCAA titles: 1943, 1947, 1948, and 1949. He captained the boxing team for three years (1947-1949).

MSC's cross country team won its second consecutive NCAA title, and third overall.

Fred Johnson, All-American track star, tied the world record in the 65-yard low hurdles, and won the NCAA outdoor long jump title at 25' 2".

Mel Stout won five NCAA gymnastics titles—flying rings, floor exercise, horizontal bar, parallel bars, and all-around (tie).

Robert Maldegan won the National AAU heavyweight wrestling title.

1950

Clarke Scholes won the NCAA 100-yard freestyle title in swimming.

Five MSC teams finished in the top ten nationally: Cross country—No.2; Boxing—No. 3, Gymnastics—No. 5, Swimming—No. 5, and Football—No. 7.

Two-Mile Relay Team sets World Record—Dave Peppard, Don Makielski, Warren Druetzler, and Bill Mack set a world record in the two-mile relay at the Los Angeles Coliseum: 7:31.8, breaking the record of 7:34.6 set in 1941.

1951

John D. Wilson, '53, won a Rhodes Scholarship in 1953. He was a defensive back on MSC's 1950, 1951 and 1952 teams which went 26-1 and won national titles in 1951 and 1952. He was senior class president and straight "A" student.

In Michigan State's first year of eligibility for competition in Big Ten Conference sports, the Spartans won two Big Ten team championships, and 17 individual Big Ten titles.

MSC's football team won its first National Championship.

MSC's boxing team won its first NCAA title.

MSC's tennis team won Michigan State's First Big Ten Title in any sport.

MSC's cross country team won the Big Ten title.

Seven MSC teams finished in the top ten nationally: Football—National Champions, Boxing—NCAA champions, Swimming No. 2, Track and Field—No. 4, Wrestling—No. 6, Fencing—No. 7, and Gymnastics—No. 7.

Mel Stout won five NCAA gymnastics titles—all-around, flying rings, floor exercise, horizontal bar, and parallel bars; and **five Big Ten gymnastics titles**—all-around, floor exercise, still rings, parallel bars, and horizontal bar.

Clarke Scholes won NCAA and Big Ten swimming titles in the 50- and 100-yard freestyle events. Big Ten 50-yard time—:23.0; 100-yard time—:50.7.

Gene Gibbons won the NCAA 167-pound wrestling title, and the Big Ten 177 pound title.

Bob Hoke won the National AAU 145-pound wrestling title.

George Bender won the Big Ten 177-pound wrestling title.

Gerald Black won the NCAA 145-pound boxing title.

Chuck Speiser won the NCAA 175-pound boxing title.

Warren Druetzler won the NCAA outdoor mile run title.

MSC won the NCAA 400-yard freestyle relay team title in swimming. Team members were: Dave Hoffman, Jim Quigley, Clarke Scholes and George Hoogerhyde.

Bert McLachlan won Big Ten swimming titles in the 220-yard freestyle in 2:10.9, and in the 440-yard freestyle in 4:41.8.

Bob Carey won the Big Ten outdoor track shot put title at 53 feet.

Jesse Thomas won the Big Ten outdoor track title in the 100-yard dash in 10.0 seconds, and the 220-yard low hurdles in 23.8.

Don Makielski won the Big Ten outdoor track 880-yard run title in 1:56.

Leonard Brose won the No. 1 Big Ten tennis singles title.

Dick Reiger won the No. 6 Big Ten tennis singles title.

Leonard Brose and John Sahratian won the No. 1 Big Ten tennis doubles title.

1952

MSC won its second consecutive football National Championship.

MSC's cross country team won its fourth NCAA title.

MSC's cross country team won its second Big Ten title.

Six MSC teams finish in top ten nationally: Football—National Champions, Cross Country—NCAA champions, Boxing—No. 2, Fencing—No. 4, Swimming—No. 4, and Gymnastics—No. 6.

Clarke Scholes won the Olympic gold medal in the 100-meter freestyle and set a new Olympic record at the 1952 games in Helsinki, Finland. **He also won his third consecutive NCAA swimming crown in the 100-yard freestyle.** He won the Big Ten 100-yard freestyle title in :49.8 seconds—one of the first 100-yard sprints under 50 seconds in the U.S.

Chuck Speiser won his second consecutive NCAA boxing title, this time at 178 pounds.

Lynn Chandnois, Pittsburgh Steeler halfback, was named National Football League Player of the Year by the Washington Touchdown Club. He played for the Steelers from 1950 to 1956, and was named to the NFL All-Pro team three times. He was a consensus All-American for State in 1949. He holds two all-time MSU football records: 7.48 yards per carry in 1948; and 20 career interceptions. He was named Michigan's Outstanding Amateur Athlete of the Year in 1950, and elected to the Michigan Sports Hall of Fame in 1988.

George Bender won the Big Ten 167-pound wrestling title.

Stan Drobac and Tom Belton won the No. 1 Big Ten tennis doubles title.

Dick Roberts and Jim Pore won the No. 3 Big Ten tennis doubles title.

Richard Berry won the Big Ten fencing title in epee.

Richard Freiheit won the Big Ten fencing title in sabre.

1953

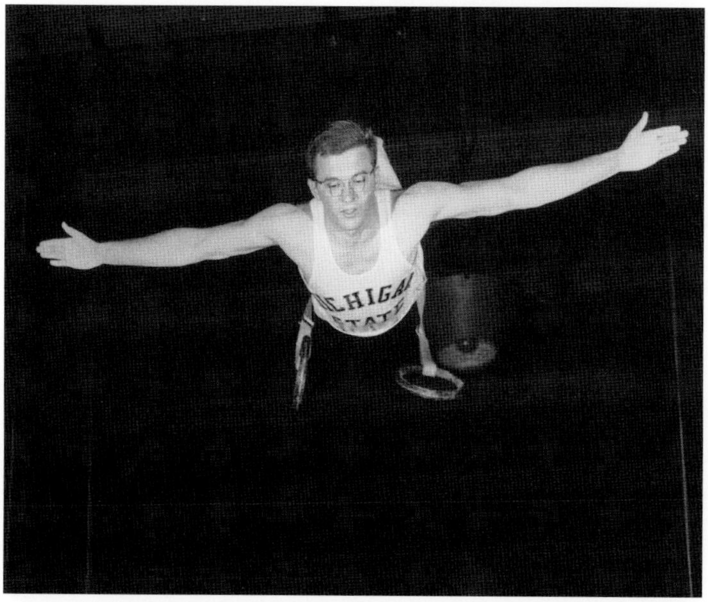

Carlton Rintz won six NCAA and ten Big Ten gymnastics titles in his three-year career, 1953-1955.

MSC's Football team won the Big Ten title.

MSC's Cross Country team won its third consecutive Big Ten title.

Six MSC teams finish in top ten nationally: Football—No. 3, Boxing—No. 4, Swimming—No. 5, Cross Country—No. 6, Gymnastics—No. 7, and Wrestling—No. 8.

Carlton Rintz won three NCAA gymnastics titles—pommel horse, horizontal bars, and floor exercise. **He also won four Big Ten titles**—still rings, horizontal bar, pommel horse, and floor exercise.

Tom Hickey won the NCAA 165-pound boxing title.

James Sinadinos won the National AAU 136-pound wrestling title.

Bert McLachlan won the Big Ten swimming 440-yard freestyle title in 4:43.9.

John Dudeck won the Big Ten swimming 100-yard breaststroke title in 1:01.1.

Bob Hoke won the Big Ten 157-pound wrestling title.

Vito Perrone won the Big Ten 167-pound wrestling title.

Jim Kepford won the Big Ten outdoor track mile run title in 4:18.4.

Stan Drobac won the No. 1 Big Ten tennis singles title.

Jim Pore won the No. 5 Big Ten tennis singles title.

Stan Drobac and Tom Belton won the No. 1 Big Ten tennis doubles title.

Dick Roberts and John Sahratian won the No. 2 Big Ten tennis doubles title.

Jim Vrooman won the Big Ten indoor track high jump title at 6' 4½".

Richard Berry won the Big Ten fencing title in foil.

John D. Wilson, football defensive back who played on the Spartans 1951 and 1952 national championship teams, won a Rhodes Scholarship in 1953. Wilson became a distinguished university administrator, capping his career as president of Washington and Lee University.

1954

MSC won its first Big Ten All-Sports title.

MSC's Baseball team won its first Big Ten title, and finished third in the NCAA.

Five MSC teams finish in top ten nationally: Baseball—No. 3, Gymnastics—No. 5, Boxing—No. 6, Wrestling—No. 6, and Swimming—No. 8.

Bob Hoke won the NCAA and Big Ten 157 pound wrestling titles.

Norman Gill won the National AAU 147-pound Greco-Roman wrestling title.

Herb Odom won the NCAA 147 pound boxing title.

John Dudeck won the Big Ten swimming 100-yard breaststroke title in :59.7.

Carlton Rintz won three Big Ten gymnastics titles—flying rings (tie), horizontal bar and all-around event.

Ken Cook tied teammate Carlton Rintz for the Big Ten gymnastics title in the rings event.

Dana Squire won the No. 6 Big Ten tennis singles title.

John Cook won the Big Ten indoor track 880-yard run title in 1:54.9, and the outdoor track mile run title in 4:14.1.

1955

MSU's cross country team won its fifth NCAA title.

MSU's boxing team won its second NCAA title.

Carlton Rintz won three NCAA gymnastics titles—horizontal bar, parallel bars, and pommel horse. **Rintz also won Big Ten titles** in the rings, pommel horse and all-around event.

Clarke Scholes won the Pan American Games gold medal and set a Pan American record in the 100-yard freestyle swimming event. He also won a gold medal as a member of the U.S. 400-meter freestyle relay team.

MSU won the Big Ten team cross country title.

Henry Kennedy became MSU's first Big Ten individual cross country champion, running the four-mile course in 19:06.

Ed Brabham won the Big Ten indoor track 60-yard dash title in 6.2 seconds, and the outdoor track long jump title at 23 feet, 8 inches.

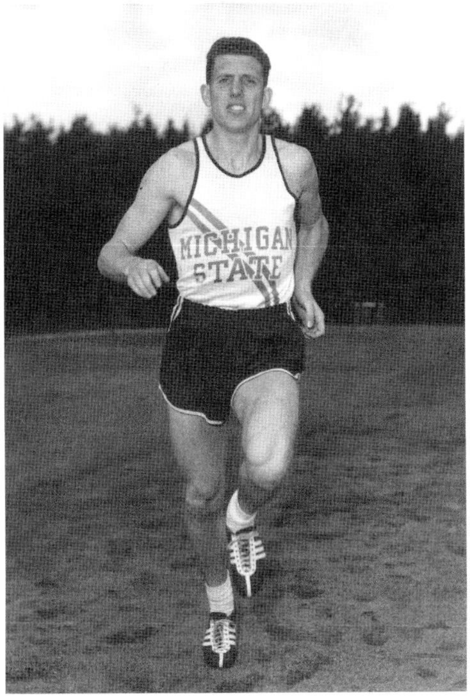

Henry Kennedy won the 1956 NCAA 3,000-meter steeplechase outdoor title. He was Big Ten Cross Country champion in 1955, and 1956 Outdoor Big Ten Two-Mile champion.

Kevan Gosper won the Big Ten indoor track 440-yard dash title in 0:48.2 seconds; and the 600-yard run title in 1:11.3. He also won the Big Ten outdoor track 440-yard run title in 47.8.

George Thomas won the Big Ten fencing title in sabre.

Vincent Magi won a silver medal as a member of the U.S. baseball team at the Pan American Games.

Ernestine Russell won a National Amateur Athletic Union (AAU) title in gymnastics.

1956

Dave Kaiser kicked a 41-yard field goal with seven seconds left in the 1956 Rose Bowl game to defeat UCLA 17-14. The game was television's all-time top-rated college football bowl game, with a 67 percent share of the TV audience. In 2000, Kaiser was inducted into the Rose Bowl Hall of Fame.

MSU's cross country team won its second consecutive NCAA title, and sixth overall.

Carol E. Heiss won the Olympic silver medal in figure skating at the Winter Olympic Games. Heiss trained at Michigan State for several consecutive summers and received fitness training at MSU. Although not an alumna, she was adopted by Spartans.

Kevan Gosper and David Lean each won silver medals at the 1956 Melbourne Olympic Games as members of the Australian 1,600-meter relay team. At MSU, Gosper won the Big Ten 440-yard title twice and the 600-yard title once.

William Steuart was a member of the South African Olympic swimming team.

Weldon Olson won a silver medal as a member of the U.S. Olympic team.

Ernestine Russell was a member of the women's Canadian Olympic gymnastics team.

Henry Kennedy won the NCAA 3,000-meter steeplechase title in outdoor track. He won the Big Ten outdoor track two-mile title in 9:19.1. He also was the Big Ten cross country champion, running four miles in 20:25.3.

Selwyn Jones won the NCAA 10,000-meter run title in outdoor track.

Jim Sinadinos won the NCAA 137-pound wrestling title, and the Big Ten 137-pound wrestling title.

Ken Maidlow won the National AAU 191-pound Greco-Roman wrestling title.

Choken Maekawa won the NCAA 119-pound boxing title.

Donald Stroud won the Big Ten 123-pound wrestling title.

Ed Brabham won the Big Ten indoor track 60-yard dash title in 6.3 seconds; the outdoor track titles in the 100-yard dash at 9.7 seconds, and the 220-yard dash in 21.2 seconds.

Joe Savoldi won the Big Ten indoor track 70-yard high hurdle title in 8.5 seconds.

Don Leas won the Big Ten gymnastics rings title.

Roland Brown won the Big Ten gymnastics floor exercise title.

1957

MSU's basketball team won the Big Ten title and went to the Final Four for the first time. The Spartans lost in the semi-final game to North Carolina, 74-70, in triple overtime.

MSU's Cross Country Team won its third consecutive Big Ten title, and sixth overall.

MSU's swimming team won the Big Ten title.

MSU won the NCAA 400-yard medley relay event in swimming. Team members were: Don Nichols, Paul Reinke, Roger Harmon, and Frank Parrish.

Tim Woodin won the National AAU 191-pound wrestling title.

Paul Reinke won the Big Ten swimming 100-yard breaststroke title in 1:03.8.

MSU won the Big Ten swimming 400-yard freestyle relay title in 3:25.

Dave Lean won the Big Ten indoor track 440-yard run title in 49.4 seconds; and the outdoor track 880-yard run title in 1:52.9.

George Thomas won the Big Ten fencing title in sabre.

1958

MSU won its seventh NCAA cross country team title and its fourth consecutive Big Ten title, which was its seventh overall.

MSU's gymnastics team won its first NCAA title.

Crawford "Forddy" Kennedy won the NCAA individual cross country title (4 miles), leading the Spartan team to the NCAA championship. He was an All-American in 1957, 1958, and 1959.

Frank Modine won two NCAA swimming titles—the 100-yard and 200-yard breaststroke events.

William Steuart won NCAA and Big Ten swimming titles in the 440-yard and 1,500-meter freestyle events. His times in the Big Ten were—4:37.5 in the 440, and 18:40.5 in the 1,500.

John Horne won the NCAA 178-pound boxing title.

Ken Maidlow won the NCAA 191-pound wrestling title.

Don Patterson won the NCAA 100-yard freestyle title in swimming.

Ted Muzyczko won the NCAA gymnastics in the parallel bars event.

Dave Lean won the Big Ten indoor track 600-yard run title in 1:10.2; and the outdoor track 880-yard title in 1:50.3.

Crawford "Forddy" Kennedy wins 1958 NCAA Cross Country title, and led the MSU team to the NCAA team title. In 1959, Kennedy won the Big Ten Cross Country title, and the outdoor two-mile run. He was an All-American in 1957, 1958, and 1959.

Tim Woodin won the Big Ten 177-pound wrestling title.

Stan Tarshis won the Big Ten gymnastics horizontal bar title.

1959

MSU won its second consecutive NCAA Cross Country title, and eighth overall, and its fifth consecutive Big Ten title, which was its eighth overall.

MSU won its second Big Ten All-Sports title.

MSU's basketball team won the Big Ten title.

MSU's ice hockey team won the Big Ten title.

Ernestine Russell Carter won four gold medals in gymnastics for her native Canada in the Pan American Games—all-around, side horse vault, balance beam, and uneven parallel bars.

Crawford "Forddy" Kennedy won the Big Ten cross country title (four miles) in 20:12.3, and the outdoor track two-mile title in 9:15.1.

John Horne won the NCAA 178-pound boxing title.

William Steuart won two NCAA swimming titles—in the 440-yard and 1,500-meter freestyle events. He also won **three Big Ten swimming titles**—220-yard freestyle in 2:04.2; 440-yard freestyle in 4:30.9; and the 1,500-meter free style in 18:36.6.

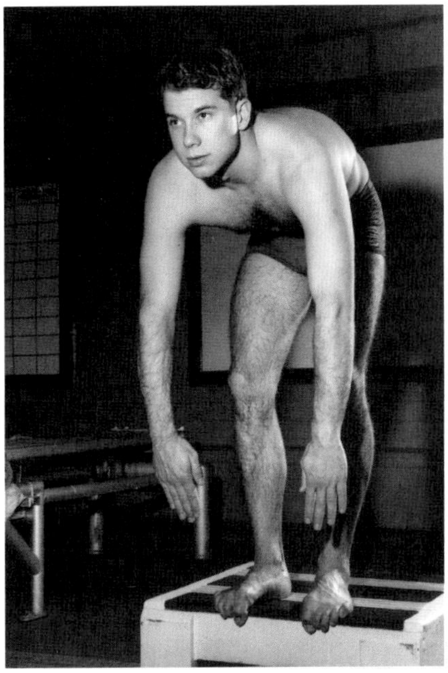

Bill Steuart won NCAA and Big Ten swimming titles in the 400-yard and 1,500-yard freestyle events in 1958 and 1959. He also won the Big Ten 220-yard freestyle in 1959.

Stan Tarshis won the NCAA and Big Ten gymnastics horizontal bar titles.

James Ferguson won a gold medal at the Pan American Games, winning the 174-pound wrestling title. He also won the Big Ten 167-pound wrestling title.

Allan S. Kwartler wins gold medal in fencing (sabre) at the Pan American Games.

Frank Modine won the Big Ten swimming 100-yard breaststroke title in 1:04.8.

Bob Lake won the Big Ten indoor track mile run title in 4:10.9; and the outdoor track mile run title in 4:09.

Norman Young won the Big Ten 130-pound wrestling title.

Tim Woodin won the Big Ten heavyweight wrestling title.

William C. Mansfield won a bronze medal as a member of the U.S. baseball team at the Pan American Games.

Carol Heiss won the 1960 Winter Olympics figure skating gold metal. She skated for several summers at MSU's ice rink in Dem Hall, and took fitness training from an MSU physical educator.

1960

MSU won its third Big Ten All-Sports title.

MSU's Cross Country team won its sixth consecutive Big Ten title, and ninth overall.

Carol E. Heiss won the Olympic gold medal in figure skating at the Squaw Valley, California Games. She trained for several summers at MSU and took fitness training from MSU's Mrs. Kerstin Radabaugh, former Swedish Olympic gymnast. Although not an alumna, Heiss nevertheless was warmly adopted by the MSU family.

Gene Grazia and Weldon Olson won gold medals as members of the U.S. Olympic champion hockey team at Squaw Valley, California, which defeated Russia.

Kevan Gosper, middle-distance sprinter, captained the Australian Olympic team at the Rome Olympic Games. He later rose to become chairman of the Australian Olympic Committee and was elected a vice president of the International Olympic Committee.

John Horne won the NCAA 178-pound boxing title.

Weldon Olson, gold medal winner on the 1960 U.S. Olympic champion hockey team, won a silver medal at the 1956 Winter Olympics. He is in the Olympic Hall of Fame. He was MSU MVP in 1953, leading scorer in 1954, and co-captain in 1955.

Stan Tarshis won NCAA and Big Ten gymnastics horizontal bar titles.

James Ferguson won the National AAU 174-pound wrestling title.

Ron Mescall won the No. 5 Big Ten tennis singles title.

Gerald Young won the Big Ten cross country title, running four miles in 19:35.3.

Willie Atterberry won the Big Ten indoor track 1,000-yard run in 2:11.7.

Mike Kleinhans tied for the Big Ten outdoor track pole vault title at 14-3 5/8ths.

Ernestine Russell was a member of the women's Canadian Olympic gymnastics team.

1961

Norm Young won the NCAA and Big Ten 137-pound wrestling titles.

MSU's football team set a school defensive season record, allowing an average of just 5.6 points per game. The team finished with a 7-2 record and a third place finish in the Big Ten.

MSU's wrestling team won the Big Ten title.

Okla Johnson won the Big Ten 115-pound wrestling title.

Gerald Young won the Big Ten indoor track two-mile run title in 9:08.1.

Don Johnson won the Big Ten fencing title in sabre.

Dick Hall won the No.2 Big Ten tennis singles title.

Jack Damson won the No. 4 Big Ten tennis singles title.

Gene Hunt reached the semi-finals of NCAA golf tournament, but lost 2-1 to Jack Nicklaus of Ohio State, the eventual champion.

1962

David Cooper won the NCAA still rings title in gymnastics.

MSU won the NCAA 400-yard freestyle relay title in swimming. Team members were: Jeff Mattson, Doug Rowe, William Wood and Mike Wood. They also won the Big Ten title in 3:14.5.

MSU's Cross Country team won the Big Ten title, their tenth.

Sherm Lewis won Big Ten indoor track titles in the long jump at 24' 6"; and the 300-yard dash in 31.2.

Gerald Young won the Big Ten outdoor track two-mile run title in 9:12.

Bob Brooks won the Big Ten fencing title in epee.

Michael Wood won the Big Ten swimming 220-yard freestyle title in 2:01.3.

Dale Cooper won the Big Ten gymnastics title in the rings event.

Gani Browsh won the Big Ten gymnastics title in floor exercise.

Steve Johnson won the Big Ten gymnastics trampoline title.

1963

MSU became the only football team in history to defeat Notre Dame in eight consecutive games, and only the second team to go eight years without losing to Michigan—recording six wins and two ties. (Minnesota beat Michigan nine consecutive times from 1934 through 1942). The Spartans beat Notre Dame 12-7, and tied Michigan 7-7 in 1963.

MSU's fencing team, led by coach Charles Schmitter, won the Big Ten title. Dick Schloemer won the foil title; and Lou Salamone was the sabre champion.

MSU's Cross Country team won the Big Ten title, MSU's eleventh.

James T. Ferguson won the gold medal in 195-pound wrestling division at the Pan American Games.

Joseph R. Puleo won the gold medal in 185-pound weightlifting division at the Pan American Games.

Willie J. Atterberry won the silver medal in the 400-meter hurdles at the Pan American Games.

Jeff Mattson won the Big Ten swimming 100-yard backstroke title in :54.6.

Robert Moreland won the Big Ten indoor track 60-yard dash title in 6.1.

Sherm Lewis won the Big Ten indoor track long jump title at 23' 8".

Jan Bowen won the Big Ten outdoor track mile run title in 4:14.3.

Richard Schloemer won the Big Ten fencing title in foil.

Dale Cooper won the Big Ten gymnastics tumbling title.

1964

Gary J. Dilley won the Olympic silver medal in the 200-meter backstroke at the Olympic Games.

Marcia Jones Smoke won the Olympic bronze medal in singles kayaking at the Olympic Games.

Solomon Akpata was a member of the Nigerian Olympic track team.

MSU's 400-Yard Freestyle Relay Team won the Big Ten swimming title in 3:13.9. The team included Dick Gretzinger, Darryle Kifer, Jim MacMillan, and Bob Sherwood.

Jim Garrett won the Big Ten indoor track long jump at 24' 7".

Mike Martens won the Big Ten indoor track 1000-yard run title in 2:10.3.

Robert Moreland won the Big Ten indoor track 60-yard dash title in 6.1.

Louis Salamone won the Big Ten fencing title in sabre.

Jim Curzi won the Big Ten gymnastics all-around, and horizontal bar titles.

Dale Cooper won the Big Ten gymnastics rings title.

1965

MSU won the National Championship in football—its third—and the Big Ten title.

Jim Curzi won two NCAA gymnastics titles—in the parallel bars and horizontal bar events.

Gary Dilley won the NCAA and Big Ten swimming 100- and 200-yard backstroke titles. His times in the Big Ten meet were :53:15 in the 100, and 1:56.28 in the 200.

Kenneth Walsh won the Big Ten swimming 100-yard freestyle title in :47.5.

MSU's 400-Yard Freestyle Relay Team won the Big Ten swimming title in 3:09.2. The team included Gary Dilley, Dick Gretzinger, Darryle Kifer, and Jim MacMillan.

Don Behm won the Big Ten 130-pound wrestling title.

Jeff Richardson won the Big Ten heavyweight wrestling title.

Gene Washington won the Big Ten outdoor track 120-yard high hurdles title in 14.2, and the indoor track 70-yard low hurdles title in 7.7.

Jim Garrett won Big Ten outdoor track titles in the long jump at 24' 5"; and the 220-yard dash in 21.6, and the indoor track long jump at 24' 11".

Keith Coates won the Big Ten outdoor track mile run title in 4:08.2, and the indoor track mile run at 4:09.5.

Daswell Campbell won the Big Ten indoor track 300-yard dash title in 30.9.

Mike Bowers won the Big Ten outdoor track high jump title at 6' 7".

Tom Hurt won the Big Ten gymnastics vaulting horse title.

Gary Dilley (L) and Ken Walsh—Olympic, NCAA and Big Ten titlists. Dilley won 4 NCAA titles (1965, 1966) and 6 Big Ten titles (1965, 1966, 1967) in the 100- and 200-yard backstroke. He won an Olympic silver medal in the 200-meter backstroke (1964), and two Big Ten 400-yard relay titles (1965, 1967). Walsh won Olympic gold (1968) in the 400-meter relay, and silver in the 100-meter freestyle. He won the NCAA 100-yard freestyle (1967), and three Big Ten titles (1967)—100- and 200-yard freestyle, and 400-yard freestyle relay.

1966

Joyce Kazmierski won the 1966 Women's National Collegiate Golf Title.

MSU football team won its fourth National Championship and the Big Ten title.

MSU won its first NCAA ice hockey championship.

Doug Volmar led MSU to the hockey title. He scored the winning goal against Boston University in the national semifinals. He led the team in goals, assists and points in 1966, and was named a first team All-American. Volmar still shares the MSU records for most goals in a period (three), and most points in a period (five). He was named to the Western Collegiate Hockey Association All-Star team in 1966, and to the 1968 U.S. Olympic hockey team.

MSU won its fourth Big Ten All-Sports title.

MSU's wrestling team won the Big Ten title, MSU's second.

MSU's track team won the Big Ten indoor, and outdoor Big Ten titles.

Joyce Kazmierski won the Women's National Collegiate Golf Title.

Gary Dilley won the NCAA and Big Ten 100- and 200-yard backstroke swimming titles. His Big Ten times were :54.2 in the 100, and 1:57.4 in the 200.

Robert Steele won the NCAA 440-yard intermediate hurdles title in outdoor track; and the Big Ten outdoor track 440-yard intermediate hurdles in :50.7.

Dick Cook won the NCAA 152-pound wrestling title.

Ed Gunny won the NCAA still rings title in gymnastics.

Dale Anderson won the Big Ten 137-pound wrestling title.

Dale Carr won the Big Ten 145-pound wrestling title.

Mike Bradley won the Big Ten 177-pound wrestling title.

Gene Washington won the Big Ten outdoor track 120-yard high hurdles title in 13.8; and won indoor track titles in the 70-yard low hurdles in 7.8, and the 70-yard high hurdles in 8.3.

John Spain won the Big Ten outdoor track 880-yard title in 1:48.

Jim Garrett won the Big Ten indoor track long jump title at 24'1".

Dick Sharkey won the Big Ten indoor track two mile run title in 9:01.4.

Dave Thor won three Big Ten gymnastics titles—all-around, pommel horse, and floor exercise.

Dave Curzi won two Big Ten gymnastics titles—horizontal bar, and parallel bars.

MSU Runners Mike Martens, Rick Dunn, Daswell Campbell, and John Spain won the Big Ten outdoor track mile relay title in 3:10.9.

Mark Haskell won the Big Ten fencing title in sabre.

Mickey Szilagyi won the No. 2 Big Ten tennis singles title.

Vic Dhooge won the No. 5 Big Ten tennis singles title.

Jim Phillips and Vic Dhooge won the No. 2 Big Ten tennis doubles title.

1967

MSU's wrestling team won its first NCAA title, and was the first Big Ten team to do so. It also won its second consecutive Big Ten title, its third overall.

MSU's soccer team won its first NCAA title.

MSU won its fifth Big Ten All-Sports title.

MSU's basketball team won the Big Ten title.

MSU's tennis team won the Big Ten title.

MSU's ice hockey team won the Big Ten title.

Robert Steele won the NCAA 440-yard intermediate hurdles title in outdoor track.

George Radman won the NCAA and Big Ten 167-pound wrestling titles.

Ken Walsh won the NCAA 100-yard freestyle title in swimming, and two gold medals at the Pan American Games—400-meter freestyle relay and 800-meter freestyle relay.

Dale Anderson won the NCAA and Big Ten 137-pound wrestling titles.

Joseph R. Puleo won the gold medal in the 181-pound wrestling division at the Pan American Games.

David Thor won four bronze medals in gymnastics at the Pan American Games—all-around, horizontal bar, side horse, and floor exercise. He also won the **Big Ten gymnastics title in the all-around event.**

Toby Towson won the Big Ten gymnastics floor exercise title.

Charles "Bubba" Smith, 1966 All-American defensive end, and **Clint Jones**, 1966 All-American halfback, were the first two players selected in the 1967 National Football League draft. **This was the first time in history that players from the same university were selected first and second.** This record was equaled by Penn State in 2000, when Courtney Brown and LaVar Arrington were selected first and second in the NFL draft.

MSU's 400-Yard Freestyle Relay Team won the Big Ten swimming title in 3:08.68. The team included: Gary Dilley, Gary Langley, Don Rauch, and Ken Walsh.

Gary Dilley won the Big Ten 100-yard backstroke swimming title in :53.10, and the 200-yard backstroke title in 1:56.23.

Kenneth Walsh won the Big Ten 100-yard freestyle swimming title in :46.17, and the 200-yard freestyle title in 1:43.45.

Mike Bowers won the Big Ten indoor track high jump title at 6' 9".

Richard Sharkey won the Big Ten indoor track two-mile title at 9:03.8.

Patrick Wilson won the Big Ten indoor track 600-yard run title at 1:11.3.

1967 NCAA Soccer Champions—Coach Gene Kenney (center) with All-American co-captains Guy Busch (L) and Peter Hens. MSU repeated as NCAA champion in 1968. In 14 years (1956-1969), Kenney led the Spartans to six Final Fours, five undefeated seasons, 120 wins, 13 losses, and 13 ties, the all-time winningest record in MSU history.

Gene Washington won the Big Ten outdoor track 120-yard high hurdles title in 13.7.

Don Behm won the Big Ten 130-pound wrestling title.

Dale Carr won the Big Ten 145-pound wrestling title.

Mike Bradley won the Big Ten 177-pound wrestling title.

Roland Carter won the Big Ten outdoor track pole vault title at 16 feet even, and the indoor track pole vault title at 15' even.

John Spain won the Big Ten outdoor track 660-yard run title in 1:16.7.

John Good won the No. 4 Big Ten tennis singles title.

Jim Phillips won the No. 6 Big Ten tennis singles title.

Rich Monan and **Chuck Brainard** won the No. 1 Big Ten tennis doubles title.

John Good and **Mickey Szilagyi** won the No. 2 Big Ten tennis doubles title.

Jim Phillips and **Vic Dhooge** won the No. 3 Big Ten tennis doubles title.

1968

MSU's soccer team won its second NCAA title.

Soccer coach Gene Kenney, later associate athletic director, led the Spartans to their second consecutive national championship. In his 14 years as soccer coach—1956-1969—Kenney's MSU soccer teams won 120 matches, lost 13 and tied 13. This 90 percent winning record is unmatched by any coach in MSU history. In addition to two NCAA titles, Kenney's teams earned appearances in six NCAA Final Fours—finishing twice as NCAA runner-up, and twice as the third place finisher. In eight consecutive appearances in the NCAA tournament—1962 through 1969—Kenney teams won 16, lost 6, and tied two, for a winning percentage of .708, the second highest in NCAA history.

MSU's wrestling team won its third consecutive Big Ten title, its fourth overall.

MSU's gymnastics team won the Big Ten title.

MSU's cross country team won the Big Ten title, MSU's twelfth.

Ken Walsh, MSU free-style swimmer, won two Olympic gold and one silver medal at the Mexico City Olympic Games—gold medals in 400-meter freestyle relay, and the 400-meter medley relay; and a silver medal in the 100-meter freestyle.

Donald R. Behm won an Olympic silver medal in the bantamweight wrestling division at the Olympic Games.

George Gonzalez was a member of the Puerto Rican Olympic swimming team.

Earl Morrall, Baltimore Colts quarterback, led the National Football League with 26 touchdown passes in 1968.

Toby Towson won the NCAA floor exercise title in gymnastics.

Dale Anderson won the NCAA and Big Ten 137-pound wrestling titles.

Mike Bradley won his third consecutive Big Ten 177-pound wrestling title.

Jeff Smith won the Big Ten heavyweight wrestling title.

Dave Thor won two Big Ten gymnastics titles—all-around, and vaulting horse.

Joe Fedorchik won the Big Ten gymnastics floor exercise title.

Doug Volmar was a member of the U.S. Olympic hockey team.

MSU's Mile Relay Team—Don Crawford, Rich Stevens, Pat Wilson, and Bill Wehrwein—won the Big Ten indoor track title in 3:14.4.

Rich Monan won the No. 2 Big Ten tennis singles title.

Steve Schafer won the No. 5 Big Ten tennis singles title.

1969

MSU's men golf team won the Big Ten title.

Toby Towson won the NCAA floor exercise title in gymnastics.

Bill Wehrwein won the NCAA indoor track 600-yard run title; the **Big Ten** outdoor track **440-yard run** title in 46.2, and the indoor track **600-yard run** in 1:09.4.

MSU's wrestling team won its fourth consecutive Big Ten title, MSU's fifth overall. Six Spartan wrestlers won individual Big Ten titles—Gary Bissell—115-pounds; **Keith Lowrance**—137 pounds; **John Abajace**—152 pounds; **Tom Muir**—160 pounds; **Jack Zindel**—177 pounds; **Jeff Smith**—Heavyweight.

MSU's Mile Relay Team—James Bastian, Roger Merchant, Pat Wilson, and Bill Wehrwein—won the Big Ten indoor track title in 3:13.4.

MSU's 400-Yard Freestyle Relay Team won the Big Ten swimming title in 3:10.99. The team included: Dick Crittenden, Mark Holdridge, Mike Kalmbach, and Don Rauch.

Bruce Richards won the Big Ten 400-yard individual medley swimming title in 4:16.4.

Norm Haynie won the Big Ten gymnastics horizontal bar title.

Toby Towson won the Big Ten gymnastics floor exercise title.

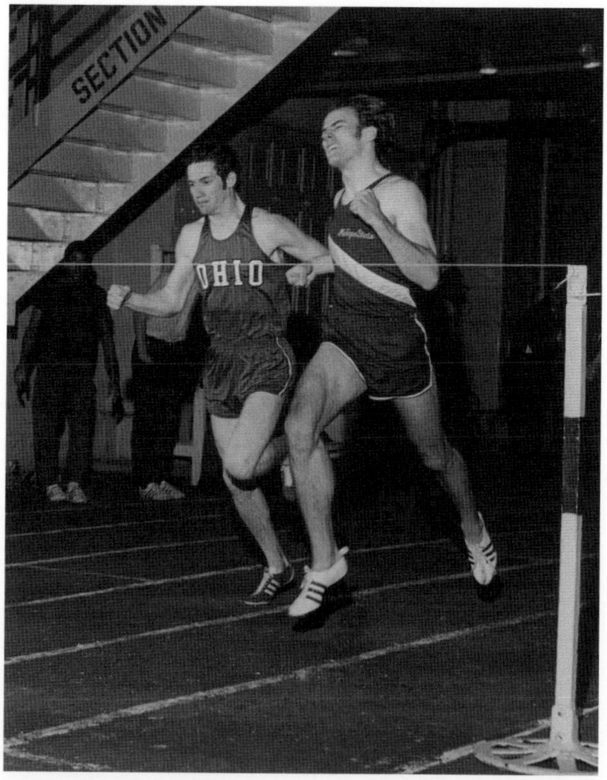

Bill Wehrwein, right, in dual meet win with Ohio State, won the 1969 NCAA and Big Ten indoor 600-yard run titles, Big Ten 440-yard outdoor title, and anchored the MSU Big Ten champion indoor mile relay team.

1970

MSU's wrestling team won its fifth consecutive Big Ten title, its sixth overall.

MSU's cross country team won the Big Ten title, MSU's thirteenth overall.

Herb Washington won the NCAA indoor track 60-yard dash title in 6.0; and the Big Ten outdoor track 100-yard dash title in 9.5.

Five Spartans won Big Ten wrestling titles--Greg Johnson won the NCAA and Big Ten 118-pound wrestling titles. Four other wrestlers won Big Ten titles—**Tom Milkovich**—134 pounds; **Keith Lowrance**—142 pounds; **Jack Zindel**—190 pounds; and **Vic Mittelberg**—Heavyweight.

Bill Wehrwein won the Big Ten indoor track 600-yard run title in 1:09.3.

MSU's Mile Relay Team—Al Henderson, Mike Murphy, John Mock, and Bill Wehrwein—won the Big Ten indoor track title in 3:15.5.

Dick Crittenden won the Big Ten 50-yard freestyle swimming title in :21.50.

1971

MSU won its sixth Big Ten All-Sports title.

MSU's wrestling team won its sixth consecutive Big Ten title, MSU's seventh overall.

MSU's cross country team won the Big Ten title, MSU's fourteenth overall.

MSU's fencing team won the Big Ten title.

MSU's baseball team won the Big Ten title.

MSU's ice hockey team won the Big Ten title.

Spartan halfback Eric "The Flea" Allen set an NCAA and Big Ten single-game rushing record of 350 yards against Purdue. The record had been held by Ron Johnson of Michigan at 347 yards. In this game, which MSU won 43-10, the Spartans set school records of 573 yards rushing and 698 total yards. Allen also set a Big Ten single-season rushing record of 1,283 yards, and the MSU career rushing record of 2,654 yards. Both records have since been surpassed.

Quarterback Earl Morrall, Spartan All-American, relieved Johnny Unitas in the second half of the Super Bowl and led the Baltimore Colts to the championship. Morrall was a member of MSU's 1954 and 1956 Rose Bowl champion teams.

MSU's 480-yard shuttle hurdle relay team tied the NCAA record and set a Florida Relays record of 56.7 seconds in Gainsville.

Five Spartans won Big Ten wrestling titles—Greg Johnson won NCAA and Big Ten 118-pound wrestling titles. Four others won Big Ten titles—**Tom Milkovich**—134 pounds; **Gerry Malecek**—167 pounds; **Dave Ciolek**—190 pounds; and **Ben Lewis**—Heavyweight.

Jeffrey Lanini won the Big Ten 100-yard breaststroke swimming title in 1:00.19.

Herb Washington won the Big Ten outdoor track 100-yard dash title in 9.4, and the indoor track 60-yard dash in 6.1.

Bob Cassleman won the Big Ten outdoor track 660-yard run title in 1:18.3, and the indoor track 600-yard run title in 1:10.3.

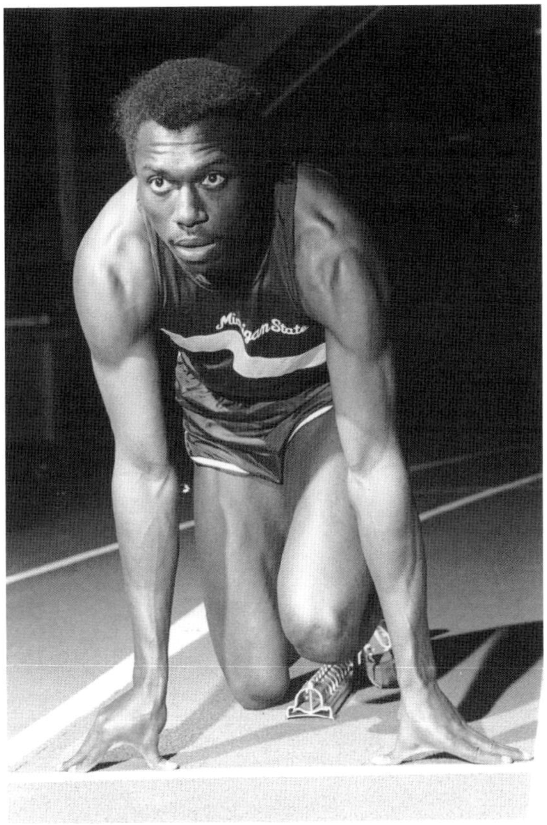

Herb Washington set world records in the 50-yard dash (5.1 seconds—1970), and 60-yard dash (5.8 seconds-1972). He won the NCAA indoor 60-yard dash titles in 1970 and 1972, Big Ten indoor 60-yard dash titles in 1971 and 1972, and three Big Ten outdoor 100-yard dash titles—1970 (9.5 seconds), 1971 (9.4), and 1972 (9.4). He won the Big Ten Medal of Honor for academics and athletics in 1972. Washington, world's fastest human (9.2 100), was a designated runner for the 1975 World Champion Oakland Athletics.

MSU's Mile Relay Team—Mike Holt, Mike Murphy, John Mock, and Bob Cassleman—won the Big Ten indoor track title in 3:12.9.

MSU's Mile Relay Team—Tom Spuller, Mike Murphy, John Mock, and Bob Cassleman won the Big Ten outdoor track title in 3:11.5.

Mike Madura won the No. 3 Big Ten tennis singles title.

Bill Mathers won the Big Ten fencing title in epee.

Women Swimmers Won Big Ten Titles in Six Events—Pam Kruse—100- and 200-yard freestyle; **Marilyn Corson**—100-yard butterfly, 100- and 200-yard individual medley; and the 400-yard freestyle relay—**Marilyn Corson, Linda Gustavson, Ellen Harrison, and Pam Kruse.**

1972

MSU's wrestling team won its seventh consecutive Big Ten title and was NCAA runner-up. It was MSU's eighth Big Ten title.

Greg Johnson won his third consecutive NCAA and third consecutive Big Ten wrestling title—all at 118-pounds.

The Milkovich brothers—Tom and Pat, won NCAA and Big Ten wrestling titles. Tom Milkovich won his NCAA title at 142. His third consecutive Big Ten title was his first at 142 pounds. Pat Milkovich won his first NCAA title and first Big Ten title at 126 pounds.

Brothers Pat and Tom Milkovich won three NCAA and seven Big Ten wrestling titles between them. Pat—NCAA (1972,1974) and Big Ten (1972, 1974, 1976); Tom—NCAA (1972) and Big Ten (1970, 1971, 1972, 1973). Pat was 4-time NCAA finalist—a Big Ten first, voted nation's outstanding wrestler three times, Big Ten Medal of Honor winner, and two-time captain. Tom, the first wrestler in history to go undefeated for four years in Big Ten competition, was a three-time All-American.

Gerry Malecek won his second consecutive Big Ten 167 pound wrestling title.

Ben Lewis won his second consecutive Big Ten Heavyweight wrestling title.

MSU's track team won the Big Ten indoor track and field title.

MSU's track team won the Big Ten outdoor track and field title.

Earl Morrall quarterbacked the Miami Dolphins to a 17-0 season and the Super Bowl championship in 1972. It was the only perfect season in modern pro football history. Morrall threw for 20,809 yards and 161 touchdowns in 23 years in the NFL.

Herb Washington won the NCAA indoor track 60-yard dash title. He also set a world record of :05.8 seconds in the 60-yard dash at the Spartan Relays in Jenison Fieldhouse, beating the record of :05.9 set by Bob Hayes in 1964. He also won the **Big Ten outdoor track 100-yard dash** title in 9.4, and the **indoor track 60-yard dash** in 5.9.

Freshman Marshall Dill set a 300-yard dash world record of :29.5, beating the old record of :29.9 at the same Spartan Relays. He also won the Big Ten outdoor track 220-yard dash title in 20.7, and the indoor track 300-yard dash title in 29.6.

These world-class sprinters led the MSU team to the Big Ten indoor title and to the runner-up position in the NCAA indoor meet, losing 19-18 to Southern California.

Spartan Ken Popejoy was the NCAA champion in the mile run, winning in 4:02.9. He also won the **Big Ten indoor track mile run** title in 4:05.4.

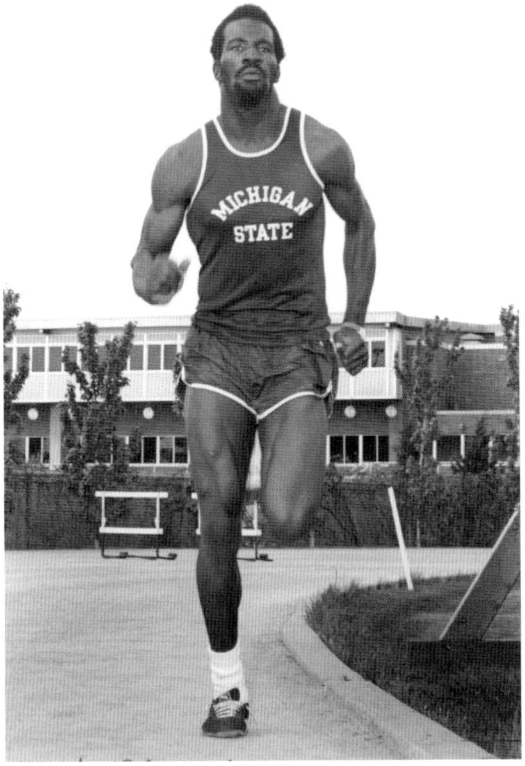

Marshall Dill, 6'2", 197-lb sprinter, set the 300-yard dash world record of 29.5 seconds in 1972. He won the NCAA outdoor 220-yard title (20.9) in 1973. Dill won three Big Ten indoor 300-yard dash titles, and three Big Ten outdoor 220-yard dash titles (1972, 1973, 1974). He also won the Big Ten outdoor 100-yard dash (9.4) in 1974.

Bob Cassleman won the Big Ten outdoor track 440-yard intermediate title in 52.4, and the indoor track 600-yard run title in 1:09.9.

John Morrison won the Big Ten indoor track 70-yard low hurdles title in 7.8.

MSU's Mile Relay Team—Alwyn Henderson, Marshall Dill, Mike Murphy, and Bob Cassleman—won the Big Ten indoor track title in 3:12.6.

MSU's 440-yard relay team—Herb Washington, LaRue Butchee, Bob Cassleman, and Marshall Dill—won the Big Ten outdoor track title in 40.2.

Sophomore basketball guard Mike Robinson won the Big Ten basketball scoring title, averaging 27.2 points per game. He was the first Spartan to win this honor and was named to the All-Big Ten team. For the entire season, he averaged 24.7 points per game.

Junior Judy Spraggs won three of five races to win the Women's North American Skating Championship. She had been the senior women's state champion the previous two years.

Women Swimmers Won Big Ten Titles in Six Events— Jane Waldie—200-yard freestyle, and 200-yard individual medley; **Marilyn Corson**—100-yard butterfly, and 100-yard individual medley; **Cheryl Solomon**—50-yard backstroke; and the 400-yard medley relay—**Marilyn Corson, Parsons, Cheryl Solomon, and Jane Waldie.**

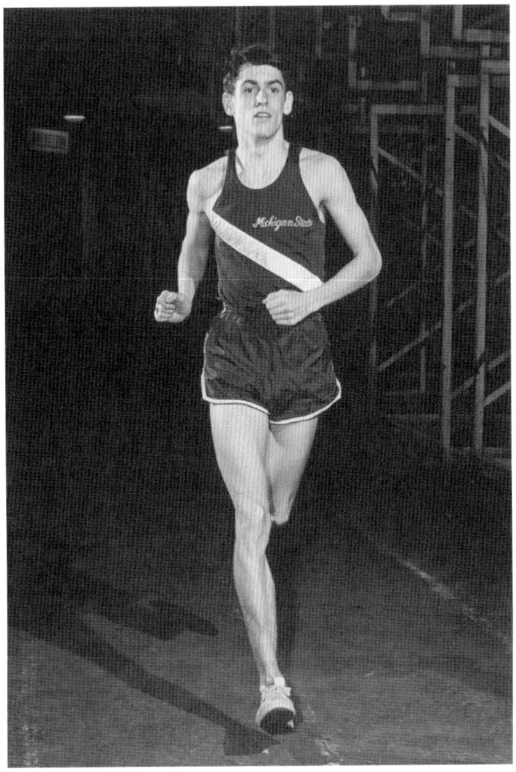

Ken Popejoy ran a 3:57 mile in 1973 in a regular meet, fastest in Big Ten history. At the Big Ten meet, he won the mile in 3:59.2. He won the 1972 NCAA (4:02.9) and Big Ten (4:05.4) mile titles.

1973

Bonnie Lauer won the 1973 NCAA Women's Golf Championship.

Bonnie Lauer won the Women's NCAA golf individual championship. During her spectacular career, she won the Michigan Amateur Championship twice—1970 and 1972; won medalist honors in four consecutive Midwest Collegiate playoffs; and was medalist in the Western Amateur in 1971. She was the first female athlete to be voted "Spartan of the Week" by the *State News*.

MSU's women's tennis team won the Big Ten title.

MSU's women's swimming team won the Big Ten title.

Jane Manchester-Meyers, All-American diver (1973, 1974 and 1976), was AIAW national three-meter diving champion; and Big Ten one-meter champion in 1973.

Women Swimmers Won Three Other Big Ten Titles—Jane Waldie—50-yard freestyle, and 100-yard breaststroke; and **Cheryl Solomon**—200-yard freestyle.

Glen Disosway won the Big Ten 50-yard freestyle swimming title in :21.48.

Bruce Wright won the Big Ten 100-yard freestyle swimming title in :46.66.

Brad Van Pelt won the Maxwell Trophy as the nation's top football player.

Mike Robinson won the Big Ten basketball scoring title for the second consecutive year. For the entire season, he averaged 25.3 points per game.

Tom Milkovich won his fourth consecutive Big Ten wrestling title, his second at 142 pounds. He scored 93 victories in four seasons, 1970 through 1973—the most in MSU history.

Marshall Dill won the NCAA outdoor 200-yard title in 20.9; the **Big Ten outdoor 220-yard dash** title in 21.1, and the **indoor track 300-yard dash** title in 30.1.

Ken Popejoy ran the fastest mile in Big Ten history: 3 minutes and 57 seconds. He won the Big Ten outdoor track mile run title in 3:59.2.

Rob Cool won the Big Ten outdoor track 3,000-meter steeplechase title in 8:49.7.

Bob Cassleman won the Big Ten outdoor track 440-yard intermediate hurdles title in 50.7, and the indoor 600-yard dash title in 1:08.8.

Sue Selke won the women's Big Ten tennis No. 1 singles title.

Cathy Stephenson won the women's Big Ten tennis No. 3 singles title.

Cathy Stephenson and **Allison Scruggs** won the women's Big Ten tennis No. 2 doubles title.

1974

MSU women athletes won Big Ten team titles in Golf, Swimming and Tennis.

Mike Robinson ended his three-year MSU basketball career by **setting a school career scoring record of 1,377 points.** He starred in the East-West College All-Star game where he received **the France Pomeroy Naismith Award as the "Nation's Most Outstanding Basketball Player Under Six Feet**." Robinson was five-foot eleven.

Jane Manchester-Meyers won four diving titles—the National AIAW and Big Ten three- and one-meter competitions. She also won the Midwest AIAW championship.

MSU's Women's Swimming 200-Yard Freestyle Relay Team--Dawn Jacobs, Lucy Johnson, Rebecca Lunsford, and Vicki Riebeling—won the women's Big Ten title.

Cheryl Solomon won the women's Big Ten swimming 50-yard backstroke title.

Pat Milkovich won his second NCAA and Big Ten 126-pound wrestling titles.

Marshall Dill won the Big Ten outdoor track 100-yard dash title in 9.4, and the 220-yard dash title in 21.0. He won the Big Ten indoor track 300-yard dash title in 30.2.

Bob Cassleman won the Big Ten outdoor track 440 intermediate hurdles title in 50.7, and the indoor track 600-yard run title in 1:10.0.

Mike Hurd won the Big Ten indoor track 70-yard high hurdles title in 8.2.

Jane Manchester-Meyers won two National AIAW 3-meter diving titles (1973, 1974), and one 1-meter title (1974). She also won two Big Ten 1-meter diving titles (1973, 1974), and one 3-meter title (1974).

MSU's Mile Relay Team—Bill Nance, Mike Holt, Bob Cassleman, and Marshall Dill—won the Big Ten indoor track title in 3:11.7.

Fred Royce won the Big Ten fencing title in sabre.

Sue Selke won the women's Big Ten tennis No. 1 singles title.

Allison Scruggs won the women's Big Ten tennis No. 4 singles title.

Allison Scruggs and Diane Suterko won the women's Big Ten tennis No. 2 doubles title.

Kathy Jo Bock and Becky Dickieson won the women's Big Ten tennis No. 3 doubles title.

1975

Los Angeles Dodge relief pitcher Mike Marshall, '65, won the coveted Cy Young Award as the best National League pitcher. He was the first relief pitcher in history to win the award. Marshall established a major league record for the most pitching appearances in a season—106. He had 15 wins, 12 losses, 21 saves, and an earned run average of 2.59.

Steve Garvey, '72, Los Angeles Dodger first baseman, was elected the National League's most valuable player (MVP), and the MVP of baseball's All-Star game. He had a spectacular season, batting .312, with 111 runs, 21 homers and 200 hits. He helped take the Dodgers to the World Series, which they lost to the Oakland Athletics.

Three Spartans played in the 1975 World Series—Mike Marshall, '65; Steve Garvey, '72; and Herb Washington, '73. For the Los Angeles Dodgers, Marshall was a relief pitcher, and Garvey played first base. Washington—the world's fastest human at 9.2 seconds in the 100-yard dash—was the designated runner for the Oakland Athletics, who won the series. Washington was the first non-baseball athlete in memory to play in a World Series.

Karen Dennis won the women's national AIAW outdoor track 220-yard dash title in 24.9.

MSU's women's golf team won the Big Ten title.

MSU's women's gymnastics team won the Big Ten title.

MSU's women's swimming team won the Big Ten title.

MSU's women's volleyball team won the Big Ten title.

Terry Furlow, 6'5" MSU forward, won the Big Ten basketball scoring title. For the season, he averaged 20.4 points per game. He scored 41 versus Detroit, and hit for 36 against Ohio State. He led MSU to an 86-78 victory over Michigan, hitting 11 for 13 from the field and 11 for 11 from the line for 33 points.

Herb Lindsay won the Big Ten indoor track two-mile run title in 8:44.8.

Marshall Dill won the Big Ten outdoor track 100-yard dash title in 9.4; and the 220-yard dash title in 21.0.

John Apsley won the Big Ten 100-yard butterfly swimming title in :50.69.

Larry Avery won the Big Ten heavyweight wrestling title.

John Moss won the Big Ten fencing title in epee.

Women Swimmers Won Big Ten Titles in Seven Events—Vicki Riebeling—100-yard butterfly; **Lynn Hughes**—50- and 100-yard backstroke; 200-yard freestyle relay—**Rebecca Hastings, Dawn Jacobs, Vicki Riebeling, and Karen Waite**; 400-yard freestyle relay—**Kathy Barrett, Rebecca Hastings, Lynn Hughes, and Vicki Riebeling;**

Mike Marshall, LA Dodgers relief pitcher, won the 1975 Cy Young Award as the best National League pitcher. (Photo—1967 with Detroit Tigers).

200-yard medley relay—**Suzy Brevitz, Lynn Hughes, Christine Swendiman, and Karen Waite**; 400-yard medley relay—**Suzy Brevitz, Lynn Hughes, Bernadine Kenny, and Vicki Riebeliing.**

Sue Selke won the women's Big Ten tennis No. 1 singles title.

June Oldman won the women's Big Ten golf title as medalist.

Ann Weaver won two women's Big Ten gymnastics titles—vault and uneven parallel bars.

Kathy Kincer won the women's Big Ten gymnastics balance beam title.

Diane Chapela won the women's Big Ten gymnastics floor exercise title.

1976

MSU women's softball team won the 1976 National Championship.

Gloria Becksford, who led and pitched MSU to the 1976 Women's National Softball Championship, was honored again in 1995 with the retirement of her jersey—# 9.

Gloria Becksford, star softball pitcher and hitter, led MSU. She won all five games at the AIAW Softball College World Series. Becksford won 17 games and lost only one during the 23-4 national title season. Becksford had an incredible earned run average of 0.56 in 137 innings, and hit .370. She became MSU's softball coach in 1980 and was Big Ten Coach of the Year in 1986. In 1995 her No. 9 MSU jersey was retired.

MSU women golfers won their third straight Big Ten team title. Coach Mary Fossom's team was composed of five freshmen, a sophomore and a senior.

MSU's women's cross country team won the Big Ten title.

MSU's women's volleyball team won the Big Ten title.

Tom Ross, MSU hockey All-American, finished his great four-year Spartan career as the most prolific scorer in NCAA Division I history—138 career goals, 186 career assists and 324 career points. All of these totals are MSU career records. By season, Ross' production looked like this: 1972-73—12 goals, 22 assists, 34points; 1973-74—37 goals, 51 assists, 88 points; 1974-75—38 goals, 59 assists, 97 points; 1975-76—51 goals, 54 assists, 105 points.

Pat Milkovich won his third Big Ten individual title, this time at 134 pounds, and became **the first Big Ten wrestler in history to make the NCAA wrestling finals four times**. He finished his career with 90 victories, second most in MSU history—second only to his brother Tom, who scored 93. (see 1973 above).

MSU forward Terry Furlow had a sensational season, averaging an MSU record 29.4 points per game, and winning the Big Ten basketball scoring title for the second consecutive year. He set MSU's all-time single-game scoring highs, hitting for 50 points against Iowa and 48 versus Northwestern. He also scored 42 against Ohio State, 41 versus Detroit, and 38 against Michigan. He set the Big Ten season scoring record with 588 points for a 32.7 average.

Quarterback Eddie Smith led the Big Ten in passing in 1976 with 94 completions, 1,142 yards and eight touchdowns. He also set five MSU single-season records: yards gained passing—1,749 yards; yards gained total offense—1,738; passes attempted—257; passes completed—132; and 13 TD passes.

Herb Lindsay won the Big Ten outdoor track 1,500-meter run title in 3:43.8.

John Moss won the Big Ten fencing title in epee.

Sue Tilden won the women's Big Ten swimming 100-yard butterfly title.

Diane Selke and Debbie Mascarin won the women's Big Ten tennis No. 1 doubles title.

Marjorie Kruger won the women's Big Ten tennis No. 5 singles title.

1977

MSU women won four Big Ten and two invitational team titles. In a superb year, women athletes won **Big Ten titles in gymnastics, softball, outdoor track and field, and golf**; and won invitational competitions in cross country and field hockey. Moreover, the Lady Spartans were runners-up in three Big Ten sports: basketball, gymnastics and swimming and diving. The tennis team placed third in the conference.

The MSU women's track and field team finished second in the U.S. Track and Field Federation Championships.

Sue Latter won the 800-meter run at the U.S. Track and Field Federation Championships in the record time of 2:04.7.

Dave Burgering won the Big Ten one- and three-meter diving titles, becoming the first Spartan to sweep both events.

Shawn Elkins won the Big Ten 200-yard butterfly swimming title in 1:50.26.

Mike Rado won the Big Ten 200-yard individual medley swimming title in 1:53.90.

Randy Smith won the Big Ten outdoor track 200-meter dash title in 21.68, and the indoor track 60-yard dash title in 6.1.

Herb Lindsay won the Big Ten outdoor track 1,500-meter run in 3:45.3, and the indoor track two-mile run in 8:42.9.

Chris Thomas won the Big Ten fencing title in sabre.

Kathy Kolon won three women's Big Ten Swimming Titles—the 50-, 100-, and 200-yard breaststroke events.

Karen Heath won the women's Big Ten swimming 200-yard backstroke title.

Sue Ertl won the women's individual Big Ten golf title.

Sue Ertl won the Big Ten women's golf titles in 1977 and 1978, leading Spartan golf teams to their fourth and fifth consecutive conference championships.

1978

The MSU Women's Golf Team won its fifth consecutive Big Ten title, and sixth consecutive Midwest AIAW title. They were coached by Mary Fossom.

Sue Ertl won the women's individual Big Ten golf title.

MSU's basketball team won the Big Ten title.

MSU's football team won the Big Ten title.

MSU's women's gymnastics team won their second consecutive Big Ten title.

MSU's women's softball team won the Big Ten title.

Steve Garvey, '72, Los Angles Dodger first baseman, was named MVP of the 1978 Baseball All-Star game. It was his second MVP award during five consecutive All-Star appearances. In the 1978 game, he slammed a two-out bases-loaded triple to tie the game. His National League team then went on to win.

Randy Smith won the Big Ten indoor track 60-yard dash title in 6.31.

Chris Thomas won the Big Ten fencing title in sabre.

Shawn Elkins won the men's Big Ten 200-yard butterfly swimming title in 1:51.49.

Jesse Griffin won the men's Big Ten three-meter diving title.

Cheryl Gilliam won the Big Ten women's track outdoor 200-meter dash.

Pam Steckroat won the Big Ten women's gymnastics uneven parallel bars title.

Melinda Whitcomb won the women's Big Ten swimming 50-yard freestyle title.

Diane Selke won the Big Ten tennis No. 5 singles title.

1979

MSU's basketball team won its first NCAA title, and the Big Ten title.

MSU's baseball team won the Big Ten title.

During the 1978-1979 school year, MSU's football, basketball and baseball teams won Big Ten titles. Only two other schools had won this triple crown: Illinois in 1914-1915 and 1951-52; and Michigan in 1925-1926 and 1947-1948.

MSU's ice hockey team won the Big Ten title.

The MSU women's Gymnastics team won their third consecutive Big Ten title.

Fifth Consecutive Big Ten Women's Golf title was won by the 1978 MSU team. Front Row, L-R: Patti Griffin, Sheila Tansey, Sue Ertl, Linda Smith, Joan Garety, Kathy Brooks, and Karen Escott. 2nd Row, L-R: Patty Caruso, Pat Trosko Fitton, Arlene Grenier, Ann McInerney, Sue Conlin, Laurie Everett, Ann Atwood, and Coach Mary Fossum.

MSU's women athletes had won Big Ten or Invitational titles in nine of ten conference sports by 1979. From the time women's sports were initiated at MSU in 1972, the Spartans had failed to win a title in only one sport—basketball. However, they had been runner-up three times in "round-ball."

Spartan Cheerleaders won the National Collegiate Cheerleading Title. Before a national audience on CBS-TV, the Spartan cheerleaders won the national title in competition with North Carolina, Mississippi, Tulsa, and Southern California. The national crown meant $10,000 for MSU's Development Fund.

Randy Smith won the Big Ten indoor track 60-yard dash title in 6.28.

Keith Moore won the Big Ten indoor track 1,000-yard run title in 2:10.2.

Shawn Whitcomb won the Big Ten heavyweight wrestling title.

Ricky Flowers won the Big Ten outdoor track 200-meter dash title in 21.20, and the 400-meter dash title in 46.13.

Charles Jenkins won the Big Ten gymnastics vaulting horse title.

Kathy Kolon won women's Big Ten swimming titles in the 100- and 200-yard breaststroke events.

Cheryl Gilliam won the Big Ten women's 200-meter indoor and outdoor track titles.

Debbie Mascarin won the women's Big Ten tennis No. 1 singles title.

Heather Mactaggart won the women's Big Ten tennis No. 5 singles title.

1980

MSU women gymnasts won their fourth consecutive Big Ten title, MSU's fifth overall.

Jay Vincent, MSU center, won the Big Ten basketball scoring title. For the season, he averaged 21.5 points per game.

Jeff Thomas won the Big Ten 126-pound wrestling title.

Randy Smith won the Big Ten outdoor track 100-meter dash title in 10.44, and the indoor track 60-yard dash title in 6.24.

MSU's Mile Relay Team—Randy Smith, Tim Kenney, Chauncy Williams, and Calvin Thomas—won the Big Ten indoor track title in 3:16.5.

Cheryl Gilliam won the Big Ten women's outdoor 200-meter dash title.

Kelly Spatz won the Big Ten women's track indoor mile and two-mile titles, and the outdoor Big Ten 3,000-meter title. She was named MSU's Sports Woman of the Year.

Bonnie Ellis won the Big Ten women's gymnastics balance beam title.

Linda Mrosko won the women's Big Ten swimming 50-yard butterfly title.

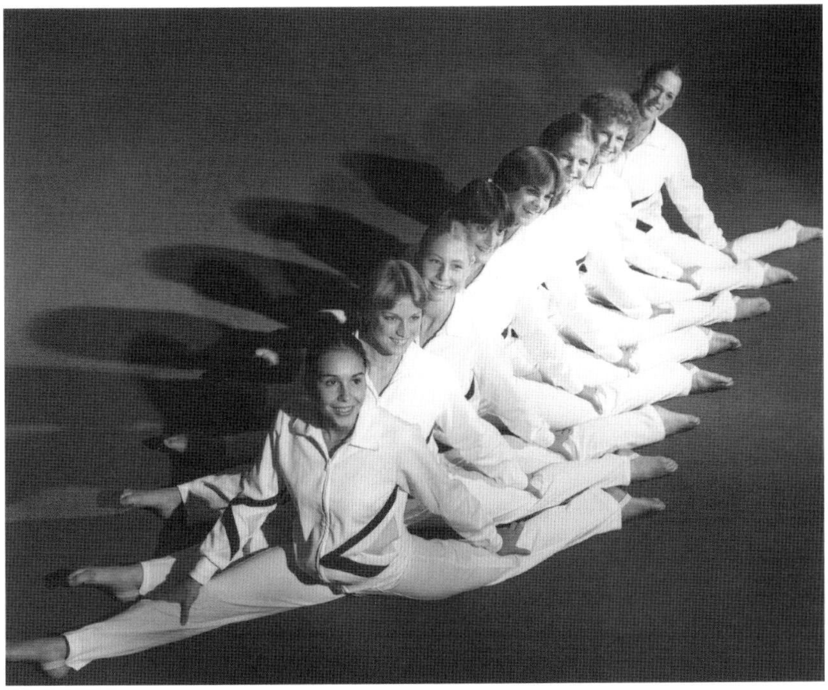

Fourth Consecutive Women's Big Ten Gymnastics title was won by the 1980 MSU team. L-R: Alice Hagan, Lori Boes, Pam Swing, Kit Bunker, Colleen Smith, Mary Beth Eigel, Bonnie Ellis, and Captain Diane Lovato.

1981

Jay Vincent, MSU center, won the Big Ten basketball scoring title for the second consecutive year, with an average of 24.1 points per game. He thus became MSU's third two-time winner of the Big Ten scoring title. For the entire season he averaged 22.6 points per game. He was voted the Big Ten's most valuable player, and was named Big Ten Player of the Year.

MSU place kicker Morten Andersen booted a 63-yard field goal against Ohio State at Columbus, an MSU and Big Ten record. MSU lost the football game 27-13.

Tony Gilbert won the Big Ten indoor track 55-meter high hurdles title in 7.4 seconds, and the triple jump title at 51'4".

Pete Roberts won the Big Ten gymnastics vaulting horse title.

Cheryl Gilliam won the Big Ten women's Big Ten outdoor 200-meter title.

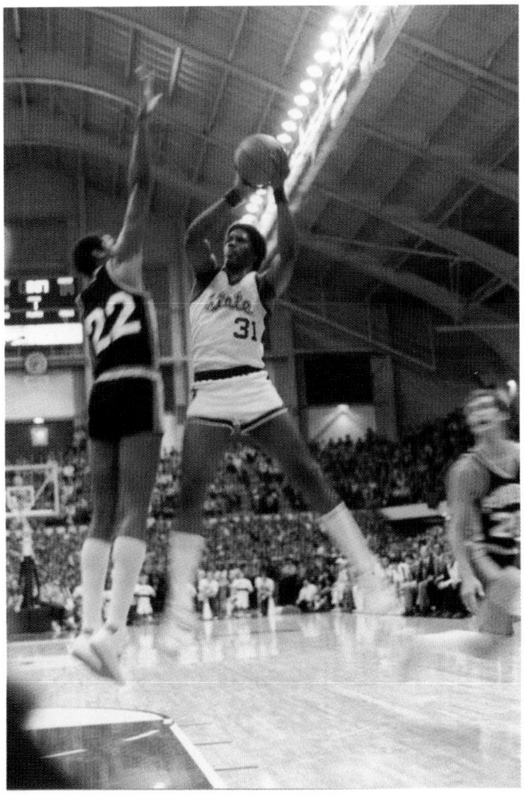

6'8" Spartan center Jay Vincent led the Big Ten in scoring in 1980 and 1981. He averaged 24.1 points per game in 1981, and was named Big Ten MVP and Player of the Year.

1982

MSU's hockey team won the CCHA Playoff title.

MSU Women's teams won Big Ten titles in Cross Country, Golf, and Outdoor Track.

Marcus Sanders won the Big Ten indoor track 600-yard run title in 1:10.19.

MSU's Mile Relay Team—Kelvin Scott, Rob Murphy, Calvin Thomas, and Marcus Sanders—won the Big Ten indoor track title in 3:13.77.

Bob Lundquist won the Big Ten 200-yard breaststroke swimming title in 2:05.4.

Eliot Tabron won the Big Ten outdoor track 400-meter dash title in 45:32.

MSU's 1,600-meter relay team—Calvin Thomas, Marcus Sanders, Kelvin Scott, and Eliot Tabron—won the Big Ten outdoor track title in 3:08.75.

Martha Jahn Won Four Women's Big Ten Swimming Titles and set Four Big Ten Records—200-yard freestyle in 1:50.83; 500-yard freestyle in 4:50.89; 200-yard butterfly in 2:02.29; and 100-yard butterfly in :56.82. At the same Big Ten Championship meet, Jahn set an MSU record in the 100-yard freestyle at :52.24; and was part of the MSU-record setting 800-yard freestyle relay team (7:35.18)—(Jahn, Karen Moskel, Beth Carmichael, and Jill Young).

Judi Brown won the Big Ten women's indoor track 440-yard title in 56:35.

Anne Pewe won the Big Ten women's indoor track two mile run in 9:57.07.

MSU's 4 x 220-Yard Relay Team—Judi Brown, Candy Burkett, Molly Brennan, and Jacqui Sedwick—won the Big Ten women's indoor title in 1:41.26, a conference record.

Martha Jahn won four Big Ten swimming titles in 1982, setting records in each event: 200- and 500-yard freestyle, and 100- and 200-yard butterfly.

Judi Brown won the Olympic silver medal in the 400-meter hurdles at the 1984 Los Angeles Games. She was 1983 NCAA 400-meter intermediate hurdle champion, three-time Big Ten 440-yard champion (conference record 54.3 seconds indoor—1983), and Big Ten 60-yard indoor hurdle, 400-meter outdoor hurdle, and 4 x 220-yard relay champion (conference record 1:41.26—1982). Named 1983 National Suzy Favor Female Athlete of the Year, and Big Ten Woman Athlete of the Year.

Judi Brown won the women's Big Ten outdoor track 400-meter hurdle title in 59.77.

Anne Pewe won the women's Big Ten outdoor track 3,000-meter run in 9:24.42.

MSU's 4 x 800-Meter Relay Team—Barb Douglas, Anne Pewe, Pam Sedwick, and Jacqui Sedwick—won the Big Ten women's outdoor track title.

1983

MSU's hockey team won the CCHA Playoff title.

Judi Brown won the NCAA 400-meter intermediate hurdles title in outdoor track. Her time of 56:44 was the fastest time posted in the nation. **She was selected the national Suzy Favor Female Athlete of the Year, and the 1982-1983 Big Ten Woman Athlete of the Year.** She also won the **Big Ten indoor track 60-yard hurdles** title in 8.11, and the **440-yard title** in 54.03, a conference record; and **the Big Ten outdoor 400-meter hurdle title** in 59.47.

Jacqui Sedwick won the Big Ten women's indoor track 880-yard run title in 2:07.30, **a conference record;** and the outdoor track 800-meter run title in 2:07.86.

MSU's 4x 440 Yard Relay Team—Jacqui Sedwick, Julie Boerman, Candy Burkett, and Judi Brown—won the Big Ten women's indoor track title in 3:41.96, **a conference record.**

Steve Garvey, Los Angeles Dodger first baseman, set the National League record by playing 1,118 consecutive games. He ultimately ran the streak to 1,207 games before a dislocated thumb stopped his run.

Marcus Sanders won the Big Ten indoor track 600-yard run title in 1:08.86.

Paul Piwinski won the Big Ten indoor track high jump title at 7-1.

MSU's Mile Relay Team—Corky Wilkins, Kelvin Scott, Marcus Sanders, and Eliot Tabron—won the Big Ten indoor track title in 3:10.20.

MSU's 1,600-meter relay team—Corky Wilkins, Kelvin Scott, Marcus Sanders, and Eliot Tabron—won the Big Ten outdoor track title in 3:09.28.

1984

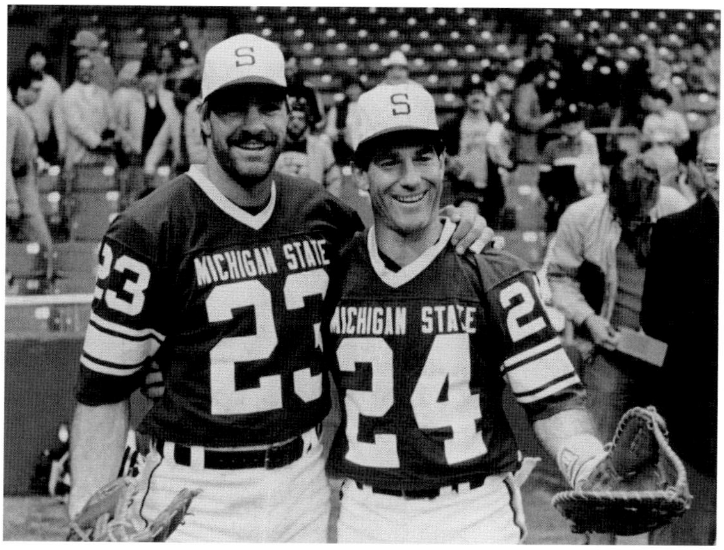

Spartans Kirk Gibson, left, and Steve Garvey met in the 1984 World Series. Gibson, Detroit Tiger outfielder, and Garvey, San Diego Padres first baseman, won the MVP awards in their respective 1984 Championship League Series. The two all-stars are shown in the jerseys they wore when playing football for MSU.

MSU hockey team won the CCHA Playoff title.

Judi Brown won an Olympic silver medal in the 400-meter hurdles at the L.A. Games.

MSU's Kirk Gibson and Steve Garvey met in the 1984 World Series. Garvey played first base for the San Diego Padres. Gibson was an outfielder for the Detroit Tigers and hit two home runs to win the series, 4-1, in the fifth game. During the series, whenever Gibson reached first base, where Garvey was stationed, TV announcers would kid about the "MSU alumni reunion."

Both Gibson and Garvey won the most valuable player awards in their respective league playoffs.

Gary Haight was a member of the U.S. Olympic hockey team.

Mike Potts won the Big Ten heavyweight wrestling title.

Marcelle Kendall won the women's Big Ten indoor track 440-yard run title in 55.18, and the outdoor 400-meter title in 52.20.

Vivian Fischer won the Big Ten women's indoor track shot put title at 52' 0".

Odessa Smalls won the Big Ten women's outdoor track 200-meter title in 23.50.

MSU's Cheerleading Squad placed second among 20 finalists in the 1984 National Cheerleading Association's national championships. The 14-member team was co-captained by **Dave Bessemer and Sharon Ferguson**.

1985

MSU's hockey team won the CCHA regular season and Playoff titles.

Sophomore halfback Lorenzo White led the nation in rushing for the regular season with more than 1,900 yards. He ran for 206 yards in the first half of the Indiana football game on November 9—the best single half performance in MSU history. In the opening seconds of the second half, he ran 73 yards, and then 7 for a touchdown. White then had 286 yards rushing in just 25 attempts, or 11.44 yards per carry average. There were 29 minutes and 30 seconds left to play. At that point, he was just 71 yards shy of the NCAA single-game rushing record of 357 yards. Coach Perles pulled him from the game. According to sports reports, Perles was concerned about overworking White, who had been carrying the ball 35 or more times per game. MSU defeated Indiana 35-16.

The 1986 MSU Football Media Guide stated it was the consensus of sportswriters and broadcasters that White would have broken the NCAA single-game record had he remained in the game a little longer. He also could have gone over 2,000 yards rushing during the regular season. In the minds of many fans, it still sits as one of the great lost opportunities in Spartan football history. In virtually every instance where a back has run more than 2,000 yards in the regular season, they have won the Heisman Trophy. As it turned out, White gained enough yards in the December 31 All-American bowl to give him 2,066 yards for the year. MSU lost that game to Georgia Tech, 17-14. White finished fourth in the Heisman balloting.

Jeff Butler won the Big Ten 100-yard butterfly swimming title in :49.27.

Mary Rozman won women's Big Ten swimming titles in the 50-yard freestyle (23.70) and the 500-yard freestyle events.

Odessa Smalls won the Big Ten women's indoor track 300-meter run title in 38.52, **a conference record;** and the outdoor track 200-meter title in 23.52.

Jacqui Sedwick won the Big Ten women's outdoor track 800-meter run title in 2:05.42.

MSU's 4 x 100 Meter Relay Team—Marcelle Kendall, Connie Burnett, Joanna Childress, and Odessa Smalls—won the Big Ten women's outdoor title in 45.03.

Allan Powers won the Big Ten gymnastics rings title.

1986

The MSU Hockey Team Won its second NCAA title, and the CCHA regular season title.

Spartan Jean Perron, age 39, in his first season as the Montreal Canadiens head coach, led his team to a Stanley Cup victory for the world hockey championship. When at MSU, Perron wrote his thesis on hockey tactics while an assistant coach at MSU under Amo Bessone. Perron credited the great season to tactics borrowed from Bessone.

Scott Skiles, All-American basketball guard, was selected Big Ten Player of the Year and National Player of the Year by *Basketball Times* and by Billy Packer of CBS-TV. Skiles led the Big Ten in scoring with a 29.1 per game average, and was second in the nation in scoring for the season with a 27.4 point per game average. His best single-game scoring performances were 43 points versus Minnesota, 40 against Michigan and 36 versus Wisconsin. Skiles also became MSU's career leader in points—2,145; assists—645; free throw percentage—.848; and steals—172.

Earvin "Magic" Johnson received a record 1,060,892 votes in the balloting for the National Basketball Association's All-Star team, which broke the record he set the previous year. Johnson also set a contract record, a 25-year deal at $1 million per year.

Jim Morrissey, former MSU football captain and rookie linebacker for the Chicago Bears, intercepted a New England Patriot's pass that **helped the Bears rout the Patriots, 46-10 in Super Bowl XX.**

1986 NCAA Ice Hockey Champions—Front Row (L-R): Norm Foster, Assistant Coach George Gwozdecky, Bill Shibicky, Mitch Messier, Rick Fernandez, Dee Rizzo, Head Coach Ron Mason, Mike Donnelly, Brad Beck, Don McSween, Jeff Parker, Assistant Coach Terry Christenson, and Bob Essensa. 2nd Row (L-R): Dr. John Downs, Tom Tilley, Danton Cole, Rick Tosto, Chris Luongo, Sean Clement, Dave Chiapelli, Bob Reynolds, Kevin Miller, Dave Arkeilpane, Student Mgr. Troy Tuggle. Back Row (L-R): Equipment Mgr. Tom Magee, Athletic Trainer Dave Carrier, Geir Hoff, Jim Lycett, Mike Dyer, Bruce Rendall, Brian McReynolds, Joe Murphy, Brad Hamilton, Student Mgr. Steve Brown.

Guy Scott won the Big Ten outdoor track 800-meter run title in 1:48.80.

MSU's 400-Yard Freestyle Relay Team—Jennifer Collette, Wendy Ingraham, Mary Rozman, and Mary Schoenle—won the women's Big Ten swimming title in 3:25.80.

Mary Schoenle won the women's Big Ten 200-yard individual medley swimming title in 2:04.95.

Kim Hartwick won the Big Ten women's gymnastics balance beam title.

Odessa Smalls won the Big Ten women's indoor track 60-yard dash in 6.87; and the indoor track 300-yard run title in 34.31; and the Big Ten outdoor track 200-meter dash title in 23.28.

Joanna Childress won the Big Ten women's indoor track 60-yard hurdles title in 7.79.

Debbie Harline won the Big Ten women's indoor track high jump title at 5'11".

1987

MSU's football team won the Big Ten title.

MSU's hockey team won the CCHA Playoff title.

Magic Johnson led the Los Angeles Lakers to the National Basketball Association championship and won the NBA league and playoff most valuable player awards. He became the first three-time winner of the NBA finals MVP award. In his spectacular season, Johnson led the NBA in assists for the fourth time in five seasons. His 977 assists established a Lakers' record.

Carl Banks, former MSU linebacker, **made a game-high ten tackles in Super Bowl XXI to help the New York Giants win the game 39-20 over the Denver Broncos.**

Marvin Parnell won the Big Ten outdoor track 400-meter hurdles title in 51.31.

Mary Rozman won the women's Big Ten swimming 50-yard freestyle title in :23.30.

MSU's 200-Yard Freestyle Relay Team—Ann Agar, Dyne Burrell, Mary Rozman, and Mary Schoenle—won the women's Big Ten swimming title in 1:33.67.

Kim Hartwick won two Big Ten women's gymnastics titles—balance beam, and floor exercise.

Odessa Smalls won the women's Big Ten indoor track 60-yard dash title in 6.86, a conference record; and the indoor track 300-yard dash title in 34.36. She also won women's Big Ten outdoor track titles in the 100-meter dash in 11.67; the 200-meter dash in 23.62; and the 400-meter run.

Mary Shea won the women's Big Ten outdoor track 10,000-meter title in 33:43.88.

1988

MSU's football team won the 1988 Rose Bowl game, 20-17 over USC.

Kirk Gibson inspired the Los Angeles Dodgers with a game-winning home run in the bottom of the ninth inning of the first game of the 1988 World Series. Gibson, who hit two home runs in the National League playoffs to help his team to the World Series, had strained a knee ligament. He limped to the plate and powered the game-winning blast with his arms and shoulders only. It was his only play in the 1988 World Series, but served as an inspiration to his team, which went on to win the series over the Oakland Athletics. **Gibson was named the National League's Most Valuable Player.** He also established a baseball scholarship at MSU.

Spartans Carl Banks, New York Giant linebacker, and Morten Andersen, New Orleans Saints place kicker, were named to the All-Pro football first team by the *Associated Press*.

Kevin Miller was a member of the U.S. Olympic hockey team.

Geir Hoff was a member of the Norwegian Olympic hockey team.

Michelle Ingalls won three Big Ten women's gymnastics titles—uneven parallel bars, balance beam, and floor exercise. She also was named **Big Ten Freshman Gymnast of the Year.**

Michael Kasavana was named **Big Ten women's Gymnastics Coach of the Year.**

Judi Brown-King was honored by *Sports Illustrated* as one of eight "Athletes Who Care." She was a silver medalist in the 1984 Olympic Games in Los Angeles and the American record holder in the 400-meter hurdles at 54.23 seconds. Brown-King, who was living in Oregon, had led a major volunteer effort to assist abused children by serving as a lay member of the Oregon State Children's Service Review Board and Lane County Juvenile Services Commission.

MSU's Baseball Team won a Spartan record 41 games during the season. Coach Tom Smith's team finished second in the Big Ten, yet weren't selected for the 48-team NCAA baseball tournament. However, the University of Michigan, which finished third in the Big Ten, was selected to participate in the NCAA tournament.

Philmore Morris won the men's Big Ten outdoor track long jump title with a leap of 25' 7."

1989

The MSU hockey team won the CCHA regular season and Playoff titles.

Percy Snow, Spartan All-American linebacker, became the first football player in history to win both The Butkus Award—given to the nation's best linebacker; and The Lombardi Award—given to the top linebacker or lineman in the country.

Earvin "Magic" Johnson was voted the National Basketball Association's Most Valuable Player for the 1988-89 season, his second MVP award. NBA commissioner David Stern said, "Earvin is at the point where his only competition is himself. Johnson had led the Los Angeles Lakers to five NBA titles in the 1980s.

Sports Illustrated named **Magic Johnson, Joe Montana and Wayne Gretzky as the Athletes of the 1980s**.

Kim Hartwick was named **Big Ten Women's Gymnast of the Year**.

Michelle Roper, '89, won the National Triathlon Federation Championship in her age bracket. She swam 1.2 miles, biked 56 miles, and ran 13.1 miles in 4 hours, 44 minutes, 2 seconds. She had been a cross country runner at MSU.

Corey Pryor won the men's Big Ten indoor track 55-meter dash title in 6.28.

Julie Farrell won the women's Big Ten one-meter diving title.

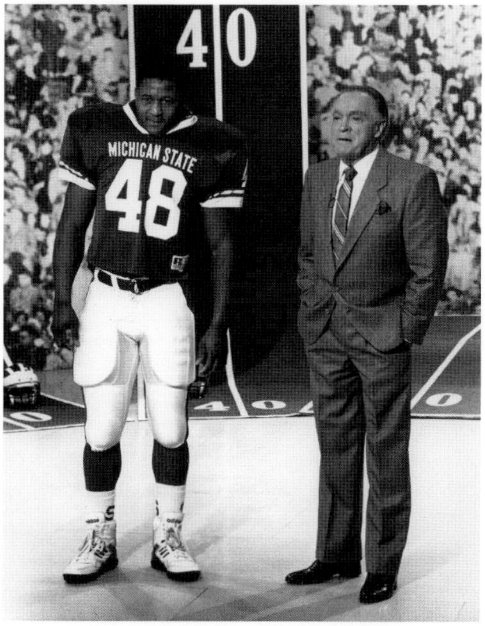

All-American Linebacker Percy Snow on Bob Hope's 1989 Christmas Special TV Show. Snow won the Butkus Award (nation's best linebacker), and the Lombardi Award (nation's best lineman or linebacker) in 1989—the first football player ever to win both awards.

All-American Kip Miller won the 1990 Hobey Baker Award, "Hockey's Heisman;" and was named Bauer College Hockey Player of the Year, and CCHA Player of the Year in 1990. He helped MSU win 3 CCHA Playoff and 2 CCHA Regular Season championships.

1990

MSU's basketball team won the Big Ten title.

MSU's football team won the Big Ten title.

MSU's hockey team won CCHA regular season and Playoff titles.

Star Spartan hockey forward Kip Miller won the Hobey Baker Award, college hockey's "Heisman Trophy." The award was presented by the Decathlon Athletic Club of Bloomington, Minnesota. He also was named **the Bauer College Hockey Player of the Year**, and the **CCHA Player of the Year**. Miller also became MSU's third two-time first team All-American. In his four-year MSU career (1986-1990), Miller was third in goals—116, fifth in assists—145, and third in points—261.

All-American basketball forward Steve Smith won the Chicago Tribune Silver Basketball Award as the Big Ten's Most Valuable Player.

Dawn Riley, '87, led the first all-female crew in the Whitbread Round-The-World Sailing Race. Riley was captain of a 12-member female crew and the only American. Their boat, *The Maiden*, finished second in its class. Riley of Grosse Pointe Park, Michigan, exhibited leadership and heroism in saving the craft during perilous weather. She was watch captain, engineer and diver. At one juncture during the race, Riley worked 50 straight hours manning the pumps and fixing a major leak while the boat was surfing at 20 knots, trying to avoid icebergs and whales. She averaged three hours sleep while helping steer the boat when some of the crew fell sick. While crashing through 20-foot waves and tornado-like winds in the Atlantic, the boat was spun 360 degrees. Riley followed in her mother Prudence's footsteps. She came to MSU and was elected captain of the Sailing Team and commodore of the Sailing Club.

1990 Big Ten Basketball Champions; First Season in the Breslin Center. Front Row (L-R): Assistant Coach Herb Williams, Jon Zulauf, Todd Wolfe, Kirk Manns, Head Coach Jud Heathcote, Mark Montgomery, Jeff Casler, Jesse Hall, Manager Erie Spiller, Assistant Coach Tom Izzo. Back Row (L-R): Trainer Tom Mackowiak, Assistant Coach Jim Boylen, Ken Redfield, Parish Hickman, Matt Hofkamp, Mike Peplowski, David Mueller, Matt Steigenga, Steve Smith, Dwayne Stephens, Graduate Assistant Coach Tom Crean.

Julie Farrell won the NCAA and Big Ten one-meter diving championships. She was the **1990 NCAA Diver of the Year, and was named the Big Ten-Jesse Owens Athlete of the Year.**

Steve Leissner won the Big Ten 200-yard individual medley swimming title in 1:48.97.

Paul Dackerman won the Big Ten gymnastics vaulting horse title.

Nancy Anderson, '74, held two world and five national records in sports for athletes with cerebral palsy. Her world records were in the 100-meter slalom and the 20-meter wheelchair dash. She held national records in the shot put, and freestyle and backstroke swimming.

1991

Carl Banks and Mark Ingram, former MSU football greats, helped lead the New York Giants to a 20-19 Super Bowl victory over the Buffalo Bills. Banks, an All-Pro linebacker, "delivered the most serious hits" on the Bills according to *Sports Illustrated*. Ingram caught a pass and made a superb run evading three tacklers for a key first down that ***Sports Illustrated*** **called "one of the greatest plays in Super Bowl history."**

Julie Farrell-Ovenhouse won the 1991 NCAA three-meter diving title with a record-setting 576.8-point performance. She also won the Big Ten one- and three-meter diving titles. She was selected the **National Suzy Favor Female Athlete of the Year.**

Magic Johnson set the National Basketball Association's all-time record for assists by making his 9,898th in a victory over Dallas.

Kelly Burke, '90, won the national dressage championship.

Anthony Hamm won the Big Ten outdoor track 10,000-meter run title in 29:11.83.

Paul Dackerman won the Big Ten gymnastics vaulting horse title.

Christine Duverge won the women's Big Ten indoor track 600-meter run title in 1:31.50.

Tracy Ames won the women's Big Ten indoor track high jump title at 5' 8".

Misty Allison won the women's Big Ten 5,000-meter title.

1992

Stu Argo, '85, and Dawn Riley, '87, helped win the America's Cup. Argo and Riley helped sail America 3 to victory in the 1992 America's Cup competition. Argo was a port sail trimmer in the final race against Il More di Venezia. Riley was the pitman on two Defender Trial races, the farthest a woman sailor had competed in America's Cup history.

Magic Johnson won an Olympic gold medal as a member of the U.S. Olympic basketball "Dream Team" that won the title at the Barcelona, Spain Games. His teammates included Pro All-Stars Michael Jordan, Charles Barkley, Karl Malone and Patrick Ewing.

Johnson scored 25 points, had nine assists, and won the MVP vote for his performance in the National Basketball Association's All-Star game. Magic hit three 3-point shots in the final two minutes to lead the West to a 151-113 victory. He did this just three months after contracting the HIV virus.

Judi Brown-King, former track star, was named MSU's Female Athlete of the 1980s. She was a two-time All-American, the winner of 12 Big Ten titles, and a silver medal winner at the 1984 Olympic Games in Los Angeles.

Julie Farrell-Ovenhouse won the three-meter springboard event at the U.S. Olympic Trials at Indianapolis. She was named **Michigan NCAA Woman of the Year**.

Misty Allison, junior cross country star, was named Big Ten Athlete of the Year for 1991-1992. She had won the 5,000-meter race at the Big Ten championships in the fall of 1991.

Barb Mucha, '84, former Spartan golfer, won the first Olds Classic Golf Tournament, which was held at East Lansing's Walnut Hills Country Club. The Ladies Professional Golf Association tournament drew 22,500 fans on the final day. ESPN-TV played the Spartan fight song as Mucha walked up the 18th fairway. The win, Mucha's second on the pro tour, was worth $75,000. MSU alum Chuck Strong, Oldsmobile assistant general sales manager, presented Mucha with her winning check.

Jason Woolley was a member of the Canadian Olympic hockey team.

Chris Brown won the Big Ten indoor track 600-meter run title in 1:18.85.

MSU's 4 x 800-Meter Relay Team—Sam Blumke, Todd Koning, Chris Rugh, and Rick Gledhill—won the Big Ten indoor track title in 7:37.30.

Anthony Hamm won the Big Ten outdoor track 10,000-meter run title in 30:02.38.

MSU's 4 x 400-Meter Relay Team—Susan Francis, Michelle Brown, Christine Duverge, and Shirley Evans—won the women's Big Ten indoor track title in 3:46.72.

Shirley Evans won the women's Big Ten outdoor track 200-meter title in 23.78.

MSU's 4 x 400-Meter Relay Team—Susan Francis, Michelle Brown, Diana Murphy, and Shirley Evans—won the women's Big Ten outdoor track title in 3:40.65.

Twenty former Spartans were playing for National Football League teams, the most for any Big Ten university. Michigan and Ohio State tied for second with 17 each.

1993

Heath Fell, Spartan golfer, won Big Ten Player of the Year honors. He was the first MSU men's golfer to win an NCAA regional tournament, winning medalist honors in Columbus, Ohio.

Dave Smith won the Big Ten outdoor track 10,000- meter run title in 30:09.71.

Nick Westermeyer, MSU gymnast who was paralyzed after a fall in practice in 1991 a week after competing in the NCAA tournament, was **the third recipient of the NCAA's Award of Courage**. The award is given each year to the student-athlete who best exemplifies

Heath Fell was 1993 Big Ten Player of the Year and the first Spartan men's golfer to win an NCAA regional tournament.

courage both on and off the field. Westermeyer graduated from MSU in construction management in 1993. He said, "I want people to know how far they can go and what they can do."

1994

John Sahratian, varsity tennis player from 1951 to 1953, **won the National 60-and-over hard-court tennis singles championship** in Santa Barbara, California. He defeated four nationally ranked players in a row to win.

Dixon Edwards and Matt Vanderbeek, former Spartan football players, were members of the Super Bowl Champion Dallas Cowboys. Edwards was a starting linebacker; Vanderbeek, a special teams player.

Geir Hoff was a member of the Norwegian Olympic hockey team.

Dwayne Norris was a member of the Canadian Olympic hockey team.

Mashiska Washington was named an All-American tennis singles player.

Susan Francis won women's **Big Ten indoor track titles in the 200-meter run** in 24.04, and the **400-meter run** in 53.96; and the **outdoor track 400-meter title** in 53.21.

Karen Winslow was named Big Ten Player of the Year in women's soccer.

Danton Cole, Spartan hockey star, 1985-1989, and Big Ten Medal of Honor winner, helped the New Jersey Devils win the 1995 Stanley Cup.

All-American Guard Shawn Respert, nicknamed "Fire" for hot scoring, was 1995 Big Ten Player of the Year. He led the Big Ten in scoring with 25.6 points per game. He was MSU's scoring leader 4 consecutive years, and set State's career scoring record—2,531 points.

1995

Kelvin Jackson won the NCAA 118-pound wrestling title.

Shawn Respert, All-American guard, was named basketball Big Ten Player of the Year.

Danton Cole, MSU ice hockey star 1985-1989, gets his name on the Stanley Cup as a member of the New Jersey Devils championship NHL team.

Brad Fields won the Big Ten indoor track 200-meter dash in 21.30.

Dan Wirnsberger won the Big Ten 160-pound wrestling title.

Wendy Minch won the women's Big Ten gymnastics uneven parallel bars title.

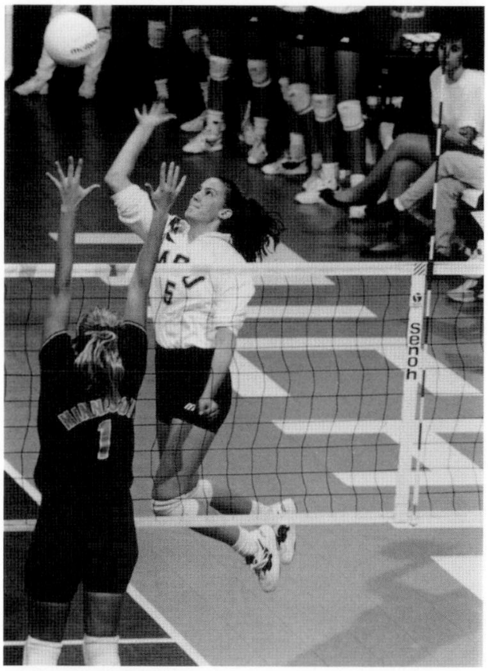

All-Americans and Co-Captains Dana Cooke (above right) and Val Sterk (below right) helped lead MSU's Volleyball team to the 1996 Big Ten title.

1996

MSU's women's volleyball team won the Big Ten title.

Kynda Kerr, baton twirler with the MSU Marching Band, **won the World Baton Twirling Championship** in Brescia, Italy, beating 32 other women from 11 nations. She was a sophomore elementary education major from Troy, Michigan.

Sevatheda Fynes, a native of the Bahamas, won an Olympic silver medal in the women's sprints at the 1996 Games in Atlanta.

Stacy Slobodnik, 24, MSU women's assistant golf coach, won the 1996 Michigan Women's amateur Golf Championship at Egypt Valley in Ada, Michigan.

Kathie Klages was named Big Ten women's Gymnastic Coach of the Year.

Sedrick Irvin, Spartan halfback, set all-time MSU freshman football record, scoring 18 touchdowns, and gaining 1,036 yards.

Chandra Burns won the women's Big Ten indoor track titles in the **200-meter dash** in 23.91, and the **400-meter run in 53.78, a conference championship record. She also won the outdoor track 400-meter title in 51.89, a conference championship record.**

David Morgan won the Big Ten 118-pound wrestling title.

Brian Picklo won the Big Ten 190-pound wrestling title.

Carolyn Hecht won the Big Ten women's gymnastic balance beam title.

1997

MSU's women's Basketball team won the Big Ten title, tying Purdue and Illinois, with a 12-4 record. The Spartans were ranked 19th in the nation.

MSU's women's Volleyball team won their second consecutive Big Ten title.

Sevatheda Fynes won three women's NCAA sprint titles—the indoor track 55-meter dash in 6.65; and two outdoor—the 100-meter dash in 11:04; and the 200-meter dash in 22.61.

Fynes also won four Big Ten track titles—two indoor— the 55-meter dash in 6.74, and the 200-meter dash in 23.65; and two outdoor—the 100-meter dash in 11:09, and 200-meter dash in 22.51. She was named **MSU's Female Athlete of the Year.**

Reid Friedrichs, Spartan soccer goalkeeper from Ann Arbor, was **selected Big Ten Player of the Year.** During the season, he scored six consecutive shutouts and had a 0.68 goals-against average. He was named **MSU's Male Athlete of the Year.**

Sedrick Irvin and Marc Renaud, Spartan running backs, **set an NCAA single-game rushing record for two players on the same team**. Against Penn State, Irvin ran for 238 yds, and Renaud for 203 to spark a 49-14 MSU victory over the Nittany Lions at Spartan Stadium. The season finale game was carried on ABC-TV.

Kasey Gant, freshman women golfer, broke the MSU three-round scoring record, shooting a 216 or 72 shot average, to win the Mary Fossom Invitational. Later in the season, the Fort Wayne native won the Lady Kat Invitational with a record low score of 69.

Kyle Baker won three men's Big Ten track titles—the indoor 3,000-meter run in 8:16.22, and the indoor 5,000-meter run in 14:23.60, and the outdoor track 5,000-meter run title in 14:06.24.

David Morgan won his second consecutive Big Ten 118-pound wrestling title, and was named **the Outstanding Wrestler at the Big Ten Championships**.

Sevatheda Fynes won 3 NCAA and 4 Big Ten sprint titles in 1997. She won Olympic gold in 2000, and Olympic silver (shown above) in 1996, running for the Bahamian 4 x 100-meter relay teams. Named MSU 1997 Female Athlete of the Year.

1997 MSU Big Ten Basketball Champions. Five senior players (L-R) standing: Alana Burns, Cheri Euler, and Paula Sanders. Sitting: Tamika Matlock (L), and Akilah Collier.

1998

MSU's basketball team won the Big Ten title.

MSU's hockey team won the CCHA regular season and Playoff titles.

Mateen Cleaves, All-American guard, was named basketball Big Ten Player of the Year.

David Morgan wrestled his way to a perfect 38-0 season and won his third consecutive Big Ten title at 118 pounds.

Morten Andersen, New Orleans Saints star placekicker and former MSU kicking star, became the **fifth player in National Football League history to surpass 1,600 points**. Andersen, 17-year NFL veteran and a native of

The "Flintstones" (Flint, Michigan natives) led MSU to 1998 Big Ten Basketball Title. L to R: Charlie Bell, Antonio Smith, Morris Peterson, and Mateen Cleaves. Cleaves was '98 and '99 Big Ten Player of the Year.

Copenhagen, Denmark, **held six NFL records**: most 100-point seasons (11); most 50-yard field goals in a career (33), season (8), and game (3); scoring in the most consecutive games (222), and the most Pro Bowl appearances by a kicker (7). Anderson still holds the MSU and Big Ten record for the longest field goal—63 yards against Ohio State at Columbus in 1981.

Barb Mucha, former MSU golfer, won the Sara Lee Classic, in Nashville. She defeated Nancy Lopez, Donna Andrews and Jenny Lidback in a playoff. Mucha's prize money of $112,500 helped put her among the Top 20 money winners in the Ladies Professional Golf Association. It was her fifth LPGA title.

Rod Brind'Amour was a member of the Canadian Olympic hockey team.

Steve Smith, former All-American in basketball and All-Star performer for the Atlanta Hawks, was **awarded the National Basketball Association's J. Walter Kennedy Citizenship Award**. Smith was recognized for his $2.5 million gift (largest ever given by a professional athlete to a university) to help create the Clara Bell Smith Student-Athlete Academic Center at MSU and the scholarship he established at Detroit Pershing High School for students who attend MSU.

Three-time All-American David Morgan won his 3rd consecutive Big Ten wrestling title in 1998. As a senior and team captain, he went 38-0 in regular season matches. In his freshmen and sophomore years, he became the 1st Spartan to win more than 40 matches in each of two years.

1999

MSU's basketball team won its second straight Big Ten title and advanced to the Final Four.

MSU's hockey team won its second consecutive CCHA regular season title, won the CCHA playoff title, and battled to the NCAA Frozen Four.

MSU became only the second university to have its basketball and ice hockey teams in their respective Final Fours at the same time. Only MSU and the University of Michigan had accomplished the feat.

MSU's track team won the Big Ten Indoor Track and Field title.

Mateen Cleaves, All-American guard, was named basketball Big Ten Player of the Year.

Dawn Riley, '87, served as captain and syndicate CEO for "America True," one of the year's entries in the America's Cup international sailing competition. **She was the first woman to head an America's Cup syndicate**.

Mike York, hockey All-American, was named CCHA Player of the Year, and conference tournament MVP.

In a *Sporting News* survey of 112 U.S. colleges that participate in NCAA Division I football and men's basketball rankings, **MSU ranked No. 10.** Penn State was No. 1, Purdue No. 7. Other Big Ten schools were: Iowa, No. 11, Wisconsin, No. 12, Michigan, No. 13, Northwestern, No. 17, Illinois, No. 18, Ohio State, No. 19, Indiana, No. 21, and Minnesota, No. 29. The survey measured standards of each school's full athletic program, including the number of teams sponsored, success rates, graduation rates for student-athletes, and Title IX compliance (support of women's athletics).

Steve Schell won the Big Ten indoor track 3,000-meter title in 8:09.45.

Jim Jurcevich won the Big Ten indoor track 5,000-meter run in 14:23.60.

Kyle Baker won the Big Ten men's outdoor track 10,000-meter run title in 29:26.68.

The MSU Motion Dance Team finished ahead of all other Big Ten teams and placed third in national championship competition at Orlando, Florida. Team captain Jenny Schultz noted that the MSU dance team achievement was accomplished without a coach, trainer, or choreographer. The team even organized its own fund-raisers to pay for operations and trips.

2000

2000 NCAA Basketball Champion Seniors—L-R: Morris Peterson, Mateen Cleaves, and A.J. Granger display season's trophies—Big 10, Spartan Classic, NCAA, Pearl Harbor Classic, and Big 10 Tournament.

MSU won its second NCAA basketball title, its third straight Big Ten title, and went to its second consecutive Final Four.

MSU's ice hockey team won the CCHA Playoff title.

CCHA Trophy Named for Ron Mason—Head coaches and athletics directors voted unanimously to name the Central Collegiate Hockey Association playoff championship trophy the Mason Cup, in honor of MSU head coach Ron Mason, the winningest hockey coach in college history.

MSU's football team won the Citrus Bowl, defeating Florida 37-34.

Karen Dennis, '77, M.A. '79, was the U.S. Women's track coach at the 2000 Olympic Games in Sydney, Australia.

Svetheda Fynes, MSU women's track star, won a gold medal as a member of the Bahamas 4 x 100-meter relay team at the 2000 Olympic Games in Sydney, Australia.

Steve Smith, MSU basketball All-American and NBA star, won a gold medal as a member of the U.S. basketball "Dream Team III" at the 2000 Olympic Games in Sydney, Australia.

Morris Peterson, star forward, was named basketball Big Ten Player of the Year.

Derrick Mason, former star Spartan wide receiver, helped the Tennessee Titans get to the 2000 Super Bowl with an 80-yard punt return to give the Titans a 26-14 win over the Jacksonville Jaguars.

Emily Bastel won the women's Big Ten individual golf title, shooting a record 288, even par. Her performance beat the previous record, set in 1995, by four strokes.

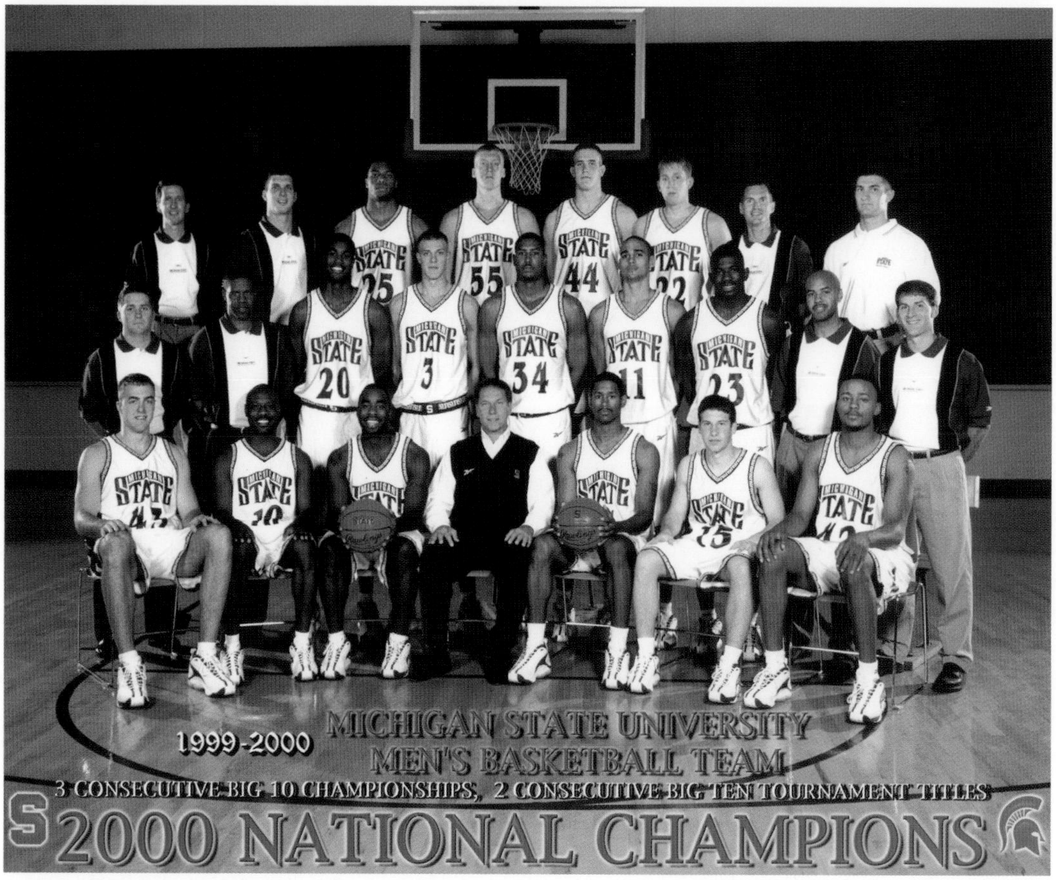

2000 NCAA Basketball Champions—Front Row (L-R): A.J. Granger, Brandon Smith, Mateen Cleaves, Head Coach Tom Izzo, Charlie Bell, Mat Ishbia, and Morris Peterson. 2nd Row (L-R): Assistant Coach Brian Gregory, Assistant Coach Mike Garland, Mike Chappell, Adam Wolfe, Andre Hutson, David Thomas, Jason Richardson, Assistant Coach Stan Heath, and Dave Owens, Assistant to Head Coach. Back Row (L-R): Trainer Tom Mackowiak, Strength and Conditioning Coach Mike Vorkapich, Aloysius Anagonye, Adam Ballinger, Jason Andreas, Steve Cherry, Equipment Mgr. Dave Pruder, and Manager Mark Armstrong.

Emily Bastel won women's Big Ten golf medalist honors for 2000, shooting a record 288 championship round, beating the conference record by 4 strokes.

MSU had produced 14 Hobey Baker Award finalists (Hockey's Heisman), more than any other university by the end of the 1999-2000 hockey season. Kip Miller won the award in 1990. Three Spartans were runners-up: Ron Scott—1982, Chad Alban—1998, and Mike York—1999. Other MSU finalists were: Ron Scott—1983, Kelly Miller—1985, Craig Simpson—1985, Mike Donnelly—1986, Bobby Reynolds—1989, Bryan Smolinski—1993, Anson Carter—1995, Mike York—1998, and Sean Horcoff—2000.

2001

All-American goalie Ryan Miller won the 2001 Hobey Baker Award, "Hockey's Heisman." He was named College Hockey and CCHA Player of the Year as well as Big Ten Male Athlete of the Year. He led the nation with a 1.32 goals against average, a .950 saves percentage, best in NCAA history. He also scored 18 shutouts in two years, breaking the NCAA career record of 16.

MSU's basketball team won its fourth straight Big Ten title and advanced to the Final Four for the third consecutive year. Winning four Big Ten titles in a row was a feat accomplished by only three other teams in conference history: Chicago (1907-1910), Ohio State (1960-1964), and Indiana (1973-1976). **In winning Big Ten titles in 1998, 1999, 2000, and 2001, the Spartans posted a record of 115 wins and 25 losses. This established a new Big Ten record for victories over four seasons**, surpassing the old mark of 108. For the 1999, 2000, and 2001 seasons, MSU won 93 games, a new Big Ten record for wins over a three-year period. By playing in three straight Final Fours, the Spartans became one of only nine schools to accomplish that feat. The others are: Cincinnati, Duke, Houston, Kentucky, North Carolina, Ohio State, San Francisco, and UCLA.

At the conclusion of the 2000-2001 season, Coach Tom Izzo led all active coaches in the U.S. with a winning percentage of .842 in NCAA tournament games (16 wins and 3 losses; minimum of 10 games).

MSU's ice hockey team won the CCHA regular season title; its second consecutive CCHA Playoff title, and advanced to the Frozen Four.

MSU became the only university in history to twice have its basketball and ice hockey teams in their respective NCAA Final Fours at the same time.

MSU Hockey Game Sets World Attendance Record of 74,554—MSU and Michigan tied 3-3 in the world's biggest ice hockey extravaganza in history. The game, held in Spartan Stadium on October 6, 2001, drew 74,554 fans, surpassing the old world record of 55,000, set in 1957 when Sweden beat Russia 3-2 for the World Championship game in Moscow Stadium.

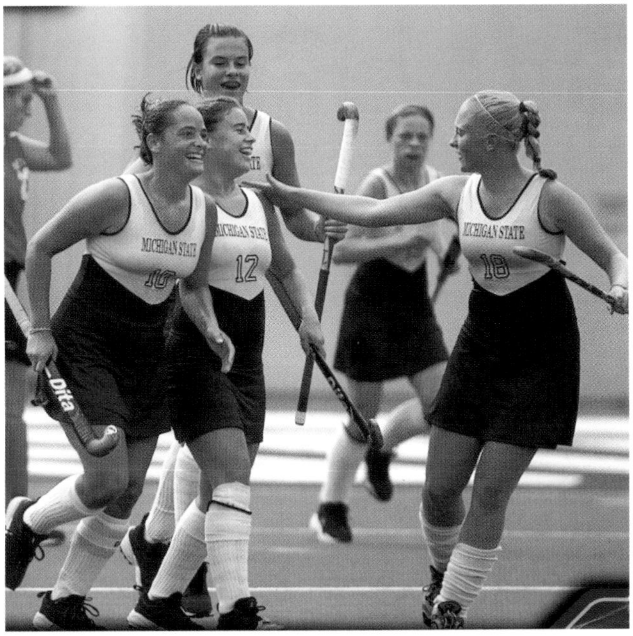

MSU 2001 Big Ten Field Hockey Champions—L-R: Bridget Cooper (10), Sophie Rosmalen (12), Alexandra Kyser (behind #12), and Jenny Sanders (18).

MSU's football team won the 2001 Silicon Valley Bowl, defeating No. 21 Fresno State, 44-35 on December 31 in San Jose State's Spartan Stadium.

MSU's women's golf team won the Big Ten title. Head coach Stacy Slobodnik was named **Big Ten Coach of the Year.**

MSU's women's cross country team won the Big Ten title.

MSU's women's field hockey team tied for the Big Ten regular season title.

Michele Madison, field hockey coach was named Big Ten Coach of the Year.

Bridget Cooper was named field hockey Big Ten Offensive Player of the Year.

Ryan Miller won the Hobey Baker award—"Hockey's Heisman." He was the second Spartan to do so. His cousin Kip won the award in 1990. Miller also **was named the Jesse Owens Male Athlete of the Year for the Big Ten Conference, and Michigan State's Male Athlete of the Year.** A two-time All-American, Miller was MSU MVP in 2001 and 2002.

Brad Van Pelt, former MSU All-American football player and NFL star, was **named to the College Football Hall of Fame.**

Paul Terek was named Big Ten Outdoor Track Athlete of the Year. He won the **Big Ten outdoor track decathlon title**, scoring 7,695 points in the ten-event competition. He also won the **Big Ten indoor track pole vault title** at 18-2.

Brad Golden won the Big Ten gymnastics floor exercise title.

Jonathon Plante won the Big Ten gymnastics pommel horse title.

Summer Mitchell won the women's Big Ten one-meter diving title.

Carly Weiden won the women's Big Ten three-meter diving title, and was **named Diver of the Championship.**

Mitchell and Weiden—both All-American divers—were named co-Big Ten Divers of the Year.

All-American Carly Weiden, 2001 Big Ten 3-Meter Diving Champion and Co-Big-Ten Diver of the Year.

All-American Summer Mitchell, 2001 Big Ten 1-Meter Diving Champion and Co-Big Ten Diver of the Year.

2002

MSU's Field Hockey Team won the Big Ten Tournament title and advanced to the NCAA Final Four. Coach Michele Madison's Spartans defeated defending national champion and No. 2 University of Michigan, 3-0 in the conference tournament. Sophomore midfielder Annebet Beerman was MSU's star, scoring on two penalty corner goals.

The field hockey team advanced to the NCAA tournament final four for the first time, losing in the quarter-finals to eventual national champion Wake Forest.

Marcus Taylor, sophomore point guard, **won the Big Ten basketball scoring and assist titles** for the 2001-2002 season, averaging 17.7 points and 5.0 assists in 14 games.

Michelle Carson won the 2002 women's Big Ten cross country championship and was named **Big Ten Cross Country Athlete of the Year**. She also earned All-American honors and was a Verizon Academic All-American first team honoree.

Eric Jorgensen, a junior, won the Big Ten individual golf title, taking medalist honors at the Big Ten championships in Iowa City, Iowa. He was the first Spartan to win the tournament.

Bob Malek was named Big Ten Baseball Player of the Year. Malek led the Spartans with 16 home runs, and set an MSU career record with 162 RBI's.

Mike York Won a Silver Olympic Medal with the U.S. ice hockey team, which was runner-up to Canada in the 2002 Salt Lake City Winter Olympics. York, a New York Rangers forward and former two-time All-American at MSU, was a Hobey Baker (Hockey's Heisman Trophy) finalist his junior and senior years.

Ryan Miller, MSU's all-star goalie, winner of the **2001 Hobey Baker Award** (ice hockey's Heisman trophy), was drafted by the Buffalo Sabre National Hockey League team. **Miller left MSU having set the NCAA record for career shutouts—26**. This performance, accomplished in just three seasons, buried the old record of 16 shutouts. Miller's career record as a goalie was 73-19-12, with a remarkable 1.53 goals against average.

Charles Rogers, MSU football wide receiver, set an NCAA record by catching a touchdown pass in a 39-24 win over Northwestern on September 28. It was his 13th consecutive regular-season game in which he caught a TD pass. He thus moved ahead of former record holders Randy Moss of Marshall, Aaron Turner of Pacific, and Desmond Howard of Michigan, who were tied at 12 straight games with touchdown catches. Including the MSU victory at the 2001 Silicon Valley Bowl, Rogers' streak was 14 consecutive TD games, breaking the Big Ten record of 13 straight games with a touchdown catch, formerly held by Michigan's Desmond Howard. Later in the season, Rogers broke the

MSU career record of 24 touchdown catches set by Kirk Gibson, 1975-1978. Rogers caught TD passes of 36 and 21 yards in a 56-21 rout of Indiana, giving him 25 career touchdown catches in 2001 and 2002. He also caught 68 passes during the season, an MSU record.

At the end of the season, **Rogers won the Biltnikoff Award** as the outstanding receiver in the nation. He also was named **Receiver of the Year by the Touchdown Club of Columbus, Ohio**.

MSU's women's basketball team defeated Kent State 85-72 on December 3rd before an all-time home crowd of 12,058, breaking the previous attendance record of 7,733 set against Michigan in 2000.

Kirk Gibson's Game-Winning Home Run for the Los Angeles Dodgers in the bottom of the ninth **in the first game of the 1988 World Series was selected by baseball fans as one of the top ten (9th) most exciting moments in baseball history**. Gibson and the other living selectees were honored prior to the third game of the 2002 World Series in San Francisco.

The MSU Dance Team placed third in national competition. Cal State finished first; Nebraska second.

2003

Joe DeLamielleure, former star lineman for the Spartan football team and All-Pro with the Buffalo Bills NFL team, was inducted into the **Professional Football Hall of Fame.**

Steve Smith (Clara Bell Smith Academic-Athletic Support Center), former MSU All-American forward, and **Kevin Willis**, former Spartan center, helped the San Antonio Spurs win the 2003 National Basketball Association championship.

Chris Hill, sophomore basketball guard, set a Big Ten and MSU record, hitting ten three-point shots in a frustrating 76-75 loss to eventual 2003 National Champion Syracuse at Breslin Arena on February 23. Hill scored a career high 34 points.

MSU's Basketball team advanced to the NCAA Elite Eight, farther than any other Big Ten team. The regular season record was 18-11. In the Big Ten, MSU finished tied for third, with a 10-6 record.

Two NCAA games were notable. At Tampa, Florida, MSU shocked a home-state crowd of 21,304, crushing the University of Florida Gators, 68-46. Coach Izzo called the game "a memory-maker." State shot 70 percent in the first half, and finished the game with a 55 percent shooting average. It was the first time in coach Billy Donovan's seven-year career that Florida scored fewer than 50 points. Freshman guard Maurice Ager led MSU scoring with 16 points, hitting on 6 of 9 shots. State held Florida freshman Anthony Roberson, former Saginaw, Michigan All-Stater, to zero points.

Next, Michigan State knocked off defending NCAA champion Maryland, 60-58, before 33,009 fans at San Antonio's Alamodome to advance to the Elite Eight. MSU was leading 54-40 with about six minutes to play, and appeared unbeatable. Then, in a 3 minute and 46 second stretch, Maryland turned up the defensive heat, causing seven turnovers, and outscored State, 15-0 to take a 55-54 lead.

Many teams would have folded after blowing a 14 point lead. But MSU responded. Freshman 6' 11" center Paul Davis slammed home a tying basket with 50 seconds left. And with 4.7 seconds left, Davis made a remarkable leaning baseline drive and caromed the ball off the glass for a 60-58 lead. Maryland All-American Steve Blake launched a long three-pointer in the final second, but missed. Davis led the Spartans with 13 points. In their game to try to advance to the Final Four, the Spartans lost to the University of Texas, 85-76.

The win improved Spartan coach Tom Izzo's NCAA tournament record to 19-4 for a winning percentage of .826—the best among all coaches with at least ten wins.

John L. Smith, head football coach, led MSU to an 8-4 regular season and was named Big Ten Coach of the Year.

Jacquie Joseph, MSU softball coach, was named **Big Ten Coach of the Year**.

Jamie Krzyminski won the Big Ten indoor track 5,000-meter title, and the outdoor track 10,000-meter title. She was named an All-American for the second straight year, and a Verizon Academic All-American second team member.

Nick Simmons, MSU 125-pound wrestler, was named **Big Ten Freshman of the Year**. He led the team with 29 wins and 11 falls.

MSU's Field Hockey Team tied for the Big Ten title, and won the Big Ten tournament. Coach Michele Madison's team posted a 17-5 record.

Bebe Bryans, MSU women's crew coach was named 2003 Big Ten Rowing Coach of the Year. She previously won the award in 2001.

The MSU-Kentucky "Basket Bowl" drew a World Record Basketball Crowd of 78,129 to the Detroit Lions' Ford Field in Detroit on December 13, 2003. The Wildcats defeated the Spartans, 79-74. The old world record attendance was 75,000 at the Berlin, Germany Olympic Stadium in 1951 when the Harlem Globetrotters played. The former national attendance record was set in the Louisiana Superdome in New Orleans when LSU and Notre Dame played before 68,000 in 1990.

Andy Ruthkoski, junior on the MSU golf team, broke the Belvedere Golf Club course record in Charlevoix at the Michigan Amateur Golf Championship by shooting a six under par 64. His June 18th round beat the old course record set by Walter Hagen in the 1930s.

MSU's Football Team Defeated Notre Dame 22-16 at South Bend for their eleventh victory in Notre Dame Stadium, more than any other team. It also was the Spartans' fourth consecutive win in Notre Dame Stadium. Purdue holds the record with five straight wins under the golden dome. No other schools have won more than two in a row at South Bend.

The World's Largest Basketball Crowd—78,129—saw Kentucky defeat MSU, 79-74, December 13, 2003 at the Detroit Lions' Ford Field in Detroit. Called the BasketBowl, the unique event sold more than 75,000 seats by mid-July, 2003. The original world record for basketball attendance was set in 1951 when the Harlem Globetrotters drew 75,000 to the Olympic Stadium in Berlin. The national attendance record was set on January 20, 1990 when LSU beat Notre Dame, 87-64, at the New Orleans' Superdome before 68,112 fans.

MSU head coach Tom Izzo declared, "Everything was awesome, except the biggest fact: we lost the game. We had the opportunity of a lifetime. This was an incredible setting. It'll be a good memory. It just won't be a good memory for a while," (*Detroit News,* December 14, 2003, story by Dave Dye).

2004

Maurice Ager, Spartan sophomore basketball forward, scored an amazing 17 points in 5 minutes and 53 seconds against Northwestern on January 21, 2004 as MSU defeated the Wildcats 73-61 at Evanston, Illinois. The scoring included five for five from the three-point line, and a layup. Overall, Ager had 24 points, his career high, on six for six shooting from 3-point land.

Miracle Win at Minnesota a hinge-point in the basketball season—After losing a heart-breaking overtime away game to Purdue, 79-74, MSU needed a victory to be a Big Ten title contender. The Gophers roared to a 23-point lead (37-14) late in the first half and they led at intermission by 16. In a remarkable resurgence, MSU tied the game at 53. With 2.8 seconds left in the game, Minnesota led 69-66. MSU took the ball out-of-bounds under the Gophers basket. A pass was fired to Paul Davis near the top of the key. He turned and rifled a pass to Maurice Ager who hit a 25-foot three-pointer to tie the game and put it into overtime. The Spartans prevailed in overtime for a miracle 78-77 win on January 28. The team record went to 9-8, and 4-2 in the Big Ten.

Spartans Shoot the Lights Out at Ohio State—In a rare shooting show, MSU hit 11 of its first 12 shots, and 21 of 26 in the first half for an unreal 81 percent. The lead was 48-30. For the entire game the Spartans shot 73 percent from the field, the second best shooting percentage in MSU history, and third best in Big Ten history. The Green and White won 84-70, running the team record to 12-8, and 7-2 in the Big Ten, putting the Spartans in undisputed first place on February 7.

MSU's Cagers Overcame a 12-Point Deficit to Beat Michigan 72-69 at Crisler Arena in Ann Arbor. Chris Hill hit a crucial 3-pointer inside the final minute to cement the win.

Izzo Wins 100th Big Ten Game—MSU defeated Minnesota 69-58 in a hard-fought basketball game at Breslin Students Events Center on Valentine's Day, 2004. Thus, Tom Izzo became only the third coach in Big Ten history to win 100 conference games within nine seasons. The others were Bobby Knight at Indiana and Gene Keady at Purdue.

Men's Basketball Team First to Lead Big Ten in Four Offensive Categories—In conference games, MSU led the Big Ten in scoring (71.3 points per game), field-goal percentage (.522), free-throw percentage (.777),and three-point percentage (.434). The Spartans finished the season tied for second in the Big Ten with a 12-4 record, and posted a 17-10 record overall.

The Spartan Basketball Team earned its seventh consecutive NCAA tournament bid, the longest current string of NCAA appearances in the Big Ten. In their first game of the tournament, MSU led Nevada by ten points with some nine minutes to play. But then the Spartans failed to score for seven minutes and lost the game 72-66, ending the season with an 18-10 record.

Women's Basketball Team Reaches a Historic High National Ranking—The Spartan women cagers were ranked No. 15 in one national poll, their highest ranking in history. Coach Joanne McCallie had the team playing high-energy defense, and aggressive offense. On February 12 at Ann Arbor, the Spartans overcame a 17-point deficit to beat Michigan 59-54, their second win over the Wolverines during the season and the fourth consecutive in the series. MSU fought back from a 13-point deficit at the half, and finished the game with an 11-0 run. State committed 14 turnovers in the first half, none in the second. Lindsey Bowen led State with 17 points. The game was played before 4,611, the largest women's basketball crowd in U-M history. The victory gave the Spartans a 19-4 overall record, and 9-3 in the Big Ten.

Twenty-Win Regular Season for Joanne McCallie's Women's Basketball Team—The Spartans beat Indiana at Bloomington, 60-51, ending the regular season with 20 wins and seven losses (10-6 Big Ten). It was just the fifth time an MSU women's basketball team won 20 games in a 32-year history of the sport.

Women's Basketball Team Advanced to the NCAA tournament second round for the first time since 1997, defeating Arizona, 72-60. Sophomore Lindsay Bowen led the Spartans with 18 points, and sophomore Liz Shimek added 16. The tournament run ended with an 80-61 loss to Texas on their home court.

Ice Hockey Team Makes NCAA Tournament for 10th Time in 11 Years. The Spartan hockey players earned a number three seed in the Midwest Region facing Minnesota-Duluth, as one of the "Sweet Sixteen." It was MSU's 23rd appearance in the NCAA tournament. The Spartans entered the tournament with a 23-16-2 record, including a 2-1-1 margin over Michigan. Freshman goalie Dominic Vicari went into the tournament with a nation-leading seven shutouts scored during the regular season.

The Women's Softball Team won its first Big Ten tournament title and earned a trip to the NCAA tournament. Senior pitcher Jessica Beech led the Spartans to victories over Michigan, 5-1; Northwestern, 2-0; and Illinois, 7-5—three of the top four teams in the conference. Brittney Green, senior third baseman, hit a three-run homer to beat Michigan, and hit two four-baggers in the championship game with Illinois. Beech finished the tournament as MSU's career leader in victories (70), strikeouts (643), and shutouts (24).

The Women's Water Polo Team (Club Sport) Won Its Fourth Consecutive Big Ten title. The team was to compete for the national championship, a title that MSU had won in 2001 and 2002.

MSU's Synchronized Skating Team (Club sport) finished fourth in the 2004 U.S. Synchronized Skating Championships in San Diego on March 6.

A Vision for the Future

President McPherson Looks Ahead

In a June 9, 2004 interview, MSU President M. Peter McPherson stated, "If in the next decade, we build like we have this past decade, we'll be one of the super strong universities in the country. We won't be as vulnerable to downturns as we have in the past." He gave great credit to MSU's officers, deans, faculty, and staff.

"Michigan State's foundation is in place. Our capital campaign ($1.2 billion) is vital to funding for faculty, facilities, and students. Our faculty and staff are strong, and are key players in MSU's continued achievements. Many faculty are building productive intellectual machines as well as winning major research grants.

"The role of the president and administration is to establish a structure and environment that provides the resources and the encouragement to create exemplary educational results. We must nurture a level of activity that sustains our greatness, internal drive, and momentum. In my estimation, we are getting there.

"Looking to the future, not everything has to be planned. Michigan State's leaders need to be ever alert and listening, to take advantage of creative ideas and targets of opportunity as they appear. This we have done in helping create the Michigan Life Sciences Corridor.

"And now, we are focused on winning the $1 billion Rare Isotope Accelerator for the State of Michigan and Michigan State University. This could mean 1,600 high-tech jobs for central Michigan, and an annual budget of $80 million.

"Moreover, we are pursuing the idea of establishing a strong presence for our College of Human Medicine in Grand Rapids, Michigan.

"The future of Michigan State looks promising. And, in our reach for excellence, we must never forget that we are a land-grant university, always seeking to provide educational access and opportunity for all classes of people."

The Next Wave: Educational Entrepreneurship

The next wave in funding for universities is educational entrepreneurship. And, Michigan State has one of the premier entrepreneurial educators in America: E. James Potchen, M.D., chair of the Radiology Department, which serves the Colleges of Human Medicine, Osteopathic Medicine, Veterinary Medicine, and many MSU scientific departments.

Educational Entrepreneur
National Leader in Developing MRI

Jim Potchen has chaired Michigan State's radiology department since 1975, and has created a leadership entrepreneurial strategy and mind-set that is the wave of the future in funding higher education.

He and his staff have created and built the finest university Magnetic Resonance Imaging and Radiology Facility in America ($35 million) at no cost to the taxpayer. They did it by borrowing the money to build facilities and equipment them, and then paying off the loans through the earnings of innovative joint ventures, business-medical consulting fees, and clinical fees. This imaginative business model is on-going, generating new facilities and equipment on a continuing basis.

E. James Potchen, M.D.
Chair, Radiology Department

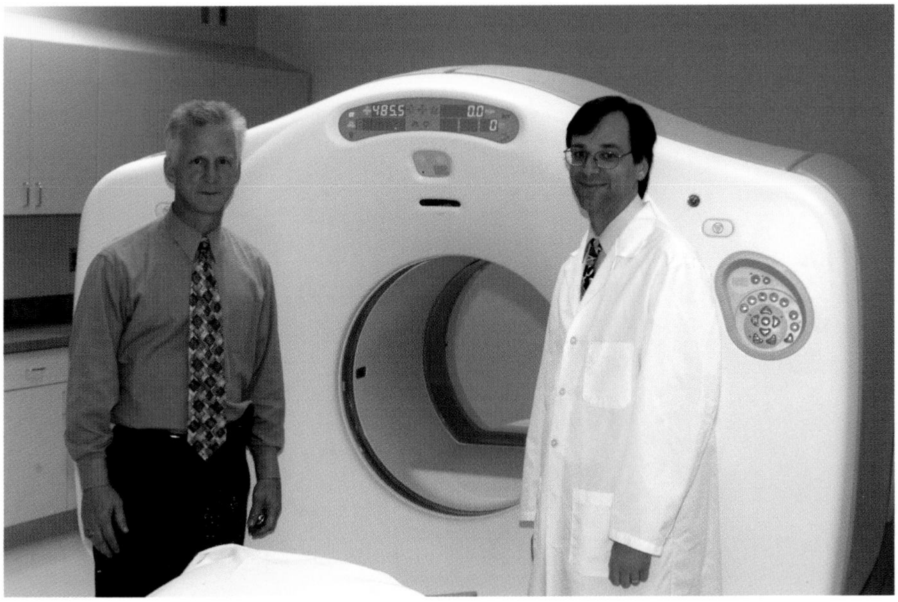

Latest PET CT radiology equipment is displayed by Thomas G. Cooper, MSEE, assistant chair, radiology department (L); and Kevin Berger, M.D., assistant professor, radiology.

Potchen declares, "If you add value to society and market it, revenue will flow. We have the intellectual and human capital here at MSU to create that value."

Under Potchen's leadership, the radiology department has developed close relationships with the world's leading producers of MRI and radiology equipment—General Electric, Phillips, and Siemens.

Since 1984, MSU radiologists have had GE's Medical Systems Division MRI equipment on site, helping to develop and improve this high-tech body-imaging capability. GE's National Demonstration Center for its MRI and CAT scanning equipment is located at MSU's Radiology Facility.

An annual Synergy Symposium—to bring together industrial and academic world leaders in radiology—is held at MSU's Department of Radiology.

Every month a top radiology expert comes to the radiology department to serve as a visiting professor. This continual renewal of the latest in radiology knowledge keeps MSU at the cutting edge of this fast-moving technology.

MSU's world leadership in radiology is exemplified by MRI angiography, which allows doctors to see human blood flow in the body without invasive catheter procedures. In 2004, a 16-slice, high-speed PET CT (Positron Emission Tomography/ Computerized Tomography) machine at MSU, allowed doctors to see the blood flow in the heart and vessels so quickly and precisely that the heart beat didn't disrupt viewing. This was a first.

Dr. Potchen and his highly educated staff have nurtured radiology leaders that now serve all over the nation. The business model he has helped create will aid MSU and universities nationwide for years to come.

Potchen's remarkable entrepreneurial leadership is underpinned with an equally remarkable set of academic credentials. He holds a bachelor's degree in horticulture from Michigan State University, an M.D. degree from Wayne State University, an MBA degree from Massachusetts Institute of Technology, and a law degree from the University of Michigan.

Magnificent botanical garden, with 3,000 species of flowers and plants, wraps around the MSU Radiology Facility; a testimony to Dr. Jim Potchen's love for horticulture, in which he received his first academic degree.

Coeds studying between the pillars of Kedzie Hall, south.

Sources

Quotations used in this book, in most cases, are credited to the authors immediately following the quote and are not documented in footnotes. Other sources are listed below chronologically.

1849-1854 *History of the Agricultural College of Michigan* by Dr. William J. Beal.
Michigan State: The First Hundred Years by Madison Kuhn.

1855 *History of the Agricultural College of Michigan* by Dr. William J. Beal.
Transactions of the State Agricultural Society (Michigan), 1855.

1856 *History of the Agricultural College of Michigan* by Dr. William J. Beal.

1857 *History of the Agricultural College of Michigan* by Dr. William J. Beal.
Transactions of the State Agricultural Society (Michigan), 1857.

1858 *History of the Agricultural College of Michigan* by Dr. William J. Beal.
Michigan State: The First Hundred Years by Madison Kuhn.
From An Oak Opening by Harold W. Lautner.

1859 *History of the Agricultural College of Michigan* by Dr. William J. Beal.
From An Oak Opening by Harold W. Lautner.

1860 *Michigan State: The First Hundred Years* by Madison Kuhn.
History of the Agricultural College of Michigan by Dr. William J. Beal.

1861 *Michigan State: The First Hundred Years* by Madison Kuhn.
History of the Agricultural College of Michigan by Dr. William J. Beal.

1862 *Annual Report of the Secretary of the State Board of Agriculture of the State of Michigan., 1862.*
(These Annual Reports hereafter will be referred to as *Annual Report of the State Board of Agriculture).*
Michigan State: The First Hundred Years by Madison Kuhn.

1863 *History of the Agricultural College of Michigan* by Dr. William J. Beal.
Michigan State: The First Hundred Years by Madison Kuhn.
Annual Report of the State Board of Agriculture, 1863.

1864 *Annual Report of the State Board of Agriculture, 1864.*
History of the Agricultural College of Michigan by Dr. William J. Beal.

1865 *Michigan State: The First Hundred Years* by Madison Kuhn.
Annual Report of the State Board of Agriculture, 1865.

1866 *Annual Report of the State Board of Agriculture, 1866.*

1867 *Annual Report of the State Board of Agriculture, 1867.*
History of the Agricultural College of Michigan by Dr. William J. Beal.

1868 *Annual Report of the State Board of Agriculture, 1868.*

1869 *Annual Report of the State Board of Agriculture, 1869.*
Michigan State: The First Hundred Years by Madison Kuhn.

1870 *Annual Report of the State Board of Agriculture, 1870.*

1871	*Michigan State: The First Hundred Years* by Madison Kuhn. *Annual Report of the State Board of Agriculture, 1871.*
1872	*Annual Report of the State Board of Agriculture, 1872.*
1873	*Michigan State: The First Hundred Years* by Madison Kuhn. *Annual Report of the State Board of Agriculture, 1873.* *History of the Agricultural College of Michigan* by Dr. William J. Beal.
1874	*Annual Report of the State Board of Agriculture, 1874.*
1875	*Annual Report of the State Board of Agriculture, 1875.* *History of the Agricultural College of Michigan* by Dr. William J. Beal.
1876	*Annual Report of the State Board of Agriculture, 1876.* *Michigan State: The First Hundred Years* by Madison Kuhn.
1877	*Michigan State: The First Hundred Years* by Madison Kuhn. MSU Archives and Historical Collections exhibit, 1993, on M.A.C.'s reforestation efforts in the 1870s. *Annual Report of the State Board of Agriculture, 1877.*
1878	*Annual Report of the State Board of Agriculture, 1878.* *History of the Agricultural College of Michigan* by Dr. William J. Beal.
1879	*Annual Report of the State Board of Agriculture,* 1879. *Michigan State: The First Hundred Years* by Madison Kuhn.
1880	*History of the Agricultural College of Michigan* by Dr. William J. Beal. *Annual Report of the State Board of Agriculture, 1880.*
1881	*Annual Report of the State Board of Agriculture, 1881.* *Michigan State: The First Hundred Years* by Madison Kuhn.
1882	*Annual Report of the State Board of Agriculture, 1882.* *From An Oak Opening* by Harold W. Lautner.
1883	*Annual Report of the State Board of Agriculture, 1883.* *Michigan State: The First Hundred Years* by Madison Kuhn.
1884	*Annual Report of the State Board of Agriculture, 1884.* *History of the Agricultural College of Michigan* by Dr. William J. Beal. *Michigan State: The First Hundred Years* by Madison Kuhn.
1885	*Annual Report of the State Board of Agriculture, 1885.* *History of the Agricultural College of Michigan* by Dr. William J. Beal.
1886	*Annual Report of the State Board of Agriculture, 1886.*
1887	*Annual Report of the State Board of Agriculture, 1887.* *Michigan State: The First Hundred Years* by Madison Kuhn.
1888	*Annual Report of the State Board of Agriculture, 1888.* *Michigan State: The First Hundred Years* by Madison Kuhn.
1889	*Annual Report of the State Board of Agriculture, 1889.* *History of the Agricultural College of Michigan* by Dr. William J. Beal. *Michigan State: The First Hundred Years* by Madison Kuhn.
1890	*Annual Report of the State Board of Agriculture, 1890.*

1891 *Annual Report of the State Board of Agriculture, 1891.*
History of the Agricultural College of Michigan by Dr. William J. Beal.
Michigan State: The First Hundred Years by Madison Kuhn.

1892 *Annual Report of the State Board of Agriculture, 1892.*

1893 *Annual Report of the State Board of Agriculture, 1893.*
A Centennial History of the Detroit College of Law by Gwenn Bashara Samuel, 1992.
Michigan State: The First Hundred Years by Madison Kuhn.

1894 *Annual Report of the State Board of Agriculture, 1894.*
Michigan State: The First Hundred Years by Madison Kuhn.

1895 *Michigan State: The First Hundred Years* by Madison Kuhn.
History of the Agricultural College of Michigan by Dr. William J. Beal.
Annual Report of the State Board of Agriculture, 1895.
A Centennial History of the Detroit College of Law by Gwenn Bashara Samuel, 1992.

1896 *Annual Report of the State Board of Agriculture, 1896.*
History of the Agricultural College of Michigan by Dr. William J. Beal.
Michigan State: The First Hundred Years by Madison Kuhn.

1897 *Michigan State: The First Hundred Years* by Madison Kuhn.
Annual Report of the State Board of Agriculture, 1897.
History of the Agricultural College of Michigan by Dr. William J. Beal.

1898 *Annual Report of the State Board of Agriculture, 1898.*
Michigan State: The First Hundred Years by Madison Kuhn.
The History of the Agricultural College of Michigan by Dr. William J. Beal.

1899 *Annual Report of the State Board of Agriculture, 1899.*
Michigan State: The First Hundred Years by Madison Kuhn.

1900 *Annual Report of the State Board of Agriculture, 1900.*
Michigan State: The First Hundred Years by Madison Kuhn.

1901 *Annual Report of the State Board of Agriculture, 1901.*
History of the Agricultural College of Michigan by Dr. William J. Beal.
Michigan State: The First Hundred Years by Madison Kuhn.

1902 *Annual Report of the State Board of Agriculture, 1902.*
History of the Agricultural College of Michigan by Dr. William J. Beal.
Michigan State: The First Hundred Years by Madison Kuhn.

1903 *Annual Report of the State Board of Agriculture, 1903.*
History of the Agricultural College of Michigan by Dr. William J. Beal.
Michigan State: The First Hundred Years by Madison Kuhn.

1904 *Annual Report of the State Board of Agriculture, 1904.*
History of the Agricultural College of Michigan by Dr. William J. Beal.
Michigan State: The First Hundred Years by Madison Kuhn.

1905 *Annual Report of the State Board of Agriculture, 1905.*
History of the Agricultural College of Michigan by Dr. William J. Beal.
Theodore Rex by Edmund Morris (Random House, 2001).

1906 *Annual Report of the State Board of Agriculture, 1906.*
Michigan State: The First Hundred Years by Madison Kuhn.
Theodore Rex by Edmund Morris (Random House, 2001).

1907	*Annual Report of the State Board of Agriculture, 1907.* *History of the Agricultural College of Michigan* by Dr. William J. Beal. *Report on M.A.C.'s 50th Anniversary Celebration.*
1908	*Annual Report of the State Board of Agriculture, 1908.* *History of the Agricultural College of Michigan* by Dr. William J. Beal.
1909	*Annual Report of the State Board of Agriculture, 1909.* *History of the Agricultural College of Michigan* by Dr. William J. Beal.
1910	*History of the Agricultural College of Michigan* by Dr. William J. Beal. *Annual Report of the State Board of Agriculture, 1910.*
1911	*History of the Agricultural College of Michigan* by Dr. William J. Beal. *Annual Report of the State Board of Agriculture, 1911.*
1912	*Annual Report of the State Board of Agriculture, 1912.* *History of the Agricultural College of Michigan* by Dr. William J. Beal.
1913	*History of the Agricultural College of Michigan* by Dr. William J. Beal. *Annual Report of the State Board of Agriculture, 1913.* *From An Oak Opening* by Harold W. Lautner.
1914	*Annual Report of the State Board of Agriculture, 1914.*
1915	*Annual Report of the State Board of Agriculture, 1915.* *A Century of Michigan State Football* by Ken Hoffman and Larry Bielat. *Alumni Patriarch Memories—50th Anniversary, 1965.*
1916	*Annual Report of the State Board of Agriculture, 1916.* *Michigan State: The First Hundred Years* by Madison Kuhn. *Alumni Patriarch Memories—50th Anniversary, 1966.*
1917	*Annual Report of the State Board of Agriculture, 1917.*
1918	*Annual Report of the State Board of Agriculture, 1918.* *Alumni Patriarch Memories—50th Anniversary, 1968.* *Lansing State Journal, November 17, 1918.*
1919	*Annual Report of the State Board of Agriculture, 1919.*
1920	*Annual Report of the State Board of Agriculture, 1920.* *Michigan State: The First Hundred Years* by Madison Kuhn. *A Century of Michigan State Football* by Ken Hoffman and Larry Bielat. *Alumni Patriarch Memories—50th Anniversary, 1970.*
1921	*Annual Report of the State Board of Agriculture, 1921.* *Michigan State: The First Hundred Years* by Madison Kuhn.
1922	*Annual Report of the State Board of Agriculture, 1922.* *Michigan State: The First Hundred Years* by Madison Kuhn. *Alumni Patriarch Memories—50th Anniversary, 1972.*
1923	*Annual Report of the State Board of Agriculture, 1923.* *Michigan State: The First Hundred Years* by Madison Kuhn.
1924	*Annual Report of the State Board of Agriculture, 1924.* *Michigan State: The First Hundred Years* by Madison Kuhn. *Alumni Patriarch Memories—50th Anniversary, 1974.*
1925	*Annual Report of the State Board of Agriculture, 1925.* *Michigan State: The First Hundred Years* by Madison Kuhn.

1926	*Annual Report of the State Board of Agriculture, 1926.* *Michigan State: The First Hundred Years* by Madison Kuhn. *Alumni Patriarch Memories—50th Anniversary, 1976.*
1927	*Annual Report of the State Board of Agriculture, 1927.* *Michigan State: The First Hundred* by Madison Kuhn.
1928	*Annual Report of the State Board of Agriculture, 1928.* *Michigan State: The First Hundred Years* by Madison Kuhn.
1929	*Annual Report of the State Board of Agriculture, 1929.* *Michigan State: The First Hundred Years* by Madison Kuhn. *University Club 75th Anniversary History.*
1930	*Annual Report of the State Board of Agriculture, 1930.* *Michigan State: The First Hundred Years* by Madison Kuhn. *Alumni Patriarch Memories—50th Anniversary, 1980.*
1931	*Annual Report of the State Board of Agriculture, 1931.* *Michigan State: The First Hundred Years* by Madison Kuhn. *Alumni Patriarch Memories—50th Anniversary, 1981.*
1932	*Annual Report of the State Board of Agriculture, 1932.* *Michigan State: The First Hundred Years* by Madison Kuhn. *Alumni Patriarch Memories—50th Anniversary, 1982.*
1933	*Annual Report of the State Board of Agriculture,* 1933. *Michigan State: The First Hundred Years* by Madison Kuhn. *Alumni Patriarch Memories—50th Anniversary,* 1983.
1934	*Annual Report of the State Board of Agriculture,* 1934. *Michigan State: The First Hundred Years* by Madison Kuhn. *Alumni Patriarch Memories—50th Anniversary,* 1984.
1935	*Annual Report of the State Board of Agriculture, 1935.* *Michigan State: The First Hundred Years* by Madison Kuhn. *Alumni Patriarch Memories—50th Anniversary, 1985.*
1936	*Annual Report of the State Board of Agriculture, 1936.* *Michigan State: The First Hundred Years* by Madison Kuhn.
1937	*Annual Report of the State Board of Agriculture, 1937.* *Michigan State: The First Hundred Years* by Madison Kuhn. *Alumni Patriarch Memories—50th Anniversary, 1991.*
1938	*Annual Report of the State Board of Agriculture, 1938.* *Michigan State: The First Hundred Years* by Madison Kuhn. *Alumni Patriarch Memories—50th Anniversary, 1988.*
1939	*Annual Report of the State Board of Agriculture, 1939.* *Michigan State: The First Hundred Years* by Madison Kuhn.
1940	*Annual Report of the State Board of Agriculture, 1940.* *Michigan State: The First Hundred Years* by Madison Kuhn. *Alumni Patriarch Memories—50th Anniversary, 1990.*
1941	*Annual Report of the State Board of Agriculture, 1941.* *Michigan State: The First Hundred Years* Madison Kuhn. *Theodore Rex* by Edmund Morris (Random House, 2001).

1942	*Annual Report of the State Board of Agriculture, 1942.* *Michigan State: The First Hundred Years* by Madison Kuhn. *Alumni Patriarch Memories—50th Anniversary, 1995.*
1943	*Annual Report of the State Board of Agriculture, 1943.* *Michigan State: The First Hundred Years* by Madison Kuhn. *President's Annual Report, 1943.*
1944	*Annual Report of the State Board of Agriculture, 1944.* *President's Annual Report, 1944.* *Michigan State: The First Hundred Years* by Madison Kuhn.
1945	*Annual Report of the State Board of Agriculture, 1945.* *President's Annual Report, 1945.* *Michigan State: The First Hundred Years* by Madison Kuhn.
1946	*Annual Report of the State Board of Agriculture, 1946.* *President's Annual Report, 1946* *From An Oak Opening* by Harold W. Lautner. *Alumni Patriarch Memories—50th Anniversary, 2000.*
1947	*Annual Report of the State Board of Agriculture, 1947.* *President's Annual Report, 1947.* *Alumni Patriarch Memories—50th Anniversary, 2000.*
1948	*Annual Report of the State Board of Agriculture, 1948.* *President's Annual Report, 1948.* *From an Oak Opening* by Harold W. Lautner. *Alumni Patriarch Memories—50th Anniversary, 2000 & 2001.*
1949	*Annual Report of the State Board of Agriculture,* 1949. *President's Annual Report,* 1949. *Michigan State: The First Hundred Years* by Madison Kuhn. *Alumni Patriarch Memories—50th Anniversary, 1999.*
1950	*Annual Report of the State Board of Agriculture,* 1950. *President's Annual Report,* 1950. *Michigan State: The First Hundred Year*s by Madison Kuhn. *Alumni Patriarch Memories—50th Anniversary,* 2000.
1951	*Annual Report of the State Board of Agriculture,* 1951. *President's Annual Report,* 1951. *Michigan State: The First Hundred Years* by Madison Kuhn.
1952	*Annual Report of the State Board of Agriculture,* 1952. *President's Annual Report, 1952.* *Alumni Patriarch Memories—50th Anniversary,* 2002. *Michigan State: The First Hundred Years* by Madison Kuhn.
1953	*Annual Report of the State Board of Agriculture, 1953.* *President's Annual Report,* 1953.
1954	*Annual Report of the State Board of Agriculture,* 1954. *President's Annual Report,* 1954.
1955	*Annual Report of the State Board of Agriculture,* 1955. *President's Annual Report,* 1955.
1956	*Annual Report of the State Board of Agriculture,* 1956. *President's Annual Report,* 1956.

1957	*Annual Report of the State Board of Agriculture,* 1957. *President's Annual Report,* 1957.
1958	*President's Annual Report,* 1958.
1959	*President's Annual Report,* 1959.
1960	*President's Annual Report,* 1960.
1961	*President's Annual Report,* 1961.
1962	*President's Annual Report,* 1962.
1963	*President's Annual Report,* 1963.
1964	*President's Annual Report,* 1964.
1965	*President's Annual Report*, 1965.
1966	*President's Annual Report*, 1966.
1967	*President's Annual Report,* 1967.
1968	*President's Annual Report,* 1968.
1969	*President's Annual Report,* 1969. (Final Report by President John A. Hannah) *From an Oak Opening* by Harold W. Lautner. *MSU Faculty News,* 1969. *MSU Alumni Association Magazine, November-December,* 1969.
1970	*MSU Faculty News,* 1970. *MSU Alumni Association Magazine, Fall 1970, February,* 1971.
1971	*MSU Alumni Association Magazine, April, September, November, 1971; January, 1972.*
1972	*MSU Alumni Association Magazine, January, May, July, September, November, 1972; January, 1973.*
1973	*MSU Alumni Association Magazine, January, March, May, July, September, November, 1973; January, 1974.*
1974	*MSU Alumni Association Magazine, January, March, May, July, September, November-December, 1974.* *MSU Alumni Association Magazine, January, 1975*
1975	*MSU Alumni Association Magazine, January-February, March-April, May-June, July-August, September-October, and November-December, 1975.*
1976	*MSU Alumni Association Magazine, January-February, March-April, Summer, September-October, November-December, 1976.*
1977	*MSU Alumni Association Magazine, March-April, May-June, July-August, September-October, November-December, 1977.*
1978	*MSU Alumni Association Magazine, January-February, March-April, Summer, September-October, 1978; December 1978-January 1979.*
1979	*MSU Alumni Association Magazine, December 1978-January 1979, February-March, April-May, Summer, 1979.*
1980	*MSU Alumni Association Magazine, Winter, Spring, Summer, Autumn, 1980.*
1981	*MSU Alumni Association Magazine, Spring, Autumn, 1981.*
1982	*MSU News Bulletin—January 7, 14, 21, 28; February 4, 11, 18,25; March 11; April 1, 8, 15, 22; May 13, 20, 27; June 3, 10, 17; July 29; August 12; September 16, 23, 30; October 7, 14, 21; November 4, 11, 18; December 2, 1982.*(No MSU Alumni Association Magazine Published in 1982).

1983 *MSU Alumni Magazine, Summer, Fall, 1983.*

1984 *MSU Alumni Magazine, Winter, Spring, Summer, Fall, 1984.*

1985 *MSU Alumni Magazine, Winter, Spring, Fall, 1985.*

1986 *MSU Alumni Magazine, Winter, Spring, Summer, Fall, 1986.*

1987 *MSU Alumni Magazine, Winter, Spring, Summer, Fall, 1987.*

1988 *MSU Alumni Magazine, Winter, Spring, Fall, 1988.*

1989 *MSU Alumni Magazine, Winter, Spring, Summer, Fall, 1989.*

1990 *MSU Alumni Magazine, Winter, Spring, Fall, 1990.*

1991 *MSU Alumni Magazine, Winter, Spring, Summer, Fall, 1991.*

1992 *MSU Alumni Magazine, Winter, Spring, Fall, 1992.*

1993 *MSU Alumni Magazine, Winter, Spring, Summer, Fall, 1993.*

1994 *MSU Alumni Magazine, Winter, Spring, Summer, Fall, 1994.*

1995 *MSU Alumni Magazine, Winter, Spring, Summer, Fall, 1995.*

1996 *MSU Alumni Magazine, Winter, Spring, Summer, Fall, 1996.*

1997 *MSU Alumni Magazine, Winter, Spring, Summer, Fall, 1997.*

1998 *MSU Alumni Magazine, Winter, Spring, Summer, Fall, 1998.*

1999 *MSU Alumni Magazine, Winter, Spring, Summer, Fall, 1999.*

2000 *MSU Alumni Magazine, Winter, Spring, Summer, Fall, 2000.*

2001 *MSU Alumni Magazine, Winter, Spring, Summer, Fall, 2001.*

2002 *MSU Alumni Magazine, Winter, Spring, Summer, Fall, 2002.*

2003 *MSU Alumni Magazine, Winter, Spring, Summer, Fall, 2003.*

2004 *MSU Alumni Magazine, Winter, Spring, 2004.*

Photographic Credits

Book Cover

Beaumont Tower—MSU University Relations.

Inside Front Cover

Red Cedar River walkway—tulips in foreground—MSU University Relations.

Introductory Pages

MSU graduates—*MSU Alumni Magazine*—vii.
King and Alice McCristal—King J. McCristal collection—viii.
Bruce and Sheryl McCristal—Dr. Robert Moran—x.
East Lansing-Michigan State University I-96 highway sign—J. Bruce McCristal—xiii.
Dr. John A. Hannah near Beaumont Tower—MSU Archives & Historical Collections—xiv.

A Sesquicentennial Salute

Cowles House—MSU University Relations—xxviii.

Overview Chapter—The Spirit of Michigan State

Campus entrance sign—J. Bruce McCristal—1.
Campus lantern against yellow leaves—MSU University Relations—2.
Library fountains—MSU University Relations—3.
Promenade between Anthony and Ericson Halls—J. Bruce McCristal—7.

MSU Historical Timeline

Joseph R. Williams, First President—1857—MSU Archives & Historical Collections—10.
College Hall—MSU Archives & Historical Collections—11.
"Saints' Rest"—first college dormitory—MSU Archives & Historical Collections—12.
Lewis R. Fisk, Second President—1859—MSU Archives & Historical Collections—15.
Class of 1861—first graduating class—MSU Archives & Historical Collections—15.
Theophilus C. Abbot, Third President—1862—MSU Archives & Historical Collections—16.
"Saints' Rest"—1865—MSU Archives & Historical Collections—17.
Dr. Manly Miles—"Father" of Scientific Agriculture—MSU Archives & Historical Collections—18.
First Williams Hall—1869—MSU Archives & Historical Collections—19.
Dr. William J. Beal in his Botanical Garden—foot on stone—MSU Archives & Historical Collections—20.
President's Home—# 1 Faculty Row—1874—MSU Archives & Historical Collections—21.
Class of 1875 at "The Rock" (Gift of Class of 1873)—MSU Archives & Historical Collections—22.
Dr. Robert C. Kedzie lecturing—MSU Archives & Historical Collections—24.
First Wells Hall—1877—MSU Archives & Historical Collections—26.
Dr. William J. Beal sitting in his Botanical Garden—MSU Archives & Historical Collections—27.
Linton Hall (First Library-Museum)—1881—MSU University Relations—28.
Class of 1883 Fountain—MSU Archives & Historical Collections—29.
College Band—1884—MSU Archives & Historical Collections—30.
Edwin Willits, Fourth President—1885—MSU Archives & Historical Collections—30.
Armory Building—1885—MSU Archives & Historical Collections—31.
ROTC cadets—Armory in background—MSU Archives & Historical Collections—31.

Coeds on campus walkway—1929—MSU Archives & Historical Collections—73.
G. Malcolm Trout—"Father" of Homogenized Milk—MSU Archives & Historical Collections—74.
Clara (Hantel) Brucker, Class of 1930, Michigan's First Lady—MSU Archives & Historical Collections—75.
First Basketball Team flight in U.S.—1931—MSU Archives & Historical Collections—75.
Michigan State College seal—J. Bruce McCristal—77.
John A. Hannah—Secretary to the Board—1935—MSU Archives & Historical Collections—78.
John W. and Elizabeth Beaumont—MSU Archives & Historical Collections—80.
Band Shell—1937—MSU Archives & Historical Collections—81.
Abbot Road campus entrance sculpture—1938—J. Bruce McCristal—82.
Harvey Woodstra—World Record hurdler—MSU Archives & Historical Collections—82.
Campus aerial view—1939—MSU Archives & Historical Collections—83.
Lyman J. Briggs—Led U.S. feasibility investigation of atomic power—MSU Archives & Historical Collections—84.
Eleanor Roosevelt & John A. Hannah—1940—MSU Archives & Historical Collections—85.
Jenison Fieldhouse basketball crowd—MSU Archives & Historical Collections—86.
Auditorium—MSU University Relations—86.
Ray Stannard Baker, Pulitzer Prize winner—1940—MSU Archives & Historical Collections—87.
John A. Hannah, Twelfth President—1941—MSU Archives & Historical Collections—88.
Robert S. Shaw and John A. Hannah—Linton Hall—1941—MSU Archives & Historical Collections—89.
Merle and Burl Jennings and Bill Maxwell—1942 NCAA wrestling champions—MSU Archives & Historical Collections—90.
Florence Hall, Class of 1909, headed Women's Land Army—1943—MSU Archives & Historical Collections—91.
Army Air Corps cadets—1943—MSU Archives & Historical Collections—92.
Russell B. Nye, English professor & Pulitzer Prize winner—1944—MSU Archives & Historical Collections—93.
Grand River Avenue, East Lansing—1945—MSU Archives & Historical Collections—94.
Spartan Statue—Laura Little—95.
Double deck beds—Jenison Gymnasium—1946—MSU Archives & Historical Collections—96.
Canoeing Red Cedar River—two couples—1946—MSU Archives & Historical Collections—97.
Students walking between classes—1946—MSU Archives & Historical Collections—98.
Coeds on central campus walkway—1946—MSU Archives & Historical Collections—99.
Canoe baseball—flooded Kobs Field—1947—MSU Archives & Historical Collections—99.
Aerial view student housing—quonset huts & barracks apartments—1947—MSU Archives & Historical Collections—100.
NCAA champions—1947—Hoogerhyde, Davey, Mikles—MSU Archives & Historical Collections—101.
Engagement bench—MSU Archives & Historical Collections—101.
"State Makes Big 10"—1948—MSU Archives & Historical Collections—102.
Macklin Stadium sellout crowd of 51,000—1948—MSU Archives & Historical Collections—103.
Barbara Tanner—National "Sweetheart of Sigma Chi"—1948—MSU Archives & Historical Collections—103.
Student protest of Dior's long skirts—1948—MSU Archives & Historical Collections—104.
Student football ticket campout, Jenison Fieldhouse steps—1949—Archives & Historical Collections—104.
Junior 500 Push Cart Derby—1949—MSU Archives & Historical Collections—105.
Shaw Hall reflected at night in Red Cedar River—1950—MSU Archives & Historical Collections—106.
Chuck Davey—1949—MSU Sports Information—107.
Biggie Munn with U of M goal post—1950—MSU Archives & Historical Collections—108.
Mary Termohlen, Homecoming queen—1950—MSU Archives & Historical Collections—108.
Two-Mile World Record Relay Team—1950—MSU Archives & Historical Collections—109.
Dick Panin 88-yard TD run vs. Notre Dame—1951—MSU Archives & Historical Collections—109.
Big Ten Tennis Champions—1951—1st Big Ten title in any sport—MSU Archives & Historical Collections—110.
NCAA Boxing Champions—1951—MSU Archives & Historical Collections—110.
Alumni Chapel reflected in Red Cedar River—MSU Alumni Relations—111.

Beaumont Tower, magnolia blossoms—George Booth—160.
Snow-covered walkway—IM Circle—J. Bruce McCristal—161.
Dr. Edgar L. Harden, Fifteenth President—MSU Archives & Historical Collections—162.
Jack Meyers, Class of 1951, publisher *Time* magazine, greets Chinese leader—MSU Archives & Historical Collections—164.
Dr. Barnett Rosenberg, "Father" of Cisplatin anti-cancer drug—MSU Archives & Historical Collections—165.
Dr. Cecil Mackey, Sixteenth President—MSU Archives & Historical Collections—166.
Magic Johnson—1979 NCAA Basketball Championship game—MSU Archives & Historical Collections—166.
MSU Cheerleaders—1979 National Champions—MSU Archives & Historical Collections—167.
Stanley O. Ikenberry, M.A. '57, Ph.D. '60, President-U. of *Illinois—MSU Alumni Magazine/MSU* Archives & Historical Collections—168.
Canoes at Red Cedar Yacht Club—MSU University Relations—169.
Sanford Natural Area—students jogging, fall color—J. Bruce McCristal—170.
Coeds strolling in campus winter wonderland—MSU University Relations—171.
David Stockman, cum laude 1968—MSU Archives & Historical Collections—172.
K500 Super Cyclotron—MSU University Relations—173.
Anthony Earl, Class of 1958, Governor of *Wisconsin—MSU Alumni Magazine/*MSU Archives & Historical Collections—174.
James Blanchard, Governor of Michigan—1982—*MSU Alumni Magazine;* MSU Archives & Historical Collections—174.
Wharton Center Catherine Herrick Cobb Great Hall—MSU University Relations—175.
Dr. Robert C. Trojanowicz, '63, M.A. '65, Ph.D. '69—"Father" of Community Policing—School of Criminal Justice—177.
Rhodes Scholars Judith Stoddart, Claudena Skran, Molly *Brennan—MSU Alumni Magazine/*MSU Archives & Historical Collections—178.
Dr. John A. DiBiaggio, Seventeenth President—MSU Archives & Historical Collections—179.
Mike Donnelly, Lorenzo White, Scott Skiles—Spartan Stars—*MSU Alumni Magazine/* MSU Archives & Historical Collections—180.
Plant & Soil Sciences Building—Laura Little—181.
Kelly Lynn Garver, Miss Michigan—1986—*MSU Alumni Magazine/* MSU Archives & Historical Collections—182.
Jim Cash, award winning movie writer—*MSU Alumni Magazine/* MSU Archives & Historical Collections—182.
Sunraycer Team, Solar Car World Champions, 1987—General Motors—183.
Norm Barkeley, Class of 1953—Norm Barkeley collection—183.
Dr. Walter Adams, 1988 Rose Bowl Parade—Harley Seeley—184.
MSU Band—1988 Rose Bowl—MSU University Relations—184.
Kevan Gosper, Class of 1955, International Olympic Committee—*MSU Alumni Magazine/* MSU Archives & Historical Collections—185.
Jack Breslin Biographical Sketch—Two photographs—MSU Sports Information—186,187.
Breslin Student Events Center—MSU University Relations—188.
Engineering Building Addition—1989—J. Bruce McCristal—188.
IM-East interior—Laura Little—189.
William R. Tiefel, Class of 1956, President-Marriott Hotels—*MSU Alumni Magazine/* MSU Archives & Historical Collections—189.
Dr. Beatrice Paolucci—MSU Archives & Historical Collections—190.
Super Conducting Cyclotron for cancer therapy, Dr. Henry Blosser—MSU University Relations—191.
Robert J. Schultz, GM Vice Chairman & Robert C. Stempel, GM Chairman—1990—General Motors—192.
Richard Barkley, Class of 1954, Ambassador to East Germany—*MSU Alumni Magazine/* MSU Archives & Historical Collections—192.
Eli Broad, Class of 1954, Gives $20 million to MSU—1991—*MSU Alumni Magazine*—193.

September 11,2001 Vigil at "The Rock"—*MSU Alumni Magazine*—222.
World Record Hockey Crowd—74,554—"The Cold War"—J. Bruce McCristal—223.
Lloyd Ward, '70, CEO U.S. Olympic Committee—*MSU Alumni Magazine/* MSU Archives & Historical Collections—224.
Ty Willingham, '77, Head Football Coach-Notre Dame—*MSU Alumni Magazine*—225.
Dr. Michael Tomashow, winner Alexander von Humboldt Award—*MSU Alumni Magazine*—226.
Biomedical & Physical Sciences Building—J. Bruce McCristal—227.
Alfred Berkowitz Basketball Complex—J. Bruce McCristal—228.
Ron Mason, MSU Athletics Director—*MSU Alumni Magazine*—229.
Nicholas Perricone, M.D. '82, $5 million gift to MSU—*MSU Alumni Magazine*—229.
Donald G. Cook, '69, Commander, U.S. Air Force Education & Training Command—*MSU Alumni Magazine*—230.
Carl Angelo, '52, winningest pitcher, U.S. amateur baseball—*MSU Alumni Magazine*—231.
M. Peter McPherson, economic rebuilding of Iraq—*MSU Alumni Magazine*—232.
Spartan Marching Band Drumline at Spartan Statue—J. Bruce McCristal—233.
Bill Brink '54, Carol Brink '55—Leaders, Detroit Area Development Council—*MSU Alumni Magazine*—234.
Lynn Myers, '64, MBA '67, with GMC Envoy XUVs—Hannah Award Winner—General Motors—235.
Magic Johnson at dedication of his statue-Breslin Center—J. Bruce McCristal—236.
Joe DeLamielleure—MSU Sports Information—237.
Lou Anna K. Simon, Twentieth President—Kim Kauffman—239.

MSU Colleges and Study Programs

Agricultural Hall—MSU University Relations—245.
Agricultural students in England—Dr. H. Paul Roberts, College of Agriculture & Natural Resources—246.
Chistiane Morel, Fine Arts' Masters' student—Lamont Clegg, Department of Theater, College of Arts & Letters—253.
Financial Analysis Laboratory—Eli Broad College of Business—255.
Kevin Sullivan, telecommunications major—College of Communication Arts & Sciences—257.
Rudy Hobbs student teaching—College of Education—259.
Andy Fedewa, graduate student in MSU Engine Research Laboratory—College of Engineering—262.
MSU's Central School Child Development Laboratories—College of Human Ecology—264.
Young child examination—College of Human Medicine—Lynne Brown—266.
Rujuta Bhatt, '93, Rhodes, Marshall, Truman Scholar—*MSU Alumni Magazine/*MSU Archives & Historical Collections—268.
Michigan State University-Detroit College of Law Moot Court—MSU-Detroit College of Law—270.
MSU-Detroit College of Law Building—J. Bruce McCristal—271.
K500 Superconducting Cyclotron, Peter Miller, Harold Hilbert—MSU University Relations—Bruce Fox photo for College of Natural Science—273.
Southern Astrophysical Research Telescope—College of Natural Science—*MSU Alumni Magazine*—274.
Nursing student with Regina Taylor, RN, MSM—College of Nursing—276.
College of Osteopathic Medicine students Eric Hawkins & Kristan Gaumer—College of Osteopathic Medicine—278.
Forensic Anthropology Laboratory—Professors Norman Sauer, Roger Hunt, and Todd Fenton, College of Social Science—Photo by Ann Cook, College of Osteopathic Medicine Graphics—281.
Veterinary students, cow surgery—College of Veterinary Medicine—283.
Eustace-Cole Hall, home of Honors College—J. Bruce McCristal—286.
Dr. Terrie Taylor attends malaria patient in Africa—Photo by Dr. Fred MacInnes, RR3, Pictou, Nova Scotia, Canada BOK 1HO, for MSU International Studies and Programs—288.

Alumni Achievement

Spencer Abraham, '74, U.S. Secretary of Energy, with MSU President McPherson—*MSU Alumni* Magazine/MSU Archives & Historical Collections—293.
George Ariyoshi, '49, Governor of Hawaii—*MSU Alumni Magazine/*MSU Archives & Historical Collections—293.

John Kornblum, '64, U.S. Ambassador to Federal Republic of Germany—*MSU Alumni Magazine*/MSU Archives & Historical Collections—294.
John Walters, '74, U.S. "Drug Czar"—*MSU Alumni Magazine*—294.
Jay Johnson, '70, Director, U.S. Mint—*MSU Alumni Magazine*—295.
Kwame Kilpatrick, MSU-Detroit College of Law '99, Mayor of Detroit—*MSU Alumni Magazine*—296.
Wallace Jefferson, '85, Texas Supreme Court Justice and Family—*MSU Alumni Magazine*—296.
Harry L. Martin, '36, Congressional Medal of Honor Winner—MSU Archives & Historical Collections—297.
Jay Schadler, '74, Emmy Award Winner—*MSU Alumni Magazine*—297.
James P. Holden, MBA '90, President of Daimler-Chrysler—*MSU Alumni Magazine*—298.
Philip E. Austin, M.A. '68, Ph.D. '69, President, U. of Alabama—*MSU Alumni Magazine*/MSU Archives & Historical Collections—299.
David C. Broski, '62, M.A. '63, Ph.D. '74, President, Bradley U.—*MSU Alumni Magazine*/MSU Archives & Historical Collections—300.
Barbara Ross-Lee, D.O. '73, first African-American to head a medical school in U.S.—*MSU Alumni Magazine*/MSU Archives & Historical Collections—300.
Gregory Josefowicz, '74, CEO Borders Group, Inc.—*MSU Alumni Magazine*—301.
Michael Budman, '68, and Donald Green, Roots Clothing founders—*MSU Alumni Magazine*—302.
Robin Richards, '78, President of MP3.Com—*MSU Alumni Magazine*—302.
Julie Aigner-Clark, '88, founder Baby Einstein Co.—*MSU Alumni Magazine*—303.
Carl T. Motteck, '51, President, Hilton Hotels—*MSU Alumni Magazine*/MSU Archives & Historical Collections—303.
Joan Sills, '75, President, Colony Hotels & Resorts—*MSU Alumni Magazine*/MSU Archives & Historical Collections—304.
Gene Jankowski, M.A. '69, President, CBS Broadcasting—*MSU Alumni Magazine*/MSU Archives & Historical Collections—305.
Anthony Heald, '71, actor in movie *Silence of the Lambs*—*MSU Alumni Magazine*—306.
James P. Hoffa, '63, President, International Brotherhood of Teamsters—*MSU Alumni Magazine*—307.
John D. Hutson, '63, Judge Advocate General, U.S. Navy—*MSU Alumni Magazine*—307.
Carole Leigh Hutton, '78, Publisher and Editor, *Detroit Free Press*—*Detroit Free Press*—308.

Academic Excellence

Mary Norton, '77, Rhodes Scholar—MSU Archives & Historical Collections—Photo, 1977 *Wolverine*—317.
Kathleen Romig, 2001, Mitchell Scholar—*MSU Alumni Magazine*—319.

Buildings & Places Named for MSU People

The first 12 photographs in this chapter are from the *MSC Record,* April 15, 1951 courtesy of MSU Archives & Historical Collections—Article by Madison Kuhn and Joseph G. Duncan.
Dr. Liberty Hyde Bailey, Class of 1882, "Father" of American Horticulture; Dean of Agriculture at Cornell University—324.
Bailey Hall at Cornell University—324.
Dr. Charles E. Bessey, Class of 1869, Dean of Agriculture, University of Nebraska—324.
Bessey Hall at University of Nebraska—324.
Burnett Hall at University of Nebraska—325.
Dr. Edgar A. Burnett, Class of 1887, Chancellor and Dean of Agriculture, University of Nebraska—325.
Dr. Eugene Davenport, Class of 1878, Dean of Agriculture, University of Illinois—325.
Davenport Hall at University of Illinois—325.
Mumford Hall at University of Illinois—326.
Dr. Herbert W. Mumford, Class of 1891, Dean of Agriculture, University of Illinois—326.
Dr. Frederick B. Mumford, Class of 1891, Dean of Agriculture, University of Missouri—326.
Mumford Hall at University of Missouri—326.
Durward "Woody" Varner, first President, MSU-Oakland University (now Oakland University)—*Wolverine,* 1962—Photo by Gerald Holmes/MSU Archives & Historical Collections—327.
Forest Akers, MSU graduate, benefactor, and board member—MSU Archives & Historical Collections—328.
The "Bricks"—Laura Little—330.

Landon Hall viewed through blossoms—J. Bruce McCristal—332.
Kellogg Center lounge—Laura Little—333.
IM-West Charles McCaffree outdoor swimming pool—J. Bruce McCristal—333.
Autumn splendor behind McDonel Hall—J. Bruce McCristal—334.
Wharton Center for Performing Arts—MSU University Relations—336.

The Campus Beautiful

Central Campus "Sacred Space"—MSU University Relations—338.
Coeds jogging—MSU University Relations—339.
Pine Grove near Demonstration Hall—J. Bruce McCristal—340.
Union Building South Entrance—Fall Color—J. Bruce McCristal—341.
Old Horticulture Gardens—behind Natural Science Building—MSU University Relations—342.
"Close Beside the Winding Cedar…"—MSU University Relations—343.
Forest Akers-West golf course signature hole—MSU University Relations—344.
Central Campus walkways—MSU University Relations—345.
Linton Hall—Laura Little—346.

Campus Living—Yesterday and Today

Golden Glow of campus autumn—MSU Alumni Association—348.

The MSU Family's Favorite Things

Water Carnival—1950—MSU Archives & Historical Collections—350.
Campus Color, walkway behind Owen Hall—J. Bruce McCristal—351.
Homecoming display—Phi Delta Theta—1950—MSU Archives & Historical Collections—352.
Contemplating the Red Cedar River—MSU University Relations—352.
Red Cedar Corridor walkway—J. Bruce McCristal—353.
Studying in the Beal Botanical Garden—MSU University Relations—353.
Spartan Marching Band practice—Kirk Stepnitz—354.
Spartan Marching Band circles Spartan Statue—J. Bruce McCristal—354.
Feeding the ducks at the Red Cedar rapids—MSU Archives & Historical Collections—355.
MSU Tailgating—J. Bruce McCristal—355.
Homecoming Parade—Governor & Mrs. Engler—MSU University Relations—356.
Coeds Canoeing on Red Cedar—1925—MSU Archives & Historical Collections—356.
Kissing in the shadow of Beaumont Tower—Wolverine, 1962—Photo by Thompson Crockett—357.
MSU Drummers—MSU University Relations—357.
Spring Blossoms at Landon Hall—Laura Little—358.
MSU Cheerleader—MSU University Relations—358.
MSU Band march to Spartan Stadium—J. Bruce McCristal—359.

Leaving A Living Legacy

New Music Complex—artist's concept—School of Music, College of Arts & Letters—360.

Michigan State and Notre Dame: A Special Relationship

Three MSU football coaches—all from Notre Dame—MSU Sports Information—368.
Charles Bachman, head football coach—1933—MSU Sports Information—370.

The Big Ten Conference: Important in MSU's Development

Big Ten logo—Big Ten Conference—372.

U.S. Presidential Visits to MSU

Presidential Debate Poster—1992—MSU Archives & Historical Collections—374.
President William J. Clinton, Tom Izzo—*MSU Alumni Magazine*—375.

East Lansing: Home of Michigan State University

Grand River Avenue downtown—J. Bruce McCristal—377.
Grand River Avenue, lamp post banners—J. Bruce McCristal—378.

Spartan Sports Success

Spartan Stadium $61 million improvement—MSU Athletic Department—381.
Jimmy Raye run in MSU-Notre Dame 10-10 tie—MSU Sports Information—382.
Magic Johnson dunk in 1979 NCAA basketball title game—MSU Sports Information—383.
World record ice hockey crowd—74,554 at Spartan Stadium—2001—J. Bruce McCristal—383.
Dave Kaiser Rose Bowl fieldgoal, 1956—MSU Sports Information—384.
Ralph H. Young, Athletic Director,1923-1954—MSU Archives & Historical Collections—387.
Biggie Munn, Athletic Director, 1954-1971—MSU Sports Information—388.
Fred W. Stabley, Sr., Sports Information Director, 1948-1980; and Edward "Bud" Erickson, Assistant Sports Information Director—MSU Archives & Historical Collections—389.
Nick Vista, Sports Information Director, 1980-1988; and Mike Pearson, Assistant Sports Information Director—Nick Vista Collection—390.

Great Spartan Individual & Team Performances

Fred Alderman wins 1927 NCAA 100-yard title—MSU Sports Information—397.
Walter Jacobs, four-time National Wrestling Champion—MSU Sports Information—398.
MSC's 1939 NCAA Champion Cross Country team—MSU Sports Information—398.
Chet Aubuchon, first basketball All-American—MSU Sports Information—399.
Swimming Seibold brothers and Charles McCaffree, swimming coach—1946—MSU Sports Information—399.
Robin Roberts—MSU Sports Information—400.
Fred Johnson, World Record in 60-yard dash; NCAA long-jump champion, 1949—MSU Sports Information—400.
John P. Wilson, defensive halfback, Rhodes Scholar—1953—MSU Sports Information—401.
Carlton Rintz, six NCAA titles and ten Big Ten titles in gymnastics, 1953-1955—MSU Sports Information—402.
Henry Kennedy, NCAA 3,000-meter steeplechase champion, 1956—MSU Sports Information—403.
Crawford "Forddy" Kennedy, NCAA cross country champion, 1958—MSU Sports Information—404.
Bill Steuart, NCAA and Big Ten champion in 400-yard & 1,500-yard freestyle events—MSU Sports Information—405.
Carol Heiss, 1960 Olympic gold medal winner in figure skating—MSU Sports Information—405.
Weldon Olson, 1960 Olympic gold medal winner with U.S. ice hockey team—MSU Sports Information—406.
Gary Dilley and Ken Walsh, NCAA & Big Ten swimming champions—MSU Sports Information—407.
Joyce Kazmierski, 1966 Women's National Golf Champion—MSU Sports Information—408.
Gene Kenney, soccer coach, with All-Americans Guy Bush & Peter Hens, 1967 NCAA champions—MSU Sports Information—409.
Bill Wehrwein, 1969 NCAA & Big Ten indoor 600-yard run champion—MSU Sports Information—410.
Herb Washington set World Records in the 50-yard dash (1970) & 60-yard dash (1972)—MSU Sports Information—411.
Pat & Tom Milkovich won three NCAA and seven Big Ten wrestling titles between them—MSU Sports Information—412.
Marshall Dill, set 300-yard dash World Record in 1972—MSU Sports Information—413.
Ken Popejoy ran a 3:57 mile in 1973, fastest in Big Ten history—MSU Sports Information—413.
Bonnie Lauer won the 1973 NCAA Women's Golf Championship—MSU Sports Information—414.
Jane Manchester-Meyers, three-time National Diving Champion—MSU Sports Information—415.
Mike Marshall, L.A. Dodgers relief pitcher won the 1975 Cy Young Award—MSU Sports Information—415.
Gloria Becksford, pitcher for MSU's 1976 National Softball Champions—MSU Sports Information—416.
Sue Ertl, Women's Big Ten Golf Champion, 1977 and 1978—MSU Sports Information—417.
Women's Golf Team wins Fifth Consecutive Big Ten title—1978—MSU Sports Information—418.

Women's Gymnastics Team wins Fourth Consecutive Big Ten title—1980—MSU Sports Information—419.
Jay Vincent, 1980 and 1981 Big Ten basketball scoring leader—MSU Sports Information—419.
Martha Jahn set four Women's Big Ten swimming records in 1982—MSU Sports Information—420.
Judi Brown, track Olympic Silver Medal winner, 1984; NCAA champion, 1983—MSU Sports Information—420.
Kirk Gibson, Detroit Tigers, and Steve Garvey, San Diego Padres, 1984 World Series—MSU Sports Information—421.
1986 MSU Ice Hockey NCAA Champions—MSU Sports Information—422.
Percy Snow, 1989 Butkus and Lombardi Award winner with Bob Hope—MSU Sports Information—424.
Kip Miller, 1990 Hobey Baker Award winner (Hockey's Heisman)—MSU Sports Information—424.
1999 Men's Basketball Big Ten Champions—MSU Sports Information—425.
Heath Fell, MSU golfer, 1993 Big Ten Player of the Year—MSU Sports Information—426.
Shawn Respert, 1995 Big Ten Basketball Player of the Year—MSU Sports Information—427.
Danton Cole, 1995 Stanley Cup winner with N.J. Devils; Big Ten Medal of Honor—MSU Sports Information—427.
Val Sterk, All-American Co-Captain, Women's Big Ten 1996 Volleyball Champions—MSU Sports Information—428.
Dana Cooke, All-American Co-Captain, Women's Big Ten 1996 Volleyball Champions—MSU Sports Information—428.
Sevatheda Fynes, track Olympic Gold & Silver Medal winner; 3 NCAA titles—MSU Sports Information—429.
1997 Women's Basketball Big Ten Champions; senior players—MSU Sports Information—429.
Four "Flintstones"—1998 Big Ten Basketball Champions—MSU Sports Information—430.
David Morgan, three-time Big Ten Wrestling Champion—MSU Sports Information—430.
Morris Peterson, Mateen Cleaves, and A.J. Granger with 2000 NCAA and other trophies—MSU Sports Information—431.
MSU 2000 NCAA Basketball Champions—MSU Sports Information—432.
Emily Bastel, 2000 Big Ten Women's Golf Champion shoots record 288—MSU Sports Information—432.
Goalie Ryan Miller, All-American, won 2001 Hobey Baker Award (Hockey's Heisman)—MSU Sports Information—433.
2001 Women's Field Hockey Champions—Bridget Cooper, Sophie Rosmalen, Alexandra Kyser, and Jenny Sanders—MSU Sports Information—433.
Carley Weiden, All-American, 2001 Co-Big Ten Women's Diver of the Year—MSU Sports Information—434.
Summer Mitchell, All-American, 2001 Co-Big Ten Women's Diver of the Year—MSU Sports Information—434.
Ford Field—Basket Bowl—MSU vs. Kentucky-2003—MSU Sports Information—436.

Vision for the Future

E. James Potchen, M.D.—MSU Radiology—438.
Radiology PET CT with Thomas G. Cooper and Dr. Kevin L. Berger—Kevin Henley, MSU Radiology—439.
Radiology gardens—Kevin Henley, MSU Radiology—439.
Coeds studying between pillars of Kedzie Hall, South—MSU University Relations—440.

Back inside cover

Central campus fall haze—MSU University Relations.

Index

B

C

D

E

F

G

H

I

J

M

N

O

P

Q

R

T

W

Y

Z